S0-BMS-351

Lecture Notes in Computer Science 1552

Edited by G. Goos, J. Hartmanis and J. van Leeuwen

Springer

Berlin
Heidelberg
New York
Barcelona
Hong Kong
London
Milan
Paris
Singapore
Tokyo

Foreword

Advances in Database Technologies (ADT) is a workshop series designed to promote interaction and discussion among researchers and practitioners in specific topics related to advanced data modeling and database technologies. The first ADT workshop was held in conjunction with the 17th International Conference on Conceptual Modeling (ER'98) in Singapore. It consisted of three small workshops, i.e., the "International Workshop on Data Warehousing and Data Mining" organized by Prof. Sham Navathe and Dr. Mukesh Mohania, the "International Workshop on Mobile Data Access" organized by Prof. Dik Lun Lee, and the "International Workshop on New Database Technologies for Collaborative Work Support and Spatio-Temporal Data Management" organized by Prof. Yoshifumi Masunaga. These three small workshops were held simultaneously on 19 and 20 November, and the papers were jointly published in this ADT'98 proceedings.

We would like to thank Prof. Sham Navathe, Dr. Mukesh Mohania, Prof. Dik Lun Lee, Prof. Yoshifumi Masunaga and their program committees for working together to insure an excellent workshop program. The program co-chair of ER'98 Prof. Tok Wang Ling and his organizing committee members gave outstanding support to the workshops with the local arrangements, registration, publicity, and the preparation of the proceedings. Our special thanks go to Prof. Stefano Spaccapietra, Chair of the ER Steering Committee, for his encouragement to make the ADT workshop an annual event to be held in conjunction with the future ER conferences. We would also like to thank Dr. Peter Chen and Dr. Bernhard Thalheim for their efforts in expanding the scope of the ER conference series. We were fortunate to have ACM, ACM SIGMOBILE, the ER Insitute and the Japanese research project on Advanced Databases (supported by the Ministry of Education, Science, Sports and Culture of Japan) as workshop sponsors. Lastly, we would also like to express our sincere thanks to all reviewers of the workshop papers.

We hope that the first ADT workshop was stimulating and enjoyable to all who attended it, and we look forward to more successful ADT workshops in the coming years.

December 1998

Prof. Yahiko Kambayashi
ER'98 Conference Chair

Dr. Ee-Peng Lim
ER'98 Workshop Chair

Workshop Chairs' Messages

Data warehousing and data mining is a recent information technology that allows electronic information to be easily and efficiently accessed for decision making activities and the automated extraction of interesting patterns and trends in the data stored in a data warehouse (called data mining).

The first international workshop on Data Warehousing and Data Mining (DWDM'98) focuses on the physical and the logical design of data warehousing and data mining systems. The scope of the papers covers the most recent and relevant topics in the areas of data and web warehousing, multidimensional databases, knowledge discovery and data mining.

We received more than 30 papers from over 15 countries and the programme committee finally selected 14 papers. A special panel on 'Data Warehousing and Data Mining - Are we working on the right things?' is included in the workshop programme to discuss the current challenges.

We would like to thank the conference general chair, workshop general chair and the organising committee of the 17th International Conference on Conceptual Modelling (ER'98) for recognising the importance of the theme of this workshop. We are very indebted to all programme committee members and the referees who have very carefully and timely reviewed the papers. We would also like to thanks all the authors who submitted their papers to this workshop.

November 1998   Sham Navathe
                                                           Workshop Chair

                                                         Mukesh Mohania
                                             Program Committee Chair

                                                  International Workshop on
                                     Data Warehousing and Data Mining

Wireless communication has added a new dimension of freedom to the Internet. It gives people truly ubiquitous access to information and computational resources, practically at any time and from anywhere in the world. In the past few years, we have witnessed the astonishing progress in both research and technological advancement in wireless communication systems. We expect to see a rapid penetration of the technology into every aspect of life, from global communication to applicance control in households. This workshop was organized with this perspective in mind to provide a forum for this timely topic. To align with the theme of the main conference (Conceptual Modelling, ER '98), this workshop was intended to focus on the data access aspect of mobile systems. I am glad that with the help of the program committee, we were able to put together an interesting program drawing papers from industry and academia around the world, with a panel on the future directions of academic research and industrial development. I am also greatly indebted to Dr. Ee-Peng Lim for his tremendous efforts in handling all the organizational aspect of the workshop and to Dr. Tok Wang Ling for making the publication of the workshop proceedings possible.

I hope this workshop is merely the very first of a continuous sequence of workshops dedicated to the data access aspect of mobile computing.

December 1998

Dik L. Lee
Chair, International Workshop on
Mobile Data Access

The International Workshop on New Database Technologies for Collaborative Work Support and Spatio-Temporal Data Management (NewDB'98) was held on November 19-20, 1998 in Singapore. The NewDB'98 was organized in conjunction with the Seventeenth International Conference on Conceptual Modeling (ER'98). These proceedings contain the technical papers accepted for presentation at the workshop.

The NewDB'98 program committee accepted 12 and 6 papers for regular and short presentation, respectively, which were selected from 28 submitted papers from various countries. It is interesting to note that the majority of the 13 accepted papers were from Japan. In Japan there is an on-going project "Research and Development of Advanced Database Systems for Integration of Media and User Environments" funded by the Ministry of Education, Science, Sports and Culture. This is a three year project started in 1996, and is directed by Prof. Yahiko Kambayashi of Kyoto University. In carrying out the project, we have recognized that the support of collaborative work and management of spatio-temporal data has become one of the most interesting and important database applications, which is due to the tremendous progress of database and its surrounding technologies in the last decade.

I believe that the future database systems in the coming twenty first century cannot survive without supporting spatio-temporal virtual database environments which users enter to work together.

Last but no least, I would like to thank you all of the NewDB'98 program committee members, Dr. Ee Peng Lim of ER'98 Workshop Chair, and Prof. Tok Wang Ling of ER'98 Program Co-Chair for their hard work.

December 1998   Yoshifumi Masunaga
                                        Chair, International Workshop on
                                           New Database Technologies for
                                          Collaborative Work Support and
                                        Spatio-Temporal Data Management

Workshop Organization

International Workshop on Data Warehousing and Data Mining
Chair: Sham Navathe (Georgia Institute of Technology, USA)
Program Chair: Mukesh Mohania (University of South Australia, Australia)

International Workshop on Mobile Data Access
Chair: Dik L. Lee (Hong Kong University of Science and Technology, Hong Kong)

International Workshop on New Database Technologies for Collaborative Work Support and Spatio-Temporal Data Management
Chair: Yoshifumi Masunaga (University of Library and Information Science, Japan)

Conference Chair, ER'98:
Yahiko Kambayashi (Kyoto University, Japan)

Program Co-Chairs, ER'98:
Tok Wang Ling (National University of Singapore, Singapore)
Sudha Ram (University of Arizona, USA)

Workshop Chair, ER'98:
Ee-Peng Lim (Nanyang Technological University, Singapore)

Publication Chair:
Chuan Heng Ang (National University of Singapore, Singapore)

Registration Chair:
Hock Chuan Chan (National University of Singapore, Singapore)

Finance Chair:
Cheng Hian Goh (National University of Singapore, Singapore)

Local Arrangements Co-Chairs:
Mong Li Lee (National University of Singapore, Singapore)
Danny Poo (National University of Singapore, Singapore)

Industrial Chair:
Kian Lee Tan (National University of Singapore, Singapore)

Publicity Chair:
Yong Meng Teo (National University of Singapore, Singapore)

Secretary:
Sew Kiok Toh (National University of Singapore, Singapore)

Steering Committee Representatives:
Stefano Spaccapietra (Swiss Federal Institute of Technology, Switzerland)
Bernhard Thalheim (Cottbus Technical University, Germany)
Peter Chen (Louisiana State University, USA)

Regional Co-ordinators:
Alberto Laender (Federal University of Minas Geras, Brazil)
Erich Neuhold (German National Research Center for Information Technology, Germany)
Masaaki Tsubaki (Data Research Institute, Japan)
Shiwei Tang (Peking University, China)

Program Committee for International Workshop on Data Warehousing and Data Mining

Sharma Chakravarthy, USA
Arbee L.P. Chen, Taiwan
Qiming Chen, USA
Anindya Datta, USA
Jonathan Gray, Australia
John Harrison, Australia
Yahiko Kambayashi, Japan
Kamal Karlapalem, Hong Kong, China
Masaru Kitsuregawa, Japan
Shin'ichi Konomi, Germany
Vijay Kumar, USA

Wolfgang Lehner, Germany
Leonid Libkin, USA
Sanjay Madria, Singapore
Wee-Keong Ng, Singapore
Maria Orlowska, Australia
Stefano Paraboschi, Italy
D. Janaki Ram, India
John Roddick, Australia
N. L. Sarda, India
Ashok Savasere, USA
Ernest Teniente, Spain

Program Committee for International Workshop on Mobile Data Access

Arbee Chen, Taiwan
Wan-Sup Cho, Korea
Pam Drew, USA
San-Yih Hwang, Taiwan
Wang-Chien Lee, USA
Bo Li, Hong Kong
Ee-Peng Lim, Singapore

Sanjay Kumar Madria, Singapore
Kimmo Raatikainen, Finland
Nobuo Saito, Japan
Kian-Lee Tan, Singapore
Martti Tienari, Finland
Guoren Wang, China
Lawrence Yeung, Hong Kong

Program Committee for International Workshop on New Database Technologies for Collaborative Work Support and Spatio-Temporal Data Management

Masatoshi Arikawa, Japan
Hiroshi Arisawa, Japan
Chin-Chen Chang, Taiwan
David Wai-lok Cheung, HK
Max Egenhofer, USA
Ramez Elmasri, USA
Burkhard Freitag, Germany
Theo Haerder, Germany
Yoshinari Kanamori, Japan
Kyuchul Lee, Korea
Wen-Syan Li, USA
Tok Wang Ling, Singapore
Akifumi Makinouchi, Japan

Songchun Moon, Korea
Yasuaki Nakamura, Japan
Anne Ngu, Australia
Shogo Nishida, Japan
Yutaka Ohsawa, Japan
Christine Parent, Switzerland
N. L. Sarda, India
Sigeru Shimada, Japan
Mark Sondheim, Canada
Katsumi Tanaka, Japan
Seiichi Uchinami, Japan
Shunsuke Uemura, Japan
Yasushi Yamaguchi, Japan

Organized By

School of Computing, National University of Singapore

Sponsored By

ACM

ACM SIGMOBILE

Research and Development of Advanced Database Systems for Integration of Media and User Environments
(Supported by the Ministry of Education, Science, Sports and Culture, Japan)

The ER Institute

In-cooperation with

School of Applied Science, Nanyang Technological University

Singapore Computer Society

Information Processing Society of Japan

Table of Contents

Part 1: Data Warehousing and Data Mining

1.1: Knowledge Discovery

Session chair: John F. Roddick, AUSTRALIA

1.2: Data Mining

Session chair: Roger Hsiang-Li Chiang, SINGAPORE

1.3: Data and Web Warehousing

Session chair: Wee-Keong Ng, SINGAPORE

Part 2: Mobile Data Access

2.1: Caching

2.2: Data Dissemination

2.3: Replication

2.4: Mobile Networks

Session chair: Stuart Jacobs, USA

2.5: Mobile Platforms

Session chair: Keizo Saisho, JAPAN

2.6: Tracking and Monitoring

Session chair: San-Yih Hwang, TAIWAN

Panel Discussion:

Part 3: New Database Technologies for Collaborative Work Support and Spatio-Temporal Data Management

3.1: Collaborative Work Support-1

Session chair: Hiroshi Arisawa, JAPAN

3.2: Collaborative Work Support-2

Session chair: Lutz Wegner, GERMANY

3.3: Temporal Data Modelling

Session chair: Stefano Spaccapietra, SWITZERLAND

3.4: Moving Objects and Spatial Indexing

Session chair: Yutaba Ohsawa, JAPAN

3.5: Spatio-Temporal Databases

Session chair: Shogo Nishida, JAPAN

3.6: Video Database Content

Session chair: Yoshinari Kanamori, JAPAN

A Fuzzy Attribute-Oriented Induction Method for Knowledge Discovery in Relational Databases

Noureddine Mouaddib and Guillaume Raschia

IRIN - Université de Nantes
2 rue de la Houssinière, BP 92208, 44322 Nantes Cedex 3, France.
{mouaddib, raschia}@irin.univ-nantes.fr

Abstract. In this paper, we propose a fuzzy attribute-oriented induction method for knowledge discovery in relational databases. This method is adapted from the DBLearn system by representing background knowledge with fuzzy thesauri and fuzzy labels. These models allow to take into account inherent imprecision and uncertainty of the domain representation. We also show the power of fuzzy thesauri and linguistic variables to describe gradations in the generalization process and to handle exceptions.

1   Introduction

The computerization of business activities produces an amount of data recorded in databases. These databases are rapidly growing and managers would like to explore this mine of information. This need leads up to researches on Knowledge Discovery in Databases (KDD), considered as *the non trivial process of identifying valid, novel, potentially usefull, and ultimately understandable pattern in data* [1].

Our approach addresses this issue: it is based on the principle of attribute-oriented induction proposed in the DBLearn system [2,3] which integrates the learning-from-example paradigm, with relational database operations. DBLearn first collects the interesting data using a SQL query. Next, it applies the generalization operator attribute by attribute on the extracted relation. Some attribute values in the relation are replaced with higher level concepts defined into a partially ordered hierarchy - general-to-specific concepts tree. On the final step, the generalized relation is transformed into rules.

Our paper is motivated by two observations. First, the user domain knowledge representation is usually vague, incomplete or uncertain, even if the user is an expert. Second, as concept trees represent preferences and points of view of the user, they are necessary to provide powerful and flexible tools to represent the knowledge about the domain. As you can see, our goal is not to solve the inherent problems of induction process, but only to take advantage of an establishment in order to improve efficiency and accuracy of attribute-oriented induction methods, by using the DBLearn algorithm as a general framework.

The remainder of this paper is organized as follows. In section 2, we show how fuzzy logic offers a framework to represent inherent uncertainty or vagueness of domain knowledge. We present the advantage of using fuzzy thesauri and fuzzy labels instead of concepts trees as it is used in DBLearn. Section 3 proposes the fuzzy attribute-oriented induction method, which adapts and improves the DBLearn algorithm. We conclude in section 4 and consider future works.

2 Background Knowledge Representation

In this paper, we propose two kinds of models which are able to represent complex (uncertain, incomplete...) information. The first one (cf section 2.1) represents symbolic values in a fuzzy thesaurus [4]. The second one represents numeric values.

2.1 Representing Symbolic Values in a Fuzzy Thesaurus

General definition : A fuzzy thesaurus is a set (C, R, L, I) where :
- C is a set of concepts (or terms) $\{c_1, \ldots, c_n\}$; e.g. $\{Boa, Oviparous, Reptile, Snake, Viper\}$.
- R is a set of relations $\{r_1, \ldots, r_m\}$; e.g. $\{isa, isn\}$ is a set of relations where *isa* means "is a" and *isn* means "is not a".
- I is a given set of degrees in $[0, 1]$.
- L is a partial function from $C \times R \times C$ into I. The function L generates a set of links $\{l_1, \ldots, l_p\}$ where l_k represents the equality $L(c_i, r_q, c_j) = \alpha$ noted :

$$l_k : c_i \xrightarrow{r_q} _\alpha c_j$$

where $c_i, c_j \in C$, $r_q \in R$ and $\alpha \in I$ (used to express the strength of link l_k). We note $origin(l_k) = c_i$ the origin of l_k, $end(l_k) = c_j$ the destination of l_k, $rel(l_k) = r_q$ the relation involved in l_k, and $strength(l_k) = \alpha$ the degree of the link. For example (cf figure 1), $Viper \xrightarrow{isa} _1 Snake$ is a link.

Paths A path from a concept c_i to a concept c_j, noted $path(c_i, c_j)$ is a set of links $\{l_{k_1}, \ldots, l_{k_q}\}$ such that :
  $l_{k_1}, l_{k_2}, \cdots, l_{k_q} \in L$, $origin(l_{k_1}) = c_i$, $end(l_{k_q}) = c_j$, $end(l_{k_m}) = origin(l_{k_{m+1}})$ for $m = 1, \cdots, q - 1$

Valid paths Some paths are not valid, for instance, "the neighbour of my neighbour is not my own neighbour". Thus, we use a grammar to define the set of valid paths.

We consider G as a Chomsky's grammar generating a set of sentences. A sentence represents an authorized sequence of relations in a path with respect to grammar G. We note this set $\mathcal{L}(G)$.

A valid path from a concept c_i to a concept c_j respecting a grammar G, noted $G-path(c_i, c_j)$, is a path $\{l_{k_1}, \ldots, l_{k_q}\}$ such that the sequence $rel(l_{k_1}), \ldots, rel(l_{k_q})$ is in $\mathcal{L}(G)$.

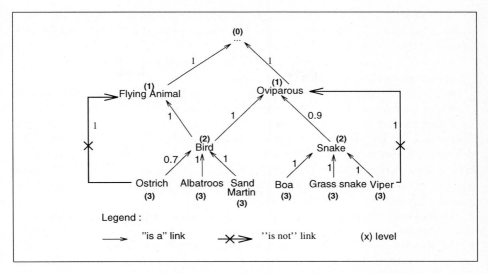

Fig. 1. An extract of the thesaurus on the attribute "type": thes1

Generalization grammar In this paper, we focus on a particular grammar used in the knowledge discovery process: generalization grammar. We consider two kinds of relations: *isa* (is a) and *isn* (is not a) like those represented in the example of figure 1. Then, to give the set of more general concepts of a concept c_i, we use a grammar defined by:

$G : X \longrightarrow isa^+(1) \mid isa^\star isn\ isa^\star(0)$

where the number between parenthesis indicates the authorization of the generated sentence (i.e. 0 for an unauthorized path and 1 for an authorized path). From the figure 1, *Albatross* can be generalized to *Bird*, *Flying Animal* and *Oviparous*. However, *Ostrich* can be generalized to *Bird* and *Oviparous* but not to *Flying Animal* because there exists an invalid path $\{Ostrich \xrightarrow{\text{isn}}_1 Flying\ Animal\}$.

Generalized concept degree A degree d is associated to each higher level concept c_j to show to which extent it generalizes the concept c_i. This degree is calculated by:

$$d = \alpha \times \gamma$$
$$\alpha = \max_{k=1,\cdots,m} \left(strength_{path}(G\text{--}path_k(c_i, c_j))\right)$$
$$\gamma = \min_{k=1,\cdots,m} \left(\max(\beta(G\text{--}path_k(c_i, c_j)),\right.$$
$$\left. 1 - strength_{path}(G\text{--}path_k(c_i, c_j)))\right)$$

where:

- $strength_{path}(p)$ gives the strength associated to path p (i.e. a kind of proximity degree between the first and the last term of the path). The strength of a path $p = \{l_{k_1}, \ldots, l_{k_q}\}$ is calculated by:

$$strength_{path}(p) = Min_{p=1,\ldots,q}(strength(l_{k_p}))$$

- $\beta(p)$ gives the authorization of a path p
- α is the degree of the best path from c_i to c_j (with the higher strength)
- γ is an aggregation of authorized level for all paths from c_i to c_j

From the previous example, *Ostrich* can be generalized to *Bird* with the degree 0.7, to *Oviparous* with the degree 0.7, and to *Flying Animal* with the degree 0. Then, we consider the set of more general concepts of a given concept c_i as a fuzzy set determined by a membership function noted μ_{c_i} where $\mu_{c_i}(c_{i'}) = d$ is the generalization degree of c_i to $c_{i'}$. For example, we have $\mu_{Ostrich}(Oviparous) = 0.7$ from figure 1.

Using fuzzy thesauri, instead of concepts trees as in DBLearn allows to represent graduations of the generalization process. For example, we can represent in the thesaurus (cf figure 1) that a concept *Ostrich* can be generalized to the concept *Bird* with a weight lower than the concept *Albatros*. If we consider the concept *Bird* as the union of the following characteristics: to fly, to have a beak, to have feathers..., an ostrich does not verify all these properties.

Exceptions are also easily taken into account with the "is not" link of fuzzy thesauri. Unlike, to represent exceptions in a hierarchy, artificial classes are introduced, for example "no flying bird", "no feathers bird"...

As the fuzzy thesaurus should be a graph, multi-generalization is allowed representing multiple points of view in the same hierarchy.

2.2 Representing Numeric Values with Fuzzy Labels

We use fuzzy labels [5] to generalize numerical values. They partition the attribute domain into fuzzy subsets. For example, the domain of the attribute "height" can be divided into three fuzzy labels "small", "medium", "tall".

In [6], a similar method is used to reduce a relation, but authors did not use the membership grade during the data reduction process to weight the generalized tuple obtained after substitution.

Compared to other approaches in KDD, fuzzy labels offer more flexibility to represent the background knowledge, particularly when dealing with values at the limit of a class. For example, the tuple $<$ *viper, 0.6 cm, ... $>$* can be generalized in $<$ *viper, small (0.8), ... $>$* and in $<$ *viper, medium (0.2), ... $>$*.

3 Fuzzy Attribute-Oriented Induction Method

The induction process is the most important part of works in machine learning. Its general principle consists in identifying symbolic concepts from observations [12]. Therefore this activity is really close from generalization process of data. Symbolic concept is characterized by an intentional description of the generated categories - concepts, or classes -, as opposed to the clustering activity [8], which only provides an extentional description of categories: the disjunction of all the instances of the class. In our point of view, summarized descriptions are built from background knowledge - fuzzy thesauri and fuzzy labels - and acquired concepts are in fact merged tuples. We could notice that the word *concept* is used both for a merged tuple and for a term of a thesaurus.

Overall, the induction method we want to use is monothetic; it only considers one property at a time for the abstraction process, as opposed to a polythetic approach, which could take into account a lot of different attributes in order to define the best data generalization. So we could roughly compare our approach with the construction of decision trees [9] in classification problems.

Finally, the learning process we propose has several features in common with constructive conceptual clustering algorithms [11] :

- the unsupervised nature of the learning task : the system must cluster and merge instances without any advice or help from a human expert;
- the nonincremental process determined by the need of data global view for the choice of future-merged tuples, but we could quite easily consider an extension of the system which will integrate an incremental process in order to deal with large and evolutive databases;
- the use of background knowledge, which allows a high level of abstraction and a relevant semantics of concept descriptions;
- the great interpretability of the acquired concepts due to the use of the same vocabulary between the domain expert and the system;

Nevertheless, the main feature of a typical conceptual clustering algorithm is the top-down construction of a concept hierarchy [10], and consequentely the definition of different abstraction levels. In our approach, there does not exist this kind of data organization, even if we could take into account different abstraction levels in the generalization process.

To apply the attribute-oriented induction, we have adapted the steps proposed in DBLearn system to use fuzzy thesauri and fuzzy labels during the generalization process. In a first step, DBLearn collects relevant data from the database using a SQL query. The second step removes attributes which have no significance in the process. In the third one, the procedure selects the attribute on which the generalization operator will be applied (step four). In step five, identical tuples are merged into an unique one. These last three steps are repeated until the number of tuples in the generalized relation is greater than a threshold set by the user.

The procedure that performs the fuzzy attribute-oriented induction method is noted:

FAOI(DB, Lat, FT, FL, thres): GR

where :

DB is the database that contains data on which the algorithm will be performed.

Lat is a list that indicates for each attribute the number of distinct values an attribute may have in the final relation GR. If a thesaurus is associated to this attribute, `Lat` indicates the maximum steps in the thesaurus the generalization process may climb. For example, if the user indicates a level 2 for the attribute "type" in the relation $\mathcal{R}_{animal}$ (cf table 1), the generalization process will actually climb until the values *Bird* or *Snake* (cf figure 1).

`FT` and `FL` which are respectively the set of thesauri and the set of fuzzy labels.

`thres` is the maximum number of distinct tuples in the generalized relation `GR`.

`GR` is the generalized relation. Its schema is adapted from the original relation by attaching a weight to each significant attribute `w_ai` and adding an extra column `count` detailed below.

To illustrate the extraction process, we use the following relation $\mathcal{R}_{animal}$.

Table 1. $\mathcal{R}_{animal}$

Ident	Type	Height	...	place
AX34	vipera	0.3	...	France
AZ65	boa	1.2	...	Nigeria
...	...	...	... ...	
AA88	ostrich	1.1	...	Australia

3.1 FAOI Algorithm

• **Procedure** `FAOI(DB,Lat,FT,FL,thres):GR`

```
IR = Collect_relevant_data(DB)
GR = Attribute_removal(IR, Lat)
While count(GR) > thres do
  ag = Attribute_selection(GR, Lat)
  GR = Generalization(GR, ag, FT, FL)
  GR = Merging(GR)
End
```

• **Procedure** `Collect_relevant_data(DB):IR`

The user enters a SQL query to collect the interesting data on which the data mining algorithm will be performed.

• **Procedure** `Attribute_removal(IR,Lat):GR`

```
GR = IR
For each attribute a in relation IR
```

```
do
   if FT[a] = {} or FL[a] = {} and
   Lat[a] < Distinct_values(Proj(IR, a))
   then GR = GR - <a>
end
```

This procedure examines all attributes in sequence. We remove those with no higher level concepts specified on them and whose the number of distinct values in the relation IR is greater than the threshold specifed in the Lat list. For example, the attribute *"ident"* that identifies animals in the relation $\mathcal{R}_{Animal}$ can be removed from the relation. In fact, this attribute provides no property that would characterize the class underlying the relation $\mathcal{R}_{Animal}$. This strategy is also used in DBLearn.

• **Procedure** `Attribute_selection(GR,Lat):ag`

```
max_value = 0
For each attribute a in relation GR
do
   value_nb = Distinct_values(Proj(GR, a))
   if value_nb > max_value
   and value_nb > Lat[a]
   then ag = a
     max_value = value_nb
end
```

This procedure chooses the next attribute on which the generalization operator will be applied. As in DBLearn, we select the attribute with the maximum number of distinct values.

• **Procedure** `Generalization(RG,ag,FT,FL):RG`

```
if ag is numeric attribute
then
   GR = generalization_FL(GR, ag, FL[a])
else
   GR = generalization_FT(GR, ag, FT[a])
end
```

According to the type of the selected attribute, two procedures are used for the generalization: **generalization_FL** if it is a numeric attribute and **generalization_FT** otherwise.

In this paper, we only explain `generalization_FT` but `generalization_FL` can be defined in the same way.

Before that, we explore several problems we encountered while using fuzzy thesauri to represent background knowledge.

The first difference with the DBLearn system is that, in databases, tuples can contain values which are not necessarily leafs of the thesaurus. For example, a database user observing a snake, does not always have necessarily information to identify to which type it belongs. If there exist different levels in the initial relation, we have to control the process applying the generalization one level at a time to avoid over-generalization.

The generalization is applied on concepts with maximum depth and climbs one level at each step. For example, table 2 contains different level concepts. In the first generalization step on the attribute "type", only the values *Ostrich* and *Albatroos* will be generalized because their depth level is the maximum in the relation (cf figure 1). This maximum defines the first generalization level, which decreases at each next step.

Table 2. An extract of the relation GR

type	wt	height	wh	...	count
ostrich	1	tall	0.9	...	30
albatross	1	tall	0.7	...	40
snake	1	small	0.8	...	10
...		... ...	...	...	...

Table 3. table 2 after one generalization and merging

type	wt	height	wh	...	count
bird	1	tall	0.78	...	70
snake	1	small	0.8	...	10
...		... ...	...	... ...	

The second difference with the DBLearn system is the multi-generalization and the use of different kinds of links to represent background knowledge, particularly the link "is not". A concept can be generalized into more than one concept or a concept can not be generalized into a higher level concept. Mistakes can be made, if we do not take some precautions. Especially, the generalization process should not leave out the previous steps as it is made in DBLearn. For example, if a generalization is performed on the attribute "type", table 3 describes the relation after merging identical tuples. When identical tuples are merged, the new weight associated to each attribute is calculated with a weighted average (cf **Merging** procedure).

After a second generalization stage on table 3, table 4 is obtained. Instead of table 4, we must obtain the relation described in table 5.

Table 4. table 3 one step after

type	wt	height	wh	...	count
flying animal	0.8	tall	0.78	...	70
oviparous	1	tall	0.78	...	70
oviparous	0.9	small	0.8	...	10
...		... ...	...	... ...	

Table 5. table 3 one step after, respecting the link "is not" in the thesaurus

type	wt	height	wh	...	count
flying animal	0,8	tall	0,7	...	40
bird	1	tall	0,9	...	30
oviparous	1	tall	0,78	...	70
oviparous	0,9	small	0,8	...	10
...		... ...	...	... ...	

To ensure the validity of the generalization, a particular procedure must be applied to process the multi-inheritance and the "is not" link cases.

The multi-generalization can generate problems only when several paths exist between a specific concept *cs* and a generic concept *cg*. So, if we adopt the strategy of generalizing at each step, *cs* will be generalized as many times as the number of paths relating it to *cg*. The strategy we adopt is to generalize *cs* directly to *cg*.

To solve the problem generated by the "is not" link, we adopted a similar strategy. We detect concepts related with this link. If there exists a link labelled "is not" between a concept *cs* and a generic concept *cg*, the concept *cs* can not be generalized into *cg*'s ancestors. *cs* is generalized into the direct *cg*'s descendants that are also ancestors of *cs*. But, this attribute value can not be generalized next and it can not be merged with other tuples. That is why the tuple representing an exception is stored in a particular relation named ER. These "exceptional" tuples can be generalized on other attributes values and they can be merged together. Then, the ER relation also stores information for each attribute indicating if the attribute value can be generalized in the future (cf table 7) or not.

For example, in the thesaurus (cf figure 1), the concept *Ostrich* is related to the concept *Flying Animal* with a link "is not". So when table 2 is generalized on the first column, *Ostrich* is directly generalized into *Bird* and this new tuple can not have new generalizations on this value afterwards. *Ostrich* is also generalized in *Oviparous* and this new tuple can handle the process further on.

Table 6. table 2 after a generalization

type	wt	height	wh	...	count
bird	1	tall	0.7	...	40
oviparous	0.7	tall	0.9	...	30
snake	1	small	0.8	...	10
...	...	...	...	...	...

Table 7. ER table generated by generalizing table 2 into table 6

type	wt	gt	height	wh	...	count
bird	0.7	false	tall	1	...	30

gt indicates if the value *Bird* can be generalized next.

The generalized relation GR is divided into two relations: ER (cf table 7) and NR (cf table 6). The procedure of generalization and merging on each relation can be processed concurrently. The generalized table GR is obtained by an union of the relation ER and NR after generalization and merging.

- **Procedure: generalization_FT(ER,NR,ag,ft): NR, ER**

```
ER_generalization_FT(ER,ag,Lat,ft): ER
NR_generalization_FT(NR,ag,LAt,ft): NR, NER
ER = Union(ER, NER)
```

The generalization GR is obtained by an union of the relation ER and NR.

```
GR = Union(NR, Proj(ER,a1,wa1,...,an,wan,count))
```

The function **general_concepts**, used below, gives for a concept (and its associated weight) the set of more general concepts taking into account problems introduced by the multi-generalization and the link "is not". Using the exemple of the table 2, **general_concepts(thes1,ostrich,1,1)**, where the third parameter represents the weight associated and the fourth the level set by the user in the list **Lat**, returns the following values: (**bird, 0.7,false**) and (**oviparous, 0.7, true**). The level set by the user indicates in the procedure if problems may occur or not in the generalization process. For example, still using the table 2, if the level set by the user is 2, **general_concepts(thes1,ostrich,1,2)** returns only (**bird,0.7,true**). Any problem can occur because the concept related with *Ostrich* by a link "is not" is at the level 1 in the thesaurus (cf figure 1). The generalization can not climb to this value.

There are actually two generalization procedures, that are slightly similar. They only differ in their target relation. **NR_generalization_FT** addresses relation **NR**, and **ER_generalization_FT** addresses relation **ER**. We describe them below.

• **Procedure: ER_generalization_FT(ER,ag,Lat,ft): ER**

```
For each t in relation ER do
 if generalizable(ft,t.ag)
 then
  Lcg = general_concepts(ft,t.ag,t.w_ag,Lat[ag])
  if Lcg = {}
  then t = update(t,g_ag,false)
   ER = update_r(ER,t)
  else
   For each e in list Lcg do
    if e.g = false
    then t = update(t,g_ag,false)
    end
    t = update(t,ag,e.cg)
    t = update(t,w_ag,e.wcg)
    ER = update_r(ER,t)
```

• **Procedure: NR_generalization_FT(NR,ag, Lat,ft): NR,ER**

```
NNR = {}
For each t in relation NR do
 if generalizable(ft,t.ag)
 then
  Lcg = general_concepts(ft,t.ag,t.w_ag,Lat[ag])
  if Lcg = {}
  then te =<t.a1,t.w_a1,true,...>
```

```
    te = update(te,t.g_ag,e.g)
    ER = ER + <t>
  else
    For each e in list Lcg do
      if e.g = false
      then te =<t.a1,t.w_a1,true,...>
        te = update(te,t.ag,e.cg)
        te = update(te,t.w_ag,e.w_cg)
        te = update(te,t.g_ag,e.g)
        ER = ER + <t>
      else t = update(t,ag,e.cg)
        t = update(t,w_ag,e.w_cg)
        NNR = NNR + <t>
NR = NNR
```

• **Procedure: Merging(GR):GR**

```
ER = Merging(ER)
NR = Merging(NR)
GR = Union(NR, Proj(ER, a1,wa1,...,an,wan,count))
```

The `Merging` procedure applied on the relation gathers identical tuples together. Two tuples are considered as being identical if they have the same value for all the columns except for `w_ai` and `count`. In the merged tuple, the weight w_ai associated to an attribute value depends on the attribute weights $t_k.w\_ai, i \in \{1..n\}$ and the coverage $t_k.count$ of all the N tuples t_k to be merged. It is calculated as follows:

$$w\_ai_{(t_1,...,t_N)} = \frac{\sum_{k \in \{1,..,N\}} t_k.w\_ai \times t_k.count}{\sum_{k \in \{1,..,N\}} t_k.count}$$

The factor $t_k.count$ allows to take into account the contribution of each tuple to the merged tuple, from a representativity point of view. The division by the sum $\sum_{k \in \{1,..,N\}} t_k.count$ normalizes the calculated weight. Finally, and as the generalization procedure, the merging procedure can be performed concurrently on each of the relations `ER` and `NR`.

3.2 Generating Rules

The interpretation stage consists of giving a set of rules to the user. A rule takes the following form:

Q are $concept_1$ (d_1) and $concept_2$ (d_2) and ...

where Q is a fuzzy quantifier, $concept_i$ are concepts (attribute values) and d_i are satisfaction degrees of concepts.

To be more useful and expressive to the user, we translate the rules into sentences. For example, the following sentence express such a rule: "most animals are apparently snakes and somewhat small". To achieve this interpretation, we procede in two steps:

First step: Final ER-NR merging. We apply the merging procedure on the relation GR (i.e. Merging(ER + NR)).

Second step: interpretation of ER and NR.

The process examines all tuples of ER and NR in sequence. For a tuple (c1, w1, ..., cn, wn, count) we can deduce the rule: "count% of relevant data are c1 (w1) and ...and cn (wn)" where count% is the percent of count with regard to the number of tuples in the initial relation (containing relevant data).

Next, a rule is converted to a sentence using a quantifier and linguistic terms to qualify each element of the rule. The quantifier Q is translated into a term taken from a given set of terms [7]. In this set, each term is represented by a fuzzy set. In the same way, the different degrees become fuzzy terms modulating the concepts. We shall not go further in this process but we illustrate it in the following example. Let table 8 be the result of the extraction process from an initial relation containing 1000 european animals.

Table 8. Final relation from an extraction process

type	wt	height	wh	...	count
oviparous	0.9	small	0.8	...	800
oviparous	1	medium	0.9	...	200
flying animal	1	small	0.9	...	200

Three rules can be deduced from this relation:
80% of european animals are oviparous (0.9) and small (0.8)
20% of european animals are oviparous (1) and medium (0.9)
20% of european animals are flying animals (1) and small (0.9)
These three rules can have the following linguistic interpretation:
"Most european animals are roughly oviparous and roughly small"
"Few european animals are oviparous and roughly medium"
"Few european animals are flying animals and roughly small"

4 Conclusion and Further Work

We presented a fuzzy attribute-oriented induction method for rules discovery in relational databases. This method adapts the one proposed in the DBLearn [2] system to handle background knowledge represented by fuzzy thesauri and fuzzy labels. Using this kind of models allowed us to take into account the inherent imprecision and uncertainty of the domain knowledge representation. Fuzzy thesauri also offers a framework for representing graduations in the generalization process. In short, valuation of links combined with "is not" relationship, and multiple inheritance enrich attribute-oriented induction methods and offer an easy way to represent exceptions.

Finally, we consider a concrete extension of this work by investigating the *data summary* issue through the construction of a fuzzy data synthesis system based on a concept formation algorithm [10].

References

1. Fayyad, U., Piatetsky-Shapiro, G., Smyth, P. Uthurusamy, R. (eds): Advances in Knowledge Discovery and Data Mining. *AAAI Press/ the MIT Press*, ch. 1, pp. 1–37 (1996)
2. Han, J., Cai, Y., Cercone, N.: Knowledge discovery in databases: An attribute-oriented approach. *18th Very Large DataBases Conference*, (Vancouver, Canada), pp. 547–559 (1992)
3. Han, J., Fu, Y., Wang, W., Chiang, J., Gong, W., Koperski, K., Li, D., Lu, Y., Xia, A.: Dbminer : a system for mining knowledge in large relational databases. *2nd International conference on knowledge discovery in databases and data mining*, (Portland, Usa), pp. 250–255 (1997)
4. Subtil, P., Mouaddib, N., Foucaut, O.: Fuzzy thesaurus for databases. *6th International Fuzzy Systems Association World Congress - Vol. 2*, (Sao Paulo, Brazil), pp. 349–352, (1995)
5. Zadeh, L.: Concept of a linguistic variable and its application to approximate reasoning (1). *Information Systems*, Vol. 8, pp. 199–249 (1975)
6. Bosc, P., Dubois, D., Prade, H.: Approximate data reduction and fuzzy functionnal dependencies. *6th International Fuzzy Systems Association World Congress - Vol. 2*, (Sao Paulo, Brazil), pp. 369 – 371, (1995)
7. Yager, R.: Linguistic summaries as a tool for database discovery. *FUZZ-IEEE'95 Worskshop on Fuzzy Databases Systems*, (Yokohama, Japan), pp. 79–84, (1995)
8. Michalsky, R.S., Stepp, R.: Learning from observation : conceptual clustering. Michalsky, R.S., Carbonell, J.G. and Mitchell T.M. eds, *Machine Learning : an Artificial Intelligence Approach*, Vol. 1, ch. 11, pp. 331–363 (1983)
9. Quinlan, J.R.: Induction of decision trees. *Machine Learning*, pp. 81–106 (1986)
10. Fisher, D.H.: Knowledge acquisition via incremental conceptual clustering. *Machine Learning*,Vol. 2, pp. 139–172 (1987)
11. Gennari, J.H., Langley, P., Fisher, D.H.: Models of incremental concept formation. In *Knowledge Acquisition and Learning*, Buchanan, B.G. and Wilkins, D.C. (eds) (1989)
12. Kodratoff, Y., Diday, E.: Induction symbolique et numérique à partir des données. Cépaduès-Editions (1991)

Fast Methods with Magic Sampling for Knowledge Discovery in Deductive Databases with Large Deduction Results

Chien-Le GOH   Masahiko TSUKAMOTO   Shojiro NISHIO

Department of Information Systems Engineering,
Graduate School of Engineering, Osaka University,
2-1 Yamadaoka, Suita, Osaka 565, Japan.
Tel: +81-6-879-7820. Fax: +81-6-877-9463.
e-mail:{tuka, nishio}@ise.eng.osaka-u.ac.jp

Abstract. The ability of the *deductive database* to handle *recursive queries* is one of its most useful features. It opens up new possibilities for users to view and analyze data. This ability to handle recursive queries, however, still cannot be fully utilized because when *recursive rules* are involved, the amount of deduced facts can become very large, making it difficult and sometimes impossible to store, view or analyze the query results. In order to overcome this problem, we have proposed the DSK method and the DSK(S) method to discover *characteristic rules* from large amount of deduction results without having to store all of them. In this paper, we propose two new methods, the DSK(T) method and the D-SK(ST) method which are faster than the DSK method and the DSK(S) method respectively. In addition, we propose a new sampling method called *magic sampling*, which is used by the two methods to achieve the improvement in speed. Magic sampling works when *linear recursive rules* are involved and the magic set algorithm is used for deduction.

1   Introduction

The ability of the deductive database to handle recursive queries is one of its most useful features. It opens up new possibilities for users to view and analyze data. For example, a user who has stored data about all the vertices and arcs of a graph in a deductive database can easily instruct the database management system to deduce all the possible paths from a certain vertex and analyze them. This ability to handle recursive queries, however, still cannot be fully utilized because when recursive rules are involved, the amount of deduced facts can become very large, making it difficult and sometimes impossible to store, view or analyze the query results.

In [10], we have proposed five methods of applying the attribute-oriented algorithm proposed by J. Han, Y. Cai, and N. Cercone[11, 12] to discover characteristic rules in large amount of deduced facts, deduced by recursive or non-recursive rules, without having to store all of them. We chose the algorithm because it has been found to be effective as a data mining [8, 9] algorithm in its implementation in DBLEARN [13]. In addition, the use of the algorithm has been extended to object-oriented databases in [14]. In [10], we view the extensional database (EDB) of a deductive database as a relational database, and apply the algorithm to deductive databases.

Comparisons among the five methods (KD, SDK, DK, DSK, DSK(S)) in terms of speed, accuracy, memory requirement, etc. have been made. From the comparisons, we realized that the two most useful methods are the DSK method and the DSK(S) method. The DSK method is reasonably fast and accurate while the DSK(S) method is slightly slower, uses a lot less memory and accurate. "D", "S", and "K" stand for "deduction", "sampling", and "knowledge discovery" respectively. The "S" in brackets stands for "space".

In this paper, we propose two new methods, the DSK(T) method and the DSK(ST) method ("T" stands for time) which are faster than the DSK method and the DSK(S) method respectively. In addition, we propose a new sampling method called *magic sampling*, which is used by the two methods to achieve the improvement in speed. Magic sampling works when linear recursive rules [4] are involved and the magic set algorithm [3, 4, 6] is used for deduction.

The organization of this paper is as follows. In section 2, an example which will be used in the explanation is presented. The DSK(T) method and the D-SK(ST) method are explained in sections 3 and 4. Qualitative comparisons among the DSK method, the DSK(S) method, the DSK(T) method, and the DSK(ST) method are presented in section 5. Section 6 is the conclusion of this paper.

2   An Example

For the purpose of explanation, let us suppose an imaginary case where we have the medical records for the last one thousand years of all the people in Japan who suffered or are suffering from at least a kind of allergies. A one thousand year period is supposed because we need medical records that cover many generations to act as a good example. The medical records are stored in deductive databases distributed all over Japan but they can be accessed as a single large database from a user's point of view. Here, a deductive database is regarded as a relational database with deduction mechanism.

The extensional database of the imaginary deductive database has the following scheme:

MEDICAL_RECORD(Patient, Parent, Allergy)

Although a more realistic medical record has more attributes such as address, height, weight, etc., we only assume three attributes in this example to make things simple. Based on the above scheme, we have a relation such as the one in Fig. 1 to store the extensional database of the deductive database.

In the intensional database (IDB), we assume that rules to deduce the ancestors of patients exist and are expressed as below. In the rules, $parent(R, S)$ is equivalent to **MEDICAL_RECORD**$(R, S, $ -$)$. Here, "-" means "not specified" and

Patient	Parent	Allergy
Masako YAMADA	Taro YAMADA	Y
Masako YAMADA	Tomoko YAMADA	Y
Taro YAMADA	Toru YAMADA	X
Taro YAMADA	Keiko YAMADA	X
Shigeo YAMADA	Masako YAMADA	Z
Hiroaki SUZUKI	Jiro SUZUKI	Z
⋮	⋮	⋮

Fig. 1. MEDICAL_RECORD(Patient, Parent, Allergy).

Patient	Ancestor
Taro YAMADA	Toru YAMADA
Taro YAMADA	Keiko YAMADA
Masako YAMADA	Toru YAMADA
Masako YAMADA	Keiko YAMADA
Masako YAMADA	Taro YAMADA
Masako YAMADA	Tomoko YAMADA
Hiroaki SUZUKI	Jiro SUZUKI
⋮	⋮

Fig. 2. A deduced relation with Patient and Ancestor.

$$ancestor(R, S) : - parent(R, S).$$
$$ancestor(R, S) : - ancestor(R, T), parent(T, S).$$

Using the rules for deducing ancestors, it is possible to deduce all the ancestors of any number of patients (Fig. 2). From the deductive database, we wish to find a previously unknown hereditary allergy. The search can be conducted by finding out the characteristic rules of all the allergies throughout the generations.

In order to use the attribute-oriented algorithm to find the characteristic rules, we need some background knowledge in the form of concept hierarchies. In our example, we assume that we have a concept hierarchy like the one shown in Fig. 3. The two layers from the bottom of the concept hierarchy can be easily constructed from the extensional database using the patients' names and the allergies they suffered from.

The concept hierarchy is used to generalize the names of **Patient** and **Ancestor** to the allergies they suffered from and then to broader terms that describe the allergies. Not all the names can be generalized because we do not know the allergies that some of the patients' parents suffered from. However, most can be generalized and this should be sufficient for our purpose of finding characteristic rules.

If we randomly sample a certain number of tuples, for example two hundred tuples, from the deduced relation which contains attributes **Patient** and **Ancestor** and generalize the instances of **Patient** and **Ancestor** using the concept hierarchy in Fig. 3, we may obtain the characteristic rules of the deduced relation in the form shown in Fig. 4 depending on the attribute thresholds and

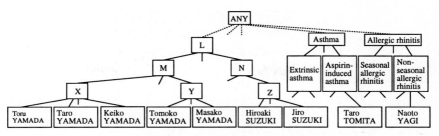

Fig. 3. A concept hierarchy used as background knowledge.

Patient	Ancestor	Count	Percentage
M	M	74	37.0%
N	N	18	9.0%
N	O	19	9.5%
⋮	⋮	⋮	⋮

Fig. 4. Characteristic rules of the deduced relation.

the table threshold values set by the user. The characteristic rules can then be processed using probabilistic and statistical methods to find hereditary allergies. The errors between characteristic rules obtained from random samples and the whole amount of deduced facts are very small. This has been shown in [15].

The way that we used above can help us find the characteristic rules. However, since the deduced facts of every patient's ancestors are often too many to be stored in the limited memory capacity we have, we are not able to obtain a random sample. We need to find a way to obtain a random sample and learn the characteristic rules without having to store all the deduced facts. The DSK(T) method and the DSK(ST) method represent two solutions.

3   The DSK(T) Method

If we take a closer look at the DSK method, we can find some redundancies in processing when we try to build the *aggregate relation* introduced and used by the DSK method. For example, when we find the number of ancestors of Masako YAMADA, we can also find the number of ancestors of Taro YAMADA; but that is not done in the DSK method. The DSK method finds the number of ancestors of Masako YAMADA and Taro YAMADA independently from scratch.

The DSK(T) method aims to increase the speed of forming the aggregate relation by utilizing the information of each query. However, it works only when linear recursive rules are involved and when the magic set algorithm is used for query processing. These restrictions are not too harsh for real life problems because there is a belief that most "real life" recursive rules are linear [4] and the magic set algorithm is popular and efficient. With the restrictions, we obtain the

Patient	Number of ancestors
Masako YAMADA	1023

Fig. 5. The aggregate relation. (Step 1a)

following lemma. We call a sampling method using the lemma magic sampling.

Lemma 1 $\forall x, x \in magic(a) \Rightarrow magic(x) \subseteq magic(a)$;
  a *is a constant and* $magic(a)$ *is the magic set of* a.

Proof sketch. A linear recursive rule has the following form.

$$P_0 : -P_1, P_2, P_3, \ldots, P_m, P_0. \quad \cdots\cdots (1)$$

For simplicity, variables have been omitted. Each literal may have different *arities* [5] but P_0 at the head and P_0 in the body must have the same arity.

From rule (1), adorned rules where only one variable is bound have the form shown below. (The lemma stands when only one variable is bound.)

$$P_0^{\cdots ffbff\cdots} : -P_1, P_2, P_3, \ldots, P_m, P_0^{\cdots ffbff\cdots}. \quad \cdots\cdots (2)$$

Although there are many ways to generate magic rules from adorned rules in the form of (2), they can be summarized into the following two forms.

$$magic.P_0^{\cdots ffbff\cdots}(X) : -P_i, P_{i+1}, \ldots P_j, magic.P_0^{\cdots ffbff\cdots}(X).$$

$$magic.P_0^{\cdots ffbff\cdots}(Y) : -P_k, P_{k+1}, \ldots P_l, magic.P_0^{\cdots ffbff\cdots}(X).$$

The first form shows that for a constant a,

$$magic.P_0^{\cdots ffbff\cdots}(a) = \{a\} \text{ or } \emptyset$$

and the lemma is correct. The second form is a rule of transitive closure and in this case too, the lemma is correct. □

This lemma means when using the magic set algorithm to process a query q involving a constant a, the magic set of a can also be used to process a query q involving x. For example, we can use $magic$(Masako YAMADA) to find the ancestors of Masako YAMADA, Taro YAMADA, etc. Finding the magic set is "expensive" and by eliminating the need to find $magic(x)$ for each x, we can have a significant gain in speed.

The DSK(T) method consists of three steps: (i) deduction, (ii) sampling and (iii) knowledge discovery. At step 1, deduction is performed and the number of deduced facts for each fact in the extensional database is calculated. Based on the example in section 2, we look at the extensional database and select the first tuple Masako YAMADA. Then we find the magic set of Masako YAMADA, $magic$(Masako YAMADA), and find her total number of ancestors (see Fig. 5).

Patient	Number of ancestors
Masako YAMADA	1023
Taro YAMADA	255
Toru YAMADA	200
Keiko YAMADA	55
⋮	⋮

Fig. 6. The aggregate relation. (Step 1b)

Patient	Number of ancestors
Masako YAMADA	1023
Taro YAMADA	255
Toru YAMADA	200
Keiko YAMADA	55
Shigeo YAMADA	1024
⋮	⋮
Hiroaki SUZUKI	2000
⋮	⋮

Fig. 7. The aggregate relation. (End of step 1)

After that, for each person x in $magic$(Masako YAMADA), we use $magic$(Masako YAMADA) to find the number of ancestors of x. Each x is checked against the aggregate relation to see whether he or she has appeared in it or not before we find the number of ancestors of x. If he or she has already appeared, we skip and go to the next x. After finding the number of ancestors of each x, we may obtain something like Fig. 6.

Then we go to the second patient, Taro YAMADA, in the extensional database. By checking the aggregate relation, we know that his total number of ancestors has been calculated. So we skip and go to the third patient, Shigeo YAMADA.

Since Shigeo YAMADA is not in the aggregate relation, we have to find the magic set of Shigeo YAMADA and calculate his total number of ancestors. Then again for each person x in $magic$(Shigeo YAMADA), we check whether he or she has already appeared in the aggregate relation before we find the total number of ancestors of x. We find that every x has already appeared and thus can skip the calculation.

The above process continues until we have calculated the total number of ancestors of every patient in the extensional database. Finally, the accumulated total number of ancestors of all the patients is calculated and we should obtain an aggregate relation like Fig. 7.

At step 2, sampling is performed in 2 stages. At the first stage, a patient is selected according to the probability p where

$$p = \frac{the\ number\ of\ ancestors\ of\ a\ patient}{the\ number\ of\ ancestors\ of\ all\ the\ patients}.$$

Then at the second stage, all the selected patient's ancestors will be deduced and one of them, which is equivalent to one tuple from the deduction results, will be sampled by random. After a tuple is sampled, the number of ancestors of the selected patient and the total number of ancestors of all the patients are each deducted by one. The two stages of step 2 are repeated many times until a user specified n number of tuples have been sampled.

The sample is passed on to step 3 where the process of discovering characteristic rules is performed using the attribute-oriented algorithm and we may obtain a relation like Fig. 4. Steps 2 and 3 of the DSK(T) method are the same as steps 2 and 3 of the DSK method. Further details of the DSK method can be found in [10].

Summarizing the DSK(T) method, we can obtain the following algorithm:

Algorithm 1. Discovery of characteristic rules using the DSK(T) method.

Input. (i) A set of concept hierarchies, (ii) a set of attribute thresholds, (iii) a table threshold, (iv) an intensional database, (v) an extensional database, and (vi) n, the number of tuples to obtain to form a sample.
Output. A set of characteristic rules of the deduced facts.

Method.

1. Collect the set of task-relevant data from the extensional database by a database query.
2. Create a view v of the attributes which bind the arguments of IDB predicates used in deduction from the set of task-relevant data.
3. **begin**
   for each tuple s in v do {
      if s is not in the aggregate relation R
      then do {
         find $magic(s)$,
         use $magic(s)$ to calculate the total number of tuples N_t that can be deduced from s,
         store s and N_t in R,
         delete the deduced tuples of s,
         for each $x \in magic(s)$ **do {**
            if x is not in R
            then do {
               use $magic(s)$ to calculate the N_t of x,
               store x and N_t in R,
               delete the deduced tuples of x }
         }
         delete $magic(s)$ }
   }
   Calculate the sum S of all N_t.
   end
4. **do {**
      Sample a tuple t from relation R based on the formula $p(t) = \frac{N_t}{S}$,
      deduce from t,
      select a result u by random from all the deduction result that can be deduced from t,
      store t (without N_t) and u together as one tuple in relation Q,
      reduce N_t by one,
      reduce S by one,
      delete all deduction results }
   until n distinct tuples have been stored in Q.
   - Comment:
   $p(t)$ is the probability for t to be selected from R.
   Distinct tuples can be obtained by avoiding deduction result selected previously.
   If this does not work, select a new t.
5. Generalize relation Q according to the set of attribute thresholds, the table threshold and the set of concept hierarchies provided.
6. Present the generalized relation as a set of characteristic rules with two additional attributes, Count and Percentage.

Like the DSK method, we have the following theorem:

Theorem 1 *The distribution of a sample obtained by the DSK(T) method from deduction results D is the same as the distribution of a sample obtained by random sampling from D.*

Proof sketch. Assuming that the total number of deduction results is S, the probability that a deduction result is sampled is $\frac{1}{S}$. Using the DSK(T) method, the probability that a deduction result is sampled is $\frac{N_t}{S} \times \frac{1}{N_t}$, which is equal to $\frac{1}{S}$. □

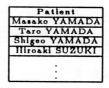

Fig. 8. A view with only the attribute Patient.

4 The DSK(ST) Method

The DSK(S) method also has some redundancies in processing when building the *buffer relation*. In this section, we propose the DSK(ST) method which does away with the redundancies and improves the speed of the DSK(S) method.

The DSK(ST) uses the idea of magic sampling to improve the DSK(S) method and has the same restrictions as that of the DSK(T) method, i.e. the DSK(ST) method can be applied when only linear recursive rules are involved and the magic set algorithm is used for query processing. With the restrictions, **Lemma 1** also stands true for the DSK(ST) method.

The DSK(ST) method consists of 2 steps: (i) deduction and sampling, and(ii) knowledge discovery. At the first step, deduction and sampling are performed together to obtain a random sample of n tuples from the deduction results. n is specified by the user. Step 1 consists of three stages. At stage 1, a sample of patients is taken. At stage 2, ancestors of each patient in the sample are deduced and one of them is selected for each patient. At stage 3, more patients and their ancestors are selected if a sample of n tuples has not yet been obtained at stages 1 and 2.

Using the example in section 2, stage 1 starts by creating a view (see Fig. 8) with only the attribute **Patient** which binds the argument of the IDB predicates. Then the first patient of the view, Masako YAMADA, is selected and her total number of ancestors, t, is calculated using the magic set algorithm and stored in a variable called *scanned_tuples*. Assuming that Masako YAMADA has 1023 ancestors (see Fig. 6), it will be "*scanned_tuples* = t = 1023".

Then Masako YAMADA is stored in a relation called *buffer relation* like what is shown in Fig. 9. The buffer relation will eventually hold a sample at the end of step 1. k, which is the number of tuples in the buffer relation, is defined as an *integer* which is equal to $n \times r$ where r, the redundancy factor, is a real number specified by the user. k is purposely made to be r times greater than n so that we can still obtain a sample of at least n number of tuples from the buffer relation after avoiding similar tuples. r must be greater than 1 and the user can set it to, for example, 1.2 to obtain enough tuples to form a sample.

After that, unlike the DSK(S) method which discards the information of Masako YAMADA's ancestors, we make use of *magic*(Masako YAMADA) to find the total number of ancestors of each x where $x \in$ *magic*(Masako YAMADA) = {Taro YAMADA, Toru YAMADA, Keiko YAMADA, ...}

Taro YAMADA in *magic*(Masako YAMADA) is first examined and the total

Variable	Patient
*selected_tuple*₁	Masako YAMADA
*selected_tuple*₂	Masako YAMADA
*selected_tuple*₃	Masako YAMADA
⋮	⋮
*selected_tuple*ᵢ	Masako YAMADA
⋮	⋮
*selected_tuple*ₖ	Masako YAMADA

Fig. 9. Selected patients after examining the first patient, Masako YAMADA.

Variable	Patient
*selected_tuple*₁	Taro YAMADA
*selected_tuple*₂	Masako YAMADA
*selected_tuple*₃	Masako YAMADA
⋮	⋮
*selected_tuple*ᵢ	Taro YAMADA
⋮	⋮
*selected_tuple*ₖ	Masako YAMADA

Fig. 10. Selected patients after examining Taro YAMADA.

number of ancestors, t, of Taro YAMADA is calculated. Then, for each variable from $selected\_tuple_1$ to $selected\_tuple_k$, modification of the content is determined by the following probability.

$$selected\_tuple_i = \begin{cases} selected\_tuple_i & \text{; with probability } \frac{scanned\_tuples}{scanned\_tuples+t} \\ \text{Taro YAMADA} & \text{; with probability } \frac{t}{scanned\_tuples+t} \end{cases}$$

The variable $scanned\_tuples$ is also updated by incrementing it by t. Assuming that t for Taro YAMADA is 255, $scanned\_tuples$ will be incremented to 1278 ($= 1023 + 255$) and we may obtain something like Fig. 10.

For the rest of the patients in $magic$(Masako YAMADA), variables $selected\_tuple_1$ to $selected\_tuple_k$ and $scanned\_tuples$ are updated accordingly until every patient in $magic$(Masako YAMADA) has been examined (see Fig. 11). We then store the elements of $magic$(Masako YAMADA) in a relation called *cache relation* (see Fig. 12). The cache relation tells us who have already been examined and should not be examined again.

After we have finished examining the first patient and the elements of its magic set, we go to the second patient, Taro YAMADA. We first have to check to see whether Taro YAMADA is in the cache relation. Since he is in there, we do not have to find his ancestors nor update the buffer relation. We just skip Taro YAMADA and delete Taro YAMADA from the cache relation because he will not appear later when we go further down the view and we thus do not need to check for his existence again in the cache relation.

The third patient, Shigeo YAMADA, is not in the cache relation. Therefore, we have to find his magic set and his ancestors and update the buffer relation.

Variable	Patient
selected_tuple$_1$	Taro YAMADA
selected_tuple$_2$	Masako YAMADA
selected_tuple$_3$	Toru YAMADA
⋮	⋮
selected_tuple$_i$	Keiko YAMADA
⋮	⋮
selected_tuple$_k$	Masako YAMADA

Fig. 11. Selected patients after examining all the elements of *magic*(Masako YAMADA).

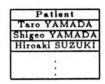

Patient
Taro YAMADA
Shigeo YAMADA
Hiroaki SUZUKI
⋮

Fig. 12. A cache relation

We then proceed to examine all the elements in the magic set of Shigeo YA-MADA. For elements which are already in the cache relation, we neither find their ancestors nor update the buffer relation. They are simply deleted from the cache relation. For elements which are not in the cache relation, we use *magic*(Shigeo YAMADA) to find their ancestors, update the buffer relation and store the elements in the cache relation for future references.

The above process is repeated until we reach the last patient of the view. Let us suppose that we have obtained something like Fig. 13 after stage 1 and we have found that there are 100,000 **Patient-Ancestor** relations (*scanned_tuples* = 100000).

At stage 2, for each selected patient, all his or her ancestors are deduced and one of them is randomly selected. The probability that an ancestor is selected is $\frac{1}{t}$ where t is the total number of ancestors. This will give us Fig. 14. From Fig. 14, we only select n number of distinct tuples to form a sample. This can be done by selecting the tuples one by one from top to bottom while ignoring the redundant tuples. For example, from Fig. 14, we may get a sample like Fig. 15, after ignoring redundant **Patient-Ancestor** relations such as the "Masako YAMADA - Toru YAMADA" relation.

If at the end of stage 2, we can find a sample of n number of tuples, then we can pass this sample to step 2 where we try to discovery of characteristic rules is carried out. However, there is a possibility that there are so many overlapping **Patient-Ancestor** relations that we cannot find enough tuples to form a sample. To solve this, we will have to go to stage 3 to find additional tuples.

Suppose we are short of m tuples to form a sample. At stage 3, m patients are selected using the same method as in stage 1 using variables *selected_tuple$_1$* to *selected_tuple$_l$* where l is equal to $m \times r$.

In order to be statistically correct, the total number of ancestors of each

Variable	Patient
$selected\_tuple_1$	Taro YAMADA
$selected\_tuple_2$	Masako YAMADA
$selected\_tuple_3$	Hiroaki SUZUKI
$\vdots$	$\vdots$
$selected\_tuple_k$	Masako YAMADA

Fig. 13. Selected patients at the end of stage 1.

Variable	Patient	Ancestor
$selected\_tuple_1$	Taro YAMADA	Keiko YAMADA
$selected\_tuple_2$	Masako YAMADA	Toru YAMADA
$selected\_tuple_3$	Hiroaki Suzuki	Jiro Suzuki
$\vdots$	$\vdots$	$\vdots$
$selected\_tuple_k$	Masako YAMADA	Toru YAMADA

Fig. 14. Selected patients and their selected ancestors.

patient, t, is reduced by the total number of **Patient-Ancestor** relations that are already in the sample and involve the patient being examined. This means, for example, if there are 10 **Patient-Ancestor** relations in the sample with Taro YAMADA as the attribute value of **Patient**, then when Taro YAMADA is examined, t of Taro YAMADA will be reduced by 10 ($t = t - 10$).

After l patients have been selected, the ancestors of each selected patient is deduced and one of them is randomly selected using the same method of stage 2. Again, to be statistically correct, **Patient-Ancestor** relations which are already in the sample must be avoided. For example, if Taro YAMADA's ancestors are {Toru YAMADA, Keiko YAMADA, ...} and the relation "Taro YAMADA - Keiko YAMADA" is already in the sample, Keiko YAMADA is deleted from the set of ancestors of Taro YAMADA before the selection of ancestor is made.

At the end of stage 3, m number of distinct tuples which are not in the sample are selected from l number of **Patient-Ancestor** relations and inserted into the sample. There is a possibility that a sample with n number of **Patient-Ancestor** relations still cannot be obtained after stage 3. In this case, we will have to execute stage 3 again until we obtain n number of **Patient-Ancestor** relations.

Finally, the sample obtained at step 1 is passed on to step 2. At step 2 characteristic rules are discovered using the attribute-oriented algorithm. Depending on the attribute threshold and the table threshold values set by the user, the characteristic rules in relevance to **Patient** and **Ancestor** can be something like Fig. 4.

Summarizing the DSK(ST) method, we can obtain the following algorithm:

Algorithm 2. Discovery of characteristic rules using the DSK(ST) method.

Input. (i) A set of concept hierarchies, (ii) a set of attribute thresholds, (iii) a table threshold, (iv) an intensional database, (v) an extensional database, (vi) r, the redundancy factor (positive real number), and (vi) n, the number of tuples to obtain to form a sample.
Output. A set of characteristic rules of the deduced facts.

Method.

Patient	Ancestor
Taro YAMADA	Keiko YAMADA
Masako YAMADA	Toru YAMADA
Hiroaki Suzuki	Jiro Suzuki
.	.
.	.
Tadashi IZUMI	Jun IZUMI

Fig. 15. A sample obtained after stage 2.

1. Collect the set of task-relevant data from the extensional database by a database query.
2. Create a view v of the attributes which bind the arguments of IDB predicates used in deduction from the set of task-relevant data.
3. Initialize variable $scanned\_tuples$ to zero.
4. **begin**
   for each tuple s in the view v do {
      if s is in the cache relation C
      then delete s from C,
      else do {
         find $magic(s)$,
         Examine$(s, magic(s))$,
         $magic\_temp = magic(s)$,
         for each element u in $magic(s)$ do {
            if u is in C
            then do {
               delete u from C,
               delete u from $magic\_temp$ }
            else Examine$(u, magic(u))$ }
         $C = C \cup magic\_temp$ }
      }
   end.
   Examine$(z, magic)$ {
      use $magic$ to calculate t, the total number of tuples that can be deduced from z,
      if $z = x$ of the "$x - y$" pairs already in the sample
      then $t = t$ - the number of "$x - y$" pairs where $z = x$,
      delete the deduced tuples of z,
      update the contents of each variable $selected\_tuple_i$ where $i = 1, 2, ..., n \times r$ using the
      following formula
      $$selected\_tuple_i = selected\_tuple_i \; ; \text{ with probability } \frac{scanned\_tuples}{scanned\_tuples + t} \text{ or}$$
      $$selected\_tuple_i = z \qquad\qquad ; \text{ with probability } \frac{t}{scanned\_tuples + t}$$
      $scanned\_tuples = scanned\_tuples + t$ }
   }
5. **begin**
   for the content x of each $selected\_tuple_i$ $(i = 1, 2, ..., n \times r)$ do {
      Perform deduction,
      if deduction result $d = y$ of the "$x - y$" pairs already in the sample
      then remove d from D, the set of deduction results,
      randomly select a deduction result y from D,
      form an "$x - y$" pair and replace $selected\_tuple_i$ with the "$x - y$" pair }
   end.
6. Select n number of distinct (ignore redundant pairs) "$x - y$" pairs from $selected\_tuple_i$ and append them to relation Q.
7. if n number of distinct "$x - y$" pairs cannot be obtained,
   then do step 3 and step 6 to obtain additional pairs, setting n to the number of pairs needed
   until n number of distinct "$x - y$" pairs have been obtained.
8. Generalize relation Q according to the set of attribute thresholds, the table threshold and the set of concept hierarchies provided.
9. Present the generalized relation as a set of characteristic rules with two additional attributes, Count and Percentage.

The following theorem shows that the distribution of the sample obtained by the DSK(ST) method is the same as the distribution of the sample obtained by the method used in the example in section 2.

Theorem 2 *The distribution of a sample obtained by the DSK(ST) method from deduction results D is the same as the distribution of a sample obtained by random sampling from D.*

Proof sketch. Assuming that the total number of tuples of D is S, the probability that a tuple is sampled is $\frac{1}{S}$. Using the DSK(ST) method, the probability p_1 that the ath tuple in the buffer relation will be selected at the end of step 4 in Algorithm 2 is shown below. In the equation, t_a is the number of deduction results of the ath tuple and $scanned\_tuples$ is the number of tuples that have been scanned until the $(a-1)th$ tuple.

$$p_1 = \frac{t_a}{scanned\_tuples + t_a} \times \frac{scanned\_tuples + t_a}{scanned\_tuples + \sum_{i=a}^{a+1} t_i} \times \cdots$$
$$\times \frac{scanned\_tuples + \sum_{i=a}^{k-2} t_i}{scanned\_tuples + \sum_{i=a}^{k-1} t_i} \times \frac{scanned\_tuples + \sum_{i=a}^{k-1} t_i}{scanned\_tuples + \sum_{i=a}^{k} t_i}$$
$$= \frac{t_a}{scanned\_tuples + \sum_{i=a}^{k} t_i} = \frac{t_a}{S}$$

At step 5, a deduction results of the ath tuple will be selected with the probability $\frac{1}{t_a}$. Therefore, we can prove that a deduced fact is selected with the probability p_2 where

$$p_2 = \frac{t_a}{S} \times \frac{1}{t_a} = \frac{1}{S}.$$
□

5   Comparisons

We can compare the DSK method, the DSK(T) method, the DSK(S) method and the DSK(ST) method in terms of the accuracy of the characteristic rules discovered, the speed of discovery, the amount of storage needed in the process of discovery, and the ease of implementation. Because of page limitation, we only mention briefly the comparison results.

The distribution of the sample obtained by any of the four methods is the same as the distribution of the sample obtained by random sampling. Therefore, they have the same accuracy.

In terms of speed, the DSK(T) method is the fastest. The DSK(ST) method has to do more complex processing than the DSK(T) method and is therefore the second fastest. The third fastest method is the DSK method. The slowest method is the DSK(S) method. However, it should be noted that the speed improvement of the DSK(T) method and the DSK(ST) method is accomplished by narrowing the problem domain of the DSK method and the DSK(S) method.

The DSK(S) method uses the least amount of memory. It is followed by the DSK(ST) method, the DSK method and the DSK(T) method. An interesting relation between memory usage and accuracy exists in the case where the amount of available memory is fixed. The method which uses less memory can collect a larger sample and this can increase the accuracy of the characteristic rules

In terms of ease of implementation, the DSK method is the easiest to implement. The hardest to implement method is the DSK(ST) method. The DSK(S) method and the DSK(T) method lie in between and they are equally complex and equally hard to implement.

Method	DSK	DSK(S)	DSK(T)	DSK(ST)
Accuracy	A	A	A	A
Speed of discovery*	B	B	A	A-
Memory usage‡	B	A	B	A-
Implementation	A	B	B	C

* : When the IDB predicates involved have 3 or more arguments, the speed decreases.
‡ : When the IDB predicates involved have 3 or more arguments, memory usage increases.

Fig. 16. Qualitative comparisons among the four methods.

The characteristics of the four methods are summarized in Fig. 16. From the table, we can see that each method has its own unique advantage. The DSK method is best when fast implementation is needed. The DSK(S) method and the DSK(T) method is good for saving space and time respectively. The DSK(ST) method saves both space and time.

6 Conclusion

In this paper, we have proposed the DSK(T) method and the DSK(ST) method that improve the DSK method and the DSK(S) method in terms of speed. The two methods use our proposed sampling method, magic sampling, to achieve the improvement in speed.

Qualitative comparisons among four methods, the DSK method, the DSK(S) method , the DSK(T) method, and the DSK(ST) method have been made and the role of each method has been pointed out. We feel that quantitative comparisons based on actual experiments are still needed to verify and to provide rigorous comparisons. Furthermore, investigation to see whether these methods can be further improved is still needed.

Other than characteristic rules, we think that discovering association rules [1, 2] and classification rules [7, 11] from large amount of deduction results are also useful and should be further investigated. As the generation of random sample in the DSK(T) method and the DSK(ST) method are not tightly coupled with the attribute-oriented algorithm used, modifications can be easily made to accomodate other data mining algorithms. Furthermore, possibilities of further improvements when using other query processing strategies should also be investigated.

We have used a typical example of analyzing the data of patients and their ancestors to find hereditary allergies in this paper. Apart from the medical field, the methods proposed are also useful in facilitating advanced analysis of data in other fields such as in anthropology and sociology to analyze the diet of people of the *same generation* [4] and their ancestors, and in fault analysis systems and circuit simulation systems where expert systems are involved.

References

1. R. Agrawal, T. Imielinski, and A. Swami, "Mining Association Rules between Sets of Items in Large Databases," *Proc. of the ACM SIGMOD International Conference on Management of Data*, vol. 22, no. 2, pp. 207-216, 1993.

2. R. Agrawal and R. Srikant, "Fast Algorithms for Mining Association Rules," *Proc. of the 20th VLDB Conference*, pp. 487-499, 1994.

3. F. Bancilhon, D. Maier, Y. Sagiv, and J. D. Ullman, "Magic Sets and Other Strange Ways to Implement Logic Programs," *Proc. of the fifth ACM SIGMOD-SIGACT Symposium on Principles of Database Systems*, pp. 1-15, 1986.

4. F. Bancilhon and R. Ramakrishnan, "An Amateur's Introduction to Recursive Query Processing Strategies," *Proc. of ACM SIGMOD'86*, vol. 15, no. 2, pp. 16-52, 1986.

5. J. Barwise and J. Etchemendy, *The Language of First-order Logic*, 3rd Edition, Revised and Expanded, CSLI, 1992.

6. C. Beeri and R. Ramakrishnan, "On the Power of Magic," *Proc. of the sixth ACM SIGMOD-SIGACT Symposium on Principles of Database Systems*, pp. 269-283, 1987.

7. Y. Cai, N. Cercone, and J. Han, "Attribute-Oriented Induction in Relational Databases," in *Knowledge Discovery in Databases*, G. Piatetsky-Shapiro and W. J. Frawley (Eds.), AAAI Press/The MIT Press, pp. 213-228, 1991.

8. U. M. Fayyad, G. Piatetsky-Shapiro, and P. Smyth, "From Data Mining to Knowledge Discovery: An Overview," in *Advances in Knowledge Discovery and Data Mining*, U. M. Fayyad, G. Piatetsky-Shapiro, P. Smyth, and R. Uthurusamy (Eds.), AAAI Press / The MIT Press, pp. 1-34, 1996.

9. W. J. Frawley, G. Piatetsky-Shapiro, and C. J. Matheus, "Knowledge Discovery in Databases: An Overview," in *Knowledge Discovery in Databases*, G. Piatetsky-Shapiro and W. J. Frawley (Eds.), AAAI Press / The MIT Press, pp. 1-27, 1991.

10. C. Goh, M. Tsukamoto, and S. Nishio, "Knowledge Discovery in Deductive Databases with Large Deduction Results: The First Step," *IEEE Trans. on Knowledge and Data Engineering*, vol. 8, no. 6, pp. 952-956, 1996.

11. J. Han, Y. Cai, and N. Cercone, "Knowledge Discovery in Databases: an Attribute-Oriented Approach," *Proc. of the 18th VLDB Conference*, pp. 547-559, 1992.

12. J. Han, Y. Cai, and N. Cercone, "Data-Driven Discovery of Quantitative Rules in Relational Databases," *IEEE Trans. on Knowledge and Data Engineering*, vol. 5, no. 1, pp. 29-40, 1993.

13. J. Han, Y. Fu, Y. Huang, Y. Cai, and N. Cercone, "DBLearn: A System Prototype for Knowledge Discovery in Relational Databases," *Proc. of ACM SIGMOD'94*, vol. 23, no. 2, pp. 516, 1994.

14. S. Nishio, H. Kawano, J. Han, "Knowledge Discovery in Object-Oriented Databases: The First Step," *Proc. of the AAAI Knowledge Discovery in Databases Workshop 1993*, pp. 299, 1993.

15. H. Kawano, K. Sonoo, S. Nishio, and T. Hasegawa, "Accuracy Evaluation of Rules Derived from Sample Data in VLKD," *Proc. of the ORSA/TIMS Joint National Meeting*, p.144, Anaheim, California, U.S.A., Nov.3-6, 1991.

A Heuristic Method for Correlating Attribute Group Pairs in Data Mining

Chua Eng Huang Cecil[1], Roger H.L. Chiang[1], and Ee-Peng Lim[2]

[1] Information Management Research Centre, School of Accountancy and Business,
Nanyang Technological University, Singapore 639798
{p7408153c, ahlchiang}@ntu.edu.sg
[2] Center for Advanced Information Systems, School of Applied Science,
Nanyang Technological University, Singapore 639798
aseplim@ntu.edu.sg

Abstract. Many different kinds of algorithms have been developed to discover relationships between two attribute groups (e.g., association rule discovery algorithms, functional dependency discovery algorithms, and correlation tests). Of these algorithms, only the correlation tests discover relationships using the *measurement scales* of attribute groups. Measurement scales determine whether order or distance information should be considered in the relationship discovery process. Order and distance information limits the possible forms a legitimate relationship between two attribute groups can have. Since this information is considered in correlation tests, the relationships discovered tend not to be spurious. Furthermore, the result of a correlation test can be empirically evaluated by measuring its significance. Often, the appropriate correlation test to apply on an attribute group pair must be selected manually, as information required to identify the appropriate test (e.g., the measurement scale of the attribute groups) is not available in the database. However, information required for test identification can be *inferred* from the system catalog, and analysis of the values of the attribute groups. In this paper, we propose a (semi-) automated correlation test identification method which infers information for identifying appropriate tests, and measures the correlation between attribute group pairs.

1 Introduction

Many algorithms have been developed to discover the extent that the values of a pair of attribute groups associate with each other. These *relationship discovery* algorithms include algorithms that mine for functional dependencies [13], association rules [1], and correlations [2].

Most of the recently developed algorithms discover relationships between attribute groups without taking into account information such as the measurement scale, or statistical significance of the results. Thus, the relationships discovered by these algorithms are often spurious or erroneous. For example, the support and confidence framework used by association rules may discover relationships that are contrary to the real world situation [3].

One type of information that can assist in relationship discovery is the *measurement scale* of the attribute group. Measurement scales specify the measurement properties (distinctiveness, order, distance, and zero value) in effect on an attribute group. Statisticians recognize four different measurement scales, the nominal, ordinal, interval, and ratio scales [2]. The nominal measurement scale indicates that the values of an attribute group are *distinct*. For example, `Religion` has a nominal measurement scale. All we know about the values 'Catholic', and 'Buddhist' is that they describe different religions. The ordinal measurement scale indicates that the values of an attribute group not only are distinct, but have an *intrinsic order* as well. For example, `School_Ranking` has an ordinal measurement scale. Being the '1st' in school is better than being the '2nd'. The interval measurement scale indicates that values are not only distinct, and have order, but also the distance between the values can be measured. For example, `Date_of_Birth` has an interval measurement scale. Someone born on September 4, 1976 was born 2 days after someone born on September 2, 1976. The ratio measurement scale has all of the properties of the interval measurement scale. In addition, one value of the ratio measurement scale conforms to a 'zero value'. This 'zero value' indicates the absence of the property that the attribute group measures. For example `No_of_Children` is on the ratio scale. If you have 0 children, you have no children.

An example of how measurement scale information is useful in determining the spuriousness of a relationship is given in Table 1. In Table 1, a one-to-one mapping can be established between the values of `Salary`, and `Time_Leave_Home`. This mapping seems to imply that a relationship exists between `Salary`, and `Time_Leave_Home`. However, `Salary`, and `Time_Leave_Home` have the interval measurement scale, and can be treated as continuous. We can therefore expect that a genuine relationship between these two attributes would be a continuous function. However, the Intermediate Value Theorem [16] states that for any continuous function, every value Y between some pair of values B_1 and B_2 will have a corresponding value X between the pair of values A_1, and A_2, where A_1 is associated with B_1, and A_2 is associated with B_2. In Table 1, we see no evidence that the Central Limit Theorem holds. Thus, we can suspect that the relationship between `Salary`, and `Time_Leave_Home` is spurious.

Table 1. An Artificial Relationship

Salary	Time_Leave_Home
10,425.00	7:45
15,492.66	6:30
20,485.42	8:15
15,628.23	7:54
27,154.21	7:05

Correlation tests employ the measurement scale to measure the relationship between two attribute groups. As they exploit the properties of measurement scales, relationships they discover tend to be less spurious than other relationship discovery algorithms which do not exploit this information. This is important, as large databases may contain many spurious relationships. In addition, the results of correlation tests can also be validated by measuring the *significance* of the results. Significance measures the probability that a relationship discovered by the correlation test is a spurious one [2].

However, there are problems with using correlation tests for data mining. These problems include: 1) the identification of the measurement scale of an attribute group, and 2) the need for more information than just the measurement scales to determine the appropriate correlation test. First, to identify the appropriate correlation test, the measurement scales of the attribute groups must be known. For example, one of the correlation tests for interval measurement scales, such as the coefficient of determination should be used to measure the correlation of an attribute group pair with interval measurement scales. The correlation coefficient of an attribute group pair with nominal measurement scales should be calculated using a correlation test such as the phi coefficient. However, because of the large number of attributes in the relation, the data mining specialist cannot be expected to determine the measurement scale for every single attribute group manually.

Also, additional information needs to be derived in order to determine the appropriate correlation test from those usable for each measurement scale. For example, both the phi coefficient, and the contingency coefficient are used on attribute group pairs with nominal measurement scales. However, the phi coefficient should be employed only when both attribute groups have at most two distinct values, and the contingency coefficient should be applied when any attribute group has three or more distinct values. This information can be inferred from the values, length, and data type of the attribute.

Finally, the problem of identifying correlation tests for relationship discovery in data mining is complicated by the need to identify the appropriate correlation tests not only for the individual attribute pairs, but also the attribute group pairs. For example, while the attributes Monthly_Salary, Bonus, Net_Yearly_-Salary, and Taxes may have no strong pair-wise relationships, the combination {Monthly_Salary, Bonus} may correlate strongly with {Net_Yearly_Salary, Taxes}, as the attributes are related to each other through the function Monthly_Salary ×12+ Bonus = Net_Yearly_Salary + Taxes.

Therefore, a (semi-)automatic method should be developed to facilitate determining the appropriate correlation tests. In this paper, we propose and discuss a (semi-)automated correlation test identification method. The result of the appropriate correlation test (i.e. correlation coefficient) measures the strength of the relationship of the attribute group pair. While our correlation test identification method assumes that the database to be mined follows the relational database model, it can be generalized to other database models as well. In this paper, the discussion of our method focuses on the attribute groups of a single relation only.

Problem Definition- Let R be a relation with attributes $A = \{A_1, A_2, \ldots, A_n\}$. $G = 2^A$ is the set of attribute groups. Let $P_{ij} = (g_i, g_j)$ be a relationship between two mutually exclusive attribute groups, i.e. $g_i \in G, g_j \in G, g_i \cap g_j = \emptyset\}$. Given a P_{ij}, calculate the *correlation coefficient* S_{ij} (which determines the strength of the relationship between the attribute groups of the pair). To calculate S_{ij}, we must first identify the appropriate correlation test T for (g_i, g_j).

2   Overview of the Correlation Test Identification Method

Attribute characteristics necessary for determining the appropriate test must be identified. We identify these characteristics and classify them into a set of *representations*. For each attribute, at most one representation should be identified. The representation can be identified by analyzing the instances, data type, and length of each attribute. We assume that the system catalog records the data types of attributes. If the system catalog does not contain information on the length of attributes, this information can be derived from the instances. In addition, the representations of the individual attributes are used to infer the representations of the attribute groups. The two representations of an attribute group pair will then determine the appropriate correlation test used to measure their relationship.

Data instances are used to infer the representation of an attribute. In a large relation, examining all data instances may take too much time. To speed up processing, a sample may be used for analysis as long as that sample is representative. Our method incorporates a formula which estimates the representative sample size.

There are four steps in the correlation test identification method:

Step 1: Take a Representative Sample. A representative sample of the relation is extracted to speed up relationship discovery. The size of the sample is determined based on the acceptable degree of error, and the acceptable probability that this degree of error will be exceeded. The formula for calculating the sample size (Step 1) is discussed in Section 3.

Step 2: Assign Representations to All Attribute Groups. Each attribute is assigned a representation based on the analysis of its data type, length of the attribute, and values. The representations of attributes are then used to determine the representations of attribute groups. The identification of representations for attributes, and attribute groups (Step 2) are discussed in Section 4, and 5 respectively.

Step 3: Select Tests. The attribute groups are paired to form all possible sets of P_{ij}. The representations of the two attribute groups in each pair are then used to identify the most appropriate correlation test. Section 6 discusses the identification of the appropriate correlation tests.

Step 4: Execute and Evaluate the Correlation Test Result. The correlation test is executed, and the result and its significance is analyzed. If the result of the test is strong and significant, it is validated by executing the correlation test on other samples in the same attribute group pair. The evaluation of correlation tests is discussed in Section 7.

3 Identifying a Representative Sample

Most of the time, the relation to be mined will contain a large number of instances. Any examination of all instances in the relation would take a very long time. If a random sample of the data in the relation is extracted, it often will be representative of the original data set. Thus, while mining the *representative* sample is quicker than mining the relation, the result of mining the sample will often be comparable to that of mining the relation.

Our method uses the worst case of the formula for calculating sample size from estimated proportions $n = \frac{p \times (1-p) \times Z(\alpha/2)^2}{\epsilon^2}$ to generate our sample size, where p is a value between 0 and 0.5 which indicates a degree of variability, n is the size of the sample, ϵ is a degree of error, α is a probability this degree of error will be exceeded, and Z is a function describing the area under the standard normal curve [10]. As we do not know the degree of variability, we set p to be the worst case value of 0.5. This formula can be used to estimate sample size in any relation with a large number of instances, as it assumes that the number of instances is *infinite*.

4 Assigning Representations to Individual Attributes

4.1 Representations

To identify the appropriate correlation test for an attribute group pair, we need to know more than just the measurement scale. The measurement scales are subdivided into a set of *representations*, which captures this additional information.

We are not aware of any correlation test which exploits zero value information to measure a relationship. Therefore, we do not differentiate between attribute groups with the ratio and interval measurement scales. For the interval measurement scale, two major characteristics of the data play a major part in determining the appropriate correlation test. First, the various tests for attributes groups with interval measurement scales can only handle attribute groups with certain numbers of attributes. For example, the coefficient of determination requires that of the two attribute groups being compared, one of them contains only one attribute. Second, dates differ from other kinds of attributes with the interval measurement scale, because multiplication, division, exponentiation, etc. cannot be performed on dates. Thus, two date attribute groups $\{X_1, X_2, \dots\}, \{Y_1, Y_2, \dots\}$ can relate to each other only through a linear functional form, i.e. $X_1 \pm X_2 \pm \dots \pm C = Y_1 \pm Y_2 \pm \dots$.

Few correlation tests exist for the ordinal measurement scale, so it is not necessary to further partition it. However, for the nominal measurement scale, special case tests exist which exploit the special characteristics of *dichotomies*. Dichotomies are attribute groups with nominal measurement scales which have only two distinct values. Since dichotomies only have two values, they have characteristics that are different from other nominal attribute groups. For example, it can be assumed that all values in the dichotomy are equidistant. In the dichotomy

Sex with values {M, F}, we can say that $|M - F| = |F - M|$. However, for a non-dichotomy like `Religion`, it cannot be assumed that $|Catholic - Buddhist| = |Buddhist - Moslem|$. We subdivide the nominal measurement scale into two scales, one scale for dichotomies, and one scale for non-dichotomies.

We take these characteristics of the measurement scales into account by partitioning the measurement scales into the following representations:

- MULTI-ATTRIBUTE NUMERIC (MAN)- An attribute group with this representation has an interval measurement scale. This attribute group contains more than one attribute.
- SINGLE-ATTRIBUTE NUMERIC (SAN)- An attribute group with this representation has an interval measurement scale. This attribute group contains only one attribute.
- SINGLE-ATTRIBUTE DATE (SAD)-This is an attribute group which represents temporal data (e.g., The attribute group {Date_of_Birth} is a SAD). This attribute group contains only one attribute.
- MULTI-ATTRIBUTE DATE (MAD)- An attribute group with this representation uses several attributes to describe a temporal 'fact'.
- ORDINAL(ORD.)- The ORDINAL representation indicates that while the values of the attribute group have a ranking order, no information is available to determine the *distance* between the values.
- CATEGORICAL(CAT.)- This representation means that the only measurement property found in the attribute group is distinctness.
- DICHOTOMOUS(DICH.)-Attribute groups with the DICHOTOMOUS representation can only contain two distinct values, e.g., {M, F}, {0, 1} etc.

The measurement scales are partitioned into the following representations: 1) The Interval measurement scale is partitioned into the MAN, SAN, MAD, and SAD representations, 2) The Ordinal measurement scale has the analogous ORDINAL representation, and 3) The Nominal measurement scale is partitioned into the CATEGORICAL and DICHOTOMOUS representations. In this paper, any discussion of a measurement scale applies to all representations with that measurement scale. In addition, when we refer to a NUMERIC representation, we mean the MAN, and SAN representations collectively. When we refer to a DATE representation, we mean the SAD and MAD representations collectively.

4.2 Data Types

The data type of an attribute is useful in determining its representation. However, different RDBMSes use different labels to describe the same data types. For the purpose of this paper, we assume that the following are the data types available in the RDBMS:

- Integers- The values of attributes with this data type differ from each other in increments of at least one unit. For example, the attribute `Years_Of_Service` is often given an Integer data type.

- Decimals - Attributes with this data type may have values which differ from each other by less than one unit. For example, the attribute `Salary` can be given the Decimal data type.
- Date- A data type where user input is restricted to specifying a day, month, and year. For example, `Date_Of_Birth` is often assigned a Date data type.
- String-Each character in this data type may have any value.

4.3 Identifying and Eliminating Representations for Single Attributes

An attribute with a particular data type can only have certain representations. The possible representations of each data type are shown in Table 2. A set of heuristic rules are then applied to the attribute to identify which of the possible representations is the correct one. Many of these heuristic rules have been adapted from rules used in SNOUT [15] to identify measurement scales from survey data.

Table 2. Initially Generated Hypotheses

Type	SAN	SAD	Ordinal	Categorical	Dichotomous
Integer	√	√	√	√	√
Decimal	√	√			
String	√	√	√	√	√
Date		√			

The heuristic rules are listed below. Each heuristic rule uses more information to determine the correct representation than the previous rule. However, the additional information used by each rule is less reliable as compared to information added by the previous rule. Thus, representations identified by an earlier rule can be said to be more accurate than representations identified by a later rule.

1. Attributes with the Date data type have the DATE representation.
2. If the attribute has a possible DICHOTOMOUS representation, and the number of distinct values of the attribute is two or less, the attribute has the DICHOTOMOUS representation. If the number of values is more than two, the attribute can not have the DICHOTOMOUS representation.
3. If the length of the attribute varies across the values, it cannot have the SAD representation.
4. If the values of an attribute with the String data type contains non-numeric characters, then the attribute cannot have the SAN representation.
5. If an attribute does not conform to an accepted date format, it cannot have the SAD representation. For example, an attribute with the instance '231297' might have the date representation, since this instance could mean December 23, 1997. However, if the same attribute had another instance '122397', it could not have the date representation, since both instances could not indicate a date under the same format.

6. If an attribute is longer than nine characters, it cannot have the ORDINAL or CATEGORICAL representations. If an attribute has more than 25 distinct values, it cannot have these two representations either. An attribute with less than 25 distinct values cannot have the SAN representation [15].

7. Attributes with the Integer data type can not have the CATEGORICAL representation if the length of the values is greater than 2. If the difference between the minimum and maximum value of attributes with the Integer data type is greater than 25, it will not have the CATEGORICAL REPRESENTATION. This rule follows as a direct consequence of rule 6. If an attribute with the String data type has only values with characters between '0' and '9', then it must also follow this rule.

8. If the first character of any value of an attribute with the String data type differs from the first character of all other values by 3 or more, (e.g., 'D' differs from 'A' by 3), then the attribute does not have an ORDINAL representation.

9. If an attribute may have both a SAD and a SAN representation, the attribute will not have the SAN representation.
   Justification: The range of values which can indicate a SAD forms only a small proportion of the range of values which can indicate a SAN. If every single value in an attribute falls into the range of values that indicate a SAD, the attribute is more likely to represent a SAD than a SAN.

10. If an attribute can have both an ORDINAL and a CATEGORICAL representation, the attribute cannot have the ORDINAL representation.
    Justification: It is often difficult to identify whether an attribute really has an ORDINAL or a CATEGORICAL representation based on the schema and instance information alone. However, a correlation test designed for attribute groups with CATEGORICAL representations can be correctly used to compare attributes with ORDINAL representations. However, the reverse is not true. By using this rule, we err on the side of caution.

11. Attributes which may have SAD, and ORDINAL, or SAD, and CATEGORICAL representations have the SAD representation. The reasoning in this rule is similar to that of rule 9.

After an attribute has been processed using these rules, it is possible for it to have no representation. This indicates that the attribute can not be analyzed using correlation tests. After the system has discovered the representations for the individual attributes, the data mining specialist may review the results, and change any representation he or she deems incorrect.

5 Identifying Representations For Attribute Groups

The representation for an attribute group which contains only one attribute is the same as the representation of that attribute. The representation for an attribute group containing more than one attribute is determined by consulting Table 3. We discuss some of the counterintuitive derivations of attribute group representations in this section.

Table 3. Representations of Attribute Groups With More Than One Attribute

Attr. Grp 1 \ Attr. Grp 2	MAN	SAN	MAD	SAD	Ord.	Cat.	Dich.
MAN	MAN	MAN	MAD	MAD	N/A	N/A	N/A
SAN	MAN	MAN	MAD	MAD	N/A	N/A	N/A
MAD	MAD	MAD	MAD	MAD	N/A	N/A	N/A
SAD	MAD	MAD	MAD	MAD	N/A	N/A	N/A
Ord.	N/A	N/A	N/A	N/A	Cat.	Cat.	Cat.
Cat.	N/A	N/A	N/A	N/A	Cat.	Cat.	Cat.
Dich.	N/A	N/A	N/A	N/A	Cat.	Cat.	Cat.

An attribute group with the NUMERIC *representation combined with an attribute group with the* DATE *representation produces an attribute group with the* MAD *representation.* This rule reflects the situations when numbers are used to increment or decrement a date. For example, when the attribute group with SAN representation {Project_Duration} is combined with the attribute group with SAD representation {Date_Started} it produces the attribute group {Project_Duration, Date_Started}. The combined attribute group identifies the date the project was completed.

An attribute group with the ORDINAL *representation combined with an attribute group with the* ORDINAL *representation produces an attribute group with the* CATEGORICAL *representation:* Intuitively, the combination of two attribute groups with ORDINAL representations should result in an attribute group with the ORDINAL representation. We do not allow this for two reasons. First, the ordering priority of the two attribute groups is often not self evident. For example, the attribute group {A$_1$, A$_2$} may be ordered as (A$_1$, A$_2$) or as (A$_2$, A$_1$). Second, we have found no correlation test which allows attribute groups with ORDINAL representations to have more than one attribute. Instead, we downgrade the representation of the combined attribute group to a CATEGORICAL representation. Similarly, an attribute group with an ORDINAL representation is treated as if it had a CATEGORICAL representation when it is combined with attribute groups having INTERVAL representations.

An attribute group with the INTERVAL *representation and an attribute group with the* NOMINAL *representation cannot be automatically combined.* For the two attribute groups to be combined, the attribute group with an INTERVAL representation would have to have its values transformed to values which can be compared using a correlation test for CATEGORICAL, or DICHOTOMOUS representations. It is not possible to perform this transformation automatically.

It is not possible to convert the values of an attribute group with the INTERVAL representation to values acceptable for the DICHOTOMOUS representation, as there are too many distinct values in an attribute group with the INTERVAL representation. While a sample of the instances of an attribute group with the INTERVAL representation does not physically capture all the distinct values, missing values can still be extrapolated from the values present in the sample. For example, while the sample may not have the value 49, the presence of 49 may still be inferred because the values 50 and 48 exist in the sample. "Dichotomization" destroys the notion of distance between values, and thus the inferred values are lost in the process. This would make the sample unrepresentative.

The conversion of an attribute with the INTERVAL representation to one with the CATEGORICAL representation cannot be automatically performed, as the appropriate categorization system, and the appropriate number of categories are often not apparent from an examination of the data. Arbitrary selection of a categorization method may lead to incorrect categorization. If categorization is performed manually, the combined representation of an attribute group with the INTERVAL representation, and one with the CATEGORICAL representation will be CATEGORICAL.

6 Measuring Relationships Between Attribute Groups

Once representations for all attribute groups have been identified, all mutually exclusive attribute groups can then be paired for analysis. Depending on the representation of each attribute group in the pair, one of the tests in Table 4 is selected to measure the correlation of the attribute groups.

Table 4. Tests to Compare Relationships Among Attribute Groups

Repr.	MAN	SAN	MAD	SAD	ORDINAL	CATEGORICAL	DICHOTOMOUS
MAN	Canon. Corr.	Box-Tidwell	Canon. Corr.	Box-Tidwell	MANOVA	MANOVA	Log. Regr.
SAN	Box-Tidwell	Box-Cox	Box-Tidwell	Box-Cox	Spearman	ANOVA	Pt. Biserial
MAD	Canon. Corr.	Box-Tidwell	Canon. Corr.	Pearson Corr.	MANOVA	MANOVA	Log. Regr.
SAD	Box-Tidwell	Box-Cox	Pearson Corr.	Pearson Corr.	Spearman	ANOVA	Pt. Biserial
ORD	MANOVA	Spearman	MANOVA	Spearman	Spearman	Cntgcy. Coeff.	Ordered Log.
CAT	MANOVA	ANOVA	MANOVA	ANOVA	Cntgcy. Coeff.	Cntgcy. Coeff.	Cntgcy. Coeff.
DICH	Log. Regr.	Pt. Biserial	Log. Regr.	Pt. Biserial	Ordered Log.	Cntgcy. Coeff.	Phi Coeff.

Most of the tests described in Table 4 are common and accepted tests for comparing attribute groups with the representations described. They are discussed in most classic statistics textbooks (e.g., [2], [9], [14]).

7 Evaluating the Correlation Tests

Once an appropriate correlation test for a pair of attribute groups has been determined, the test is performed against the representative sample extracted from the instances of the attribute group pair. The test will yield two values, the correlation coefficient, and the statistical significance. The correlation coefficient measures the degree to which the values of one attribute group predict the values of another. The value of the ANOVA which is comparable to the correlation coefficient is the *F-ratio*, which measures the difference in the distribution of interval values associated with each categorical value.

The *statistical significance* indicates the probability that the relationship being discovered occurred as a result of chance. The smaller the significance value, the more certain we are that the correlation test found a genuine relationship.

A maximum significance threshold, and minimum correlation coefficient threshold for each test can be specified by the mining specialist prior to relationship discovery. Only attribute group pairs which have correlation coefficient values above the coefficient threshold, and significance values below the significance threshold will then be confirmed.

Like other kinds of knowledge discovered by data mining, relationships discovered by correlation tests should not be taken as gospel until they are verified and validated. While setting the significance threshold to a low value would reduce the number of discovered relationships that are spurious, some spurious relationships will still be discovered. Furthermore, setting the significance threshold to an extremely low value will cause the method to reject many genuine relationships, thus rendering the method less effective.

The results of correlation tests can be validated empirically in several ways. A quick, and reliable way would be to first re-sample values from the attribute group pair identified as having a strong correlation, and then run the same correlation test again. If repeated tests on different samples produce high correlation coefficients, and low significance values, then we are more certain that a genuine relationship exists between the two attribute groups. Of course, if time permits, the best validation would be to perform the correlation test on *all* the values of the attribute group pair.

8   Conclusion

In this paper, we propose and discuss a heuristic method for identifying correlation tests to measure the relationship between attribute group pairs. We have also discussed how correlation tests can provide information not only on the strength, but also the significance of a relationship. We are currently attempting to extend our research in several directions.

First, are in the process of standardizing the results of the various correlation tests. The possible results of the various correlation tests vary widely. For example, the Spearman's Rho, Box-Tidwell, and Canonical Correlation tests have scores ranging from -1 to 1. The minimum score of the contingency coefficient is 0, but the maximum score varies according to the sample size. The result of the F-ratio has a minimum value of 1, and a theoretically infinite maximum. We cannot expect that an untrained user will be able to interpret these varied scores.

Second, we are attempting to apply this method to the database integration problem. In developing this method, we have noted the similarity between data mining, and the attribute identification problem in database integration. Attribute identification is the sub-problem of database integration which not only deals with identifying equivalent attributes (i.e. attribute equivalence [12]), but sets of attributes as well. Finding representations for attribute identification is a problem of significantly larger scope than finding representations for data mining, since relationships between attribute groups with STRING and KEY representations must also be accounted for. We are currently investigating the applicability of an extended version of our correlation test identification method to the attribute identification problem.

Finally, we are looking for ways to validate our method. As it is difficult to mathematically validate heuristic methods, we are attempting to validate the heuristics employed against real world databases. Currently, we are acquiring a large variety of data sets to validate our method against. Results from preliminary tests on small, publicly available data sets (e.g., [4], [8]) are encouraging. However, further tests still need to be performed.

References

1. R. Agrawal, T. Imielinski, A. Swami. *Mining Association Rules Between Sets of Items in Large Databases.* Proc. of the ACM SIGMOD Conference on Management of Data. pp. 207-216.
2. R.B. Burns. *Introduction to Research Methods - Third Edition.* Addison-Wesley. 1997.
3. S. Brin, R. Motwani, C. Silverstein. *Beyond Market Baskets: Generalizing Association Rules to Correlations.* Proceedings of the 1997 ACM SIGMOD International Conference on Management of Data. 1997. pp. 265-276.
4. T.J. Biblarz, A.E. Raftery. *The Effects of Family Disruption on Social Mobility.* American Sociological Review. 1993.
5. B. Everitt. *Cluster Analysis.* Heinemann Educational Books. 1980.
6. J.E. Freund, R.E. Walpole. *Mathematical Statistics- Fourth Edition.* Prentice-Hall. 1987.
7. J.D. Gibbons. *Nonparametric Methods for Quantitative Analysis (Second Edition).* American Sciences Press Inc. 1985.
8. V. Greaney, and T. Kelleghan. *Equality of Opportunity in Irish Schools.* Dublin: Educational Company. 1984.
9. J.F. Hair Jr., R.E. Anderson, R.L. Tatham, and W.C. Black. *Multivariate Data Analysis with Readings.* Prentice Hall. 1995.
10. D.V. Huntsberger, and P.P. Billingsley. *Elements of Statistical Inference.* Allyn and Bacon Inc. 1987.
11. J.S. Long. *Regression Models for Categorical and Limited Dependent Variables.* Sage Publications. 1997.
12. J.A. Larson, S.B. Navathe, R. Elmasri. *A Theory of Attribute Equivalence in Databases with Application to Schema Integration.* IEEE Transactions on Software Engineering. April 1989. pp. 449-463.
13. H. Mannila, and K.J. Raiha. *Algorithms for Inferring Functional Dependencies From Relations.* Data and Knowledge Engineering. February, 1994. pp. 83-90.
14. J. Neter, W. Wasserman, M.H. Kutner. *Applied Linear Regression Models. 2nd Edition.* Irwin Homewood. 1989.
15. P.D. Scott, A.P.M. Coxon, M.H. Hobbs, R.J. Williams. *SNOUT: An Intelligent Assistant for Exploratory Data Analysis.* Principles of Knowledge Discovery and Data Mining. 1997. pp. 189-199.
16. G.B. Thomas, and R.L. Finney. *Calculus and Analytic Geometry.* Addison-Wesley. 1996.

Incremental Meta-Mining from Large Temporal Data Sets[1]

Tamas Abraham and John F. Roddick

Advanced Computing Research Centre
School of Computer and Information Science,
University of South Australia
The Levels Campus, Mawson Lakes, Adelaide,
South Australia 5095
{abraham, roddick}@cis.unisa.edu.au

Abstract. With the increase in the size of datasets, data mining has become one of the most prevalent topics for research in database systems. The output from this process, the generation of rules of various types, has raised the question of how rules can be considered interesting. We argue that, in many cases, it is the meta-rule that holds the most interest. That is, given a set of known rules about a dataset, it is the confluence of rules relating to a small subset of characteristics that commonly becomes the focus of interest. In earlier work, we investigated the manner in which meta-rules, rules describing rules, could be discovered and used within a data mining system. In this paper we extend this and present an approach that enable meta-rules to be found incrementally. The emphasis of the work is on temporal data mining as we find that temporal data readily lends itself to data mining techniques, however, as can be seen from the paper, the temporal component can easily be abstracted out and the results are thus also applicable in a non-temporal domain.

1   Introduction

Data mining has recently become a common research topic in the field of database systems partly due to the increase in interest in size of datasets, and partly due to the maturity of current database and machine learning technology. The output from this process, the generation of rules of various types, has raised the fundamental question of how the generation (or at least the presentation) of a potentially limitless number of rules can be restricted to those that are in some way *interesting*. We argue that, in many cases, it is the meta-rule that holds the most interest. That is, given a set of known rules about a dataset, it is the confluence of rules relating to a small subset of characteristics that commonly becomes the focus of interest. In earlier work (Abraham and Roddick 1997a) we investigated the manner in which meta-rules - rules describing rules, could be discovered and used within a data mining system. In this paper we extend this and present an approach that enable meta-rules to be found incrementally.

---

[1] This paper is an abstract of a longer Technical Report CIS-98-010 available from the School of Computer and Information Science at the address above.

In this respect, it parallels the incremental data mining work done on normal data although some interesting differences have been found and are discussed.

For many reasons, the emphasis of much of our work (q.v. Rainsford and Roddick 1996; Abraham and Roddick 1997b, 1998b) relates to temporal data mining as we find that temporal data readily lends itself to non-trivial data mining techniques that commonly suggest cause and effect – one of the most useful, yet most difficult connections to make manually. However, as can be seen from the paper, the temporal component can easily be abstracted out and the results are thus also applicable in a non-temporal domain. Our framework includes the following:

♦ Definitions of the elements within the framework (in this case, meta-rules and other supporting components).

♦ Naming conditions that enable the meta-rule mining process to take place (the environment and the existence of pre-compiled rule sets).

♦ Describing the process itself.

Throughout this paper, we will refer to meta-rules as rules that express changes in two or more rule sets possibly compiled by different methods at different times. This concept of examining changes in evolving rule sets is dissimilar to previous efforts such as rule maintenance (Cheung, *et al.* 1996; Cheung, Ng and Tam 1996), which generally do not retain earlier versions of an updated rule, and thus no comparison between new and old versions is possible. The term meta-rule has been chosen to describe the fact that we are constructing rules about already existing rules (or even meta-rules), by way of describing the variation of patterns between rule set layers.

The paper is sub-divided as follows. The remainder of the introduction introduces meta-rules and discusses the meta-rule set base and the definition of difference measures. Section 2 discusses the processing of the meta-rule set base and the meta-mining process itself. This is a synopsis of the work formerly presented in (Abraham and Roddick 1997a) and is included here (and in more detail in (Abraham and Roddick 1998a)) for completeness. Section 3 looks at the applications of meta-rules and meta-mining in a number of different application domains while Section 4 presents a framework for mining evolution patterns in spatio-temporal data.

1.1   Meta-Rules and the Meta-Rule Set Base

Many of the terms used in data mining and knowledge discovery literature have many meanings and a number of terms need to be clarified.

Definition 1. A *rule r* in rule set R on data set D describes a characterisation of the contents of D in an *If A then B with caveat c* format, where A and B are concepts/patterns represented or implied in D and caveat c may be a probability or some other kind of expression indicating rule feasibility. A *meta-rule m* in meta-rule set M on rule set R then describes a characterisation of the contents of R in the same fashion.

As this definition is very general (and can be extended to define meta-meta-rules etc.), we give an interpretation of it for the snapshot data case. By allowing the data set D to be a collection of snapshots $\{D_1, ..., D_n\}$ over the same domain with their corresponding homogenous rule sets compiled into $R = \{R_1, ..., R_n\}$, R_i being the rule set extracted for D_i, $i = 1,...$, n, a meta-rule set $M_{i,j}$ relates to rules belonging to rule set layer pairs (R_i, R_j) of R and will express differences between the two rule set layers forming the pair. The collection of all $M_{i,j}$, $i, j = 1,...$, n, makes up the meta-rule set M over R. This can be viewed as a restriction of the original definition of meta-rules as characterisation (in this case, difference description) is only performed for pairs of selected subsets and not for R as a whole, but it is a convenient and capable way to handle the snapshot nature of the original data.

Definition 2. Given two rule sets R_1 and R_2 of the same rule type, compiled on the same data domain but registered at different times, with set R_2 being for the later time, we define four categories of rule to make up the *meta-rule set base* between R_1 and R_2:
- New Rules. Rules in rule set R_2 that do not themselves or, in some variant (modified) form, appear in R_1.
- Expired Rules. Rules in rule set R_1 that do not themselves or, in a variant form, appear in R_2.
- Unchanged Rules. Rules that appear in both R_1 and R_2 in the same form.
- Changed Rules. Rules that appear in both R_1 and R_2, but in a different form.

Depending on the rule type, the extent of modification necessary to change an existing rule is determined by some predefined difference measure.

2 Processing the Meta-Rule Set Base and the Meta-Mining Process

The new, expired, unchanged and changed rule categories can be obtained by an appropriate separation algorithm and are presented in the same normalised format as the input rule sets, except for the changed category. This happens because the change in a given rule must be explicitly recorded to facilitate later processing. Therefore, rules in the changed category of the meta-rule set base will have an *extended* normalised format, recording both the old and new values of the designated difference measures. For example, for association rules, two new columns are added to the original four to record the antecedent, consequent, old and new confidence and support values. Alternatively, if the interest measures are quantitative and we are only interested in the deviation in the difference measures, the magnitudal change from the original values can be stored instead of new values (or may be omitted altogether). An *altered* normalised form would be used in such cases instead of an extended one. In the association example, columns to be used form a set containing the {antecedent, consequent, confidence and support percentage *deviation*}. Note that this differs from the original format of {antecedent, consequent, confidence and support} in that the confidence and support deviations can be negative as well as positive, while the original confidence and support values are always non-negative.

In processing the categorised meta-rule set base, we mentioned general descriptions, or generalisation as the obvious choice. Alternatives may exist (such as mining associations within each group), but we shall concentrate on the individual generalisation of the four categories in further discussions. Three of these categories (new, expired and unchanged) are in the original normalised rule input format. Processing them can therefore be done in the same fashion. Because the rules are normalised, the contents of each category can be treated as the data source for the particular mining algorithm employed. In addition, if the original rules were derived using some kind of background knowledge, typically conceptual hierarchies, then they can be re-utilised by the algorithm, e.g. the previously mentioned attribute-oriented induction technique of Han, *et al.* (Han, Cai and Cercone 1992). Thus, higher level conceptualisations of the rules in each category can be attained for both the constant rule parts and difference measures. Of course, if no conceptual hierarchies were available at the time of generating the original rule sets, then they may need to be provided before induction can take place.

In the case of the changed rules category, we may employ the same above strategy when extracting general descriptions for the constant rule parts. On the other hand, to measure and generalise change in the difference measures, separate *change magnitude hierarchies* must be introduced. This, in fact, is the area where the most powerful observations can be made.

Whilst meta-rules are capable of expressing the general characteristics of the meta-rule set base categories, some obvious questions remained unanswered in previous sections. Three of these issues are listed below and are discussed in more detail in (Abraham and Roddick 1998).

- **Identification**. A meta-rule, as stated above, relates to rules in different rule sets, or more strictly, different layers of a given rule set. Therefore, it must be identifiable with these rule set layers.

- **Existence**. The four categories in the meta-rule set base may or may not exist for every rule type. For example, spatial dominant generalisation of geo-referenced data, (qv. Lu, Han and Ooi 1993) does not have new or expired rules as rules in both sets relate to the same generalised spatial areas determined by the generalisation thresholds.

- **Feasibility**. In the case of some rule types we may not require the use of meta-rules if the rule sets are small and comparison is easy by other means. A typical example could be the extraction of general descriptions for only a limited number of spatial areas. Association rule sets, on the other hand, are often quite large (Klemettinen, *et al.* 1994), and are therefore one of the possible areas where meta-rule discovery can be most beneficial.

2.1 The Meta-Rule Mining Process

Meta-rule mining is only one component of the process. The typical meta-rule extraction process consists of four steps (Abraham and Roddick 1997a).

- **Rule set generation**. In this step, we select and mine individual snapshots and collect the associated rules into separate rule sets (timestamped for identification). The rules that are generated are commonly of the same rule type, and the same hierarchies for background knowledge, also including possible generalisation thresholds, etc., must be used to ensure full compatibility between the resulting rule set layers.
- **Input preparation**. This is the stage of preparation before meta-rule mining. If necessary, we convert the contents of the snapshot rule set layers into a consistent format to facilitate rule processing.
- **Meta-rule set base generation**. A separation algorithm that takes two rule set layers as input, compares them and produces the four categories of the meta-rule set base: *new*, *retired*, *unchanged* and *changed* rules, some of which may be null.
- **Processing of categories**. The meta-rule mining process is concluded by individually processing each meta-rule set base category to derive general characterisations for the contents of each of the four (or possibly only some selected, e.g. *new* and *expired*) categories. This step is the one that constitutes the second level of abstraction described by the term *meta-rule*.

3 Applying Meta-Rules in Different Domains

In the previous section we concentrated on extracting meta-rules from a number of rule sets compiled on time-stamped data layers. In this section, we demonstrate this process by providing a specific example and discuss modifications to the original concept to accommodate the incremental update of the meta-rule set as the data eventually gets refreshed.

We shall use and extend the example used in (Lu, Han and Ooi 1993), in which temperature data is generalised for regions of British Columbia, Canada. Spatially distributed data collection points are allocated to regions that are obtained by conceptual hierarchy ascension and generalisation thresholds.

Area	*Temperature*
Mid-Central	Hot
...	...
North-Central	Mild
North-Central	Mild
North-Central	Mild
...	...
South-West	Moderate

Table 1 : Generalised region temperatures

For each region, temperature data values are averaged and generalised to higher-level temperature concepts. The resulting table contains (*region, temperature*) pairs with values such as (North-West, mild) and (Mid-Central, hot), see Table 1. Thus, stage 1 of the meta-rule generation process starts with two spatial-data dominant generalisations of the same spatial area, using the same conceptual hierarchies and generalisation thresholds, but for temperature attribute data registered at two different times.

Stage 2 of the meta-rule mining process, input preparation, can be omitted as the rules are expressed in a two-column tabular format by default.

Area	*Temperature*
North-Central	Mild
North-Central	Mild
North-Central	Mild

Area	*Old Temperature*	*New Temperature*
Mid-Central	Hot	Warm
Mid-East	Warm	Moderate
Mid-West	Moderate	Warm
South Central	Mild	Cool
South-East	Warm	Cool
South-West	Moderate	Cool

Table 2: Unchanged and changed generalised temperatures: An example

The next step (Stage 3) is to use a merge-and-split algorithm with the region description being the constant part of the rules and the temperature concept the difference measure. Because we required the use of the same conceptual hierarchies and generalisation thresholds for the regions, this ensures that they remain the same for both data layers, ie. there is a one-to-one correspondence between regions in the two tables. Therefore, there will not be any new and expired rule categories. The unchanged category contains (*region, temperature*) pairs as in Table 1 that have the same temperature concept in both sets, e.g. (Mid-West, mild), while the changed category holds (*region, old temperature, new temperature*) triplets such as (Mid-East, hot, moderately hot), see Table 2, with the total number of entries in the two groups equalling the number of existing generalised regions.

The final step in the meta-rule mining process describes further the contents of these two categories. In the unchanged case, climbing the spatial conceptual hierarchy may merge adjoining regions. This may be done even if the temperatures are different for the merged regions. In this case, the resulting meta-rule may state '*The temperature of the North region remained the same between the surveys*'. In the database, this can be represented by a (*region, temperature set*) pair such as (North, {mild, moderately cold}). Notice that the constancy of the temperature is implied by the membership in the appropriate meta-rule set base category and does not have to be explicitly stated. Furthermore, if the temperature set contains a single entry, the resulting meta-rule can be even more specific, '*The temperature in the North remained mild*'. Similar results can be achieved for the regions in the changed category. Merging them may immediately produce descriptions such as '*The temperature has changed in the South*'. However, investigating the direction of change may further enhance this. For this purpose, rules may be applied to the (*old temperature, new temperature*) pairs, replacing them with concepts such as 'moderate increase', 'steep decline', and so on, that can be associated with each region producing rules like '*The Mid-East experienced a moderate temperature decrease*', in the case of the above example triplet. Furthermore, regions may be merged using a set of change concepts in a similar fashion to the unchanged case, by applying a restriction on the direction of the change. This may produce a database entry such as (South, {moderate decrease, steep decrease}) that can be interpreted as '*The temperature decreased in the South*', after the change values are further generalised.

3.1   Incremental Maintenance

Until now, we have discussed generating meta-rules for snapshot data. The database used for this purpose does not, however, need to use the snapshot model: snapshots can be taken of continuously changing databases at certain time points and mined. In some circumstances, only the rules generated need to be preserved for meta-mining and there may be no need to store the earlier versions of the database itself.

Certain database types (transaction databases, for example) only allow a limited set of operations such as insertion of new records or the reversal of existing records. This makes it relatively easy to keep track of modifications within the database. Clearly, as their contents change, so may the rules that are implied by the data. In order to adjust the rules to reflect the database contents at any given time, the rule generation algorithm could simply be run again. This, however, presents a number of questions. Firstly, when do we run the rule generation algorithm again? Should it be done after each new insertion, or should it wait until a certain threshold is reached? Secondly, is it necessary to re-run the algorithm on the whole data set when only a relatively small number of records may have been inserted (at least, a small number compared to the total number of records)? These questions are addressed by Cheung, *et al.* (1996). Their *rule maintenance* algorithm focuses on the contents of newly inserted data and their effects on already existing rules and reduces processing requirements dramatically.

Another example can be found in Rainsford, *et al.* (Rainsford, Mohania and Roddick 1996), which successfully manages to apply rule maintenance to another data mining technique, in this case, classification. Subsequent work concentrates on enhancing existing algorithms, such as Cheung, Ng and Tam. (1996), to handle multi-level associations, or Cheung, Lee and Kao (1997) to allow maintaining association rules with more versatile changes permitted in the database, such as modifications or deletions. In addition to describing incremental mining algorithms, the question of when it is appropriate to initiate the maintenance process has received attention (Lee and Cheung 1997).

We now discuss the benefits of maintaining meta-rules. The points to be investigated include:

- The possibility of utilising some of the earlier results or develop new techniques to maintain meta-rules;
- The possibility of maintaining meta-rules – at which level will this happen? Is the maintenance restricted to the incremental updates of the underlying rules or can meta-rules be also incrementally maintained?
- If it is possible to maintain meta-rules, is it viable and/or useful to use this method? Can we show that maintaining meta-rules is more efficient than the direct extraction and generation of rules and meta-rules?
- Finally, if all of the above are possible, can an efficient algorithm to perform incremental maintenance of meta-rules be derived?

To answer these questions, we separate our investigation into two parts: the examination of maintaining the rule sets used as input in the meta mining process and the inspection of possible methods to use to maintain the meta-rules themselves.

Initially, it appears that the use of incremental updates for the input rule sets is indeed an option: because snapshots are taken of the same database, only the difference between these snapshots determines the effectiveness of incremental algorithms. This has been extensively studied for association rules in transaction databases with deletions and insertions allowed by Cheung, *et al.* (Cheung, Lee and Kao 1997) (a modification of an existing record can be treated as a deletion followed by an insertion). They have shown that as long as the changes between the data sets do not exceed a certain limit then incremental updating works faster than re-running existing extraction algorithms. This means, that if appropriate measures are installed to trace the number of updates between snapshots, it becomes possible to select the most efficient algorithm to generate the next rule set, be that either an incremental updating technique or re-running the original extraction algorithm.

Figure 1 contrasts changes that occur in data and rules from one time instance to another. The superscript E (expired) has been used to denote data/rules that exist is the earlier sets but not in the later ones. Similarly, the superscript N (new) has been used to denote data/rules that exist in the later sets but not in the earlier ones.

The main difference that can be observed between the data and rule sets for times T_1 and T_2 in the figure is that we must explicitly mark the rules that changed over time. This can be avoided for raw data as any modification can be treated as a deletion followed by an addition. We cannot, however, allow the same for rules, because one of the major benefits of meta-level discoveries lies in inferring regularities of change. Thus, one of the additional tasks of incremental meta-rule maintenance should be the handling of changed rules from one rule set to another.

The aim of maintaining rules from dynamically changing data is to bring the rules describing the data up to date. The database is constantly updated while the rules are extracted only when this is considered to be important, such as significant change in the data or an upcoming scientific analysis. This means that there is normally some difference between the current contents of the rule set and those that are implied within the present data, unless there have not been any changes to the database since the last rule set generation/update. Meta-rules, on the other hand, describe events in the environment for selected time periods, ie. there is a *from* rule set and a *to* rule set, the two sets used to generate one set of meta-discoveries. In other words, a discovery is tied to a certain period of time and when we maintain meta-rules, we need to consider what happens to both the starting and ending rule set of the period to be updated. Meta-rules will always, at least implicitly, reference the two rule sets that are used to generate them, in order to provide the time frame in which the rules are valid. There is a possible exception to this, though, namely those meta-rules that are valid *now*, ie. are extracted between an old and the current rule set, because these latter observations can be viewed as still in the process.

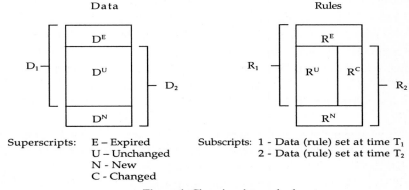

Figure 1: Changing data and rule sets

Figure 2 illustrates some example rule sets and the meta-rule sets that can be generated upon them. Suppose there are some previously compiled rule sets, and a new one is generated. New sets of meta-rules can be generated between this new rule set and any of the previous ones. If there are n previous sets and we add a new one, n new meta-rule sets $M_{i(n+1)}$, $i = 1, ..., n$ can be extracted in all. The following two scenarios exist for creating these meta-rule sets:

a). We extract the meta-rule set for the new and immediately preceding rule sets, ie. $M_{n(n+1)}$. No previous meta information is available for this process, meaning that no incremental procedures can be employed at the meta-level and full extraction needs to be performed. In this kind of meta-mining, the advantage gained can only be in the production of R_{n+1} from R_n, by using incremental rule maintenance.

b). We extract the meta-rule set for the new and older rule sets, $M_{i(n+1)}$, $1 \leq i < n$. In any of these cases, a meta-rule set can already exist between the starting rule set R_i and the old ending rule set R_n. Therefore, it may become possible to use the contents of M_{in} in the production of $M_{i(n+1)}$.

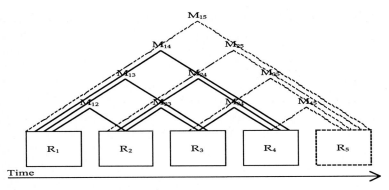

Figure 2: Rule and meta-rule sets

The observation we made in scenario B above presumes that previous meta-rule sets are available. This may not always be the case and depends on the mining strategy employed by the meta-miner. A possible preference might be that meta-rules are mined between an *elected* starting rule set (say R_1 of Figure 2) and the current one. Thus, one new meta-rule set is generated every time the current rule set is updated. In this case, scenario B still applies, as the meta-rule set between the starting rule set and the preceding one is available (for example, if R_5 is the new rule set and we are extracting M_{15}, the meta-rule set M_{14} is available). Problems can arise when in addition to this simplified meta-mining technique we also employ a 'time windowing' approach.

The time windowing approach to incremental rule updates was initially proposed by Rainsford, *et al.* (Rainsford, Mohania and Roddick 1997). Its purpose is to discard some old data during the generation of the current rule set, ensuring that its contents more closely represent the presently prevailing regularities in the environment. This addition to the incremental updating process can be viewed as an improvement on earlier work such as Cheung, *et al.* (1996), who highlight the need for statistically significant amounts of data. The time windowing approach retains this important aspect but maintains that some of the old data should no longer contribute to the current rules. We wish to follow a similar approach in producing meta-rule sets. That is, we would no longer keep meta-rules that span over a very long period of time.

In addition to applying time windowing, we may also request that to justify a meta-rule update we must have an appropriately significant change between the newly generated rule set and the previous one. For example, if a meta-rule set M_{ij} exists and there is very little change observed between rule sets R_j and its current successor R_{j+1}, then there might be very little advantage gained by extracting $M_{i(j+1)}$. User defined thresholds may be used to control this process. For instance, a delta-file can be kept to store rules that have changed since the last meta-rule update, and a threshold (e.g. the percentage of changed rules compared to the total number of rules must exceed a given value) has to be reached to trigger the meta-rule update.

4   Discussions on a Framework for Mining Evolution Patterns in Spatio-Temporal Data

In earlier discussions, we gave a definition for a rule in knowledge discovery terms. The description *If A then B with caveat c* can be easily converted into more appropriate formats used in conjunction with popular data mining techniques, such as generalisation and association. An even simpler description is to express a general rule as a function of the data itself, e.g. *R(X)* where X represents the domain or the data set being mined and *R* is a data mining function. By extrapolating this train of thought, a meta-rule would then be a function of this function, e.g. *M(R(X))*. Using Clausal Form Logic and omitting the uncertainty measure *c* for the moment, a rule can be written as

$$A \Rightarrow B$$

or more specifically,

$$\{p_1, ..., p_m\} \Rightarrow \{q_1, ..., q_n\} \tag{1}$$

where $p_1, ..., p_m$ and $q_1, ..., q_n$ ($n, m \geq 0$) are atomic logical expressions, ie. either true or false values, or predicates with at least an argument each. In a spatial (and hence also spatio-temporal) environment, we can distinguish between three classes of predicates that describe attributes of spatial objects, their location and spatial relationships:

attribute predicates   *a_predicate(o, v)*
positional predicates   *p_predicate(o, v)*
relationship predicates   *r_predicate(o, o')*

where *o* and *o'* denote spatial objects and *v* attribute values or positional references. We treat the first two types in the same way since for our purposes positional information can be managed as another set of attributes. A fourth type of predicate that is introduced by the temporal dimension concerns the existence of objects over time. At any given time,

existential predicates   *e_predicate(o)*

describe the status of object *o* with regards to its presence in the corresponding temporal snapshot of the data.

Suppose that there exists a set of rules about the spatio-temporal environment at time T_1. As data collection continues, at time T_2 another set of rules may be extracted. A simple rule of the form:

$$p \Rightarrow q$$

where *p* and *q* are predicates of the above four classes may change in several different ways. In Table 3 existential, value related and relationship predicates are separated because changes in values and object identities as well as the predicate itself indicate different forms of evolution in a rule. Notice that it is possible to use the same four groups to categorise rule sets at times T_1 and T_2 as has been done while discussing meta-rules. Rows with no explanations in Table 3 contain *new* rules with their *expired* counterparts in the earlier rule set, while the other explanations indicate *changed* rules unless it is explicitly stated that they are *unchanged*.

Predicate	Object	Value	Object	Explanation
U	U	-	-	Unchanged (existential) rule
U	C	-	-	-
U	U	U	-	Unchanged (value) rule
U	U	C	-	Value evolution
U	C	U	-	Object substitution
U	C	C	-	
U	U	-	U	Unchanged (relationship) rule
U	U	-	C	Object substitution
U	C	-	U	Object substitution
U	C	-	C	
C	U	-	-	Existential change
C	C	-	-	
C	U	-	U	Relationship change
C	U	-	C	
C	C	-	U	
C	C	-	C	

Table 3: Changes in rule description over time

It is also possible to observe other types of change in Equation 1. Instead of a variation in the descriptions, the structure of the antecedent or consequent may evolve. Suppose, for instance, that another term is added to the antecedent at time T_2 while the rest of the formula remains intact. Equation 1 can then be written as

$$\{p_1, ..., p_m, p_{(m+1)}\} \Rightarrow \{q_1, ..., q_n\} \tag{2}$$

This equates into a more specific description of the rule, or *specialisation*. For instance, an additional observation can be made regarding the object in the rule. When this is incorporated into the rule, our knowledge about the object is increased and hence becomes more specific. Similarly, if a term is removed from either the antecedent or the consequent, the expression becomes more general, ie. the evolution we observe is a form of *generalisation*.

Another aspect of evolution within a predicate term is the *rate of change* in the attribute value of an object. The multi-valued predicates that can be used are often qualitative (*e.g.* colour can be blue, white, direction can be north, north-east, etc.) and are not immediately quantifiable. It is nevertheless important to note just how much an attribute has changed from one time to another, *ie.* to define the proximity between two predicate values. A range of different norms can be employed to define distances between values, both for numeric attributes and qualitative descriptions. An example for the qualitative attribute colour is to convert colour names to numbers on the hue palette using an auxiliary reference look-up table that uses a 360 degree disk representation for all allowed colours and take the difference of the angles corresponding to two colours.

In spatial and spatio-temporal information systems quantitative (and sometimes derived qualitative) data often contain measurement errors making subsequent observations for the same set of objects vary. Thus, rules that may indicate minor change over time should be treated with care if change does not exceed some given thresholds. In addition, change in a particular attribute may not be considered interesting. For example, a drop in the average temperature from summer to winter may be sizeable but not necessarily interesting. The determination of the attributes where change carries a high level of significance hence remains an important aspect of spatio-temporal evolution mining. We propose that the specification of these attributes be, at least partially, the a user responsibility since their relative importance is commonly application dependent. Moreover, the attributes relevant to interesting discoveries may change over time, and therefore need to be maintained between data mining processes. This observation is underlined by a discussion in (Silberschatz and Tuzhilin 1996) which highlights the relevance of objective and subjective interestingness measures and their tendency to evolve over time.

Furthermore, when an object parameter changes in a predicate expression, it may not necessarily imply a drastic deviation from the original rule. In a spatio-temporal environment, objects are not just related by spatial relationships and their positional characteristics, but depending on the model employed they often belong in a class structure of types. This means that when an object is replaced in a predicate by one of its descendants in a particular class structure, the rule becomes more *refined*, because more information is available about the object type. Conversely, if an object is replaced by one of its ancestors, the description becomes *coarser*. A paradox of these changes is that the particularity of an object and its support are inversely related, *ie.* the more refined a description the less likely that the corresponding object occurs in the database and hence some of the strength of the associated rules may diminish. On the other hand, other types of uncertainty measures, such as confidence values, may be unaffected or even improved.

In summary, a spatio-temporal rule extracted by data mining techniques can change in time, space, description and structure. If a rule contains an antecedent and a consequent, there are in total 2^8 possible combinations, some of which are not valid. For example, it is safe to require that both sides of the rule have to change in time in order to constitute any kind of change in the rule. On the other hand, if a rule does not change in time, then no other component should be allowed to change either. This "*no alternate realities*" requirement does not, however, exclude that two rules in a particular rule set cannot be very similar. For instance, it is possible that rule A of the set is a refined version of another rule B of the set, but as far as their membership in the rule set goes, they are considered different. For the remaining combinations, most constitute change to a degree where rules would be regarded as new and not altered, leaving only a small number of options interesting from the knowledge discovery point of view (although the fact that a rule has not changed but was replaced entirely could be an interesting observation in itself).

This paper outlines the work in progress of a part of a research project investigating the applicability of data mining in a variety of domains. It is our contention that many of the useful aspects of data mining are in the mining of the rules themselves and we argue that meta-mining can yield useful results in this area.

Further work is progressing in the areas of temporal, spatio-temporal, incremental and meta-mining and results to date can be found at http://www.cis.unisa.edu.au.

5 References

Abraham, T. and Roddick, J.F. 1997a. 'Discovering Meta-rules in Mining Temporal and Spatio-Temporal Data'. In *Proc. Eighth International Database Workshop*, 30-41.

Abraham, T. and Roddick, J.F. 1997b. 'Research issues in spatio-temporal knowledge discovery'. In *Proc. SIGMOD'97 Workshop on Data Mining*, 85.

Abraham, T. and Roddick, J.F. 1998a. 'Incremental meta-mining from large temporal data sets: extended report'. Technical Report University of South Australia.

Abraham, T. and Roddick, J.F. 1998b. 'Opportunities for knowledge discovery in spatio-temporal information systems'. *Australian Journal of Information Systems.* 5(2):3-12.

Cheung, D.W., Han, J., Ng, V.T. and Wong, C.Y. 1996. 'Maintenance of Discovered Association Rules in Large Databases: An Incremental Updating Technique.'. In *Proc. International Conference on Data Engineering (ICDE'96)*, New Orleans, Louisiana, USA.

Cheung, D.W., Lee, S.D. and Kao, B. 1997. 'A General Incremental Technique for Maintaining Discovered Association Rules'. In *Proc. Fifth International Conference on Database Systems for Advanced Applications*, Melbourne, Australia.

Cheung, D.W., Ng, V.T. and Tam, B.W. 1996. 'Maintenance of Discovered Knowledge : A Case in Multi-level Association Rules'. In *Proc. Second International Conference on Knowledge Discovery and Data Mining (KDD-96)*, Portland, Oregon. AAAI Press, Menlo Park, California. 307-310.

Han, J., Cai, Y. and Cercone, N. 1992. 'Knowledge Discovery in Databases: An Attribute-Oriented Approach'. In *Proc. Eighteenth International Conference on Very Large Data Bases*, Vancouver, Canada.

Klemettinen, M., Mannila, H., Ronkainen, P., Toivonen, H. and Verkamo, A.I. 1994. 'Finding interesting Rules from Large Sets of Discovered Association Rules'. In *Proc. Third International Conference on Information and Knowledge Management*, Gaithersburg, Maryland. ACM Press. 401-407.

Koperski, K. and Han, J. 1995. 'Discovery of Spatial Association Rules in Geographic Information Databases'. In *Proc. Fourth International Symposium on Large Spatial Databases*, Maine. 47-66.

Lee, S.D. and Cheung, D.W. 1997. 'Maintenance of Discovered Association Rules: When to update?'. In *Proc. 1997 SIGMOD Workshop on Research Issues on Data Mining and Knowledge Discovery (DMKD'97)*, Tucson, Arizona. 51-58.

Lu, W., Han, J. and Ooi, B.C. 1993. 'Discovery of General Knowledge in Large Spatial Databases'. In *Proc. 1993 Far East Workshop on GIS (IEGIS 93)*, Singapore. 275-289.

Rainsford, C.P., Mohania, M.K. and Roddick, J.F. 1996. 'Incremental maintenance techniques for discovered classification rules'. In *Proc. International Symposium on Cooperative Database Systems for Advanced Applications*, Kyoto, Japan. World Scientific Publishing Co. 302-305.

Rainsford, C.P., Mohania, M.K. and Roddick, J.F. 1997. 'A temporal windowing approach to the incremental maintenance of association rules'. In *Proc. Eighth International Database Workshop (IDW'97)*, 78-94.

Rainsford, C.P. and Roddick, J.F. 1996. 'Temporal data mining in information systems: a model'. In *Proc. Seventh Australasian Conference on Information Systems*, Hobart, Tasmania. 2:545-553.

Silberschatz, A. and Tuzhilin, A. 1996. 'What Makes Patterns Interesting in Knowledge Discovery Systems'. *IEEE Trans. Knowl. and Data Eng.* 8(6):970-974.

On the Suitability of Genetic-Based Algorithms for Data Mining*

Sunil Choenni

Nat. Aerospace Lab., NLR, P.O. Box 90502, 1006 BM Amsterdam, The Netherlands,
and
Univ. of Twente, P.O. Box 217, 7500 AE Enschede, The Netherlands
email: choenni@nlr.nl

Abstract. Data mining has as goal to extract knowledge from large databases. A database may be considered as a search space consisting of an enormous number of elements, and a mining algorithm as a search strategy. In general, an exhaustive search of the space is infeasible. Therefore, efficient search strategies are of vital importance. Search strategies on genetic-based algorithms have been applied successfully in a wide range of applications. We focus on the suitability of genetic-based algorithms for data mining. We discuss the design and implementation of a genetic-based algorithm for data mining and illustrate its potentials.

1 Introduction

Research and development in data mining evolves in several directions, such as association rules, time series, and classification. The latter field has our attention. We have developed an algorithm to classify tuples in groups and to derive rules from these groups. In our view, a user formulates a mining question and the algorithm selects the group(s) that satisfy this question. For example, in an insurance environment, a question may be to identify persons with (more than average) chances of causing an accident. Then, the algorithm searches for the (group) profiles of these persons.

In general, the search spaces that should be inspected in order to find answers on mining questions are very large, making exhaustive search infeasible. So, heuristic search strategies are of vital importance to data mining. Genetic algorithms, which are heuristic search strategies, have been successfully used in a wide range of applications. A genetic algorithm is capable of exploring different parts of a search space [10].

In this paper, we discuss the applicability of a genetic-based algorithm to the search process in data mining. We show how a genetic algorithm can be suited for data mining problems. In our approach, a search space consists of expressions. An expression is a conjunction of predicates and each predicate is defined on a database attribute. Initially, a random number of expressions, called initial population, is selected. Then, the initial population is manipulated

---

* This research has been sponsored by the Dutch Ministry of Defense.

by applying a number of operations. The best individuals are selected to form the next generation and the manipulation process is repeated until no significant improvement of the population can be observed.

In general, data mining algorithms require a technique that partitions the domain values of an attribute in a limited set of ranges, simply because considering all possible ranges of domain values is infeasible. Suppose that we have an attribute *age* which has a domain between 18 to 65, and an expression of the form *age* **in** $[v_i, v_k]$, in which v_i and v_k are values from the domain of *age*, defining a range of values. The problem is how to choose the values for v_i and v_k. As illustrated in [11], this is in general an NP-complete problem. Our solution to this problem is based on a suitable choice of the mutation operator (see Section 3.3). Furthermore, we have chosen a representation for individuals that seamlessly fits in the field of databases. The same holds for the manipulation operators and the function to rank individuals (fitness function). The fitness function discussed in this paper is close to our intuition and gives rise to a speed up of the optimization process. Based on our approach, we have implemented a (prototype) tool for data mining, and have performed a preliminary evaluation. The results will be presented in this paper.

A genetic approach has been proposed in [2] to learn first order logic rules and in [7] a framework is proposed for data mining based on genetic programming. However, the authors neither come up with a implementation nor with experiments. The effort in [2] is focussed towards machine learning, and the important data mining issue of integration with databases is superficially discussed. The effort in [7] describes a framework for data mining based on genetic programming, and stresses on the integration of genetic programming and databases. However, an elaborated approach to implement and evaluate the framework is not presented. Other related research has been reported in [1, 8, 9]. While in [8, 9] variants of a hill climber are used to identify the group(s) of tuples satisfying a mining question, the approach in [1] is based on decision trees. However, the problem of partitioning attribute values has not been discussed in these efforts. We note that a genetic-based algorithm has, by nature, a better chance to escape from a local optimum than a hill climber.

The remainder of this paper is organized as follows. In Section 2, we outline some preliminaries and problem limitations. In Section 3, we identify the issues that play a role in genetic-based algorithms and adapt them in a data mining context. In Section 4, we point out a number of rules that may speed up the search process of a genetic-based algorithm. Section 5 is devoted to an overall algorithm for data mining. In Section 6, we discuss the implementation of the algorithm and some preliminary results. Finally, Section 7 contains conclusions and further work.

2 Preliminaries & problem limitations

In the following, a database consists of a universal relation [6]. The relation is defined over some independent single valued attributes, such as $att_1, att_2, ..., att_n$, and is a subset of the Cartesian product $\mathrm{dom}(att_1) \times \mathrm{dom}(att_2) \times ... \times \mathrm{dom}(att_n)$, in which $\mathrm{dom}(att_j)$ is the set of values that can be assumed by attribute att_j. A tuple is an ordered list of attribute values to which a unique identifier (tid) is associated. So, we do not allow missing attribute values. Furthermore, we assume that the content of the database remains the same during the mining process.

An expression is used to derive a relation, and is defined as a conjunction of predicates over some attributes. The length of an expression is the number of attributes involved in the expression. An example of an expression of length 2 is (*age* **in** [19, 24] $\wedge$ *gender* **is** 'male'), representing the males who are older than 18 and younger than 25. An expression with length 1 is called an *elementary* expression. In this paper, we deal with search spaces that contain expressions.

3 Data Mining with Genetic algorithms

Initially, a genetic algorithm [10] randomly generates an initial population. Traditionally, individuals in the population are represented as bit strings. The quality of each individual, i.e., its fitness, is computed. On the basis of these qualities, a selection of individuals is made (an individual may be chosen more than once). Some of the selected individuals undergo a minor modification, called mutation. For some pairs of selected individuals a random point is selected, and the substrings behind this random point are exchanged; this process is called cross-over. The selected individuals, modified or not, form a new population and the same procedure is applied to this generation until some predefined criteria are met.

In the following, we discuss the issues that play a role in tailoring a genetic algorithm for data mining. Section 3.1 is devoted to the representation of individuals and Section 3.2 to the fitness function. Finally, in Section 3.3, we discuss the two operators to manipulate an individual.

3.1 Representation

An individual is regarded as an expression to which some restrictions are imposed with regard to the the notation of elementary expressions and the number of times that an attribute may be involved in the expression. The notation of an elementary expression depends on the domain type of the involved attribute. If there exists no ordering relationship between the attribute values of an attribute *att*, we represent an elementary expression as follows: *expression* := *att* **is** $(v_1, v_2,...,v_n)$, in which $v_i \in \mathrm{dom}(att)$, $1 \leq i \leq n$. In this way, we express that an attribute *att* assumes one of the values in the set $\{v_1, v_2,...,v_n\}$. If an ordering relationship exists between the domain values of an attribute, an elementary expression is denoted as *expression* := *att* **in** $[v_i, v_k]$, $i \leq k$, in which $[v_i, v_k]$ represents the values within the range of v_i and v_k. An attribute is allowed to participate at most once in an individual. This restriction is imposed to prevent the exploration of expressions to which no tuples satisfy. In the following, an expression to which no tuples qualify will be called an *empty* expression. Consider a database in which, among others, the age of persons is recorded. Then, the expression *age* **in** [19,34] $\wedge$ *age* **in** [39,44] represents the class of persons whose

$p_1 = gender$ **is** ('male') $\wedge$ age **in** [19,34]
$p_2 = age$ **in** [29,44] $\wedge$ $town$ **is** ('Almere', 'Amsterdam', 'Weesp') $\wedge$ $category$ **is** ('lease')
$p_3 = gender$ **is** ('male') $\wedge$ age **in** [29,34] $\wedge$ $category$ **is** ('lease')
$p_4 = gender$ **is** ('female') $\wedge$ age **in** [29,40] $\wedge$ $category$ **is** ('lease') $\wedge$ $price$ **in** [50K, 100K]
$p_5 = gender$ **is** ('male') $\wedge$ $price$ **in** [20K,45K]

Fig. 1. Example of a population

age is between 19 and 34 as well as between 39 and 44. It should be clear that no persons will satisfy this expression, since *age* is a single-valued attribute.

In the following, a population is defined as a set of individuals. As a running example, we use a database that keeps record of cars and their owners. This artificial database consists of the following universal relation[2]: *Ex(gender, age, town, category, price, damage)*, in which the attributes *gender, age*, and *town* refer to the owner and the remainder of the attributes refer to the car. Attribute *category* records whether a car is leased or not, and *damage* records whether a car has been involved in an accident or not. An example of a population consisting of 5 individuals is given in Figure 1.

3.2 Fitness function

A central instrument in a genetic algorithm is the fitness function. Since a genetic algorithm is aimed to the optimization of such a function, this function is one of the keys to success. Consequently, a fitness function should represent all issues that play a role in the optimization of a specific problem. Before enumerating these issues in the context of data mining, we introduce the notion of cover.

Definition 1: Let D be a database and p an individual defined on D. Then, the number of tuples that satisfies the expression corresponding to p is called the cover of p, and is denoted as $\|\sigma_p(D)\|$. The set of tuples satisfying p is denoted as $\sigma_p(D)$.

Note that p can be regarded as a description of a class in D and $\sigma_p(D)$ summarizes the tuples satisfying p. Within a class we can define subclasses. In the following, we regard classification problem as follows: *Given a target class t, search interesting subclasses, i.e., individuals, within class t.* We note that the target class is the class of tuples in which interesting knowledge should be searched for. Suppose we want to expose the profiles of risky drivers, i.e., the class of persons with (more than average) chances of causing an accident, from the database *Ex(gender, age, town, category, price, damage)*. Then, these profiles should be searched for in a class that records the characteristics of drivers that caused accidents. Such a class may be described as *damage* = 'yes'.

We feel that the following issues play a role in classification problems.

− The cover of the target class. Since results from data mining are used for informed decision making, knowledge extracted from databases should be

---

[2] We note that a universal relation can be obtained by performing a number of joins between the relations involved in a database.

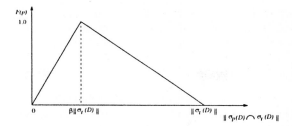

Fig. 2. Shape of the fitness function

supported by a significant part of the database. This increases the reliability of the results. So, a fitness function should take into account that small covers are undesired.

- The ratio of the cover of an individual p to the cover of the target class t, i.e., $\frac{\|\sigma_p(D) \cap \sigma_t(D)\|}{\|\sigma_t(D)\|}$. If the ratio is close to 0, this means that only a few tuples of the target class satisfy individual p. This is undesired for the same reason as a small cover for a target class. If the ratio is close to 1, almost all tuples of the target class satisfy p. This is also undesired because this will result in knowledge that is often known. A fitness function should take these properties into account.

Taking into account above-mentioned issues, we have defined the following fitness function:

$$
F(p) = \begin{cases} \frac{\|\sigma_p(D) \cap \sigma_t(D)\|}{\beta \|\sigma_t(D)\|} C(t) & \text{if } \|\sigma_p(D) \cap \sigma_t(D)\| \le \beta \|\sigma_t(D)\| \\ \\ \frac{\|\sigma_p(D) \cap \sigma_t(D)\| - \|\sigma_t(D)\|}{\|\sigma_t(D))\|(\beta - 1)} C(t) & \text{otherwise} \end{cases}
$$

in which $0 < \beta \le 1$, and

$$
C(t) = \begin{cases} 0 & \text{if } \frac{\|\sigma_t(D)\|}{\|\sigma(D)\|} \le \alpha \\ 1 & \text{otherwise} \end{cases}
$$

and $0 \le \alpha \le 1$.

We note that the values for α and β should be defined by the user and will vary for different applications. The value of α defines the fraction of tuples that a target class should contain in order to be a candidate for further exploration. The value β defines the fraction of tuples that an individual should represent within a target class in order to obtain the maximal fitness. In Figure 2, the shape of the fitness function is presented.

The fitness grows linearly with the number of tuples satisfying the description of an individual p as well as satisfying a target class t, i.e., $\|\sigma_p(D) \cap \sigma_t(D)\|$, above a user-defined value α, and decreases linearly with $\|\sigma_p(D) \cap \sigma_t(D)\|$ after reaching the value $\beta \|\sigma_t(D)\|$.

It should be clear that our goal is to search for those individuals that approximate a fitness of $\beta \|\sigma_t(D)\|$. Consider the target class *damage* = *yes* that consists of 100.000 tuples. Assume that a profile is considered risky if about 30.000 out of 100.000 persons satisfy this profile. This means that $\beta \approx 0.3$. Assuming that 33.000 of the persons caused an accident are young males, the algorithm should find individuals like (*gender* **is** ('male') $\land$ *age* **in** [19,28]).

3.3 Manipulation operators

Mutation As stated in the introduction of this section, a mutation modifies an individual. In defining the mutation operator, we take into account the domain type of an attribute. If there exists no ordering relationship between the domain values, then we select randomly an attribute value and replace it by another value, which can be a NULL value as well, in an expression that contains this attribute. For example, a mutation on attribute town of individual p_2 (see Figure 1) may result into $p_2' = age$ **in** [29,44] $\land$ *town* **is** ('Almere', 'Den Haag', 'Weesp') $\land$ *category* **is** ('lease').

If there exists a relationship between the domain values of an attribute, the mutation operator acts as follows in the case that a single value is associated with this attribute in an expression, i.e., the expression looks as *att* **is** (v_c). Let $[v_b, v_e]$ be the domain of attribute *att*. In order to mutate v_c, we choose randomly a value $\delta_v \in [0, (v_e - v_b)\mu]$, in which $0 \leq \mu \leq 1$. The mutated value v_c' is defined as $v_c' = v_c + \delta_v$ or $v_c' = v_c - \delta_v$ as long as $v_c' \in [v_b, v_e]$. The parameter μ is used to control the maximal increase or decrease of an attribute value.

To handle overflow, i.e., if $v_c' \notin [v_b, v_e]$, we assume that the successor of v_e is v_b, and, consequently the predecessor of v_b is v_e. To compute a mutated value v_c' appropriately, we distinguish between whether v_c will be increased or decreased, which is randomly determined.

In the case that v_c is increased

$$v_c' = \begin{cases} v_c + \delta_v & \text{if } v_c + \delta_v \in [v_b, v_e] \\ v_b + \delta_v - (v_e - v_c) & \text{otherwise} \end{cases}$$

and in the case v_c is decreased

$$v_c' = \begin{cases} v_c - \delta_v & \text{if } v_c - \delta_v \in [v_b, v_e] \\ v_e - \delta_v + (v_c - v_b) & \text{otherwise} \end{cases}$$

Let us consider the situation in which more than one value is associated with an attribute *att* in an expression. If a list of non successive (enumerable) values is associated with *att*, we select one of the values and compute the new value according to one of the above-mentioned formulas. If a range of successive values, i.e., an interval, is associated with *att*, we select either the lower or upper bound value and mutate it. A potential disadvantage of this strategy for intervals is that an interval may be significantly enlarged, if the mutated value crosses a domain boundary. Suppose that the domain of *age* is [18,60], and we mutate the upper bound value of the expression *age* **in** [55, 59], i.e., the value 59. Assume that the value 59 is increased by 6, then 59 is mutated in the value 23. The new expression becomes *age* **in** [23, 55].

We note that the partitioning of attribute values, i.e., the selection of proper intervals in an expression, is simply adjusted by the mutation operator.

Cross-over The idea behind a crossover operation is as follows; it takes as input 2 expressions, selects a random point, and exchanges the subexpressions behind this point. In general, not all attributes will be involved in an expression. This may have some undesired effects for a cross-over. First, a cross-over may produce individuals in which an attribute is involved more than once. For example, a cross-over between the individuals $p_1 = $ *gender* **is** ('male') $\wedge$ *age* **in** [19,34] and $p_2 = $ *age* **in** [29,44] $\wedge$ *town* **is** ('Almere', 'Amsterdam', 'Weesp') $\wedge$ *category* **is** ('lease') after the first attribute results into the following individuals: $p_1' = $ *gender* **is** ('male') $\wedge$ *town* **is** ('Almere', 'Amsterdam', 'Weesp') $\wedge$ *category* **is** ('lease') and $p_2' = $ *age* **in** [19,34] $\wedge$ *age* **in** [29,44]. As we can see, the attribute *age* appears twice in p_2'.

Second, a cross-over may result in an offspring that is exactly the same as the parents with probability 1.0. For example, a cross-over between p_1 and p_2 that occurs on a point that is beyond the last elementary expression of p_2, i.e., *category* **is** ('lease'), will result into the equal new individuals.

To prevent the above-mentioned effects, we apply the following technique to perform cross-overs. Consider two individuals p_i and p_j that have been selected for crossover. Let A_i be the set of attributes that is not involved in p_i but is involved in p_j and A_j the set of attributes that is not involved in p_j but is involved in p_i. Then, for each attribute in A_i, we generate an empty elementary expression using this attribute and add it to p_i. The same procedure is applied to the attributes of A_j. This procedure has as effect that the lengths of p_i and p_j become equal. Finally, we regard an individual as a sequence of elementary expressions, and order these in p_i and p_j according to the rule that elementary expressions having the same attribute will appear at the same position in p_i and p_j. Then, the cross-over between p_i and p_j can be performed. We note that the cross-over point should be chosen between the first and final position of p_i or p_j. The following example illustrates this technique.

Example 1 Consider the individuals $p_1 = $ *gender* **is** ('male') $\wedge$ *age* **in** [19,34] and $p_2 = $ *age* **in** [29,44] $\wedge$ *town* **is** ('Almere', 'Amsterdam', 'Weesp') $\wedge$ *category* **is** ('lease') again. Then, $A_1 = \{town, category\}$ and $A_2 = \{gender\}$. So, we extend p_1 with the following expression *town* **is** ('') $\wedge$ *category* **is** ('') and p_2 is extended with *gender* **is** ('').

After ordering the elementary expressions p_1 and p_2 look as follows:
$p_1 = $ *gender* **is** ('male') $\wedge$ *age* **in** [19,34] $\wedge$ *town* **is** ('') $\wedge$ *category* **is** ('')
$p_2 = $ *gender* **is** ('') $\wedge$ *age* **in** [29,44] $\wedge$ *town* **is** ('Almere', 'Amsterdam', 'Weesp')
$\qquad \wedge$ *category* **is** ('lease')
Now, a cross-over at position 2 results into
$p_1' = $ *gender* **is** ('male') $\wedge$ *age* **in** [19,34] $\wedge$ *town* **is** ('Almere', 'Amsterdam',
$\qquad$ 'Weesp') $\wedge$ *category* **is** ('lease')
$p_2' = $ *gender* **is** ('') $\wedge$ *age* **in** [29,44] $\wedge$ *town* **is** ('') $\wedge$ *category* **is** ('')
Note that p_2' is equal to *age* **in** [29,44]. $\square$

In the next section, we introduce a number of rules that may prevent the exploration of unpromising individuals.

4 Optimization rules

In this section, we discuss two propositions that may be used to prevent the exploration of unprofitable individuals. These propositions are derived from the shape of the fitness function. The complexity of a genetic-based algorithm for data mining is determined by the evaluation of the fitness function [5], since this is computationally the most expensive operation. Before presenting these propositions, we introduce the notion of a similar of an individual.

Definition 2: Let length(p) be the number of elementary expressions involved in p. An individual p_{sim} is a *similar* of p if each elementary expression of p_{sim} is contained in p or p_{sim} contains each elementary expression of p and length(p_{sim}) $\neq$ length(p).

As stated in the foregoing, we search for individuals with high values for the fitness function F, see section 3.2. for F.

We note that the computation of $F(p)$ requires the number of tuples that satisfy individual p. So, these tuples should be searched for and retrieved from the database, which is a costly operation [6]. Although several techniques may be used to minimize the number of retrievals from a database, still large amounts of tuples have to be retrieved from the database in mining applications. The techniques to minimize retrievals are mainly based on storing frequently used tuples in an efficient way in main memory [4]. In this way, disk accesses are reduced.

In the following, two propositions will be presented that may be used to avoid the computation of fitness values of unprofitable individuals. These propositions decide if the fitness value of a similar of an individual p is worse than the fitness of p. If this is the case, this similar can be excluded from the search process.

Proposition 1: Let p_{sim} be a similar of p. If $\|\sigma_p(D) \cap \sigma_t(D)\| \leq \beta \|\sigma_t(D)\|$ and length(p_{sim}) $>$ length(p) then $F(p_{sim}) \leq F(p)$.

Proof. From length(p_{sim}) $>$ length(p) follows that $\sigma_{p_{sim}}(D) \subseteq \sigma_p(D)$. As a consequence, $\|\sigma_{p_{sim}}(D) \cap \sigma_t(D)\| \leq \|\sigma_p(D) \cap \sigma_t(D)\|$. Since $\|\sigma_p(D) \cap \sigma_t(D)\| \leq \beta \|\sigma_t(D)\|$, it follows $F(p_{sim}) \leq F(p)$. $\square$

Proposition 2: Let p_{sim} be a similar of p. If $\|\sigma_p(D) \cap \sigma_t(D)\| \geq \beta \|\sigma_t(D)\|$ and length(p_{sim}) $<$ length(p) then $F(p_{sim}) \leq F(p)$.

Proof. Similar to the proof of Proposition 1. $\square$

Note that the propositions do not require additional retrievals from a database to decide if $F(p_{sim}) \leq F(p)$.

We discuss an alternative how these propositions at cross-over level may contribute in optimizing the search process. As stated in the foregoing, a cross-over is applied on a mating pair and results into two offsprings. Suppose that a mutation is performed after a cross-over, and the parent and the offspring with the highest fitness values are eligible to be mutated (see Section 5). Consider an offspring p_o resulted from a cross-over, and let p_o be a similar of p, one of its parents. If we can decide that $F(p_o) \leq F(p)$, then it is efficient to mutate p_o. The reason is that computation on an unmutated p_o will be a wasting of effort.

In the next section, we propose an overall algorithm, in which we apply the two propositions.

5 Algorithm

The previous section was devoted to the major issues that play a role in designing a genetic-based algorithm for data mining. In this section, we describe the overall algorithm. Before starting this description, we discuss a mechanism to select an individual for a next generation.

The mechanism to select individuals for a new generation is based on the technique of elitist recombination [12]. According to this technique, the individuals in a population are randomly shuffled. Then, the cross-over operation is applied on each mating pair, resulting into two offsprings. The parent and the offspring with the highest fitness value are selected for the next generation. In this way, there is a direct competition between the offsprings and their own parents. Note, the offspring provides the possibility to explore different parts of a search space.

The elitist recombination technique has been chosen for two reasons. First, there is no need to specify a particular cross-over probability, since each individual is involved in exactly one cross-over. Second, there is no need for intermediate populations in order to generate a new population as is the case in a traditional genetic algorithm. These properties simplify the implementation of a genetic algorithm. Let us outline the overall algorithm.

The algorithm starts with the initialization of a population consisting of an even number of individuals, called $P(t)$. The individuals in this population are shuffled. Then, the cross-over operation is applied on two successive individuals. After completion of a cross-over, the fitness values of the parents are compared[3]; the parent with the highest value is selected and it may be mutated with a probability c. This parent, p'_{sel}, is added to the next generation, and in case it is mutated its fitness value is computed. Then, for each offspring, p_o, we test if this offspring is a similar of p'_{sel} and if its fitness value is worse or equal than p'_{sel}. If this is true, p_o is an unpromising individual, and, therefore, we always mutate p_o. Otherwise, we mutate p_o with probability c. Note, to compare the fitness value between p'_{sel} and p_o, the propositions of the previous section are used. So, no additional fitness values are computed for this comparison. After possible mutation of the offsprings, their fitness values are computed, and the most fittest offspring is added to the new generation. This process is repeated for all individuals in a generation.

Once the new population has been built up, the total fitness of the existing as well as of the new population is computed, and compared. The algorithm

---

[3] These values are already computed and stored by the algorithm.

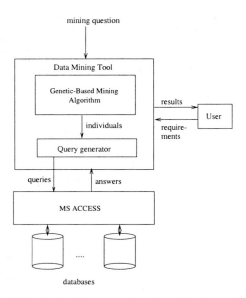

Fig. 3. Architecture of a data mining tool

terminates if the total fitness of the new population does not significantly improve compared with the total fitness of the existing population, i.e., that the improvement of the total fitness of the new population is less than a threshold value ϵ. For a detailed discussion with regard to the algorithm, we refer to [5].

6 Implementation and preliminary results

Based on the algorithm described in Section 5, we have built a re-targetable prototype of a data mining tool, which means that the tool can be coupled to different databases. The main goal of the current effort is to determine if the genetic-based algorithm is able to find hidden knowledge.

Let us continue with the description of the tool. The tool takes as input a mining question and produces a set of answers for the question. The prototype is running in a Microsoft Access 97 environment that uses the Microsoft Jet Engine[4]. The genetic-based algorithm is implemented in Visual Basic. We have chosen this environment for two reasons. First, this environment is available at our laboratory. Second, the database that we want to mine is a Microsoft database.

In Figure 3, the architecture of our tool is represented. Once the tool receives a mining question, it runs the genetic-based mining algorithm, which generates, among others, a population. The individuals of the population are passed to the Query Generator. For each individual a corresponding SQL query is generated.

---

[4] Within the scope of a feasibility study, a previous version of the algorithm was implemented in C and connected to the Monet Database Server [3].

These queries are passed to the MS ACCESS DBMS, which on its turn processes the queries and passes the results to the data mining tool. These results are used to compute the fitness of each individual. Upon request of the user individuals and their associated fitness values can be shown. The user has the possibility to modify the initial mining question or to specify additional requirements with regard to the question. We note that this is a very useful feature of a mining tool, since, in practice, a user starts a mining session with a rough idea of what information might be interesting, and during the mining session (with help of the results provided by the system) the user specifies more precisely what information should be searched for.

The generation of a query corresponding to an individual p is straightforward. Recall that an individual is a conjunction of predicates. So, this forms the major part of the WHERE clause of a query corresponding to p. Since we require the number of tuples satisfying p and a target class t, the query corresponding to p is: *select count(*) from* database *where* $p \wedge t$.

We have applied the tool on an artificial database, and are currently applying it on a real-life database. In the following, we describe the databases and the results obtained so far.

Artificial database This database consists of the relation *Ex(gender, age, town, category, price, damage)*. For this database 100.000 tuples have been generated, of which 50% have a value "yes" for *damage*, i.e., 50% of the tuples relate to an accident. Furthermore, the fact that young men in lease cars have more than average chances to cause an accident was hidden in the database. The goal of mining this database was to determine whether the tool is capable to find the hidden fact. Therefore, we have set the target class as *damage* = 'yes', and we searched for the profile of risky drivers. We note that the expression for the hidden profile is: *age* **in** [19,24] $\wedge$ *category* **is** ('lease') $\wedge$ *gender* **is** ('male').

We have mined the database with varying initial populations, consisting of 36 individuals. The following three classes of initial population were distinguished: (1) random: the populations contained a few individuals that could set the algorithm quickly on a promising route, (2) modified random: individuals that could apparently set the algorithm on a promising route were replaced by other (not promising) individuals, and (3) bad converged: the populations contained individuals with low fitness values.

We have observed that the algorithm usually finds near optimal solutions, i.e., profiles that look like the hidden one, in less than 1000 fitness evaluations. The differences between the hidden profile and profiles found by the algorithm (for different initial populations) were mainly caused by variations in the range of attribute *age*.

With regard to the settings of the parameters α and β, we note that appropriate values could be easily selected, since the content of the database is precisely known. $\square$

Real-life database Currently, we are mining a real-life database, the so-called

FAA incident database, which is available at our aerospace laboratory. This database contains aircraft incident data that are recorded from 1978 to 1995. Incidents are potentially hazardous events that do not meet the aircraft damage or personal injury thresholds as defined by American National Transportation Safety Board (NTSB). For example, the database contains reports of collisions between aircraft and birds while on approach to or departure from an airport. The FAA database consists of more than 70 attributes and about 80.000 tuples.

The initial mining task on the FAA database was: search for the class of flights with (more than average) chances of causing an incident, i.e., profiles of risky flights. This search resulted in (valid) profiles but which could be easily declared. An example of such a profile is that aircraft with 1 or 2 engines are more often involved in incidents. The explanation for this profile is that these types of aircraft perform more flights.

During the mining process the mining question was refined in the following three more specific questions: (1) given the fact that an incident was due to operational defects not inflicted by the pilot, what is the profile of this type of incident?, (2) given the fact that an incident was due to mistakes of the pilot, what is the profile of this type of incident?, and (3) given the fact that an incident was due to improper maintenance, what is the profile of this type of incident?

We have proposed these questions to our tool with the following values for the parameters, $\alpha = 0$, $\beta = 0.25$, mutation probability (c) $= 0.3$, and $\epsilon = 0.1$. Furthermore, the population size was set on 50. On the first glance, the results of the tool appear to be promising. Safety experts at our laboratory are analysing the results. On the basis of their analysis, we will set up a plan to mine the database more systematically, and to study the impact of different parameter values on the results provided by the tool. The goal of the latter study is to formulate some guidelines for selecting parameter values for similar type of databases, such as an aircraft accident database. □

Although our evaluation is not completed yet and a significant amount of research has to be done, e.g., on performance issues, in order to build an adequate genetic-based data mining tool, the preliminary results are promising. A second observation is that the range interval of an attribute in an expression may significantly enlarged, if a mutation occurs on a domain boundary. An interval that consists of (almost) the whole the domain slows down the search process. In a next version of the tool, we will enhance the mutation operator. An alternative is to clip on boundary values in cases of overflow.

7 Conclusions & further research

In order to answer mining questions, very large search spaces should be inspected, making an exhaustive search infeasible. So, heuristic search strategies are of vital importance in searching such spaces. We have discussed a genetic-based algorithm that may be used for data mining. Contrary to the conventional bit string representation in genetic algorithms, we have chosen a representation that fits better in the field of databases. The fitness function discussed in this paper is close to our intuition and gives rise to an optimization of the search process.

A genetic-based algorithm for data mining has two major advantages. First, the problem of partitioning attribute values in proper ranges could be solved by choosing a suitable mutation operator. Second, a genetic-based algorithm is able to escape a local optimum and does not pose any restrictions on the structure of a search space.

By means of a (prototype) implementation and a preliminary evaluation, we have shown the potentials of a genetic-based data mining tool. Since the preliminary results of the tool appear to be promising, we are setting up a research plan to evaluate this tool thoroughly. The outcome of the evaluation will determine our future research activities in this field.

Acknowledgements The author is grateful to Wim Pelt from the Dutch Ministry of Defense, who made this research possible. Hein Veenhof and Egbert Boers from NLR are thanked for their valuable comments on earlier drafts of this paper. Finally, Leo de Penning and Martijn Suurd from the Univ. of Twente are thanked for their implementation efforts.

References

[1] Agrawal, R., Ghosh, S., Imielinski, T., Iyer, B., Swami, A., An Interval Classifier for Database Mining Applications, Proc. 18th Int. Conf. Very Large Data Base, pp. 560-573.

[2] Augier, S., Venturini, G., Kodratoff, Y., Learning First Order Logic Rules with a Genetic Algorithm, Proc. 1st Int. Conf. on Knowledge Discovery and Data Mining, pp. 21-26.

[3] Boncz, P., Wilschut, A., Kersten, M., Flattening an Object Algebra to Provide Performance, Proc. 14th Int. Conf. on Data Engineering, pp. 568-577.

[4] Choenni, R., Siebes, A., Query Optimization to Support Data Mining, Proc. DEXA '97 8th Int. Workshop on Database and Expert Systems Applications, pp. 658-663.

[5] Choenni, R., On the Suitability of Genetic-Based Algorithms for Data Mining, extended version, to appear as NLR technical publication.

[6] Elmasri, R., Navathe, S., Fundamentals of Database Systems, The Benjamin/Cummings Publishing Company, 1989.

[7] Freitas, A., A Genetic Programming Framework for two Data Mining Tasks: Classification and Generalized Rule Induction, Proc. Int. Conf on Genetic Programming 1997, pp. 96-101.

[8] Han, J., Cai, Y., Cerone, N., Knowledge Discovery in Databases: An Attribute-Oriented Approach, in Proc. 18th Int. Conf. Very Large Data Base, pp. 547-559.

[9] Holsheimer, M., Kersten, M.L., Architectural Support for Data Mining, Proc. AAAI-94 Workshop on Knowledge Discovery, pp. 217-228.

[10] Michalewicz, Z., Genetic Algorithms + Data Structures = Evolution Programs. Springer-Verlag, New York, USA.

[11] Srikant, R., Agrawal, R., Mining Quantitative Association Rules in Large Relational Tables, Proc. ACM SIGMOD'96 Int. Conf. Management of Data, pp. 1-12.

[12] Thierens, D., Goldberg, D., Elitist Recombination: an integrated selection recombination GA, 1st IEEE Conf. on Evolutionary Computing, pp. 508-512.

Data Visualization in a Web Warehouse*

S. S. BHOWMICK   S. K. MADRIA   W. -K. NG   E.P. LIM
{sourav,askumar,wkn,aseplim}@cais.ntu.edu.sg

Center for Advanced Information Systems, School of Applied Science,
Nanyang Technological University, Singapore 639798, SINGAPORE

Abstract

The effective representation and manipulation of web data is currently an active area of research in databases. In a web warehouse, *web information coupling* provides the means to derive useful information from the WWW. Web information is materialized in the form of *web tuples* and stored in *web tables*. In this paper, we discuss web data visualization operators such as *web nest*, *web coalesce*, *web pack* and *web sort* to provide users with the flexibility to view sets of web documents in perspectives which may be more meaningful.

1 Introduction

Currently, web information may be discovered primarily by two mechanisms; browsers and search engines. This form of information access on the Web has a few shortcomings [6]. To resolve these limitations, we introduced Web Information Coupling System (WICS) [6], a database system for managing and manipulating coupled information extracted from the Web. WICS is one of the component of our web warehouse, called WHOWEDA (*Warehouse of Web Data*) [1, 5, 14]. In WICS, we materialize web information as *web tuples* and store it in a *web table*. We equip WICS with the basic capability to manipulate web tables and correlate additional, useful, related web information residing in the web tables [17]. Note that a web table is a collection of directed graphs (i.e., web tuples). The following example briefly illustrates query graph and web table, and provides the motivation for our work in this paper.

Example 1. Suppose a user Bill wish to find a list of drugs and their side effects on diseases from the WWW. We assume that there is a web site at http://www.panacea.org/ which provides drug related information. Bill figured that there could be hyperlinks with anchor labels 'side effects' in http://www.pana-cea.org/ that might be useful. To couple these related information from the

---

* This work was supported in part by the Nanyang Technological University, Ministry of Education (Singapore) under Academic Research Fund #4-12034-5060, #4-12034-3012, #4-12034-6022. Any opinions, findings, and recommendations in this paper are those of the authors and do not reflect the views of the funding agencies.

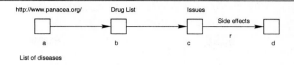

Fig. 1. Web schema (query graph) of 'Drugs' web table.

WWW, Bill constructs a *coupling framework* (*query graph*) as shown in Figure 1[1].

The global web coupling operator [6] can be applied to retrieve those set of related documents that match the coupling framework. Each set of inter-linked documents retrieved for the coupling framework is a directed graph (also called web tuples) and is materialized in web table called **Drugs**. A small portion of the web table is shown in Figure 2(a). Each web tuple in **Drugs** contains information about the side effects of a drug on a disease. ∎

The above approach of storing web information in a web table has the following shortcomings:

- It does not provide us with the ability to see the overall structure of the information captured in the web table. It is not possible for a user to visualize how one web tuple in a web table is related to another.
- The set of web tuples in a web table may contain duplicate web documents. For example, documents at `http://www.panacea.org/` (denoted by a_1) in all the web tuples in Figure 2(a) are identical. Similarly documents (denoted by b_1) in the first two web tuples are identical. Thus, a web table may contain duplicate documents and there is no mechanism to provide a *coalesced view* of the set of web tuples. A coalesced view allows a user to browse lesser number of directed connected graphs when locating information.
- It does not allow a user to group web tuples based on *related information content*, or *similar (or identical)* web sites. A user has to manually probe each web tuple to find these information. For example, the fifth, seventh and eighth web tuples in Figure 2(a) deal with the side effects of the drug **Beta Carotene**. However, these information cannot be grouped together in our web table.
- The set of web tuples are materialize in web tables. There is no other materialized representation of these web tables. For example, the collective view of these web tuples can be stored as a set of directed graphs having lesser number of nodes or links as compared to the original web table. This can optimize the query, storage and maintenance cost.

---

[1] In the figures, the boxes and directed lines correspond to *nodes* (Web document) and *links* respectively. Observe that some nodes and links have keywords imposed on them. These keywords express the content of the web document or the label of the hyperlink between the web documents.

In this paper, we introduce some *data visualization operators* to resolve the above difficulties. These operators take as input a set of web tuples of a web table and provide a different view of the tuples as output. This gives users the flexibility to view documents in different perspectives that are more meaningful. Formally, we illustrate some data visualization operators and provide formal algorithm for these operators.

These operators provide different storage representation of web tuples which will help in optimizing the query, storage and maintenance cost. These different representations may also lead to inconsistency problems with respect to the original web table. Due to space limitations, we have not discussed the above problems in this paper.

2 Related Work

There has been considerable work in data model and query languages for the World Wide Web [11–13, 16]. For example, Mendelzon, Mihaila and Milo [16] proposed a WebSQL query language based on a formal calculus for querying the WWW. The result of WebSQL query is a set of web tuples which are flattened immediately to linear tuples. Konopnicki and Shmueli [12] proposed a high level querying system called the W3QS for the WWW whereby users may specify content and structure queries on the WWW and maintain the results of queries as database views of the WWW. In W3QL, queries are always made to the WWW. Fiebig, Weiss and Moerkotte extended relational algebra to the World Wide Web by augmenting the algebra with new domains (data types) [11], and functions that apply to the domains. The extended model is known as RAW (Relational Algebra for the Web). Inspired by concepts in declarative logic, Lakshmanan, Sadri and Subramanian designed WebLog [13] to be a language for querying and restructuring web information. Other proposals, namely Lorel [2] and UnQL [9], aim at querying heterogeneous and semistructured information. However, none of these systems discuss data visualization operators similar to ours.

3 Background

Since our goal is to discuss data visualization operators in WICS, we use as a starting point the *Web Information Coupling Model* (WICM), designed as part of our Web Warehousing project (WHOWEDA). We describe WICM briefly, only to the extent necessary to understand the concept of data visualization operators. A complete description of the data model and its usefulness is given in [6, 17].

3.1 Web Objects

It consists of a hierarchy of web objects. The fundamental objects are *Nodes* and *Links*. Nodes correspond to HTML or plain text documents and links correspond to hyper-links interconnecting the documents in the World Wide Web. We define a Node type and a Link type to refer to these two sets of distinct objects. These objects consist of a set of attributes as shown below:

```
Node = [url, title, format, size, date, text]
Link = [source-url, target-url, label, link-type]
```

For the `Node` object type, the attributes are the URL of a `Node` instance and its title, document format, size (in bytes), date of last modification, and textual contents. For the `Link` type, the attributes are the URL of the source document containing the hyperlink, the URL of the target document, the anchor or label of the link, and the type of the link. Hyperlinks in the WWW may be characterized into three types: *interior*, *local*, and *global* [16].

The next higher level of abstraction is a `web tuple`. A web tuple is a set of connected, directed graphs each consisting of a set of `nodes` and `links` which are instances of `Node` and `Link` respectively. A collection of web tuples is called a `web table`. If the table is materialized, we associate a `name` with the table. There is a *schema* (see next section) associated with every web table. A `web database` consists of a set of web schemas and a set of web tables.

3.2   Web Schema

A web schema contains meta-information that binds a set of web tuples in a web table. Web tables are materialized results of web queries. In WICS, a user expresses a web query by describing a *query graph*.

When the query graph in Figure 1 is evaluated, a set of web tuples each *satisfying* the query graph is harnessed from the WWW. By collecting the tuples as a table, the query graph may be used as the table's schema to bind the tuples. Hence, the web schema of a table is the query graph that is used to derive the table. Formally, a web schema is an ordered 4-tuple $M = \langle X_n, X_\ell, C, P \rangle$ where X_n is a set of node variables, X_ℓ is a set of link variables, C is a set of connectivities (in Disjunctive Normal Form), and P is a set of predicates (in Disjunctive Normal Form).

Observe that some of the nodes and links in the figures have keywords imposed on them. To express these conditions, we introduced *node* and *link variables* in the query graph. Thus, in Figure 1 node d represents those web documents which contains the words 'side effects' in the text or title. In other words, variables denote arbitrary instances of `Node` or `Link`. There are two special variables: a node variable denoted by the symbol '#' and a link variable denoted by the symbol '-'. These two variables differ from the other variables in that they are never *bound* (these variables are not defined by the predicates of the schema).

Structural properties of web tuples are expressed by a set of *connectivities*. Formally, a connectivity k is an expression of the form: $x\langle\rho\rangle y$ where $x \in X_n, y \in X_n$, and ρ is a regular expression over X_ℓ. (The angle brackets around ρ are used for delimitation purposes only.) Thus, $x\langle\rho\rangle y$ describes a path or a set of possible paths between two nodes x and y.

The last schema component is the set of predicates P. Predicates provide a means to impose additional conditions on web information to be retrieved. Let p be a predicate. If x, y are node or link variables then the following are possible forms of predicates: $p(x) \equiv [x.\texttt{attribute CONTAINS "}A\texttt{"}]$ or $p(x) \equiv [x.\texttt{attribute}$ $\texttt{EQUALS "}A\texttt{"}]$ and $p(x, y) \equiv [x.\texttt{attribute} = y.\texttt{attribute}]$. where `attribute` refers to an attribute of `Node`, `Link` or `link_type`, A is a regular expression over the ASCII character set, x and y are *arguments* of p.

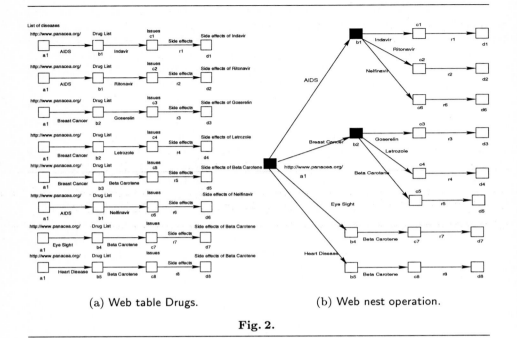

(a) Web table Drugs. (b) Web nest operation.

Fig. 2.

4 Web Data Visualization Operators

A query graph returns a set of web tuples which are stored as a web table. However, a user may wish to view these web tuples in different framework. In this section, we introduce some data visualization operators to add flexibility in viewing query results coupled from the WWW. Within this context, we propose an algorithm for each operator and illustrate each operator with an example.

4.1 Web Nest

Web tuples in a web table may be topically related. However, the relationship is not explicit from the way we store tuples in a web table. A visualization of this relationship gives an overview of the information space harnessed from the WWW and how these information are topically related. The **web nest** operator achieve this. It is an unary operator whose operand is a web table and whose output is a set of directed connected graphs condensed from the web table. Formally, let W be a web table with schema $M = \langle X_n, X_\ell, C, P \rangle$. Then, $G_n = \text{Nest}(W)$ where G_n is the set of condensed graphs.

Algorithm Nest Algorithm nest is used to determine the topical relationship between a set of web tuples in a web table. It takes a web table as an input and produce a set of graphs as output. In WHOWEDA, a set of instances of a node variable may appear in more than one tuple in a web table. For example, in Figure 2(a) the node b_1 (an instance of node variable b) appears in first, second and sixth tuple. This indicates that the URLs of the instances of b in

---

Input: Web table W with schema $M = \langle X_n, X_\ell, C, P \rangle$.
Output: A set of directed connected graphs G_n.

Retrieve the first web tuple (denoted as t_i) from W;
Store the tuple t_i in G_n;
for each of the remaining web tuples (denoted as t_j) in W **do** {
    $Z = 0$;   **for each** directed connected graph in G_n {
        for each node $x_j \in t_j$ {
            Get the URL of x_j;
            for each node $x_i \in t_i$ {
                if (URL of x_j = URL of x_i) {
                    Remove x_j;
                    Concatenate the out-bound and/or in-bound links
                    of x_j with the node x_i in G_n;
                    $Z = Z + 1$;
                }
                else {
                    Add x_j in G_n;
                    Retrieve the next node in t_i;
                }
            }
            Retrieve the next node in t_j;
        }
        if ($Z = 0$) /* None of the nodes in t_j are identical to t_i */
            Add t_j in G_n as a seperate directed connected graph;
    }
}

Fig. 3. Algorithm nest.

these web tuples are identical. Algorithm nest identifies multiple occurence of such identical nodes (by comparing the URLs of these nodes) in a set of web tuples and concatenate these tuples to one another over these identical nodes. Execution of this algorithm eliminates such replicated nodes in a web table. The formal description of the algorithm is given in Figure 3.

Example 2. Consider the web table in Figure 2(a). Application of web nest operator on the web table Drugs will result in a directed connected graph as shown in Figure 2(b) . Note that in Figure 2(b) none of the instances of node variables are replicated. The darkened boxes in the figure represents nodes over which web tuples are concatenated. ∎

4.2 Web Coalesce

The set of web tuples in a web table may contain duplicate web documents. For example, documents denoted by b_1 in the first two web tuples in Figure 2(a) are identical. The number of duplicate nodes (documents) increases with the number of outgoing links of each nodes that satisfies the query graph. Thus, the size of a web table is proportional to the number of outgoing links satisfying the

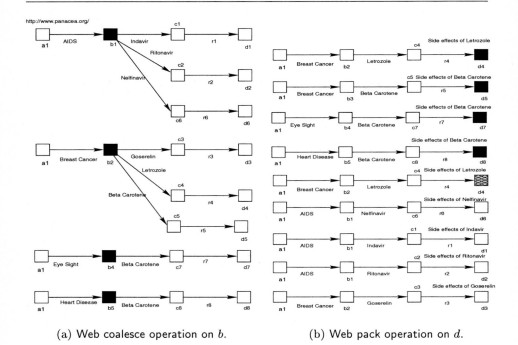

(a) Web coalesce operation on b. (b) Web pack operation on d.

Fig. 4. Web coalesce and web pack operation.

schema in each nodes. For reasonably small size of the web tables, browsing each web tuples for information of interest is a feasible option. However, browsing web tables of significant size may be tedious and inefficient way of locating information of interest. This problem may be minimized by coalescing duplicate nodes to reduce the size of the number of directed connected graphs in a web table. A coalesced web table results in a set of directed connected graphs and allows the user to browse lesser number of graphs (web tuples) compared to the original web table to locate desired information. To achieve this, we define the `web coalesce` operator. It takes a web table and a node variable as input and produce as ouput a set of directed connected graphs. It combines those web tuples in a web table which contains identical instances of the input node variable. Note that web coalesce is a specialization of web nest operation. Web nest coalesce web tuples by removing all duplicate nodes, whereas web coalesce operation coalesce a web table based on a node variable explicitly specified by a user. Formally, the web coalesce operation on node variable $x \in X_n$ is defined as $G_c = \texttt{Coalesce}(W, x)$.

Algorithm Coalesce The objective of Algorithm coalesce is similar to that of Algorithm nest. Analogous to Algorithm nest, it concatenates a set of web tuples in a web table. However, Algorithm coalesce only eliminates identical instances of a *specified* node variable from a set of web tuples as opposed to removal of all

---

Input: Web table W with schema $M = \langle X_n, X_\ell, C, P \rangle$, Node variable x
such that $x \in X_n$.
Output: A set of directed connected graphs G_c.

Retrieve the first web tuple (denoted as t_i) from W;
Get the URL of the instance of the node variable x (denoted as u_i) in t_i;
Store the tuple t_i in G_c;
Remove t_i from W;
for each of the remaining web tuples (denoted as t_j) in W {
    Get the URL of the instance of node variable x (denoted as u_j) in t_j;
    for each directed connected graph in G_c {
        if $(u_i = u_j)$ {
            Concatenate tuple t_j with t_i when the URL of nodes
            in t_j is identical to the corresponding URL of the nodes in t_i;
            Denote the concatenated directed graph in G_c as t_i;
            Remove the web tuple t_j from W;
        }
        else {
            Add t_j in G_c as a separate directed graph;
            Retrieve the next graph in G_c and denote it as t_i;
        }
    }
    Retrieve the next web tuple from W;
}

Fig. 5. Algorithm coalesce.

identical nodes in web nest operation. Algorithm coalesce takes as input a web table and a specified node variable based on which web coalesce operation is to be performed and produce a set of coalesced graph as output. First, it identifies multiple occurence of identical instances (same URL) of specified node variable by comparing the URLs of these nodes. Then, it concatenate the web tuples over these identical nodes to produce a set of coalesced graphs. The formal description of the algorithm is given in Figure 5.

Example 3. Consider the web table in Figure 2(a). Suppose Bill wish to coalesce the web tuples in `Drugs` on node variable b. This query will create a set of directed connected graphs as shown in Figure 4(a). The darkened boxes in the figure represents nodes over which web coalesce is performed. Note that each graph describes side effects of various drugs for a particular disease. ∎

4.3 Web Pack

The `web pack` operator groups the web tuples in a web tables based on *similar criteria*. It provides the flexibility to view web tuples containing *similar* nodes together. A user explicitly specifies the node variable and the criteria based on which web pack operation is performed. The criteria based on which packing of web tuples can be performed is given below:

- `Host name`: Web tuples containing instances of specified node variable with identical host name are packed together.
- `Domain name`: Web tuples containing instances of specified node variable with identical domain names (.com, .edu, .org, .gov, .net, .mil etc) are grouped together.
- `Keyword content`: Packing may be performed by grouping web tuples whose instance of specified node variable contains user-specified keyword(s).

Note that in the case of packing based on keywords, the packed web table may contain duplicate web tuples since two different keywords may appear in the same node in a web tuple. Furthermore, tuples containing the keyword are displayed as top results and the remaining web tuples are pushed down in the packed web table. Formally, the web pack operation on node variable $x \in X_n$ is defined as $W_p = \texttt{Pack}(W, x, criteria)$ where W_p is the packed web table.

Algorithm Pack The objective of Algorithm pack is to group a set of web tuples (on a specified node variable) based on identical host name, domain name or keyword set. It takes as input a web table W with schema $M = \langle X_n, X_\ell, C, P \rangle$, a node variable $x \in X_n$ and packing condition P (P may be domain name, host name or keyword set) and produces as ouput a collection of packed web tuples W_p based on the packing condition P. If the packing condition is host name or domain name then Algorithm pack retrieve the domain name or host name of instances of x (by checking the URLs of these nodes) in each web tuple and compare them to find if they are identical. Tuples with identical host or domain names are grouped together and stored in W_p. The remaining web tuples with distinct host or domain names are appended at the end of W_p. This displays of the group of web tuples with identical domain or host names as top results in W_p.

If the packing condition is a keyword set then Algorithm pack first checks the existence of the keyword(s) in each instance of x. Then, all the web tuples in W with identical keyword(s) (each keyword must be an element of the specified keyword set) are packed together and displayed as top results in W_p. Note that Algorithm pack may create duplicate web tuples when the packing condition is a keyword set. This is because different keywords may appear in the same document. The formal description of the algorithm is given in Figure 6.

Example 4. Continuing with the web table in Figure 2(a), suppose Bill wish to group all the web tuples in `Drugs` on node variable d which contains the keywords "Beta Carotene" or "Letrozole". The result of this query is shown in Figure 4(b). Note that the group of web tuples whose instance of node variable d contains the keyword "Beta Carotene" or "Letrozole" is displayed as top query results and remaining web tuples in `Drugs` are pushed down. The tuples whose instances of node variable d (the first four tuples) are filled with black are grouped together since they contain the keyword "Beta Carotene". The tuples whose instances of node variable d (fifth tuple) are filled with a pattern, are grouped together because they contain the keyword "Letrozole". Note that the node d_4 contains both the keywords. Thus, tuple containing d_4 is replicated (1st and 5th web tuples are identical) in the web table created after web pack operation. ∎

Input: Web table W with schema $M = \langle X_n, X_\ell, C, P \rangle$, Node variable x
such that $x \in X_n$,
Pack condition $P \in \{\texttt{host\_name}, \texttt{domain\_name}, \texttt{keyword\_set}\}$.
Output: Web table W_p.

(1) $Z = 0$;
(2) if $(P = \texttt{host\_name}$ or $P = \texttt{domain\_name})$ {
(3)   Get the first web tuple (denoted as t_1) in W;
(4)   Get the instance of node variable x in t_1;
(5)   Get the host name (denoted as h_1) or domain name (denoted as d_1)
(6)   depending on P from the URL of the node;
(7)   **for each** of the remaining web tuples in W {
(8)   Get the instance of node variable x;
(9)   if $(P = \texttt{host\_name})$
(10)   Get the host name from the URL of the node;
(11)   else
(12)   Get the domain name;
(13)   if (host name of the node instance $= h_1$ or domain name $= d_1$) {
(14)   Append the web tuple at the end of W_p;
(15)   Remove the tuple from W;
(16) $Z = Z + 1$;
(17)   }
(18)   else
(19)   ;
(20)   }
(21)   Append t_1 at the end of W_p;
(22)   if $(Z = 0)$
(23)   Mark the tuple t_1;
(24)   Remove t_1 from W;
(25)   Repeat steps (1) to (24) for the remaining web tuples in W;
(26)   Move the set of marked web tuples at the end of W_p;
(27) }
(28) else {
(29)   **for each** keyword or combination of keywords in the keyword set {
(30)   **for each** web tuples in W {
(31)   Get the instance of node variable x;
(32)   Check if the keyword or set of keywords exist in the node;
(33)   if (keyword exists) {
(34)   Append the web tuple at the end of W_p;
(35) $Z = Z + 1$;
(36)   Mark the web tuple in W;
(37)   }
(38)   Get the next web tuple in W;
(39)   }
(40)   }
(41) }
(42) Get the set of web tuples which are unmarked in W;
(43) Append these web tuples at the end of W_p;

Fig. 6. Algorithm pack.

Input: Web table W with schema $M = \langle X_n, X_\ell, C, P \rangle$,
Sort condition $S_c \in \{\text{node}, \text{local}, \text{global}, \text{interior}\}$, Ordering type $O_t \in \{\text{asc}, \text{desc}\}$
Output: Web table W_s.

```
(1)    Z = 0;
(2)    if (S_c = node) {
(3)    for each web tuple in W {
(4)          Calculate total number of nodes N;
(5)          Store N;
(6)    }
(7)    else {
(8)        for each web tuple in W {
(9)            Z = 0;
(10)          for each link {
(11)              Get the link-type of the link;
(12)              if (S_c = local) {
(13)                  if (linktype is local)
(14)                      Z = Z + 1;
(15)                  else
(16)                      ;
(17)              }
(18)              else {
(19)                  if (S_c = global) {
(20)                      if (link-type is global)
(21)                          Z = Z + 1 ;
(22)                      else
(23)                          ;
(24)                  }
(25)                  else {
(26)                      if (link-type is interior)
(27)                          Z = Z + 1 ;
(28)                      else
(29)                          ;
(30)                  }
(31)              }
(32)          }
(33)          Store Z for each tuple;
(34)      }
(35)    }
(36)    if (O_t = asc)
(37)        Sort the tuples in ascending order based on N or Z;
(38)    else
(39)        Sort the tuples in descending order;
(40)    Store the sorted web tuples in W_s;
```

Fig. 7. Algorithm sort.

4.4 Web Sort

`Web sort` operator sort web tuples based on given *conditions*. The conditions to sort the web tuples in a web table in ascending or descending order are given below:

- Total number of nodes in each web tuple.
- Total number of specified link-type (local, global or interior) in each web tuple. This allows a user to measure the frequency of local, interior and global links in the web tuples returned in response to his query.

Web sort enables us to rearrange the tuples in ascending or descending order based on the number of occurrences of local, global or interior links in each tuple or total number of nodes in each tuple. Formally, web sort operation on a web table W with schema $M = \langle X_n, X_\ell, C, P \rangle$ is $W_s = \text{Sort}(W, \text{sort\_condition}, \text{order}$ $\text{\_type})$ where *sort_condition* is the condition based on which sorting is performed and *order_type* specifies the ordering method (ascending or descending) of the sorted web tuples.

Algorithm Sort Algorithm sort rearranges the web tuples in ascending or descending order based on the sorting condition. It takes as input a web table W, sort condition S_c and ordering type O_t (ascending or descending order) and produces as output a sorted web table W_s based on the sorting condition. For each tuple in W, Algorithm sort calculates the total number of nodes or total number of local, global or interior links (depending on the sort condition S_c) and arranges these tuples in ascending or descending order. The formal description of the algorithm is given in Figure 7. Due to space limitations, we do not provide an example for web sort here. Refer to [8] for details.

5 Conclusion

In this paper, we have motivated the need for the data visualization operators and introduced some operators such as web nest, web coalesce, web pack and web sort that provides different flavors of visualizing web tables. Due to space limitations, we have not reported inverse operators like *web unnest, web expand, web unpack*. Refer to [8] for details. Currently, we are implementing these web operators as a part of a web query language.

References

1. http://www.cais.ntu.edu.sg:8000/~ whoweda/.
2. S. ABITEBOUL, D. QUASS, J. MCHUGH, J. WIDOM, J. WEINER. The Lorel Query Language for Semistructured Data. *Journal of Digital Libraries*, 1(1):68-88, April 1997.
3. G. AROCENA, A. MENDELZON. WebOQL: Restructuring Documents, Databases and Webs. *Proceedings of ICDE 98*, Orlando, Florida, February 1998.
4. S. BHOWMICK, S. K. MADRIA, W.-K. NG, E.-P. LIM. Web Bags: Are They Useful in A Web Warehouse? *Proceedings of 5th International Conference of Foundation of Data Organization (FODO'98)*, Kobe, Japan, November 1998.

5. S. BHOWMICK, S. K. MADRIA, W.-K. NG, E.-P. LIM. Web Warehousing: Design and Issues. *Proceedings of International Workshop on Data Warehousing and Data Mining (DWDM'98) (in conjunction with ER'98)*, Singapore, 1998.

6. S. BHOWMICK, W.-K. NG, E.-P. LIM. Information Coupling in Web Databases. *Proceedings of the 17th International Conference on Conceptual Modelling (ER'98)*, Singapore, 1998.

7. S. S. BHOWMICK, W.-K. NG, E.-P. LIM, S. K. MADRIA. Join Processing in Web Databases. *Proceedings of the 9th International Conference on Database and Expert Systems Application (DEXA)*, Vienna, Austria, 1998.

8. S. BHOWMICK, S. K. MADRIA, W.-K. NG, E.-P. LIM. Data Visualization Operators in A Web Warehouse. *Technical Report,*CAIS-TR-98-20, Center for Advanced Information Systems, Nanyang Technological University, Singapore, 1998.

9. P. BUNEMAN, S. DAVIDSON, G. HILLEBRAND, D. SUCIU. A query language and optimization techniques for unstructured data. *Proceedings of the ACM SIGMOD International Conference on Management of Data*, Canada, June 1996.

10. M. FERNANDEZ, D. FLORESCU, A. LEVY, D. SUCIU. A Query Language for a Web-Site Management Systems *SIGMOD Record*, 26(3), Sept, 1997.

11. T. FIEBIG, J. WEISS, G. MOERKOTTE. RAW: A Relational Algebra for the Web. *Workshop on Management of Semistructured Data (PODS/SIGMOD'97)*, Tucson, Arizona, May 16, 1997.

12. D. KONOPNICKI, O. SHMUELI. W3QS: A Query System for the World Wide Web. *Proceedings of the 21st International Conference on Very Large Data Bases*, Zurich, Switzerland, 1995.

13. L.V.S. LAKSHMANAN, F. SADRI, I.N. SUBRAMANIAN. A Declarative Language for Querying and Restructuring the Web *Proceedings of the Sixth International Workshop on Research Issues in Data Engineering*, February, 1996.

14. E.-P. LIM, W.-K. NG, S. BHOWMICK, F.-Q. QIN, X. YE. A Data Warehousing System for Web Information.*Proceedings of 1st Asia Digital Library Workshop*, Hong Kong, August 5–7, 1998.

15. M. LIU, T. GUAN, L. V. SAXTON. Structured-Based Queries over the World Wide Web. *Proceedings of the 17th International Conference on Conceptual Modeling (ER'98)*, Singapore, 1998.

16. A. O. MENDELZON, G. A. MIHAILA, T. MILO. Querying the World Wide Web. *Proceedings of the International Conference on Parallel and Distributed Information Systems (PDIS'96)*, Miami, Florida,

17. W. K. NG, E.-P. LIM, C. T. HUANG, S. BHOWMICK, F. Q. QIN. Web Warehousing: An Algebra for Web Information. *Proceedings of IEEE International Conference on Advances in Digital Libraries (ADL'98)*, Santa Barbara, California, April 22–24, 1998.

Recent Advances and Research Problems in Data Warehousing

Sunil Samtani[1] Mukesh Mohania[2] Vijay Kumar[1] Yahiko Kambayashi[3]

[1] Dept. of Computer Science Telecommunications, University of Missouri-Kansas City, Kansas City, MO 64110, U.S.A. Email: ssamtani@cstp.umkc.edu
[2] Advanced Computing Research Centre, School of Computer and Information Science, University of South Australia, Mawson Lakes 5095 , Australia. Email: mohania@cis.unisa.edu.au
[3] Department of Social Informatics, Kyoto University, Kyoto 606-8501, Japan. Email: yahiko@kuis.kyoto-u.ac.jp

Abstract. In the recent years, the database community has witnessed the emergence of a new technology, namely *data warehousing*. A data warehouse is a global repository that stores pre-processed queries on data which resides in multiple, possibly heterogeneous, operational or legacy sources. The information stored in the data warehouse can be easily and efficiently accessed for making effective decisions. The On-Line Analytical Processing (OLAP) tools access data from the data warehouse for complex data analysis, such as multidimensional data analysis, and decision support activities. Current research has lead to new developments in all aspects of data warehousing, however, there are still a number of problems that need to be solved for making data warehousing effective. In this paper, we discuss recent developments in data warehouse modelling, view maintenance, and parallel query processing. A number of technical issues for exploratory research are presented and possible solutions are discussed.

1 Introduction

A data warehouse is an integrated repository that stores information which may originate from multiple, possibly heterogeneous operational or legacy data sources. The contents of a data warehouse may be a replica of a part of data from a source or they may be the results of *preprocessed* queries or both. This way of storing data provides a powerful tools to business organizations for making business decisions. The architecture of a data warehousing system allows a number of ways to integrate and query (such as *eager* or *in-advance*) information stored in it. This approach of integrating data from distributed data sources pays rich dividends when it translates into calculated decisions backed by sound analysis. Thus, the *Data warehousing* coupled with *On-Line Analytical Processing (OLAP)* enable business decision makers to creatively approach, analyze and understand business problems. The data warehouse system is used to provide solutions for business problems since it transforms operational data into strategic decision making information. The data warehouse stores summarized information over operational data. This summarized information is time-variant and provides effective answers to queries like "what are the supply patterns of 'toy' product in California in 1997 and how were they different from last year?" To extract this information from a distributed relational model, we would require to query multiple data sources and integrate the information at a particular point before presenting the answers to the user. This requires time and it is not *online*. In a data warehousing scenario, such queries find their answers in a central place, thus reducing the processing and management costs.

[Wid95] proposed a number of technical issues in data warehousing which needed the immediate attention of the research community. A lot of work has been done in many areas since then and new issues have come to the fore. [CD97] presents the state of art in data warehousing and OLAP, with emphasis on new requirements. The work presented serves as a very good overview and is an excellent survey in this area. However, there is a need to initiate a discussion on the impending research problems in the above mentioned fields. We need to delve into each research problem minutely rather than adopting a global approach. In this paper, we attempt to give new direction in some of these problems by providing insight for developing efficient solutions and by discussing some of the well known solutions.

The rest of the paper is organised as follows. In Section 2, we give an architecture of a data warehousing system. We discuss the multidimensional model and the implementation schemes in Section 3. In Section 4 we highlight the need for constraints in the multidimensional environment and its proposed uses. A promising challenge in data warehousing is how to maintain the materialized views. The view maintenance has branched into a number of sub-problems like self maintenance, consistency maintenance, update filtering and on-line view maintenance In Section 5, we investigate these sub-problems. We also discuss the issues of parallelism in data warehousing in Section 6. We mention the other areas of active research in Section 7. Section 8 concludes the paper with a discussion on possible future work.

2 Data Warehousing System

The data warehousing system architecture is illustrated in Figure 1. Warehouse data is derived from the data contained in operational data systems. These operational data sources are connected to the *wrappers/monitors*, whose main function is to select, transform and clean data. It also monitors changes to the source data and propagates them to the integrator. The integrator's job is to combine data selected from different data sources. It resolves conflicts among data and brings data in consistent form. After integration, data is propagated into warehouse storage. Many commercial analysis and development tools are available for data selecting, filtering, transforming, and loading. Examples include Platinum InfoRefiner and InfoPump, SAS Access, IBM Data joiner.

There are two approaches to creating the warehouse data, namely, bottom-up approach and top-down approach, respectively. In a bottom-up approach,

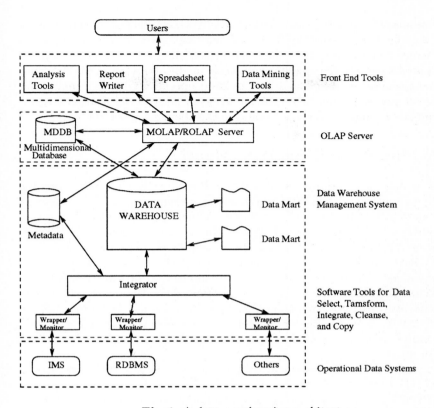

Fig. 1. A data warehousing architecture

the data is obtained from the primary sources based on the data warehouse applications and queries which are typically known in advance, and then data is selected, transformed, and integrated by data acquisition tools. In a top-down approach, the data is obtained from the primary sources whenever a query is posed. In this case, the warehouse system determines the primary data sources in order to answer the query. These two approaches are similar to *eager* and *lazy* approaches discussed in [Wid95]. The bottom-up approach is used in data warehousing because user queries can be answered immediately and data analysis can be done efficiently since data will always be available in the warehouse. Hence, this approach is feasible and improves the performance of the system. Another approach is a hybrid approach, which combines aspects of the bottom-up and top-down approaches. In this approach, some data is stored in a warehouse, and other data can be obtained from the primary sources on demand [HZ96].

The metadata contains the informational data about the creation, management, and usage of the data warehouse. It serves as a bridge between the users of the warehouse and the data contained in it. The warehouse data is accessed by OLAP server to present the same in a multidimensional way to the front end tools (such as analytical tools, report writer, spreadsheets, data mining tools) for analysis and informational purposes. Basically, OLAP server interprets client queries (the client interacts with front end tools and pass these queries to the OLAP server) and converts them into complex SQL queries (indeed extended SQL) required to access the warehouse data. It might also access the data from the primary sources if the client's queries need operational data. Finally, the OLAP server passes the multidimensional views of data to the front end tools, and these tools format the data according to the client's requirements.

3   The Multidimensional Data Model

The data models for designing traditional OLTP systems are not well-suited for modelling complex queries in data warehousing environment. The transactions in OLTP systems are made up of simple, pre-defined queries. In the data warehousing environments, queries tend to use joins on more tables, have a larger computation time and are ad-hoc in nature. This kind of processing environment warrants a new perspective to data modelling. The *multidimensional* data model i.e., the *data cube* turned out to be an adequate model that provides a way to aggregate facts along multiple attributes, called *dimensions*. Data is stored as *facts* and *dimensions* instead of rows and columns as in relational data model. Facts are numeric or factual data that represent a specific business activity and a dimension represent a single perspective on the data. Each dimension is described by a set of attributes.

The conceptual multidimensional data model can be physically realized in two ways, (1) by using trusted relational databases (*star schema/snowflake schema* [CD97]) or (2) by making use of specialised multidimensional databases. In this section we briefly describe multidimensional scheme.

Multidimensional Scheme

This scheme stores data in a matrix using array-based storage structure. Each cell in the array is formed by the intersection of all the dimensions, therefore, not all cells have a value. For example, not all database researchers publish in all journals. The multi-dimensional data set requires smaller data storage since the data is clustered compactly in the multidimensional array. The values of the dimensions need not be explicitly stored. The n-dimensional table schema is used to support multidimensional data representation which is described next.

n-dimensional Table Schema An n-dimensional table schema is the fundamental structure of a multidimensional database which draws on terminology of the statistical databases. The attribute set associated with this schema is of two kinds: *parameters* and *measures*. An n-dimensional table has a set of attributes R and a set of dimensions D associated with it. Each dimension is characterized by a distinct subset of attributes from R, called the parameters of that dimension. The attributes in R which are not parameters of any dimension are called the measure attributes. This approach is a very unique way of *flattening* the data cube since the table structure is inherently multidimensional. The actual contents of the table are essentially orthogonal to the associated structure. Each *cell* of the data cube can be represented in an n-dimensional table as table entries. These table entries have to be extended by dimensions to interpret their meaning. The current literature on n-dimensional table however does not give an implementation of the MDDB which is different from the implementation suggested by the already existing schemas. This implementation breaks up the n-dimensional table into dimension tables and fact tables which snowballs into snowflake schema and traditional ROLAP. The challenge with the research community is to find mechanisms that translate this multidimensional table into a true multidimensional implementation. This would require us to look at new data structures for the implementation of multiple dimensions in one table. The relation in relational data model is a classic example of 0-dimensional table.

4   Constraints on the Multidimensional Databases

In a relational schema, we can define a number of integrity constraints in the conceptual design. These constraints can be broadly classified as key constraints, referential integrity constraints, not null constraint, relation-based check constraints, attribute-based check constraints and general assertions (business rules). These constraints can be easily translated into triggers that keep the relational database consistent at all times. This concept of defining constraints based on dependencies can be mapped to a multidimensional scenario.

The current literature on modelling multidimensional databases has not discussed the constraints on the data cube. In a relational model, the integrity and business constraints that are defined in the conceptual schema provide for efficient design, implementation and maintenance of the database. Taking a cue from the relational model, we need to identify and enumerate the constraints that exist in the multidimensional model. An exploratory research area would be to categorise the cube constraints into classes and compare them with the relational constraints. The constraints can be broadly classified into two categories: *intra-cube* constraints and *inter-cube* constraints.. The intra-cube constraints define constraints within a cube by exploiting the relationships that exist between the various attributes of a cube. The relationships between the various dimensions in a cube, the relationships between the dimensions and measure attributes in a cube, dimension attribute hierarchy and other cell characteristics are some of the key cube features that need to formalised as a set of intra-cube constraints. The inter-cube constraints define relationships between two or more cubes. There are various considerations in defining inter-cube constraints. Such constraints can be defined by considering the relationships between dimensions in different cubes, the relationships between measures in different cubes, the relationships between measures in one cube and dimensions in the other cube and the overall relationship between two cubes, i.e., two cubes might *merge* into one, one cube might be a *subset* of the other cube, etc.

Using Constraints The cube constraints will facilitate the conceptual schema design of a data warehouse and allow us to provide triggers in a multidimensional scenario. In a relational database system, triggers play a very important role by enforcing the constraints and business rules in a very effective manner. The UPDATE, INSERT and DELETE triggers in the relational model have provided the robustness by allowing least manual intervention. The current data warehouse maintenance algorithms have neglected the role of triggers in designing effective view maintenance paradigms. The research community needs to envision the new types of triggers which would be needed for effective data warehousing. The constraint set will be of vital importance to this faculty.

The constraint set can also be used to solve the existing problems like view maintenance. In [MKK97, RSS96], the authors have proposed the view maintenance techniques based on the view expression tree that is used for evaluating the view as a query. The auxiliary relations are materialized for each node in the tree in addition to the materialized view. The updates to nodes in the expression tree are calculated and propagated in a bottom-up fashion. The update to each node in the tree is derived from the updates to its children nodes and the auxiliary relations materialized for the children and the node itself. If the constraints are defined on the view, then they can be broken down into smaller components (i.e. sub-constraints) and these sub-constraints can be pushed down into the expression tree to provide new efficient mechanisms for view maintenance and aggregate query optimization. That is, the constraints can be defined at each node in the tree. In this case, the updates to each node can be checked using these constraints before propagating them to the parent node. If some of the updates violate constraints, then there is no need to propagate these updates to the parent node. This method of decomposing the constraints and pushing them down along the edges of the expression tree can effectively reduce the communication and computation costs. The constraint set acts like a sieve which effectively filters the updates that do not affect the view.

Further, the constraint set will be an very effective tool that can be used in every aspect of data warehousing. The constraint set will enable us to define a complete algebra for the multidimensional data model which is independent of the underlying schema definitions. Also, the constraint set will allow evolution of new attributes in the multidimensional scenario. Some of these constraints can be used to map the multidimensional world into the relational world. We can view the data model as a soccer ball and the constraints can help us get an impression of that ball from a certain perspective. The constraint set will enable us to seek new, improved implementation mechanisms that are able to conserve the multidimensionality of data. Our first task is to define a constraint set on the multidimensional data model which is complete in any implementation scheme. The constraints need to be formally defined and the precedence order for the constraints needs to be decided. We hope that the discussion we have initiated will spark off hectic activity in the research community.

5   View Maintenance

A *data warehouse* (DW) stores integrated information from multiple data sources in *materialized views* (MV) over the source data. The data sources (DS) may be heterogeneous, distributed and autonomous. When the data in any source (base data) changes, the MVs at the DW need to be updated accordingly. *The process of updating a materialized view in response to the changes in the underlying source data is called View Maintenance.* The view maintenance problem has evoked great interest in the past few years. This view maintenance in such a distributed environment gives rise to inconsistencies since there is a finite unpredictable amount of time required for (a) propagating changes from the DS to the DW and (b) computing view updates in response to these changes. Data consistency can be maintained at the data warehouse by performing the following steps:

- propagate changes from the data sources (ST_1 - current state of the data sources at the time of propagation of these changes) to the data warehouse to ensure that each view reflects a consistent state of the base data.
- compute view updates in response to these changes using the state ST_1 of the data sources.
- install the view updates at the data warehouse in the same order as the changes have occurred at the data sources.

The inconsistencies at the data warehouse occur since the changes that take place at the data sources are random and dynamic. Before the data warehouse is able to compute the view update for the *old* changes, the *new* changes change the state of the data sources from ST_1 to ST_2. This violates the consistency criterion that we have listed. Making the MVs at the data warehouse self-maintainable decimates the problem of inconsistencies by eliminating the finite unpredictable time required to query the data source for computing the view updates. In the next subsection, we describe self-maintenance of materialized views at the data warehouse.

Self-Maintenance Consider a materialized view MV at the data warehouse defined over a set of base relations $R = \{R_1, R_2, ..., R_n\}$. MV stores a pre-processed query at the data warehouse. The set of base relations R may reside in one data source or in multiple, heterogenous data sources. A change ΔR_i made to the relation R_i might affect MV. MV is defined to be self-maintainable if a change ΔMV in MV, in response to the change ΔR_i can be computed using only the MV and the update ΔR_i. But the data warehouse might need some additional information from other relations in the set R residing in one or more data sources to compute the view update ΔMV. Since the underlying data sources are decoupled from the data warehouse, this requires a finite computation time. Also the random changes at the data sources can give rise to inconsistencies at the data warehouse. Some data sources may not support full database functionalities and querying such sources to compute the view updates might be a cumbersome, even an impossible task. Because of these problems, the preprocessed query that is materialized at the warehouse needs to be maintained without access to the base relations.

One of the approaches is to replicate all base data in its entirety at the data warehouse so that maintenance of the MV becomes local to the data warehouse. [GM95, Küc91, GMS93]. Although this approach guarantees self-maintainability at the warehouse, it creates new problems. As more and more data is added to the warehouse, it increases the space complexity and gives rise to information redundancy which might lead to inconsistencies. This approach also overlooks the point that the base tuples might be present in the view itself, so the view instance, the base update and a subset of the base relations might be sufficient to achieve self-maintainability in the case of SPJ (Select-Project-Join) views [Huy97]. *But how can the subset of the base relations that is needed to compute the view updates be stored at DW ?* This question was addressed in [QGMW96], which defines a set of minimal *auxiliary views (AVs)* to materialize that are sufficient to make a view self-maintainable. Although materializing auxiliary views at the DW was a novel concept, the minimality of auxiliary views defined was still questionable since the MV instance was never exploited for self-maintenance. Most of the current approaches maintain the MVs separately from each other using a separate *view manager* for each view and such approaches fail to recognize that these views can be maintained together by identifying the set of related materialized views. This issue of multiple-view self-maintenance was addressed for the first time in [Huy97].

In some approaches to multiple-view self-maintenance, a set of auxiliary views (AV) are stored at the data warehouse along with the set of materialized views (MV) such that together $MV \cup AV$ is self-maintainable. The research challenge lies in finding the most *economical AVs* in terms of space complexity and computational costs. The view self maintenance is still an active research problem. It is not always feasible to provide self-maintainability of the views at the data warehouse. When the cost of providing self-maintainability exceeds the cost of querying data sources for computing view updates, it is profitable to allow querying of data sources instead.

Update Filtering The changes that take place in the source data need to be reflected at the data warehouse. Some changes may create view updates that need to installed at the data warehouse; some changes leave the views at the data warehouse unchanged. If we are able to detect at the data sources that certain changes are guaranteed to leave the views unchanged, we need not propagate these changes to the data warehouse. This would require checking of distributed integrity constraints at a single site. As many changes as possible can be filtered at the sources and only the changes that result in view updates may be propagated to the warehouse. The update filtering will reduce the size of the maintenance transactions at the data warehouse, thus minimizing the time required to make the data warehouse consistent with the data sources. The side effect of update filtering is that we need to make our data sources (and the wrapper/monitor) components more intelligent. They need to know about their participation in the data warehouse and the data warehouse configuration so that the updates can be checked against the constraint set before propagating them. To be able to realize this, the data sources cannot be decoupled from the data warehouse anymore. This would give rise to new problems like configuration management i.e., if there is a change in the schema at any data source or at the data warehouse, all the participating entities need to be informed of this change so that they can modify the constraint set to reflect this change. The view maintenance strategies would now be based on the constraint set and any change to the constraint set would warrant a change in the existing view maintenance transaction.

On-Line View Maintenance Warehouse view maintenance can be either done *incrementally* or by queueing a large number of updates at the data sources to be propagated as a *batch* update from the data sources to the data warehouse. In current commercial systems, a batch update is periodically sent to the data warehouse and view updates are computed and installed. This transaction is called the *maintenance transaction*. A user typically issues read-only queries at the data warehouse and a long-running sequence of user queries is called a *reader session*. The batch maintenance transaction is typically large and blocks the reader sessions. This makes the data warehouse *offline* for the duration of the maintenance transaction. The maintenance transaction typically runs at night. With the advent of the internet and global users, this scheme will have to give way. The $24 - hour$ shop concept is what most companies are striving for and the data warehouse to be online 24 hours to allow the company to be competitive in its strategies. Incremental view maintenance which updates the data warehouse instantaneously in response to every change at the data source is expensive and gives rise to inconsistent results during the same reader session. An update from the data source will change the results a user might see over a sequence of queries. We need to get around these problems. [QW97] discusses a possible approach to this problem by maintaining two versions of each tuple at the data warehouse simultaneously so that the reader sessions and the maintenance transactions do not block each other. A possible solution may need the integration with self maintenance techniques, where auxiliary views can be used to answer queries during maintenance transactions.

6   Parallelism in Data Warehousing

In this paper, we have discussed every possible technique to evaluate OLAP queries faster. All these techniques are restricted in their ways. The precomputation strategy needs to anticipate queries so that it can materialize them in the data warehouse. OLAP queries are of adhoc nature and restricts precomputing to the imagination of the designer. The indexing schemes we have discussed provide faster access to the data stored in the warehouse, but does not reduce the size of tables stored at the data warehouse. One can say that the strategies presented provide faster query processing, but they need not be fast enough as perceived by the user. One mechanism that is recently being exploited by vendors to compute queries quickly is to execute the query in parallel by partitioning data among a set of processors. This can potentially achieve *linear speedup* and can significantly improve query response times. However to exploit this technology we need to address a few key issues like parallel data placement and parallel join.

The existing data warehouse schema design strategies is not catered to parallel data placement, although the star schema suggests implicitly the need of partitioning the data into a set of dimension tables and fact tables. Many DBMS vendors claim to support parallel data warehousing to various degrees. Most of these products, however, do not use the dimensionality of data that exists in a data warehouse. The effective use of parallel processing in this environment can be achieved only if we are able to find innovative techniques for parallel data placement using the underlying properties of data in the warehouse. [DMT98] use the data indexing strategy to provide efficient data partitioning and parallel resource utilization. Effective algorithms that split the data among n parallel processors and perform parallel join operation have been illustrated. We need to take a cue from this work and find more effective solutions.

7 Other Research Challenges

The research challenges discussed so far are directly concerned with the problem of faster data integration. There are other challenges which are a result of the data warehousing concept. Here we mention a few such challenges which are currently active. One such problem arises due to the changing user requirements. As the requirements of the user changes, the view definitions at the data warehouse change dynamically. We need to develop view adaptation techniques that do not need the entire recomputation of the materialized view at every change. In [GMR95, MD96, Moh97], the authors have presented the view adaptation techniques for a data warehouse that recompute only parts of the view (if any) which cannot be derived from the existing materialized views. These techniques are applicable for SPJ queries. However, there is a need to devise adaptation algorithms for aggregated queries.

One issue which has seen little investigation is the fragmentation of a multi-dimensional database. Fragmentation plays an important role in the design of a distributed database system, it enables the definition of appropriate units of distribution which enhance query performance by enabling concurrent and parallel execution of queries. The requirement for parallel processing of OLAP operations to achieve quick response times is also important [DMT98]. This can be acheived by fragmenting multidimensional database into number of fragments. We identify two types of possible fragmentation; (1) *slice 'n dice* that selects subsets of data by 'cutting up' the multidimensional hypercube representation of the global data into sub-cubes. This strategy is currently employed by vendors of multidimensional databases that support fragmentation; for example the Essbase OLAP Server Partitioning option. (2) *severing* that divides the global data by removing dimensions from a hypercube. This method may be used to divide a cube into two cubes with different dimensions from each other. Operations performed during severing ensure that the original cube may be reconstructed from the two severed cubes.

Another interesting problem is the problem of data expiry in the warehouse. Data that is materialized in the warehouse may not ne needed after a point. We need to devise efficient schemes that determine the data expiry point and do effective garbage collection by removing the unnecessary tuples.

8   Conclusions

This paper brings together under one roof all the techniques of integrating data quickly to help effective decision making. The data warehousing phenomenon, which has grown from strength to strength in the last few years presents new challenges everyday as we find new applications where warehousing can play a crucial role. In this paper, we have discussed the recent advances and research problems in three different areas, namely, data warehouse modeling, view maintenance, parallel query processing. Since the four areas discussed in this paper directly contribute in a large way to the *warehousing* phenomenon, there is a need to integrate the research work that is done in these different areas under one umbrella. This paper serves as a stepping stone in this direction.

Further, we have exploited the multidimensionality of data in the warehouse to introduce the concept of constraints on the data cube. We highlight the usefulness of the constraint set in every aspect of data warehousing, that is, design, implementation and maintenance. This paper also underlines the need for dynamic self-maintainability of materialized views and discusses the issues involved. In this paper, new areas for exploratory research have been presented and we hope that the issues presented will invoke keen interest from the data warehousing community.

References

[CD97]   S. Chaudhuri and U. Dayal. An overview of data warehousing and OLAP technology. In *ACM SIGMOD Record*, volume 26, pages 65–74. 1997.

[DMT98]   A. Datta, B. Moon, and H. Thomas. A case for parallelism in data warehousing and olap. Technical report, Dept. of MIS, University of Arizona, Tucson, AZ URL: http://loochi.bpa.arizona.edu, 1998.

[GM95]   A. Gupta and I. S. Mumick. Maintenance of materialized views: problems, techniques, and applications. *IEEE Data Engineering Bulletin, Special Issue on Materialized Views and Warehousing*, 18(2), 1995.

[GMR95]   A. Gupta, I.S. Mumick, and K.A. Ross. Adapting materialized views after redefinitions. In *Proc. ACM SIGMOD International Conference on Management of Data, San Jose, USA*, 1995.

[GMS93]   A. Gupta, I. S. Mumick, and V. S. Subrahmanian. Maintaining views in-
          crementally. In *Proc. ACM SIGMOD Int. Conf. on Management of Data*,
          pages 157–166, 1993.

[Huy97]   N. Huyn. Multiple view self-maintenance in data warehousing environ-
          ments. In *To Appear in Proc. Int'l Conf. on Very Large Databases*, 1997.

[HZ96]   R. Hull and G. Zhou. A framework for supporting data integration using
          the materialized and virtual approaches. In *Proc. ACM SIGMOD Conf.
          On Management of Data*, pages 481–492, 1996.

[Küc91]   V. Küchenhoff. On the efficient computation of the difference between
          consecutive database states. In C. Delobel, M. Kifer, and Y. Masunaga,
          editors, *Proc. Second Int. Conf. on Deductive Object-Oriented Databases*,
          volume 566 of *Lecture Notes in Computer Science, Springer-Verlag*, pages
          478–502. Springer-Verlag, 1991.

[MD96]   M. Mohania and G. Dong. Algorithms for adapting materialized views
          in data warehouses. In *Proc. of International Symposium on Cooperative
          Database Systems for Advanced Applications, Kyoto, Japan*, pages 62–69,
          1996.

[MKK97]   M. Mohania, S. Konomi, and Y. Kambayashi. Incremental maintenance of
          materialized views. In *Proc. of 8th International Conference on Database
          and Expert Systems Applications (DEXA '97)*. Springer-Verlag, 1997.

[Moh97]   M. Mohania. Avoiding re-computation: View adaptation in data ware-
          houses. In *Proc. of 8th International Database Workshop, Hong Kong*,
          pages 151–165, 1997.

[QGMW96] Dallan Quass, Ashish Gupta, Inderpal Singh Mumick, and Jennifer
          Widom. Making views self-maintainable for data warehousing. In *Proc. of
          International Conference on Parallel and Database Information Systems*,
          1996.

[QW97]   D. Quass and J. Widom. On-line warehouse view maintenance for batch
          updates. In *Proc. ACM SIGMOD Int. Conf. on Management of Data*,
          1997.

[RSS96]   K.A. Ross, D. Srivastava, and Sudarshan S. Materialized view mainte-
          nance and integrity constraint checking: Trading space for time. In *Proc.
          ACM SIGMOD International Conference on Management of Data, Mon-
          treal, Canada*, 1996.

[Wid95]   Jennifer Widom. Research problems in data warehousing. In *Proc. Fourth
          Intl. Conference on Information and Knowledge Management*, 1995.

Web Warehousing: Design and Issues*

S. S. BHOWMICK   S. K. MADRIA   W. -K. NG   E.P. LIM
{sourav,askumar,wkn,aseplim}@cais.ntu.edu.sg

Center for Advanced Information Systems, School of Applied Science,
Nanyang Technological University, Singapore 639798, SINGAPORE

Abstract

The World Wide Web is a distributed global information resource. It contains a large amount of information that have been placed on the web independently by different organizations and thus, related information may appear across different web sites. To manage and access heterogeneous information on WWW, we have started a project of building a web warehouse, called WHOWEDA (*W*are*h*ouse *o*f *Web* *D*ata). Currently, our work on building a web warehousing system has focused on building a data model and designing a web algebra. In this paper, we discuss design and research issues in a web warehousing system. The issues include are designing algebraic operators for web information access and manipulation, web data visualization and web knowledge discovery. These issues will not only overcome the limitations of available search engines but also provide powerful and friendly query mechanisms for retrieving useful information and knowledge discovery from a web warehouse.

1 Introduction

Most users obtain WWW information using a combination of search engines and browsers. However, these two types of retrieval mechanisms do not necessarily address all of a user's information needs and have the following shortcomings:

- Web browsers fully exploit hyperlinks among web pages, however, search engines have so far made little progress in exploiting link information. Not only do most search engines fail to support queries on the web utilizing link information, they also fail to return link information as part of a query's result.
- The search is limited to string matching. Numeric comparisons, as in conventional databases, cannot be done.
- Queries are evaluated on the index data rather than on the original and up-to-date data.

---

* This work was supported in part by the Nanyang Technological University, Ministry of Education (Singapore) under Academic Research Fund #4-12034-5060, #4-12034-3012, #4-12034-6022. Any opinions, findings, and recommendations in this paper are those of the authors and do not reflect the views of the funding agencies.

- The accuracy of results is low as there is an almost unavoidable repetition of information and existence of non-relevant data in the results.
- From the query's result returned by the search engines, a user may wish to couple a set of related Web documents together for reference. Presently, he may only do so manually by visiting and downloading these documents as files on the user's hard disk. However, this method is tedious, and it does not allow a user to retain the *coupling framework*.
- The set of downloaded documents can be refreshed (or updated) only by repeating the above procedure.
- If a user has successfully coupled a set of Web documents together, he may wish to know if there are other Web documents satisfying the same coupling framework. Presently, the only way is to request the same or other search engines for further Web documents and probe these documents manually.
- Over a period of time, there will be a number of coupled collections of Web documents created by the user. As each of these collections exists simply as a set of files on the user's system, there is no convenient way to manage and infer further useful information from them.

To overcome the limitations explained above and provide the user with a powerful and friendly query mechanism for accessing information on the web, the critical problem is to find the effective ways to build web data models of the information of interest, and to provide a mechanism to manipulate these information to garner additional useful information. The key objective of our web warehousing project, called WHOWEDA (*Warehouse of Web Data*), at the Centre for Advanced Information Systems in Nanyang Technological University, Singapore is to design and implement a web warehouse that materializes and manages useful information from the Web [22]. To meet the warehousing objective, we materialize coupled web information in the form of *web tuples* and store them in *web tables*. We define a set of web operators with web semantics to equip the warehouse with the basic capabilities to manipulate web tables and couple additional, useful, related web information residing in the web tables [9, 22]. These operators include web algebraic operations such as web select, web join, web union, web intersection, and so on [22]. In this paper, we present an overview of a web warehouse and highlight new research directions in some of the important areas of building a web warehousing system.

1.1 Related Work

There has been considerable work in data model and query languages for the World Wide Web [13, 15, 16, 20]. For example, Mendelzon, Mihaila and Milo [20] proposed a WebSQL query language based on a formal calculus for querying the WWW. The result of a WebSQL query is a set of web tuples which are flattened immediately to linear tuples. Konopnicki and Shmueli [15] proposed a high level querying system called the W3QS for the WWW whereby users may specify content and structure queries on the WWW and maintain the results of queries as database views of the WWW. In W3QL, queries are always made to the WWW. Fiebig, Weiss and Moerkotte extended relational algebra to the

World Wide Web by augmenting the algebra with new domains (data types) [13], and functions that apply to the domains. The extended model is known as RAW (Relational Algebra for the Web). Inspired by concepts in declarative logic, Lakshmanan, Sadri and Subramanian designed WebLog [16] to be a language for querying and restructuring web information. Other proposals, namely Lorel [2] and UnQL [11], aim at querying heterogeneous and semistructured information. These languages adopt a lightweight data model (based on labeled graphs) to represent data, and concentrate on the development of powerful query languages for these structures.

2 Web Information Coupling Model

In Web Information Coupling System (WICS) [9], we materialize web information as web tuples stored in web tables. Each web table is associated with a web schema. We equip the WICS with the basic capability to manipulate web tables and correlate additional useful and related web information residing in the web tables [22]. We proposed a Web Information Coupling Model (WICM) which describe web objects, web schema and a web algebra for retrieving information from the web and manipulating these information to derive additional information.

2.1 Web Objects

It consists of a hierarchy of web objects. The fundamental objects are *Nodes* and *Links*. Nodes correspond to HTML or plain text documents and links correspond to hyper-links interconnecting the documents in the World Wide Web. We define a Node type and a Link type to refer to these two sets of distinct objects. These objects consist of a set of attributes as shown below:

```
Node = [url, title, format, size, date, text]
Link = [source-url, target-url, label, link-type]
```

For the Node object type, the attributes are the URL of a Node instance and its title, document format, size (in bytes), date of last modification, and textual contents. For the Link type, the attributes are the URL of the source document containing the hyperlink, the URL of the target document, the anchor or label of the link, and the type of the link. Hyperlinks in the WWW may be characterized into three types: *interior*, *local*, and *global* [20].

The next higher level of abstraction is a web tuple. A web tuple is a set of connected, directed graphs each consisting of a set of nodes and links which are instances of Node and Link respectively. A collection of web tuples is called a web table. If the table is materialized, we associate a name with the table. There is a *schema* (see next section) associated with every web table. A web database consists of a set of web schemas and a set of web tables.

2.2 Web Schema

A web schema contains meta-information that binds a set of web tuples in a web table. Web tables are materialized results of web queries. In WICS, a user expresses a web query by describing a *query graph*.

When the query graph is evaluated, a set of web tuples each *satisfying* the query graph is harnessed from the WWW. By collecting the tuples as a table, the query graph may be used as the table's schema to bind the tuples. Hence, the web schema of a table is the query graph that is used to derive the table. Formally, a web schema is an ordered 4-tuple $M = \langle X_n, X_\ell, C, P \rangle$ where X_n is a set of node variables, X_ℓ is a set of link variables, C is a set of connectivities (in Disjunctive Normal Form), and P is a set of predicates (in Disjunctive Normal Form).

Observe that some of the nodes and links in the figures have keywords imposed on them. To express these conditions, we introduced *node* and *link variables* in the query graph. Thus, in Figure **??** node d represents those web documents which contains the words 'side effects' in the text or title. In other words, variables denote arbitrary instances of `Node` or `Link`. There are two special variables: a node variable denoted by the symbol '#' and a link variable denoted by the symbol '-'. These two variables differ from the other variables in that they are never *bound* (these variables are not defined by the predicates of the schema).

Structural properties of web tuples are expressed by a set of *connectivities*. Formally, a connectivity k is an expression of the form: $x\langle\rho\rangle y$ where $x \in X_n, y \in X_n$, and ρ is a regular expression over X_ℓ. (The angle brackets around ρ are used for delimitation purposes only.) Thus, $x\langle\rho\rangle y$ describes a path or a set of possible paths between two nodes x and y.

The last schema component is the set of predicates P. Predicates provide a means to impose additional conditions on web information to be retrieved. Let p be a predicate. If x, y are node or link variables then the following are possible forms of predicates: $p(x) \equiv [x.\texttt{attribute}\ \texttt{CONTAINS}\ "A"]$ or $p(x) \equiv [x.\texttt{attribute}$ $\texttt{EQUALS}\ "A"]$ and $p(x, y) \equiv [x.\texttt{attribute} = y.\texttt{attribute}]$. where `attribute` refers to an attribute of `Node`, `Link` or `link_type`, A is a regular expression over the ASCII character set, x and y are *arguments* of p.

3   Web Algebra

The web algebra provides a formal foundation for data representation and manipulation for the web warehouse. It supports structured and topological query with sets of keywords specified on multiple nodes and on hyperlinks among the nodes. The user query is a graph-like structure and it is used to match the portions of WWW satisfying the conditions. The query result is a set of graphs called web tuples. We then define a set of web operators with web semantics to manipulate web tuples stored in a web table. The basic algebraic operators include global and local web coupling, web select, web join, web intersection, web union, etc. These operators are implemented as a part of our web query language. Briefly, these operators are discussed below. More details can be found in [5, 9, 22].

3.1   Information Access Operator

Global Web Coupling Global coupling enables a user to retrieve a set of collections of inter-related documents satisfying a web schema or coupling framework, regardless of the locations of the documents in the Web. To initiate global coupling, the user specifies the coupling framework in the form of a *query graph*. The coupling is performed by the WIC system and is transparent to the user. Formally, the global web coupling operator Γ takes in a query (expressed as a schema M) and extracts a set of web tuples from the WWW satisfying the schema. Let W_g be the resultant table, then $W_g = \Gamma(M)$. Each web tuple matches a portion of the WWW satisfying the conditions described in the schema. These related set of web tuples are coupled together and stored in a web table. Each web tuple in the web table is structurally identical to the schema of the table. The formal details appear in [9].

3.2 Information Manipulation Operators

Web Select The `select` operation on a web table extract web tuples from a web table satisfying certain conditions. However, since the schema of web tables is more complex than that of relational tables, selection conditions have to be expressed as predicates on node and link variables, as well as connectivities of web tuples. The `web select` operation augments the schema of web tables by incorporating new conditions into the schema. Thus, it is different from its relational counterpart.

Let W be a web table with schema $M = \langle X_n, X_\ell, C, P \rangle$. Selection condition(s) on that table is denoted by another schema $M_s = \langle X_{s,n}, X_{s,\ell}, C_s, P_s \rangle$ where C_s contains the selection criteria on connectivities, and P_s contains predicates on node and link variables in $X_{s,n}$ and $X_{s,\ell}$ respectively. Formally, we define web select as follows: $W_s = \sigma_{M_s}(W)$ where σ is the select operator.

Web Project The web project operation on a web table extract portions of a web tuple satisfying certain conditions. However, since the schema of web tables is more complex than that of relational tables, *projection conditions* have to be expressed as node and link variables and/or connectivities between the node variables. The web project operation reduces the number of node and link variables in the original schema and the constraints over these variables. For more details, refer to [5].

Given a web table W with schema $M = \langle X_n, X_\ell, C, P \rangle$, a web projection on W computes a new web table W' with schema $M_p = \langle X_{n_p}, X_{\ell_p}, C_p, P_p \rangle$. The components of M_p depends on the project conditions. Formally, we define web project as follows: $W' = \pi_{\langle project\_condition(s) \rangle}(W)$ where π is the symbol for project operation.

A user may explicitly specify any one of the conditions or any combination of the three conditions discussed below to initiate a web project operation.

- **Set of node variables:** To project a set of node variables from the web table.
- **Start-node variable and end-node variable:** To project all the instances of node variables between two node variables.
- **Node variable and depth of links:** To restrict the set of nodes to be projected within a limited number of links starting from the specified node variable.

Web Cartesian Product A web cartesian product, denoted by $\times$, is a binary operation that combines two web tables by concatenating a web tuple of one web table with a web tuple of other. If W_i and W_j are web tables with n and m web tuples respectively, the resulting web table W created by web cartesian product consists of $n \times m$ web tuples.

Local Web Coupling Given two web tables, local coupling is initiated explicitly by specifying a pair(s) of web documents (*coupling node variables*) and a set of keyword(s) to relate them. The result of local web coupling is a web table consisting of a set of collections of inter-related Web documents from the two input tables. To elaborate further, let W_i and W_j be two web tables with schemas $M_i = \langle X_{i,n}, X_{i,\ell}, C_i, P_i \rangle$ and $M_j = \langle X_{j,n}, X_{j,\ell}, C_j, P_j \rangle$ respectively. Let w_i and w_j be two web tuples from W_i and W_j, and $n_c(w_i)$ and $n_c(w_j)$ are instances of node variables n_{c_i} and n_{c_j} respectively. Suppose documents at `http://www.virtualdisease.com/cancer/index.html` (represented by node $n_c(w_i)$) and `http://www.virtualdrug.com/cancerdrugs/index.html` (represented by node $n_c(w_j)$) contain information related to cancer and appears in w_i and w_j respectively. Tuples w_i and w_j are *coupling-compatible locally* on $n_c(w_i)$ and $n_c(w_j)$ since they both contain similar information (information related to cancer).

We express local web coupling between two web tables as follows:

$$W = W_i \otimes_{(\{\langle node\_pair\rangle, \langle keyword(s)\rangle\})} W_j$$

where W_i and W_j are the two web tables participating in the coupling operation and W is the coupled web table satisfying a schema $M = \langle X_n, X_\ell, C, P \rangle$. In this case, $\langle node\_pair\rangle$ specifies a pair of coupling node variables in the web table W_i and W_j, and $\langle keyword(s)\rangle$ specifies a list of keyword(s) on which the similarity between the coupling node variable pair is evaluated.

Web Join The web join operator combines two web tables by *concatenating* a web tuple of one table with a web tuple of other table whenever there exists *joinable nodes*. Let W_i and W_j be two web tables with schemas $M_i = \langle X_{i,n}, X_{i,\ell}, C_{i,p}, P_i \rangle$ and $M_j = \langle X_{j,n}, X_{j,\ell}, C_j, P_j \rangle$ respectively. Then W_i and W_j are *joinable* if and only if there exist at least one node variable in M_i and in M_j which refers to identical (having the same URL) node or web document.

Consider the following predicates of the node variables c and z where $c \in X_{i,n}$ and $z \in X_{j,n}$:

$$p_{i_4}(c) \equiv [c.\texttt{url EQUALS "http://www.singapore.com/area/"}],$$
$$p_{j_4}(z) \equiv [z.\texttt{url EQUALS "http://www.singapore.com/area/"}]$$

Since the node variables c and z of M_i and M_j respectively refers to the same web document at URL '`http://www.singapore.com/area/`', the web tables W_i and W_j are joinable. The joinable nodes are c and z.

Formally, we define $W = W_i \bowtie W_j$ is a set of web tuples satisfying schema $M = \langle X_n, X_\ell, C, P \rangle$ where X_n is the set of node variables appearing in P, X_ℓ is the set of link variables appearing in P, C and P are obtained from M_i and M_j. We discussed web join operator in detail in [10].

Schema Tightness In a web warehouse, a user expresses a web query by describing a query graph or coupling framework. The query graph is used as the schema of the web table to bind the web tuples. In reality, it is unrealistic to assume from the (naive) user complete knowledge of the structure of the query graph. The user may express some incomplete graph structure based on the partial knowledge. Thus, such query graphs, if used as schema of the web table, may contain unbound nodes and links. Furthermore, a web schema serves two important purposes: First, it enables users to understand the structure of the web table and form meaningful queries over it. Second, a query processor relies on the schema to devise efficient plans for computing query results. Both the tasks become significantly harder when the schema contains unbound nodes and links.

To address these challenges, we design and implement a web operator called *schema tightness operator*. The schema tightness operator takes as input a web table containing unbound nodes and links and web schema and *tighten* the web schema of the web table by imposing constraints on the unbound nodes and links in the web table.

4 Web Data Visualization

A query graph returns a set of web tuples which are stored in a web table. However, a user may wish to view these web tuples in different framework. Here we present some data visualization operators to add flexibility in viewing query results coupled from the WWW and to generate some additional useful information.

4.1 Web Ranking Operators

Presently, in the WICM we have web operators to manipulate information from the WWW globally and locally. A crucial problem that a WIC system faces is extracting *hot tuples* for a user query (the most relevant web tuples). This problem is challenging because hot tuples might not be displayed at the beginning of the web table. We are developing two web ranking operators; *global ranking* and *local ranking* operators to rank web tuples generated by global and local web coupling respectively. The ranking operators are based on the following factors:

- Number of occurrence of a keyword in a document.
- Location of occurrence of a keyword in a document, i.e.,whether the keyword occurs in the title, text or anchor of a document.
- Overlap between all pairs of web documents, i.e., if A, B and C are documents in three web tuples considered relevant (in that order) to a user query, then we believe that the "interestingness" of B is lower than C if B overlaps with A significantly, while C is a distinct result. Thus, our ranking function will rank web tuple containing C before the web tuple containing B.

4.2 Data Visualization Operators

Presently, in the WICM we have a set of web operators to manipulate information from the WWW. Web information is materialized and displayed in the form of web tuples stored in a web table. This approach of displaying information to the user has few shortcomings:

- It does not provide us with the ability to see the overall structure of the information captured in the web table. It is not possible for a user to visualize how one web tuple in a web table is related to another.
- The set of web tuples in a web table may contain duplicate web documents. There is no mechanism to provide a *coalesced view* of the set of web tuples. A coalesced view allows a user to browse lesser number of directed connected graphs when locating information.
- It does not allow a user to group web tuples based on *related information content*, or *similar (or identical)* web sites. A user has to manually probe each web tuple to find these information. However, these information cannot be grouped together in our web table.
- The set of web tuples are materialize in web table. There is no other representation of these web tables. For example, the collective view of these web tuples can be stored as a set of directed graphs having lesser number of nodes or links as compared to the original web table.

To resolve the above difficulties, we have introduced to following data visualization operators:

- `Web Nest`: This operator allows one to visualize relationships between web tuples in a web table. It provides an overview of the information space harnessed from the WWW and shows how these information are topically related.
- `Web Unnest`: This operator returns the original web table from a set of directed connected graphs created by the web nest operation.
- `Web Coalesce`: This operator coalesces duplicate nodes to reduce the size of the number of directed connected graphs in a web table. A coalesced web table is a set of condensed graphs and allow a user to browse lesser number of graphs (web tuples).
- `Web Expand`: This operator expands a coalesced web table to recover the original set of web tuples.
- `Web Pack`: This operator groups a web tuples based on related (or similar) information content, and similar (or identical) web sites.
- `Web Unpack`: This operator returns the original set of web tuples from the packed web table.
- `Web Sort`: This operator sorts web tuples in *ascending* or *descending* order based on the total number of nodes or link types (local, global or interior) in a web tuple.

These web operators take as input a set of web tuples of a web table and provide a different view of the tuples as output. This gives users the flexibility to view documents in perspectives that are more meaningful. These operators provide different storage representation of web tuples which will help in optimizing the query, storage and maintenance cost. These different representations may also lead to inconsistency problems with respect to the original web table. Currently, we are investigating these problems.

5 Web Data Mining

The resulting growth in on-line information combined with the almost unstructuredness of web data necessitates the development of powerful yet computationally efficient web mining tools. Web mining can be defined as the discovery and analysis of useful information from WWW data. Web mining involves three types of data; data on the WWW, web documents structure and the data on users who browse web pages. Thus, web data mining should focus on three issues; content-based mining [17], web usage mining [23] and web structure mining. Web content mining describes the automatic search of information resources available on-line. Web usage mining includes the mining of data from the server access logs, user registration or profiles, user sessions or transactions, etc. Web structure mining involves mining web document's structures and links. A survey of some of the emerging tools and techniques for web usage mining is given in [21]. One of the important areas in WHOWEDA involves the development of tools and techniques for mining useful information from the web.

The web contains a mix of many different data types, and in a sense subsumes text data mining, database data mining, image mining, and so on. The web contains additional data types that are not available in a large scale before, including hyperlinks and massive amounts of (indirect) user usage information. Spanning across all these data types is the dimension of time, since data on the web changes over time. Finally, there is data that are generated dynamically, in response to user input and programmatic scripts. In WHOWEDA, we primarily focus on mining useful information from these different data types. For further information related to web mining in WHOWEDA refer to [7].

5.1 Web Bags and Knowledge Discovery

Most of the search engines fail to handle the following knowledge discovery goals:

- From query results returned by search engines, a user may wish to locate the most *visible* Web sites [4] or documents for reference. That is, sites or documents which can be reached by many paths (high fan-in).
- Reversing the concept of visibility, a user may wish to locate the most *luminous* Web sites [4] or documents for reference. That is, web sites or documents which have the most number of outgoing links.
- Furthermore, a user may wish to find out the most traversed path for a particular query result. This is important since it helps the user to identify the set of most popular interlinked Web documents which are traversed frequently to obtain the query result.

We have introduced the concept of web bag in [5] and used web bags for knowledge discovery. Informally, a web bag is a web table containing multiple occurrences of the identical web tuples. A web tuple is a set of inter-linked documents retrieved from the WWW that satisfy a query graph. A web bag may only be created by projecting some of the nodes from the web tuples of a web table using the web project operator. A web project operator is used to isolate data of interest, allowing subsequent queries to run over a smaller, perhaps more structured web data. Unlike its relational counterpart, a web project operator does not eliminate identical web tuples autonomously. The projected web table may contain identical web tuples, thus forming a web bag. The duplicate elimination process is initiated explicitly by a user. Autonomous duplicate elimination may hinder the possibility of discovering useful knowledge from a web table. This is due to the fact that these knowledge may only be discovered from the web bags.

5.2 Warehouse Concept Mart (WCMart)

Due to the large amount of data on the WWW, knowledge discovery from web data becomes more and more complex. We propose the building of concept hierarchies from web documents and use them in discovering new knowledge. We call the collection of concepts a Warehouse Concept Mart (WCMart). Concept marts are built by extracting and generalizing terms from web documents to represent classification knowledge of a given class hierarchy. For unclassified words, they can be clustered based on their common properties. Once the clusters are decided, the keywords can be labeled with their corresponding clusters, and common features of the terms are summarized to form the concept description. We may associate a weight at each level of concept marts to evaluate the importance of a term with respect to the concept level in the concept hierarchy. Concept marts can be used for the following:

- *Intelligent answering of web queries:* Knowledge discovery using concept marts facilitates querying web data and intelligent query answering in web warehousing system. A user can supply the threshold for a given key word in the concept mart and the words with the threshold above the given value can be taken into account while answering the query. The query can also be answered using different levels of concept marts [14] or can provide approximate answers [19].
- *Ranking result tuples of a query:* In our model, tuples returned as a result of a web query are stored in a web table. We use warehouse concept marts for ranking these tuples so that the most relevant tuples are returned in response to a user's query. The user may rank tuples interactively by specifying various threshold values and concept levels.
- *Global information coupling across the WWW:* In our model, we introduce the concept of web information coupling. It refers to an association of related web documents. We use concept marts to define this "association" among web documents. Since the coupling is initiated by the user, he may supply threshold values for keywords in the concept mart to be used in the coupling.
- *Web mining:* Concept marts can also be used for web data mining. Web mining so far in the literature is restricted to mining web access patterns and trends by examining the web server log files [23]. An alternative is to make use of web concept marts in generating some useful knowledge. We may use association rule techniques to mine associations between words appearing in the concept mart at various levels, and the query graph. Mining knowledge

at multiple levels may help WWW users discover interesting rules which are
difficult to find otherwise.

- *Characterization of web tables:* In a web warehouse, we store tuples in web
  tables. We need to categorize these tables so that a user's query can be directed to the appropriate table(s). Based on the classification of web tables,
  a user may also specify tables to be used for evaluating his query. We categorize the web tables using the concept marts. We generate concept marts
  from web tables and classify a set of tables by known classes or concepts.

6   Conclusions

In this paper, we have reported an overview of a Web Warehousing Project
(WHOWEDA) [22] at the Nanyang Technological University, Singapore and discussed some interesting research ideas in that context. Building a warehouse that
accommodates data from the WWW has required us to rethink nearly every aspect of conventional data warehousing and relational technology. This paper
brings together some of the important techniques required for designing a web
warehouse and generating useful knowledge. In particular, our focus is on web
data model and an algebra for web information access, manipulation and visualization. We have also discussed the motivation for developing a Web Concept
Mart and its application in web warehousing. Furthermore, we have outline the
problem of web mining and maintenance of web information. We believe that
issues presented here will serve as an interesting example for further discussion.

References

1. http://www.cais.ntu.edu.sg:8000/~ whoweda/.
2. S. ABITEBOUL, D. QUASS, J. McHUGH, J. WIDOM, J. WEINER. The Lorel Query
   Language for Semistructured Data. *Journal of Digital Libraries*, 1(1):68-88, April
   1997.
3. G. AROCENA, A. MENDELZON. WebOQL: Restructuring Documents, Databases
   and Webs. *Proceedings of International Conference on Data Engineering* , Orlando,
   Florida, February 1998.
4. T. BRAY. Measuring the Web. *Proceedings of the 5th International World Wide
   Web Conference (WWW)*, Paris, France, 1996.
5. S. BHOWMICK, S. K. MADRIA, W.-K. NG, E.-P. LIM. Web Bags: Are They Useful
   in A Web Warehouse? *Proceedings of 5th International Conference of Foundation
   of Data Organization (FODO'98)*, Kobe, Japan, November 1998.
6. S. BHOWMICK, S. K. MADRIA, W.-K. NG, E.-P. LIM. Data Visualization in a Web
   Warehouse. *Proceedings of International Workshop on Data Warehousing and Data
   Mining (DWDM'98) (in conjunction with ER'98)*, Singapore, 1998.
7. S. BHOWMICK, S. K. MADRIA, W.-K. NG, E.-P. LIM. Web Mining in WHOWEDA:
   Some Issues.*PRICAI'98 Workshop on Knowledge Discovery and Data Mining*, Singapore, 1998.
8. S. BHOWMICK, S. K. MADRIA, W.-K. NG, E.-P. LIM. Bags in A Web Warehouse:
   Design and Analysis. *Submitted for publication.*

9. S. Bhowmick, W.-K. Ng, E.-P. Lim. Information Coupling in Web Databases. *Proceedings of the 17th International Conference on Conceptual Modelling (ER'98)*, Singapore, 1998.

10. S. S. Bhowmick, W.-K. Ng, E.-P. Lim, S. K. Madria. Join Processing in Web Databases. *Proceedings of the 9th International Conference on Database and Expert Systems Application (DEXA)*, Vienna, Austria, 1998.

11. P. Buneman, S. Davidson, G. Hillebrand, D. Suciu. A query language and optimization techniques for unstructured data. *Proceedings of the ACM SIGMOD International Conference on Management of Data*, Canada, June 1996.

12. M. Fernandez, D. Florescu, A. Levy, D. Suciu. A Query Language for a Web-Site Management Systems *SIGMOD Record*, 26(3), Sept, 1997.

13. T. Fiebig, J. Weiss, G. Moerkotte. RAW: A Relational Algebra for the Web. *Workshop on Management of Semistructured Data (PODS/SIGMOD'97)*, Tucson, Arizona, May 16, 1997.

14. J. Han, Y. Huang, N. Cercone, Y. Fu. Intelligent Query Answering by Knowledge Discovery Techniques. *IEEE Transactions of Knowledge and Data Engineering.*, 8(3):373 – 390, 1996.

15. D. Konopnicki, O. Shmueli. W3QS: A Query System for the World Wide Web. *Proceedings of the 21st International Conference on Very Large Data Bases*, Zurich, Switzerland, 1995.

16. L.V.S. Lakshmanan, F. Sadri., I.N. Subramanian. A Declarative Language for Querying and Restructuring the Web *Proceedings of the Sixth International Workshop on Research Issues in Data Engineering*, February, 1996.

17. S. H. Lin, C. S. Shih, M. C. Chang Chen et al. Extracting Classification Knowledge of Internet Documents with Mining Term Associations: A Semantic Approach. *Proceedings of the Sixth International Workshop on Research Issues in Data Engineering*, February, 1996.

18. M. Liu, T. Guan, L. V. Saxton. Structured-Based Queries over the World Wide Web. *Proceedings of the 17th International Conference on Conceptual Modeling (ER'98)*, Singapore, 1998.

19. S. K. Madria, M. Mohania, J. F. Roddick. A Query Processing Model for Mobile Computing using Concept Hierarchies and Summary Databases. *Submitted for publication.*

20. A. O. Mendelzon, G. A. Mihaila, T. Milo. Querying the World Wide Web. *Proceedings of the International Conference on Parallel and Distributed Information Systems (PDIS'96)*, Miami, Florida.

21. B. Mobasher, R. Cooley, J. Shrivastava. Web Mining: Information and Pattern Discovery on the World Wide Web. *Proceedings of the 9th IEEE International Conference on Tools with Artificial Intelligence (ICTAI'97)*, November 1997.

22. W. K. Ng, E.-P. Lim, C. T. Huang, S. Bhowmick, F. Q. Qin. Web Warehousing: An Algebra for Web Information. *Proceedings of IEEE International Conference on Advances in Digital Libraries (ADL'98)*, Santa Barbara, California, April 22–24, 1998.

23. O. R. Zaine, M. Xin, J. Han. Discovering Web Access Patterns and Trends by Applying OLAP and Data Mining Technology on Web Logs. *Proceedings of IEEE International Conference on Advances in Digital Libraries (ADL'98)*, Santa Barbara, California, April 22–24, 1998.

Extending the E/R Model for the Multidimensional Paradigm

Carsten Sapia, Markus Blaschka, Gabriele Höfling, Barbara Dinter

FORWISS (Bavarian Research Center for Knowledge-Based Systems)
Orleansstr. 34, D-81667 Munich, Germany
Email: {sapia, blaschka, hoefling, dinter}@forwiss.tu-muenchen.de

Abstract. Multidimensional data modeling plays a key role in the design of a data warehouse. We argue that the Entity Relationship Model is not suited for multidimensional conceptual modeling because the semantics of the main characteristics of the paradigm cannot be adequately represented. Consequently, we present a specialization of the E/R model - called Multidimensional Entity Relationship (ME/R) Model. In order to express the multidimensional structure of the data we define two specialized relationship sets and a specialized entity set. The resulting ME/R model allows the adequate conceptual representation of the multidimensional data view inherent to OLAP, namely the separation of qualifying and quantifying data and the complex structure of dimensions. We demonstrate the usability of the ME/R model by an example taken from an actual project dealing with the analysis of vehicle repairs.

1 Introduction

Multidimensional data modeling plays a key role during the design of a data warehouse. The multidimensional warehouse schema offers an integrated view on the operational data sources. Consequently, it serves as the core of the data warehouse and as the basis for the whole warehouse development and maintenance cycle. Due to this central role sufficient attention should be paid to the development of this schema. Figure 1 sketches the process of the schema design in data warehousing environments. The schema is mainly influenced by user requirements and the availability and structure of the data in operational systems. Most warehousing projects take an evolutionary approach[1], i.e. start with a prototype providing a certain functionality and set of data. This prototype will be further adopted according to the changing and growing requirements gained from users' feedback. Thus the user requirements are subject to frequent changes making schema evolution an important issue. To assure the flexibility and re-usability of the schema in such an environment, the model must be specified on a conceptual level (e.g. using the Entity Relationship Model). This means especially that it must not assume any facts that are the result of further design steps

---

[1] both in our experience from industrial projects [9] and in the warehouse literature, see e.g. [11]

e.g. the decision which database technology is to be used (multidimensional vs. relational).

For OLAP and data warehouse systems this is even more important as the most common design methodologies mix up the conceptual and the logical/physical design. Currently the state of art in dimensional modeling is the use of implementation (mostly even tool specific) formalisms for data modeling. For example, the ubiquitous star schema is not conceptual in the sense that it assumes the relational implementation and contains further decisions (e.g. denormalization) that should be subject of the physical design phase.

There is a consensus ([11], [13], [15]) that the multidimensional paradigm comes very close to the inherent structure of the problem domain (decision support systems). In this paper we investigate the special requirements of the multidimensional paradigm. We argue that the established conceptual design methods used for relational (e.g. the Entity Relationship Model [4]) or object-oriented systems do not offer the necessary support to reflect the multidimensional data model in a natural and intuitive way. Moreover, some of the multidimensional semantics is lost when expressing a multidimensional schema with these techniques. This means that the semantics must be represented informally which makes them unusable for the purpose of automatic generation (e.g. automatic generation of database schemes or query tools).

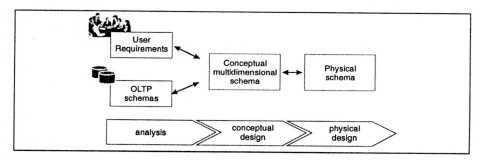

Fig. 1. Schema design process in data warehousing environments

Possible approaches to an expressive conceptual multidimensional model are to build a new model from scratch (which also means additional effort for its formal foundation) or to use an existing, general-purpose model and modify it so that the special characteristics of the multidimensional paradigm can be expressed.

Consequently, this paper presents a multidimensional specialization of the E/R model - called Multidimensional E/R Model (ME/R Model). By basing our approach on an established model we enable the transfer of the research results published in the context of the E/R model. This includes especially the work about automatic schema generation and formal foundation of the semantics. Furthermore, it is possible to make use of the proven flexibility of the well accepted E/R model.

The remainder of this paper is structured as follows: section 2 informally introduces the multidimensional paradigm and states the special requirements of OLAP applications regarding the data model. Section 3 describes the specializations of the E/R model that are necessary to fulfil these requirements and defines the ME/R model. In section 4 we investigate the expressive power of the ME/R model. To demonstrate the feasibility of our approach we model a real world example (section 5). Finally, we present related (section 6) and future work (section 7).

2   The Multidimensional Paradigm

The multidimensional paradigm is useful for a multitude of application areas (e.g. GIS, PACS, statistical databases and decision support). For the purpose of this paper we focus on typical OLAP applications. For example a vehicle manufacturer might want to analyze the vehicle repairs to improve his product, define new warranty policies and to get information about the quality of the garages.

Often a cube metaphor ([3]) is used to represent this data view as shown in figure 2. Such a cube corresponds to a subject of analysis called *fact* (e.g. vehicle repair). The cells of the data cube contain the (mostly numerical) *measures* (also called *quantifying data*) describing the fact (e.g. costs and duration of the vehicle repair). The axes of the cube (called *dimensions* or *qualifying data*) represent different ways of analyzing the data (e.g. vehicle and time of the repair).

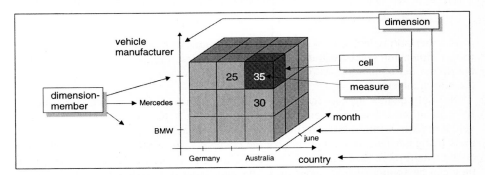

Fig. 2. A visualization of a multidimensional schema using the cube metaphor

This data view is similar to the notion of arrays. However, with arrays the dimensions of the multidimensional data space are only structured by a linear order defined on the indexes. For OLAP applications this is not sufficient because from the point of view of the OLAP end-user, the elements (respectively instances) of an OLAP dimension (called dimension members) are normally not linearly ordered (e.g. garages)[2].

Instead classification hierarchies containing levels are used for the structuring of dimensions. A hierarchy level contains a distinct set of members. Different levels correspond to different data granularities (e.g. daily figures vs. monthly figures) and ways of classification (e.g. geographic classification of garages vs. classification of garages by type). Level A is classified according to level B if a classification of the elements of A according to the elements of B is semantically meaningful to the application (e.g. the level 'days' are classified according to 'month').

---

[2] A prominent exception to this rule is the time dimension that possesses an inherent order

A level can be classified according to any number of levels thus forming multiple hierarchies on a single dimension. For example, garages can be classified by their geographical location and their type (see example in section 5). Another special case of hierarchies are alternative paths. This type of hierarchy occurs if several classification paths exist between two levels. An example for this is the classification of cities by geographical regions and federal districts (see figure 3).

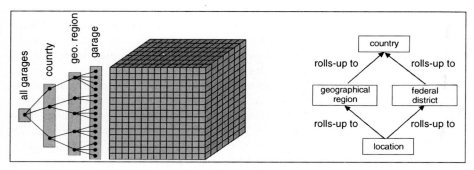

Fig. 3. Hierarchy levels structure the dimensions(left). Alternative pathes within a dimension(right)

Another orthogonal way of structuring dimensions from a users point of view is the use of dimension level attributes. These attributes describe dimension level members but do not define hierarchies (e.g. the name and address of a customer or the name of the region manager).

Not only qualifying data but also quantifying data possesses an inherent structure. In most applications different measures describing a fact are common (e.g. for a vehicle repair it might be useful to measure the duration of the repair, the costs for parts being exchanged and the cost for the wages). That means that a cell of the cube does contain more than one numeric value. Some of these measures are derived, i.e. they can be computed from other measures and dimension attributes (e.g. total repair cost is the sum of part costs and costs for wages).

A complex schema can contain more than one cube. This becomes necessary if an application requires the analysis of different facts (e.g. vehicle sales and repairs) or if not all of the measures are dependent on the same set of dimensions.

These multiple cubes can share dimensions (e.g. the time dimension). This does not necessarily mean that these cubes measure data using the same granularity. For example vehicle sales might be recorded and analyzed on a weekly basis, while the vehicle repairs are recorded daily (see section 5).

Regarding the multidimensional paradigm it is obvious, that the E/R model is not very well suited for the natural representation of multidimensional schemas. The inherent separation of qualifying and quantifying data cannot be expressed as all entity sets are treated equally by the E/R model. Furthermore the semantics of the complex structure of the dimensions (classification relationship between dimension levels) is an integral part of the multidimensional paradigm that is too specific to be modeled as a general purpose relationship.

3   The Multidimensional E/R Model

In order to allow the natural representation of the multidimensional semantics inherent to OLAP schemas, the E/R model is specialized. Of course, there are several possible ways to achieve this goal. Our design was driven by the following key considerations:

- *Specialization of the E/R model*: All elements that are introduced should be special cases of native E/R constructs. Thus, the flexibility and expressiveness of the E/R model is not reduced.
- *Minimal extension of the E/R model*: The specialized model should be easy to learn and use for an experienced E/R modeler. Thus, the number of additional elements needed should be as small as possible. A minimal set of extensions ensures the easy transferability of scientific results (e.g. formal foundations) from the E/R model to the ME/R model by discussing only the specific extensions.
- *Representation of the multidimensional semantics*: Despite the minimality, the specialization should be powerful enough to express the basic multidimensional semantics, namely the separation of qualifying and quantifying data and the hierarchical structure of the qualifying data.

A lot of variations of the E/R model (for an overview see e.g. [18]) have been published since the first proposal of Chen. For the purpose of this paper we use a very basic version of the E/R model. We formally describe our specialized E/R model using the meta modeling approach. We adhere to the four layer technique of the ISO/IRDS standard for metadata [12]. Figure 4 shows the meta model of our M/ER model (Dictionary Definition Layer of the IRDS). The part with the white background shows the meta model of the E/R model we use as a foundation. For the purpose of describing the meta model, we make use of an extended version of the E/R model which allows the concept of generalization. This is done to increase the readability of the meta model. However, the decision which type of constructs are allowed in the E/R model itself (and thus the ME/R model) is left open to the modeler.
Following our key considerations we introduce the following specialization:
- a special entity set: dimension level,
- two special relationship sets connecting dimension levels:
  - □ a special n-ary relationship set: the *'fact'* relationship set and
  - □ a special binary relationship set: the *'classification'* relationship set.

Since the semantic concept 'dimension level' is of central importance, we introduce a special entity set for dimension levels.

To model the structure of qualifying data we introduce a special binary relationship set: the classification relationship. It relates a dimension level A to a dimension level B representing concepts of a higher level of abstraction (e.g. city *is classified* according to country). The classification graph is defined as follows: $RG = (E,V)$ with E being the finite set of all dimension levels $e_1,...,e_k$ and $V = \{ (e_i,e_j) \mid i \neq j \wedge 1 \leq i,j \leq k \wedge e_i$ *is classified according to* $e_j \}$. Due to the special semantics of the classification relation, no cycles must be contained in the graph as this could lead to semantically not reasonable infinte roll-up pathes (e.g. day is classified according to month and month is classified according to day). This means the following global integrity constraint must be fulfilled (→* denotes the transitive closure of the *classification relation*):

$$\forall\ e_1, e_j \in E : e_i \rightarrow^* e_j \Rightarrow i \neq j$$

Thus the classification graph *RG* is a directed acyclic graph (DAG). The name attribute of the classifiaction relation set describes the criteria of classification. (e.g. 'lives in' for the classification relationship set connecting 'customer' and 'geographical region')

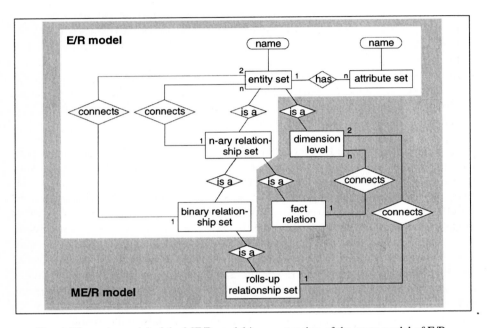

Fig. 4. The meta model of the ME/R model is an extension of the meta model of E/R.

The fact relationship set is a specialization of a general n-ary relationship set. It connects n different dimension level entities. Such a relation represents a fact (e.g. vehicle repair) of dimensionality n. A description of the fact is used as the name for the set. The directly connected dimension levels are called *atomic* dimension levels.

The fact relationship set models the inherent separation of qualifying and quantifying data. The attributes of the fact relationship set model the measures of the fact (quantifying data) while dimension levels model the qualifying data.

To distinguish our specialized elements from the native E/R modeling elements and to enhance the understandability of the graphical model, we use a special graphical notation for dimension level sets, fact relationship sets, and classification relationship sets (figure 5).

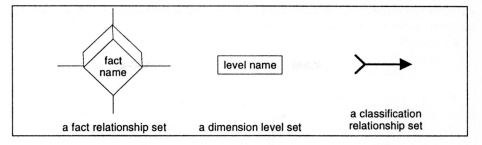

Fig. 5. The graphical notation of the ME/R elements.

4   Distinctive Features of the ME/R model

After having introduced the ME/R model, we now investigate how the ME/R model fulfills the requirements of the multidimensional paradigm. An example for modeling a real-world scenario can be found in the next section.

A central element in the multidimensional paradigm is the notion of dimensions that span the multidimensional space. The ME/R model does not contain an explicit counterpart for this concept. This is not necessary because a dimension consists of a set of dimension levels. The information which dimension-levels belong to a given dimension is included implicitly within the structure of the classification graph. Formally, the fact relationship identifies the n atomic dimension levels $e_{i_1},..e_{i_n}$. The according dimensions D_k are the set of the dimension levels that are included in the subgraph of the classification graph $RG(E,V)$ defined by the atomic level.

$$D_k = \left\{ e \in E \mid e_{i_k} \rightarrow^* e \right\} \quad 1 \leq k \leq n$$

The hierarchical classification structure of the dimensions is expressed by dimension level entity sets and the classification relationships. As previously noted, the classification relationship sets define a directed acyclic graph on the dimension levels. This enables the easy modeling of multiple hierarchies, alternative paths and shared hierarchy levels for different dimensions (e.g. customer and garage in figure 7). Thus no redundant modeling of the shared levels is necessary. Dimension level attributes are modeled as attributes of dimension level entity sets. This allows a different attribute structure for each dimension level.

By modeling the multidimensional cube as a relationship set it is possible to include an arbitrary number of facts in the schema thus representing a 'multi-cube model'. These different cubes and their shared dimensions can be expressed as shown in figure 7. Notably the schema also contains information about the granularity level on which the dimensions are shared. This information is for example necessary for the design of multidimensional joins during further development steps.

Regarding measures and their structure the ME/R model allows record structured measures as multiple attributes are possible for one fact relationship set. The semantic information that some of the measures are derived cannot be included in the model. Like the E/R model the ME/R model captures the static structure of the application domain. The calculation of measures is a functional information and should not be included in the static model. An orthogonal functional model should capture these dependencies.

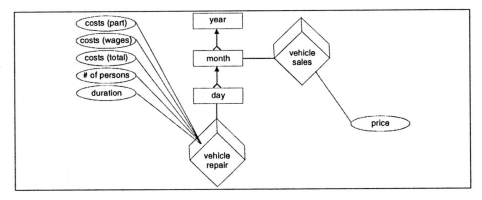

Fig. 6. Multiple cubes sharing a dimension on different levels

5   Applying the ME/R Model (Case Study)

To demonstrate the feasibility of our ME/R model, we present a real application. The following example is taken from a project with an industrial partner [10]. An automobile manufacturer stores data about repairs of vehicles. Among other, the date of repair, properties of the vehicle (e.g. model), information about the specific repair case (e.g. costs, number of garage employees involved, duration of the repair), data about the garage doing the repair, and data about the customer who owns the vehicle are stored.

Typical examples queries for this scenario are: "Give me the average total repair costs per month for garages in Bavaria by type of garage during the year 1997" or "Give me the five vehicle types that had the lowest average part costs in the year 1997"

The first design step is to determine which data are dimensions and which are facts. We assume that the repair costs (broken down by part costs, wages and total) for a specific vehicle (owned by a customer) for a specific garage are given on a daily basis. Then the facts (quantifying data) are the repair costs (parts, wages, total). Vehicle, customer, garage and day are the corresponding dimensions (qualifying data) and because they are at the finest granularity also the atomic dimension levels. Thus, the *fact* relationship connects the *vehicle repair fact* with the dimensions vehicle, customer, garage and day. The *classification relation*ships are shown in figure 7 which contains the complete ME/R diagram for this case study. The *fact* relationship in the middle of the ME/R diagram connects the atomic dimension levels. Each dimension is represented by a subgraph that starts at the corresponding atomic level (e.g. the time dimension starts at the dimension level day and comprehends also month and year). The actual facts (part costs, wages, total costs, number of persons involved and duration of the repair) are modeled as attributes of the *fact* relationship. The dimension hierarchies are depicted by the *classification* relationships (e.g. vehicle *is classified* according to model and brand). Additional attributes of a dimension level (e.g. age or income of a customer) are depicted as dimension attributes of the corresponding dimension level.

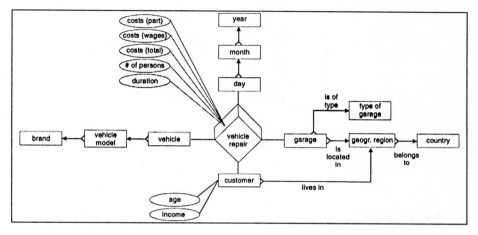

Fig. 7. The ME/R diagram for the analysis of vehicle repairs

Notably, the schema contains a *classification relation*ship between the entities *'customer'* and *'geographic region'* and between *'garage'* and *'geographic region'*. This shows a distinctive feature of our model: levels of different dimensions may by classified according to a common parent level. This might imply that the dimensionality of the cube is reduced by one when executing a roll-up operation along this classification. However, this is not the case as the model only captures the semantical fact, that the same type of classification (geographical classification) is used in both dimensions. During later phases of the development cycle this information can be used to avoid redundancies as the geographical regions only have to be stored once. The corresponding data cube however still contains two dimensions that contain the same members (customer geographical region and garage geographical region).

Since our ME/R model is a **specialization** of the E/R model, regular E/R constructs can also be used in ME/R diagrams. In our example, the entity *vehicle* can be extended e.g. to distinguish between cars and trucks. This scenario is shown in figure 8. We use the *isa* relationship to model the categorization of vehicles. The extended diagram (i.e. with 'regular' E/R constructs and special ME/R constructs) further allows us to model additional features of the subtypes of our entity *vehicle*. Features [14] are attributes that are only meaningful in a subclass but not in a superclass. Different subclasses may have different features. For example, for a *vehicle* in general one might store attributes like *length, width, height, colour,* or *horse power*, but a feature like *loading capacity* or *loading area* in m² is only meaningful for trucks. For a car on the other hand, it might be useful to store the *number of seats* or the *type of gear* (i.e. manual or automatic). Thus, using these combined E/R and ME/R modeling technique, features as introduced in [14] can be modeled on a conceptual level.

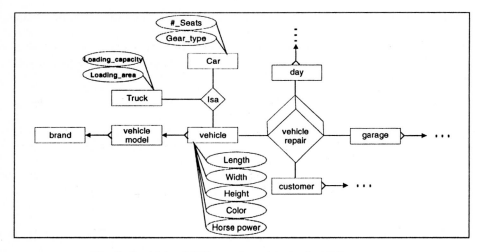

Fig. 8. Combining ME/R notation with classical E/R constructs

6   Related Work

A lot of publications are available concerning 'multidimensional data modeling'. Unfortunately only very few recognize the importance of the separation of conceptual and logical/physical issues. This is largely because the development in this area has so far been driven by the product vendors of OLAP systems. To our knowledge only very few papers investigating a graphical conceptual (i.e. implementation independent) data modeling methodology for multidimensional database have been published. Ralph Kimball proposes the design of Data Warehouses using a multidimensional view of the enterprise data. He presented a 'multidimensional modeling manifesto' [13]. However, his approach is not conceptual in the sense that it is not independent of the implementation (a relational implementation in the form of a 'star schema' is assumed).

In the area of statistical databases, graphical conceptual models to capture the structure and semantics of statistical tables have been proposed (e.g. [16], [17]) for a long time. The data warehouse research community focused mainly on physical issues (e.g. [9]) of data warehouse design. Quite a lot of work has also been done to formalize or extend ([7],[14]) the multidimensional data model (see [2] for a comparison) and to define query languages for these data models ([1]). However, these formalisms are not suited for conceptual modeling of user requirements. Our work supplements these papers by providing a graphical conceptual layer (as the E/R model provides for the relational paradigm).

Nevertheless, recently the deficit in conceptual models has been recognized. [6] proposes a formal logical model for OLAP systems and showed how it can be used in the design process. The paper suggests a bottom-up approach to data warehouse design. The authors assume an integrated E/R schema of the operational data sources and give a methodology to transform this schema into a dimensional graph which can be translated into the formal MD model. Our model is more suited to a top-down approach modeling the user requirements independently from the structure of the operational systems.

[8] also proposes a conceptual model called dimensional fact (DF) scheme. They give a graphical notation and a methodology to derive a DF model form the E/R models of the data sources. Although the technique supports semantically rich concepts it is not based on a formal data model. Our approach is to specialize a well researched and formally founded model. Furthermore, the notation does not allow the modeling of alternative paths which we believe is an important requirement.

In [14] Lehner et al. present a conceptual multidimensional data model. They argue that the common classification hierarchies are not sufficient for all types of applications. Therefore, they propose feature descriptions as a complementary mechanism for structuring qualifying information. As the main focus of the paper is the extension of the paradigm, no graphical notation (apart from the cube visualization) is provided.

7   Conclusions and Future Work

We started from the fact that the multidimensional paradigm plays a central role in the data warehouse and OLAP design process. However the fundamental semantics of this paradigm cannot be adequately expressed using the E/R model. Consequently, we proposed ME/R, a specialization of the E/R model especially suited for the modeling of OLAP applications. We also defined a graphical notation for the new elements which allows intuitive graphical diagrams. Our technique supports the easy modeling of multidimensional semantics (namely the separation of qualifying and quantifying data and the complex structure of dimensions). Multiple hierarchies, alternative paths and shared dimension levels can be naturally expressed. By designing ME/R as a specialization of the common E/R model we ensure a shallow learning curve and a high intuitivity of the diagrams. Since the modeler can combine ME/R elements with classical E/R elements semantically rich models can be built. Finally, we demonstrated the flexibility and usefulness of our approach by modeling a real world example.

The ME/R model can serve as the core of a full scale data warehouse design methodology. Using the ME/R model it is possible to capture the multidimensional application semantics during the conceptual design phase of a data warehouse. This information can be used during later phases (physical design and implementation) of the data warehouse process for (semi-) automatic system generation. A first step in this direction will be the mapping of the ME/R model to the formal logical multidimensional data models that were proposed recently.

The ME/R model allows to capture the static data structure. The modeling of dynamical (e.g. anticipated query behavior) and functional (e.g. the additivity of measures along dimensions or the functional relationship between hierarchy levels) aspects deserve a deeper study. Currently we are investigating a dynamic and a functional model supplementing the static model (analogous to the OMT) and study the interrelationship between those models. Additionally, we are working on a classification of multidimensional schema evolution operations (e.g. 'add dimension level') and examine the impacts of these operations. To this end, we evaluate schema evolution approaches from object-oriented databases and investigate their feasibility in the multidimensional case.

References

[1] A, Bauer, W. Lehner: *The Cube-Query-Language (CQL) for Multidimensional Statistical and Scientific Database Systems,* Proc. of the 5th CIKM, Melbourne 1997.

[2] M. Blaschka, C. Sapia, G. Höfling, B. Dinter: Finding Your Way through Multidimensional Data Models, DWDOT Workshop (DEXA 98), Vienna

[3] S. Chaudhuri, U. Dayal: *An Overview of Data Warehousing and OLAP Technology.* SIGMOD Records 26(1), 1997

[4] P.P-S. Chen: The Entity Relationship Model – Towards a Unified View of Data. ACM TODS Vol. 1, No. 1, 1976

[5] E. F. Codd: Extending the Database Relational Model to Capture More meaning. ACM TODS Vol. 4, No. 4 (December 1979)

[6] L. Cabibbo, R. Torlone: *A Logical Approach to Multidimensional Databases.* EDBT 1998.

[7] S. Dekeyser, B. Kuijpers, J. Paredaens, J. Wijsen: *The nested datacube model for OLAP* in Advances in Database Technology, LNCS, Springer Verlag

[8] M. Golfarelli, D. Maio, S. Rizzi, *Conceptual design of data warehouses from E/R schemes,* Proc. 31st Hawaii Intl. Conf. on System Sciences, 1998.

[9] V. Harinarayan, A. Rajaraman, J. D. Ullman: *Implementing Data Cubes Efficiently.* Proc. SIGMOD Conference, Montreal, Canada, 1996

[10] G. Höfling, M. Blaschka, B. Dinter, P. Spiegel, T. Ringel: *Data Warehouse Technology for the Management of Diagnosis Data* (in German), in Dittrich, Geppert (eds.): *Datenbanksysteme in Büro, Technik und Wissenschaft* (BTW), Springer, 1997.

[11] W. H. Inmon: *Building the Data Warehouse,* 2nd edition, John Wiley &Sons, 1996

[12] IRDS Framework ISO/IEC IS 10027, 1990

[13] R. Kimball: *A Dimensional Modeling Manifesto,* DBMS Magazine, August 1997,

[14] W. Lehner, T. Ruf, M. Teschke: CROSS-DB: *A Feature-Extended Multidimensional Data Model for Statistical and Scientific Databases*, Proc. of the CIKM'96, Maryland.

[15] Micro Strategy Inc.: The Case For Relational OLAP, White Paper. 1995,

[16] M. Rafanelli, A. Shoshani: *STORM : A Statistical Object Representation,* SSDBM 90

[17] S.Y.W. Su : SAM*: *A Semantic Association Model for Corporate and Scientific-Statistical Databases,* in: Journal of Information Sciences 29, 1983

[18] T.J. Teorey: *Database Modeling and Design,* 2nd edition, Morgan Kaufmann 1994

Numerical Aspects in the Data Model of Conceptual Information Systems

Gerd Stumme[1] and Karl Erich Wolff[2]

[1] Technische Universität Darmstadt, Fachbereich Mathematik, Schloßgartenstr. 7, D–64289 Darmstadt; stumme@mathematik.tu-darmstadt.de
[2] Fachhochschule Darmstadt, Fachbereich Mathematik und Naturwissenschaften, Schöfferstr. 3, D–64295 Darmstadt; wolff@mathematik.tu-darmstadt.de

Abstract. While most data analysis and decision support tools use numerical aspects of the data, Conceptual Information Systems focus on their conceptual structure. This paper discusses how both approaches can be combined.

1 Introduction

The data model of Conceptual Information Systems relies on the insight that concepts are basic units of human thinking, and should hence be activated in data analysis and decision support. The data model is founded on the mathematical theory of *Formal Concept Analysis*. Conceptual Information Systems provide a multi-dimensional conceptually structured view on data stored in relational databases. They are similar to On-Line Analytical Processing (OLAP) tools, but focus on qualitative (i. e. non-numerical) data. The management system TOSCANA visualizes arbitrary combinations of conceptual hierarchies and allows on-line interaction with the database to analyze and explore data conceptually.

Data tables are usually equipped with different types of structures. While most data analysis tools use their numerical structure, Conceptual Information Systems are designed for conceptually structuring data. As concepts are the basic units of human thought, the resulting data model is quite universal — and is also able to cover numerical aspects of the data. However, up to now, the model does not have any features which support techniques specific to numerical data.

Many applications indicate the need for not only using tools which operate only on numerical or only on conceptual aspects, but to provide an integrative approach combining both numerical and conceptual structures for data analysis and decision support in one tool. In this paper we discuss how the data model of Conceptual Information Systems can be extended by numerical aspects. The developments discussed in the sequel arose mostly from scientific and commercial applications, but for sake of simplicity, we start with a small demonstration application: a Conceptual Information System for a private bank account. But first, we provide some basics about Formal Concept Analysis.

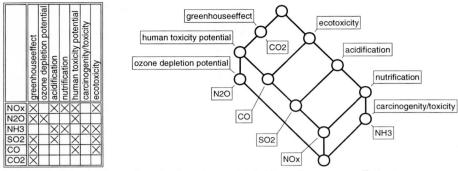

Fig. 1. Formal context and concept lattice of gaseous pollutants

2 The Mathematical Background: Formal Concept Analysis

Concepts are necessary for expressing human knowledge. Therefore, the process of knowledge discovery in databases benefits from a comprehensive formalization of concepts which can be activated to represent knowledge coded in databases. *Formal Concept Analysis* ([10], [1], [13]) offers such a formalization by mathematizing concepts which are understood as units of thought constituted by their extension and intension. For allowing a mathematical description of extensions and intensions, Formal Concept Analysis always starts with a *formal context*.

Definition. A *formal context* is a triple (G, M, I) where G is a set whose elements are called (*formal*) *objects*, M is a set whose elements are called (*formal*) *attributes*, and I is a binary relation between G and M (i. e. $I \subseteq G \times M$); in general, $(g, m) \in I$ is read: "the object g *has* the attribute m".

A *formal concept* of a formal context (G, M, I) is defined as a pair (A, B) with $A \subseteq G$ and $B \subseteq M$ such that (A, B) is maximal with the property $A \times B \subseteq I$; the sets A and B are called the *extent* and the *intent* of the formal concept (A, B). The *subconcept-superconcept-relation* is formalized by $(A_1, B_1) \leq (A_2, B_2) :\Longleftrightarrow A_1 \subseteq A_2 \ (\Longleftrightarrow B_1 \supseteq B_2)$. The set of all concepts of a context (G, M, I) together with the order relation $\leq$ is always a complete lattice, called the *concept lattice* of (G, M, I) and denoted by $\mathfrak{B}(G, M, I)$.

Example. Figure 1 shows a formal context about the potential of gaseous pollutants. The six gases NO_x, ..., CO_2 are the objects, and the seven listed perils are the attributes of the formal context. In the line diagram of the concept lattice, we label, for each object $g \in G$, the smallest concept having g in its extent with the name of the object and, for each attribute $m \in M$, the largest concept having m in its intent with the name of the attribute. This labeling allows us to determine for each concept its extent and its intent: The extent [intent] of a concept contains all objects [attributes] whose object concepts [attribute concepts] can be reached from the concept on a descending [ascending] path of

no.	value	paid for	objective	health	date
3	42.00	Konni	ski-club	s	03.01.1995
20	641.26	Konni, Florian	office chairs	/	23.01.1995
27	68.57	Family	health insurance	hi	02.02.1995
34	688.85	Tobias	office table	/	06.02.1995
37	25.00	Father	gymn. club	s	08.02.1995
52	75.00	Konni	gymn. club	s	24.02.1995
73	578.60	Mother	Dr. Schmidt	d	10.03.1995
77	45.02	Tobias	Dr. Gram	d	17.03.1995
80	77.34	Parents	money due	/	21.03.1995

Fig. 2. Withdrawals from a private bank account

straight line segments. For instance, the concept labeled with CO has $\{$CO, SO_2, $NO_x\}$ as extent, and {human toxicity potential, greenhouse effect, ecotoxicity} as intent. The concept lattice combines the view of different pollution scenarios with the influence of individual pollutants. Such an integrated view can be of interest for the planning of chimneys for plants generating specific pollutants.

In the following, we distinguish, for each formal concept c, between its *extent* (i. e., the set of all objects belonging to c) and its *contingent* (i. e., the set of all objects belonging to c but not to any proper subconcept of c). In the standard line diagram, the contingent of a formal concept c is the set of objects which is represented just below the point representing c. The extent of the largest concept is always the set of all objects. The extent of an arbitrary concept is exactly the union of all contingents of its subconcepts.

In many applications, the data table does not only allow Boolean attributes as in Fig. 1, but also many-valued attributes. In the next section, we show by means of an example how such *many-valued contexts* are handled by formal concept analysis.

3   The Conceptual Aspect of the Bank Account System

The basic example underlying this paper consists of a table of all withdrawals from a private bank account during several months. A small part of this table is shown in Fig. 2. As an example, the row numbered 20 contains information about a withdrawal of 641.26 DM for office chairs for the sons Konni and Florian paid on January 23, 1995. In formal concept analysis, data tables such as the one in Fig. 2 are formalized as *many-valued contexts*.

Definition. A *many-valued context* is a tuple $\mathbb{K} := (G, M, (W_m)_{m \in M}, I)$, where G, M, and W_m, $m \in M$, are sets, and $I \subseteq \{(g, m, w) \mid g \in G, m \in M, w \in W_m\}$ is a relation where $(g, m, w_1) \in I$ and $(g, m, w_2) \in I$ implies $w_1 = w_2$. Thus, each $m \in M$ can be seen as a partial function. For $(g, m, w) \in I$ we say that "object g has value w for attribute m" and write $m(g) = w$.

	sport	doctor	health insurance	health
health= "s"	×			×
health= "d"		×		×
health= "hi"			×	×
health= "/"				

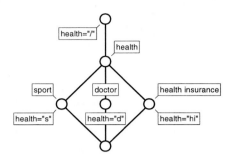

Fig. 3. The scale "health"

Clearly each finite many-valued context can be represented as a relational database table where the set G of objects occurs in the first field chosen as primary key.

In the following we construct a conceptual overview with the purpose to answer questions like "How much has been paid for health for each family member?". Therefore we first introduce a conceptual language representing the meaning of the values occuring in the column health of Fig. 2. This language is represented by the formal context in Fig. 3. For example, the withdrawals labeled "s" in column health of Fig. 2 are assigned to "sport" and to "health", while the withdrawals labeled "/" are not assigned to any attribute of this scale. The concept lattice of this formal context is represented by the line diagram in Fig. 3 which demonstrates graphically the intended distinction between the withdrawals not assigned to "health" and those assigned to "health" and the classification of these into three classes. This is an example of a conceptual scale in the sense of the following definition.

Definition. A *conceptual scale* for an attribute $m \in M$ of a many-valued context $(G, M, (W_m)_{m \in M}, I)$ is a formal context $\mathbb{S}_m := (W_m, M_m, I_m)$.

Conceptual scales serve for "embedding" the values of a many-valued attribute in a conceptual framework describing the aspects the user is interested in. But to embed also the original objects, in our example the withdrawals, into this framework we have to combine the partial mapping of the many-valued attribute m and the embedding of the values. This is done in the following definition of a realized scale.

Definition. Let $S_m = (W_m, M_m, I_m)$ be a conceptual scale of an attribute m of a many-valued context $(G, M, (W_m)_{m \in M}, I)$. The context (G, M_m, J) with $gJn : \iff \exists w \in W_m : (g, m, w) \in I \wedge (w, n) \in I_m$ is called the *realized scale* for the attribute m.

To construct the concept lattice of the realized scale we assign to each value w of m, hence to each object of the scale S_m, an SQL-query searching for all objects

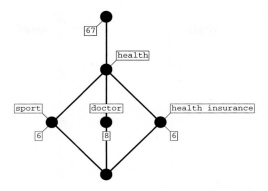

Fig. 4. Frequencies of withdrawals related to "health".

g in the given many-valued context such that $m(g) = w$. The concept lattice of the realized scale for "health" is shown in Fig. 4 where the contingents are replaced by their cardinalities, called *frequencies*.

Reading example: There are exactly six withdrawals assigned to "sport" and exactly 67 withdrawals not assigned to "health". Finally we remark that there are no withdrawals which are assigned to "health" but neither to "sport", "doctor" or "health insurance".

In TOSCANA, the user can choose conceptual scales from a menu. The database is queried by SQL-statements for determining the contingents of the concepts. Finally the results are displayed in a line diagram representing the embedding of the concept lattice of the realized scale in the concept lattice of the scale.

The line diagram in Fig. 4 is unsatisfactory insofar as we would like to see not only the frequencies of withdrawals but the amount of money paid. In the next section we shall discuss how this can be visualized.

4   The Numerical Aspect of the Bank Account System

For an efficient control of the household budget, the user needs an overview over the distribution of the money, and not of the number of withdrawals. Hence, for each contingent S, we display the sum over the corresponding entries in the column "value" instead of the frequency of S. The result of this computation is the left line diagram in Fig. 5. We can see for example that the withdrawals for "sport" sum up to 383 DM and the withdrawals not concerning "health" sum up to 41538 DM. The right line diagram shows, for each formal concept, the sum over the values of all withdrawals in the extent (instead of the contingent) of this concept, for instance the total amount of 45518 DM for all withdrawals in the given data table and the amount of 3980 DM for "health". To visualize also the amount of money paid for the family members (and for relevant groups

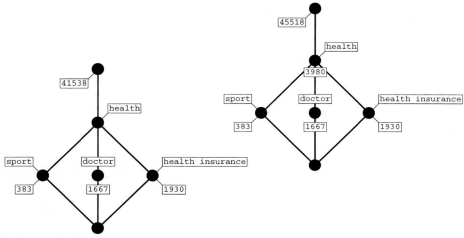

Fig. 5. Summing up book-values over contingents (left) and extents.

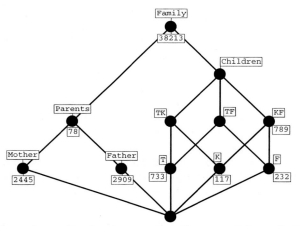

Fig. 6. Summing up book-values over contingents of the scale "family".

of them), we use the scale "family" in Fig. 6. This diagram shows for instance that there are withdrawals of 2445 DM for "Mother", that 78 DM are classified under "Parents", but not under "Mother" or "Father" (this is the "money due" in the last row of Fig. 2) and that 38213 DM appear for withdrawals classified under "Family" which are not specified further.

Next we combine the scales "family" and "health". The resulting *nested line diagram* is shown in Fig. 7. Now the withdrawals are classified with respect to the direct product of the scales for family and health. For instance, 733 DM expended for Tobias split into 45 DM for a doctor and 688 DM not concerning health, i.e., the amount spent on his office table (see Fig. 2). This nested line

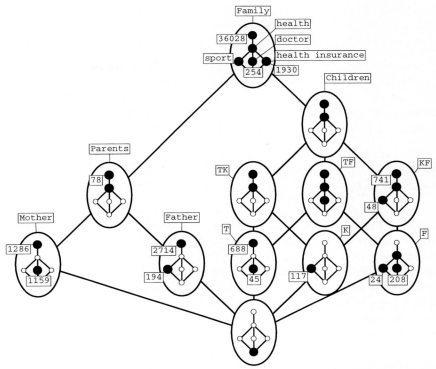

Fig. 7. Summing up over contingents in the nested line diagram of the scales "health" and "family".

diagram shows also that the withdrawals for health insurance (which amount to 1930 DM) are all summarized under the concept "Family" and are not specified further.

In the next section, we describe the formalization of numerical structures. This is the basis for generalizing the example in Section 6.

5   Relational Structures

In Section 2, we have seen how conceptual structures are formalized. Let us now consider the numerical aspect of the data. In fact, the formalization is a bit more general, such that it covers arbitrary relations and functions on arbitrary sets. It is based on the mathematical notion of *relational structures*.

In the bank account example, the bankbook values are real numbers, for which addition is defined. In general, for each $m \in M$, there may be functions and relations on the set W_m.

Definition. A *relational structure* $\mathbb{R} := (W, \mathcal{R}, \mathcal{F})$ consists of a set W, a set $\mathcal{R}$ of relations $R \subseteq W^{ar(R)}$ on W, and a set $\mathcal{F}$ of functions $f : W^{ar(f)} \to W$, where ar assigns to each relation and function its arity.

For instance, the data types implemented in the database management system (e. g., `Integer`, `Real`, `Boolean`, `Currency`, or `Datetime`) are relational structures. Hence, for each attribute $m \in M$, we can capture the algebraic structure of its possible attribute values by a relational structure $\mathbb{R}_m := (W_m, \mathcal{R}_m, \mathcal{F}_m)$, just as we captured their hierarchical relationships by a conceptual scale $\mathbb{S}_m$.

Definition. A *conceptual-relational scheme* of a family $(W_m)_{m \in M}$ of sets is a family $(\mathcal{R}_m, \mathbb{S}_m)_{m \in M}$ where, for each $m \in M$, $\mathbb{R}_m := (W_m, \mathcal{R}_m, \mathcal{F}_m)$ is a relational structure and $\mathbb{S}_m = (W_m, M_m, I_m)$ is a conceptual scale.

Here we should mention, that sometimes conceptual and relational aspects overlap. Depending on the purpose, they should be covered by a relational structure or by a conceptual scale, or by both. Time, for instance, can be captured by a linear order in a relational structure or by some scale (e. g., an inter-ordinal scale, if only certain time intervals are of interest).

Relational structures can be used for creating new scales. This *logical scaling* was developed by S. Prediger (cf. [5]). In this paper, however, we discuss only how relational structures may affect the data analysis process once the conceptual scales are created.

6 Conceptual Scaling Supported by Relational Structures

The bank account example and other applications show that it is useful not to analyze numerical and conceptual aspects of the data independently, but to combine them. In this section, we discuss how Conceptual Information Systems can be extended by a numerical component. Since the required functionalities differ from application to application, the idea is to delegate application-specific computations to an external system (e. g., book-keeping system, CAD system, control system, etc.). TOSCANA already provides an SQL-interface to the relational database management system in which the many-valued context is stored, so that we can use the numerical tools of the relational database system (as, for instance, in the bank account example).

In the process of going from the request of the user to the diagram shown on the screen, we can distinguish two consecutive, intermediary subprocesses. First, the chosen scale is imported from the conceptual scheme, and to each of its concepts, a subset of objects is assigned (by default, its extent or contingent). Second, for each of these sets, some algebraic operations may be performed. Most of the implemented Conceptual Information Systems only activate the first step. Our bank account system is an example where the second step is also activated. In the first step, we also can identify two actions where a numerical component can influence the analysis or retrieval process: the import of scales from the conceptual scheme, where parameters can be assigned to parametrized scales, and the import of objects from the database, which can be sorted out by filters. Finally, we can imagine a further action, following the display of the line diagram, which results in highlighting interesting concepts. These four activities which make an interaction between conceptual and numerical component possible now shall be discussed in detail.

6.1   Adapting Conceptual Scales to the Data

A conceptual scale represents knowledge about the structure of the set W_m of possible values of the attribute m. In general, it is independant from the values $m(G)$ that really appear in the database. In some situations however, it is desirable to construct the scale automatically depending on $m(G)$.

Inter-ordinal scales are typically used when a linear order (e. g., a price scale, a time scale) is divided into intervals with respect to their meaning. The boundaries of the intervals are usually fixed by a knowledge engineer. However, the range of possible attribute values is not always known a priori. Hence, for a first glance at the data, it has proved useful to query the database for the minimal and the maximal value and to split up this interval into intervals of equal length. Depending on the application, it might also be useful to fix the boundaries on certain statistical measures, as for instance average, median, quantiles. These "self-adapting scales" reduce the effort needed to create the conceptual scheme, since they are re-usable. It is planned to implement a user interface by means of which the user can edit parameters at runtime. For instance, he could first invoke an inter-ordinal scale with equidistant boundaries and then fine-tune it according to his needs.

This user interface leads to the second example, an application in control theory: Process data of the incineration plant of Darmstadt were analyzed in order to make the control system more efficient (cf. [2]). Process parameters like `ram velocity` and `steam` are stored in a database. The ram velocity does not influence the steam volume directly, but only with a certain time delay. When the time delay is kept variable, the user can change it via the interface during the runtime of TOSCANA. That can be used, for instance, for determining the time delay of two variables experimentally: The engineer examines the nested line diagram of the corresponding scales for ordinal dependencies. By varying the shift time, he tries to augment the dependencies, and to determine in this way the time delay.

The possibility of using parameters is also of interest for filters that control the data flow from the database to TOSCANA. They are discussed in the next subsection.

6.2   Filtering the Objects of the Many-valued Context

In many applications, users are interested in analyzing only a specific subset of objects of the many-valued context; for instance, if one is interested in the withdrawals from the bank account during the past quarter only. If such a subset is determined conceptually, being the extent (more rarely the contingent) of a concept of a suitable combination of conceptual scales, TOSCANA provides for the possibility of "zooming" into that specific concept by mouse click. In the sequel of the analysis only objects belonging to that concept are considered.

But if the interesting subset is not available as extent or contingent of some combinations of earlier constructed scales it is often easier to use a filter. Filters are designed to generate one single interesting subset of the set of objects while conceptual scales generate a whole set of interesting extents and all their intersections and contingents.

For such applications, the conceptual scheme should be extended by *filters*. In addition to conceptual scales, the user can choose filters from a menu. When a filter is activated, then objects are only considered for display if they pass the filter. A filter is realized as an SQL-fragment that is added by AND to the conditions provided by the chosen scales.

The remarks about parameters in the previous subsection apply to filters as well. An example for the use of parameters in filters is again the system of Sects. 2 and 3. As described above, we can construct a filter that only accepts withdrawals effected in a certain period, e. g., the last quarter. The interface for editing parameters introduced in Sect. 5.1 provides the possibility of examining the withdrawals of any period required. When the user activates the filter, he is asked for start and end date.

6.3 Focussing on Specific Aspects of the Objects

The bank account system is an example of focussing on different aspects of the data. There we focus not only on withdrawal numbers, but also on the sum of bankbook values. Now we discuss how this example fits into the formalization described in Sect. 4. Once the user has chosen one or more scales, TOSCANA determines for each concept of the corresponding concept lattice a set S of objects – in most cases its extent or its contingent. In Sect. 1 we mentioned that the user can choose for each concept whether all names of the objects in S shall be displayed or only the cardinality of S. A third standard aspect in TOSCANA is the display of relative frequencies. The last two aspects are examples of algebraic operations.

The focussing in the example of Sects. 2 and 3 can be understood as being composed of two actions: Firstly, instead of working on the set S, the sequence $(m(g) \in W_m)_{g \in S}$ is chosen. In the bank account example, this *projection* assigns to each withdrawal from S the corresponding book-value. Secondly, the sum $\sum(m(S)) := \sum_{g \in S} m(g)$ is computed (and displayed). The latter is done in the relational structure assigned to the corresponding attribute. In TOSCANA, this is realized by a modification of the way the SQL-queries are generated: the standard COUNT-command used for the computation of the frequency of S is replaced by a SUM-command operating on the column "value".

6.4 Highlighting Interesting Concepts

Focussing also can be understood in a different setting. It also means drawing the user's attention to those concepts where the frequency of objects (or the sum of book-values, etc.) is extraordinarily high (or low). The determination of these concepts is based on the frequency distribution of the nested line diagram. This distribution can be represented – without its conceptual order – by a contingency table with entry n_{ij} in cell (i, j) where i (j, resp.) is an object concept of the first (second) scale. As a refinement of Pearson's Chi- Square calculations for contingency tables we recommend calculating for each cell (i, j) the *expected frequency* $e_{ij} := (n_i n_j)/n$ ("expected" means "expected under independence assumption") where n_i (n_j, resp.) is the frequency of object concept i (j, resp.) and n is the total number of all objects. To compare the distribution of the observed frequencies n_{ij} and the expected frequencies e_{ij}, one should study the *dependency double matrix* (n_{ij}, e_{ij}). Pearson's Chi-Square calculations reduce the dependency double matrix to the famous $\chi^2 := \sum_{ij}((n_{ij} - e_{ij})^2/e_{ij})$. But the matrix also can be used as a whole in order to highlight interesting places in a nested line diagram:

- If the user wants to examine the dependency double matrix in detail, then he may choose to display their entries at the corresponding concepts. Additionally, one of the matrices of differences $n_{ij} - e_{ij}$, quotients $(n_{ij} - e_{ij})/e_{ij}$, or quotients n_{ij}/e_{ij} may be displayed in the same way. The conceptual structure represented by the line diagram helps us to understand the dependency double matrix.
- If a less detailed view is required, then the calculation component can generate graphical marks which indicate those concepts where the matrix entries are above or below a given threshold. A typical condition in applications is "$e_{ij} > k$ and $n_{ij}/e_{ij} > p$" where k and p are parameters which can be chosen on a suitable scale.

The Chi-Square formula is a very rough reduction of the information about dependencies, but, clearly, the degree of reduction depends on the purpose of the investigation. If one is interested not only in having an index showing whether there is a dependency, but in understanding the dependencies between two many-valued attributes with respect to chosen scales in detail, then one should carefully study the distribution of observed and expected frequencies. This can be done with the program DEPEND developed by C. Wehrle in his diploma thesis ([9], supervised by K. E. Wolff).)

7 Outlook

The connections between conceptual scales and relational structures should be studied extensively. Therefore, practical relevant examples containing both parts should be considered.

It is of particular interest to examine the compatibility of various conceptual scales and relational structures on the same set of attribute values. From a formal point of view both structures are of the same generality in the sense that each conceptual scale can be described as a relational structure and vice versa. But they are used differently: conceptual scales generate overviews for knowledge landscapes, while relational structures serve for computations.

This paper discussed how numerical components can support conceptual data processing. One should also investigate how, vice-versa, results of data analysis and retrieval activities in Conceptual Information Systems can be made accessible to other systems. This discussion may lead to hybrid knowledge systems composed of conceptual, numerical and also logical subsystems, each focussing on different aspects of the knowledge landscape inherent in the data.

References

1. B. Ganter, R. Wille: Formale Begriffsanalyse: Mathematische Grundlagen. Springer, Heidelberg 1996 (English translation to appear)
2. E. Kalix: Entwicklung von Regelungskonzepten für thermische Abfallbehandlungsanlagen. TH Darmstadt 1997
3. W. Kollewe, C. Sander, R. Schmiede, R. Wille: TOSCANA als Instrument der bibliothekarischen Sacherschließung. In: H. Havekost, H.-J. Wätjen (eds.): *Aufbau und Erschließung begrifflicher Datenbanken.* (BIS)-Verlag, Oldenburg 1995, 95–114
4. W. Kollewe, M. Skorsky, F. Vogt, R. Wille: TOSCANA — ein Werkzeug zur begrifflichen Analyse und Erkundung von Daten. In: R. Wille, M. Zickwolff (eds.): *Begriffliche Wissensverarbeitung — Grundfragen und Aufgaben.* B. I.–Wissenschaftsverlag, Mannheim 1994
5. S. Prediger: Logical scaling in formal concept analysis. LNAI **1257**, Springer, Berlin
6. P. Scheich, M. Skorsky, F. Vogt, C. Wachter, R. Wille: Conceptual data systems. In: O. Opitz, B. Lausen, R. Klar (eds.): *Information and classification.* Springer, Heidelberg 1993, 72–84
7. F. Vogt, C. Wachter, R. Wille: Data analysis based on a conceptual file. In: H.-H. Bock, P. Ihm (eds.): *Classification, data analysis, and knowledge organization.* Springer, Heidelberg 1991, 131–140
8. F. Vogt, R. Wille: TOSCANA — A graphical tool for analyzing and exploring data. LNCS **894**, Springer, Heidelberg 1995, 226–233
9. C. Wehrle: *Abhängigkeitsuntersuchungen in mehrwertigen Kontexten.* Diplomarbeit, Fachhochschule Darmstadt 1997
10. R. Wille: Restructuring lattice theory: an approach based on hierarchies of concepts. In: I. Rival (ed.): *Ordered sets.* Reidel, Dordrecht–Boston 1982, 445–470
11. R. Wille: Lattices in data analysis: how to draw them with a computer In: I. Rival (ed.): *Algorithms and order.* Kluwer, Dordrecht–Boston 1989, 33–58
12. R. Wille: Conceptual landscapes of knowledge: A pragmatic paradigm of knowledge processing. In: *Proc. KRUSE '97*, Vancouver, Kanada, 11.–13. 8. 1997, 2–14
13. K. E. Wolff: A first course in formal concept analysis – How to understand line diagrams. In: F. Faulbaum (ed.): *SoftStat '93, Advances in statistical software* **4**, Gustav Fischer Verlag, Stuttgart 1993, 429–438

Nested Data Cubes for OLAP

(extended abstract)

Stijn Dekeyser, Bart Kuijpers,* Jan Paredaens, and Jef Wijsen**

University of Antwerp (UIA), Dept. Math. & Computer Sci.,
Universiteitsplein 1, B-2610 Antwerp, Belgium
Email: {dekeyser,kuijpers,pareda,jwijsen}@uia.ua.ac.be

Abstract. *Nested data cubes* (NDCs in short) are a generalization of other OLAP models such as f-tables [4] and hypercubes [2], but also of classical structures as sets, bags, and relations. This model adds to the previous models flexibility in viewing the data, in that it allows for the assignment of priorities to the different dimensions of the multidimensional OLAP data.
We also present an algebra in which most typical OLAP analysis and navigation operations can be formulated. We present a number of algebraic operators that work on nested data cubes and that preserve the functional dependency between the dimensional coordinates of the data cube and the factual data in it. We show how these operations can be applied to sub-NDCs at any depth, and also show that the NDC algebra can express the SPJR algebra [1] of the relational model. Importantly, we show that the NDC algebra primitives can be implemented by linear time algorithms.

1 Introduction and Motivation

Since the 1993 seminal paper of Codd et al [6], *on-line analytical processing* (OLAP) is recognized as a promising approach for the analysis and navigation of data warehouses and multidimensional data [5, 7, 12, 13, 16, 28]. Multidimensional databases typically are large collections of enterprise data which are arranged according to different dimensions (e.g., time, measures, products, geographical regions) to facilitate sophisticated analysis and navigation for decision support in, for instance, marketing. Figure 1 depicts a three-dimensional database, containing sales information of stores. A popular way of representing such information is the "data cube" [9, 17, 28]. Each dimension is assigned to an axis in n-dimensional space, and the numeric values are placed in the corresponding cells of the 'cube.'

The effectiveness of analysis and the ease of navigation is mainly determined by the flexibility that the system offers to rearrange the perspectives on different dimensions and by its ability to efficiently calculate and store summary information. A sales manager might want to look at the sales per store, or he might

---

* Post-doctoral research fellow of the Fund for Scientific Research of Flanders (FWO).
** Affiliated to the University of Brussels (VUB) at the time this research was done.

Day : day	Item : item	Store : store	
Jan1	Lego	Navona	→ 32
Jan1	Lego	Colosseum	→ 24
Jan1	Scrabble	Navona	→ 13
Jan1	Scrabble	Colosseum	→ 14
Jan1	Scrabble	Kinderdroom	→ 22
Jan2	Lego	Kinderdroom	→ 2
Jan2	Lego	Colosseum	→ 21

Fig. 1. A multidimensional database.

want to see the total number of items sold in all his stores in a particular month. OLAP systems aim to offer these qualities.

During the past few years, many commercial systems have appeared that offer, through ever more efficient implementations, a wide number of analysis capabilities. A few well-known examples are Arbor Software's *Essbase* [10], IBM's *Intelligent Server* [19], Red Brick's *Red Brick Warehouse* [24], Pilot Software's *Pilot Decision Support Suite* [23], and Oracle's *Sales Analyzer* [25]. Some of these implementations are founded on theoretical results on efficient array manipulation [21, 22, 26].

In more recent years, however, it has become apparant that there is a need for a formal OLAP model that explicitly incorporates the notion of different and independent views on dimensions and also offers a logical way to compute summary information. Lately, a number of starting points for such models have been proposed (an overview is given in [3]). Gyssens et al. [14] have proposed the first theoretical foundation for OLAP systems: the *tabular database* model. They give a complete algebraic language for querying and restructuring two-dimensional tables. Agrawal et al. [2] have introduced a *hypercube* based data model with a number of operations that can be easily inserted into SQL. Cabibbo and Torlone [4] have recently proposed a data model that forms a logical counterpart of multidimensional arrays. Their model is based on dimensions and *f-tables*. Dimensions are partially ordered categories that correspond to different ways of looking at the multidimensional information (see also [9]). F-tables are structures to store factual data functionally dependent on the dimensions (such as the one depicted in Figure 1). They also propose a calculus to query f-tables that supports multidimensional data analysis and aggregation.

In this paper, we generalize the notions of f-tables and hypercube by introducing the *nested data cube model*. Our data model supports a variety of nested versions of f-tables, each of which corresponds to an assignment of priorities to the different dimensions. The answer to the query *"Give an overview of the stores and their areas together with the global sales of the various items,"* on the data cube of Figure 1, for instance, is depicted in Figure 2 by a nested data cube. We also present an *algebra* to formulate queries, such as the one above, on nested data cubes. This query language supports all the important OLAP analysis and navigational restructuring operations on data cubes. There are a number of operations whose aim lies purely in rearranging the information in the cube in order to create different and independent views on the data. These include, for instance, nesting and unnesting operations, factual data collection in bags, duplication, extention of the cube with additional dimensions, and renaming. The algebra also contains selection, aggregation, and roll-up operations, which support data analysis.

Motivation. The model we propose offers a natural paradigm for perceiving large data cubes, as it adds to previously mentioned models mainly flexibility in viewing the data by assigning priorities to different dimensions. Put another way, grouping on values of an attribute is made explicit. As is shown in the next section, the NDC model can also be used to represent common data structures such as sets, bags, and relations. Furthermore, our model generalizes and improves upon a number of other OLAP models, as discussed later in this paragraph.

Let us first come back to the problem of perceiving large data cubes. Traditional data cubes are "flat" in the sense that they treat each dimension in the same way. This causes two kinds of perceptional difficulties. Firstly, the *dimensionality* can be too high to be practically visualizable in a 'cubic' format. Secondly, the *cardinality* (the number of tuples in the database) is typically very high. Our approach can be used to decrease both measures.

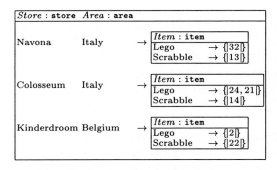

Fig. 2. A three-dimensional data cube containing sales information.

We now turn to the comparison of our approach to other OLAP models. While the query language for the tabular data model proposed by Gyssens et al. [14] only covers restructuring of tables, ours supports both restructuring and complex analysis queries. Their model, although generalized for an arbitrary number of dimensions [15], is mainly suited for two-dimensional spreadsheet applications. The NDC model, however, offers a theoretical framework for "cube viewers" where users navigate through a space of linearly nested n-dimensional cubes.

Our model is based on a simple hypercube model such as the one proposed by Agrawal et al. [2]. Their approach primarily deals with the insertion of their alebra into SQL, while this paper proposes an independent implementation of nested data cubes.

The NDC model most closely resembles the f-tables proposed by Cabibbo et al. [4]. Like their model, ours contains explicit notions of dimensions and describes hierarchies of levels within dimensions in a clean way. However, the model we propose also allows the construction of a hierarchy of the dimensions in an NDC. This does not only make viewing very large cubes easier, it also gives semantics to the scheme of a data cube. Different end-users will typically prefer different schemes for the same underlying data.

An important problem with the calculus for f-tables as proposed by Cabibbo et al. is that in at least two cases it is necessary to leave the model temporarily. Firstly, when aggregate functions are used, the result of a query may no longer be functional. In contrast, the NDC model has the ability to collect factual data in bags which allows us to stay within our model after grouping and before aggregation. Once data is collected in bags, a wide variety of aggregate functions can be performed on them by reusing the constructed bags.

Secondly, in the f-table model, it is not clear where in the system the information for the roll-up function is to be found. It is assumed that it is known for every value in any level how to roll-up to a value in a higher level from the hierarchy. Conversely, our operator that is used for roll-up takes any relation as input, meaning that roll-up information can be stored in another NDC.

While our model clearly shares similarities with the nested relational model [11, 18, 27], it is not a generalization of it. Importantly, our model imposes linear nesting which only allows for the construction of a linear hierarchy of dimensions. Finally, Lehner [20] considered a Nested Multidimensional Data Model where nesting, however, mainly applies to the modeling of dimensional levels. Furthermore, their approach does not formalize the content of the cube and permits only single numerical values as cube entries. Also, it does not allow for user defined aggregation, nor does it treat dimensions and measures symmetrically.

Organization. Section 2 introduces *nested data cubes* (NDCs). Section 3 introduces the operators of the NDC algebra and illustrates them by presenting an extensive example. Section 4 contains two results concerning the expressive power of the NDC algebra. Section 5 shows how our algebra can be implemented efficiently. For formal definitions and the proofs of the theorems, we refer to [8].

2   Nested Data Cubes

In this section, we formally define the nested data cube model and illustrate the definitions using the data cube of Figure 2. After giving additional examples, we show that the set of NDCs over a given scheme is recursively enumerable. Algebraic operators that work on NDCs are presented in the next section.

In what follows, we use the delimiters $\{\!|\cdot|\!\}$ to denote a bag. We assume the existence of a set $\mathcal{A}$ of *attributes* and a set $\mathcal{L}$ of *levels*. In Figure 2, the attributes are *Store*, *Area*, and *Item*, and the levels are store, area, item, and num (the set of natural numbers). Every level l has a recursively enumerable set $dom(l)$ of atomic values associated to it. For technical reasons, the set $\mathcal{L}$ contains a reserved level, λ, which has a singleton domain: $dom(\lambda) = \{\top\}$, with $\top$ the Boolean true value. We define $\mathbf{dom} = \bigcup\{dom(l) \mid l \in \mathcal{L}\}$.

For certain pairs (l_1, l_2) of $\mathcal{L} \times \mathcal{L}$, there exist a *roll-up function*, denoted $\text{R-UP}_{l_1}^{l_2}$, that maps every element of l_1 to an element of l_2. Further requirements may be imposed on the nature of roll-up functions, as is done in [4].

Definition 1. (Coordinate).

- A *coordinate type* is a set $\{A_1 : l_1, \ldots, A_n : l_n\}$ where $A_1, \ldots, A_n$ are distinct attributes, $l_1, \ldots, l_n$ are levels, and $n \geq 0$.
- A *coordinate* over the coordinate type $\{A_1 : l_1, \ldots, A_n : l_n\}$ is a set $\{A_1 : v_1, \ldots, A_n : v_n\}$ where $v_i \in dom(l_i)$, for $1 \leq i \leq n$.

The set of attributes appearing in a coordinate (type) γ, is denoted $att(\gamma)$. □

The NDC of Figure 2 has two coordinate types; i.e., $\{Store : \texttt{store}, Area : \texttt{area}\}$ and $\{Item : \texttt{item}\}$. An example of a coordinate over the former coordinate type is $\{Store : \text{Navona}, Area : \text{Italy}\}$.

Definition 2. (Scheme). The abstract syntax of a *nested data cube scheme* (NDC *scheme*, or simply *scheme*) is given by:

$$\tau = [\delta \to \tau] \quad | \quad \beta \tag{1}$$
$$\beta = l \quad | \quad \{\!|\beta|\!\} \tag{2}$$

where δ is a coordinate type, and l is a level. Throughout this paper, the Greek characters δ, τ, and β consistently refer to the above syntax. □

The nested data cube of Figure 2, for example, is

$$\tau_0 = [\{Store : \texttt{store}, Area : \texttt{area}\} \to [\{Item : \texttt{item}\} \to \{\!|\texttt{num}|\!\}]].$$

As another example, the scheme of Figure 1 is $[\{Day : \texttt{day}, Item : \texttt{item}, Store : \texttt{store}\} \to \texttt{num}]$.

Definition 3. (Instance). To define an instance (*nested data cube*) over a scheme τ, we first define the function $dom(\cdot)$ as follows:

$$dom(\delta) = \text{the set of all coordinates over coordinate type } \delta$$
$$dom([\delta \to \tau]) = \{\{v_1 \to w_1, \ldots, v_m \to w_m\} \mid m \geq 0, \text{ and}$$
$$v_1, \ldots, v_m \text{ are pairwise distinct coordinates of } dom(\delta), \text{ and}$$
$$w_i \in dom(\tau) \text{ for } 1 \leq i \leq m\}$$
$$dom(\{\!|\beta|\!\}) = \{\{\!|v_1, \ldots, v_m|\!\} \mid v_i \in dom(\beta) \text{ for } 1 \leq i \leq m\}$$

An NDC over the scheme τ is an element of $dom(\tau)$. □

Figure 2 is a representation of an instance of the NDC with scheme τ_0.

Definition 4. (Depth). The *depth* of a scheme τ, denoted $depth(\tau)$, is defined as the number of occurences of δ in the construction of τ by applying rule (1) of Definition 2.

The notion of depth is extended to NDCs in an obvious way: if C is an NDC over the scheme τ, then we say that the depth of C is $depth(\tau)$. The notion of *subscheme* of a scheme τ at depth n is assumed to be intuitively clear. □

The NDC with scheme τ_0 is of depth 2. The subscheme at depth 2 is [{*Item* : item} → {|num|}].

We now give some additional examples.

Example 1. Note that [{} → num] is a legal scheme. Its depth is equal to 1. All NDCs over this scheme can be listed as follows (assume $dom(\text{num}) = \{1, 2, \ldots\}$): {} (the empty NDC), {{} → 1}, {{} → 2}, and so on.

Importantly, num itself is also a legal scheme. Its depth is equal to 0. The NDCs over num (as a scheme) are 1,2, ... □

Example 2. NDCs can represent several common data structures, as follows.

Bag: An NDC over a scheme of the form {|β|}.
Set: An NDC over a scheme of the form [{$A : l$} → λ].
Relation: An NDC over a scheme of the form [δ → λ]. The NDC called C_0 in Section 3 represents a conventional relation.
F-tables [4]: An NDC over a scheme of the form [δ → l]. □

Example 1 shows that the NDCs over the scheme [{} → num] are recursively enumerable. The following theorem generalizes this result for arbitrary schemes.

Theorem 1. *The set of all NDCs over a given scheme τ is recursively enumerable.*

3   The NDC Algebra

The NDC *algebra* consists of the following eight operators:

bagify This operator decreases the depth of an NDC by replacing each innermost sub-NDC by a bag containing the right-hand values appearing in the sub-NDC;

extend This operator adds an attribute to an NDC. The attribute values of the newly added attribute are computed from the coordinates in the original NDC;

nest *and* unnest These operators capture the classical meaning of nesting and unnesting;

duplicate This operator takes an NDC and replaces the right-hand values by the attribute values of some specified attribute;

select *and* rename These operators correspond to operators with the same name in the conventional relational algebra;

aggregate This operator replaces each right-hand value w in an NDC by a new value obtained by applying a specified function to w.

Furthermore, the NDC algebra also allows for the use of these operators at arbitrary depths. For instance, the use of **nest** at depth 2, will be denoted by nest^2. For more details, we refer to Section 4.1.

These operators are illustrated in the following extensive example, which is purely designed to contain all operators (and thus contains redundant steps). Readers interested in the formal definitions of the operators and the details of their semantics, are refered to [8].

Before turning to the example, we make the following remarks. Due to space restrictions, we omit several intermediate NDCs. Also, to make the tables smaller in size, we have used abbreviations for the attributes. It should be noted that the size of the tables printed below is big because we chose to show all sub-cubes at once. However, in interactive cube-viewers, sub-cubes will only "open" when clicked upon, thus reducing the size profoundly. Finally, the reader should understand that the definitions of the operators are formed such that the result of an operation always retains functionality.

The query used in the example is

Give an overview per (area, country) pair and per item of the amounts of toys sold over all shops and all time, in the area of Europe.

We start from raw data in a relation C_0 containing information about toy shops. Typically, such tables contain more than one attribute that can be seen as a measure. In C_0, for instance, both the number of items sold (So) as well as the number of damaged or lost items (Lo) can serve as a measure.

Da : day	It : item	St : store	So : num	Lo : num	Co : country	
Jan1	Lego	Colosseum	35	4	Italy	→ T
Jan1	Lego	Navona	12	1	Italy	→ T
Jan1	Lego	Kindertuin	31	6	Belgium	→ T
Jan1	Lego	Toygarden	31	1	USA	→ T
Jan1	Scrabble	Atomium	11	2	Belgium	→ T
Jan1	Scrabble	Colosseum	15	2	Italy	→ T
Jan1	Scrabble	Funtastic	22	0	Canada	→ T
Jan1	Scrabble	Kindertuin	19	5	Belgium	→ T
Jan1	Scrabble	Navona	17	3	Italy	→ T
Jan2	Lego	Kindertuin	42	5	Belgium	→ T
Jan2	Lego	Navona	28	7	Italy	→ T

$$C_0$$

Cube C_1 is obtained after selecting one attribute (So) from C_0 to be used as a measure, i.e., $C_1 = \text{duplicate}(C_0, So)$. After chosing this measure for the OLAP analysis, a logical next step would be to remove this and all other measures from the coordinate type of the NDC. This projection can be simulated in our NDC algebra by the following three steps; first the measures are put in a seperate sub-cube by using the **nest** operator, then the information is collapsed in bags, and finally the aggregate **sum** is computed.

However, to save space, we temporarily leave the measures in the coordinate type. In later steps, they will disappear.

$$C_1 = [\{Da : \text{day}, It : \text{item}, St : \text{store}, So : \text{num}, Lo : \text{num}, Co : \text{country}\} \rightarrow \text{num}].$$

In order to satisfy the query, we have to add the **area** attribute to the coordinate type. This is done by applying **extend**, i.e.,

$$C_2 = \text{extend}(C_1, Ar, \text{area}, \text{R-UP}^{\text{area}}_{\text{country}}).$$

Thus, the scheme of C_2 is $[\{Da : \text{day}, It : \text{item}, St : \text{store}, So : \text{num}, Lo : \text{num}, Co : \text{country}, Ar : \text{area}\} \rightarrow \text{num}]$.

We now nest in two steps. Thus, $C_3 = \text{nest}(C_2, Ar)$ and $C_4 = \text{nest}^2(C_3, Co)$. The scheme of C_3 then is

$$[\{Ar : \text{area}\} \rightarrow [\{Da : \text{day}, It : \text{item}, St : \text{store}, So : \text{num}, Lo : \text{num}, Co : \text{country}\} \rightarrow \text{num}]].$$

Ar : area							

	Co : country						
Europe →	Belgium →	Da : day	It : item	St : store	So : num	Lo : num	
		Jan1	Lego	Kindertuin	31	6	→ 31
		Jan1	Scrabble	Atomium	11	2	→ 11
		Jan1	Scrabble	Kindertuin	19	5	→ 19
		Jan2	Lego	Kindertuin	42	5	→ 42
	Italy →	Da : day	It : item	St : store	So : num	Lo : num	
		Jan1	Lego	Colosseum	35	4	→ 35
		Jan1	Lego	Navona	12	1	→ 12
		Jan1	Scrabble	Colosseum	15	2	→ 15
		Jan1	Scrabble	Navona	17	3	→ 17
		Jan2	Lego	Navona	28	7	→ 28

	Co : country						
America →	USA →	Da : day	It : item	St : store	So : num	Lo : num	
		Jan1	Lego	Toygarden	31	1	→ 31
	Canada →	Da : day	It : item	St : store	So : num	Lo : num	
		Jan1	Scrabble	Funtastic	22	0	→ 22

$$C_4 = [\{Ar : \text{area}\} \rightarrow [\{Co : \text{country}\} \rightarrow [\{Da : \text{day}, It : \text{item}, St : \text{store}, So : \text{num}, Lo : \text{num}\} \rightarrow \text{num}]]]$$

We now decrease the number of tuples in the cube by performing a selection. Cube $C_5 = \text{select}(C_4, Ar, \text{Europe})$. The scheme of C_5 is the same as that of C_4. To obtain the pairs of (area, country) requested in the query, unnesting is applied to the cube. Cube $C_6 = \text{unnest}(C_5)$, and its scheme is

$$[\{Ar : \text{area}, Co : \text{country}\} \rightarrow [\{Da : \text{day}, It : \text{item}, St : \text{store}, So : \text{num}, Lo : \text{num}\} \rightarrow \text{num}]].$$

We now need to nest on the **item** attribute (as mentioned in the statement of our example query), appearing in the second level of grouping. Cube $C_7 = \text{nest}^2(C_6, It)$, with scheme

$[\{Ar : \textbf{area}, Co : \textbf{country}\} \rightarrow [\{It : \textbf{item}\} \rightarrow$
$\quad [\{Da : \textbf{day}, St : \textbf{store}, So : \textbf{num}, Lo : \textbf{num}\} \rightarrow \textbf{num}]]]$.

Since we have now obtained the necessary grouping, all attributes remaining at the deepest level of nesting are not needed anymore. Their data is collapsed into bags, i.e., $C_8 = \texttt{bagify}(C_7)$. Note that we are now removing the measures from the coordinate type, and are also putting all information over all dates together.

$C_8 = [\{Ar : \textbf{area}, Co : \textbf{country}\} \rightarrow [\{It : \textbf{item}\} \rightarrow \{\!|\textbf{num}|\!\}]]$.

As a last step in the process of realizing our example query by using the NDC algebra, we perform the $\texttt{sum}$ aggregate on the bags of cube C_8 to obtain the totals of sold items. This yields the desired result.

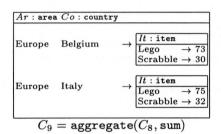

$$C_9 = \textbf{aggregate}(C_8, \textbf{sum})$$

4 The Expressive Power of the NDC Algebra

In this section, we show some properties concerning the expressiveness of the NDC algebra. We first show that the NDC algebra is sufficiently powerful to capture algebraic operations working directly on sub-NDCs over a subscheme of a scheme. Next, we show that the NDC algebra can express the SPJR algebra [1]. We refer to [8] for the proofs of the theorems in this section.

4.1 Applying Operators at a Certain Depth

The recursion in the definition of NDC is a "tail recursion." Consequently, the "recursion depth" can be used to unequivocally address a sub-NDC within an NDC. This is an interesting and important property of NDCs. It is exploited by defining operators that directly work on sub-NDCs at a certain depth. Such operators reduce the need for frequent nesting and unnesting of NDCs.

Definition 5. Let C be an NDC over the scheme τ. Let $1 \leq d \leq \textit{depth}(\tau)$. Let $\text{op}(C, a_1, \ldots, a_n)$ be any operation of the NDC algebra.

Let $\tau' = \textit{subscheme}(\tau, d)$. Then $\text{op}^d(C, a_1, \ldots, a_n)$ is defined iff $\text{op}(\tau', a_1, \ldots, a_n)$ is defined. $\square$

The details of the impact on schemes and NDCs are omitted. They can be found in [8].

In the example of Section 3, cube C_4 was obtained from C_3 by using the nest operator at depth 2.

The following theorem states that $\mathsf{op}^d(C, a_1, \ldots, a_n)$ is not a primitive operator; i.e., it can be expressed in terms of the operators of the NDC algebra.

Theorem 2. *Let C be an NDC over the scheme τ.*
The operator $\mathsf{op}^d(C, a_1, \ldots, a_n)$ with $d \geq 2$ is redundant.

As an example of this theorem, cube C_4 of the previous section can be obtained from cube C_3 by applying the following expressions at depth 1:

$$C_4 = \mathsf{nest}(\mathsf{nest}(\mathsf{unnest}(C_3), \mathit{It}), \mathit{Ar}).$$

4.2 The SPJR Algebra

Theorem 3. *The NDC algebra expresses the SPJR [1] algebra.*

The proof for Theorem 3 (see [8]) shows how the **extend** operator can be used to simulate the relational join.

5 Implementing the NDC Algebra

The operations of Section 3 can be implemented by algorithms that run in linear time with respect to the number of atomic values that appear in the data cube. We assume that each aggregate function is computable in polynomial time.

We introduce two new constructs: the iCube which holds the actual data in an n-dimensional array, and the iStruct, essentially a string representing the structure behind the data.

For example, consider the scheme $[\{A_1 : a_1, A_2 : a_2\} \rightarrow [\{B_1 : b_1, B_2 : b_2\} \rightarrow c]]$. It can be implemented by the iCube *cube* of type $\mathsf{c}[\#\mathsf{b}_1][\#\mathsf{a}_2][\#\mathsf{d}_1][\#\mathsf{b}_2][\#\mathsf{a}_1]$ (the array type of the Java language is used for simplicity) together with the iStruct $[5, 2 \rightarrow [1, 4 \rightarrow \cdot]]$. In the iCube's type, $\#\mathsf{a}_1$ denotes the cardinality of $dom(\mathsf{a}_1)$ plus one. That is, there is one entry for each element of $dom(\mathsf{a}_1)$ (indexes $1, 2, \ldots, \#\mathsf{a}_1 - 1$) on top of the entry with index 0. The numbers in the iStruct denote positions in the array type. For example, "5" refers to the fifth dimension, which ranges to $\#\mathsf{a}_1$. A possible member of an NDC over the given scheme is $[\{A_1 : u_1, A_2 : u_2\} \rightarrow [\{B_1 : v_1, B_2 : v_2\} \rightarrow w]]$ which will be represented in the iCube as $cube[v_1][u_2][0][v_2][u_1] = w$.

Note that an extra, unused dimension is present in the iCube (namely, the third dimension ranging to $\#\mathsf{d}_1$). This is necessary in case the **extend** operation is used, as we require the types of iCubes to remain the same throughout the computation of the query. This dimension will then be used to store the attribute created by the **extend** operator.

A final remark relates to the use of bags in our model. The implementation should support fast access to the elements in a bag of an NDC, to facilitate the computation of aggregate functions. Consider, for example, the scheme $[\{A : a\} \to \{|c|\}]$. NDCs over this scheme contain bags. One possible implementation uses the iCube $cube$ of type c$[\#a][\#d]$ and the iStruct $[1 \to \{|2|\}]$. A member $[\{A : v\} \to \{|w_1, w_2|\}]$ of an NDC over this scheme, for example, is represented by $\{|cube[v][i] \mid 1 \le i < \#d|\} = \{|w_1, w_2|\}$.

The operations of the NDC algebra are implemented in such a way that the type of the iCube never changes. Importantly, the **nest**, **unnest**, and **bagify** operations only change the iStruct, leaving the iCube unaffected. The other operations also change the content of the iCube. Based on this, we can implement an expression in the NDC algebra in linear time. We now give a concrete example.

Let *revenue* be an NDC over the scheme

$$[\{Store : \text{store} \to [\{City : \text{city}\} \to [\{Product : \text{product}\} \to \text{num}]]]$$

We want to answer the query *"For each city, give the maximal total revenue realized by any store in that city."* The iCube and initial iStruct implementing the NDC are *revenue* = num$[\#\text{store}][\#\text{city}][\#\text{product}]$ and $[1 \to [2 \to [3 \to \cdot]]]$, respectively. The algebraic expression for the query is

$$\text{aggregate}(\text{bagify}(\text{aggregate}(\text{bagify}(\text{nest}(\text{unnest}(revenue), City)), \text{sum})), \text{max})$$

A Java-like linear program implementing the expression is

```
for (int c = 1; c ≤ #city; c++) {
    revenue[0][c][0] = 0;
    for (int s = 1; s ≤ #store; s++) {
        revenue[s][c][0] = 0;
        for (int p = 1; p ≤ #product; p++) {
            revenue[s][c][0] += revenue[s][c][p];
        }
        revenue[0][c][0] = max(revenue[0][c][0], revenue[s][c][0]);
    }
}
```

References

1. S. Abiteboul, R. Hull, V. Vianu. *Foundations of Databases.* Addison-Wesley, 1995.
2. R. Agrawal, A. Gupta, and S. Sarawagi. Modeling multidimensional databases. In *Proc. IEEE Int. Conf. Data Engineering (ICDE '97)*, pages 232–243, 1997.
3. M. Blaschka, C. Sapia, G. Höfling, and B. Dinter. Finding Your Way through Multidimensional Data Models. In *DWDOT Workshop (Dexa 98)*, Vienna, 1998.
4. L. Cabibbo and R. Torlone. Querying multidimensional databases. In *Sixth Int. Workshop on Database Programming Languages (DBPL '97)*, pages 253–269, 1997.
5. S. Chaudhuri and U. Dayal. An overview of data warehousing and olap technology. *SIGMOD Record*, 26(1):65–74, 1997.
6. E. Codd, S. Codd, and C. Salley. Providing OLAP (On-Line Analytical Processing) to user-analysts: An IT mandate. *Arbor Software White Paper.*

7. G. Colliat. Olap, relational, and multidimensional database systems. *SIGMOD Record*, 25(3):64–69, 1996.

8. S. Dekeyser, B. Kuijpers, J. Paredaens, and J. Wijsen. Nested Data Cubes. *Technical Report 9804*, University of Antwerp, 1998. ftp://wins.uia.ac.be/pub/olap/ndc.ps

9. C. Dyreson. Information retrieval from an incomplete data cube. In *Proc. Int. Conf. Very Large Data Bases (VLDB '96)*, pages 532–543, Bombai, India, 1996.

10. Essbase. *Arbor Software*, http://www.arborsoft.com/OLAP.html.

11. P.C. Fischer, and S.J. Thomas. Nested Relational Structures. In *The Theory of Databases, Advances in Computing Research III*, PC. Kanellakis, ed., pages 269–307, JAI Press, Greenwich, CT, 1986.

12. J. Gray, A. Boswirth, A. Layman, and H. Pirahesh. Data cube: A relational aggregation operator generalizing group-by. In *Proc. IEEE Int. Conf. Data Engineering (ICDE '97)*, pages 152–159, 1997.

13. J. Gray, S. Chaudhuri, A. Boswirth, A. Layman, D. Reichart, F. Pellow, and H. Pirahesh. Data cube: A relational aggregation operator generalizing group-by, crosstab, and sub-totals. *Data Mining and Knowledge Discovery*, 1:29–53, 1997.

14. M. Gyssens, L. Lakshmanan, and I. Subramanian. Tables as a paradigm for querying and restructuring. In *Proc. Symposium on Principles of Database Systems (PODS '96)*, pages 93–103, Montreal, Canada, 1996.

15. M. Gyssens and L. Lakshmanan. A Foundation for Multi-Dimensional Databases. In *Proc. VLDB '97*, pages 106–115, Athens, Greece, 1997.

16. J. Han. OLAP mining: An integration of OLAP with data mining. In *Proceedings of the 7th IFIP 2.6 Working Conf. on Database Semantics (DS-7)*, pages 1–9, 1997.

17. V. Harinarayan, A. Rajaraman, and J. D. Ullman. Implementing data cubes efficiently. In *Proc. ACM SIGMOD International Conference on Management of Data (SIGMOD '96)*, pages 205–216, Montreal, Canada, 1996.

18. G. Jaeschke, and H.-J. Schek. Remarks on the Algebra on Non First Normal Form Relations. In *Proceedings first Symposium on Principles of Database Systems (PODS '82)*, pages 124–138, Los Angeles, CA, 1982.

19. Intelligent server. *IBM*, http://www.software.ibm.com/data/pubs/papers.

20. W. Lehner. Modeling Large Scale OLAP Scenarios. In *Proceedings of EDBT '98*, pages 153–167, Valencia, Spain, 1998.

21. L. Libkin, R. Machlin, and L. Wong. A query language for multidimensional arrays: Design implementation, and optimization techniques. In *Proc. Int. Conf. Management of Data (SIGMOD '96)*, pages 228–239, Montreal, Canada, 1996.

22. A. Marathe and K. Salem. A language for manipulating arrays. In *Proc. Int. Conf. Very Large Data Bases (VLDB '97)*, pages 46–55, Athens, Greece, 1997.

23. Pilot decision support suite. *Pilot Software*, rickover.pilotsw.com/products/.

24. Red brick warehouse. *Red Brick*, www.redbrick.com/rbs-g/html/plo.html.

25. Sales analyzer. *Oracle*, http://www.oracle.com/products/olap/html/.

26. S. Sarawagi and M. Stonebraker. Efficient organization of large multidimensional arrays. In *Proc. Int. Conf. Data Engineering*, pages 328–336, Houston, TX, 1994.

27. H. J. Schek, and M. H. Scholl. The Relational Model with Relation-Valued Attributes. In *Information Systems* **11:2**, pages 137–147, 1986.

28. A. Shoshani. OLAP and statistical databases: Similarities and differences. In *Proc. ACM SIGACT-SIGMOD-SIGART Symposium on Principles of Database Systems (PODS '97)*, pages 185–196, Tucson, AZ, 1997.

Data Warehousing and Data Mining:
Are We Working on the Right Things?

John F. Roddick

School of Computer and Information Science,
University of South Australia
The Levels Campus, Mawson Lakes, Adelaide,
South Australia 5095
roddick@cis.unisa.edu.au

Abstract. This paper is a report of the panel session of the same name held at the 1st International Workshop on Data Warehousing and Data Mining (DWDM'98) held in Singapore in November 1998. The purpose of the panel was to discover the views of researchers in the field in order to encourage research in data warehousing and data mining to be directed in the most profitably manner and to discuss issues relating to the open problems in the area.

1   Introduction

It is essential for all scientific areas to occasionally reflect on the current state of their endeavours to ensure that effort is being directed in the most appropriate directions. This is especially so for rapidly moving areas such as computing and even more so for emergent areas such as data warehousing and data mining. The panel session held as part of the 1st International Workshop on Data Warehousing and Data Mining (DWDM'98) in Singapore focused on these issues and this paper provides the results of that panel.

The panel was structured around three prime questions:

- ◆ What areas should be considered as solved problems, or are problems which are not worth working on?
- ◆ What areas should we, as researchers in the data warehousing / data mining area, be concentrating on?
- ◆ Which areas are unlikely to yield results in the near future (say, 10 years)?

For each question in turn, the three panelists, Gerd Stumme from the Technical University, Darmstadt, Tetsuya Furukawa from Kyushu University in Japan and myself as chair, presented an initial list of answers to these questions that were then discussed, modified and augmented by the workshop delegates. In the end, almost half of the issues raised came from the workshop delegates themselves and the debate was both open and constructive.

At the end of the panel session a number issues had been suggested (although, as can be seen from the results of the questionnaire, not necessarily universally endorsed); 11 as solved problems, 16 as active research areas and 4 as areas that were unlikely to yield results in the near future (although these may still be considered worthy of research effort). The panel delegates then ranked the issues through the use of a

Likert-scale questionnaire giving each issue within each question a mark ranging from 3 (strongly agree) through 0 (neutral) to –3 (strongly disagree). 31 delegates took the time to complete the questionnaire and the results are shown and discussed in the next three sections. Given this sample size, only questions with answers more than about 0.8 above or below the neutral mark of zero can be considered significant.

2 What areas should be considered as solved problems, or are not worth working on?

As would be expected, this question generated a significant amount of debate and as the results in Table 1 indicate, overall consensus on these issues was low and the difference of opinions was marked with an average standard deviation of 2.0. Three items only can be considered to be identified. Firstly, there was some consensus on the need to acknowledge work already completed in other areas although the particular needs of data mining systems may necessitate a further look at their applicability. Secondly, the development of algorithms that cannot be scaled up was generally thought to be of concern as was the emphasis on problems which were extremely dependent on local characteristics and which cannot be applied widely. It is interesting to note that some issues raised by some were considered by the group as a whole not to be solved.

Issue	Average (Max 3, Min –3)	Standard Deviation	Negative Votes (Max 31)
Reinvention of algorithms and techniques already formulated by statisticians and artificial intelligence researchers over many years	1.2	2.1	6
Development of algorithms that cannot be scaled up	1.0	2.1	7
Emphasis on localised problems which cannot be applied widely	0.8	1.8	6
Mining from object-oriented databases	0.5	2.2	8
Small-scale views of the nature of knowledge	0.4	1.4	5
Development of data warehouse architectures	0.1	2.3	11
RDBMS-specific data mining	0.1	2.0	10
Mining of data histories	0.0	1.7	8
Investing special algorithms for web	-0.1	2.2	9
Schema integration	-0.2	2.0	8
Proofs of correctness of algorithms	-0.4	2.2	13
Average	0.3	2.0	

Table 1 – Aggregated Response to the question "What areas should be considered as solved problems, or are not worth working on?"

3 What areas should we, as researchers in the data warehousing / data mining area, be working on?

When the group debated the list of active issues, there was far more consensus on those confronting the field. By far the most important area identified was that of data mining techniques being applied to data warehouses. In discussing this, the distinction between current information retrieval techniques, sometimes referred to as data mining, and full data mining was emphasised. Indeed, the need to promote the correct terminology was also strongly supported. It was also suggested that while data warehouses provided some of the motivation for data mining, much of the effort to date has been directed at simpler database or flat file organisations. Other issues included the mining of more complex forms of data such as multidimensional, temporal, spatio-temporal, etc. as was the need to develop models and scalable mining techniques applicable to very large data warehouses.

Issue	Average (Max 3, Min −3)	Standard Deviation	Negative Votes (Max 31)
Data mining with data warehousing	2.4	0.9	0
Multi-dimensional and advanced data semantics (temporal, spatio-temporal etc)	2.0	1.1	0
Scalability of Mining / VLDW	2.0	1.5	1
Query Optimisation / Updates	1.9	1.3	2
Meta-Data Issues and Meta data Models for DW	1.9	1.6	2
Getting the terminology straight, particularly DM .v. IR and working with people from other areas such as AI/Stats.	1.8	1.6	1
Interestingness Measures	1.8	1.5	2
Gathering and using real data and data acquisition methods	1.7	1.6	2
Materialised View Maintenance	1.7	1.6	2
Warehousing of semi-structured data	1.6	1.6	3
Human-centred mining - algorithms that support rather than replace humans	1.3	1.6	3
Concept hierarchy construction for WWW	0.8	1.7	5
Mining of web data/structure	0.0	2.0	11
One model for WWW	-0.2	2.1	9
Numerical computation on web	-0.3	2.1	10
Mining RDBMS with OODBMS	-0.3	1.7	7
Average	1.3	1.6	

Table 2 – Aggregated Response to the question "What areas should we, as researchers in the data warehousing / data mining area, be working on?"

The area of query optimisation, felt by many to be a solved area for many years, was also considered in need of further work in the light of recent research in this area[1]. There was also significant discussion on the development of better measures for measuring the quality and interestingness of data mining results.

---

[1] Similar comments on this issue were also discussed at the 1997 SIGMOD Conference in Tucson, Arizona [1].

4   Which areas are unlikely to yield results in the near future (say, 10 years)?

Just four issues were raised in this category and there was general consensus on at least two. Firstly, totally autonomous knowledge discovery was felt to be unrealistic (and by some even to be undesirable) and secondly, the concept of a general knowledge discovery algorithm applicable to a large range of data was felt to be optimistic at best. It is interesting to note that, in common with the first question, the standard deviation for these questions was high.

Issue	Average (Max 3, Min −3)	Standard Deviation	Negative Votes (Max 31)
Human-less Knowledge discovery	1.4	1.6	3
General KD algorithm	1.1	2.0	6
Internet "Mining" (as opposed to internet IR)	0.8	2.0	5
Legacy Data Mining	0.5	2.1	7
Average	1.0	1.9	

Table 3 – Aggregated Response to the question "Which areas are unlikely to yield results in the near future (say, 10 years)?"

5   Conclusions

For an area as young as the fields of data warehousing and data mining there was a remarkable unanimity in the direction the field should be taking, particularly in respect to the answers to Question 2, the active research issues. Differences of opinion are to be expected when identifying areas to be abandoned or which may not yield immediate results and previous surveys of these sorts of questions have shown similar divergence of opinion [2, 3]. Importantly however, the issues were raised for further thought and debate and consideration of these issues is likely to be a topic for discussion at future workshops.

References

[1]   S. Chaudhuri, "Panel on "Query Optimisation at the Crossroads"", in *Proc. ACM SIGMOD International Conference on the Management of Data*. Tucson, Arizona, pp. 509, 1997.

[2]   Laguna Beach Report, "Future directions in DBMS research". *SIGMOD Rec.* vol. 18, no. 1, pp. 17-26, 1989.

[3]   M. Stonebraker, R. Agrawal, U. Dayal, E.J. Neuhold and A. Reuter, "DBMS research at the crossroads: the Vienna update", in *Proc. Nineteenth International Conference on Very Large Databases*. Dublin, Ireland, Morgan Kaufmann, Palo Alto, CA, pp. 688-692, 1993.

The Design of an Engineering Data Warehouse Based on Meta-Object Structures

F. Estrella[1], Z. Kovacs[1], J-M. Le Goff[2], R. McClatchey[1], and I. Willers[2]

[1]Centre for Complex Cooperative Systems, UWE, Frenchay, Bristol BS16 1QY UK
{Florida.Estrella, Zsolt.Kovacs, Richard.McClatchey}@cern.ch
[2]CERN, Geneva, Switzerland
{Jean-Marie.Le.Goff, Ian.Willers}@cern.ch

Abstract. Large scale engineering and scientific projects demand product and workflow management which may require integration and/or distribution over many separate organisations. The integration of such 'islands of information', which ultimately forms the basis of so-called 'virtual enterprises', is heavily dependent on the flexibility and accessibility of the data model describing the enterprise's repository. The model must provide interoperability and reusability so that a range of applications can access the enterprise data. Making the repository self-describing ensures that knowledge about the repository structure is available for applications to interrogate and to navigate around for the extraction of application-specific data. Herein a large application is described which uses a meta-object based repository to capture product and workflow data in an engineering data warehouse. It is shown that adopting a meta-object approach to repository design provides support for interoperability and a suitable environment on which to build data mining applications.

1. Background

The Compact Muon Solenoid (CMS experiment [1]) will comprise several complex detectors for fundamental particle physics. Each detector will be constructed out of, potentially, over a million parts and will be produced and assembled during the next decade by specialised centres distributed world-wide. Each constituent part of each detector must be accurately measured and tested locally prior to its ultimate assembly at the European Centre for Particle Physics at CERN, Geneva. Much of the information collected during the construction phase will be needed for detector calibration, to facilitate accurate simulation of its performance and to assist in its maintenance.

In the construction of previous generations of detectors, this data gathering process was rather ad-hoc, with engineers using CAD/CAM tools for design and databases, file-based systems or logbooks to record construction details. The overall effect of this was to create disparate and unconnected 'islands of information' specific to mechanical design, calibration, maintenance etc. When it was necessary to combine information from design for assembly or from construction for calibration, there were no transparent methods for relating information between these separate systems and no management techniques which could span those systems. Developers of CMS require a *data warehouse* to capture all salient detector engineering data and a set of methods by which this data warehouse can be *mined* to extract information from a variety of viewpoints (e.g calibration and maintenance). Each centre gathers information on the assembly and testing of CMS parts and the warehouse is established centrally at CERN to capture the complete construction data.

The CRISTAL [2] system is a prototype being developed to monitor and control the production and assembly process of the 87,000 lead tungstate mono-crystals, and their fast electronics, to be installed in the CMS Electromagnetic Calorimeter detector at CERN. CRISTAL employs workflow (WfMS) and product data management (PDM) techniques to provide an infrastructure in which the engineering data can be warehoused. A distributed object-oriented database, Objectivity [3], is used to hold both the engineering data and the definitions of the detector components and the tasks which are performed on the components. This paper advocates such a meta-object design approach to developing a warehouse model and shows how this facilitates data mining.

2. Design Constraints in CRISTAL

The CRISTAL project has been described elsewhere from a standpoint of workflow and product data management [4]. In developing a model [5] which integrates product- and process-related data, *definitions of workflow and product data elements are captured in addition to actual instantiations of those elements*. This fundamental design approach reduces complexity and maximises flexibility in the data model of the CRISTAL data warehouse. Additional design constraints are detailed below.

The data warehouse must support long-running (and potentially nested) workflow activities. The environment at CERN is research-based and both process and data-related definitions tend to evolve rapidly over time. The CRISTAL software must cater for the development of CMS which will take place over an extended period of time (1999-2005) and whose design will naturally advance as time elapses.

Schema evolution must be allowed to take place as the construction continues. The construction of CMS is a once-off process, so versions of workflow activities and product definitions must co-exist in the production process for the duration of construction. In addition, users of CRISTAL must ultimately be able to handle the ad-hoc definition and execution of processes, as and when required in CMS construction.

Distribution must be supported in CRISTAL. Production of (versions of) CMS products will take place in areas as disparate as China and Russia, their testing will be undertaken in Italy, CERN and the UK and assembly will largely take place at CERN. Each of these 'Centres' must cater for multiple versions of evolving product and process definitions autonomously but be centrally coordinated from CERN.

The data collected in the CRISTAL data warehouse must be reliable, secure and easily accessible. Many different users require access to the CRISTAL data from a variety of viewpoints: construction engineers interpret data using an assembly-oriented view whereas physicists see the detector in terms of a set of electronically-decoded channels and mechanical engineers view the detector in terms of constituent 3-dimensional volumes aligned in space.

The CRISTAL system must co-exist with other systems during its lifetime. For example, at the outset it must exchange information with a legacy Product Data Manager and, as time elapses, it must act as a source of data for Calibration, Alignment and Maintenance systems, as yet unspecified.

These design constraints cannot currently be satisfied by any commercial offering. The team charged with designing the CRISTAL data model could consequently develop an open and flexible solution. An approach has been adopted in which a model was developed that provided genericity through the use of *meta-objects*, describing general structures, rather than specifying a restricted view onto the process or product-specific data. The particular constraints of time, evolution and viewpoint support quickly led to the adoption of an object-oriented approach to data and process modelling. The Unified Modeling language (UML) [6] methodology of Booch, Rumbaugh & Jacobson has been followed; the result being a detailed UML model, presented elsewhere [5].

3. Meta Models and Self-Description

The main feature of the CRISTAL data model resulting from the use of a meta-object design approach is its self-describing nature. CRISTAL objects retain knowledge both about their dynamic structure and how they are related and this knowledge is the basis

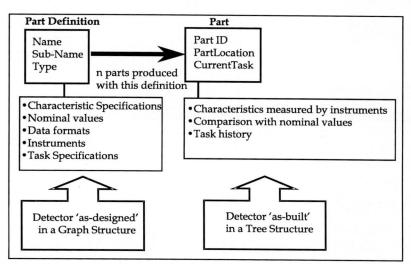

Fig 1. An example of a Meta-Object: Part Definitions for Parts.

for navigating the CRISTAL database. This aspect of the data model design is crucial to the development of a model which facilitates data mining - the mining for data is catered for by saving knowledge about the model itself, and potentially how it has been accessed, alongside the data.

For each class of significance in the data model, a meta-class is defined: e.g part definitions for parts, activity definitions for activities, and agent definitions for agents (see figure 1). This meta-object mechanism reduces system complexity by promoting object reuse and translating complex hierarchies of object instances into graphs of object types. Meta-models allow the capture of knowledge alongside the objects, enriching them and facilitating self-description and data independence. It is believed that the use of meta-object structures provides the flexibility needed to cope with their evolution over the extended timescales of CRISTAL production and the flexibility required to cope with ad-hoc workflow specification.

A simplified subset of the CRISTAL meta model, described using UML, is shown in figure 2. This model describes relationships, types, inheritance, containment and other associations between the meta objects in the system. The meta objects in the model are definitions, for example, part definitions or activity definitions and the definitions are either elementary or composite in nature. CompositeMember objects capture the membership of objects in other objects. The data description world of, in this example, parts and the process description world of, in this case activities, displays an elegant symmetry with respect to compositeness.

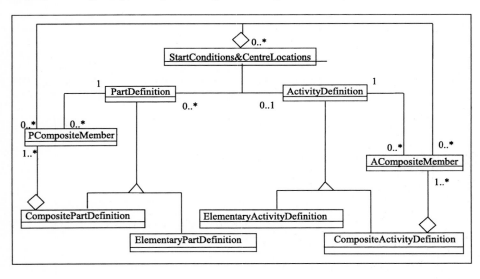

Fig. 2. A simplified subset of the CRISTAL UML Object (Meta-)Model

Figure 2 shows that there is an association between a given activity meta-object definition and a named part meta-object definition. The CRISTAL data model has been designed so that each assignment of a Part Definition to an Activity Definition is declared for a specific purpose. In detector construction, the assignment is made to indicate the activity to be instantiated for the assembly of a particular instance of a part of a given part definition. Each assignment has associated with it some *Conditions*: in detector construction, the data model captures the definition of the conditions required for each assignment of an activity definition to a part definition.

This technique can be generalised for other applications. For example, the association of a maintenance activity to a part will require quite different conditions to be captured than when the detector was constructed. Also, the association of a calibration activity to a part would require calibration-specific conditions to be captured. In other words, the identified association between the process and part description worlds carries rich semantics. This method of integrating PDM and WfMS through the definition of meta-objects and their mutual assignment is very powerful. It allows many other links to be made between aspects of the overall CRISTAL data model: the same mechanism can be used to assign agents to activity definitions for the purposes of enactment or the assignment of agents to part definitions for the purposes of resource management.

Over time, new distributed computing systems will need to interoperate with the CRISTAL production system in unforseeable ways. Interoperability is maximised by building flexibility and expandability into the data model. To facilitate interoperability, the CRISTAL developers have taken advantage of the meta-object nature of the CRISTAL -model.

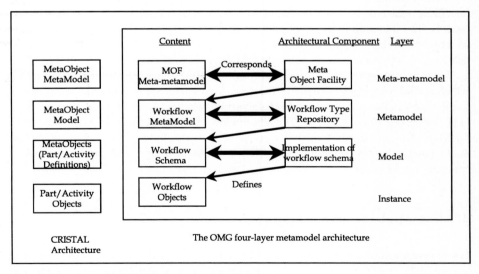

Fig. 3 Workflow Facility Meta-model Architecture

Figure 3 compares the CRISTAL architecture, based on meta-objects, to the emerging OMG four layer meta-data model. The proposal for this type of architecture, which itself is similar to previous multi-layer meta-models [7], was first advocated by Schultz [8] at a recent OMG technical meeting. In the OMG model the highest level, meta-modeling layer is responsible for defining a generic modeling language for the specification of meta-models. Examples of meta-meta objects in this meta-metamodeling layer are MetaClass, MetaAttribute and MetaOperation. At the next layer down a metamodel is an *instance* of a meta-metamodel. This layer defines a language (e.g UML [6]) for specifying models, examples of objects at this layer are Class, Attribute, Operation. A model at layer two is an instance of a meta-model. The primary responsibility of the model layer is to describe a particular information domain. At the lowest level user objects are an instance of a model and describe a specific information and application domain, in the example of figure 3 that of workflow objects.

By way of comparison, the CRISTAL architecture is shown alongside the OMG model. At the lowest level CRISTAL handles workflow objects such as parts and activities. These objects are instances of the definition meta-objects such as part definitions and activity definitions (as noted earlier). The metaobjects, themselves, can be related through a model which constitutes a third layer in the CRISTAL architecture. The highest level in the CRISTAL architecture is a metaobject metamodel i.e. a layer which describes how metaobjects are modeled. Clearly there is much overlap in architectural components between this model and the four-layer model of the OMG.

A considerable amount of interest has been generated in meta-object description languages elsewhere. The OMG Meta Object facility (MOF) [9], which is located at the highest layer of figure 3, is potentially capable of describing all the types used in the CRISTAL metamodel. The purpose of the MOF is to provide a set of CORBA interfaces that can be used to define and manipulate a set of interoperable meta-models. The intention is that the meta-metaobjects defined in the MOF will provide a general modelling language capable of specifying a diverse range of metamodels designed to support aspects of generality, extendability, reuse and reflection (see [10]).

Work is in progress within the OMG on the MOF that will manage meta-models which are relevant to the OMG Architecture. Two which are of particular significance to the views in this paper are the Manufacturing's Product Data Management Enablers [11] and Work Flow Facility[12] meta-models. This meta-modelling approach will facilitate further integration between product data management and workflow management thereby providing consistency between design and production and a speeding up the process of implementing design changes in a production system.

4. Meta-Models and Viewpoints

For the purposes of optimisation and analysis, physicists and engineers must be able to extract data from the general CMS construction data warehouse from numerous viewpoints. It must be inherently simple for users to extract sets of data from the terabyte-sized warehouse, according to defined criteria, for subsequent analysis. The use of an object database and a dynamic object model together with so-called meta-query facilities provides this functionality as demonstrated in this section.

As the CMS production process evolves more data, together with the relationships between different aspects of the data, must be permanently recorded in the CRISTAL data warehouse. Different groups of users will require flexible ways to locate, access and share this production data. The actual information required will depend on the *viewpoint* and the role of the user in the organisation. User groups may well require a maintenance, a geometry, an alignment or an experiment slow-controls *viewpoint*. The physicist therefore needs to define a viewpoint in terms of 'physics elements' (or sets of detector components) which are derived from the tree of physical locations of detector components resulting from detector assembly. Figure 4 shows how a matrix of physics elements can be extracted from the 'as-built' detector construction hierarchy by providing software which can traverse the construction tree and can query and extract the construction data for a selected set of detector components.

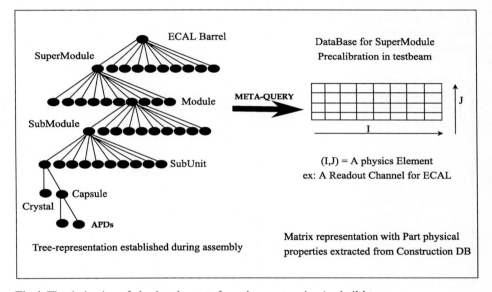

Fig 4. The derivation of physics elements from the construction 'as-built' tree.

Meta-modelling will assist the extraction of data for physics elements provided a *meta-query* mechanism is developed which can navigate the warehouse meta-model, can interpret the structures in the warehouse and can present the data in a form meaningful to the end-user. The meta-query facility comprises a set of software processes (or Agents) which can be invoked either by a viewpoint-specific application (e.g. calibration) or by a viewpoint non-specific application. The agents either navigate a generalised warehouse meta-model to project out viewpoint-specific data (i.e. 'looking in' the meta-model) or they navigate the meta-model to correlate effects between viewpoints (i.e. 'looking out' from the data model). In the 'looking in' (viewpoint-specific) case the agents perform the traversal of the detector description, following selected physics elements in the construction tree and extract the relevant physics data for the application. In the 'looking out' case (viewpoint non-specific), the agents are used to determine the effect of a system-wide change on individual viewpoints or sets of viewpoints i.e across viewpoints. As an example of cross-viewpoint navigation consider a request to determine the effects of a detector temperature variation: this will effect multiple viewpoints such as calibration and slow controls. In this case, the meta-query facility must traverse the meta-model and determine for each effected channel the set of viewpoints it contributes to and reflect the change in those viewpoints. A meta-query facility is currently under development for CRISTAL [13].

Figure 5 shows the architecture of a meta-model based system for CMS which encompasses multiple viewpoint databases (e.g Geometry, Calibration, Construction). In each case data has been extracted from a general CMS meta-model (or detector description database) via the meta-query facility. This generalised extraction facility can navigate the detector description, from a physicist-defined viewpoint, looking for specific data associated with a set of defined physics elements. The result is a totally integrated set of collaborating databases which, as the next section relates, can be *mined* for data from a selection of viewpoints.

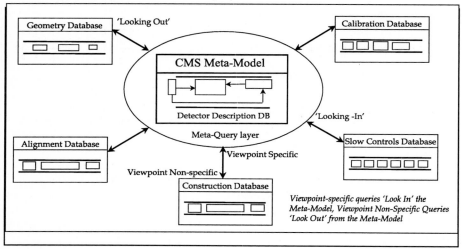

Fig 5. A generalised meta-query facility for CMS based on a central meta-model.

5. Data Architecture & Data Mining

The CRISTAL architecture must support autonomous data collection in remote Centres with secure storage in the central data warehouse at CERN. New versions of product and workflow definitions are defined centrally at CERN and are farmed out to each Centre by the warehouse Coordinator. Facilities are therefore required to share configuration data between the independent data acquisition Centres. Remote Centres must also be allowed to continue data gathering even when the network connection to the warehouse is down. Data is duplicated from the Centres to the warehouse when network connections allow. Once written into the warehouse, the data is thereafter mined by read-only processes running centrally.

Figure 6 shows the database architecture selected for CRISTAL. It is based on the Objectivity federated database concept in which multiple autonomous databases co-operate. The Central warehouse holds the federation configuration files and any changes in the schema take place centrally and are dispatched to the Centres via a small, shared configuration database (*the Configuration DB*). Production data is gathered at the Centres and copied remotely to the warehouse.

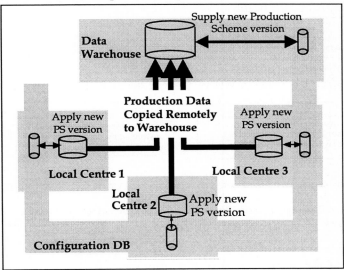

Fig 6. The CRISTAL data warehouse and data distribution.

Data mining takes place only at the data warehouse. One example of mining the construction data warehouse is for the extraction of detector calibration data. For physicists calibration data is required for each electronic readout channel of the detector. The structure of readout channels, however, is necessarily different to the assembly structure of the detector. In essence, the calibration system must be able to *mine* subsets of physics data from the construction database for the calibration of particular components even if these components are specified in a manner which is different to that in the construction database. This is facilitated in CRISTAL through the use of the self-describing nature of the warehouse meta-model.

As an example, calibration data can be mined from the warehouse using meta-queries by navigating the meta-model according to a user-defined set of parameters. For each member of the set of physics elements the meta-query facility mines the warehouse and projects out the set of (in this case calibration) data. As stated earlier, other applications will also need to extract sets of data e.g. for control and monitoring of the equipment and, ultimately, for physics reconstruction programmes and, in each case, sets of physics elements can be specified for that purpose.

In CRISTAL physics element definitions, themselves meta-objects, are captured in the data model. They reside alongside the detector description as pre-defined 'routes' to sets of components of interest to the physicist. When specifying a new viewpoint from which data is to be mined, the physicist can define new physics elements either from scratch or by reusing existing physics elements definitions (see figure 7). Therefore physics elements can be nested and are mined for a specific purpose which is captured in the data model. Data mining from different viewpoints is supported through the capture of reusable physics elements definitions and through the provision of a meta-query extraction facility.

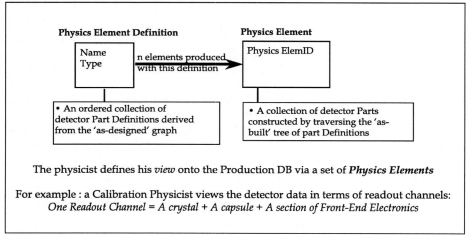

Fig 7. The definition of physics elements as data-mining viewpoints.

6. Conclusions

The experience of using meta models and meta objects at the analysis and design phase in the CRISTAL project has been very positive. Designing the meta model separately from the runtime model has allowed the design team to provide consistent solutions to dynamic change and versioning and to support data mining via user-defined viewpoints. The object models are described using UML which itself can be described by the OMG Meta Object Facility and is the candidate choice by OMG for describing all business models.

The concept of using meta-data to reduce complexity and aid navigability of data resident in a database is well known [14]. Also its use in minimising the effect of schema evolution in object databases has been stated many times elsewhere [15]. In the CRISTAL project *meta-data* are used for these purposes and, in addition, *meta-models* are used to provide self-description for data and to provide the mechanisms necessary for developing a meta-query facility to navigate multiple data models. (compare this approach to that in [16]). Using meta-queries, data can be extracted from multiple databases and presented in user-defined viewpoints.

The CMS meta-model of figure 5 therefore acts as a repository of knowledge against which meta-queries are issued to locate and extract data across multiple databases. Agent processes are used to 'look in' the meta-model and mine for data from a user-specified viewpoint and to 'look out' from the model to correlate effects between viewpoints. The overall effect is to produce an integrated set of cooperating databases accessed through a meta-query facilitry. Hence 'islands' of disparate information (such as maintenance, calibration, alignment) are eliminated. Such an approach could reasonably be applied to organisations developing technologies for 'virtual enterprises' (such as in [17], [18]) where collections of autonomous databases could be related via a central enterprise meta-model. Furthermore, in the area of standardisation, the Meta Data Coalition (MDC [19]) is working towards a Metadata Interchange Specification [20] which aims to tackle the exchange, sharing and management of metadata in industry. In another direction groups are now investigating data warehouse applications of the OMG MOF and coming to similar conclusions to those in this paper [21]. The experiences of CRISTAL in providing viewpoint access (and location and application transparency) to enterprise data through the use of meta-queries is clearly relevant to the work in these areas.

The current phase of CRISTAL research aims to adopt an open architectural approach, based on a meta-model and a meta-query facility to produce an adaptable mining system capable of interoperating with future systems and of supporting views onto an engineering data warehouse. The meta-model approach to design reduces system complexity, provides model flexibility and can integrate multiple, potentially heterogeneous, databases into the enterprise-wide data warehouse. A first prototype for CRISTAL based on CORBA, Java and Objectivity technologies has been deployed in the autumn of 1998 [22]. The second phase of research will culminate in the delivery of a production system in 1999 supporting meta-queries and the definition, capture and extraction of data according to physicist-defined viewpoints.

7. Acknowledgments

The authors take this opportunity to acknowledge the support of their home institutes, In particular, the support of P. Lecoq, J-L. Faure and M. Pimia is greatly appreciated. Richard McClatchey is supported by the Royal Academy of Engineering. N. Baker, A. Bazan, T. Le Flour, S. Lieunard, M. Zsenei, S. Murray, G. Organtini and G. Chevenier are thanked for their assistance in developing the CRISTAL prototype.

References

1 CMS Technical Proposal. The CMS Collaboration, January 1995. Available from ftp://cmsdoc.cern.ch/TPref/TP.html

2 J-M Le Goff et al.,"Detector Construction Management and Quality Control: Establishing and Using a CRISTAL System". CERN CMS Note 1998/033, May 1998. Available from ftp://cmsdoc.cern.ch/documents/98/note98_033.pdf

3 Objectivity, an object-oriented database product see http://www.objy.com.

4 R. McClatchey et al., "The Integration of Product and Workflow Management Systems in a Large Scale Engineering Database Application". Proc of the 2nd IEEE IDEAS Symposium. Cardiff, UK July 1998.

5 N. Baker et al., "An Object Model for product and Workflow Data Management". Workshop proc. At the 9th Int. Conference on Database & Expert System Applications. Vienna, Austria August 1998.

6 M. Fowler & K. Scott: "UML Distilled - Applying the Standard Object Modelling Language", Addison-Wesley Longman Inc., 1997

7 B. Byrne., "IRDS Systems and Support for Present and Future CASE Technology". Proc of CAiSE'96 DC, W4, Heraklion, Crete, 1996.

8 W. Schulze., "Fitting the Workflow Management Facility into the Object Management Architecture". Proc of the Business Object Workshop at OOPSLA'97.

9 Object Management Group Publications, Common Facilities RFP-5 Meta-Object Facility TC Doc cf/96-02-01 R2, Evaluation Report TC Doc cf/97-04-02 & TC Doc ad/97-08-14

10 S. Crawley et al., "Meta-Information Management". Proc of the Int Conf on Formal methods for Open Object-based Distributed Systems (FMOODS), Canterbury, UK. July 1997

11 Object Management Group Publications, Product Data Management Enablers RFP, Manufacturing Domain Task Force Docs mfg/96-08-01, mfg/98-01-01 & mfg/98-02-02

12 W. Schulze, C. Bussler & K. Meyer-Wegener., "Standardising on Workflow Management - The OMG Workflow Management Facility". ACM SIGGROUP Bulletin Vol 19 (3) April 1998.

13 N. Baker & J-M Le Goff., "Meta Object Facilities and their Role in Distributed Information Management Systems". Proc of the EPS ICALEPCS97 conference, Beijing, November 1997. Published by Science Press, 1997.

14 Selected papers from the proceedings of the 1st IEEE Metadata conference, Silver Spring, Maryland, 1996.

15 W. Kim., "Modern Database Systems". ACM Press / Addison Wesley Publishers, 1995

16 B. Kerherve & A. Gerbe., "Models for Metadata or Metamodels for Data?". Proc of the 2nd IEEE Meta-Data Conference, Silver Spring, Maryland, 1997.

17 M. Hardwick, D. Spooner, T. Rando & K. Morris., "Sharing Manufacturing Information in Virtual Enterprises", Communications of the ACM 39 (2) pp 46-54, 1996.

18 B Gaines, D Norrie & A. Lapsley., "An Intelligent Information System Supporting the Virtual manufacturing Enterprise". Proc of the IEEE Int Conf on Systems, Man & Cybernetics, Vancouver, Canada. October 1995.

19 The Meta Data Coalition. An industry led consortium for standardising meta data interchange. See URL http://www.MDCinfo.com

20 The Meta Data Interchange Specification (MDIS v1.1). Available from the Meta Data Coalition. See URL http:// 207.33.3.206/standards/toc.html

21 OMG Common Warehouse Metadata Interchange (CWMI) RFP. OMG technical document ad/98-09-02, September 1998

22 A. Bazan et al., "The Use of Production Management Techniques in the Construction of Large Scale Physics Detectors". Accepted at the IEEE Nuclear Science Symposium and Medical Imaging conference, Toronto, Canada. November 1998.

Two Version Concurrency Control Algorithm with Query Locking for Decision Support[1]

Hoewon Kim

Information & Communication,
Samsung Electronics, Korea
hwkim@khgw.info.samsung.co.kr

Seog Park

Dept. of Computer Science,
Sogang University, Korea
spark@dblab.sogang.ac.kr

Abstract. In decision supporting environments, a legacy operational system is needed to provide the additional facilities in order to manage the transaction that has the different characteristic from the traditional transaction. The most transactions that are used for decision support have a long-term read operation accessing a considerable portion of database. Therefore, the traditional concurrency control methods that are optimized to the on-line transaction processing cause the serious problem to the transaction management. The long delay of transaction processing cannot be avoided in those methods because of the lock conflict between the read operation of a decision supporting query and the write operation of an OLTP transaction. In this paper, transactions can be classified into two groups in decision supporting environment. One is the query session that consists of only read operations for decision support. The query session does not mind reading a possibly slightly old, but still consistent, version of the database. The other is the OLTP transaction that can have write operations for on-line transaction processing. According to our classification of transactions, we present a concurrency control algorithm that is called 'Two Version Query Locking (2VQL)'. The 2VQL algorithm prevents a query session from blocking the operation of other transactions. It can be achieved by delaying the refresh process that exchanges old and new versions of an updated data. By our performance evaluation, the 2VQL algorithm is proved to be better than other legacy algorithms in the decision supporting of operational system.

1. Introduction

In decision supporting environments, legacy operational systems should satisfy the requirements of new jobs [9,11]. For example, whenever data warehouse system periodically extracts the snapshots of operational data, the operational system should put up with the extraction job that has the long running read operation accessing the considerable portion of the source database. Again, a user may wish to give some real-time analyses of the operational system for uncovering the present conditions in a banking or billing system. When the operational systems simply take charge of these

[1] This work was supported in part by the KOSEF under the contract 96-0101-06-01-3.

decision-supporting jobs as well as the legacy transactional job, they cause very poor performance because these new jobs have very different characteristics with the legacy online transaction processing (OLTP). So these jobs have been processed during the night. In other words, data warehouse management would be processed in off-line without any user's requests, and real-time analysis jobs were carried with partially pardoning the consistency of the analysis result.

In this paper, we propose a new concurrency control method processing the decision supporting jobs in consistent and timely manner as well as the legacy transactional job efficiently. For this new concurrency control, we classify these operational jobs as following two groups.

- The OLTP transaction – It is the traditional OLTP job that reads and writes a few data items of database.
- The query session – It's a set of successive read-only queries that must see a consistent view of data for correct analysis. It typically reads the considerable portion of whole database. Because it has only read operations that cannot modify the state of database, we don't have to exactly preserve the currency of the data that is read by the query session. So it reads the old version of data in the tolerable bound to its application.

2. Related Works

Traditional concurrency control algorithms are designed for the transactional jobs of the OLTP environment. In the case of 2PL algorithm, since the read lock doesn't have the compatibility with the write lock, the long-term read operation fiercely causes the delay of the short-term write operations of other OLTP transactions [3]. In the MV2PL algorithm, however, read-only transaction causes no effect to the other transactions, and reads the correct version of data selected in the version pool that is a special storage for keeping the old versions of data items [1]. When the MV2PL algorithm is applied to the query session for decision supporting job that accesses very large data volume, the size of version pool becomes also large. Therefore the MV2PL algorithm is not suitable, because of the high cost of the exploring and managing the version pool. To overcome the problem of multi-version algorithm, Mohan proposed the transient versioning scheme whose read-only transactions do not mind reading a possibly slightly old, but still consistent version of the database [7].

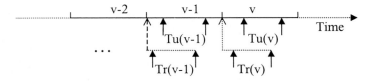

Fig. 1. Version Periods and Association of Transactions in Transient versioning algorithm

Fig. 1 illustrates database versions and transaction types. The time axis is divided into version periods, which are numbered v-2, v-1, v, and so on. It runs simultaneously update transactions that update some data more or less randomly (call the transactions of type Tu) and read-only transactions that access a large quantity of data (type Tr). The version of a Tu transaction is v iff it commits during version period v. The version of Tr transaction is v iff it arrives during version period v. Tr transactions of version v see the results of only Tu transactions whose version is less than v. New version period is built periodically, thus the subsequently arriving Tr transactions are allowed to see the more recently committed data. This is called a refresh operation. The transient versioning scheme may keep the smaller size of the old version data than the multi-version algorithm, since all Tr transactions of version v need only one version. Since the decision-supporting query may read the huge size of data, it is not appropriate to keep the data more than two versions in consideration of storage overhead. When only two versions are available, the system should switch to a new version period only when no Tr transaction is active. Otherwise, the refresh operation takes away the consistent version of data from the Tr transaction. When a Tr transaction lose the consistent version of data, we call the transaction is expired. Furthermore, since the decision supporting query sessions access the considerable portion of database for a long time, the expiring problem is more serious.

3. 2VQL(2 Version Query Locking) algorithm

3.1. Example and Motivation

It is the minimal overhead to allow two versions of database in order to avoid the undesirable interference between the query sessions and the short OLTP transaction that may cause unnecessary delays. Since the original 2V2PL algorithm does not consider the read-only transactions, it must convert the write lock that is compatible with the read lock into the exclusive certifying lock. It causes that the commit operation is delayed until all the conflicting read locks are released. In the OLTP environment, such delay has a trivial effect to the performance. But if the read-only transaction is the long-running decision-supporting job, it is even impossible for other OLTP transaction to write some conflicting data items. However Fig. 2 illustrates the possibility to solve thus delaying problem in only two-version.

	1	2	3	4	5	6	7	8	9	10	11	12
Q1	$R(X_0)$					$R(Y_0)$	C					
T2		$W(X_2)$	$W(Y_2)$	C								
Q3					$R(X_0)$					$R(Y_0)$	C	

Fig. 2. A possible schedule in two-version algorithm

The schedule of Fig. 2 has an equivalent serial schedule "Q1->Q3->T2". Although Q3 begins to running after the commitment of T2, it can not see the modification of

T2. However, in our assumption, query session does not mind reading the old version of data in a tolerable bound. If Q3 is an OLTP transaction in the schedule of Fig. 2, it should read the X_2 instead of X_0 at the time slot 5. Therefore two versions of data can be readable at the same time in this scheme. We call them as the old version and the new version respectively. Since the state that the both versions are readable exists, we need an additional protocol to select the consistent version for readers. Although [6] presents a work to use both readable versions in 2V2PL, it needs a critical overhead maintaining the dependency graph. The 2VQL algorithm proposed in this paper uses both readable versions without such overhead. In other words, query sessions always read the old version with no relation to the availability of the new version, and OLTP transactions always read the most recently committed version. When the old version becomes useless, it performs the refresh operation by switching the old version with the new version.

3.2. The lock compatible matrix

The 2VQL algorithm use NM (the new version available mark), as well as RL (the read lock of the lately committed version) and WL (the write lock) for OLTP transactions. Query session uses its own read lock QL (the query lock) that is the read lock of the old version. As mentioned above, the major object of the 2VQL algorithm is to solve the interference between RL and QL. Our idea is that OLTP transactions use only the new version for the data whose old version is held by any QL. So, the 2VQL algorithm seems to be a mixture of 1V2PL and 2V2PL schemes. Fig. 3 presents the lock compatibility matrix of the 2VQL algorithm.

Lock holder

	QL	RL	WL
QL	O	O	O
RL	O	O	-
WL	O	-	X
NM	O	X	✕

(Lock requester — row labels QL, RL, WL, NM)

Fig. 3. The compatibility matrix of 2VQL

In Fig. 3, the mark '**O**' indicates the compatibility and the mark '**X**' indicates the incompatibility. Yet the mark '-' indicates the conditional compatibility as follows.
- When NM is checked, the mark '-' indicates the incompatibility. In other words, when the new version is readable, RL is not compatible with WL that is the write lock of the new version, since the RL is the read lock of the new version of data.
- When NM isn't checked, the mark '-' indicates the compatibility. In other words, when the new version is not readable, RL is compatible with WL that is the write lock of the new version, since the RL is the read lock of the old version of data.

In Fig. 3, we realize that QL has no interference with other lock, since the QL has no conflict relation. Yet, since QL may delay the refresh operation that updates the old version, it may press other query sessions to see the same old version.

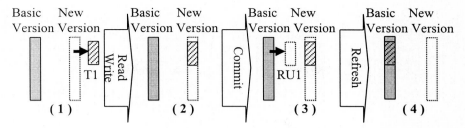

Fig. 4. The life-cycle of an OLTP transaction.

3.3. The life-cycle of a query session

Query sessions acquire the QL of the data items to read, and always read the old version of the data. After all the read operations are completed, it releases its QLs.

3.4. The life-cycle of a OLTP transaction

3.4.1. The processing steps of an OLTP transaction

An OLTP transaction goes through more complex steps than a query session as presented in Fig. 4. The area that is filled with a slash pattern indicates the data written by a transaction T1, and an arrow means that an operation is blocked. The part (1) of the Fig. 4 shows that a transaction T1 submitted by a user waits to acquire some locks. The part (2) shows that T1 makes new version of data by read and write operations after it required those locks. After it completes all operations and commits, it constructs the refresh unit (RU) that contains the information for the delayed refresh operation. The part (3) shows that the RU waits until the refresh condition is satisfied. In the last, The part (4) shows the data written by T1 is applied to the old version.

When some data are updated but not yet refreshed, if another transaction requests a write lock on the same data, we would encounter the fundamental limits of the two-version. If we simply delay such lock requests, it causes the problem that a long-lived query session blocks other short OLTP transaction. On the contrary, if we simply pardon the existence of such write-write conflicting RU, query sessions may lose the consistent view of database. In Fig. 5, The part (1) shows that another transaction T2 requests WL on the data whose new version is made by T1, before the RU1 is refreshed. So, the write set of T1 may be partially overwritten by the write set of T2. When RU1 is refreshed after that, the write set of T2 is partially refreshed as presented in the part (3)a. It causes that the analysis-result of other query session loses the consistency, since the old version that is used as the source of the analysis is corrupted. Therefore the RUs that have the W-W conflicts with other OLTP transaction must not be individually refreshed. So, when each OLTP transaction acquires a WL, we mark the RUs that have W-W conflict with the transaction.

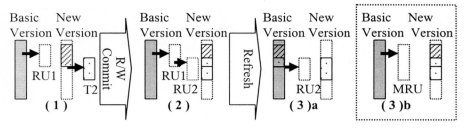

Fig. 5. The Write-Write conflict of RUs and MRU(merged refresh unit)

We call this work as the freezing operation and attach a freezing mark (FM) to each RU, and when the transaction that freezes other RUs, we construct the merged refresh unit (MRU) that merges the contents of the freezing RU and the frozen RUs as showed in the part (3)b.

3.4.2 The read and write operation of OLTP transaction

The algorithm that an OLTP transaction processes the read operation on a data item x can be outlined as follows.

```
IF NM(x) IS SET THEN
            IF WL(x) IS HELD THEN WAIT
            ELSE ACHIVE RL(x)
                  READ THE NEW VERSION OF x
            END IF
ELSE        ACHIVE RL(x)
            READ THE OLD VERSION OF x
END IF
```

The algorithm that an OLTP transaction performs the write operation on a data item x is outlined as follows.

```
IF WL(x) IS HELD THEN WAIT
ELSE IF NM(x) IS SET THEN
            IF RL(x) IS HELD THEN WAIT
            ELSE ACHIVE WL(x)
                  SET THE FM OF THE FORMER WRITER
                  WRITE THE NEW VERSION OF x
            END IF
ELSE        ALLOCATE A STORAGE FOR THE NEW VERSION OF x
            ACHIVE WL(x)
            WRITE THE NEW VERSION OF x
END IF
```

3.4.4 The commitment of OLTP transaction

The committing process of a query session is simply the releasing of all own QLs. But, that of an OLTP transaction has a step of acquiring all NMs on its own write set firstly. So, the commit time is delayed until all the RLs that other OLTP transaction acquires are released. As showed in Fig. 3, since QL has no effect on the acquirement of NM, the commit time of an OLTP transaction is not directly affected by other query sessions. When all the NMs that are required to commit are acquired, the commit operation is performed as follows.

1. Construct the RU. It contains the write set and the information to test the refresh condition. If it freezes some RUs, also construct the MRU that merges those RUs.
2. Release all the locks of the transaction except NMs.

3.4.5 The refreshment of OLTP transaction

The refresh operation is one of the most complex parts of 2VQL algorithm. In this verse, we describe the refresh condition and refresh process, and the structure of RU. In the first place, we define some terminology as follows.

- Set_after(i) – the set of all the transactions that follow Ti in serializable order.
- Set_before(i) – the set of all the transactions that precede a transaction Ti.
- Set_subsequent(i) – the subset of the Set_after(i) that has no direct conflict with Ti.
- Set_previous(i) – the subset of the Set_before(i) that has no direct conflict with Ti.
- Set_write(i) – the write set of a transaction Ti.
- RUi – the refresh unit of Ti.

Then, the condition that RUi can be refreshed is equivalent to the satisfaction of the following three requirements.

- All transactions that are contained in Set_before(i) should be refreshed. This makes the processing order of conflict write operations also kept in the old version.
- All the QLs of the data in Set_after(i) should be released. So, the refresh operation is delayed until all the query session that read the data complete their analyses.
- The freezing mark (FM) of RUi should be reset. When the write set of RUi is overwritten by other transaction, this prohibits query sessions from reading the inconsistent data refreshed partially by forbidding RUi to be refreshed independently.

When such three conditions are satisfied at the same time, the refresh operation is done as following order.

Acquire the exclusive short-term latches on the write set.

1. Replace the old version with the new version (version switching).
2. Reset the values of NMs of the data in the write set.
3. Release the exclusive short-term latches.
4. Free the storage allocated for the original old version.

RUi should maintain the write set to refresh and the information to check the condition of refresh. So, it contains following information.

- The number of RUs in the SET_previous(i) that are not refreshed yet.
- Set_write(i)
- FM (freezing mark)

3.4.6 The construction method of the merged refresh unit (MRU)

IF a committing OLTP transaction have set the FM of other RU because of W-W conflicts, it should perform the constructing operation of MRU.

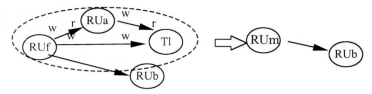

Fig. 6. An example of the construction of MRU

Fig. 6 illustrates that a transaction Tl makes the MRU RUm instead of RUl since Tl has a W-W conflict with RUf. Clearly, all the transactions located between Tf and Tl according to the serializable order should be merged into RUm. The following statement is the method to check the condition.

- "Tk locates between Tf and Tl in the serializable order" if and only if **"Tk ∈ SETbefore(Tl) AND Tk ∈ SETafter(Tf)"**

Yet, to maintain Set_before and Set_after costs higher than to maintain Set_previous and Set_subsequent since the latter two sets are directly obtained from the lock table. In verse 3.4.7, we present a method to only use Set_previous and Set_subsequent.

3.4.7 The implementation of 2VQL

2VQL uses the locking based structure like the original 2V2PL. Yet, to refresh the committed transaction later, we maintain Set_write and Set_previous after commit. It's not the additional overhead of 2VQL, since 2V2PL maintain all the data structure of a transaction till the refresh time. We present a simple data structure called RU table. RU table has columns named RU ID, Set_write, Set_previous, Set_subsequent obtained from the lock table and an additional column Mark. For example, Fig.7 illustrates the RU table when all the transactions are committed and make own RUs.

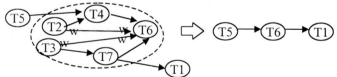

RU ID	Set_write	Set_previous	Set_subsequent	Mark
1	D	7	Null	6
2	X	Null	4, 6	6
3	Y	Null	6, 7	6
4	A	2, 5	6	6
5	B	Null	4	
6	X, y	2, 3, 4, 7	Null	6
7	C	3	1	6

Fig. 7. An example conflict relationships and an example RU table

The MRU construction algorithm consists of two parts. First part is to fill the column Mark of RUs visited while scanning from all the former writers following all the nodes in the Set_subsequent with the unique id of MRU. In Fig. 7, RU2 and RU3 are the former writers and RU6 is the latter writer. If the id of MRU is 6, the result of above operation is the same as the column Mark of the RU table of Fig. 7. Second part is to make the set of RU IDs visited while scanning from the latter writer following all the nodes of the Set_previsous whose Mark column has the same value of MRU. In Fig. 7, we obtain a set of RU IDs {2, 3, 4, 6, 7} that should be merged into the MRU. After we obtain the set of RU IDs, we make Set_write, Set_previous, and Set_subsequent of MRU.

4. Evaluation

4.1 The Evaluation model

The 2VQL algorithm we present solves the conflict relationship between query sessions and OLTP transactions, but the query sessions may obstruct other query session in reading the more current data. Therefore we evaluate the currency of data read by query sessions as well as the processing performance.

We compares the 2VQL algorithm with are the original 2V2PL and the two versions transient versioning algorithm (2VTV). We adopt the general system model that is similar with the existing approaches. Fig. 8 illustrates the system model using a queuing model.

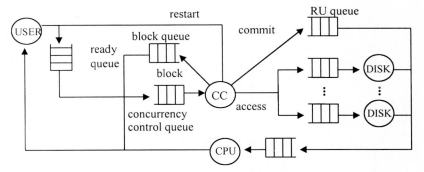

Fig. 8. The simulation queuing model

To detect deadlocks, we use the continuous deadlock detection scheme [6]. The refresh operation is performed immediately in the original 2V2PL, and periodically in the 2VTV, but it is deferred in 2VQL until the refresh conditions are satisfied. Fig. 9 presents the value of each system parameter used in our simulation model. We refer to [2] for the database size and the relative size of OLTP transaction. And we assume that the size of query session is average ten times of the size of OLTP transaction. Also, we refer to [2] for the write probability that is the probability of write operation among all operations.

Parameter	Description	Value
Database Size	Number of Objects in database	1,000 pages
OLTP Max Size	Max number of operations in OLTP transaction	12
OLTP Min Size	Min number of operations in OLTP transaction	4
Query Max Size	Max number of operations in Query session	120
Query Min Size	Min number of operations in Query session	40
Write Probability	Pr(write operation)	25 %
Restart Delay	Mean transaction restart delay	20 ms
MPL	Multiprogramming level	50
IO Time	I/O time for accessing an object	2 ms
Disk Entry Size	Number of operations accessing disk in parallel.	30

Fig. 9. The simulation parameters

4.2 Analysis of Evaluation

Fig. 10 illustrates the transformation of the average processing time of OLTP transaction while the ratio of query session increases. In 2V2PL, As the ratio of query session increases, the processing time of OLTP transaction also increases explosively. In 2VQL and 2VTV, the processing time of OLTP transaction is hardly changed, since the OLTP transaction is not directly affected by query sessions.

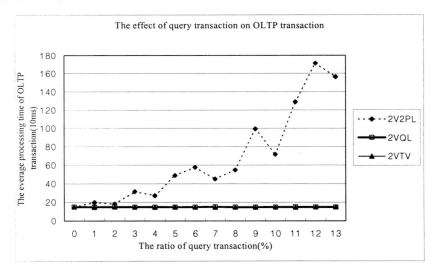

Fig. 10. The processing time of OLTP transaction

Fig. 11 illustrates the effect that the ratio of query session leads to on the average processing time of query sessions.

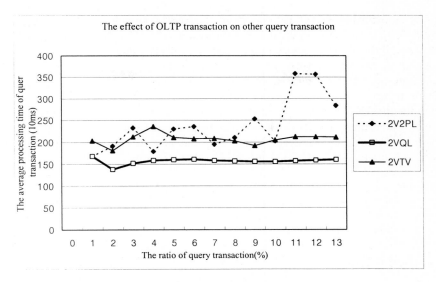

Fig. 11. The processing time of query session.

Query session should not see the boundlessly old data. So we should select the tolerable bound of aging of data. In these simulations, we fix the version period of 2VTV as 400 unit times (10ms). On the balance, we also fix the maximum delay time of refreshing of RU as 400 unit times (10ms) in 2VQL. If a RU can not be refreshed in 400 unit times (10ms), we refresh the RU oppressively and immediately. So, the query sessions that read the oppressively refreshed data also are aborted. In Fig. 11, the operations of query sessions of 2VQL are not blocked by the write operations of other OLTP transactions at all. So, we cannot find any outstanding decline of processing performances of the 2VQL algorithm. But, In 2VTV, whenever the version period is ended and the old version should be used for the update transactions, all the query sessions that read old version are aborted and restarted.

In conclusion, 2VQL occupies higher grade than other two algorithms in the performance of OLTP transaction and the currency of data read by query session.

5. Conclusion

In decision supporting environment, operational system should process efficiently the extraction job of snapshots and the query for real time analysis that have typically the complex and long-term read operations. Yet, since the legacy concurrency control schemes lead to the long delay, we use the offline time at night or endure the somewhat inconsistency.

The 2VQL proposed in this paper is the new concurrency control scheme for decision support queries in the consistent and timely manner. 2VQL solve the conflict between the write operations of OLTP transactions and the read operations of query sessions by deferring the refresh operations that replace the old version of data with the new version. In other words, we offer the new state of data that query sessions can read the slightly old but consistent data and the OLTP transaction can build a new version at the same time. Since we keep the information to refresh after commit of a transaction, we propose a data structure named RU(refresh unit) and an algorithm to maintain it.

As mentioned above, the proposed algorithm shows the better performance than the legacy algorithm. Yet, 2VQL have an additional overhead to maintain query lock. To reduce the locking overhead, it is a splendid idea to apply the multi-granules locking scheme to 2VQL. This is a topic for further research.

References

[1]   A. Chan, S. Fox, W. Lin, A. Nori, and D. Ries, "The Implementation of an Integrated Concurrency Control and Recovery Scheme," in Proce. of the ACM SIGMOD, pp. 184-191, Jun. 1982.

[2]   R. Agrawal, M. J. Carey, and M. Livny, "Concurrency Control Performance Modeling: Alternatives and Implications," ACM Transaction on Database Systems, vol. 12, no. 4, pp. 609-654, Dec. 1987.

[3]   P. A. Bernstein, V. Hadzilacos, and N. Goodman. *Concurrency Control and Recovery in Database Systems.* Reading, MA: Addison-Wesley, 1987.

[4]   P. M. Bober, and M. J. Carey, "On Mixing Queries and Transactions via Multiversion Locking," in Proc. of the IEEE Data Engineering, pp. 535-545, Feb. 1992.

[5]   Paul M. Bober, and M. J. Carey, "Multiversion Query Locking," in Proc. of the VLDB, pp. 497-510, Aug. 1992.

[6]   B. Claybrook. *OLTP online transaction processing systems.* Reading, MA: John Wiley & Sons, 1992.

[7]   C. Mohan, H. Pirahesh, and R. Lorie, "Efficient and Flexible Methods for Transient Versioning of Records to Avoid Locking by Read-Only Transactions," in Proc. of the ACM SIGMOD, pp. 124-133, Jun. 1992.

[8]   I. S. Mumick, "The Rejuvenation of Materialized Views," in Proc. of 6th Int. Conf. on Information Systems and Data Management, pp. 258-264, Nov. 1995.

[9]   W. H. Inmon. *Building the Data Warehouse 2nd Edition.* Reading, MA: John Wiley & Sons, 1996.

[10]   V. Kumar. *Performance of Concurrency Control Mechanisms in Centralized Database Systems.* Reading, MA: Prentice Hall, 1996.

[11]   R. C. Barquin, and H. A. Edelstein. *Planning and Designing the Data Warehouse.* Reading, MA: Prentice Hall PTR, 1997.

[12]   D. Quass and J. Widom, "On-Line Warehouse View Maintenance," in Proc. of the ACM SIGMOD, pp. 393-404, May. 1997.

An Efficient View Maintenance Algorithm for Data Warehousing

Tok Wang Ling and Ye Liu
email: {lingtw, liuye}@comp.nus.edu.sg

School of Computing, National University of Singapore,
Lower Kent Ridge Road, Singapore 119260

Abstract. We first present a brief analysis of current issues on view maintenance problem for data warehousing. Then, we present an efficient view maintenance algorithm to maintain the materialized view of a data warehouse system. In our approach, a mechanism is provided to detect maintenance anomaly even if messages are delivered in a different order from their generated order. Our approach enforces *complete consistency* of the materialized view in the sense that every logical state of base relations is reflected as a distinct state of the materialized view. We conclude that our approach is efficient in two aspects: (1) maintenance queries for multiple update transactions are executed in parallel instead of in sequential approach; (2) any *maintenance anomaly* occurs during the maintenance query execution for some update transaction is removed locally at the data warehouse and no extra queries need to be sent to any base relation.

1 Introduction and Related Work

A materialized view in a data warehouse system is a relation, which is derived from a set of base relations of multiple data sources. Once the data warehouse is initialized, any update to a base relation needed to be propagated to the materialized views at the data warehouse. This is called as view maintenance for data warehousing. Incremental view maintenance is to find an optimized solution to maintain a materialized view without re-computing it from the base relations. A view maintenance operation in response to an update transaction is completed in two steps: (1) *maintenance query execution*: where the view maintenance engine of the data warehouse composes a maintenance query according to that update and then executes the query through base relations to get the change to the view caused by that update; (2) *view refreshment*: where the view maintenance engine incorporates the change into the materialized view. During the step (1), the answer of the maintenance query may include the changes caused by further update transactions of base relations. This is referenced as *maintenance anomaly*. This anomaly must be removed from the answer before the answer is incorporated into the materialized view. Some application domains (e.g., banking, billing and network management) require *complete consistency* of the data warehouse. That is, the data warehouse is required to reflect each state of the base relations of the data sources. For example, in a telephone billing application, the summary of charges reported to a user must match the detailed call data.

Previous works [2–10] have given various view maintenance algorithms for data warehousing. However, they are inadequate in the following aspects: ECA [2] and Strobe [7] only enforce *strong consistency* of the data warehouse in the sense that some states of the base relations may be lost. ECA restricts all the base relations to be from the same data source site. Strobe [7] does compensation for maintenance anomaly by the all-key preserving assumption of the materialized view. Although C-Strobe [7] enforces complete consistency, its remote compensation strategy causes too much communication cost and renders it an intractable algorithm. Besides, the three algorithms require the *quiescence assumption* of the data sources for the changes to be incorporated into the materialized view. If there are update transactions committed at their corresponding sources forever, the view may not have chance to be refreshed. SWEEP and the algorithm of [10] enforce complete consistency. They handle maintenance anomaly by local compensation. The problem of these two is that they all totally **sequential** approaches: they perform view maintenance for each update transactions one by one; they do not start to execute maintenance query for an update transaction until they complete all the view maintenance operations for the transaction ordered before it. Besides, SWEEP and ECA make the FIFO assumption of message transmissions between the data warehouse and a data source site. However, *message transmission disorder problem* [10] may occur because of the network delay.

We observe that to enforce complete consistency, it is not necessary for the view maintenance engine to execute maintenance query for each update transaction in sequential approach; on the contrary, what the view maintenance engine needs to do is to guarantee that the changes of the update transactions are incorporated into the view according the logical order of the update transactions. We provide our view maintenance approach, which is referred as a **parallel** approach in that it enables the view maintenance engine to execute maintenance queries for multiple update transactions in parallel, while complete consistency is still enforced. In execution of maintenance query for each update, our approach handles possible maintenance anomaly with local compensation. A detailed analysis table on the properties of our approach compared to some other algorithms is given in Figure 1. The rest part is organized as follows: we give some preliminaries in section 2; then in section 3, we provide a mechanism according which the view maintenance engine performs view maintenance operations and the message transmission disorder problem is taken into consideration; in section 4, we present our view maintenance algorithm based on the mechanism of section 3; in section 5, we give a simulation system of our approach; finally, we conclude the paper with section 6.

Algorithm	Sequential / Parallel	Consistency	Require Quiescence	Message Cost per Update	Handling Anomaly	Communication assumption	Data Source(s)	View Definition
ECA	Parallel	Strong	Yes	O(1)	Remote Compensation	FIFO	Single Site	SPJ-Expression
Strobe	Parallel	Strong	Yes	O(n)	Removal of Duplicates By Key Enforcement	FIFO	Multiple Sites	Unique Key Assumption
C-Strobe	Sequential	Complete	No	O(n!)	Remote Compensation	FIFO	Multiple Sites	Unique Key Assumption
SWEEP	Sequential	Complete	No	O(n)	Local Compensation	FIFO	Multiple Sites	SPJ-Expression
[CM97]	Sequential	Complete	No	O(n)	Local Compensation	None Lost	Multiple Sites	SPJ-Expression
Our Approach	Parallel	Complete	No	O(n)	Local Compensation	None Lost	Multiple Sites	SPJ-Expression

Fig. 1. Comparison of Various View Maintenance Algorithms

2 The Data Warehouse with Independent Update Transactions

The architecture of the data warehouse is described as follows. The warehouse is connected with each data source with some communication channel, while there is no communication channel between any two data sources. Each communication channel is assumed to be non-lost in the sense that messages will finally arrive the object sites, but their arrival order may be different from their generated order. The data sources are assumed to be n sites of independent RDBMS. Each data source i may store any number of relations, but conceptually we assume only one base relation R_i contributes the materialized view at the data warehouse. At the warehouse, a materialized view V is defined as: $V = \pi_\alpha \sigma_p(R_1 \bowtie R_2 \bowtie ... \bowtie R_n)$, where α is the set of projection attributes and p is the set of predicate conditions. Each update transaction only involves one base relation of the corresponding data source site by insertions and/or deletions. Update transactions of different data sources are not related and therefore not synchronized. As update transactions are committed, there are transmitted to the data warehouse from their sources to the warehouse; an update transaction is sent as a single unit. In our approach, all the update transactions are serialized in the logical sequence $\mathcal{L}$ [11] that the update transactions committed from the same source keep their committed order and the update transactions from different sources are ordered according to the order in which the update transactions arrives at the warehouse. For each update $\mathcal{T}_k$ ($k = 1, 2, ...$) there is a *logical state* of the base relations denoted as: $R_i(\mathcal{T}_k)$ ($i = 1, 2, ..., n$), which is obtained by completing exactly those updates ordered before $\mathcal{T}_k$ ($\mathcal{T}_k$ is included). We denote that V is in state $V(\mathcal{T}_k)$ if V is computed against the base relations of state $R_i(\mathcal{T}_k)$ ($i = 1, 2, ..., n$). Our approach guarantees that each logical state of the base relations be reflected as a distinct state of the materialized view V and the state transformation order of the base relations be preserved. Hence, complete consistency is enforced.

3   Synchronization of the Communication Messages

Two types transactions of each data source are involved in view maintenance: (1) execution of an update transaction and (2) evaluation of a maintenance sub-query. Note that evaluation of a maintenance sub-query must be executed as a read-only transaction. Corresponding to the two transactions, two types of messages are generated by the data source to the warehouse: reporting an update transaction and returning the answer to a maintenance sub-query and the order of the messages must keep the executed order of their corresponding transactions. Notice that the messages may arrive at the warehouse in a different order from their generated order because of data communication problem, i.e., two update transactions arrive at the warehouse in the different order from their committed order. This is referred as *message transmission disorder*. Basically, our solution to problem is that if each message carries a *version number* to indicate the execution order of that message, then, in spite of message transmission disorder problem, the data warehouse can then detect a missing message and wait for it before processing any later messages from that source.

For each data source site i, we build a **update/query monitor** as the interface with the data warehouse. The monitor maintains an *update counter*, uc_i to indicate the number of update transactions committed at base relation R_i since the data warehouse is initialized. At the initialization of the data warehouse, uc_i is set to zero. uc_i is employed to provide the value of the version number for each message. Each data source i executes update transactions and maintenance sub-queries and forwards the committed update transaction or the answer of a maintenance sub-query to the monitor in a first-come-first-serve mode. The monitor generates a message for each committed transaction or each answer of a maintenance query in first-come-first-serve mode as they are forwarded to the monitor by the data source. For an update transaction $\mathcal{T}$ from R_i, the monitor increases uc_i by one, then sets the version number of the committed update transaction as the current value of uc_i; after that the monitor sends $\mathcal{T}$ with its version number to the data warehouse. Such a committed transaction $\mathcal{T}$ is a record $(source(\mathcal{T}), uc(\mathcal{T}), < \Delta(\mathcal{T}), \nabla(\mathcal{T}) >)$, where $source(\mathcal{T})$ denotes the base relation id, $uc(\mathcal{T})$ denotes the version number of the message and $< \Delta(\mathcal{T}), \nabla(\mathcal{T}) >$ denotes the inserted tuples and deleted tuples of the update transaction. On the other hand, for an answer of a maintenance sub-query, the monitor sets the version number of the answer as the current value of uc_i and sends the answer to the data warehouse as the answer message. An answer message A is a record $(< \Delta(A), \nabla(A) >, uc(A))$, where $uc(A)$ is the version number and $< \Delta(A), \nabla(A) >$ is an answer of a maintenance sub-query. Notice that as the monitor processes the committed update transactions and the answers of maintenance sub-queries in first-come-first-serve mode as their arrival order from the data source, the version number of each message can always reflect the message execution order at the data source.

At the data warehouse, we build a **pre-processor** to synchronize the message transmission. The pre-processor orders all the update transactions and their changes to the view into the *Ordered Update Message Queue, $OUMQ$,* and the *View Change Queue, VCQ* respectively according to sequence $\mathcal{L}$. At initialization of the data warehouse, both $OUMQ$ and VCQ are set empty. For each R_i, the pre-processor maintains a *process index, $index(R_i)$,* to indicate that the update transaction $\mathcal{T}$ from R_i with version number equal to $index(R_i)$ can be ordered into $OUMQ$. Each $index(R_i)$ is set to one when the data warehouse system is initialized. Suppose a committed update transaction $\mathcal{T}$ whose $source(\mathcal{T}) = i$ is sent to the data warehouse, when there are $k-1$ entries in $OUMQ$ and in VCQ respectively. If $uc(\mathcal{T})$ is equal to $index(R_i)$, then the pre-processor appends that update into the end $OUMQ$ as the kth entry, denoted as $\mathcal{T}_k$; at the same time, the pre-processor also appends an entry E_k, to the end of VCQ as its the kth entry and marks E_k as an *incomplete entry*; and then the pre-processor increases $index(R_i)$ by one. Notice that these operations are completed atomically. If $uc(\mathcal{T}) > index(R_i)$, the pre-processor concludes that there are some update transactions which are committed earlier than $\mathcal{T}$ but have not been ordered in $OUMQ$ yet. $\mathcal{T}$ must be held in the buffer until those transactions have been ordered into $OUMQ$ and $index(R_i)$ is updated equal to $uc(\mathcal{T})$. On the other hand, if an answer message A from data source i is delivered to the data warehouse, whose $uc(A) \leq index(R_i) - 1$, the pre-processor concludes that all the transactions committed earlier than the evaluation of A have been ordered into $OUMQ$, then the pre-processor passes A to the view maintenance engine. If $uc(A) > index(R_i) - 1$, that means that, there are some transactions committed earlier than the evaluation of A have not been ordered in $OUMQ$ yet. The pre-processor holds A in the buffer until those transactions have been ordered into $OUMQ$ and $index(R_i)$ is updated equal to $uc(A)+1$. Until then, the pre-processor passes A to the view maintenance engine. Notice that if the pre-processor creates a new process for each received message, concurrency control facilities are required for $OUMQ$, VCQ and each $index(R_i)$.

4 A Parallel Algorithm for View Maintenance

In this section, we present an algorithm for view maintenance (Figure 2). In our approach, the view maintenance engine employs two processes: **CompChange** and **Refresh** to perform view maintenance. When an update transaction is ordered into the end of VCQ, the view maintenance creates a new thread of process **CompChange** to execute the maintenance query of that transaction. Therefore, multiple maintenance queries are executed in parallel. The process **Refresh** incorporates the changes of the update transactions into the view according to the order of the update transactions in $OUMQ$. During each maintenance query execution, the view maintenance engine handles each possible maintenance anomaly with local compensation, and the process **Refresh** enforces the complete consistency of the materialized view V.

4.1 Maintenance Query Evaluation with Local Compensation

In this subsection, we describe how the view maintenance engine handles the maintenance anomaly by local compensation when executing a maintenance query for an update transaction ordered in $OUMQ$. If an update transaction from R_i is ordered by the pre-processor into $OUMQ$ as the kth entry, $\mathcal{T}_k$, the view maintenance engine creates a new process **CompChange**$(\Delta(\mathcal{T}_k), \nabla(\mathcal{T}_k),$ $source(\mathcal{T}_k),\ uc(\mathcal{T}_k),\ k)$ to compute the change $< \Delta V(\mathcal{T}_k), \nabla V(\mathcal{T}_k) >$ by executing the maintenance query $\mathcal{Q}_k$ of $\mathcal{T}_k$. The process **CompChange** computes the change by executing the *forward phase* and the *backward phase* in parallel [11]. Let us consider the forward execution phase. Suppose the procedure sends the sub-query $Q_{kj} = < \Delta V^{j-1}(\mathcal{T}_k) \bowtie R_j, \nabla V^{j-1}(\mathcal{T}_k) \bowtie R_j)$ (where $i + 1 \leq j \leq n$), where $< \Delta V^{j-1}(\mathcal{T}_k), \nabla V^{j-1}(\mathcal{T}_k) >$ is the consistent answer of the sub-query $Q_{k,j-1}$. Notice that $\Delta V^i(\mathcal{T}_k)$ and $\nabla V^i(\mathcal{T}_k)$ are $\Delta(\mathcal{T}_k)$ and $\nabla(\mathcal{T}_k)$ respectively. When the procedure receives the answer message A_{kj} of the sub-query Q_{kj} of $\mathcal{T}_k \in OUMQ$, from the pre-processor, the pre-processor of the data warehouse ensures that all the update transactions committed at R_j before Q_{kj} is executed have been already ordered into $OUMQ$. Therefore, all the update transactions which may interfere the execution of Q_{kj} are available in $OUMQ$. They can be detected by the following theorem.

Theorem 1. For any $\mathcal{T}_m \in OUMQ$, $\mathcal{T}_m$ interferes the execution of maintenance sub-query Q_{kj} of a given update transaction $\mathcal{T}_k \in QUMQ$, if and only if $\mathcal{T}_m$ is satisfied with all the three conditions $(1) k < m$; $(2) uc(\mathcal{T}_m) \leq uc(A_{kj})$, where A_{kj} is the answer message of Q_{kj}; and $(3) source(\mathcal{T}_m) = j$.

    Proof: If part. Since $\mathcal{T}_m \in OUMQ$ and $k < m$, the base relations state corresponding to $\mathcal{T}_k$, $\mathcal{T}_k$, is corresponding to a earlier state of the warehouse than that of $\mathcal{T}_m$. At the same time, $\mathcal{T}_m(source) = j$ and $uc(\mathcal{T}_m) \leq uc(A_{kj})$, that is $\mathcal{T}_m$ is committed at R_j earlier than when Q_{kj} is executed, and Q_{kj} is a maintenance sub-query of $\mathcal{T}_k$. Therefore, $\mathcal{T}_m$ interferes the execution of Q_{kj} of $\mathcal{T}_k$.

    Only if part. Since $\mathcal{T}_m$ interferes the execution of maintenance sub-query Q_{kj} of $\mathcal{T}_k \in OUMQ$, that is, $k < m$, $source(\mathcal{T}_m) = j$ and $\mathcal{T}_m$ is committed earlier than when Q_{kj} is executed, therefore, $uc(\mathcal{T}_m) \leq uc(A_{kj})$. ∎

    Therefore, compensation is computed as the following pseudocode.

$\Delta R_j = \emptyset;\ \nabla R_j = \emptyset;$
IF$(\mathcal{T}_m \in UMQ) \wedge (m < k) \wedge (source(\mathcal{T}_m) = j) \wedge (uc(\mathcal{T}_m) \leq uc(A_{kj}))$ THEN
    $\Delta R_j = \Delta R_j + \Delta R(\mathcal{T}_m);\ \nabla R_j = \nabla R_j + \nabla R(\mathcal{T}_m);$
END-IF;
$\Delta V^j(\mathcal{T}_k) = \Delta(A_{kj}) + \Delta V^{j-1}(\mathcal{T}_k) \bowtie \nabla R_j - \Delta V^{j-1}(\mathcal{T}_k) \bowtie \Delta R_j;$

$$\nabla V^j(\mathcal{T}_k) = \nabla(A_{kj}) + \nabla V^{j-1}(\mathcal{T}_k) \bowtie \nabla R_j - \nabla V^{j-1}(\mathcal{T}_k) \bowtie \Delta R_j;$$

Therefore, the maintenance anomaly is removed and the intermediate result $< \Delta V^j(\mathcal{T}_k), \nabla V^j(\mathcal{T}_k) >$ can be used to construct the next sub-query $Q_{k,j+1}$ in the next iteration until the result $< \Delta V^n(\mathcal{T}_k), \nabla V^n(\mathcal{T}_k) >$ is evaluated. In the backward, the engine can compute $< \Delta V^1(\mathcal{T}_k), \nabla V^1(\mathcal{T}_k) >$ in a very similar approach. Notice that the two phases are executed in parallel. Then, the change of $\mathcal{T}_k$ to V can be computed by: $\Delta V(\mathcal{T}_k) = \Delta V^1(\mathcal{T}_k) \bowtie \Delta V^n(\mathcal{T}_k)$ and $\nabla V(\mathcal{T}_k) = \nabla V^1(\mathcal{T}_k) \bowtie \nabla V^1(\mathcal{T}_k)$. Finally, the view maintenance engine updates the corresponding entry E_k with $< \Delta V(\mathcal{T}_k), \nabla V(\mathcal{T}_k) >$ and marks E_k as a *complete entry*. The execution of maintenance query $\mathcal{Q}_k$ is completed.

4.2 Complete Consistency

In our approach, the view maintenance engine executes the maintenance query of each update transaction as soon as it is ordered in $OUMQ$. That is, all the maintenance queries of the update transactions in $OUMQ$ may be completed asynchronously. However, in order to keep complete consistency of V, the changes of the update transactions must be incorporated into V according to the order of the transactions in $OUMQ$: when the change $< \Delta V(\mathcal{T}_k), \nabla V(\mathcal{T}_k) >$ of transaction $\mathcal{T}_k \in OUMQ$ is incorporated V, the view maintenance engine must ensure that V is in $V(\mathcal{T}_{k-1})$, when all the changes of the update transactions in front of $\mathcal{T}_k$ in $OUMQ$ have been incorporated into the view, so that V can be updated to $V(\mathcal{T}_k)$ as: $V(\mathcal{T}_k) = V(\mathcal{T}_{k-1}) + \Delta V(\mathcal{T}_k) - \nabla V(\mathcal{T}_k)$. Our method enforces complete consistency as follows:

Remember that for a given $\mathcal{T}_k \in OUMQ$, there is a corresponding entry E_k in VCQ and E_k preserves the order of $\mathcal{T}_k$ in $OUMQ$. Before maintenance query $\mathcal{Q}_k$ is executed, E_k is marked as an incomplete entry. When $\mathcal{Q}_k$ is completed, the view maintenance engine updates the corresponding E_k with $(\Delta V(\mathcal{T}_k), \nabla V(\mathcal{T}_k))$ and marks it as a complete entry. Then the view maintenance engine invokes the process **Refresh** to manipulate VCQ.

The process **Refresh** reads the first entry E_h of VCQ, notice that E_h is the change for the update transaction $\mathcal{T}_h$, which is ordered as the first entry of $OUMQ$. If E_h is a complete entry, then the process incorporates the change of $\mathcal{T}_h$ into the view and removes E_h and removes $\mathcal{T}_h$ from VCQ and $OUMQ$ respectively. If the first entry is an incomplete entry, the process **Refresh** is blocked. That is, for any $\mathcal{T}_k$ in $OUMQ$, the change of $\mathcal{T}_k$ is incorporated into V only when the corresponding enrty E_k of $\mathcal{T}_k$ in VCQ is a complete entry and this entry appears as the first entry of VCQ, that means, all the changes of the transactions which are in front of $\mathcal{T}_k$ in $OUMQ$ have been already incorporated into V and V is in the state $V(\mathcal{T}_{k-1})$. In this way, although maintenance queries for update transactions of $OUMQ$ are executed asynchronously, the changes of the update transactions are incorporated into V according to their order in $OUMQ$.

```
Algorithm View_Maintenance_Engine;
GLOBAL DATA
    OUMQ: Ordered Update Message Queue;
    VCQ: View Change Queue;
    h: INTEGER; /* h points to the first entry of OUMMQ and VCQ */
    PROCESS CompChange(ΔR(𝒯_k), ∇R(𝒯_k), source(𝒯_k), uc(𝒯_k), k) /* execution of maintenance query Q_k */
    BEGIN
        PAR BEGIN /* Forward phase and backward phase are executed in parallel */
            BEGIN /* The forward execution phase begins.*/
                i = source(𝒯_k); ΔV^i(𝒯_k) = ΔR(𝒯_k); ∇V^i(𝒯_k) = ∇R(𝒯_k);
                FOR j = i + 1 TO n DO
                    Send maintenance sub-query Q_kj =< ΔV^{j-1}(𝒯_k) ⋈ R_j, ∇V^{j-1}(𝒯_k) ⋈ R_j > to data source j;
                    Receive answer message (< Δ(A_kj), ∇(A_kj) >, uc(A_kj)) from the pre-processor;
                    /* Local compensation begins */
                    ΔR_j = ∅; ∇R_j = ∅;
                    IF(∃𝒯_m ∈ UMQ) ∧ (source(𝒯_m) = j) ∧ (m > k) ∧ (uc(𝒯_m) ≤ uc(A_kj)) THEN
                        ΔR_j = ΔR_j + ΔR(𝒯_m); ∇R_j = ∇R_j + ∇R(𝒯_m); END IF;
                    ΔV^j(𝒯_k) = Δ(A_kj) + ΔV^{j-1}(𝒯_k) ⋈ ∇R_j − ΔV^{j-1}(𝒯_k) ⋈ ΔR_j;
                    ∇V^j(𝒯_k) = ∇(A_kj) + ∇V^{j-1}(𝒯_k) ⋈ ∇R_j − ∇V^{j-1}(𝒯_k) ⋈ ΔR_j;
                    /* Local compensation ends */
                END FOR;
            END /* The forward execution phase ends*/
            BEGIN /* The backward execution phase begins*/
                i = source(𝒯_k); ΔV^i(𝒯_k) = ΔR(𝒯_k); ∇V^i(𝒯_k) = ∇R(𝒯_k);
                FOR j = i − 1 DOWN TO 1 DO
                    Send maintenance sub-query Q_kj =< ΔV^{j+1}(𝒯_k) ⋈ R_j, ∇V^{j+1}(𝒯_k) ⋈ R_j > to data source j;
                    Receive answer message (< Δ(A_kj), ∇(A_kj) >, uc(A_kj)) from the pre-processor;
                    /* Local compensation begins */
                    ΔR_j = ∅; ∇R_j = ∅;
                    IF (∃𝒯_m ∈ UMQ) ∧ (source(𝒯_m) = j) ∧ (m > k) ∧ (uc(𝒯_m) ≤ uc(A_kj)) THEN
                        ΔR_j = ΔR_j + ΔR(𝒯_m); ∇R_j = ∇R_j + ∇R(𝒯_m); END IF;
                    ΔV^j(𝒯_k) = Δ(A_kj) + ΔV^{j+1}(𝒯_k) ⋈ ∇R_j − ΔV^{j+1}(𝒯_k) ⋈ ΔR_j;
                    ∇V^j(𝒯_k) = ∇(A_kj) + ∇V^{j+1}(𝒯_k) ⋈ ∇R_j − ∇V^{j+1}(𝒯_k) ⋈ ΔR_j;
                    /* Local compensation ends */
                END FOR;
            END /* The backward execution phase ends*/
        PAR END;
        ΔV(𝒯_k) = ΔV^1(𝒯_k) ⋈ ΔV^n(𝒯_k); ∇V(𝒯_k) = ∇V^1(𝒯_k) ⋈ ∇V^n(𝒯_k);
        Update the corresponding entry E_k in VCQ of 𝒯_k with < ΔV(𝒯_k), ∇V(𝒯_k) >;
    END CompChange;
    PROCESS Refresh /* view refreshment process */
    BEGIN
        Read the first entry E_h from VCQ; /* h indicates the first entry of VCQ */
        WHILE E_h is not an incomplete entry DO /* Block itself if E_h is an incomplete entry */
            Incorporate < ΔV(𝒯_h), ∇V(𝒯_h) > into the view V;
            Remove E_h from VCQ;
            Remove 𝒯_h from OUMQ;
            h = h + 1; /* Read the next entry of VCQ */
        END WHILE;
    END Refresh;
    BEGIN /* Start view maintenance engine */
        h = 0; /* Initially, VCQ and OUMQ are empty */
        StartProcess(Refresh);
        FOR any new entry 𝒯_k in OUMQ
            StartProcess(CompChange(ΔR(𝒯_k), ∇R(𝒯_k), source(𝒯_k), uc(𝒯_k), k));
    END View_Miantenance_Engine.
```

Fig. 2. A Parallel View Maintenance Algorithm

4.3 An Example

In this subsection, we will show our algorithm for view maintenance with the following example. Consider a data warehouse is derived from three base relations $R_1(A, B)$, $R_2(B, C)$, $R_3(C, D)$ of three data source sites. The materialized view V is defined as:

$$V(A, B, C, D) = R_1 \overset{R_1[B]=R_2[B]}{\bowtie} R_2 \overset{R_2[C]=R_3[C]}{\bowtie} R_3.$$

The initial state of each base relation and the materialized view is shown in Figure 3. We now consider three update transactions have been commit-

Update Message Queue					States of the Data Sources			States of the Data Warehouse V
					R_1	R_2	R_3	
Initial State					{(1,3),(2,3)}	{(3,7)}	{(5,6),(7,8)}	{(1,3,7,8), (2,3,7,8)}
T_k	$\Delta(T_k)$	(T_k)	source(T_k)	uc(T_k)	$R_1(T_k)$	$R_2(T_k)$	$R_3(T_k)$	$V(T_k)$
T_1	{(3,5)}	{(3,7)}	2	1	{(1,3),(2,3)}	{(3,5)}	{(5,6),(7,8)}	{(1,3,5,6), (2,3,5,6)}
T_2	{(5,9)}	{(7,8)}	3	1	{(1,3),(2,3)}	{(3,5)}	{(5,6),(5,9)}	{(1,3,5,6), (2,3,5,6), (1,3,5,9), (2,3,5,9)}
T_3	{(7,3)}	{(2,3)}	1	1	{(1,3),(7,3)}	{(3,5)}	{(5,6),(5,9)}	{(1,3,5,6), (1,3,5,9) (7,3,5,6), (7,3,5,9)}

Fig. 3. The State Transformations of the Data Warehouse

ted at the the data sources and the maintenance notifications are ordered into $OUMQ$ by the pre-processor of the data warehouse as $\mathcal{T}_1$, $\mathcal{T}_2$ and $\mathcal{T}_3$ and VCQ is set as E_1, E_2 and E_3, where each E_k ($k = 1, 2, 3$) is an incomplete entry. The resulting state transformation of the view V are shown in Figure 3. Any algorithm that ensures is complete consistency must reflect all of the above state transformations. We now show how our approach enforces complete consistency while executing maintenance queries for these three update transactions in parallel.

Let us consider the execution of maintenance query $\mathcal{Q}_1$ by **CompChange(** $\Delta R(\mathcal{T}_1)$, $\nabla R(\mathcal{T}_1)$, $source(\mathcal{T}_1)$, $uc(\mathcal{T}_1)$, 1) individually. In the forward execution phase, the view maintenance engine sends maintenance sub-query Q_{13}; then, the view maintenance engine receives the answer message ($<$ $\{(3, 5, 6), (3, 5, 9)\}, \emptyset >$, 1) of Q_{13} from the pre-processor and concludes that $\mathcal{T}_2$ interferes Q_{13}, since $\mathcal{T}_2 \in OUMQ$, $1 < 2$, $source(\mathcal{T}_2) = 3$ and $uc(\mathcal{T}_2) \leq uc(A_{13})$. The compensation is computed at the warehouse and the view maintenance engine gets $< \Delta V^3(\mathcal{T}_1), \nabla V^3(\mathcal{T}_1) >$ as: $\Delta V^3(\mathcal{T}_1) = \{(3, 5, 6)\}$, $\nabla V^3(\mathcal{T}_1) = \{(3, 7, 8)\}$. In the backward execution phase, the view maintenance engine sends maintenance sub-query Q_{11} to data source 1; after the answer A_{11} is sent back, the view maintenance engine detects that $\mathcal{T}_3$ has interfered execution of Q_{11}, so it performs compensation locally and gets $< \Delta V^1(\mathcal{T}_1), \nabla V^1(\mathcal{T}_1) >$. After the two execution phases are completed, the view maintenance engine computes the change of $\mathcal{T}_1$ as: $\Delta V(\mathcal{T}_1) = \{(1, 3, 5, 6), (2, 3, 5, 6)\}$ and $\nabla V(\mathcal{T}_1) = \{(1, 3, 7, 8), (2, 3, 7, 8)\}$. Then, the view maintenance engine updates the corresponding entry E_1 with $< \{(1,3,5,6),$ $(2,3,5,6)\}, \{(1,3,7,8), (2,3,7,8)\} >$ and marks E_1 a complete entry. The execution of Q_1 is completed.

Suppose the three maintenance queries are completed in the order that the execution of Q_2 is first completed, then Q_1 and then Q_3. We will show how the view V is updated by the process **Refresh** of the view maintenance engine. At first, the execution of Q_2 is completed and E_2 of VCQ is updated to $< \{(1,3,5,9), (2,3,5,9)\}, \emptyset >$ and set to an complete entry, **Refresh** is invoked. Because the first entry E_1 is an incomplete entry, **Refresh** is blocked. Then, the execution of Q_1 is completed and **Refresh** is invoked again. The first entry E_1 of VCQ is a complete entry, **Refresh** updates the view by: $V(T_1) = \{(1,3,5,6),(2,3,5,6)\}$ and removes T_1 and E_1 from $OUMQ$ and VCQ respectively. Therefore, E_2 appears as the first entry of VCQ, **Refresh** updates the view V as: $V(T_2) = \{(1,3,5,6),(2,3,5,6),(1,3,5,9),(2,3,5,9)\}$. T_2 and E_2 are removed from $OUMQ$ and VCQ respectively. Finally, the execution of Q_3 is completed and E_3 is updated to $< \{(7,3,5,9), (7,3,5,6)\},$ $\{(2,3,5,6), (2,3,5,9)\} >$. **Refresh** is invoked for the third time to update V into $V(T_3)=\{(1,3,5,6), (1,3,5,9), (7,3,5,6), \{(7,3,5,9)\}$ and removes T_3 and E_3 from $OUMQ$ and VCQ respectively. Therefore, although the execution of the maintenance query for each update transaction is completed asynchronously, the complete consistency of the view V is still enforced.

5 Performance Evaluation

In this section, we compare our view maintenance strategy against the sequential view maintenance strategies with a simulation system. We will measure the **time latency** which is from when an update request occurs at its corresponding data source to when the update is incorporated into the materialized view. We make the following assumptions in our simulation: (1) The tuple size of each base relation is some constant and the number of tuples of each base relation is some constant. The selectivity of the joined attribute is some constant. (2) The server of each data source has similar processing ability and similar workload. Compared the data sources, the server of the data warehouse has a much stronger processing ability. Each data source communicates with the data warehouse in a similar data transmission speed. (3) The update transactions are distributed uniformly both by time and by location. Each update transaction include a set of deleted tuples and/or a set of inserted tuples, and the window size of the each update transaction is some constant.

In our system, there are three base relations: $R_1(W, X)$, $R_2(X, Y)$ and $R_3(Y, Z)$; each is modeled as a plain file in a Digital Personal Workstations 433au, Digital Unix 4.0D, with 128MB SDRAM, 2.1GB Ultra-SCSI Hard Disk. The tuple size of each table is 64Bytes and each base relation is 1M Bytes. We model the data warehouse with a Dec AlphaServer 8400 with 4 A

XP CPUs running at 350MHz each, 1GB of RAM and 50 GB of disk space, where the materialized view is defined as: $V = \pi_{W,Z}((R_1 \bowtie R_2 \bowtie R_3))$. The three data sources communicate with the data warehouse through 10Base-T Ethernet by using connected TCP socket.

At the initialization, the three base relations are transmitted to the data warehouse and the data warehouse will in term compute the materialized view and store it as a plain file. After that, the data warehouse will send synchronization signal to the three data sources. When a data source receives the synchronization message, it invokes the process to execute update requests and to evaluate the maintenance sub-queries sent from the data warehouse in a first-come-first-serve mode. Before any update transaction or any maintenance sub-query is executed, the process must get an exclusive lock of the base relation. The process will not release the lock until it commits the update transaction or completes the evaluation of the maintenance sub-query. The data source employs another process to transmit the update notifications and the answer messages to the data warehouse according to their completed order. Figure 4 shows the latency time of each update transaction by using the sequential approach and the parallel approach, when the update transaction sequence is as shown in Figure 4. The selectivity of the joined attribute is 4.0×10^{-6} and each update transaction includes 2 deleted tuples and 2 inserted tuples. In each data source, there is no time latency between two neighboring update requests. From our simulations, we can find that: (1)In the sequential approach, the latency time of the update transaction is added up. The longer time latency an update transaction has, the more concurrent updates it may has and these concurrent updates will prolong the time latency. (2) Although our approach has some overhead in forking for a new process the concurrent control mechanism, our approach always has a shorter latency time for each update.

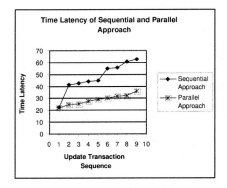

The First 9 update Transactions in OUMQ

update transactions	source	version
1	0	1
2	1	1
3	2	1
4	0	2
5	1	2
6	2	2
7	1	3
8	2	3
9	1	4

Fig. 4. A Simulation Result

6 Conclusion and Future Work

We present an efficient view maintenance algorithm for a data Warehouse system with multiple data sites. Our approach has the following properties: (1) the view maintenance executes the maintenance query for each update transaction in parallel; (2) the maintenance anomaly is handled by local compensation and no further queries need to be sent to the data sources; (3) Our approach can enforce the complete consistency of the view at the warehouse; (4) the materialized view is defined SPJ-expression; (5) the message transmission disorder is considered; (6) Our approach does not require the data sources be quiescent.

References

1. S. Grumbach and T. Milo. Towards tractable algebra for bags. In *PODS'93*.
2. Yue Zhuge, Hector Garcia-Molina, Joachim Hammer, and Jennifer Widom. View Maintenance in a Warehousing Environment. In *Proceedings of the ACM SIGMOD International Conference on Management of Data*, pages 316-327, May 1995.
3. J. Hammer, H. Garcia-Molina, J. Widom, W. Labio, and Y. Zhuge. The Stanford Data Warehousing Project. *IEEE Bulletin of the Technical Committee on Data Engineering*, 18(2):41-48, June 1995.
4. A. Gupta and I. S. Mumick. Maintenance of Materialized Views: Problems, Techniques, and Applications. in *IEEE Bulletin of the Technical Committee on Data Engineering*, 18(2):3-18, June 1995.
5. L. S. Colby, T. Griffin, L. Libkin, I. S. Mumick, and H. Trickey. Algorithms for Deferred View Maintenance. In *Proceedings of the ACM SIGMOD International Conference on Management of Data*, pages 469-492, 1996.
6. Richard Hull and Gang Zhou. A Framework for Supporting Data Integration Using the Materialized and Virtual Approaches. In *Proceedings of the ACM SIGMOD International Conference on Management of Data*, pages 481-492, June 1996.
7. Yue Zhuge, Hector Garcia-Molina, and Janet L. Wiener. The Strobe Algorithms for Multi-Source Warehouse Consistency. In *Proceedings of the International Conference on Parallel and Distributed Information Systems*, December 1996.
8. Richard Hull and Gang Zhou. Towards the Study of Performance Trade-offs Between Materialized and Virtual Integrated Views. In *Workshop on VIEWS'96*, 1996.
9. D. Agrawal, A. El Abbadi, A. Singh, and T. Yurek, Efficient View Maintenance at Data Warehouses. In *Sigmod Conference 1997*, Pages 417-427.
10. Rongquen Chen, Weiyi Meng, Precise Detection and Proper Handling of View Anomalies in Multidatabase Environment. In *DASFAA 97*, 391-400.
11. Ye Liu, An Efficient View Maintenance Algorithm for Multidatabase Environment. Thesis for master degree, School of Computing, National University of Singapore.

Adaptive Cache Validation for Mobile File Systems

Simon Cuce[1] and Arkady Zaslavsky[2]

[1] simon.cuce@csse.monash.edu.au
[2] arkady.zaslavsky@csse.monash.edu.au
Department of Computer Science and Software Engineering, Monash University
900 Dandenong Road, Caulfield East 3145, Australia;
Phone: +61 3 9903 2479; Fax: +61 3 9903 1077;

Abstract. The uneven advancement in computing hardware components has restricted the development of mobile computing technology. Key components like bandwidth and battery life have only improved slightly over the last decade. Compounding this problem, systems are failing to address these constraints, focusing on cache consistency rather than accessibility. We propose a system that refocuses the design methodology towards file accessibility by offering a means of cache validation while disconnected. By using file information in the form of a file map stored locally, the likely status of a file can be determined. Thus the system can decide on an appropriate course of action without the associated cost of full validation of files. By offering a secondary means of validation, resources can be utilised more efficiently by directing tasks to processors rather than bandwidth.

1 Introduction

With most mobile file systems, files are assumed as either valid or invalid. Determining the status primarily depends on connection with the server and the systems ability to validate the two. However, the characteristics of mobile computing do not allow for this process to operate constantly. When disconnected, the client has no physical means of determining the validity of the cache's contents. This problem has given rise to the partial cache consistency model, which uses client side secondary information to determine the likely status of a file.

The proposed system focuses on two areas, the first being the resulting problems associated with distributed system assumptions and the second being the failure not to exploit access patterns of average users. The major distributed system assumption, which is in direct conflict with mobility issues is that disconnected operations are treated as failures, assuming all files cached locally are invalid. By providing additional information, a state can "most likely" be determined without the need for the server to be contacted. How this information is created is by studying file access patterns to determine the likely status of a file after a period of time. With this system, a balance can be struck between file integrity and validation overhead cost, resulting in less bandwidth usage and with only a possible minimal reduction in cache consistency.

This paper firstly discusses the reasons why mobility has suffered as a result of distributed system assumptions and the motivation behind this approach. The second section discusses the design of the partial cache consistency model and how normal mobile operations are handled. The next section then argues the benefits this type of technique offers, with a description of the implementation. The final section justifies the usefulness of this approach and discusses possible problems that may arise.

2 Background

The need for variable cache consistency is due in part to the evolution of mobile computing and the assumptions which accompany these systems. Most mobile systems are either a hybrid of a distributed system or loosely based on the distributed system paradigm [15]. As a result, systems are implementing distributed system assumptions that are in direct conflict with mobile and mobility aware systems [2]. Mobile environments cannot accept these assumptions as their own, as the nature of mobile computing is not consistency but rather accessibility. The distributed system assumptions that have affected mobile system development are:

- Nodes are constantly connected - The concept of nodes constantly connected in a mobile environment is not possible as many external factors can effect connection.
- Disconnection is a failure - Treating disconnection as a failure is not always possible, as the disconnection phase is not always the result of a failure.
- Nodes are connected with ample bandwidth - Current infrastructure does not allow for nodes to be connected with ample bandwidth.

The original version of the CODA file system [12, 6] illustrates this conflict. The CODA file system, which was based on the Andrew File System (AFS) [5], is the most advanced work with mobility and disconnection operations at present. The way AFS handles disconnection is to invalidate all locally stored files when the connection is severed, thus rendering the unit inoperable. The CODA system took the opposite approach, assuming all files are valid, postponing the validation task until reintegration. The decision was made that full data integrity should be maintained at the expense of bandwidth usage. This meant that during the reintegration period all files are checked to ensure data integrity. As a result the reintegration process was a lengthy and complex event. This became prominent when the system started to use a SLIP connection. The time taken to validate the client's files over a limited bandwidth system rendered the mobile unit useless until complete. The limitations of a SLIP connection required the reworking of the system design, converting the reintegration event into a background process. Even with the use of granularity for data validation and the redesign of the reintegration event, full cache consistency is still maintained at the expense of bandwidth.

The reason for full consistency is that it is the best way of ensuring that the client's copy is the most up-to-date, thus helping to avoid write-write conflicts. Where mobile and distributed systems diverge is in relation to write-write conflict handling. There are many techniques used by distributed systems for handling file concurrency, many based on the database concurrency control [3]. The mobile environment does not readily accept this classic method of avoiding conflicts. Rather, conflicts are igno red until reintegration. However, the need for full consistency is not justified, as case studies [6, 11] have shown the chance of conflicts occurring is low. As a result file systems like CODA which offer full consistency are unnecessarily over utilising resources, when only partial consistency would be sufficient.

A system that understands the complexity of user patterns and consistency constraints is the Sprite operating system [9, 10]. The aims of this system are different to that of CODA, where efficiency is predominant to design rather than disconnection operations. Instead of using call-back for cache validation, Sprite uses version numbering. Validation is done upon a file request rather than a periodical broadcast message. Efficiency is improved by validating files only when required. Our system shares similar goals as the Sprite system, ensuring efficiency by capitalising on file access patterns. However, where our system differs is that operating disconnected is of paramount importance.

3 System Design

3.1 Overview

The general structure of our system is similar to Tait's Mobile File System [13], where integrity can be adjusted depending on the resources. On each server is an Observer, which supplies the file system interface to the clients. Every Observer has a client interface and Analyser. The client interface handles the transmissions of files, while the Analyser creates the secondary validation information depending on the clients' needs.

The client side of this system has two components. The main component is the cache manager, which handles the communication between the application and the local or remote file systems. The other component is the file map process, which handles the testing and validation of files (Figure 1).

3.2 File Map

The foundation of the proposed system is the file map. This is the secondary validation information used by the cache manager for integrity measurement. The file map contains an entry for every file on the client's file system. Each entry contains the file name, the directory where the file resides, its size, date of last modification and user's rights. Additional information that is used for validation includes, longevity (seconds), and importance (Figure 2).

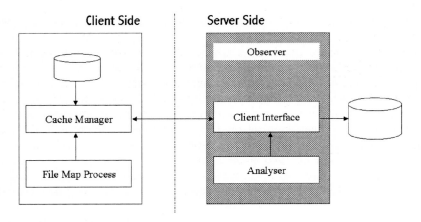

Fig. 1. The Partial Cache Consistency Design

Longevity is the cache manager's means of determining if the file currently cached has become invalid. By setting a likely time when the file will become invalid, the cache manager does not need to be concerned when disconnected. The importance factor of a file is a user determined status that gives the cache manager a view of how important a file is to the whole system. For example, a highly used database, where data consistency is paramount, would be graded as very important. The cache manager then dictates what operations are allowed to ensure that the importance is not compromised. This mechanism allows the user to set the concurrency level for every file within the system. This in turn reduces the need for complex reintegration algorithms, as conflicts are avoided before they occur.

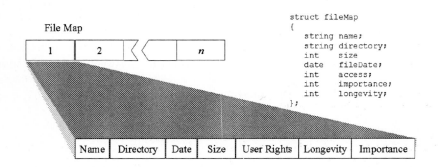

Fig. 2. File Map Contents

File Map Contents The actual data that comprises of the file map has numerous sources. Arbitrary information can easily be determined from the server's file system, whereas the longevity and importance information requires additional effort to determine their value. This information is derived from two sources, they are static (user specified) and dynamic (learned). The static sources include user working set patterns, known application behaviour and specific file requirements. These are set by the system administrator or user and remain relatively constant throughout the file's life. By allowing manual control of validation information, consistency can be refined for user requirements, giving a mechanism for adjusting consistency control.

Dynamic sources are generated after every disconnection session. To handle cache misses, a disconnection log is checked. Files that were required but which were not found are automatically added to the file map. These files are inserted first into the file map ensuring that when the next file collection event occurs, they are first to be propagated. Currently only cache misses are derived from dynamic means, but other advanced prefetching algorithms can be incorporated into the design. Systems like SEER [7] and Tait's File Working Set system [14] can provide more intelligent file management, thus reducing the amount of cache misses that occur.

File Map Ordering In distributed systems atomicity is assumed, as the network connection rarely fails. However, in a mobile system the chance of a disconnection event occurring is higher. The file map then must be ordered so the chance of the most important information reaching its destination is increased. Whereas most systems disregard incomplete files, this system loosens the rule for the file map only. As the data is entering the client, the properties are instantly accessed, regardless of whether the file is complete or not. For this reason the file map contents will be structured, with the most important data placed first.

The criterion on which this ordering is based depends on changes from the last file map sent. This requires the server to keep a copy of the past file map and recreate the new one based on this information. The criterion is based on:

1. Cache Missed Files - These are inserted first in the list, so that the client knows to collect these files first on the next collection.
2. Importance Change - The change in Importance is the foremost indication of a file usage changing.
3. Size Change - The Size change indicates the magnitude of the modification to the file.
4. Longevity Change - If the characteristics of the file have changed, the files with the greatest deviation are placed first.

This ordering criterion purpose is to allow a means of supplying the most up to date information on validity to the client. As there is high correlation between disconnection periods, this mechanism only attempts to support clients in gaining all the information required to preformed disconnection validation. This ordering scheme can have problems in relation to ensuring important files are also sent. For this to be resolved issues like longevity factors and time until invalidation are considered.

Using this criterion ensures that even in the face of disconnection operations during transfer, the chance that the most updated information will be present on the client is greatly improved.

3.3 File Validation

When a file request is made by a client application, the first step is to determine the status of the file. At this point cache misses are detected and handled, with all appropriate responses made. These responses depend on the current status of the mobile unit (connected or disconnected). If the file is present locally, the cache manager then consults the analyser, asking for the validation status of the file. This procedure consists of a number of steps:

1. The application that requires the file is queried. Depending on the application type the process will abort or continue. The reason the application is analysed first is because some application types can not work if disconnected. This step catches these applications and returns a response accordingly.

2. If it is concluded that the application can operate in this current environment (disconnected), then the importance factor of the file is tested. If the importance factor is high, the chance that either a change has happened or changes must be propagated instantly is assumed. As a result, the cache manager will invalidate the file.

3. As most files have little importance to the distributed system in general, longevity is then used. The time the file has been on the client machine is calculated, re-evaluated after every successful file map transfer. This is then compared with the longevity of the file. If it is determined that the file has been on the client machine for longer than the longevity period, it is said that the original copy has most likely changed and that the file is invalid.

4. The last measure used to determine file validation is user access privileges (private, shared or public). If a file is read all and write private, then the validation status of the file can easily be determined. If the world has write access, assuming validation is harder.

Determining Status Determining the final status of a file is done via a points system. If the file value is under 100 points then it is deemed as safe, else the file is invalid. The choice of 100 as a threshold point was beacuse it was an easy way to calculate invalidation. Depending on the results of each validation task a value is returned, this is accumulated over the life of the test. The reason for using summation for each test, is if all test just pass and thus the likelihood of the file being invalid is close, then this calculation will detect it. Any test showing that the file is certain to be invalid would increase the total by a minimum of 100, thus ensuring the invalidation of the file.

3.4   Connection Phase

When an application requires a file, a call is made to the client side cache manager. At this point the currently existing file map is checked. Depending on the properties of the file, the cache manager will determine if:

- A cache miss has occurred.
- The file is "most likely" out-of-date and needs to be fetched.
- Or the currently existing file is valid.

If the file residing locally is deemed valid, then that file is returned to the application that required it. When the file needs to be fetched, a similar approach to the CODA threshold mechanism is used. Once complete the newly created file map is downloaded, with the file that was fetched being the first entry in the list. File maps created as a result of a fetch override current ordering procedures. This is only a temporary arrangement to ensure that the cache manager has some validation information for this file. The file map is then integrated into the client's list with the file's age adjusted. When the client cache records a cache miss, the event is recorded in a log. This event log is used for post disconnection analysis to ensure future sessions do not have this recurring situation.

The ACID rule for transactions might be loosened for the file map, but must be strictly enforced for all other file down-loads. To ensure this, the Ficus shadow copy approach is used [4]. This approach involves files being transferred into a shadow cache area under another name. When download is complete and the integrity of the file is assured, the original is removed and the replacement renamed, taking over its role. If the downloaded file fails then the shadow copy is rendered useless and removed, with the original copy left unaltered.

Most of the transactions described have been as a result of file request failures. It is also possible to gain new files periodically, in a manner similar to CODA's hoard walk. This event occurs in times of low network traffic, with file collection based on file map order. As the priority of the files lessens further down the file map, the user has the option to restrict the depth the hoard walk can go. By setting less important files to be collected only when required, files that are not integral to the client will not hinder performance.

3.5   Disconnection Phase

The nature of mobile computing means that disconnection is a normal part of operation. There are two types of disconnection that can occur in a mobile computing environment, elective and non-elective. In this system both can be handled.

Elective When a user knows that they will disconnect, the system can be informed of this event and thus handled in an efficient way. How this is achieved is via a disconnection command. This informs the cache to collect the files required for the disconnection period and set the cache manager to handle cache misses and invalid files. One assumption made is the most users will accept some delay from when the disconnection command is made, to the actual time when physically disconnected from the network. For this reason the cache will iterate through the file map, fetching all out of date files to its local cache. This ensures that the cache has the most up to date files possible before disconnection. The threshold policy is still in place here. If the file takes too long to download, then the user will be given an option to continue or ignore. If continued, the file will be downloaded, else the currently existing file will be used. All events are now recorded in the log, with cache misses returned as errors and the file map used for validation.

Two aspects of the client's cache manager differ in a disconnection mode compared to normal operations. When a cache miss occurs, instead of fetching the file, a message is displayed indicating that the process must abort. The other difference is that an option is given to the user when a file exists but is invalid. The user can abort the process or continue, knowing that there may be problems upon reintegration.

Non-elective Non-elected failures can occur at any time, so different techniques are required to handle different events. If a failure occurs when no file operations are taking place, the clean-up process is simple. The client unit will detect the failure (no periodical heartbeat from the server) and enter the disconnected mode. If a failure occurs during a file download (not a file map), the file is removed, then the disconnected mode is automatically initiated.

Where disconnection clean up procedures become complicated is when the disconnection occurs before or during the file map download. If the event happens before the file map starts, the cache manager can only rely on the previous file map. If the event happens while the file map is downloading, the new records that have made it to the client are integrated separately. This means that correct information can be gained even when a file map is only partially downloaded. This unforeseen failure restricts the reuse factor within the client's machine, but if file patterns analysis has been correct, then this degrade in system performance will be minimal.

3.6   Reintegration

When the disconnection period is over, the files must be re-integrated back into the system. How this is done is that the client sends the disconnection log to the server. The server views this list and compares it to the newly constructed file map and actual files. This moves most of the reintegration processing to the server. The server determines the files that need to be updated on the system.

The server requests all the files that have been modified during the disconnection period. This assumes that the user will handle some waiting before full connection is returned. If any major conflicts occur, the client is informed. When complete a new file map is created, with the files that need to be downloaded having their longevity set to zero. This will force the client to download the new files when required (Figure 3).

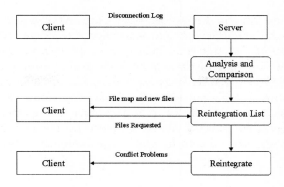

Fig. 3. The Reintegration Process

4 Implementation

To determine the feasibility of this approach, a simulation will be used to test the success of secondary cache validation. The simulation will consist of three primary components, the Client Process (CP), Bandwidth Control System (BCS) and the Server Process (SP) (see Figure 4).

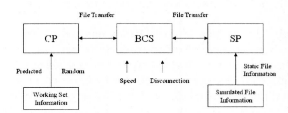

Fig. 4. Simulation Program

The Client Process is the portion of the simulation that mimics the client side and the Server Process simulates the server side of this model. The CP and SP will implement the major portions of our design. Minor procedures like threshold calculation will be ignored as their success have been proven on numerous occasions

As this simulation will not be implemented over a network, no actual file transfers will occur. Rather, network bound events will be passed to the BCS. This BCS will act as a broker for the client and server, simulating different network conditions. By creating a separate process impersonating the wireless link, connection speed and disconnection events can be recreated by the user when appropriate.

To replicate user actions in a mobile environment, two opposing file access patterns are defined in the CP. These two patterns are predictive (file access rarely diverge) and random (file access pattern are unknown). The nature of the file accesses for the predictive pattern will reflect the usage pattern concluded from case studies by [6] and [11]. This type of pattern usually consists of a predefined set of files that rarely change from previous sessions. Applications used by these patterns predominantly use read operations and occasionally write operations. The random file pattern will consist of randomly generated events, with no predefined quota for types of applications and operations used. As a result of using these extremes of file access patterns, not only is the feasibility determined, but also the domain in which this approach is best suited can be concluded.

5   Related Work

One of the few papers in which cache validation is based on contents, rather than conventional means is the quasi-copy approach [1]. This approach weakens the consistency rule for copies of data, depending on the operations required. Cached data is allowed to deviate from the central record to a certain degree. Once exceeding the specified amount, the cached version is deemed invalid. By allowing the user to set the degree of consistency, less emphasis is placed on the link compared with other database consistency systems. This approach is ideologically similar to our system, as file variation is allowed. However, validation techniques for database systems and file systems are different, as their scopes are very different.

Isolation-Only Transaction [8] is CODA's method of handling the complex task of reintegration when write-write conflicts occur. This concept consists of allowing only those operations that satisfy certain serialisation constraints. This is similar in approach to our system, as the user can set consistency levels. Where the two systems differ is that consistency control is given to the user as a means of avoiding and handling conflicts. With our system, the resulting benefit from providing validation information is a less complex reintegration procedure.

6   Conclusion

There are a number of associated benefits with the partial cache consistency model for cache management in a mobile environment. These include fewer bandwidth-consuming messages and less server-initiated transactions. Our approach views bandwidth utilisation and consistency control as a balance, where consistency can be reduced resulting in improved performance. Whether the conflict rates for this approach are high still need to be tested, but from previous case studies, the probability would indicate a low chance.

Much of the success this system promotes is determined by the variable information (longevity and importance factors). Currently, the system administrator sets such information. This in turn places the responsibility on the user, as incorrect information can erode the benefits this system promotes. At this early stage, more research is required to understand what are appropriate values for a file to have. However, some general rules have been determined. What is hoped is that an automated process will lessen the responsibility on the system administrator, by monitoring and recording patterns of access, frequency of accesses and active interval of files. Based on this information, an adaptive mechanism can reduce the need of external adjustment.

This approach has still to be implemented in a working system, but the design structure invites efficient bandwidth utilisation, while not greatly affecting data consistency. Currently there is a lack of research in the area of variable consistency, as most systems that promote anything less than full consistency are deemed as unsafe. Whether this is really the case is still to be proven, but by focusing the design towards the end-user, beneficial results are certain.

7 Acknowledgment

We wish to thank Peter Stanski for his valuable time and effort for fine tuning portions of this design. Also Peter Granville and Harriet Searcy for work done on the draft copies.

References

[1] Alonso, R., D. Barbara, and H. Garcia-Molina (1990, September). Data caching issues in an information retrieval system. *ACM Transactions on Database Systems 15*(3), 359–384.

[2] Beigl, M. and R. Rudisch (1996). Transparent extention of existing applications for mobile computing. Technical Report iratr-1995-52, Universität Karlsruhe, Institut für Telematik.

[3] Date, C. (1995). *An Introduction to Database Systems.* (Sixth ed.). Addison-Wesley Publishing Company.

[4] Guy, R. G., J. S. Heidemann, W. Mak, T. W. Page, Jr., G. J. Popek, and D. Rothmeier (1990, June 11-15). Implementation of the ficus replicated file system. In *Proc. 1990 Summer USENIX Conf.*, Anaheim.

[5] Huston, L. B. and P. Honeyman (1993, August). Disconnected operation for AFS. In USENIX Association (Ed.), *Proceedings of the USENIX Mobile and Location-Independent Computing Symposium: August 2–3, 1993, Cambridge, Massachusetts, USA*, Berkeley, CA, USA, pp. 1–10. USENIX.

[6] Kistler, J. J. and M. Satyanarayanan (1991, October). Disconnected operation in the Coda file system. In *Proceedings of 13th ACM Symposium on Operating Systems Principles*, pp. 213–25. Association for Computing Machinery SIGOPS.

[7] Kuenning, G. H. and G. J. Popek (1997, October5–8). Automated hoarding for mobile computers. In *Proceedings of the 16th Symposium on Operating Systems Principles (SOSP-97)*, Volume 31,5 of *Operating Systems Review*, New York, pp. 264–275. ACM Press.

[8] Lu, Q. and M. Satyanarayanan (1995, March). Improving data consistency in mobile computing using isolation-only transactons. Technical Report CS-95-126, Carnegie Mellon University, School of Computer Science.

[9] Nelson, M. N., B. B. Welch, and J. K. Ousterhout (1998, February). Caching in the sprite network file system. *ACM TOCS 6*(1), 134–154.

[10] Ousterhout, J. K., A. R. Cherenson, F. Douglis, M. N. Nelson, and B. B. Welch (1988, February). The Sprite network operating system. *Computer 21*(2), 23–36.

[11] Ousterhout, J. K., H. D. Costa, D. Harrison, J. A. Kunze, M. Kupfer, and J. G. Thompson (1985, April). A trace-driven analysis of the UNIX 4.2BSD file system. Technical Report UCB/CSD 85/230, University of California.

[12] Satyanarayanan, M. (1993). Mobile computing. *IEEE Computer 26*(9), 81–82.

[13] Tait, C. D. (1993, August). *A File System for Mobile Computing.* Ph. D. thesis.

[14] Tait, C. D. and D. Duchamp (1991, May). Detection and exploitation of file working sets. In *11th International Conference on Distributed Computing Systems*, Washington, D.C., USA, pp. 2–9. IEEE Computer Society Press.

[15] Zaslavsky, A. and Z. Tari (1998, May). Mobile Computing: Overview and Current Status. *The Australian Computer Journal.* Vol. 30, No. 2.

Broadcast Strategies to Maintain Cached Data for Mobile Computing System[1]

Kam-yiu Lam, Edward Chan and Joe Chun-Hung Yuen
Department of Computer Science
City University of Hong Kong
83 Tat Chee Avenue, Kowloon
Hong Kong
Fax: 852-2788-8614
Email: {cskylam|csedchan|csjyuen}@cityu.edu.hk

Abstract.
Although data broadcast has been shown to be an efficient data dissemination technique for mobile computing systems, many issues such as selection of broadcast data and caching strategies at the clients are still active research areas. In this paper, by examining the dynamic properties of the data items in mobile computing systems, we define the validity of a data item by its absolute validity interval (avi). Based on the avi of the data items, we propose different broadcast algorithms in which the selection of data items for broadcast will be based on the avi of the data items and their access frequencies. The purpose of the AVI algorithms is to increase the client cache hit probability so that the access delay for a data item will be much reduced. Simulation experiments have been conducted to compare the AVI algorithms with the algorithm which only considers the popularity of the data items. The results indicate that the AVI algorithms can significantly improve the mean response time and reduce the deadline missing requests.

1 Introduction

The research in mobile computing systems has received a lot of interest in recent years. A key element in many of these mobile computing systems is the need to distributed real-time information from a database server to mobile clients. Recent research has focused on one of the most important issues: supporting efficient data retrieval and dissemination to the requests from mobile clients [1,2,7,11,12]. The performance objective is to reduce the mean access delay for data items and minimize the response times of the requests from the mobile clients. Generally speaking, the proposed mechanisms for data dissemination to the requests from mobile clients fall into one of two main approaches: the *on-demand* approach and the *broadcast* approach (also called the *pull* and *push* approach respectively) [1].

In the on-demand approach, the data items required by the requests from mobile clients will be sent from the information server on request. This approach is simple but does not scale well with the number of mobile client requests [1,13]. In the broadcast approach, the information server periodically and continuously broadcasts data items to the mobile clients. If there is a request waiting for a data item, it will get the data item from the "air" while it is being broadcast. Under the broadcast approach, the cost for data dissemination is independent of the number of requests since a broadcast can satisfy multiple requests for the same data item, resulting in much more efficient utilization of the bandwidth. Hence, most of the previous work on data dissemination in mobile systems is based on the broadcast approaches [1,2,4,5,8,9,10,13].

In this paper, we focus on the data dissemination problem using the broadcast approach. An important design issue in this approach is the algorithm used for selecting data items from the database for broadcast. Although a number of algorithms which aims to minimize the average delay for data items [1,5, 8,10,13] have been proposed, most of them are based on the

---

[1] This work was supported in part by City University Strategic Grant #700584.

popularity, or the access frequencies, of the data items. They have ignored the impact of the timing constraints of the client requests and the temporal properties of the data items on the performance of the algorithms.

In many mobile computing systems, many data items in a mobile computing system are status information, for instance the last traded price of a stock and the current traffic situation of a road. Their values are highly dynamic as they are used to represent the current situations in the external environment. The validity of the current values of the data items is associated with temporal constraints. They may become out-dated and useless with the passage of time. The dynamic properties of the data items can greatly affect the management of data items at the client caches. Maintaining data items at the client caches is critical to the performance of a mobile computing system. If a request can find its required data items at the client cache, the request can be served immediately and its response time can be greatly reduced. Otherwise, it has to wait until the server broadcast the data items. However, the data items at the client cache will become out-dated. A request still has to wait for its data items even though it can find the data items at the client cache but they are out-dated.

Although a lot of work has been done on data dissemination for mobile computing systems, the temporal properties of data items have been largely ignored in the research literature. In this paper, we introduce a new data model to characterize the temporal properties of the data items. Based on the this temporal data model, we propose new broadcast algorithms, we call them AVI algorithms, in which the temporal properties of the data items will also be considered to select the data items for broadcast. The purpose of the AVI algorithms is to maintain the data items at the client caches so that the cache hit probability can be improved and consequently, the access delay for the data items can be much reduced.

2 Temporal Data Model for Mobile Computing Systems

When we examine the properties of the data items in a mobile computing system, we can find that many data items in the database are used to record the "real-time" information of the objects in the external environment. Some of the examples are the last traded stock prices, news updates, as well as traffic and weather conditions. Since they track external events, this information may change quite rapidly. In order to maintain the consistency of the data items with the status of their corresponding objects in the external environment, an immediate update approach may be used in which updates are generated to "refresh" the data items in the database whenever the status of the external objects have changed.

Although this approach can provide a tight consistency between the data items in the database and the actual status of the objects in the external environment, tracking every change in the status of the external objects will create a large number of update transactions. For many data items, such as the weather condition, news updates and traffic situations, their updates may be performed periodically. There are two reasons for this design. Firstly, for many mobile computing systems, the value of a data item that models an object in the external environment cannot, in general, be updated continuously to perfectly track the dynamics of the real-world object as the update process itself requires time to complete. Thus, there already exists a discrepancy between the value of the data item and the "real-time" status of its corresponding object such as the traffic status of a particular road. When this information is reported to the information, the traffic status of the road will already change to another status. Secondly, it is often unnecessary for data values to be perfectly up-to-date or precise to be useful. In particular, values of a data item that are slightly different are often interchangeable and the mobile clients will consider them to be the same. For example, the traffic condition at one minute past noon can be considered to be the same as the traffic condition at noon to most drivers.

The dynamic properties of the data items make the management of cached data a difficult problem. Whenever a new version of a data item has been created in the database, all the cached version of the data item has to be invalidated. Traditionally, the invalidation is done by sending invalidation messages to the clients which have cached the data item [6]. Due to the delay in invalidation as a result of the slow bandwidth, maintaining a tight consistency between the data items at the client cache and the database is not easy. When a request finds that its required data item is at the client cache, it is not able to determine whether this is the most updated version without incurring heavy overhead.

In order to resolve the problem in accessing the data items at the client cache and to improve the probability of cache hit probability, we introduce a new temporal model to characterize the temporal properties of the data items in mobile computing systems. In the temporal data model, it is assumed that the data items are classified into different *data groups* based on their temporal properties, e.g., their values will change in similar rate. Within each data group, the data items are assigned a time frame, called *absolute validity interval (avi)*, to characterize their temporal properties.

Different types of data items may have different *avi* values. The definition of the avi for a data group can be based on how the users will use the data items in that group or their update periods. For example, the generation of news report is every 30 minutes. Thus, the avi for the news reports can be defined as 30 min. For some information, which update period may not be fixed, i.e., stock data, their avi can be defined based on the user requirements. For example, the stock data will be defined with an avi of 10 min. as most of the investors will consider the stock information to be out-dated if it is recorded at ten minutes ago. The avi for traffic information may be longer as it is not as dynamic as the stock data.

In the temporal data model, formally, each data item can be defined as a 3-tuple:

$$D_1 \quad = (V_i, avi_i, TS_i) \tag{1}$$

where V_i is the value for data item D_i, avi_i is the absolute validity interval of D_i and TS_i is the update time-stamp of D_i. Each transaction update, which captures the "real-time" status of an external object, is associated with a time-stamp, called *update time-stamp (TS)* which indicates at which time the update transaction is created. Whenever an update transaction is completed, the update time-stamp will also be recorded in the database associated with the data value. A data item, D_i, is *invalid* if $avi_i + TS_i <$ current time. In this case a new value of the data item is required.

The advantage of using avi to define the validity of a data item is that no invalidation message will be required to invalidate the data items in the client caches as the validity of the data items is explicitly defined by their avi and their last update time-stamps. When a request has found that its required data item is at the client cache, it can determine the validity of the data item immediately by checking the data item's time-stamp and avi. Another advantage of the avi approach is that it can help us to design the broadcast algorithms so that the validity of the cached data items can be better maintained.

3 AVI Approaches

In this section, we present the AVI approaches in which the avi of the data items will be considered explicitly in selecting the data items for broadcast in addition to the access frequencies of the data items. The purpose of considering the avi of the data items is to increase the probability of finding valid data items at the client cache of the mobile clients. Under the temporal data model, a data item may become invalid while it is in the client cache. Without a suitable cache refreshment policy, the probability of cache hit (finding valid data items in the cache) will decrease over time, leading to an increase in access delay. However, if the data items are not selected for broadcast, it is not possible to refresh their validity them in the client cache under the broadcast approach. The AVI approaches consist of two main parts:

(1) Selection of data items: determination of which data items should be selected for broadcast in each broadcast cycle; and

(2) Broadcast skipping: even if a data item has been selected for broadcast, its broadcast

may be skipped if it has been broadcast in the recent broadcast cycles. The reason is that it may still be valid in the client caches. The purpose of broadcast skipping is to save broadcast bandwidth so that more data items can be broadcast in the same period of time.

3.1 Selection of Data items in the AVI Approaches

The primary issue in the design of broadcast algorithms is to determine which client requests should be served first under the limited bandwidth. As there are a large number of requests waiting for different data items, the server may not be able to satisfy all the requests before their deadlines with the limited bandwidth. Even though, as assumed in many previous work, the server knows the previous data access patterns of the requests and which data items are waiting by the current requests (e.g., by sampling or by asking the mobile clients to periodically generate request reports to the server), it is still not easy to determine an optimal schedule to broadcast the data items so that all the requests can be served before their deadlines or the number of deadline missing requests can be minimized.

To solve the problem, different approaches have been proposed to select the data items for broadcast. One of the most common approaches is based on the access frequencies of the data items [5,9,10] in which it is assumed that the data requirements of the requests from a mobile client have locality. It is expected that the broadcast of "hot" data items will serve more client requests and these data items are given higher priorities for broadcast.

In the AVI approaches, both the access frequencies and avi of the data items will be considered in selecting the data items.

3.1.1 Access Frequencies (AF)

In this approach, each data item is assigned an access score based on its access frequency. The statistics can be obtained by sampling or by asking the mobile clients to generate access reports periodically to the server. In the calculation of access scores, we use a method similar to the EWMA as suggested in [10]. The EWMA method uses a weighed moving average to calculate the access scores of the data items. It gives highest weight to the data items currently requested and the weights assigned to the previously requested data items tail off as they become aged. Data items requested in the current cycle has a weight of one; and they age by a factor α ($\alpha<1$) for each successive cycle. The final access score of a data item is obtained by summing up of all its scores in each broadcast cycle and then normalized through dividing the sum of all the weights used such as:

$$f_{x,n} = (f_{x,n} + \alpha f_{x,n1} + \alpha^2 f_{x,n2} + \ldots + \alpha^{nl} f_{x,1}) / S \qquad (2)$$

where S is the sum of the weights $(1 + \alpha + \alpha^2 + \ldots + \alpha^{n-1})$

3.1.2 Static AVI Approach (SAVI)

Basically, there are two ways to include the avi of data items into the AVI approaches. The first one is a static approach in which a fixed bandwidth, defined in terms of number of data items, is reserved for the data items in each data group based on the *avi* value of the data group. The selection of data items from a data group is then based on their access scores. The second approach is a dynamic approach in which a weighting factor, based on the *avi* of the data items, is included in the calculation of the access score for each data item.

In the Static AVI approach, the selection of data items for broadcast is divided into two steps. Firstly, the broadcast cycle is divided into n partitions, C_1 to C_n, where n is the number of data groups in the database. B_i is the size of partition C_i. The value of B_i is defined according to the value of avi_i. It is defined to be proportional to $1/avi_i$. A larger B_i will be assigned to the data group with a smaller avi_i.

$$B_i = DS \times (\frac{\frac{1}{avi_i}}{\sum\limits_{j=1}^{k} \frac{1}{avi_j}}) \times \frac{S_i}{DB} \qquad\qquad (3)$$

where k is the number of data groups in the system. DS is the size of a broadcast cycle, DB is the size of the database and S_i is the size of the data group i. All of them are defined in terms of number of data items.

After the bandwidth to be assigned to a data group has been determined, the selection of the data items from a data group will be based on their access scores. The data item with a higher score will be selected first until the bandwidth (the value of B) assigned to the data group has been filled up.

In the SAVI, the data items having shorter avi will have a higher chance to be selected for broadcast. The purpose is to maintain their validity in the client caches Since these item become invalid quicker. It is expected that this approach can improve the client cache hit rate can be improved.

3.1.3 Dynamic AVI Approach

According to the above equation, if the avi of the data groups are very different, the bandwidth (in terms of the number of data items to be selected from that group) assigned to the data groups will also be very different. It is possible that the bandwidth allocated to a data group with a very large avi will be very small especially when the length of the broadcast cycle is short. Thus, only a few data items can be selected from this group for broadcast in each broadcast cycle even though the access scores of the data items in that group are very high comparing with the data items in the other groups which have a much smaller avi.

In the Dynamic AVI approach, the above problem is solved as the bandwidth allocated to each data group is not fixed. In the selection of data items for broadcast, both the avi of different data groups and the access frequencies of the data items will be considered at the *same time*. They are used to calculate a final access score for a data item, D_i:

$$Score(D_i) = f(D_i) \times (1 + (\frac{\frac{1}{avi_i}}{\sum\limits_{j=1}^{k} \frac{1}{avi_j}})^w) \times \frac{S_i}{DB} \qquad\qquad (4)$$

where $f(D_i)$ is a function which is used to calculate the access score of the data item D_i based on its access frequency from the mobile clients and w is a tunable parameter to define the weighting (importance) of the avi of the data items as compared with the access frequency function $f(D_i)$.

3.2 Broadcast Skipping

If a data item has been broadcast in the last broadcast cycle, it may not be necessary to broadcast it again in the current broadcast cycle if it is still valid at the end of the current cycle. The new requests still can find a valid version of the data item in the client caches if the data item has been cached in the client caches in the previous broadcast cycles. This technique, which we call it *broadcast skipping*, can be exploited to save bandwidth by reducing unnecessary broadcast.

However, if a data item has not been cached at a mobile client, the use of the broadcast skipping may cause the requests from the mobile client to wait for a long period of time as their data items may be skipped in the current broadcast cycle. To prevent this, we stipulate that a data item will be skipped for broadcast only if there is no request waiting for it:

```
For each data group
    Number of selected data item from the data group = 0
    While number of selected data item from the data group <
        no of data item to be selected from the data group Do
```

Get the data item with highest score from the unselected data item set
If   ((the completion time of this broadcast cycle –
       last broadcast time of the data item) >
              Avi of the data item) or
       (the number of requesting waiting for the data item > 0)
       Select the data item into the broadcast data item set
       Number of selected data item increment by one
Endif
Remove the data item from the unselected data item set
End While
End For

4 Performance Study

4.1 Simulation Model

Figure 1 depicts the model of the mobile computing system used in our simulation experiments. It consists of an information server and a number of mobile clients. The mobile clients are connected through a wireless network to the information server which maintains a database to record different real-time information of the external environment. It is assumed that the data items in the database are classified into N data item groups based on their avi. The data items belonging to the same group will have the same *avi* value.

The information server is connected directly to a number of update processes which generate updates to refresh the validity of the data items in the database. It is assumed that each update process is responsible for the update of the data items in a data group. An update randomly selects a data item in the group to update. The creation time of the update will also be recorded in the data item. The generation of the updates is periodic.

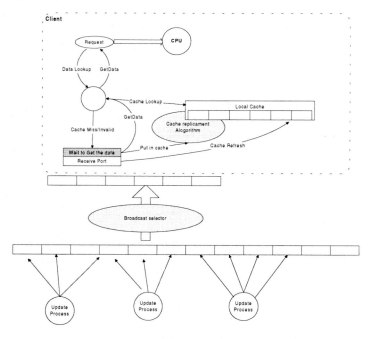

Figure 1. Model of the Mobile Computing System

The information server broadcasts data items from the database one by one until the end of a broadcast cycle. Then, it starts another broadcast cycle immediately. The selection of data items is performed by the broadcast selector in which a broadcast selection approach is implemented.

It is assumed that each request requires access to one data item. After the completion of a request, the mobile client will generate the next request after a think time. A client cache is maintained at each mobile client. In processing a request, the cache of the mobile client will be searched first. If the required data item is found in the cache and it is valid, the request will access the data item at the client cache and will be served immediately by the CPU of the mobile client. If the required data item is not in the cache or the data item at client cache is invalid, the request will be blocked until the required data item is being broadcast. After getting the required data item, the request will be processed by the CPU. After the request is served, the data item will also be put in the cache and hence it will be available for future requests. If the cache is full, a cache replacement algorithm will be invoked to free some space for the incoming data item. In our model, we use a modified version of Least Recent Used (I-LRU) for cache replacement. In I-LRU, the invalid data items will be selected for replacement first. If all the data items are valid, the original LRU principle will be used to select the data items. Note that if the data item, which is being broadcast, also exists in the cache, the copy in the cache will be refreshed by the new version.

It is assumed that the requests from a mobile client have locality in the references to data items. The locality of a mobile client is defined by two variables, *DataRange* and *AccessProbability*. *DataRange* defines the set of hot data items of a mobile client. *AccessProbability* defines the access probability of the mobile client on the hot data items. Each client has a different set of hot data items and the hot data items of different clients are evenly distributed among different data groups in the database.

4.2 Model Parameters
The following lists the model parameters and their baseline values:

Parameters	Baseline values
Broadcast cycle length	200 data items
Database size	4000 data items
Number of data item groups	4
Avi of the group 1 data items	350 sec
Avi of the group 2 data items	750 sec
Avi of the group 3 data items	1400 sec
Avi of the group 4 data items	2800 sec
Number of mobile clients	400
Broadcast bandwidth	18kbps
Size of a data item	1.8kbit
CPU service time for a request	1.0 – 5.0 ms (uniformly distributed)
Think time	0 second
Cache size	25 data items
Weighting factor, α, for calculating access frequency	0.5
w, weighting factor for the DAVI	1
Proportion of hot data items	0.001
Access probability	0.8
Drop period	7.5 sec

4.3 Performance Measures
We use the following four performance measures in our experiments:

R_R : mean response time of a request
D_R : dropped rate

C_H : cache hit rate
C_I : cache invalid rate

D_R is defined as the number of dropped requests divided by the total number of requests generated. C_H is defined as the number of requests, which requesting data items are located in the client caches at the arrival time of the requests and are valid, divided by the total number of requests generated. C_I is defined as the number of requests, which required data items are in the client caches but are invalid, divided by the sum of the number of cache hit and the number cache invalid.

4.4 Results and Discussions

In this section, we report the performance of the avi approaches. Our simulation program is implemented in CSIM [3]. Due to the limitation of space, we cannot include all the tested performance results. In the following sub-sections, we only show their performance at difference broadcast cycles, avi values and data groups. We have tested the performance of the avi approaches under different deadline constraints of the requests and client cache sizes. The results are consistent with those shown in sections 4.4.1 and 4.4.2.

4.4.1 Impact of Broadcast Cycle Length

Figure 2 to Figure 5 show the results for the three broadcast approaches at different broadcast cycle lengths. In Figure 2 and Figure 3, it can be observed that the AVI approaches consistently give a better performance than the AF in terms of mean response time, R_R, and drop rate, D_R. Amongst the three approaches, SAVI gives the best performance. When we compare the performance of SAVI with AF, we can observe that R_R for SAVI is about 15% (e.g., R_R for AF is around 1.85 sec and R_R for SAVI is around 1.5 sec.) smaller than that for AF. D_R for the SAVI is also consistently about 4% smaller than that for the AF. Although the performance of DSAVI is not as good as SAVI, its R_R is also about 10% smaller than that for AF when the broadcast length is smaller than 75 data items.

The better performance of the AVI approaches, especially SAVI, is due to higher cache hit rate, C_H, and smaller cache invalid rate, C_I, as can be observed in Figure 4 and Figure 5. The lower C_H for AF is due to higher C_I as can be observed in Figure 5. In DAVI and SAVI, due to the additional consideration given to the avi of the data items in selecting the data items for broadcast, the data items with smaller avi values will have higher chances to broadcast than the data items with larger avi values. Thus, the validity of the data items in the client caches can be better maintained. As shown in Figure 5, C_I for the SAVI is almost zero. Although the cache invalid rate for AF is also very small, however, a few percent decrease in cache invalid rate can greatly improve the system performance as the access delay for cache data items is much shorter than the access delay for data broadcast. These results confirm our belief that including the factor of the avi of the data items in the broadcast selection approaches can significantly improve the overall system performance.

When we compare the performance of SAVI with DAVI as in Figures 2 to 6, it can be seen that the performance of SAVI is better than DAVI especially when the broadcast cycle length is long. Although the DAVI approach has more freedom in choosing data items for broadcast, it is difficult to define what should be the contribution of the avi of the data items in calculating the score for a data item as compared with the access frequencies of the data items. As observed in Figure 4, when the broadcast cycle is very small (e.g., the broadcast cycle length is smaller than 25), the performance of DAVI is marginally better than SAVI. It is because if the broadcast cycle length is very small, the bandwidth (defined in terms of number of data items) assigned to a data group will be very small especially for the data group with a large avi. Thus, a "hot" data item may not be selected for broadcast even though its access score is very high. Thus, the performance of SAVI is affected. This effect is smaller when the broadcast cycle length is increases.

4.4.2 Impact of avi Values and Number of Data Groups

In this set of experiments, we increase the avi of the four data groups to be 700sec, 1400sec, 2800sec and 5600sec. The impact of the broadcast cycle length on the performance of the three approaches is presented in Figures 6 to 8. It can be seen from Figures 6 and 7 that the performance of the three broadcast approaches is similar. It is because when the avi of the data items are large, the cache invalid problem is less serious and the probability of finding an invalid data item at the client cache is low. Thus, C_I for the three broadcast approaches are about the same and approach zero as shown in Figure 8. C_I for AF is slightly greater than that for DAVI and SAVI.

The impact of the number of data groups on the performance of the broadcast approaches is shown in Figures 9 to 11. (When the number of data group is varied, the avi of the new data groups are defined based on largest and smallest avi values used in the baseline setting. For example, when two data groups are used, their avi are 350 sec and 2800 sec.). Consistent with the results in section 4.4.1, the performance of the AVI approaches is better than the AF and SAVI gives the best performance as shown in Figure 9 and Figure 10. Again, the better performance of SAVI is due to low cache invalid rate as shown in Figure 11. C_I for SAVI remains zero but C_I for AF is more than 2.5% when the number of data group is two. The poor performance of AF when two data groups are used is due to large number of data items having a small avi value. Thus, the cache invalid problem becomes more serious.

5 Conclusions

The importance of mobile computing systems has resulted in much research in this area recently. An important scenario which has not received adequate treatment in the literature is the case where the mobile clients requests real-time information from the information server. Although the broadcast approach has been shown to be a good choice as it can utilize the limited bandwidth more effectively, we have shown in this paper that new strategies need to be devised when the temporal constraints on the validity of the data are considered. We have developed a data model which considers the temporal properties of the data items explicitly, and have designed new data selection algorithms using the concept of absolute validity interval based on how the users use the data items, their update periods and their dynamic properties. In these approaches, the selection of data items for broadcast to satisfy the requests from the mobile clients consider both the access frequencies of the data items and their avi which characterize their validity. The purpose of including the avi of the data items in selecting the data items is to increase the cache hit probability and thus reduce the access delay for the data items. At the same time, it can eliminate the requirement of invalidation message to invalidate the cache data items whenever the value of the data items have been updated in the database server.

Two AVI approaches are proposed: static and dynamic. The simulation results show that by incorporating the avi of the data items in the selection of data for broadcast with the dynamic and static approaches, the system performance is significantly better than just considering the access frequencies of the data items. SAVI gives a better performance comparing with DAVI as it can maintain the validity of the data items in the client cache in a better way. However, if the broadcast cycle is very small, DAVI may be able to give a better performance.

References

1. Acharya, S., Franklin, M., Zdonik, S., "Dissemintanig Updates on Broadcast Disks, in Proceedings of 22nd VLDB Conference, India, 1996.
2. Acharya, S., Franklin, M., Zdonik, S., "Balancing Push and Pull for Data Broadcast", in *Proceedings of ACM SIGMOD*, Tucson, Arizona, May 1997.
3. *CSIM 18 User Guide*, Mesquite Software, Inc. (URL: http://www.mesquite.com/ 1_intro.html).

4. Chan, B.Y.L, Si, A. and Leong, H.V, "Cache management for mobile databases: design and valuation", in *Proceedings of the 14th International Conference on Data Engineering*, pages 54-63, February 1998.
5. Datta, A., Celik, A., Kim, J. and VanderMeer, D.E., "Adaptive Broadcast Protocol to Support Power Conservant Retrieval by Mobile Users*", in Proceedings of 13th International Conference on Data Engineering*, 1997.
6. Hu, Q. and Lee, D.L., "Adaptive Cache Invalidation Methods in Mobile Environments", *Proc. 6th IEEE Intl. Symposium on High Performance Distributed Computing Environments*, 1997.
7. Imielinski, T. and Badrinath, B.R., "Mobile Wireless Computing: Challenges in Data Management," *Communications of the ACM*, vol. 37, no. 10, Oct. 1994.
8. Leong, H.V. and Si, A, "Data broadcasting strategies over multiple unreliable wireless channels", in *Proceedings of the 4th International Conference on Information and Knowledge Management*, pages 96-104, November 1995.
9. Leong, H.V., Si, A., Chan, B.Y.L., "Caching Data over a Broadcast Channel", in *Mobile Communications*, ed. J.L. Encarnacao and J.M. Rabaey, Chapman and Hall, 1996.
10. Leong, H.V. and Si, A., "Database Caching over the Air-Storage", The Computer Journal. Volume 40, number 7, pages 401-415, 1997.
11. Pitoura, E. and Bhargava, B. "Dealing with Mobility: Issues and Research Challenges," *Technical Report*, Purdue Univ., Nov. 1993.
12. Pitoura, E. and Samaras, G., *Data Management for Mobile Computing*, Kluwer Academic Publishers, 1997.
13. Xuan, P., O. Gonzalez, J. Fernandez & Ramamritham, K., "Broadcast on Demand: Efficient and Timely Dissemination of Data in Mobile Environments", in *Proceedings of 3rd IEEE Real-Time Technology Application Symposium*, 1997.

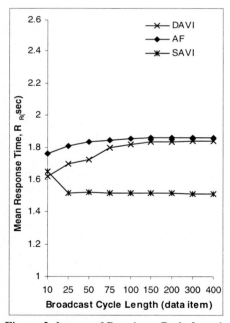

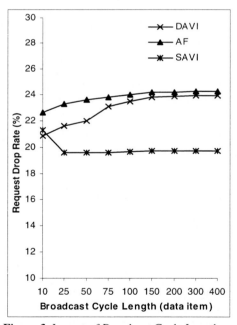

Figure 2. Impact of Broadcast Cycle Length on Mean Response Time

Figure 3. Impact of Broadcast Cycle Length on Drop Rate

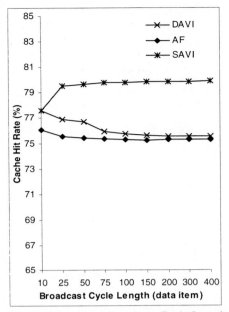

Figure 4. Impact of Broadcast Cycle Length on Cache Hit Rate

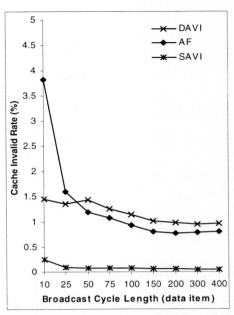

Figure 5. Impact of Broadcast Cycle Length on Cache Invalid Rate

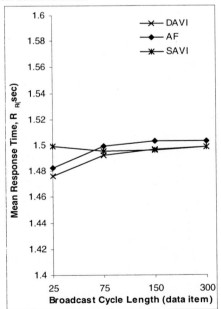

Figure 6. Impact of Broadcast Cycle Length on Mean Response Time

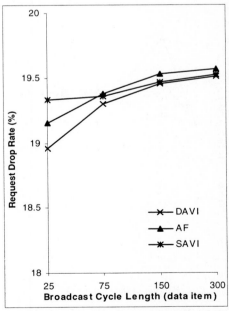

Figure 7. Impact of Broadcast Cycle Length on Drop Rate

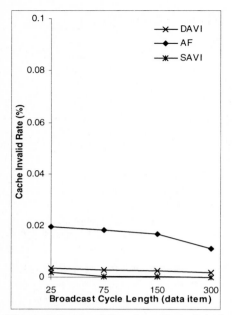

Figure 8. Impact of Broadcast Cycle Length on Cache Invalid Rate

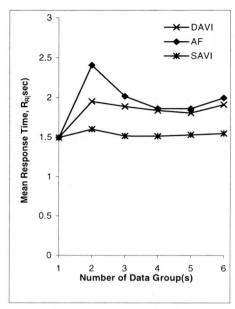

Figure 9. Impact of Number of Data Groups on Mean Response Time

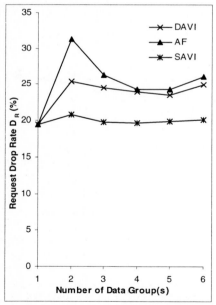

Figure 10. Impact of Number of Data Groups on Request Drop Rate

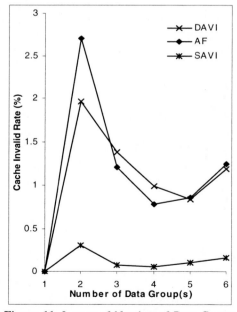

Figure 11. Impact of Number of Data Groups on Cache Invalid Rate

Web Content Delivery to Heterogeneous Mobile Platforms

Martin Gaedke, Michael Beigl, Hans-Werner Gellersen, Christian Segor

Telecooperation Office (TecO), University of Karlsruhe
Vincenz-Prießnitz-Str. 1, 76131 Karlsruhe, GERMANY
Ph. +49 (721) 6902-79, Fax +49 (721) 6902-16

{gaedke, michael, hwg, segor}@teco.edu

Abstract. It is widely acknowledged that information such as web content should be adapted for mobile platforms to account for restrictions in mobile environments. As emerging mobile platforms such as different kinds of Personal Digital Assistant (PDA) tend to vary largely in their capabilities, we suggest that adaptation should be platform-specific. Common approaches for content adaptation are automated conversion and explicit specification of adapted content, with a trade-off between quality and development/maintenance effort. As alternative avoiding this trade-off, we propose a simple object-oriented framework for content adaptation. To facilitate the use of this framework in the Web, we base our approach on the object-oriented WebComposition model and its XML-based implementation WCML. We apply our object-oriented approach to an example application to demonstrate how object-oriented specification of platform-adapted content reduces development/maintenance effort.

Information Access from Mobile Devices

Information access from mobile devices has to take a range of restrictions into account, which exists in mobile computing environments in comparison to desktop environments. Both, properties of wireless networks and of mobile devices have to be considered. Regarding mobile devices, most notably screen real estate, computing power and power consumption are relevant. In this article, we refer to Personal Digital Assistants (PDA) with their largely varying properties to motivate the need to adapt information for delivery to mobile devices. The proposed solution though does not merely apply to PDAs but to heterogeneous mobile devices in general.

Several restrictions influence whether and how information can be presented on PDA devices. Each of these restrictions has to be taken into account when building content that should be delivered to and viewed on a PDA, or other mobile devices. Below, the most important restrictions are discussed.

- *Power Consumption.* Many researchers have indicated that battery live and power consumption are an essential constraint that mobile devices struggle with; special care has to be taken that applications save these important resource. For example, power consuming output methods such as audio should be avoided on mobile devices.
- *Computing Power.* Mobile devices usually have less computing power than stationary computers; computing power also varies largely among PDAs or more generally among mobile devices. Therefore, content requiring a lot of computing power, for example compressed video, is usually not suited for display on PDAs.
- *Display Properties.* PDAs and other mobile devices have very little screen real estate compared to desktop computers. Furthermore, display properties among different PDAs vary too a large extent. Table 1 shows a comparison of resolution, size and colour depth supported by different PDAs. This table indicates clearly a quite impressive difference of the display possibilities of different devices: the resolution ranges from 160x98 to 640x480 (factor 20), the size from 3,3x2,1 cm to 13x8 cm (factor 15), and the colour depth from 1 bit grey scale displays to TFT with 16 Millions of colours.

Table 1. Display Properties

Device	Display resolution	Display Size	Capability
Franklin Rex	160x98	3,3x2,1 cm	2 grey scale
3Com PalmPilot	160x160	6x6 cm	2 grey scale
Nokia Communicator	640x200	11,43x3,6 cm	8 grey scale
Psion 5	640x240	5,1x13,5 cm	16 grey scale
WindowsCE PalmPC	240x320$^+$	Ca. 8x6 cm	Grey scale
Windows CE Handheld	640x240	Ca. 16x6 cm	Grey scale or colour
Apple Newton 2000	480x320	12,98x8,32 cm	16 grey scale
Toshiba Libretto	640x480	6,1''	16,7 Mio colours

$^+$ Except Casio PA-2400 Cassiopeia 420x240

- *Communication.* Beside the characteristics of the mobile device itself, restrictions in the communication infrastructure are quite important. Table 2 gives a general overview of different options for wireless communication and their characteristics. Information to be delivered to mobile devices may have to be adapted to bandwidth availability and transmission cost.

Table 2. Communication Properties

Type of Communication	Connection Cost	Bandwidth
I/R Communication	-	115 kbit
Radio Communication	-	2 Mbit
GSM Modem/Phone	1,20$/60sec (in Germany)	9,6 kbit

The above consideration of constraints that apply to information delivery to mobile devices shows the need for adaptation to more than one parameter. For example, web content may have to be adapted regarding the choice of media, the layout of pages, and the overall volume of data, depending on computing power, display properties and available bandwidth.

The remainder of this paper is structured as follows. In the next section, we will discuss two common approaches for adaptation of information, more specifically web content, to mobile platforms. In section 3, we will propose a new approach based on an object-oriented framework for content adaptation. Section 3 also introduces an XML-based markup language based on WebComposition, an object-oriented model for web applications. Finally, section 4 illustrates an example-application applying the framework

Approaches to Web Content Adaptation for Mobile Platforms

In the remainder of the paper, we discuss information access from mobile devices in the context of the World-Wide Web as primary information medium. The World-Wide Web as such has a very simple model for content delivery to clients and does not provide for adaptation to different clients or to clients on mobile platforms in particular. HTML as dominant document type does only support the adaptation of image resolution to low-resolution browsers. For further adaptation of web content, in particular with respect to clients on mobile platforms, two different approaches are common:

- Automated conversion
- Explicit specification of adapted content

Automated Conversion. This approach is based on the use of filters for conversion of web content to a presentation suited for mobile devices. *PocketWeb*, the first PDA browser for the WWW presented in 1994 at WWW-2 was based on this approach, for example to convert images to bitmap in adaptation to the capabilities of the first Newton MessagePad [4]. In PocketWeb, adaptation is primarily based on display properties. In contrast, *MobileWWW* and *MobileODBC* [1] adapt the transmitted content volume automatically to the available bandwidth, based on measuring the QoS of the available network and comparing it to the user preferences regarding download-time and maximal costs. According to these preferences the content was compressed with loss for audio, video and pictures and then transferred.

Automated conversion and adaptation of content is quite advantageous for creators of applications or content, because in an optimal case no additional effort has to be taken to adapt content for mobile devices. The disadvantage of the approach is that the semantics of the content is not taken into account. While automated conversion may yield acceptable results in many cases, it is not reliable and can lead to delivery of content that is not useful anymore. For example, compression can lead to unreadable output of graphics that are indispensable for the understanding of displayed content. In addition, after automated conversion, content media may be scaled appropriately but still the content layout may prove awkward, for example forcing the user to scroll on the small display.

Specification of Adapted Content. As automated conversion is often unacceptable, it is quite common to explicitly specify adapted content for mobile devices. For example, in ESPRIT project MILLION, mobile information access to a web-based application was realised by specifying HTML documents following style guidelines for HTML delivery to a PDA [7]. Instead of style guidelines, specific description languages have been proposed for content delivery to small mobile devices. These efforts are driven by large consortia, for example the WAP forum proposing the *Wireless Markup Language* (WML) [9], and the W3C consortium suggesting *Compact HTML* (CHTML) [10]. With a language like WML or CHTML, content can be designed in a way optimised for mobile devices. This is a good solution for content and applications created exclusively for one class of mobile devices. The solution degrades though, if the goal is to gain access from heterogeneous platforms, for example from desktop browsers and different kinds of mobile browsers, because then all content has to be build several times (for each type of browser, and in addition maybe even for different communication bandwidth).

Both proposed methods, automated conversion and special language, have their trade-offs regarding content development for heterogeneous mobile platforms. In the following section, we propose to use object-oriented techniques for specification of adapted content, aimed at reduced effort for building and maintaining content for heterogeneous platforms.

Object-Oriented Development of Web Content

An Object-Oriented Framework for Content Adaptation

We propose an object-oriented approach to provide information for heterogeneous browser platforms. The approach aims at provision of content adapted to specific browsers but uses object-oriented concepts to avoid replicated content definition. The idea is based on the well-known model-view concept (or *Observer* pattern [2]) to maintain different views of the same content. In this case, different views being content presentations are adapted to specific browser platforms. Besides model-view, the idea is to capture commonalties among different views in generalised views, and to apply object-oriented inheritance to derive specifie views.

While it is straightforward to devise an object-oriented model or framework for the given problem, it is unfortunately not easily applied to web-based information delivery. The Web implementation model is based on the notion of resources, which have a unique address, and which are delivered on request to clients, where they can be rendered in a browser. Resources can be static and file-based, or dynamically generated from a script. They are meant to capture specific rather self-contained chunks of information. While the simplicity of this web implementation model largely contributed to the phenomenal success of the Web as information medium, it is very limiting from a software engineering perspective. It does especially not provide support for basic engineering concerns such as composition, reuse, and modifiability. Resources are both too coarse-grained and too specific to facilitate the construction of frameworks like the one suggested above. The coarse granularity of resources makes it impossible to implement a separation of concerns, for instance to separate content from layout. The inherent specificity of resources implies that there is no support for generalisation and hence no support for reuse-by-inheritance.

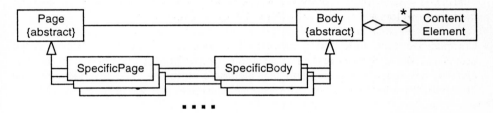

Fig. 1. Object-oriented framework for content adaptation to different platforms

In order to facilitate the use of the above-described framework, we build our approach on WebComposition, an object-oriented model for web applications. In the following subsection, the model is described briefly, for more detail see [3]. Following this, an XML-based implementation is introduced.

The WebComposition Model

WebComposition defines an object-oriented component model, which abstracts from the web implementation model. The Component Model is based on components as a uniform concept for modelling web entities at arbitrary granularity and level of abstraction. In contrast to resources, components are not fixed to a certain grain size but designed to capture design artefacts at their natural granularity. For example, in contrast to resources, components can capture a content unit as design artefact independent of a web page, which itself is a separate design artefact. Support of arbitrary grain-size means that components may model web entities as small as individual links or layout resource fragments. Of course, a component may also be associated with a complete resource, for instance an HTML document or a script generating a web document.

Components can reference other components to model aggregation (*has-part*) or specialisation (*inherits-from*). For example, a component modelling a page can reference components modelling parts of that page; and a component modelling a navigation structure can reference the components that model the involved links and anchors. By means of a special reference type, components can reference so-called prototypes components from which they inherit state and behaviour. Any component can act as prototype, following the prototype-instance model as opposed to a class-based object-oriented model. In the prototype-instance model, there is no distinction between instances and classes, and hence no distinction between the *relationships is-instance-of* and *is-subtype-of* [8]. We find the prototype-instance model naturally suited for web application modelling, because many web entities, namely those modelling content, are rather unique, and because prototyping reflects the copy-and-modify type of reuse typically applied in web development. Components may be abstract, i.e. function only as prototype for specific components. Abstract components are one mechanism to realise code sharing among objects. Another mechanism for code sharing is to allow multiple references on the same component, e.g. for a component modelling an HTML fragment that is replicated in multiple HTML pages. Sharing is fundamental for reuse but also for maintainability as it helps keeping modifications local.

Components have state and behaviour. The state is defined by a list of typed properties (name-value-pairs). For example, a component modelling an HTML element has properties relating to that element's attributes. The behaviour can be influenced by a set of services. All components have to provide at least a persistency service and an implementation service. The persistency service allows the component state to read from and to write to persistent storage. The implementation service is responsible for mapping the component state to a representation in the Web, for instance a mapping to HTML code or to script code.

General WebComposition Implementation Concepts

The WebComposition component model is an abstraction from the web implementation model, facilitating the object-oriented description of web applications or frameworks in terms of components. The implementation of the model is based on two concepts: a *component store* for persistent storage of the model to enable lifecycle-spanning maintenance of components, and automated *resource generation* from the component model. Both concepts are supported by the principle that each component has to provide a persistency service and an implementation service, as described above.

- **Component Store.** The component store can be implemented in a standard RDBMS, as the prototype-instance model can be mapped in a straightforward way to tables and relationships. Access to stored components is implemented in a transaction-oriented protocol supporting checkin, checkout, lock, unlock, set and get operations. Stored components are uniquely identified through a UUID and a version number. Access to stored components would typically be through engineering tools such as property editors and GUI builders.
- **Resource Generator.** The resource generator creates resources from the component model of a web application. The mapping is facilitated by the

components' implementation service. Starting from a root component, the implementation service is invoked top-down from composite components to atomic components. The resource generator can perform both a complete installation and an incremental update of a web application. For a complete installation, the resource generator proceeds top-down through the component hierarchy, top-down making directories, opening files and filling files with code. For incremental code generation, the resource generator makes use of the component store's revision control. In this process, it generates those resources that contain components that have been modified. As resources themselves are represented by components, component dependencies can be evaluated to identify dependent resources.

An XML-based Implementation of WebComposition

In this section, we describe an open implementation based on the object-oriented WebComposition approach. Our main goal is to provide a possibility, that enables component developer to describe and even exchange components whatever type of component store is in use. Furthermore, by making available a system-independent description language for WebComposition components mobile-device companies could support a well-known set of layout components that ideally solve display limitations of their devices.

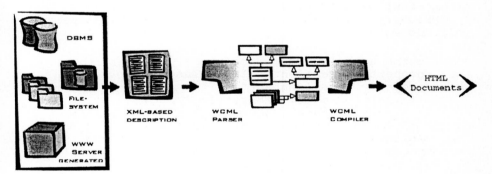

Fig. 2. Generating Components

This goal is achieved by using the eXtended Markup Language (XML) developed by the Standard Generalized Markup Language (SGML) working group of the W3C [11]. XML allows the definition for a tag-based textual format for semantic mark-up of documents or data. Parsers are widely available for almost any important platform, like Unix and WindowsNT, providing the web application or the content. Beside the fact, that we prefer the Web as application platform, the semantic mark-up enables a resource generator to create content even for non HTML-enabled devices (e.g. Mobile Phones may receive SMS messages).

Turning back to the WebComposition approach we can say that a set of components described in an XML-based language is equivalent to the "component store". This idea is shown in figure 2.

A resource generator accesses a component store by an URI and retrieves a description of the components that need to be transformed into the implementation model of the target system (the Web implementation model). The components and their states represented by their properties are described in an XML-based language, called WebComposition Markup Language. This view on the WebComposition approach doesn't assume a client-server content delivery model, as shown in the above figure.

WebComposition Markup Language

The WebComposition Markup Language (WCML) describes an XML vocabulary for WebComposition that allows the definition of (web-) components, properties, and relationships between these components.

The following code shows a typical structure of a WCML document with some components:

```
<wcml>
  <component uuid='CVersion'>
    <property name='content'>Version 1.122.58</property>
  </component>

  <component uuid='CVersionNice'>
      <property name='fontstyle' value='B'/>
      <property name='content'>
        < <refprop name=' fontstyle '/>  >
          <refprop name='content' from='Cversion'/>
        </ <refprop name=' fontstyle '/> >
      </property>
  </component>

  . . .

</wcml>
```

Each component is identified by a universally unique identifier (UUID); in our example the UUIDs *CVersion* and *CVersionNice*. The current state of *CVersion* is defined by the value of the 'content'-property. The property is evaluated by the resource generator to create the presentation of the component. It is the representative for the presentation interface/service described in the WebComposition approach. The second component *CVersionNice* references the *CVersion* component (by referencing the 'content'-property with the *refprop*-tag) and adds layout information to the content. In this code-sharing example the generation of the component *CVersion* would be "Version 1.122.58" and *CVersionNice* would result in "**Version 1.122.58**".

Components can be derived from other components based on the prototype-instance model. The description of a prototype-instance relationship is given by the *prototype*-tag. A component referencing a prototype-component possesses all prototypes and properties of the prototype-component, which may be redefined by the latest declaration of a property. The following code-segment shows a component deriving from the *CVersionNice*-component:

```
<component uuid='CversionNice2'>
   <prototype is='CversionNice'/>
   <property name='fontstyle' value='I'/>
</component>
```

The *CversionNice2* derives the 'content'- and the 'fontstyle'-property. By declaring an own 'fontstyle'-property, the value of the derived 'fontstyle'-property is redefined. The presentation of the new component would be: "*Version 1.122.58*". This example shows the difference between class-based and prototype-instance inheritance. Following the prototype-instance model, a component may be an instance (like *CVersionNice*), but may also serve as prototype describing properties for an inheriting component.

In summary it has be pointed out that an XML-based description language allows to exchange components between different operating system. XML based upon proven SGML technology is rigorous in terms of *well-formed* and *valid* documents and therefore it is easy to parse XML-documents, which is important for making good use of WCML. WCML abstracts from the actual Component Store in use. This abstraction extends the WebComposition approach by making the actual Component Store unnecessary, giving the WebComposition approach more flexibility.

The following section shows how to use WCML to provide access to a web application for different PDAs.

Example application

In this section, we will apply the component model as described in section 0 to support different views to the content of an application. This example will show how to develop an ideally adapted web application for mobile devices. We also demonstrate how prototyping helps extending an application for additional devices.

General description for implementing the Login-Screens with WCML

Mobile device users suffer from display limitations and bandwidth restriction as shown in section 1. The example shows a typical login screen for accessing the TravelAssistant-System, an information system, which supports customers with travel planning like flight schedules etc. The use of WCML will only deal with the Login-Screen, but the results can easily be adopted for other pages.

The following figure shows the desktop version of the Login-Screen displayed for a 20"-Monitor.

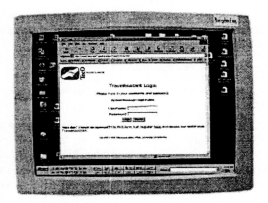

Fig. 3. Login-Screen for 20"-Monitor

The page contains five major elements. The top left element shows an image of the system provider and the applications version number. The middle of the page presents the application name, followed by a form and some text explaining what the user has to do to access the information system. User new to system may register to get instant access. A copyright notice is given at the end of the page.

Following this scenario and reusing some existing components by code sharing the following code segment gives a component description for the above figure.

```
<component uuid='CDesktopContent'>
  <property name='image' value='tecologo.gif'/>
  <property name='version'>Version 1.122.58</property>
  <property name='content'>
    <refprop name='content' from='CLogo'
     prototype='CDesktopContent'/>
    <refprop name='content' from='CApplicationName'/>
    <refprop name='content' from='CForm'/>
    <refprop name='content' from='CRegister'/>
    <refprop name='content' from='CCopyright'/>
  </property>
</component>
```

The CDesktopContent-component references the Logo-component, which itself derives the image and version properties from the CDesktopContent-component (prototype element in *refprop*-tag). The next four tags reuse the content of the existing components by simple code sharing without inheritance.

The following component is used for displaying the Login-page on a WindowsCE device. To avoid scrolling forced by the half size display resolution the important components are reordered from left to right. The possibility to register from a mobile device will not be supported. The ordering is done by adding simple HTML-code

(Table-tags) to the existing component references. In addition, the image-property value is changed to a WindowsCE suitable image filename.

```
<component uuid='CWindowsCEContent'>
  <property name='image' value='tecologo256Color.gif'/>
  <property name='version'>Version 1.122.58</property>
  <property name='content'>
    <table border="0" cellspacing="5"><tr><td>
      <refprop name='content' from='CLogo'
      prototype='CDesktopContent'/>
    </td><td>
      <refprop name='content' from="CApplicationName"/>
    </td><td>
      <refprop name='content' from="CForm"/>
    </td></tr></table>
    <refprop name='content' from="CCopyright"/>
  </property>
</component>
```

The result is shown in comparison to the Desktop page in the following figure:

Fig. 4. Login-Screen for WindowsCE device

Extending for low Bandwidth devices

In this last example, we will show how easily the model can be extended using existing components as prototypes. In case one needs to provide the WindowsCE page for access by low bandwidth, the following component uses the *CWindowsCEContent*-component as prototype but redefining the image-filename. The generator will create the same content (ordered from left to right), but linking to a picture of smaller size. The second (for Psion devices) and third (for Pilot devices) components also reuse the code by prototyping, but linking to images capable by the devices. Due to the small display of the Pilot, the image is cut out of the page.

```
<component uuid='CWindowsCEContentLowBandwidth'>
  <prototype is='CWindowsCEContent'/>
  <property name='image'
   value='tecologoCELowBandwidth.gif'/>
</component>

<component uuid='CPsion'>
  <prototype is='CWindowsCEContent'/>
  <property name='image' value='tecologo16Gray.gif'/>
</component>

<component uuid='CPilot'>
  <prototype is='CWindowsCEContent'/>
  <property name='image' value=''/>
</component>
```

This example shows how easily the model of a web application can be extended to support different platforms. The content is reused on basis of inheritance facilitating further maintenance tasks.

Conclusion

In this paper, we have proposed an object-oriented approach to development of web content adapted to mobile platforms. Our approach is based on the observation even seemingly similar devices such as Personal Digital Assistants vary largely regarding constraints effecting content delivery. Further, it is based on the experience that automated conversion of web content in general does not yield satisfying results. The alternative to automated conversion is development of explicitly adapted content for each platform, which of course imposes replicated development effort, not to speak of the maintenance problems. To reduce the development and maintenance effort we propose to use an object-oriented framework based on the well-known model-view concept. This framework ensures, that content is only specified once and then referenced by different views which are optimised for the different target platforms.

While the proposed framework as such is straightforward, its application in the Web unfortunately is not, as the web implementation model does not support the required object-oriented concepts such as abstraction, delegation, and inheritance. To close this gap, we have applied the WebComposition model for which we have presented an XML-based implementation, the WebComposition Markup Language. This language enables object-oriented specification of web content that can be deployed to different platforms. For a small example application, we have demonstrated code reuse based on delegation, and extensibility based on inheritance.

References

[1] Beigl, M. MODBC - A Middleware for Accessing Databases from Mobile Computers. *Proceedings of 3rd Cabernet Plenary Workshop*, Rennes, France, 1997

[2] Gamma, E., Helm, R., Johnson, R. and Vlissides, J. *Design Patterns: Elements of Reusable Object-Oriented Software*, Addison-Wesley, 1994.

[3] Gellersen, H.-W., Wicke, R. and M. Gaedke. WebComposition: an object-oriented support system for the Web engineering lifecycle. In *Computer Networks and ISDN Systems 29 (1997)*, Special Issue on the 6th Intl. World-Wide Web Conference, Santa Clara, USA, April 1997, p. 1429-1437.

[4] Gessler, S. and Kotulla, A. PDAs as Mobile WWW Browsers. In *Computer Networks and ISDN Systems 28 (1995)*, Special Issue on the 2nd Intl. World-Wide Web Conference, Chicago, USA, Oct. 1994, p. 53-59

[5] Imielinski, T. and Badrinath, B. Mobile Wireless Computing. *In Communications of the ACM* No.37 (1994), p. 18-28

[6] Kristensen, A. Developing HTML based Web Applications. Workshop on Web Engineering (WebE 98), 7th Intl. World-Wide Web Conference, Brisbane, Australia, April 1998

[7] Lauff, M. and Gellersen, H.-W. Multimedia Client Implementation on Personal Digital Assistants. In *Proceedings of Interactive Distributed Multimedia Systems and Telecommunication Services (IDMS'97)*, Darmstadt, Sept. 1997, Lecture Notes in Computer Science, Springer-Verlag 1997

[8] Ungar, D. and Smith, R.B. Self: The Power of Simplicity. In *Proceedings of OOPSLA '87*, p. 227-242, 1987.

[9] WAP Forum. Wireless Application Protocol: Wireless Markup Language Specification, WAP Forum, 1998

[10] World-Wide Web Consortium (W3C). Compact HTML for Small Information Appliances, W3C NOTE 09-Feb-1998

[11] World-Wide Web Consortium. XML: eXtensible Markup Language. http://www.w3c.org/XML/

Dynamic Data Delivery in Wireless Communication Environments

Qinglong Hu[1], Dik Lun Lee[1], and Wang-Chien Lee[2]

[1] University of Science and Technology, Clear Water Bay, Hong Kong,
qinglong@cs.ust.hk dlee@cs.ust.hk,
[2] GTE Laboratories Incorporated, 40 Sylvan Road, Waltham, MA 02254,
wlee@gte.com

Abstract. Information broadcasting, caching of frequently accessed data, and pull-based data delivery are commonly used techniques to reduce data access time of wireless information services. Most of the studies in the literature focused either on individual technique or a combination of them with some restrictive assumptions. In this paper, we propose a dynamic data delivery model where these three techniques work together in an integrated manner. A particular feature of our model is that data are disseminated through various storage mediums according to the dynamically collected data access patterns. Performance evaluation of the model is conducted by simulation studies.

1 Introduction

A criterion often used to evaluate the data access efficiency of a mobile system is *access time* which is the average time from a mobile computer requests a data item until the data is received. To reduce access time in a mobile environment, three major classes of techniques, namely, caching, push-based information broadcast and pulled-based data delivery have been investigated in the literature [IVB94,AAFZ95,AFZ97,SRB97].

To reduce the disadvantages of the above three techniques and to achieve efficient information retrieval in a wireless communication environment, most frequently accessed data should be cached in the client, the less frequently accessed data subset is temporarily stored on the air (through broadcast channels), and the rest of the data can be pulled from the server via explicit client requests. Data caching and push-based data dissemination can alleviate pull-based request considerably, as most frequently access data can be retrieved either from the client cache or the broadcast channel. Since the client cache and wireless broadcast channel are both limited resources in a mobile environment and their efficiency depends heavily on the preciseness of the data set, data distribution should be managed carefully to achieve high utilization of the resources. The key point is to dynamically decide which subset of data should be cached, which subset should be broadcast on the air.

This paper investigates the methods to integrate data caching, information broadcast, and pull-based techniques to achieve efficient information dissemination by continuously adjusting the client cache and the broadcast schedule to match the access patterns. In mobile systems, the clients can either monitor the broadcast channel for the arrival of the desired data or issue a pull request to the server for the data and respectively, the server can either broadcast data according to broadcast schedule or broadcast pulled data instead. The clients manage the cache via traditional page replacement policy (i.e., LRU). The hot spot of the uncached data can be obtained by client monitoring the *cache misses*. Our simulation study shows that the access patterns can be accurately estimated and based on it the server can dynamically construct broadcast program to optimize system performance. The resulting performance is consistent with the ideal case in which the server knows the exact client access patterns and is better than pure pull-based data service.

Our work is based on the assumption that the server does not know the data access patterns, which is different from the work in [AAFZ95]. In [AAFZ95], Acharya et al assumed that the data access patterns are known and remain unchange. Therefore, a fixed broadcast schedule, which is organized according to the user access patterns, is repeated in every broadcast cycle. The cached data should be tailored according to the broadcast schedule in addition to the LRU policy: data set whose local probability of access is significantly greater than their broadcast frequency. By taking those two factors into consideration, Achaya et al [AAFZ95] developed a page replacement policy called HIX and showed that HIX is superior for caching in the broadcast systems compared with other schemes. [SRB97] investigated the dynamic adjustment of the hotspot for the broadcast program. However, data caching and multiple disks of different sizes and speeds for the broadcast program were not considered.

The rest of the paper is organized as follows. Section 2 proposes dynamic data dissemination methods. Section 3 describes the simulation model developed for the evaluation of the data delivery system. Section 4 presents experiments and the results derived from this model. Finally, Section 5 concludes the paper.

2 Dynamic Data Broadcast Scheduling

Our system model is based on the satellite broadcast scenario (i.e., one shared downlink channel for all the clients and an shared uplink channel for requests) and *asymmetric communication* (i.e., the downlink channel from server to clients has far more capacity than the reverse direction).

For pull-based data delivery, clients compete for the uplink channel to send the pull requests to the server. Once a client is allocated the uplink channel, it will occupy the channel until the service ends. Upon receipt of the pull request, the server broadcast the answer to the client. Pull-based data delivery can guarantee all requested data to be finally obtained. However, bandwidth may be wasted because the pulled pages are usually of interest to only one client[1]. With a large client population, the downlink channel can easily get congested with separate pulled pages. In addition, the server must be interrupted continuously to deal with client requests.

---

[1] Although, this problem is mitigated to some extent, by the factor that any page which is pulled by one client can be accessed on the broadcast channel by any other client.

The model extends the *broadcast disk* model proposed in [AFZ97]. The differences are that the client access patterns are unknown initially or can change with time. Therefore, client access patterns must be collected dynamically. Based on the access patterns, the server constructs the broadcast program.

Similar to [AFZ97], we assume that the server has limited throughput in handling client pull requests which is imitated by a finite queue in the server. The queue is serviced in a FIFO fashion and the service rate is determined by the pull bandwidth of the system. Whenever the queue is full, all clients are blocked and pull requests will be accepted by the server only when the queue has space available again. The request for a page that is already in the queue is dropped because the processing of the earlier message will also satisfy the new request.

In order to realize dynamical selection between push-based and pull-based data delivery, the complete broadcast schedule (i.e., a list of data identifiers and the cycle version), is broadcast at the beginning of each cycle. Each active client keeps on monitoring the schedules and retrieves the broadcast schedule into its cache[2]. Based on the schedules, the client can choose the optimal data delivery method. That is, if the desired data items will appear within a certain broadcast slots, then the client keeps on monitoring the broadcast channel; otherwise, the client issues a pull request to the server and monitors the channel for the arrival of the data item. The server determines the next data item for broadcast from either the broadcast program or the pull requests waiting in the queue. We adopt a *random slot* allocation scheme proposed in [AFZ97], in which before every page is broadcast, a coin weighted by the percentage of pull bandwidth is tossed and depending on the outcome, either the requested page at the head of the queue is broadcast or the regular broadcast program continues. If the queue is empty (i.e., no pull requests from the clients), the next candidate for broadcasting is a page from broadcast program despite that it is the turn for pulled pages. Therefore, the percentage of bandwidth allocated for pull requests is an upper bound.

To efficiently utilize the broadcast channel, the broadcast schedule is tailored according to data cached and pulled requests, it is the second hot spot besides the cached data. To improve the hit ratio of the cache, we adopt LRU-K scheme [EPW93] in the model. In LRU-K scheme, the cache management keeps track of the times of last K references to popular data items and selection is based on the past K hits history. In [HLL98] we show that HIX policy does worse than LRU-K police when dynamic broadcast programs are used in the system.

To be concentrated on the issues we like to address in this paper, we assuming that there are no updates either by the server or at the clients. As a result, issues such as cache invalidation which is closely related to data updates, are not discussed in the paper. Readers interested in this subject may refer to [BI94,HL98,WYC96].

---

[2] Notice that monitoring the schedules can be quite power consumption and is not flexible, in a later study [HLL98], we introduce indexing mechanisms to avoid client keeping on monitoring the channel for the schedules.

2.1 Broadcast Scheduling

Since broadcast data can be accessed concurrently by an arbitrary number of clients without any performance degradation, it is well suited for disseminating data to many clients. The broadcast channel is a linear medium: a client waits for the desired data on the channel. Hence, the access latency depends on the volume of data broadcast. To maintain short access latency, the amount of broadcast data needs to be small (i.e., only the most frequently accessed data which are not cached should be provided for broadcasting).

Once the data set for broadcast is determined, a broadcast schedule (program) needs to be constructed. Such that the server periodically broadcasts data according to this broadcast schedule. A simple method called *flat broadcast* is to broadcast each data only once in each cycle. Note that the clients access patterns are usually skewed (i.e., some data are accessed more frequently while the others are less frequently accessed), another scheduling method for data broadcast called *broadcast disks* was proposed in [AAFZ95]. For broadcast disks, the server divides the file into groups of data items with different broadcast frequencies to imitate multiple disks spinning at different speeds. The fastest disk is closest to the clients, the expected wait time for a data item on that disk is the shortest. The data items on the slowest disk are farthest since it will take a longer time for clients to access them. The broadcast frequencies of disks are in proportion to the probability of access in order to gain the optimal access time of the system. To retrieve data from broadcast disks, the clients must know the *broadcast program* of the server. According to the program, clients monitor the broadcast and retrieve desired data items from the channel. Broadcast disks are efficient for asymmetric communication environments where the client access patterns are skewed. Data on the air can further be organized as broadcast disks with fast disks containing frequently accessed data and slow disks for less frequently accessed data.

Flat broadcast can be regarded as a special broadcast disks where the number of disks is one. Hereafter, the term *broadcast program* refers to both broadcast disks (B_DISK) and flat broadcast ($FLAT$), while data delivery system which adopts B_DISK or FLAT approach is denoted as BP. We assume that the dynamic broadcast program changes only the content of the program, while all other parameters remain fixed.

A special scenario appears when the broadcast program is empty. Therefore, all broadcast bandwidth is dedicated to pulled pages. On a cache miss, the client immediately sends a pull request for the page to the server and then waits for the arrival of the desired data item. It is called *Pure-Pull.* Obviously no access pattern information is required by the server and the server works in a passive way. This approach is simple but the server and the uplink channel may be easily congested by a lot of separate pull requests.

2.2 Collection of Client Access Patterns

Bit vector is a widely used method in delivering compact information in asymmetric environments [JBEA97,WYC96]. To record client access information, each client maintains a bit vector in which each bit represents a data item in the

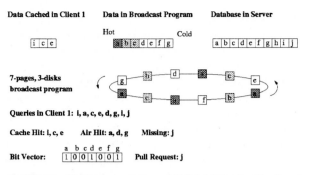

Fig. 1. Example of a Data Storage.

current broadcast program (Figure 1). Whenever a new broadcast program is retrieved (i.e., at the beginning of a broadcast cycle), the clients update the new cycle version number and resets their bit vectors for the current cycle. Every data item on the channel is marked to indicate whether it is from the broadcast program or it is from the pull requests. If there is a query answered by broadcast data (referred to *air hit*), then the corresponding bit is set. Retrieving data from the client cache (referred as *cache hit*) and pulled data on the broadcast channel have no influence on the bit vector. However, when the desired data cannot be found from both the cache and the broadcast program (called *air miss*), an explicit pull request will be issued by the client via the uplink channel. Thus, the client access statistics is piggybacked at the same time. Note that if the requests of a client all can be answered either by cached data or by broadcast data, the client access pattern will not be delivered to the server.

The pull request consists of the desired data item ID, the cycle version, and the bit vector. Since the length of the bit vector equals to the number of data items in the broadcast program which is quite small, the overhead for the uplink bandwidth is low. After this bit vector is piggybacked to the server, its content is reset and it is ready for the collection of future client access.

Using the received cycle version number, the server knows the bit vector corresponding to which broadcast program. In addition, each data item is associated with a *most frequently accessed (MFA)* counter which is initially reset. The counter of a data item is incremented by one whenever the data item is pulled by a client or the bit corresponding to that data item in the received bit vector is set. As a result, the server collects statistical information about the client access patterns. This statistics helps the server dynamically build the broadcast program according to the system workload. In this paper, the server selects pages with high MFA values for broadcast. Note that a *cache hit* has no influence on the MFA value. Therefore, once a data item is cached in the client, any further requests for it from the client will have no contribution to its MFA value in the server. Hence, cached data normally have low MFA values, though they are most frequently retrieved by the client. As the access statistics is accumulated, cached data will eventually not be selected into the broadcast program or only be placed on a slower spinning disk. Intuitively, only those data items which are accessed by a large number of the clients that occasionally make query for them will have high MFA values. In this way, the server can tailor the broadcast program to the need of a particular client.

3   Simulation Modeling

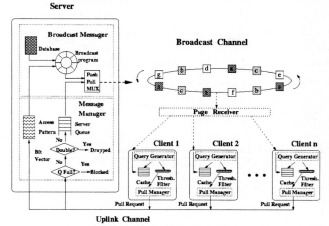

Fig. 2. Simulation Model.

In this paper, a simulation model shown in Figure 2 is used. Each client is modeled by a process[3]. The process consists of two sub-processes, namely the *Query Generator* and the *Pull Manager*. The *Query Generator* runs a continuous loop that randomly requests a page according to a specific distribution. It first checks the client's cache to see whether a valid copy of the desired data items exists there. If the answer is yes, an immediate reply is delivered to the user. Otherwise a sub-process *Pull Manager* is activated. We assume that the client has a fixed-size cache and *LRU-K* page replacement policy is adopted. After each request, the *Query Generator* waits for a period of *Thinktime* long and then makes the next request. *ThinkTime* is a parameter used to model workload processing as well as the relative speeds of the CPU and the broadcast medium. After activated, the *Pull Manager* issues a pull request to the server for the needed data item if the data item can not be obtained from the broadcast disks or the cost of access data item from the disks exceeds a cut-off value specified by the system. In either case, the client monitors the broadcast channel until the desired page arrives. A single process, called *Page Receiver*, is used to model all clients in the system. The *Page Receiver* continuously monitors the broadcast channel and becomes active when a page arrives. It checks each client in turn to see whether the incoming page is the desired page of that client. If the page is the requested one, it is brought into the client's cache.

For the data access patterns, we use two different distributions: *Zipf* (also used in [Knu81]) and *Gaussian* (used in [SRB97] as well). The *Zipf* distribution (with parameter θ) is frequently used to model skewed access patterns where θ is a parameter named *access skew coefficient* and can vary from zero to one.

---

[3] In [AFZ97], the entire client population was modeled by two client processes, a real client and a virtual client. Since the client-server model is not memoryless because of data caching, the interleaving of push and pull slots, and the bounded server queue. Using a single client process (i.e., virtual client) may not exactly reflect the true contention on the uplink channel among the clients.

The distribution becomes increasingly "skewed" as θ increases. The *Gaussian* distribution, $Normal(\mu, \sigma)$, is used to model the dynamic changes in the access patterns with the center of hot-spot μ and the width of hot-spot σ. During the experiments, the value of μ can vary to create the effect of dynamic workload and the value of σ reflects the skew of client access patterns. Table 1 summarizes the parameters used to model the resource and the data access pattern of each client.

Table 1. Client Parameter Setting.

CacheSize	Client cache size (in data items)
PullReqSize	Size of a pull request in bytes
ThinkTime	Mean think time (in seconds) between queries for each client
ThreshFactor	Value for client to select between broadcast and on-demand
θ	Zipf distribution parameter
μ	Width of hot-spot
σ	Center of hot-spot

The server is modeled by two processes: *Broadcasting Manager* and *Message Manager*. A bounded queue is built for the uplink request message. When the arrival rate of uplink requests exceed the service rate of the server, (e.g. the queue is full), all requests are blocked. Requests for pages that are already requested in the queue are dropped. The queue is served in a FIFO fashion and the service rate is determined by the parameter, *PullBW*. *PullBW* determines the percentage of the broadcast slots allocated for pages explicitly pulled by the clients. The broadcast program is dynamically determined by the *Broadcasting Manager* per cycle. Only the content of the broadcast program is tailored to meet the access patterns collected from the clients via the uplink channel. In this model, the next broadcasting page is selected alternately from either the broadcast program or the queue. However, when the queue is empty, all broadcast pages are selected from the broadcast program. The *Message Manager* receives pull requests from the clients. From these pull messages, client access patterns can be obtained from the server.

Table 2. System Parameter Setting.

DataItemSize	Size of a data item in bytes
NumClient	Number of clients in a cell
DatabaseSize	Size of database in data items
DownlinkBW	Downlink from the server to the client channel bandwidth
UplinkBW	Uplink from the client to the server channel bandwidth
PullPercentage	Percentage of broadcast slots allocated for pull requests
QueneSize	Size of downlink channel queue (in data ietms)
ProgramSize	Number of distinct data items in broadcast program
DiskNum	Number of disks for *B_DISK*
$DiskSize_i$	Size of disk i (in data items)
$DiskFreq_i$	Relative broadcast frequency of disk i

Parameters which describe the server resource and the structure of the broadcast program are listed in Table 2. Additionally, the parameters that describe the configuration and the physical resource in a cell are also included in the table. We assume that there is a uplink channel from the clients to the server and a shared downlink channel (also called broadcast channel) for the reverse communication. The database is modeled as a collection of *DatabaseSize* data items of *DataItemSize* bytes each. There are *NumChannel* channels in a cell. For the exclusive channel allocation approach, all *NumChannel* channels work in either on-demand mode or broadcast mode. For BP approach, the channel allocation made between broadcast and on-demand modes is fixed such that the ratio between the number of broadcast channels and the number of on-demand channels is *pullVSpush*. The communication is asymmetric, i.e., the bandwidth of downlink from the server to the client *DownlinkBW* is greater than that of uplink from the client to the server *UplinkBW*.

4 Experiments and Results

Table 3. System Parameter Setting.

Parameters	Values	Parameters	Values
$DataItemSize$	1000 bytes	$NumClient$	$10, \cdots, 2000$
$DatabaseSize$	3000 data items	$QueueSize$	100
$PullReqSize$	10 bytes	$PullPecentage$	1/3
$DownlinkBW$	100000 bps	$UplinkBW$	1 % of downlink bandwidth
$ThinkTime$	10 seconds	$ThreshFactor$	100%
$ProgramSize$	500 data items	$DiskSize_i$	$DiskSize_1=100, DiskSize_2=400$
$DiskNum$	2	$DiskFreq_i$	$DiskFreq_1=2, DiskFreq_2=1$
$CacheSize$	50 data items	θ	0.95
μ	300 data items	σ	randomly selected in the database

In this section, we investigate the performance of simulated *BP* together with *Pure-Pull* approach. The primary performance metric is the average client access time. The simulation is implemented using CSIM [Sch92]. Table 3 defines the system parameter setting for the experiments. The server contains a collection of self-identifying data items of equal size. The client access patterns are skewed, (i.e., either *Zipf* or *Gaussian* distribution) and the requested data sets among the clients are largely overlapped. The client population varies from 10 to 2000. The server database consists of 3000 data items (or pages), each data item is 8192 bytes in size. The broadcast rate is 100Kbps, while the uplink rate is 1Kbps (1% of the broadcast rate). The client cache size is 50 pages. The back-channel queue can hold up to 100 distinct requests. The mean think time between two consecutive queries is 10 seconds. The number of distinct pages in the broadcast program (for both B_DISK and FLAT) is 500 pages. Two-disk broadcast is used for broadcast-disk where the size of the faster disk is 100 pages, while the slower disk is 400 pages, with relative spin speeds being 2 and 1, respectively.

We examine the performance of the *Pure-Pull* approach and *BP* with emphasis on the dynamic workload environments. There are two circumstances when dynamic workload can occur. The first case is when the clients join the system with an empty cache and the server does not know the client access patterns. In the second case, an existing client changes its access hot-spot with time. Obviously, dynamic workload only affects the client cache for the pure pull approach.

For *BP* (FLAT or B_DISK), dynamic workload has effects on not only the client cache but the content of the broadcast program as well.

For *BP*, one third of the broadcast slots are allocated for pulled pages, while the entire broadcast slots are dedicated to the pulled pages in Pure-Pull approach. For both FLAT and B_DISK approaches, the threshold is set to 100%. That is, the client first checks the whole broadcast program to see whether the desired pages will appear within the remining part of the current broadcast program. If the answer is no, then the client issues an explicit pull request to the server. Otherwise, the client keeps on monitoring the broadcast channel for the desired data.

4.1 Performance for Changing User Population Size

In the first set of experiments we assume that the client access patterns follow the *Zipf* distribution and evaluate the adaptiveness of *BP* for different client populations. The Zipf distribution parameter is set to 0.95. We define a client to be at *stable stage* which is achieved by waiting 2000 accesses more after the client cache filled and a system is at stable stage when all clients in the system are at stable stage. For a system at stable stage, the warm-up effects in the client cache and the broadcast program are eliminated, such that the client caches contain the hottest access spot and the server has information on the access patterns. In the contrast, the *initial stage* of the system is from the time when the system begins to work to the time when the system is at stable stage. Hence a system at initial stage, both the clients and the server have no knowledge of the client access patterns.

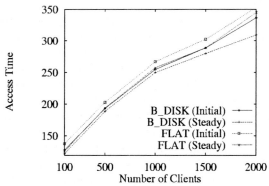

Fig. 3. Access Time VS Client Population.

To see the adaptability of *BP*, we compare the system performance for *BP* approaches at stable stage with that at initial stage in Figure 3. Obviously, both FLAT and B_DISK at steady state always perform better than at initial stage. This indicates that after a certain period of "*learning*" stage both the clients and the server have the knowledge of access probability information, which, in turn, guarantees the clients to cache important pages and the server to tailor the broadcast program according to client demand. B_DISK always gives a better performance than FLAT approach at both stable and initial stage. This is consistent with the results obtained for static broadcast program [AFZ97].

To provide comparison baselines, we introduce the ideal *BP*: *ideal flat* and *ideal broadcast disks* with respect to FLAT and B_Disk. For the ideal ones, the system (both the clients and the server) knows the exact client access patterns. *BP* disseminates information according to the optimal access distribution such that the most frequently accessed data subset is cached in the client, the less frequently accessed data subset is provided by broadcast, and the rest is pulled from the server by explicit requests. The broadcast program for broadcast disks is also constructed according to the access probability of the data subset. The ideal *BP* is the ultimate performance goal of our system.

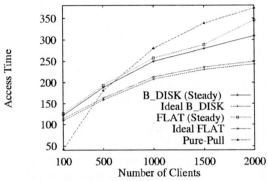

Fig. 4. Access Time VS Client Population.

The experimental results for the three data delivery methods: Pure-Pull, FLAT, and B_DISK, are shown in Figure 4. Note that the results shown are obtained when the system is at stable stage. As expected, the Pure-Pull approach is good only when the system workload is light (left side of the figure). The access time for this method increases rapidly as the client population grows. When the number of clients is beyond 600, Pure-Pull performs worse than B_DISK, and when the system becomes even more heavily loaded (i.e., the number of clients is greater than 700), Pure-Pull gives worse performance than FLAT and B_Disk. However, as client populations become large, the curve for Pure-Pull becomes flat. The reason is as the number of clients increases the pulled data set in the broadcast channel forms a hot-spot. As a result, one pulled data item can satisfy a large number of client requests. Since the basic page replacement algorithm for client caching is the same for *BP* and Pure-Pull, the improvement of the performance for *BP* over Pure-Pull is a result of the tailored broadcast program.

It is obvious that both FLAT and B_DISK can manage to follow the ideal ones very well. There is a certain gap between the real approaches with the ideal approaches. The difference is due to the imprecise access patterns collected by the server and the inaccurate LRU_K page replacement strategy. Though, FLAT and B_DISK may never achieve the ideal performance, the dynamic broadcast program is still an effective approach because of its adaptiveness to the system.

4.2 Performance for Changing Hot-Spot

To evaluate the performance of *BP* in dynamic workloads, we assume that the client access patterns follow the *Gaussian* distribution. such that μ varies to create the effect of dynamic workload and σ which reflects the skew of client access patterns is 100 or 300. In this way, we can model the elimination of access hot-spots and the generation of a new one in another part of the database (randomly selected). To interpret the impact of such hot-spot migration on the system performance, we assumed that all clients have the same hot-spots and they change access demand at the same time. Clients stay with each hot-spot for *Duration* periods of simulation time.

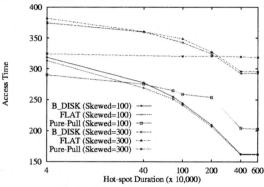

Fig. 5. Migration of Hot-spot.

In Figure 5, we show the results obtained as a function of *Duration*, where the client population is 1000. Two set of curves, labeled as *Skewed 100* and *Skewed 300*, show two different data access patterns. For more dynamic workload (left side of the figures where duration is short), Pure-Pull outperforms both B_DISK and FLAT. Since with smaller duration, the broadcast program of *BP* may not reach steady state or the steady broadcast program is obtained shortly before the clients change access hot-spot to another new one. As a result, the benefit of the air cache doesn't have enough time to become effective. Only when the system reaches steady state and stay there long enough, would *BP* give better performance than the Pure-Pull method, which can be observed in the right part of the figure. However, as the duration increases to 4×10^6, any further increase of the duration won't improve the performance of both *BP* and Pure-Pull. It is because that the system reaches the steady state after that duration period. Compared with Pure-Pull, *BP* improves the system performance more for the access pattern $\sigma = 100$ than the access pattern $\sigma = 300$, because for $\sigma = 100$ there are more air hits than $\sigma = 300$.

5 Conclusions

In this paper, we proposed a dynamic data delivery system for asymmetric communication environments, where information can be retrieved by different means (i.e., client cache, broadcast channels, or the server database by explicit pull requests), to achieve the maximum advantages. The way data are stored is determined dynamically by the access patterns of the clients, not by precompiled user profiles. The broadcast program is tailored according to access frequencies so that only the most desired data subset is scheduled to broadcast. Pull requests are needed only when the desired data cannot be found in the client cache or the broadcast program.

A simulation model has been developed to evaluate the performance of the data delivery system. We found that the system (clients and server) can adapt to the dynamically changing workload very well. Generally, broadcast disks and flat broadcast have better performance than pure pull approach when data access patterns are skewed. For skewed data access patterns and less dynamic workloads, Broadcast disks outperform flat broadcast. However, pure pull technique is a better choice for random data access patterns or highly dynamic workloads.

As future work, we will investigate ways to dynamically adjust the ratio between pull and push bandwidth according to the server workload and the impact of different broadcast program structure (i.e., the size of broadcast program etc.) on the performance of data delivery. Moreover, we will include the dissemination of updates in the hierarchical data caching system.

References

[AAFZ95] S. Acharya, R. Alonso, M. Franklin, and S. Zdonik. Broadcast disks: Data management for asymmetric communications environments. In *Proceedings of the ACM SIGMOD Conference on Management of Data*, San Jose, California, 1995.

[AFZ97] S. Acharya, M. Franklin, and S. Zdonik. Balancing push and pull for data broadcast. In *Proceedings of the ACM SIGMOD Conference on Management of Data*, pages 183–194, Tuscon, Arizona, May 1997.

[BI94] D. Barbara and T. Imielinksi. Sleepers and workaholics: Caching strategies for mobile environments. In *Proceedings of the ACM SIGMOD Conference on Management of Data*, pages 1–12, 1994.

[EPW93] E.J.O'Neil, P.E.O'Neil, and G. Weikum. The lru-k page replacement algorithm for database disk buffering. In *Proceedings of the ACM SIGMOD Conference on Management of Data*, May 1993.

[HL98] Q. L. Hu and D. L. Lee. Cache algorithms based on adaptive invalidation reports for mobile environments. *Cluster Computing*, 1(1):39–48, Feb. 1998.

[HLL98] Q. L. Hu, D. L. Lee, and W.-C. Lee. Hierarchical data caching in asymmetric communication environments. In *Under Preparation*, 1998.

[IVB94] T. Imielinski, S. Viswanathan, and B. R. Badrinath. Energy efficiency indexing on air. In *Proceedings of the International Conference on SIGMOD*, pages 25–36, 1994.

[JBEA97] J. Jing, O. Bukhres, A. K. Elmargarmid, and R. Alonso. Bit-sequences: A new cache invalidation method in mobile environments. *ACM/Baltzer Mobile Networks and Applications*, 2(II), 1997.

[Knu81] D. Knuth. *The Art of Computer Programming*, volume 3. Addison-Wesley, CA, 1981.

[Sch92] H. Schwetman. *Csim user's guide (version 17)*. MCC Corporation, 1992.

[SRB97] K. Stathatos, N. Roussopoulos, and J. S. Baras. Adaptive data broadcast in hybrid networks. In *Proceedings of the 23rd VLDB Conference*, pages 326–335, Athens, Greece, 1997.

[WYC96] K.-L. Wu, P. S. Yu, and M.-S. Chen. Energy-efficient caching for wireless mobile computing. In *12th International Conference on Data Engineering*, pages 336–345, Feb. 26-March 1 1996.

Scalable Invalidation-Based Processing of Queries in Broadcast Push Delivery

Evaggelia Pitoura

Department of Computer Science, University of Ioannina, GR 45110 Ioannina, Greece
pitoura@cs.uoi.gr, http://www.cs.uoi.gr/~pitoura

Abstract. Recently, push-based delivery has attracted considerable attention as a means of disseminating information to large client populations in both wired and wireless environments. In this paper, we address the problem of ensuring the consistency and currency of client's read-only transactions in the presence of updates. Our approach is based on broadcasting invalidation reports and is scalable, i.e., its performance and associated overhead is independent of the number of clients. Caching is also considered to improve the latency of queries. Preliminary performance results show the relative advantages of the proposed techniques.

1 Introduction

In traditional client/server systems, data are delivered on demand. A client explicitly requests data items from the server. Upon receipt of a data request, the server locates the information of interest and returns it to the client. This form of data delivery is called *pull-based*. In an increasingly important class of networked environments, such as in satellite broadcast networks and in wireless networks with mobile clients, communication is asymmetric. In particular, the server machines are provided with a relative high-bandwidth channel which supports broadcast delivery to all clients located inside a specific geographical region. This facility provides the infrastructure for a new form of data delivery called push-based delivery.

In *push-based* data delivery, the server repetitively broadcasts data to a client population without a specific request. Clients monitor the broadcast and retrieve the data items they need as they arrive on the broadcast channel. Push-based delivery is important for a wide range of applications that involve dissemination of information to a large number of clients. Dissemination-based applications include information feeds such as stock quotes and sport tickets, electronic newsletters, mailing lists, road traffic management systems, and cable TV. Important are also electronic commerce applications such as auctions or electronic tendering.

Recently, information dissemination on the Internet has gained significant attention (e.g., [8, 17]). Many commercial products have been developed that provide wireless dissemination of Internet-available information. For instance, the AirMedia's Live Internet broadcast network [3] wirelessly broadcasts customized news and information to subscribers equipped with a receiver antenna connected to their personal computer. Similarly, Hughes Network Systems' DirectPC [16] network downloads content directly from web servers on the Internet to a satellite network and then to the subscribers' personal computer. Broadcast has also received considerable attention in the area of mobile wireless computing because of the physical support for broadcast in both satellite and cellular networks. Broadcast delivery in this setting faces additional restrictions. Mobile clients are resource-poor in comparison to stationary servers. Furthermore, energy conservation is a major concern.

In this paper, we address the problem of preserving the consistency of clients' queries, that is clients' read-only transactions, when the values of the data that are being broadcasted are updated at the server. Providing transaction support tailored to read-only transactions is important for many reasons. First, a large number of transactions in dissemination systems are read-only. Then, even if we allow update transactions at the client, it is more efficient to process read-only transactions with special algorithms, since their consistency can be ensured without contacting the server. This is important because even if a backchannel exists from the client to the server, this channel typically has small communication capacity. Furthermore, since the number of clients supported is large, there is a great chance of overwhelming the server with clients' requests. In addition, avoiding contacting the server decreases the latency of client transactions.

Our approach is based on broadcasting invalidation reports, that is a list of the items that were updated. Broadcasting additional information in the form of a serialization graph is also exploited to increase the concurrency of the scheme in the expense of additional processing at both the client and the server. Consistency is preserved without contacting the server thus the approach is scalable; i.e., performance is independent of the number of clients. This property makes the approach appropriate for highly populated service areas. Both the invalidation-based approaches are extended to support caching at the client. Preliminary performance results show the relative advantages of the invalidation-based approaches in terms of the percentage of acceptable queries.

The remainder of this paper is organized as follows. In Section 2, we introduce the problem of supporting consistent read-only transactions in the presence of updates. In Section 3, we present two invalidation-based schemes: one based on broadcasting invalidation lists and one that in addition broadcasts serialization information. In Section 4, we consider client disconnections, i.e., non-continuous access to the broadcast, and other possible extensions of the schemes. Caching is considered in Section 5, while in Section 6, we present preliminary performance results. In Section 7, we discuss related work and offer our conclusions.

2   Processing Client Queries

The server periodically broadcasts items to a large client population. Each period of the broadcast is called a broadcast *cycle* or *bcycle*, while the content of the broadcast is called a *bcast*. Each client listens to the broadcast and fetches data of interest as they arrive. This way data can be accessed concurrently by any number of clients without any performance degradation. However, access to data is strictly sequential, since clients need to wait for the data of interest to appear on the channel. We assume that all updates are performed at the server. Any updates are applied at the server and disseminated from there.

The smallest logical unit of a broadcast is called a *bucket*. Buckets are the analog to blocks for disks. Each bucket has a header that includes useful information. The exact content of the bucket header depends on the specific broadcast organization. Information in the header usually includes the position of the bucket in the bcast as an offset from the beginning of the bcast as well as the offset to the beginning of the next bcast. This offset can be used by the client to determine the beginning of the next bcast when the size of the broadcast is not fixed. Data items correspond to database records (tuples). We assume that users access data by specifying the value of one attribute of the record, the search key. Each bucket contains several items.

We assume that the server broadcasts the content of a database. A database consists of a finite set of data items. A database state is typically defined as a mapping of every data to a value of its domain. Thus, a databases state, denoted DS, can be defined as a set of ordered pairs of data items in D and their values. In a database, data are related by a number of restrictions called integrity constraints that express relationships of values of data that a database state must satisfy. A database state is consistent if it does not violate the integrity constraints [7]. While data items are being broadcasted, transactions are executed at the server that may update the values of the items being broadcasted. We assume that the contents of the broadcast at each cycle is guaranteed to be consistent. In particular, we assume that the values of data items that are broadcasted during each bcycle correspond to the state of the database at the beginning of the broadcast cycle, i.e., the values produced by all transactions that have been committed by the beginning of the cycle. We make this assumption for clarity of presentation, we later discuss how it can be raised.

A read-only transaction that reads all its data within a single cycle can be executed without any concurrency overhead at all. However, since the set of items read by a transaction is not known at static time and access to data is sequential, transactions may have to read data items from different bcasts, that is, values from different database states. As an example, say T be a transaction that corresponds to the following program: " *if $a > 0$ then read b else read c* " and that b and c precede a in the broadcast. Then, a client's transaction has to read a first and wait for the next cycle to read the value of b or c. We define the *span* of a transaction T, $span(T)$, to be the maximum number of different bcasts from which T reads data.

We define the *readset* of a transaction T, denoted $Read\_Set(T)$, to be the set of items it reads. In particular, $Read\_Set(T)$ is a set of ordered pairs of data items and their values that T read. Our correctness criterion for read-only transactions is that each transaction reads consistent data. Specifically, the readset of each read-only transaction must form a subset of a consistent database state [14]. We assume that each server transaction preserves database consistency. Thus, a state produced by a serializable execution (i.e., an execution equivalent to a serial one [7]) of a number of server transactions produces a consistent database state. The goal of the methods presented in this paper is to ensure that the readset of each read-only transaction corresponds to such a state.

3 Invalidation-Based Query Processing

3.1 Invalidation-Only Scheme

Each bcast is preceded by an invalidation report in the form of a list that includes all data items that were updated during the previous bcycle. For each active read-only transaction R, the client keeps a set $RS(R)$ of all data items that R has read so far. At the beginning of each bcast, the client tunes in and reads the invalidation report. A read transaction R is aborted if an item $x \in RS(R)$ was updated, that is, if x appears in the invalidation report. Clearly,

Theorem 1. *The invalidation only method produces correct read-only transactions.*

Proof. In [10]. □

In the invalidation-only scheme, a read-only transaction R reads the most current values, that is the values produced by all transactions committed at the beginning of the bcycle at which R commits. The increase in the size of the broadcast is equal to $u\,d$, where u is the number of items that were updated and d is the size of the key.

Bounded Inconsistency. An approach to increase concurrency and reduce the overhead of transmitting and processing control information is to provide queries that tolerate inconsistency. One formal characterization of inconsistency is provided by *epsilon-serializability* (ESR) [13]. In epsilon-serializability, each read-only transaction has an import-limit that specifies the maximum amount of inconsistency that it can accept. Let R be a read-only transaction and c_0 be the cycle at which R starts. The import limit for R can be quantified on a per data item basis. Let $x \in RS(S)$, then the inconsistency associated with x can be defined as the distance between the current value of x and the value of x at c_0 say x_0. R can tolerate reading x_0, and thus import inconsistency equal to this distance, if the distance is within a specified import limit. The inconsistency imported by R depends on the number of concurrent updates, i.e., the number of server transactions that commit while R is in progress. One way to support this form of imported inconsistency is to extend the validation report for a data item x to include the number of transactions that have updated x during the previous bcycle. There are other ways to quantify import inconsistency [4]. For example, for a data item x that takes numerical values, instead of transmitting an invalidation report each time it is updated, we may transmit an invalidation report only when the difference of its new value from the old one falls outside a specified range of values.

3.2 Serialization Graph Testing

If additional information is broadcasted, it should be possible to accept more read-only transactions. To this end, we develop a serialization graph testing (SGT) method. The serialization graph for a history H, denoted $SG(H)$, is a directed graph whose nodes are the committed transactions in H and whose edges are all $T_i \rightarrow T_j$ $(i \neq j)$ such that one of T_i's operations precedes and conflicts with one of T_j operations in H [7]. According to the serialization theorem, a history H is serializable iff $SG(H)$ is acyclic. We assume that each transaction reads a data item before it writes it, that is, the readset of a transaction includes its writeset. Then, in the serialization graph, there can be two types of edges $T_i \rightarrow T_j$ between any pair of transactions T_i and T_j: *dependency* edges that express the fact that T_j read the value written by T_i and *precedence* edges that express the fact that T_j wrote an item that was previously read by T_i.

In brief, the SGT method works as follows. Each client maintains a copy of the serialization graph locally. The serialization graph at the server includes all transactions *committed* at the server, while, in addition, the local copy at the client includes any active read-only transactions that were issued at this site. At each cycle, the server broadcasts any updates of the serialization graph. Upon receipt of the updates, the client integrates them into its local copy of the graph. A read operation at a client is executed only if it does not create a cycle in the local serialization graph. We describe next, an efficient implementation of the SGT methods for strict histories. A history is *strict* if no data may be read or overwritten until the transaction that previously wrote into it terminates. The SGT method is applicable to other cases as well, but its implementation requires additional overhead. Note that the serialization graph at the server is not necessarily used for concurrency control at the server, instead a more practical method, most probably two-phase locking, may be employed.

Implementation of the SGT Method. At the beginning of each bcast, the server broadcasts the following control information:

- the *difference from the previous serialization graph*
  In particular, for each transaction T_i that was committed during the previous cycle, a list of the transactions with which it conflicts, i.e., it is connected through a direct edge.
- an *augmented invalidation report*
  The report includes all data written during the previous bcycle along with an identification of the first transaction that wrote each of them.

In addition, the content of the broadcast is augmented so that an identification of the last transaction that wrote a data item is broadcasted along with the item.

Each client tunes in at the beginning of the broadcast to obtain the control information. Upon receipt of the graph difference, the client updates its local copy of the serialization graph SG to include any additional edges and nodes. Let SG^i be the subgraph of SG that includes only the transactions that were committed during cycle i. Since all transactions in SG^i are committed prior to any transactions committed in subsequent bcycles and histories are strict, it holds:

Claim. There cannot be any incoming edges to transactions in SG^i from transactions committed in subsequent bcycles $m > i$.

The client also adds precedence edges for all its active read-only transactions as follows. Let R be such an active transaction and $RS(R)$ be the set of items that R has read so far. For each item x in the invalidation report such that $x \in RS(R)$, the client adds a precedence edge $R \to T_f$, where T_f is the first transaction that wrote x during the previous cycle. Although R conflicts with all transactions that wrote x during the previous cycle, it suffices to add just a single edge to T_f (see [10] for a proof).

When R reads an item y, a dependency edge $T_l \to R$ is added in the local serialization graph, where T_l is the last transaction that wrote y. The read operation is accepted, only if no cycle is formed. It can be shown that it suffices to add just a single edge $T_l \to R$ instead of adding edges $T' \to R$ from all transactions T' that wrote y. To prove that the SGT method detects all cycles that include a read-only transaction R, we will use the following lemma:

Lemma 1. *Let o be the first bcycle during which an item read by R is overwritten.*

(a) During bcycle m, any cycle that includes R is of the form $R \to T_{i_1} \to T_{i_2} \to \ldots T_{i_k} \to R$, where for any $T_{i_j} \in SG^l$, it holds $o \le l < m$.
(b) The SGT algorithm detects all such cycles.

Proof. In [10]. □

Theorem 2. *The SGT method produces correct read-only transactions.*

Proof. In [10]. □

Regarding the currency of read-only transactions, each read-only transaction R that performs its first read at c_0 reads values that correspond to a database state between the state at the beginning of bcycle c_0 and the current database state.

Space Efficiency. Instead of keeping a complete copy of the serialization graph locally at each client, by Lemma 1, it suffices to keep for each query R only the subgraphs SG^k with $k \ge c_o$, where c_o is the bcycle when the first item read by R is invalidated, i.e., overwritten. Thus, if no items are updated, there is no space or processing overhead at the client. Furthermore, at most S subgraphs are maintained, where S is the maximum transaction span of the queries at the client. By Lemma 1, we may also keep only the outgoing edges from R; there is no need to store the incoming edges to R.

However, the volume of the control information that is broadcasted is considerable. Let tid be the size of a transaction identifier, c be the maximum number of transactions committed during a broadcast cycle, and N be the maximum number of operations per transaction at the server. We assume that transaction identifiers are unique within each bcycle, thus it suffices to allocate $log(c)$ bits per transaction identifier. Then, when there is a need to distinguish between transactions at different cycles, we also broadcast a version number indicating the bcycle during which the transaction was committed. The size of the invalidation report is: $u(i + log(c))$. Since, there are at most N operations per transaction, each transaction may participate in at most N conflicts with other transactions. Thus, the difference from the previous graph has at most cN edges. The total size of the difference is: $cN(2log(c) + 2v)$, assuming that along with each transaction we broadcast the bcycle during which it was committed. Finally, the size of the broadcast is further augmented, since along with each item, we broadcast the identifier of the last transaction that wrote it.

4 Discussion

Disconnections. Listening to the broadcast consumes energy. In addition, access to the broadcast data may be monetarily expensive. Thus, clients may voluntary skip listening for a number of broadcast cycles. Besides this voluntary form of disconnection, client disconnections are very common when data are delivered wirelessly. Wireless communications face many obstacles because the surrounding environment interacts heavily with the signal, thus in general wireless communications are less reliable and deliver less bandwidth than wireline communications. Thus, a desirable requirement from a broadcasting scheme is to allow clients to continue their operation after periods during which some clients miss listening to the broadcast signal.

The techniques presented require active clients to monitor the broadcast continuously. In the invalidation-only scheme, a client has to tune-in at each and every cycle to read the invalidation report. Otherwise, the client cannot ensure the correctness of any active read-only transaction. Similarly, the SGT method does not tolerate any client disconnection. If a client misses a bcycle, serializability cannot be guaranteed. Thus, any active read transactions must be reissued anew. An enhancement of the scheme to increase tolerance to disconnections would be to broadcast along with items version numbers. Then, a read operation would be accepted as long as its version number was smaller than the version of the last broadcast that the transaction has listen to. This guarantees that the client has all the information required for cycle detection. In both schemes, periodic retransmission of control information would increase their tolerance to intermittent connectivity. For instance, an invalidation report of the items updated during the last w bcycles may be broadcasted to allow clients to resynchronize.

Other Extensions. Instead of the invalidation reports being broadcasted at the beginning of each broadcast cycle, such reports can as well be broadcasted at other pre-specified intervals h, $h \leq T$, where T is the duration of the broadcast. In this case, the invalidation report must include all items updated during h. The values being broadcasted correspond to the values produced by all transactions committed by the beginning of the current interval.

Another way to extend the scheme is to increase its granularity. For example, invalidation reports may include buckets instead of items. A bucket is considered updated when any of the items that it includes has been updated. Instead of maintaining for each transaction R the set of items it has read, the set of buckets is maintained. Then, a query is aborted if one of the buckets it has read is subsequently updated. This scheme may lead to aborting queries that normally should not have been aborted, since the invalidation of a bucket does not necessarily means that the specific item read has also been updated. However, only correct queries are accepted and less overhead is imposed.

5 Caching

To reduce latency in answering queries, clients can cache items of interest locally. Caching reduces not only the latency but also the span of transactions, since transactions find data of interest in their local cache and thus need to access the broadcast channel for a smaller number of cycles. We assume that each page, i.e., the unit of caching, corresponds to a bucket, i.e., the unit of broadcast. When broadcast items are updated, the value of cached items become stale. There are various approaches to communicating updates to the client. Two basic techniques are invalidation and propagation. For *invalidation*, the server sends out messages to inform the client of which pages are modified. The client removes those pages from its cache. For *propagation*, the server sends the updated values. The client replaces its old copy with the new one. Invalidation combined with a form of *autoprefetching* has been shown to perform well in broadcast delivery [2]. At the beginning of each bcycle (or at other pre-defined points), the server broadcasts an invalidation report, which is a list of the pages that have been updated. This report is used to invalidate those pages in cache that appear in the invalidation report. These pages remain in cache to be autoprefetched later. In particular, when the new value of an invalidated page appears in the broadcast, the client fetches this new value and replaces the old one. Thus, a page in cache either has a current value (the one in the current broadcast) or is marked for autoprefetching.

The cache invalidation report is similar to the invalidation report used in our schemes. However, the two reports differ in granularity. The cache invalidation report includes the pages (or buckets) that have been updated, whereas the query-processing invalidation report includes the data items that have been updated. As discussed, the query processing techniques can be modified to work on pages or buckets rather on items. We describe next how our query processing techniques can be extended to work in conjunction with caching, while keeping their granularity at the item level. For the invalidation only scheme, each read first checks whether the item is in cache. If it is found in cache and the page is not invalidated, then it is read from the cache. Otherwise, the item is read from the broadcast. For the SGT method, the cache is extended to include for each item the last transaction that wrote it; information that is broadcasted anyway.

Each time an item is read from the cache, the same test for cycles as when the item is read from the broadcast is executed.

To enhance the invalidation-only scheme, the cache may be extended to include along with each item version numbers that correspond to the bcycle during which it was inserted in the cache. Let R be a query and u be the first bcycle at which an item $x \in RS(R)$ is invalidated. Instead of aborting R, R is marked abort and continues operation as long as old enough values for all future reads are found in cache. In particular, R continues its read operations as long as the items it wants to read exist in the cache and have versions $c < u$. We call this method, invalidation-only with versioned cache.

Theorem 3. *The invalidation-only with versioned cache method produces correct read-only transactions.*

Proof. In [10].

6 Performance Evaluation

The Model. Our performance model is similar to the one presented in [1]. The server periodically broadcasts a set of data items in the range of 1 to $BroadcastSize$. We assume for simplicity a flat broadcast organization in which the server broadcasts cyclicly the set of items. Each client accesses items from the range 1 to $ReadRange$, which is a subset of the items broadcasted ($ReadRange \leq BroadcastSize$). Within this range, the access probabilities follow a Zipf distribution. The Zipf distribution with a parameter *theta* is often used to model non-uniform access. It produces access patterns that become increasingly skewed as *theta* increases. The client waits $ThinkTime$ units and then makes the next read request. The local cache maintained at the client can hold up to $CacheSize$ pages. The cache replacement policy is LRU: when the cache is full, the least recently used page is replaced. When pages are updated, the corresponding cache entries are invalidated and subsequently autoprefetched.

Table 1. Model parameters

Server Parameters		Client Parameters	
BroadcastSize	1000	ReadRange (range of client reads)	250
UpdateRange	500	theta (zipf distribution parameter)	0.95
theta (zipf distribution parameter)	0.95	Think Time (time between client reads in broadcast units)	2
Offset (update and client-read access deviation)	0 - 250 (100)	Number of Reads per Query	5 - 50 (10)
ServerReadRange	1000	Cache	
N (number of server transactions)	10	CacheSize	125
Offset (update and server-read access deviation)	0	Cache replacemnt policy	LRU
UpdateNumber	20 - 500 (100)		
ReadNumber	4*UpdateNumber		

Updates at the server are generated following a Zipf distribution similar to the read access distribution at the client. The write distribution is across the range 1 to *UpdateRange*. We use a parameter called *Offset* to model disagreement between the client access pattern and the server update pattern. When the offset is zero, the overlap between the two distributions is the greatest, that is the client's hottest pages are also the most frequently updated. An offset of k shifts the update distribution k items making them of less interest to the client. We assume that during each *bcycle*, N transactions are committed at the server. All server transactions have the same number of update operations and read operations, where read operations are four times more frequent than updates. Read operations at the server are in the range 1 to *BroadcastSize*, follow a Zipf distribution, and have zero offset with the update set at the server. Table 1 summarizes the model parameters. Values in parenthesis are the default.

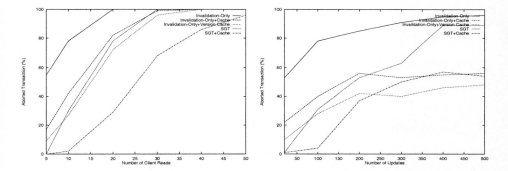

Fig. 1. Transaction aborted with the number of: (left) reads per query (right) updates

Experimental Results. To evaluate the various schemes, we considered the percentage of transactions that are aborted. First, we varied the number of read operations per query (Figure 1(left)). Whereas the SGT method with caching outperforms all other schemes, the invalidation-only scheme with versioned cache seems to offer an attractive alternative for queries with less than 30 reads, thus avoiding the considerable overhead of the SGT method. Caching reduces the number of transactions aborted since it reduces their span and thus the probability of invalidation. Then, we considered the number of updates (Figure 1 (right)). In this case, the invalidation-only scheme with versioned cache outperforms all other schemes for a large number of updates (over 1/4 of the *BroadcastSize*). This is because the possibility of cycles in the serialization graph increases with the number of operations at the server. In general, the SGT methods are less attractive than the invalidation-only methods when there is a lot of activity in the server. Thus, while for a small number of operations at the server the SGT methods more than doubles the number of queries that are accepted, when the number of operations at the server increases, the increase of the accepted transaction decreases to 10% (Figure 1(right)). Finally, we considered the overlap between the client read and the server update pattern (Figure 2). As expected, when the overlap is the maximum, that is the client's hot data are those that are most frequently updated, all schemes have the highest abort rates. When the overlap is small (less than 50%), the SGT methods accept all transactions.

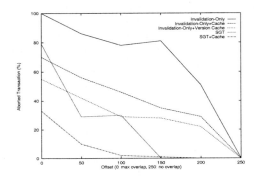

Fig. 2. Transaction aborted with the offset, i.e., update and read access deviation

7   Conclusion and Related Work

We have presented a set of invalidation-based methods that provide support for consistent queries. The methods are scalable in that their performance is independent of the number of clients. The methods were presented for a flat broadcast organization, in which all items are broadcasted with the same frequency. One possible extension is to consider a broadcast-disk organization [1], where specific items are broadcasted more frequently than others, i.e., are placed on "faster disks". An interesting problem related to the query processing methods is determining the optimal frequency for transmitting control information. We are also investigating the deployment of multiversion schemes for increasing the concurrency of queries.

Although, recently, there has been considerable interest in broadcast delivery, (for a review, see for example [9] and Chapter 4 of [12]), updates have been mainly treated in the context of caching, see for instance [6] and [2]. In this setting, updates are treated in terms of local cache consistency; there are no transaction semantics. In [11], we have first introduced the problem of maintaining the consistency of queries. In the current paper, we present specific invalidation-based techniques, prove their correctness, relate them to caching and present preliminary performance results. A weaker alternative to serializability for transactions in broadcast systems is proposed in [15]. In this work, read only transactions have similar semantics with queries in the SGT approach. However, the emphasis is on developing and formalizing a weaker serializability criterion rather than on protocols for enforcing them. Finally, broadcast in transaction management is also used in the certification-report method [5]. Read-only transactions in the certification-report method are similar to transactions in the invalidation-only method. However, in the certification-report method, data delivery is on demand, the broadcast medium is mainly used by the server to broadcast concurrency control information to its clients.

References

1. S. Acharya, et. al.: Broadcast Disks: Data Management for Asymmetric Communications Environments. Proceedings of the ACM SIGMOD Conference (1995)
2. S. Acharya, et. al.: Disseminating Updates on Broadcast Disks. Proceedings of the 22nd VLDB Conference (1996)
3. AirMedia. AirMedia Live. www.airmedia.com.
4. R. Alonso, et. al.: Data Caching Issues in an Information Retrieval System. ACM Transactions on Database Systems, 15(3) (1990) 359–384
5. D. Barbará: Certification Reports: Supporting Transactions in Wireless Systems. Proceedings of the IEEE International Conference on Distributed Computing Systems (1997)
6. D. Barbará and T. Imielinski: Sleepers and Workaholics: Caching Strategies in Mobile Environments. Proceedings of the ACM SIGMOD Conference (1994)
7. P. A. Bernstein, et. al.: Concurrency Control and Recovery in Database Systems. Addisson-Wesley (1987)
8. A. Bestavros and C. Cunha: Server-initiated Document Dissemination for the WWW. IEEE Data Engineering Bulletin 19(3) (1996)
9. M. J. Franklin and S. B. Zdonik: A Framework for Scalable Dissemination-Based Systems. Proceedings of the OOPSLA Conference (1997) 94–105
10. E. Pitoura: Scalable Invalidation-Based Processing of Queries in Broadcast Push Delivery (extended version). Technical Report 98-21, Univ. of Ioannina, Computer Science Dept (1998). Also available at: www.cs.uoi.gr/~ pitoura/pub.html.
11. E. Pitoura: Supporting Read-Only Transactions in Wireless Broadcasting. Proceedings of the DEXA98 International Workshop on Mobility in Databases and Distributed Systems (1998)
12. E. Pitoura and G. Samaras: Data Management for Mobile Computing. Kluwer Academic Publishers (1998)
13. K. Ramamritham and C. Pu: A Formal Characterization of Epsilon Serializability. IEEE Transactions on Knowledge and Data Engineering 7(6) (1995) 997–1007
14. R. Rastogi, et. al.: On Correctness of Non-serializable Executions. PODS Proceedings (1993)
15. J. Shanmugasundaram, et. al.: Transaction Processing in Broadcast Disk Environments. In S. Jajodia and L. Kerschberg, (eds.): Advanced Transaction Models and Architectures. Kluwer (1997)
16. Hughes Network Systems: DirectPC Homepage. www.direcpc.com (1997)
17. T. Yan and H. Garcia-Molina: SIFT – A Tool for Wide-area Information Dissemination. Proceedings of the USENIX Technical Conference (1995)

Timestamps to Detect R-W Conflicts in Mobile Computing

SANJAY KUMAR MADRIA

Centre for Advanced Information Systems, Division of Software System
School of Applied Sciences, Nanyang Technological University, Singapore
askumar@ntu.edu.sg

Abstract. In mobile computing, it is desirable to allow read and write accesses to occur on replicated copies of the file at MH (mobile host) and MSS (mobile service station) to increase availability. However, the read-write conflicts among the copies of the database file are to be detected when MH gets connected to MSS. We present a timestamp based technique for the detection of read-write conflicts for a single file in mobile computing. In our model, we detect and resolve read-write conflicts with the help of stored timestamps along with some additional information. We assume updates at MH and MSSs as blind writes (do not read data before updating) common in mobile computing environment. Blind writes do not cause write-write (W-W) conflicts and therefore, we deal with only read-write (R-W) conflicts.

1 Introduction

The ability to replicate the data is essential in mobile computing [2] to increase availability and performance. Replicated systems need to provide support for disconnected mode, data divergence, application defined reconciliation procedures, optimistic concurrency control, etc. Replication is a way by which the system ensures transparency for mobile users. There are many issues such as how to manage data replication, providing the levels of consistency, durability and availability needed. [22] consider a general model for maintaining consistency of replicated data in distributed applications. In [1], a new replication protocol and Software-architecture for data processing on mobile platforms including transaction processing, synchronization, reintegration, and management of mobile data objects is discussed. [9] discuss the data replication in mobile computing. In [7], it has been argued that traditional replica control methods [8] are not suitable for mobile databases and the authors have presented a virtual primary copy method. In Coda [10,24], during the disconnected operation, a client continues to have read and write accesses to data in its cache. When connectivity is restored, the system propagates the modifications and detects update conflicts. Many transaction processing models have been designed [4,6,13,16,17,18,19,23,25] to increase the availability in mobile computing environment. A survey is given in [15].

In mobile computing, it is desirable to keep the mobile host functioning in the presence of disconnection by replicating the database files over MH and MSS. The operations may be allowed to execute independently on replicated copies at MH and MSS to increase availability. However, the actual commit of transaction will be delayed until a reconnection is made with the MSS. This is because there is a possibility of backing out some of the transactions on reconnection. When the MH is disconnected, each MH and MSS maintains the consistent data but cannot make sure that their operations do not conflict with the operations in the other MSSs and the MH. Therefore, global inconsistencies across the MH and MSS may occur. There are two types of conflicting operations read-write and write-write [3] depending upon the order of read and write operations. When connection is established between the MH and the MSS, read-write and write-write conflicts among the copies of the database files are to be detected.

The algorithm [20] proposed for the detection of write-write conflicts for a single file using version vectors can be adopted for mobile computing. However, the algorithm detects only write-write conflict, where as in our mobile computing scenario the detection of read-write conflict is more important. Moreover in [20], resolving inconsistency is not straight-forward and is essentially left to the user. This scheme has also been extended to the transactions that access more than one file [21]. However, it does not detect all inconsistencies and in fact, detect some false inconsistencies [5]. The precedence graph technique [5] for detecting write-write and read-write conflicts can be used in mobile databases. However, it needs to detect cycles in the global transaction graph and has to keep track of all the reads and writes which occur at MH and MSSs. Thus, the algorithm has a high cost associated. Our motivation is to detect the conflicts by keeping minimum amount of information and moreover, use timestamps to detect possible conflicts.

One might think that with a simple timestamp scheme using synchronized clocks [11,12] at each MH and MSS, it would be possible to detect conflicts among the copies of a single file. However, this is not possible as the operations (read and write) execute independently at MH and MSSs. Therefore, the conflicts may or may not occur even if the reading or writing time of a file in MH may be less than the writing time of the same file at MSS. Hence, the detection of conflicts using simple timestamp scheme is not possible. This has been stated in [20] for the case of simple network partitions. In an earlier attempt [20], the following strategy has been mentioned (no algorithm was given) for the detection of only write-write conflicts using timestamps for a single file in case of network partitions. Whenever a file is modified, one marks it with the two update times namely the previous and the last. When two partitions merge, a check is made to find whether no update in the file has occurred or one copy of the file differs from the other by a single update. In such cases no conflict occurs, but in many complex situations, the approach fails [14].

The timestamp approach in this paper permits the read and write operations to execute independently at MH and MSSs and thus, allows possible inconsistencies to occur at the cost of more availability. We assume in our work here that updates that occur are blind writes. In mobile computing, files that keep data such as stock indices, currency rates, etc. can be updated without necessarily reading their earlier values and hence, are considered blind writes. We allow such blind writes and reads in mobile computing applications to improve availability. However, we validate reads that occur at both the places while disconnection, on reconnection.

We think that timeliness of read operations in mobile database computing is more important than response time (final commit). That is, final commit of read transactions can be delayed until a connection is established between the MH and MSSs but operations should be allowed to occur both at MH and MSS. In our model, we detect read-write conflicts when a connection is established between MH and MSS. Since we consider only blind writes, write-write conflicts do not arise. As we have seen earlier, timestamps alone are not enough to detect conflicts. Therefore, in our approach, we use read and write timestamps along with some additional information to detect and reconcile read-write conflicts for a single file. The additional information is in the form of a row-vector and each read and write timestamp is attached with this row-vector. These row-vectors are also compared to detect conflicts while comparing read and write timestamps. Our technique for resolving read-write conflicts does not take into account the semantics of the operations that manipulated the file, and the semantics of the data being stored.

Assumptions

- transactions do not read the data object before write; that is, we consider blind writes only. In mobile computing environment, blind writes occur very frequently. For example, if one would like to update the latest stock indices, or wants to update the latest traffic or weather information. These information can be updated without reading previous data. In all such situations, updates are blind write only. Therefore, while reading, we need to determine whether the reads return the consistent value or not. Therefore, we mainly focus on detecting read and write conflict. Note that in case of blind writes, write-write conflicts do not occur.

- read-only transactions commit only after a connection is established between the MH and MSS.

- no network partition occurs which can isolate these physically connected MSSs. Thus, at any time, there are no conflicts among copies of the file at MSSs.

- the physical clocks are synchronized at each MH and MSS, i..e, the time drifts among the clocks are uniform (or negligible). Our focus in this paper is towards finding a timestamp based solution for detection of read-write conflicts in wireless computing framework, that itself is a non-trivial problem. We are not concerned here to solve the problem of synchronising clocks across the MH and MSS. However, for implementation, we can use physical clocks at each MH and MSS that are only allowed to drift marginally [12].

- We also assume "read-one and write-all" approach among MSSs and thus, no conflicts of any kind are allowed among MSSs.

- Our conflict detection technique works only for a single file.

2 Our Model

In this section, we formalize some definitions and discuss some data structures to be used in the model.

Definition 1: Two operations in two different transactions are said to be in **read-write conflict** if both the operations access the same data file simultaneously and one of the two operations is a write operation and the other is a read. Note that in our discussion we consider only read-write conflict.

Definition 2: A **first update time** is the time when the first update takes place at MH (MSS) after it is disconnected with the MSS (MH). When the MH (MSS) is disconnected, the time of the first update at MH (MSS) is stored. This defines the first update time at MH (MSS). For next update, its time is stored but is updated for subsequent updates. The time of second or subsequent updates will become the **last update time** at the MH (MSS) before it moves to the new cell and starts receiving the updates consistent with the MSS. See more details in section 3.2.

Definition 3: A **W-timestamp** vector for a file f is defined as a sequence of $n + 1$ write timestamp elements where n is the number of MSSs in the system and we assume that there is one MH. Each timestamp element can be at the most two tuples where the first value is the first update time and second value is the last update time at the MH or MSS. After a disconnection, a new W-timestamp vector is to be formed both at the MH and MSSs provided some updates occur in the copy of the file at the MH and MSSs. When an update occurs at the MSS (MH), only the timestamp elements corresponding to the MSSs (MH) present is updated and the other corresponding to MH (MSSs) remains the same. The W-timestamp vector is stored in the form of the following template: $< \{MSS_1\}, \{MSS_2\},....\{MSS_n\},\{MH\}>$.

For example, suppose A and B are two MSS in the system and C is the MH. Let wT_i and wT_j be the initial and final update times at the MSS and MH for a file f before a disconnection, respectively. The W-timestamp vector, when both the MSS and MH are connected will be $<\{ wT_i, wT_j \}, \{wT_i, wT_j \}, \{wT_i, wT_j \}>$. After a disconnection, suppose mobile host C is disconnected from the MSS. If the first update occurs at C at time wT_k and the last at wT_m then the new W-timestamp vector of C will be $<\{wT_i, wT_j \},\{wT_i, wT_j\}, \{wT_k, wT_m\}>$. That is, only the timestamp element of the MH is updated and the others remain the same. Similarly, if the first update at the MSS occurs at WT_1, then the W-timestamp vector will become $< WT_1 , WT_1 , \{wT_i, wT_j\}>$.

Definition 4: A **disconnection row-vector** for a copy of the file f is an ordered tuple of flag values 0 or 1. Initially, the flag value is set to 1 for all the MSS and the MH. Note that we have assumed that all the MSSs are connected all time, therefore, entries in the row-vector corresponding to the MSSs will always be 1. Whenever an update occurs at the MH during a disconnection, the flag value corresponding to the MH is changed to 1 and for all others is set to 0. Similarly, if an update occurs at the MSSs, the row-vector has 0 entry for the MH and 1 for others. These row-vectors move with the MH from one cell to the other and are attached with each W-timestamp vectors and read timestamps. The row-vector keeps the information in the form of the following template: $<MSS_1, MSS_2,.... MSS_n, MH>$.

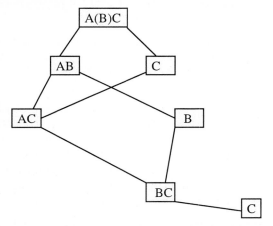

Figure 1. Mobile Disconnection Graph

Definition 5: A **mobile *disconnection graph*** PG(f) for any file f is a directed graph where the source node is labelled with the names of all the MSSs and the MH in the system having a copy of the file f and all the other nodes are labelled with a subset of this set of names. Each node (other than the source) can only be labelled with the one of the names of the MSS and the MH appearing in its ancestor nodes in the graph; conversely every MSS or MH on a node must appear on exactly one node of its descendants.

Example: Consider a disconnection graph DG(f) with two mobile service stations A and B and a mobile host C where each MSS and the MH has a copy of the file f as shown in Figure 1. Initially, MSS B and MH C are connected. After a disconnection, C is isolated and later on, gets connected with A. Next C is again connected with B, and then C is again isolated. We need to determine the conflicts each time C is connected with a MSS after it gets isolated.

3 Properties

In this section, we list some of the properties of our model.

- For the detection of read-write conflicts, we need only the first and the last write timestamps in each W-timestamp vector.

- We also need all the timestamps corresponding to the read operations performed at the MH and MSS. Therefore, we store one read timestamp per read operation both at the MH and MSSs.

- We also need to store at the most two W-timestamp vectors at MH and MSSs; initial and the one may be after the disconnection.

- Initially, the W-timestamp vector consists of the first and the last write timestamps corresponding to MSSs and the MH while connected. Later, the MH may have one new W-timestamp vector and all the MSSs collectively may have another new W-timestamp vector.

- If a write operation occurs after a disconnection at the MH (MSSs) then the write timestamp entries at the MH (all MSSs) is updated. This gives one new W-timestamp vector at MH and another at MSSs.

- Read and write timestamps are kept at the MH and MSSs until the MH establishes the connection with the MSS.

Some Observations

- MH and each MSS will have one new W-timestamp vector corresponding to each disconnection provided that the value of the file is updated during that disconnection. That is, each disconnection corresponds to one new W-timestamp vector in case there is an update.

- If there is no update during a disconnection, there will not be any new W-timestamp vector. Thus, the value returned by the read operation will be the last updated value when the MH and the MSS were connected.

3.1 Processing of Row-vectors

We associate a disconnection row-vector with each W-timestamp vector and with each read timestamp at the MH and MSSs. The row-vector gives some additional information and is associated with the timestamp of read and writes both at the MH and MSS. The first update on being disconnected in an old cell or new cell will update the entry in the row-vector corresponding to the MH to 1 and for all the MSSs to 0. The subsequent updates at the MH while disconnected will not change the row-vector entries. Note that in a new cell, if there is no new update, a read operation will return the last updated value at the MH in the previous cell. Therefore, the row-vector attached with the read timestamp will be the row-vector attached with the W-timestamp vector of the corresponding old cell. On the other hand, if there is an update in the new cell, a read operation will return the new value and the row-vector associated with the read timestamp will be the row-vector attached with the W-timestamp vector of the new cell. Similarly, when there is an update at MSSs only while the MH is disconnected, the row-vector entries remains 1 while the row-vector entry corresponding to the MH is changed to 0. In case updates or reads take place at both MSSs and the MH, all the entries in the associated row-vector will be 1.

When a write operation wants to update the file at MSSs, it first checks the row-vector associated with the W-timestamp vector at its home site. It updates the copies of the file at all the MSSs (write-all approach) and the MH having entry as 1 in the row-vector. In case the write operation is not able to update the copy of the file at the MH, it writes the copies of the file at all MSSs. It then update the row-vector entry corresponding to the MH as 0 at all the MSSs. Similarly when a write operation occurs at the MH, it first establishes a connection to the MSS in its cell. If it is successful, it updates the file and also sends the updates to its co-ordinating MSS, which in turn sends the updates to all the other MSSs. Otherwise, the MH updates the copy of its own file and change the row-vector entries to 0 for all the MSSs. However, a read transaction at the MH (MSS) will not be able to find out if there is an update at the MSS (MH) as it reads the value only at its home site. Therefore, it may return an old value. However, it will be detected later as it will generate a read-write conflict with respect to consistent updates.

3.2 First and Last Write Timestamps

When a write operation performs the first update on the file (the file may have some initial value before) at the MSSs and the MH, the time of this write operation is stored. This point onwards the write timestamp of the next write will be stored but this will be updated for subsequent writes. In general, when a disconnection is detected and a write operation's is performed independently at the MH or MSSs, it will be the first operation that will update the file at the MH or MSSs. Therefore, its time will be stored as the first update time. For the next write either at the MSSs or MH, its write time will be stored but will be updated for subsequent writes. This will determine the first and the last update time at the MH or MSSs.

4 Detection of Read-Write Conflicts

Suppose we detect first R-W conflicts between the read timestamps stored at the MH and the write timestamp elements from the W-timestamp vectors stored at the MSS. Note that there may be at the most two W-timestamp vectors at the MH or MSS; one is initial when all the MSSs and the MH were connected and the other may be created on disconnection. First, we compare the latest read timestamp available at the MH with the write timestamp of the file from the last W-timestamp vector at the MSS. Suppose the latest read timestamp of the file at the MH is less than the corresponding write timestamp element of the file at the MSS. In this case, we compare the read timestamp with the write timestamp elements from the previous W-timestamp vectors at the MSS. While comparing, on of the conditions given below will be satisfied. Similar conditions will hold for comparing reads at the MSS with the writes at the MH.

Conditions for the Detection of Read-Write Conflicts

Condition 1: If $\mathrm{Min} \{wT_m, wT_n\}_{mss} < [rT_k]_{mh} < \mathrm{Max} \{wT_m, wT_n\}_{mss}$
and the row-vectors attached with read and write timestamps differ
then R-W conflict
else no R-W conflict

Condition 2: If $[rT_k]_{mh} = \mathrm{Max} \{wT_m, wT_n\}_{mss}$ or
$[rT_k]_{mh} = \mathrm{Min} \{wT_m, wT_n\}_{mss}$
then R-W conflict

Condition 3: If $[rT_k]_{mh} > Max \{wT_m, wT_n\}_{mss}$ and
the row-vectors attached with read and write timestamps differ and the
row-vector attached with the write timestamp is not the initial row-
vector then R-W conflict
else no R-W conflict

Condition 4: If $[rT_k]_{mh} > Max \{wT_m, wT_n\}_{mss}$ and the row-vectors
attached with the write timestamp is the initial row-vector
then no R-W conflict.

Note: Condition 4 is different from 3 since it takes care of the case when there is an
update at MSS after a read has occurred at MH. In this case, the row-vectors are
different but no conflict occurs as the read returns the value before the first update at
MSS after the MH was disconnected.

$[rT_k]_{mh}$ indicates the read at k_{th} time at MH.

$\{wT_m, wT_n\}_{mss}$ indicates that wT_m is the initial and wT_n is the final update
times at MSS.

Min $\{wT_m, wT_n\}_{mss} = \{wT_m\}_{mss}$ and Max $\{wT_m, wT_n\}_{mss} = \{wT_n\}_{mss}$.

4.1 New W-timestamp Vector

When a R-W conflict is detected between the MH and MSS, we simply discard the
read timestamps in conflict with the write timestamp from the W-timestamp vector. All
the old valid reads after detecting the conflicts are committed and their read
timestamps are also discarded. Timestamps of reads now onwards are again stored.
Note that since reading is performed at only one place, any disconnection is only
detected while writing since we use "read-one and write-all" approach.

After the read-write conflicts have been detected, there are two different W-
timestamp vectors exist; one at the MH and the other at the MSS. Since the MH and
MSS are now connected, there should be only one W-timestamp vector. To do this, we
take the maximum of corresponding write timestamps in the two W-timestamp vectors
and use the corresponding last value of the copy of the file at that MSS or MH (as the
case may be) as the current value of the file. We use this value to make all the copies
of the file consistent. In case the last updated value is as occurred at the MH, the
copies of the file at all the MSSs also need to be made consistent. Otherwise, only the
copy of the file at the MH needs to be updated. The new W-timestamp vector now acts
as the initial W-timestamp vector for all the MSSs and the MH. Now onwards, the
write timestamp entries are updated as before. The associated row-vector entries are
then changed to 1 for all the MSSs and the MH. Now onwards, the new write
timestamp can be stored as next write timestamp in the new installed W-timestamp
vector but will be updated for subsequent writes as before.

5 Snapshot of Our Model

Case 1: Consider the case when only reads are allowed at the MH while disconnected. R-W conflicts are to be detected between the reads that occur at the MH and writes that occur at the MSS while in disconnection mode. Conflicts are detected when the MH is connected to the MSS. We consider two MSSs A and B, and one MH C.

Let the W-timestamp vectors and read timestamps at MSS A and MH C be as follows:

At A
W-timestamp vectors
$<wT_1, w\,T_1, w\,T_1> <111>_A$
$<\{wT_5, wT_7\}, \{wT_5, wT_7\}, wT_1> <110>_A$
At C
read timestamps
$rT_4 <111>_c$
$<rT_6, rT_{10}> <111>_c$

1. W-timestamp vector $<\{wT_5, wT_7\}, \{wT_5, wT_7\}, wT_1> <110>_A$ gives the following information:

- about the writes which occur at MSS A. It says that the first write has occurred at wT_5 whereas the last write at wT_7 while the MH C was disconnected.

- The row-vector $<110>_A$ gives the information that only MSSs have received those writes.

2. A row-vector attached with a W-timestamp vector gives the information about the MSSs and the MH present when the updates start occurring.

3. The read timestamp $<rT_6, rT_{10}> <111>_c$ denotes the following :

- first read at the MH C has occurred at time rT_6 and the last read is at time rT_{10}.

- The row-vector $<111>_c$ attached with the read timestamp implies that both the read operations have returned the values correspond to the last write when the MH and MSS were connected, and these reads have occurred at MH C.

Conflict Detection : When the wireless connection is established, the read timestamps at MH are compared with the write timestamps at MSS to detect the possible read-write conflicts.

- rT_4 is a valid read as this has occurred before the first write at wT_5 at the MSS after disconnection. Since the row-vectors attached with read timestamp and the W-timestamp vectors are identical, read has returned the last write value. This is according to the condition 3 in section 4. Thus, the read that occurred at the MH while disconnected does not conflict with the writes at the MSSs.

- rT_6 and rT_{10} both are rejected as their attached row-vectors are different. That is, these reads have been performed after some updates have taken place at MSSs. This is according to the condition 1 in section 4.

Case 2: Here we consider the case where reads and blind writes both occur at MH and MSSs. Read-write conflicts are to be determined when the MH is connected to the MSS.

At A

W-timestamp vectors   read

timestamps

$<wT_1, wT_1, wT_1> <111>$ $rT_2 <111>_A$

$<\{wT_4, wT_7\}, \{wT_4, wT_7\}, wT_1> <110>$ $<rT_5, rT_8> <110>_A$

At C

$<wT_1, wT_1, wT_1> <111>$ $rT_3 <111>_C, rT_5 <111>_C$

$<wT_1, wT_1, wT_6> <001>$ $<rT_8, rT_{10}> <001>_C$

Reads performed at MH and writes at MSS: First we compare all the read timestamps at MH with the update timestamps at MSS.

- rT_3 is a valid read (though it has occurred while the MH is disconnected) as it returns the consistent value; the value before an independent update has occurred at the MSS. The row-vector $<111>_C$ informs that the returned value is the last updated value at the MSS and the MH while both were connected.

- rT_5 is not a valid read as there is an update at wT_4 at the MSS. Note that this information is only known by comparing the row-vectors attached, which are different. Otherwise, it may be possible that this read might have occurred when the MH was connected to the MSS, so it must have received the consistent update. For similar reasons, rT_8 and rT_{10} are also rejected.

Reads performed at MSS and writes at MH: Now we compare reads performed at MSS with the updates at MH.

- rT_2 is a valid read as it has occurred before an update took place at the MH and the attached row-vector is same as attached with the first W-timestamp vector at the MH. This is according to the condition 1 in section 4.

- rT_5 is also a valid read as the first update at the MH after disconnection took place after the read has been performed though the row-vectors attached are different. This case is covered in the condition 4 in section 4.

- rT_8 is rejected as it has occurred after an update has been performed at the MH at wT_6. This is by condition 3 in section 4.

Once the conflicts are determined, the W-timestamp vector will be $<wT_7, wT_7, wT_7> <111>$. This will be the new W-timestamp vector. The new value of the file at the MSSs and the MH will be the value as exists at the MSS as the last update has occurred at wT_7 at the MSSs. In case, the last update value is taken as exists at MH, then the copies of the file at all the MSSs are to be made consistent. This is because in case the MH moves to the new cell, the false conflicts should not be detected.

6 Conclusions

In this paper, we have presented an efficient and useful technique for detecting and resolving read-write conflicts in mobile computing using the timestamps and some additional information. In our model, an inconsistency has been assumed due to multiple users modifying different copies of the same file both at the MSSs and the MH to improve availability. Conflicts have been detected when the MH is connected to the MSS by validating all the reads that occur at the MSSs and the MH. We assume blind writes in our model, thus, write-write conflicts do not arise. Our model increases the availability by allowing reads and writes to occur while there is no wireless connection. This work needs to be extended for multiple files.

References

1. Alonso, L., Data Sharing on Mobile Platforms, in Proceedings of the IASTED International Conference on Parallel and Distributed Computing and Networks (PDCN'97), Singapore, Aug. 1997.
2. Badrinath, B.R. and Imielinski, T., Replication and Mobility, in 2nd Workshop on the Management of Replicated Data, pages 9 -12, IEEE, Nov.1992.
3. Bernstein, P., Hadzilacos, V. and Goodman, N., Concurrency Control and Recovery in Database systems, Reading, MA: Addision-Wesley, 1987.
4. Chrysanthis, P.K., Transaction Processing in a Mobile Computing Environment, Proceedings of IEEE workshop on Advances in Parallel and Distributed Systems, pp.77-82, Oct.1993.
5. Davidson, S.B., Optimism and Consistency in Partitioned Distributed Database Systems, ACM Transactions on Database Systems, Vol. 9, No. 3, pp. 456-481, Sept., 1984.
6. Eich, M.H. and Helal, A., A Mobile Transaction Model That Captures Both Data and Movement Behaviour, to appear in ACM/Baltzer Journal on Special Topics on Mobile Networks and Applications, 1997.
7. Faiz, M. and Zaslavsky, A., Database Replica Management Strategies in Multidatabase Systems with Mobile Hosts, in 6th International Hong Kong Computer Society Database Workshop, 1995.
8. Helal, A., Heddaya, A., and Bhargava, B., Replicated Techniques in Distributed Systems, Kluwer Academic Publishers, 1996.
9. Huang, Y., Sistla, P. and Wolfson, O., Data Replication for Mobile Computers, in Proceedings of the ACM SIGMOD International Conference on Management of Data, 1994.
10. Kisler J. and M. Satyanarayanan, Disconnected Operation in the Coda File System, ACM Transactions on Computer Systems, 10(1), 1992.
11. Lamport L., Time, Clocks, and the Ordering of Events in a Distributed System, Communication of ACM, Vol. 21, pp. 558-565, July, 1978.
12. Liskov, B., Practical Uses of Synchronised clocks in Distributed Systems, in proceedings of 10th ACM Symposium on Principles of Distributed Computing, Aug., 1991.

13. Lu Q. and Satyanaraynan, M., Improving Data Consistency in Mobile Computing Using Isolation-Only Transactions, in proceedings of the fifth workshop on Hot Topics in Operating Systems, Orcas Island, Washington, May 1995.

14. Madria, S. K., Timestamp Based Detection and Resolution of Mutual Conflicts in a Distributed Systems, in the proceedings of IEEE Computer Society for the 8th International Conference and Workshops for the Database and Expert System Applications (DEXA, 97), Sept. 1997. Extended version to appear in The Computer Journal.

15. Madria, S. K., Transaction Models for Mobile Computing, in proceedings of 6th IEEE SICON, Singapore, World Scientific Pub., July, 1998.

16. Madria, S.K. and B. Bhargava, A Transaction Model for Mobile Computing, in proceedings of IEEE CS for 2nd International Database Engineering and Application Symposium (IDEAS'98), Cardiff, U. K, July, 1998.

17. Madria, S.K. and B. Bhargava, Improving Availability in Mobile Computing Using Prewrite Operations, Technical Report, CSD-TR 97-032, Department of Computer Science, Purdue University, IN, USA, June, 1997.

18. Madria, S. K. and Bhargava, B., On the Correctness of a Transaction Model for Mobile Computing, 9th International Conference and workshop on Database and Expert Systems (DEXA,98). Also, in Lecturer Notes in Computer Science,Vol 1460.

19. Pitoura E. and B. Bhargava, Maintaining Consistency of Data in Mobile Computing Environments, in proceedings of 15th International Conference on Distributed Computing Systems, June,1995.

20. Parker D.Scott, Gerald J., and Popek et al., Detection of Mutual Inconsistency in Distributed Systems, IEEE Transactions on Software Engineering, Vol. SE-9, No.3, May, 1983.

21. Parker, D. S. and Ramos, R.A., A Distributed File System Architecture Supporting High Availability, in Proceedings of 6th Berkeley Workshop on Distributed Data Management and Computer Networks, pp. 161-183, 1982.

22. Ravindran, K. and Shah, K., Casual Broadcasting and Consistency of Distributed Data, in 14th International Conference on Distributed Computing Systems, pages 40-47, June, 1994.

23. Rasheed, A. and Zaslavsky, A., Ensuring Database Availability in Dynamically Changing Mobile Computing Environment, in Proceedings of the 7th Australian Database Conference, Melborne, Australia, 1996 .

24. Satyanarayanan, M., Kistler, J.J., Kumar, B., et al., Coda: A Highly Available File System for a Distributed Workstation Environment, IEEE Transaction on Computers, 39(4), April, 1990.

25. Walborn, G. D., Chrysanthis, P.K., Supporting Semantics-Based Transaction Processing in Mobile Database Applications, in proceedings of 14th IEEE Symposium on Reliable Distributed Systems, pp.31-40, Sept.1995.

Rumor: Mobile Data Access Through Optimistic Peer-to-Peer Replication

Richard Guy[1], Peter Reiher[1], David Ratner[2], Michial Gunter[3], Wilkie Ma[1],
and Gerald Popek[4]

[1] University of California, Los Angeles, Los Angeles, CA 90095-1596, USA
http://fmg-www.cs.ucla.edu/rumor98/replication.html
rumor-report@fmg.cs.ucla.edu
[2] currently with Software.com
[3] currently with Silicon Graphics, Inc.
[4] also affiliated with PLATINUM *technology, inc.*)

Abstract. [1] Rumor is an optimistically replicated file system designed for use in mobile computers. Rumor uses a peer model that allows opportunistic update propagation among any sites replicating files. The paper outlines basic characteristics of replication systems for mobile computers, describes the design and implementation of the Rumor file system, and presents performance data for Rumor. The research described demonstrates the feasibility of using peer optimistic replication to support mobile computing.

1   Introduction

Mobile computers typically suffer from weaker connectivity than that enjoyed by wired machines. Latencies are significantly higher, bandwidth is limited, power conservation requirements discourage communication, some communications media cost money to use, and long-duration disconnections are the norm. In this context, data management techniques that dramatically reduce the need for continuous connectivity are highly desirable.

One such potential class of solutions is data replication, in which copies of data are placed at various hosts in the overall network, generally 'near' to users and often local to users. In the extreme, a data replica is stored on each mobile computer that desires to access (read or write) that data, so all user data access is local. Ideally, all replicas of a data item should have the same value at all times, and it is the responsibility of the replication system to maintain consistency in the face of updates. Specific goals for a replication system often include improved reliability, availability, data autonomy, host and network traffic load balancing, and data access performance.

[1] This work was supported by the United States Defense Advanced Research Projects Agency under contract number DABT63-94-C-0080.

This paper describes the Rumor replicated file system, which was designed for use in a mobile environment. The goal of mobility led to development decisions focusing on availability, autonomy, and network traffic reduction from the mobile machine's point of view. The paper discusses design alternatives for replicated file systems, the decisions made for the Rumor system, the architecture of that system, performance of the Rumor system, and lessons learned in developing Rumor.

2 Replication Design Alternatives

Replication systems can usefully be classified along several dimensions: conservative vs. optimistic update, client-server vs. peer-to-peer, and immediate propagation vs. periodic reconciliation.

2.1 Conservative vs. optimistic update

A fundamental question in replicated data systems is how to handle updates to multiple copies of the same data item. If the copies cannot communicate instantaneously, then concurrent updates to different replicas of the same data item are possible, violating the ideal semantics of emulating single copy data storage.

Conservative update replication systems prevent all concurrent updates, causing mobile users who store replicas of data items to have their updates rejected frequently, particularly if connectivity is poor or non- existent. Even when connected, mobile users will spend bandwidth to check consistency at every update. Conservative strategies are often appropriate in the wired world, but they work poorly in most mobile environments.

Optimistic replication allows any machine storing a replica to perform an update locally, rather than requiring the machine to acquire locks or votes from other replicas. Optimistic replication minimizes the bandwidth and connectivity requirements for performing updates. However, optimistic replication systems can allow conflicting updates to replicated data items. Both simulation results [17] and extensive actual experience [7], [14] have shown that conflicts are rare and usually easy to resolve.

2.2 Client-server vs. peer-to-peer

In client-server replication, all updates must be propagated first to a server machine that further propagates them to all clients. Peer-to-peer systems allow any replica to propagate updates to any other replica. Client-server systems simplify replication systems and limit costs (partially through imposing a bottleneck at the server), but slow propagation of updates among replicas and are subject to failure of the server. Peer systems can propagate updates faster by making use of any available connectivity, but are more complex both in implementation and in the states they can achieve. Hybrid systems use peer replication among servers, with all other machines serving as clients. These hybrid systems typically try to avoid the disadvantages of peer systems by requiring tight connectivity among all servers, implying that none of them can be disconnected mobile machines.

Client-server replication is a good choice for some mobile systems, such as mobile computers that disconnect from a central network and remain disconnected until they return. Workers who take their machines home at night, or go on trips with their portable computer and only connect to the home machine via modem while away, are examples of mobile computing suitable for client/server replication. Peer replication is a good choice when the connectivity patterns of the mobile computers are less predictable. Environments suited to peer replication include disaster relief teams that must carry their own infrastructure or a wireless office of cooperating workers.

2.3 Immediate propagation vs. periodic reconciliation

Updates to data replicas must be propagated to all other replicas. Update propagation can be attempted immediately when the update occurs, or at a later time. Immediate propagation notifies other replicas of the new state of the data as quickly as possible, when it works. However, it may use scarce, expensive resources to do so, perhaps when immediate propagation was not very important. Alternatively, updates can be propagated at a later, more convenient time, typically batched. This option of periodic reconciliation does not spread updates as quickly, but allows propagation to occur when it is cheap or convenient. In systems permitting disconnected operation, some form of periodic reconciliation must be supported, since immediate propagation will fail when machines are disconnected. Both options can be supported, at the cost of extra complexity and possibly higher use of scarce, expensive resources.

3 Rumor Design and Architecture

Rumor is an optimistic, peer-to-peer, reconciliation-based replicated file system. Rumor is built at the user level, which has advantages in portability and limiting replication costs. It has been operational for several years in our research laboratory and other sites worldwide, and runs on several Unix systems.

To achieve higher portability, Rumor is built strictly at the application level. Rumor has its intellectual roots in the Ficus replicated file system [2], which was an in-kernel, SunOS 4.0.3-based implementation of an optimistic, peer-to-peer replication system that used immediate propagation with reconciliation as a fall-back. Rumor borrows much of the internal consistency policies and algorithms from Ficus. Both systems allow updates whenever any replica is available. The reconciliation algorithms of both systems reliably detect concurrent file system updates and automatically handle concurrent updates to directory replicas. Both Rumor and Ficus permit users to write tools to automatically reconcile concurrent file updates for other kinds of files [13].

Rumor operates entirely at the application level. Rumor requires no kernel modifications or dynamically loadable libraries. Installation is accomplished entirely without super-user (root) privileges, allowing anyone to install or upgrade Rumor. The benefits of this application-level implementation include being easily portable across different systems and platforms, free distribution of Rumor source code with no license restrictions, and no Rumor performance overhead during the normal operation of the host machine. Nothing is installed in the critical path of the user's operations, so Rumor users pay no performance cost except when they choose to reconcile.

Rumor is purely optimistic, and uses peer replication. While Rumor's peer replication mechanically permits any replica to reconcile with any other replica, mechanisms exist to effectively constrain the patterns of reconciliation. Thus, Rumor can emulate a client-server system or any other constrained topology of update propagation suitable for particular situations. Rumor maintains consistency purely by a periodic process called *reconciliation*. Rumor does not attempt instant update propagation. Periodic reconciliation makes the problems of temporary network and machine failures easier to solve, as reconciliation guarantees to maintain consistency when communication can be restored. Additionally, multiple updates to a single file can often be batched and transmitted as one update, with the usual batching performance improvement. Furthermore, the costs of communicating with other replicas are amortized, since updates to multiple files are handled in a single reconciliation.

Rumor operates on file sets known as *volumes*. A volume is a continuous portion of the file system tree, larger than a directory but smaller than a file system. For example, a user's mail directory might constitute a volume. Volumes have been used in many systems because they offer several key benefits. They take advantage of locality for performance by grouping logically connected files into a single physical location. Performance-intensive tasks are initiated once for the volume entity, instead of once per volume member. Volumes provide natural firewalls that prevent the propagation of errors and help establish fundamental security barriers. Volumes also assist in naming, by allowing a collection of logically connected files to be identified and acted upon with a single name.

Reconciliation operates at the volume granularity. At reconciliation time, replicas synchronize a single volume. When machines store multiple volumes, reconciliation periodically executes separately on each volume. The reconciliation interval controls the balance point between consistency and system load. Users are free to customize or add intelligence such as load-threshold values to the reconciliation interval.

A disadvantage of pure volume replication is that entire volumes must be stored at each replica and reconciled as a whole. This is a significant disadvantage for a mobile computing system, where disk space available for storage may be limited, and small quantities of bandwidth suitable for propagating only very important updates might be available. Rumor overcomes this problem by *selective replication* [10] and a per-file reconciliation mechanism. Selective replication allows particular replicas to store only portions of a volume, while still guaranteeing correct operation. Per-file reconciliation permits individual files to be reconciled, rather than the entire volume, at much lower costs.

Reconciliation operates between a pair of communicating replicas in a one-way, pull-oriented fashion. A one-way mode is more general than a two-way model, and lends support for inherently uni-directional forms of communication, such as floppy-disk transfer. At reconciliation time, the target replica selects a source replica with which to reconcile; selection is based on a number of criteria, described below. Once a source replica has been identified and contacted, reconciliation ensures that the target learns all information known by the source. This information includes *gossip*: the source replica transfers not only its local updates, but also all updates it has learned of from previous reconciliations with other replicas. For instance, two machines that rarely or never directly communicate can still share data if a mutually-accessible third machine gossips on the others' behalf.

Reconciliation involves only pairs of replicas, rather than all replicas, because there is no guarantee that more than two will ever be simultaneously available. For example, mobile computers operating in a *portable workgroup* mode may only be connected to a single other computer. Additionally, operating in a point-to-point mode, with an underlying gossip-based transfer mechanism, allows a more flexible and dynamically changeable network configuration in terms of the machines' accessibility from each other. Broadcast or multicast reconciliation will often save significant amounts of bandwidth, but they are not yet implemented in Rumor.

Reconciliation is responsible for maintaining data consistency on all user-nameable files. Rumor uses Parker's *version vectors* [8] to detect updates and update/update *conflicts* (concurrent updates). A version vector is a dynamic vector of counters, with one counter per replica. Each counter i tracks the total number of known updates generated by replica i. Each replica independently maintains its own version vector for each replicated file; by comparing two version vectors, the update histories of the corresponding file replicas can be compared.

The particular choices of communication partners between sites forms the *reconciliation topology*. While the reconciliation algorithms are topology independent, the actual topology can affect both the number of messages exchanged between all replicas and the time required to reach consistency. Rumor utilizes an *adaptive ring* between all volume replicas, which reconfigures itself in response to current replica availability and provides that reconciliation occurs with the next accessible ring member. In the extreme, if only two replicas are in communication, the adaptive nature of the ring allows them to reconcile with each other. The adaptive ring requires only a linear complexity in the number of volume replicas to propagate information to everyone, and additionally is robust to network failures and reconfigurations. Due to its adaptive nature, the ring does not require point-to-point links interconnecting all members, and thus allows sharing to occur between rarely or never-communicating participants by relying on third-party replicas to gossip on their behalf. However, the ring does not scale well in number of replicas.

Rumor is designed to handle arbitrary numbers of replicas and correctly manage data consistency between all of them. Performance, rather than correctness, dictates replication factor scaling for Rumor. Rumor scales gracefully to approximately 20 replicas of any given volume. An extension to Rumor, called Roam, allows an order of magnitude better scaling [11].

Replicated systems face special problems when handling deallocation of system resources (such as disk space) held by unnamed file system objects. This deallocation process is called *garbage collection*. In a centralized system, garbage collection is relatively simple. Whenever the last name for a file is deleted, all of the file's resources can be reclaimed. Garbage collection is harder in a distributed, replicated environment due to dynamic naming. Dynamic naming allows users to generate new names for existing files; since a file should not be removed until all names have been removed, including new names at remote replicas, local removal of the last name may not indicate that the resources should be reclaimed. Rumor uses a fully distributed, two-phase, coordinator-free algorithm to ensure that all replicas learn of the garbage collection process and eventually complete it, even though any given set of participants may never be simultaneously present. Rumor enforces the Ficus *no lost updates* semantics [7], which guarantees that the most recent data version will be preserved so long as the file is globally accessible.

3.1 Rumor architecture

Rumor needs to manage attributes above and beyond the standard file system attributes, such as version vectors. All replication state is maintained by Rumor in a lookaside database hidden within the volume. Currently, Rumor uses a specially formatted file for this database, but it could use any general database facility that supports transactions, which are required to recover from failures and unexpected terminations during execution.

The attribute database is not updated at file modification time, since Rumor contains no kernel code and does not trap updates. Instead, updates are detected at reconciliation time. By comparing file modification times, and occasionally resorting to checksum comparisons, Rumor is guaranteed to detect all file updates. In the case of directories, a list of directory entries is utilized instead of a checksum; in general, checksum comparisons are rare and only required in special circumstances involving explicit manipulation of timestamps or updates that occur during reconciliations. Because the attribute database is only periodically updated, transient files created and removed between reconciliation executions are never even noticed by Rumor. Such temporary files are by definition unimportant, and periodic database updates saves the user the expense of replicating such files.

Reconciliation can be separated into three distinct phases: *scan, remote-contacting*, and *recon*. Figure 1 shows data and control flows during reconciliation. The scan phase is responsible for determining the set of files in the volume, including detecting new files, updating the attributes of existing files, and noticing the removal of previously managed files. The remote-contacting phase finds a remote replica, informs it of the reconciliation, and performs a scan

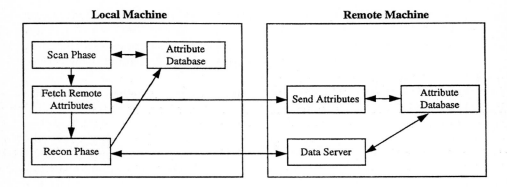

Fig. 1. Overall Rumor architecture, indicating control and data flow.

at that remote replica. The recon phase takes the list of local file attributes and the list of remote file attributes received from a remote replica during the remote-contacting phase and compares the two, taking the appropriate action (e.g., update the local replica) as determined by a comparison of the two sets of attributes.

The scan phase reads the previous set of file attributes from the database and recursively traverses the volume, detecting new files and modifying the attributes for previously known files if they have been updated. Updates are detected by examining modification timestamps and occasionally checksums, or a list of directory entries for directories. If an update has occurred, Rumor increments the version vector, obtains a new checksum, and updates the remaining attributes. The scan phase detects files that have been removed by the user by comparing the output traversal with the list of files from the previous scan, stored in the attribute database. When the scan phase completes, Rumor writes the new list of files and attributes into the lookaside database and provides them to the recon phase for processing.

The remote-contacting phase locates a remote replica of the volume according to the reconciliation topology and obtains a list of that replica's files and attributes. The remote site generates its list of files and attributes simply by initiating a scan phase on its volume. File data is not transferred during this phase, unless reconciliation is using a uni-directional transport mechanism, such as floppy disks. In this case, data must be sent by the remote site because there will be no further communications.

The recon phase performs the majority of the reconciliation work. Given the two lists of files and attributes, one local and one remote, file versions are compared and reconciliation actions are taken when appropriate. The comparison can yield four different results:

– The local version dominates (is more recent than) the remote version; no action need be taken, because the remote site will obtain the new version when it initiates a reconciliation.

- The remote version dominates; a request for file data is made of the remote site.
- The two versions are equivalent; no action need be taken.
- The two versions conflict (they each received concurrent updates); conflict-resolving and processing actions are taken. Often the conflict can be automatically resolved [13], but when it cannot, the user is notified of the conflict by email along with instructions on how to resolve it.

The recon phase also detects new files and deletions of old files. Data is requested for the new files, and they are created locally. File removals are processed by removing the appropriate local object and participating in the garbage collection algorithm.

Data requests are serviced by an asynchronous server at the remote site. Data requests are generated by the recon phase and are asynchronously processed by the remote server, which returns file data via the transport mechanism. Performing the data request and transfer asynchronously allows the recon phase to perform useful work during what would otherwise be wasted time waiting on network transmissions.

Rumor interacts with the specific data transport mechanism with very simple operations. Currently supported transport mechanisms include NFS, rshell, email, and floppy-disks.

The asynchronous data server receives data requests and processes them by performing a limited rescan of the file to ensure that the attributes to be sent with the file data are up to date. File updates could have been generated between the time that the list of files was sent and the data request was received, and Rumor does not trap such updates. Unless Rumor checks the attributes again before sending the data, updates might not be propagated correctly in some complex cases. Any new attributes are both written into the attribute database and shipped to the recon phase on the other machine. Similarly, before installing updates on the machine pulling the updates, Rumor must check the attributes of the file to ensure that simultaneous user activities have not updated them. Otherwise, Rumor would not always propagate data properly and might miss conflicting updates.

Rumor contains a selective replication facility that allows users to specify which files in a volume should be stored in a particular replica. Reconciliation does not transport updates to files that are not stored at the pulling site. However, such files are scanned locally during each reconciliation, allowing the local attribute database to be updated.

Reconciling an entire volume may be very costly when bandwidth is limited. Rumor permits users to specify individual files to be reconciled, giving the user more control over the costs paid to maintain file synchronization. This option limits the costs of reconciliation to the costs of shipping metadata related to the particular file and, if necessary, the file's contents. Basically, single-file reconciliation applies the Rumor reconciliation mechanism to one file instead of an entire volume.

Rumor itself provides no data transmission security, nor does it enforce policies on who may replicate particular files. The Truffles system [12] works with Rumor to provide those protections. Rumor provides the mechanism for portable computer users to store local replicas of files, but does not help them decide which files should be replicated. The Seer system [5] provides automatic file hoarding for this purpose, using Rumor as a replication mechanism to enforce Seer's decisions about which files to hoard. Better secondary storage space management is a growing requirement for portable computers.

4 Performance

Determining the overall performance of an optimistically replicated system is not easy [4]. In particular, determining the degree to which the system achieves the same semantics as a single-copy file system can be very difficult. The best available data of this kind comes from [13] and [17]. While not directly measuring Rumor, this data is suggestive of this aspect of Rumor's performance.

Space permits only limited discussion of Rumor performance, but we include data on two of the most important metrics: the run time to perform reconciliation on realistically large volumes and the disk storage overheads required to support Rumor. Rumor's design is such that both time and space overheads are more visible with larger numbers of smaller files, and so the data reported here focus on that portion of the exploration space.

We ran experiments on reconciling updates to a large volume replicated on two machines. The machines were Dell Latitude portable computers running 486 processors at 100 MHz, with 48 Mbytes of main memory. The communications media was a dedicated Ethernet running no other traffic. The test volume used 8 Mbytes of disk space to store 1779 files; the median file size was 3 Kbytes, and the maximum file size was 116 Kbytes.

In the experiments, various percentages of files in the volume were updated on one replica, and the other replica invoked reconciliation to pull the updated versions across. Figure 2 shows the resulting elapsed time to perform these reconciliations. These measurements represent five runs at each graphed point, with 95% confidence intervals displayed.

Reconciling a large volume with no updates thus took around 2 1/2 minutes. Reconciling the same volume with 10% of its files (by number, not by size of data) updated took a little less than 4 minutes. As Figure 2 shows, the increase in run time is close to linear. Running a minimal recursively executed command that only printed file names on the same volume took 6.3 seconds. The reconciliation times shown here are reasonable for periodic reconnections, such as via modem, but ideally they should be shorter.

The disk overhead to store Rumor attributes and other necessary information was 7.8% at each replica.

Figure 3 shows the number of bytes transported across the wire to perform the reconciliations. These figures include both the actual changed user data and Rumor's exchange of file lists, as well as any other communications overheads

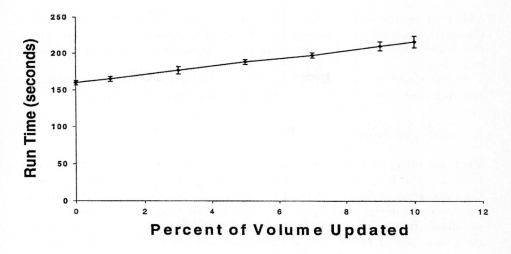

Fig. 2. Rumor Reconciliation Times

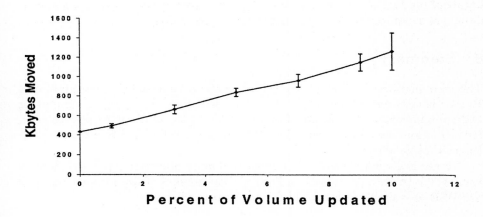

Fig. 3. Data Transferred During Reconciliation

added by Rumor. The maximum amount of data transferred was 1.2 Mbytes. Given the times required to perform reconciliation, even a modem could handle the data transfer rate required by Rumor without further slowing down the process.

Rumor has not been fully optimized for either space or time. The overheads reported here could be improved significantly with more optimization.

5 Related Work

There are many replicated file systems and database systems. Rumor's ancestor Ficus [2], which in turn was strongly influenced by Locus [9], shares many of the same goals as Rumor, but did not address mobility concerns. CMU's Coda [14] is an optimistic, client-server replication system targeted at mobility. The optimistic Bayou [16] system from Xerox PARC provides peer replication, but requires application-aware conflict detection and resolution, and does not yet provide selective replication. Mitsubishi's *reconcile* [3] facility was designed to support multiplatform (DOS and Unix) replicated directories, but is not currently available.

A number of commercial filesystem and database products support optimistic replication to varying degrees. Novell Replication Services [6] supports reconciliation-based, optimistic file replication with selective replication. Sybase's Replication Server [15] supports optimistic database replication, but the supporting documentation discourages such usage. Similarly, Oracle's Oracle7 relational database product allows optimistic updates, and provides semantic tools to help designers avoid conflicting updates wherever possible [1].

6 Summary

The combination of principles embedded in the design and implementation of Rumor is essential to effective mobile data access in the emerging computing and communications environment of the 21st century. Optimistic, peer-to-peer, reconciliation-based data replication techniques are well-suited to meet the challenges that lie ahead.

Rumor is a working system, implemented in an object-oriented style largely using C++ (with support code in Perl). A beta version of Rumor for Linux and FreeBSD is available at http://ficus-www.cs.ucla.edu/rumor.

References

1. Alan R. Downing. Conflict resolution in symmetric replication. In *Proceedings of the European Oracle User Group Conference*, 1995.
2. Richard G. Guy, John S. Heidemann, Wai Mak, Thomas W. Page, Jr., Gerald J. Popek, and Dieter Rothmeier. Implementation of the Ficus replicated file system. In *USENIX Conference Proceedings*, pages 63–71, Anaheim, CA, June 1990. USENIX.

3. John H. Howard. Using reconciliation to share files between occasionally connected computers. In *Proceedings of the Fourth Workshop on Workstation Operating Systems*, pages 56–60, Napa, California, October 1993. IEEE.

4. Geoffrey H. Kuenning, Rajive Bagrodia, Richard G. Guy, Gerald J. Popek, Peter Reiher, and An-I Wang. Measuring the quality of service of optimistic replication. In *Proceedings of the ECOOP Workshop on Mobility and Replication*, Brussels, Belgium, July 1998.

5. Geoffrey H. Kuenning and Gerald J. Popek. Automated hoarding for mobile computers. In *Proceedings of the 16th Symposium on Operating Systems Principles*, pages 264–275, St. Malo, France, October 1997. ACM.

6. Novell, Inc. Novell Replication Services white paper. unpublished, http://www.novell.com/whitepapers/nrs, 1997.

7. Thomas W. Page, Jr., Richard G. Guy, John S. Heidemann, David H. Ratner, Peter L. Reiher, Ashvin Goel, Geoffrey H. Kuenning, and Gerald J. Popek. Perspectives on optimistically replicated, peer-to-peer filing. *Software—Practice and Experience*, 27(12), December 1997.

8. D. Stott Parker, Jr., Gerald Popek, Gerard Rudisin, Allen Stoughton, Bruce J. Walker, Evelyn Walton, Johanna M. Chow, David Edwards, Stephen Kiser, and Charles Kline. Detection of mutual inconsistency in distributed systems. *IEEE Transactions on Software Engineering*, 9(3):240–247, May 1983.

9. Gerald J. Popek and Bruce J. Walker. *The Locus Distributed System Architecture*. The MIT Press, 1985.

10. David H. Ratner. Selective replication: Fine-grain control of replicated files. Technical Report CSD-950007, University of California, Los Angeles, March 1995. Master's thesis.

11. David Howard Ratner. *Roam: A Scalable Replication System for Mobile and Distributed Computing*. PhD thesis, University of California, Los Angeles, Los Angeles, CA, January 1998. Also available as UCLA CSD Technical Report UCLA-CSD-970044.

12. P. Reiher, T. Page, S. Crocker, J. Cook, and G. Popek. Truffles—a secure service for widespread file sharing. In *Proceedings of the The Privacy and Security Research Group Workshop on Network and Distributed System Security*, February 1993.

13. Peter Reiher, John S. Heidemann, David Ratner, Gregory Skinner, and Gerald J. Popek. Resolving file conflicts in the Ficus file system. In *USENIX Conference Proceedings*, pages 183–195, Boston, MA, June 1994. USENIX.

14. Mahadev Satyanarayanan, James J. Kistler, Puneet Kumar, Maria E. Okasaki, Ellen H. Siegel, and David C. Steere. Coda: A highly available file system for a distributed workstation environment. *IEEE Transactions on Computers*, 39(4):447–459, April 1990.

15. Sybase, Inc. Sybase SQL Anywhere and Replication Server: The enterprise wide replication solution. White paper, http://www.sybase.com:80/products/system11/repserv.html, 1998.

16. Douglas B. Terry, Marvin M. Theimer, Karin Petersen, Alan J. Demers, Mike J. Spreitzer, and Carl H. Hauser. Managing update conflicts in Bayou, a weakly connected replicated storage system. In *Proceedings of the 15th Symposium on Operating Systems Principles*, pages 172–183, Copper Mountain Resort, Colorado, December 1995. ACM.

17. An-I A. Wang, Peter L. Reiher, and Rajive Bagrodia. A simulation framework for evaluating replicated filing environments. Technical Report CSD-970018, University of California, Los Angeles, June 1997.

A Copy Update Mechanism for a Mobile Information Announcement System
— Transmitting Non-storage Type Resources with Redundancy —

Shigeaki Tagashira, Keizo Saisho, Fumitake Inada, and Akira Fukuda

{shigea-t, sai, fumuta-i, fukuda}@is.aist-nara.ac.jp

Graduate School of Information Science, Nara Institute of Science and Technology
8916-5 Takayama, Ikoma, Nara, 630-0101, Japan

Abstract. In this paper, the bandwidth problem between a mobile computer and an access point is discussed, and a copy update mechanism, which can make the best use of the limited bandwidth, has been proposed. If the bandwidth of a network is not sufficient, a mobile computer cannot announce all resources, and cannot update some copies on fixed computers. To announce non-storage type resources, which include time-constraint resources, as high quality as possible, the proposed mechanism limits traffic of storage type resources and announces non-storage type resources with redundancy. Traffic is controlled by limiting the number of concurrent update operations for announcing storage type resources, and packet loss of non-storage type resources is recovered using a parity packet. We implement the prototype and evaluate it. The results show that it can announce non-storage type resources with high quality.

1 Introduction

The improvement of packaging and low power technologies makes mobile computers popular. Generally, a mobile computer is used to make, keep, and modify personal information. Thus, the newest personal information usually exists on the mobile computer. Although there are many studies dealing with mobile computing environment, they regard a mobile computer as a client, and are mainly dedicated to give information to mobile computers (information acquisition). It is also, however, important to announce information from a mobile computer. If a mobile computer can announce information held on it, it is possible to provide the newest personal information.

We aim at constructing a mobile information announcement system, which can enables a mobile computer to announce the newest information independently of whether it is connected to a network or not. We already proposed an announcement method to resolve the problems of mobile information announcement systems; (1) Disconnection of a mobile computer, (2) Movement of a mobile computer, and (3) Announcement of multimedia information. We also implemented a prototype of the system and confirmed the effectiveness of the method[1].

In this paper, we discuss the bandwidth problem between a mobile computer and an access point. A mobile computer can be connected to a network at various places using various media, such as telephone circuit, wireless LAN, ethernet, and so on. The difference of media influences the bandwidth and characteristics in communication. For

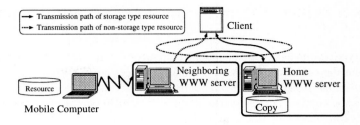

Fig. 1. An overview of the information announcement system for mobile computers

example, an ethernet has enough bandwidth for announcing information, but wireless LAN has insufficient bandwidth and communication on it is often interrupted by noise. If the bandwidth of a network is not sufficient and requests issued from clients are processed with equal priority all requested information (resources) could not be announced.

We propose a copy update mechanism that can make the best use of the limited bandwidth. The method tries to satisfy requests issued from clients with given bandwidth as much as possible. In our system, resources are classified into two types; the storage type that would be reused, and the non-storage type that is used only one time. We think that users of mobile comuoters want to obtain resources with the following priority.

Non-storage type Resource: Time-constraint resources are the non-storage type. The users want to announce such resources in the best quality.

Storage type Resource: Since the users want to provide the newest resource, a frequently accessed storage type resource should be provided as fast as possible.

The proposed copy update mechanism is designed based on the following policies:

- Announcing a non-storage type resource prior to a storage type resource,
- Handling storage type resources unequally to transmit important storage type resources as fast as possible,
- Maximizing the throughput of storage type resources, and
- Append redundancy to transmission for non-storage type resources to keep quality.

We implement a prototype of the copy update mechanism and evaluate it.

2 Information Announcement System for Mobile Computers

2.1 Overview

Fig. 1 shows an overview of our information announcement system for mobile computers. In the system, we classify resources into the storage type and the non-storage type. A mobile computer announces resources with the suitable announcement method according to the type of them.

A mobile computer is associated with the Home WWW server that manages location of the mobile computer and keeps copies of storage type resources on it. The copies are created on the Home WWW server when the mobile computer is connected to a network. They are used to announce while the mobile computer is disconnected from a network. They also work as cache during connection period. Therefore, transmission of storage type resources between a mobile computer and the Home WWW server only occurs when the coherence between original resources on the mobile computer and their copies on the Home WWW server is broken.

When a non-storage type resource is announced using the storage type announcement method, the following overheads are generated:

- It always goes and comes through the Home WWW server, and
- The copy, which is never used, is created on the Home WWW server.

These overheads increase response time and reduce the throughput of non-storage type resources. It is important to reduce latency through a transmission route for non-storage type resources. In order to alleviate these overheads, we introduced a Neighboring WWW server. The Neighboring WWW server is the nearest WWW server to the place where the mobile computer is connected to. A non-storage type resource is provided for a client through route of the mobile computer, the Neighboring WWW server, and the client. If the same request has been already issued from other clients, the request can be merged with the preceding request at the Neighboring WWW server. As the result, the request generates no additional traffic on the mobile computer. Another benefit is that it is possible to assign private address to a mobile computer.

2.2 Problems in Limited Bandwidth Networks

Some copies of storage type resources on the Home WWW server are updated as described in Section 2.1. By updating multiple copies simultaneously, total update time is expected to be reduced because protocol overhead of each update, such as open connection and wait for acknowledgment, reduces. Increase of simultaneous update, however, reduces bandwidth allocated to each connection, and then it lengthens individual update time. This also influences announcing non-storage type resources, and the deadlines of time-constraint resources cannot be guaranteed[2].

In order to confirm the above discussion, we measure elapsed update time of all the copies of storage type resources and the received throughput of the non-storage type resource on the WWW server using the following network and resources.

- The mobile computer communicates with the WWW server using 1Mbps wireless LAN whose effective throughput is about 50Kbytes per second.
- The mobile computer updates 40 copies of the storage type resources whose size is 50K bytes varying the number of connections, which is equal to the number of simultaneous update, using TCP.
- The mobile computer concurrently sends the non-storage type resource, whose throughput is 11,025 bytes per second, using UDP.

Fig. 2 shows the result of the experiment. The received throughput of the non-storage type resource decreases as the number of connections increases. Thus, the number of

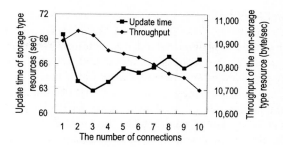

Fig. 2. The number of connections vs. update time and throughput

connections must be limited to keep some received throughput. For example, to keep the received throughput more than 10,800 bytes per second which is 98 percentage of the throughput issued from the mobile computer, the number of connections must be less than seven.

There also exist the optimal number of connections, we call the number OPTN, for storage type resources. In this experiment, OPTN is three. Thus, the number of connections must be controlled to make shortest update time of storage type resources while the throughput of the non-storage type resource is more than the requested throughput.

3   The Copy Update Mechanism

3.1   Update Method

Time-constraint resources should be transmitted before its deadline, and copies of frequently accessed resources should be updated as fast as possible. In order to satisfy these requests, we design the copy update mechanism based on the following policies:

– Transmit non-storage type resources prior to storage type resources,
– Update important storage type resources prior to other storage type resources, and
– Maximize the update throughput.

It is possible to realize a mechanism considering the above policies by limiting the number of connections. The number of connections is decided by the following policies.

(1) The policy to announce a non-storage type resource :   Allocate sufficient bandwidth to the requested resource.
(2) The policy to update a copy of a storage type resource :   Maximize the total throughput of updating copies.

Th policy (1) is prior to the policy (2). When no non-storage type resource is transmitted, the policy (2) is only used.

3.2 Parity Packet Method

There are many methods to append redundancy to transmission such as duplication, parity, ECC, and so on. We use a parity packet method, because it is easy to apply the method to existing applications and increase rate of traffic is low.

The parity packet method employs concept of RAID (Redundant Array of Inexpensive Disks). Several packets are grouped and a parity packet is appended to the group. One packet loss per group can be recovered by the method. Assume that data packets A_1, A_2, ..., and A_n are grouped (n is the number of data packets in one group) and the parity packet A_p ($= A_1 \oplus A_2 \oplus \cdots \oplus A_n$) is appended to the group. If A_k is lost, A_k is recovered by the formula $A_1 \oplus \cdots \oplus A_{k-1} \oplus A_{k+1} \cdots \oplus A_n \oplus A_p$. The traffic increases $(n + 1)/n$ times. If packet loss occurs randomly, packet loss rate is reduced from p (original packet loss rate) to $p - p(1 - p)^n$[3].

3.3 Implementation Method

Traffic on a mobile computer must be controlled in order to give higher priority to transmit non-storage type resources. Traffic control mechanism can be realized at network level or application level.

Network level

Network level implementation is classified into two categories; (1) hardware level and (2) kernel level.

(1) Hardware Level: By using the networks which can control traffic by hardware, such as ATM (Asynchronous Transfer Mode)[4, 5] and Admission Control[6, 7], allocates requested bandwidth to communications. Non-storage type resources are transmitted with requested QoS (Quality of Service) using this facility.

(2) Kernel Level: By controlling bandwidth of each applications at packet level, total amount of traffic can be restricted not to exceed the upper bound of network[8]. Each application can obtain requested bandwidth when all applications reserve bandwidth using the mechanism[9].

Application level

By controlling the number of network applications or traffic issued from each application, it is possible to control traffic at application level. Although the method realized at application level does not guarantee complete QoS, it has the following advantages.

- It is easy to adapt it to many kind of networks, e.g. ethernet, wireless LAN, and telephone circuit.
- It is easy to implement it on many kind of operating systems.

Since mobile computers move to various places and will be connected to various networks, connectivity is the most important thing for mobile computers. Thus, we adopt the controlling methods in the application level.

271

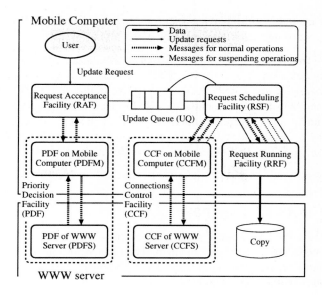

Fig. 3. Structure of the copy update method

4 Implementation of the Copy Update Mechanism

4.1 Structure of the Copy Update Mechanism

The structure of the proposed copy update mechanism is shown in Fig. 3. This mechanism consists of one update queue and five modules.

- Update Queue (**UQ**) holds update requests. An update request is issued from a user via **RAF** or returns from **RSF** caused by suspending operation.
- Priority Decision Facility (**PDF**) decides the priority of storage type resources.
- Request Acceptance Facility (**RAF**) stores an update request in **UQ**. The position of the request in **UQ** is decided according to its priority given by **PDF**.
- Connections Control Facility (**CCF**) decides OPTN according to communication condition described in Section 4.4.
- Request Scheduling Facility (**RSF**) asks **RRF** to process the request at the top of **UQ** when **UQ** is not empty and new connection can be made.
- Request Running Facility (**RRF**) processes an update request from **RSF**. **RRF** sends the requested resource to the WWW server using the copy update protocol described in Section 4.6.

The bold solid arrow, the thin solid arrows, the bold dotted arrows, and the thin dotted arrows show the flow of data, the flow of update requests, the flow of messages for normal operations, and the flow of messages for suspending operations, respectively. While the system updates copies, OPTN may change. When OPTN changes, **CCF** sends

RSF the message that notifies to change the number of connections. **RSF** processes the following two messages according to the type of them.

Increase of connections: **RSF** only increases OPTN, because the number of connections increases when it is less than OPTN and there are any requests in **UQ**.

Decrease of connections: **RSF** decreases OPTN. If the new OPTN becomes less than the number of current connections, **RSF** selects the connection, which has the lowest priority among current connections, and asks **RRF** to suspend the connection in order to decrease the number of current connections. **RRF** suspends the asked connection, and then, **RSF** returns the suspended request to **UQ**.

The following subsections describe details of each facility.

4.2 Priority Decision Facility (PDF)

A storage type resource is assigned priority according to the importance of it. The order of updating copies follows priority of them. The chance for clients to get the newest resource depends on priority of resources. We introduce A/U which is the ratio of access frequency to updating frequency:

$$A/U = \frac{\text{Access Frequency}}{\text{Update Frequency}} \, .$$

When a copy of a resource, which has a large value of A/U, is late for updating, a probability that a client gets the newest one decreases. Thus, a resource that has a large value of A/U should be set high priority.

Since the Home WWW server has information of access and update frequency, and the mobile computer uses A/U of resources, we partition **PDF** into two modules and put them into a mobile computer (**PDFM**) and a Home WWW server (**PDFS**). **PDFS** observes access and update frequency, calculates A/U, and sends it to corresponding **PDFM**. **PDFM** returns received A/U to **RAF** when **RAF** asks the priority of a resource.

4.3 Request Acceptance Facility (RAF)

A user on a mobile computer issues an update request to **RAF**. **RAF** asks **PDFM** the priority of the requested resource. After receiving the priority, **RAF** stores the request in **UQ** into priority sequence.

4.4 Connections Control Facility (CCF)

CCF decides OPTN. When the number of connections changes, **CCF** informs **RSF** of the change. We partition **CCF** into two modules, and put them into a mobile computer (**CCFM**) and a Home WWW server (**CCFS**). **CCFS** observes the throughput of transmission of resources, and sends it to corresponding **CCFM**. **CCFM** checks change of OPTN using received information. When OPTN changes, it sends the changing message to **RSF**.

Before describing the decision algorithm, we show the conditions to change the number of connections.

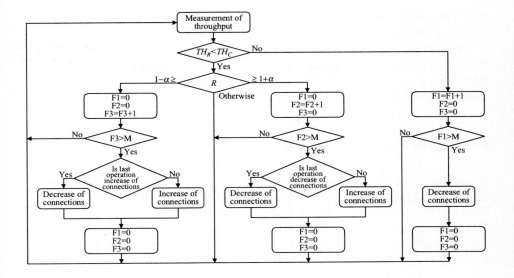

Fig. 4. OPTN decision algorithm

(1) The condition of non-storage type resource: $TH_R < TH_C$

    TH_R is the requested throughput. TH_C is the measured throughput.

(2) The condition of storage type resource: $1 - \alpha < R < 1 + \alpha$

    R is ratio of the current throughput to the preceding throughput. α is the margin for suppression of changing connections. When the value of α is too small, the influence of fluctuation of traffic is large, and then changing messages are frequently issued. Although the large value of α reduces the influence, the response to change of throughput becomes slow or smooth change is ignored.

Fig. 4 shows the decision algorithm. There are three states:

State (a): the condition (1) is not satisfied,
State (b): the condition (2) is not satisfied due to increase of throughput, and
State (c): the condition (2) is not satisfied due to decrease of throughput.

F1, F2, and F3 counters correspond to State (a), (b), and (c), respectively. When the same state repeats M times, **CCF** sends **RSF** the request to change OPTN. M is also the margin for suppression of changing throughput as time passes. If State (a) repeats M times, decrease of OPTN is sent. If State (b) repeats M times, the same request as the last request is sent. And, if State (b) repeats M times, the opposite request of the last request is sent.

4.5   Request Scheduling Facility (RSF)

When the number of current connections is smaller than OPTN, **RSF** picks out the request at the top of **UQ** and asks **RRF** to process the request. The number of current connections is increased by one. When **RSF** receives the end message from **RRF**, the number of current connections is decreased by one.

When **RSF** receives the decrement request messages from **CCF** it checks whether the number of current connections exceeds new OPTN or not. If it exceeds new OPTN, **RSF** selects a victim connection and sends the suspend message to **RRF** with the victim connection, and the suspended request is stored in **UQ** with priority sequence again.

4.6   Request Running Facility (RRF)

When **RRF** receives the request from **RSF**, it updates the copy of the requested resource, and **RRF** replies the end message to **RSF** after finishing the update. The requested resource is sent to the Home WWW server using the copy update protocol. This protocol consists of START, END, SUSPENDING, and RESUMING operations. The protocol is effective even when a mobile computer is frequently disconnected and quality of communication path is bad. The followings show operations of the protocol.

START or RESUMING
RESUMING operation is identical to START operation, except that RESUMING operation sends the resource from suspended position suspended by preceding SUSPENDING operation.
(1) A START message, which indicates start of update, is sent from the mobile computer to the Home WWW server.
(2) The name and size of the resource is attached to the START message.
(3) When the Home WWW server receives the START message, it prepares to update the copy. Since the copy update mechanism stores received resource in a buffer in order to continue the suspended update, the part of the resource updated by suspended connection is stored in the buffer. Thus, it checks the buffers whether part of the requested resource is stored or not. If the buffer that includes it exists, the Home WWW server replies the ACK message with the size of buffer (OFFSET) which indicates offset of resuming position. Otherwise, OFFSET is set to be zero.
(4) The mobile computer sends the resource from the point indicated by OFFSET.

END or SUSPENDING
SUSPENDING operation is identical to END operation, except that SUSPENDING operation does not update the copy and keeps the buffer.
(1) When a mobile computer ends or suspends the update, the connection for the update is cut off.
(2) When the Home WWW server finds out the cutoff of the connection, it checks completion of transmission. If whole resource is transmitted (END operation), the copy is atomically updated using the buffer, and the buffer is deleted. Otherwise (SUSPENDING operation), the copy is not updated and the buffer is remained.

Table 1. Parameters of experiments

Network media and Speed	Wireless LAN, 1Mbps
Effective throughput	$\simeq$ 50Kbytes/sec
The size of storage type resource	50Kbytes
The number of storage type resources	40
Basic throughput of non-storage type resource	8,000, 11,025, and 22,050 bytes/sec
Group per data packets	2, 3, 4, and without parity
Initial number of connections	1
Suppression Margin (α)	0.2

Table 2. OPTN decided by the copy update mechanism

Group/packets	OPTN		
(Label in Graphs)	8,000	11,025	22050
real OPTN	5.0	3.0	3.0
without parity packet (NO)	5.0	3.5	3.0
4 (G4)	4.0	3.5	2.0
3 (G3)	4.0	3.0	2.5
2 (G2)	4.5	2.5	2.0

5   Evaluation of the Copy Update Mechanism

We evaluate the proposed copy update mechanism using DEC HiNote UltraII (as mobile computer), 166MHz Pentium Machine (as Home WWW server), and wireless LAN. Multiple storage type resources and one non-storage type resource are sent simultaneously from the mobile computer to the Home WWW server with the parameters as shown in Table 1. The total transmission time of storage type resources is mesured and the received packets of the non-storage type resource are recorded.

Fig. 5 shows the results of experiments. Left and right vertical axes denote elapsed update time of all copies of storage type resources and packet loss rate of the non-storage type resource. The horizontal axis denotes the number of connections or the number of packets in one group. The results with fixed number of connections are shown at labels "1" to "10" which denote the number of connections. We call the fixed number of connections, which gives minimal update time, real OPTN. The results on the copy update mechanism shown at labels "NO", "G4", "G3" and "G2". "NO" shows no parity packet is appended and n in "Gn" shows the number of packets in one group. Thus, the result at "NO" shows the OPTN obtained by the copy update mechanism. Sub-captions show the basic requested throughput of the non-storage type resource. The throughput with parity packet becomes the product of the basic requested throughput and (Group per packets + 1)/(Group per packets).

Table 2 shows average OPTN decided by the copy update mechanism varying the throughput of non-storage type resources; 8,000, 11,025, and 220,50 bytes per second, and the number of data packets in one group; 2, 3, 4, and without parity packet.

OPTN without parity packet shows OPTN decided by the copy update mechanism. OPTN selected by the copy update mechanism is just or almost equal to real OPTN. For

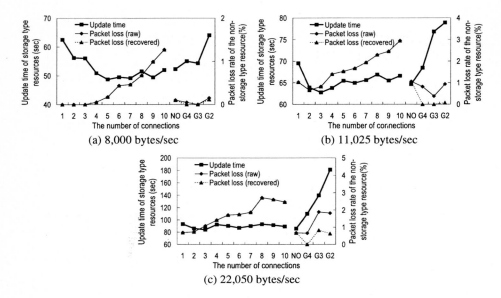

Fig. 5. The number of connection vs. update time and packet loss rate

example, both real OPTN and decided by the copy update mechanism are three with the non-storage type resource which throughput is 220,50 bytes per second. This shows that the OPTN decision algorithm is available and proposed copy update mechanism works well. Update time using the copy update mechanism is, however, longer than that with the fixed number of connections; OPTN. Two reasons for the performance degradation are thinkable. One is that data transmission in the transition period is not optimal. The other is the protocol overhead such as communication between **CCFM** and **CCFS**.

Now, we examine effectiveness of parity packet. By decreasing the number of data packets in one group that is increasing the real requested throughput of the non-storage type resource, update time of storage type resources increases in all cases. Raw packet loss rate, however, does not so increase because the number of connections is limited by the copy update mechanism. The effect of parity packet is appears in all cases. Especially, all lost packets are recovered with G4 at all basic requested throughput. In the experiments, light redundancy, that is the number of packets in one group is large, is effective because raw packet loss is low.

6   Conclusion

In this paper, the copy update mechanism, which can make the best use of the limited bandwidth, has been proposed. In order to announce non-storage type resources prior to storage type resources, the copy update mechanism controls traffic of storage type resources. Traffic is controlled by adjusting the number of connections for announcing storage type resources.

We also have implemented the prototype of the copy update mechanism and evaluated it. The results show the usefulness of the copy update mechanism and parity packet method. The copy update mechanism selects the optimal number of connections which gives enough bandwidth to transmission of non-storage type resources and gives almost short time to updating copies of storage type resources, and parity packet recovers almost lost packets.

The followings are future works:

- Apply the real multimedia data to the copy update mechanism.
- Expand the copy update mechanism.

  We append the mechanism that groups related storage type resources and updates them atomically. For example, HTML (HyperText Markup Language) shows the total relationship.

  We append the mechanism that handles layered priority. Some resources can be divided into layers based on QoS. Layers in such resource are assigned some priority.

- Provide the library of the connection administrator functions and communication functions of the system for other applications.

  We don't consider transmission from other applications. This transmission gives bad influences to the copy update mechanism. If the other applications are controlled by the mechanism, it is possible to control the number of connections including their connections.

- Implement practical applications for our mobile information announcement system with proposed copy update mechanism.

References

1. S.Tagashira, K.Nagatomo, K.Saisho, and A.Fukuda, "Design and Evaluation of a Mobile Information Announcement System Using WWW," Proc. the IEEE Third Int. Workshop on Systems Management (SMW'98), pp.38–47, 1998.
2. A.S.Tanenbaum, "Distributed Operating Systems," Prentice-Hall, 1995.
3. K.Saisho, "Highly Reliable Multimedia Data Transmission with Redundancy," Advanced Database Systems for Integration of Media and User Environments '98, Ed. Y.Kambayashi et al., World Scientific, pp.61–65, 1998.
4. H.Saito, "Teletraffic Technologies in ATM Networks," Artech House, 1994.
5. M.Prycker, "Asynchronous Transfer Mode — solution for broadband ISDN —," Ellis Horwood, 1991.
6. A.Pitsillides, P.Ioannou, and D.Tipper, "Integrated Control of Connection Admission, Flow Rate, and Bandwidth for ATM based Networks," Proc. INFOCOM'96, pp.785–794, 1996.
7. S.Jamin, S.J.Shenker, and P.B.Danzig, "Comparison of Measurement-based Admission Control Algorithms for Controlled-Load Service," Proc. INFOCOM'97, pp.973–980, 1997.
8. T.Nakano, M.Iwasaki, M.Nakahara, and T.Takeuchi, "Design and Implementation of a QoS Assurance Mechanism on an Ethernet," The Special Interest Group symposium, OS98, pp.35–42, 1997 (In Japanese).
9. S.Floyed and V.Jacobson, "Link-sharing and Resource Management Models for Packet Networks," IEEE/ACM Trans. on Networking, Vol.3 No.4, pp.365–386, 1995.

Toward Optimal Replication for Hierarchical Location Management in Wireless Systems

San-Yih Hwang and Jeng-Kuen Chiu

Department of Information Management, National Sun Yat-Sen Univeristy, Kaohsiung, Taiwan 80424
syhwang@mis.nsysu.edu.tw, jkchiu@ms17.hinet.net

Abstract. The location information of users can be replicated at various databases in a hierarchy to improve the efficiency of call lookups at the expense of increase in update and storage cost. In this paper, we systematically investigate this problem and propose two solutions. The first solution has optimal lookup and update cost, but the execution time could be exponential to the number of databases. The second solution makes some assumptions and then uses dynamic programming to tackle this problem. Its execution time is dramatically reduced with the result being less optimal. Finally, to further improve efficiency and reducing storage requirements, we propose the incorporation of clustering techniques.

1. Introduction

Establishing a connection in a wireless environment requires the location information of the callee, who may be on the move. While this problem is mostly encountered at the data link or networking layer transparently from the layers above it, applications may also need the location information at times, for instance, to contact or move a mobile agent, to answer queries that involve locations, or to update environmental parameters. This implies that future personal communication services (PCS), with high user populations and numerous customer services, will incur heavy signaling and database traffic for locating users [16]. Thus, deriving efficient strategies for location management is an important issue to mobile computing research.

In essential, there are two primitive operations for location management: lookups, or searches, for the current location of a user when a call to her/him is required, and updates when a user moves to a new location. Two kinds of architectures for location databases are widely discussed in existing researches: the two-tier architectures based on a pair of HLR/VLR and the hierarchical architectures composed of a number of location registers connected through the intelligent network, such as SS7 [13]. In the following, we extract the significant approaches that have been proposed to reduce the cost of lookups and updates in both architectures.

HLR/VLR schemes

In the basic two-tier scheme, as applied in IS-41 and GSM systems [10], each zone is equipped with two databases, namely *Home Location Register* (HLR), which contains the information of users who subscribed at the zone, and *Visitor Location Register* (VLR), which stores location information of those users who currently visit the zone but subscribed elsewhere. When a call is originated, the VLR of the caller is always queried first before consulting the HLR of the callee. When a user moves across zones, the entry for the user is deleted from the old VLR in addition to updating the user's record in the HLR, and a new entry for the user is created in the VLR of the newly arrived zone.

To provide faster lookup, [4] and [15] propose to *cache* or *replicate* the location information of a user in the databases of additional zones, so that subsequent calls from these zones can reuse this information. User i's location information is dynamically determined to store in the database of zone j if her Local Call to Mobility Ratio $LCMR_{i,j}$ is larger than a threshold [2].

Rather than dynamically deciding where to cache a user's location information, [15] suggests a static way in determining where to replicate the location information, given that the call rates and mobile rates of each user will not make abrupt change between the adjacent invocations of their algorithm. In this case, the location information of a user is replicated at some databases only if these replications bring more savings on the lookup cost than the increase on the update cost. It has been shown that off-line replication assignment problem can be reduced to a maximum-flow problem of a network.

While the previous two schemes help to reduce the lookup cost for those who receive more calls but do less move, those who receive calls less frequently relative to their moving rate do not benefit. As opposed to caching or replication, *forwarding pointers* is proposed with the aim to reduce the update cost [5]. In this scheme, each time a mobile user moves to a new location, a forwarding pointer is installed on its old VLR to point to the new VLR without the change to its HLR. Thus subsequent consulting to the HLR will refer to the first VLR at which the user was registered, and a chain of forwarding pointers to the user's current VLR is followed.

Hierarchical schemes

To improve scalability, hierarchical location management extends the two-tier schemes by maintaining a hierarchy of location databases. In its basic form, a leaf location database contains entries for all users registered in its cell, and the one at a higher level summarizes the location information (pointers) for users located at levels below it. When it comes to call a user currently located in zone i from zone j, the databases along the path from zone j to i via their least common ancestor (LCA) are all traversed.

As in the HLR/VLR schemes, the ideas of pointer forwarding, caching, and replication can also be applied in variant hierarchical schemes, as described below.

Pointer forwarding

In the basic scheme, when a mobile user i moves from zone j to k, the insertion of entries for i in all databases on the path from k to LCA_{jk} and the deletion in the databases on the path from LCA_{jk} to j are required. Rather than updating all databases on the path from j through LCA_{jk} to k, the pointer forwarding strategy updates only the databases up to a predefined level m [9]. Besides, a pointer is set from node s to node t, where s and t are the ancestors of j and k respectively at level m. To avoid long chains of forwarding pointers, mechanisms such as periodical purging proposed in [12] can be employed.

Caching location information

As in the two-tier schemes, caching techniques can be deployed in the tree-structured hierarchy to facilitate localities of calls. In [6], a pair of bypass pointers is created to support caching. When a mobile user i moves from zone j to k, a forward bypass pointer can be established. A forward bypass pointer is an entry at an ancestor of j, say s, that points to an ancestor of k, say t; the reverse bypass pointer is from t to s for the return path. During the next call from zone j to user i, the search message traverses the tree upwards until s is reached. And then, this message travels to the first database that caches the location information for user i either via LCA_{jk} or via a shorter route that consists of bypass pointers. However, s and t are nodes belonging to any level and possibly each to a different one. Several strategies have been proposed to determine when to cache the exact location information at an internal node [6].

User profile replication

Similar to the strategy used in the 2-tier schemes, replicating the location information of users at additional nodes in a hierarchy is allowed only when it is judicious, that is, the benefit of replication exceeds its cost. In this context, replication of the location information may occur at leaf nodes as well as the nodes at higher levels in the hierarchy. At each node, two numbers, R_{min} and R_{max}, where $R_{min} < R_{max}$, are derived. The call to mobility ratio of user i at zone j, $LCMR_{i,j}$, is measured such that if $LCMR_{ij} < R_{min}$, replication of user i's location information should never be done at database j, and if $LCMR_{ij} \geq R_{max}$, such replication should be always conducted. In case $R_{min} \leq LCMR_{ij} < R_{max}$, there is no clear conclusion whether the replication of user i's location information at database j should be performed. In [7], an off-line algorithm is proposed to determine the sites for replicating the profile of a user i. This algorithm proceeds in two phases. In the first phase, all databases are traversed in a bottom-up fashion, and replicas of user i's profile is stored in a database j only if $LCMR_{ij} \geq R_{max}$. As there is a limit on the maximum number of replicas a user profile can have, the second phase allocates the remaining replicas to databases with the largest non negative $LCMR_{ij} - R_{min}$, in a top-down fashion.

Motivation and Paper Organization

This paper focuses on the hierarchical scheme with user profile replication. The two-phase algorithm proposed in [7], though simple, does not provide insights on whether or why it works well. We discuss the nature of the replica assignment problem in the context and propose an optimal solution to it. As the optimal solution takes a long time to compute, we make further assumptions to simplify the problem and then solve it via dynamic programming. Finally, rather than determining the replica assignment on a per-user basis, we propose to first cluster mobile users based on their calling and moving patterns and then perform the replica assignment for each group. This will further improve the efficiency of replica assignment, in addition to reducing the storage requirements.

The remainder of this paper is organized as follows. In Section 2, we describe the nature of the problem and show how to achieve the optimal placement of profile replicas for each user in terms of the cost of updates and queries to the location information. Motivated by the high complexity of the optimal solution, in Section 3 we offer an approximate solution through a dynamic programming approach. In Section 4, we present the idea to incorporate off-line clustering technique to further reduce the complexity. Section 5 summarizes the current results and points out our future work.

2. The Replica Assignment Problem

We follow the general hierarchical model as proposed in [7]. The problem is to assign the profile replicas to a number of databases such that the overhead incurred due to calling and moving is minimized. To simplify the problem, we consider the communication overhead as the primary performance metric, as it is the main concern in most distributed environments. Specifically, minimizing the total communication cost it takes during a time unit is our goal. Deciding which databases to store the replicas of a user's profile has to take into account a number of factors. To capture these factors, we decide on several parameters. The following lists the notations of these parameters and their meaning:

$C_{i,j}$: Number of calls to user i from zone j during a time unit.
M_i : Number of moves (across zones) of user i during a time unit.
b_l : Look up message cost.
b_u : Update message cost.
N : Number of maximum profile replicas of each user.
K : Number of total databases in the hierarchy.
K' : Number of databases in leaf level of the hierarchy.
D : Number of children of each non-leaf node in the hierarchy.
L : Number of levels in the hierarchy.

Our goal is to find the replica assignment with the minimum cost for each user. Thus, a straightforward approach is to first enumerate all possible assignments. And, for each assignment, we calculate its message cost during a time unit. The assignment with the minimum message cost is finally identified. For a given replica assignment of user i's profile, the message cost during a time unit, g, can be calculated as follows:

$$g = \Sigma_{j \in \text{leaves of the hierarchy}} C_{ij} * hops_j * b_l + M_i * b_u * N',$$

$$(1)$$

where $hops_j$ is the number of hops it requires to get the location information for a call (to user i) from the zone of database j, and N' the number of replicas in the assignment. The first term in g is the total communication cost caused by looking up the user's profile for the calls from every zone, and the second term is that for updating the user's profile due to her/his moving. $hops_j$ can be determined by the given replica assignment and the way pointers are organized. Let us first consider the pointer organization used in the basic hierarchical scheme. Suppose among a set of profile replicas one copy is assigned as the primary profile. A pointer in a non-leaf database always points to the next lower level database that stores either the primary profile or the pointer to the next lower level database. We can recursively define $hops_j$ as follows:

$$hops_j = 0 \ \text{, if database } j \text{ stores the user's profile,}$$
$$= L \ \text{, if database } j \text{ is the root of the hierarchy and does}$$
$$\text{not store the user's profile,}$$
$$= 1 + hops_{parent(j)} \ \text{, otherwise.}$$

$$(2)$$

In a given replica assignment, let x_j denote whether user i's profile is replicated in database j. Solving the above recurrence equation, we obtain

$$hops_j = \Sigma_{l=0 \text{ to } L-1} \prod_{k=0 \text{ to } l} (1-x_{parent^k(j)}) + \prod_{k=0 \text{ to } L} (1-x_{parent^k(j)}) L,$$

$$(3)$$

where $parent^k(j)$ denotes the ancestor of database j that is k level higher in the hierarchy. The complexity of computing $hops_j$ is $O(L^2)$. It follows that computing g for an assignment takes $O(K'L^2)$.

Let us now consider another pointer organization that, given a replica assignment, carefully arrange the pointers so as to shorten the search path. In each database j, the shortest path to the database that stores a replica can be identified, and a pointer to the next database along the path is stored. In this case, $hops_j$ becomes the length of the shortest path to any of the profile replicas. Given an assignment, $hops_j$ can be determined through breadth first search (BFS). The complexity of BFS is $O(K)$. Thus, computing g for an assignment takes $O(K'K)$.

The number of replica assignments is equivalent to that of combinations for choosing at most N databases out of K databases, which is

$$C(K, N) + C(K, N-1) + \ldots + C(K,0) = \Sigma_{y=0 \text{ to } N} C(K, y).$$

$$(4)$$

When $N=K$, the complexity becomes $O(2^K)$, exponential to K, the total number of databases. If the basic pointer organization is employed, the total time complexity for the above brute force approach becomes $O(\Sigma_{y=0 \text{ to } N} C(K,y)K'L^2)$.

3. A Dynamic Programming Approach

We consider in this section a simpler approach in deciding where to replicate a given user's profile. Let $RA(z, K)$ be the optimal replica assignment problem in the hierarchy rooted at z such that the number of replicas is no more than K and the total benefit of replicating becomes maximum. $RA(z, K)$ achieves the maximum replication benefit of all databases rooted at z. The benefit of replicating the profile at the database j can be defined as the difference between the decrease of total lookup time and the increase of update time during a time unit. The total lookup time is in turn determined by the number of hops a lookup takes before reaching the database that stores the profile. Consider a call placed from the zone of a leaf k in the sub-tree rooted at database j. If any database along the path between k and j replicates the location information, the replication in database j does not help at all. By contrast, if none of them ever replicates the location information, the amount of benefit depends on where the profile is replicated along the path between j and the root. Therefore, the decrease of total lookup time because of database j's replication depends on the replication of databases of its descendants as well as its ancestors. This makes the principle of optimality non-applicable, and we are unable to express this problem recursively for dynamic programming.

We therefore assume the average number of hops a call takes to be a constant, denoted as H, the same assumption made in [7]. Let $level(j)$ be the level of database j in the hierarchy. For each call made from a leaf k in the sub-tree rooted at database j, if none of databases along the path from k to j ever replicates the location information, the decrease of total hops due to the replication on database j is $H - level(j)$. We then try to quantify those calls whose lookups require the traversal to database j. Let $C_{i,j}$ be the number of these calls. Clearly, $C_{i,j} = \Sigma_{k \in D(j)} C_{i,k}(1 - X_{i,k})$, where $D(j)$ denotes the (direct) children of j, and $X_{i,k} = 1$ if database k contains the location information of user i and $X_{i,k} = 0$ otherwise. The benefit of replicating user i's profile at database j, B_{ij}, becomes

$$C_{i,j} * b_l * (H - level(j)) - M_i * b_u. \tag{5}$$

Let $O_{i,j}$ be an optimal solution for $X_{i,k}$. If $O_{i,j} = 0$, then all proper descendants of j must constitute an optimal solution for the problem $RA^*(j_l, N_l)$, $RA^*(j_2, N_2)$, ..., and $RA^*(j_d, N_d)$, where $j_i \in D(j)$ and $\Sigma_{i=1}^{d} N_i = N$. If $O_{i,j} = 1$, then all proper descendants of j must constitute an optimal solution for the problem $RA^*(j_l, N_l)$, $RA^*(j_2, N_2)$, ..., and $RA^*(j_d, N_d)$, where $j_i \in D(j)$ and $\Sigma_{i=1}^{d} N_i = N-1$. Let $g_j(y)$ be the value of an optimal solution to $RA^*(j, y)$. Clearly $g_r(N)$ is the value of an optimal solution to $RA^*(r, N)$. From the principle of optimality it follows that

if $O_{i,j} = 0$, $\hfill$ (6)
$$g_j(n) = \max\{ \Sigma_{k \in D(j)} g_k(n_k): 0 \le n_k \le N \text{ for } k \in D(j), \text{ and } \Sigma_{k \in D(j)} n_k = N \},$$
and if $O_{i,j} = 1$, then

$$g_j(n) = \max\{ b_j + \Sigma_{k \in D(j)} g_k(n_k): 0 \le n_k < N \text{ for } k \in D(j), \text{ and } 1 + \Sigma_{k \in D(j)} n_k = N \},$$

where b_j is benefit of replicating the location information in database j given that all of j's children are optimally assigned its replicas. We now can use dynamic programming to compute the benefit $g_j(y)$ of all database j, $y=0$, ..., N. The algorithm is shown below:

```
(* L is the level of the root in the hierarchy *)
(* Given y is the number of maximum replicas, *)
(* x_j[y] is the 0/1 assignment to database j ,*)
(*g_j[y] is the benefit of the hierarchy rooted at j , and *)
(*c_j[y) is the number of calls that are from the zone of
   database j and cannot find the user profile before reaching
   database j *)

For each database j in level 0 do
 Begin
    Benefit = C_ij * bl * H - Mi * bu.;
    g_j[0] = 0; x_j[0] = 0;
    if Benefit > 0 then (* user i's profile is replicated
                                  on j for 1 <= y <= N *)
        For y=1 to N do
         Begin
            x_j[y] = 1;  g_j[y] = Benefit;  c_j[y] = 0;
         End
    else (* user i's profile is not replicated on j
                                  for 1 <= y <= N *)
        For y=1 to N do
         Begin
            x_j[y] = 0;  g_j[y] = 0;  c_j[y] = C_ij;
         End
 End

For l = 1 to L do
 Begin
    For each database j in level l do
        For y=0 to N do
         Begin
            Max0 = 0;
            For each combination (y1, y2, ..., yd) such
               that Σyi = y do
               Begin
                  Child_Benefit = 0;
                  For each child ci of j do
                     Child_Benefit=Child_Benefit+g_ci(y_i);
                     If Child_Benefit > Max0 then
```

```
                    Begin
                        Max0 = Child_Benefit;
                        Call0 = 0;
                        For each child ci of j do
                                Call0= Call0 + c_ci[yi];
                    End
                End
            Max1 = 0;
            For each combination (y1, y2, ..., yd) such
              that Σyi = y-1 do
              Begin
                Child_Benefit = 0;
                For each child ci of j do
                    Child_Benefit=Child_Benefit+g_ci(y_i);
                If Child_Benefit > Max1 then
                  Begin
                    Max1 = Child_Benefit;
                    Call1 = 0;
                    For each child ci of j do
                        Call1= Call1 + c_ci[yi];
                End
              End
            Benefit_j = Call1*bl*(H-1) - Mi*bu;
            If Max1 + Benefit_j > Max0 then
                Begin
                  c_j[y] = 0;
                  g_j[y] = Max1 + Benefit_j;
                  x_j[y] = 1;
                End
              else Begin
                  C_j[y]=Call0;   g_j[y]=Max0;   x_j[y]=0;
                End
        End
    End
```

Note that the number of all permutations $(y_1, y_2, \dots y_d)$ such that $\Sigma y_i = y$ is $C(y+d, d\text{-}1)$. Thus, the time complexity for the above algorithm is $O(K \cdot \Sigma_{y=0 \text{ to } N} C(y+d, d\text{-}1))$, which is $O(K \cdot C(N+d+1, d)) \approx O(K \cdot N^d)$. This complexity is much better than that of the brute-force approach shown in the Section 2.

However, as the area covered by the hierarchy is usually huge, the number of users could be quite large. Deciding the replicas on a per-user basis is thus very time-consuming. We notice that some users could have similar behavior in their calling and moving patterns, especially when bigger zones, as covered by the databases at higher levels in the hierarchy, are considered. Next section describes an approach that incorporates clustering techniques in determining the replica assignment.

4. Incorporating Clustering Techniques

Clustering techniques arise naturally in several ways where the process to create partitions or clusters is required. To convey clustering to computers, the vague concept of association for partitioning in human behavior must be translated into a numeric measure of the degree of similarity or dissimilarity [Berry97]. Various suggestions to measure the similarity between objects of various types have been proposed [14]. In practice, the Minkowski metric (L_q), as described below, is used to measure the similarity between two interval or ratio vectors, with the distances of Manhattan ($q=1$) and Euclidean ($q=2$) as special cases. That is, the distance between vectors $<X_{i1}, X_{i2}, ..., X_{ip}>$ and $<X_{j1}, X_{j2}, ..., X_{jp}>$ in p-dimensional space is:

$$L_q = (|X_{i1} - X_{j1}|^q + |X_{i2} - X_{j2}|^q + |X_{i3} - X_{j3}|^q + ... + |X_{ip} - X_{jp}|^q)^{1/q} \qquad (7)$$

Based on the measure of similarity, existing algorithms for clustering can be classified into two categories: hierarchical clustering and partitioning clustering [8]. The former organizes objects as a nested sequence of groups. An important characteristic of this method is visual impact of the dendrogram, which enables a data analyst to see how objects are to be merged into clusters or splitted at successive levels of proximity. Thus, the analyst can try to decide how many clusters to be generated at some fixed level of proximity, which makes most sense for the application in hand. It can be progressed either agglomerative or divisive in the variant linkage methods [3].

Given the number of partitions k, a partitioning method tries to find the best k partitions. It attempts to determine a cluster in which the objects are more similar to each other than in another clusters. There are many clustering techniques based on this kind of approaches, such as K-means, K-medoid and fuzzy analysis [1, 11]. It has been shown that the clusters produced in partitioning methods depend on the initial values for the means and group numbers [8]. To avoid this weakness, two-phase clustering has been suggested to take advantage of both schemes, as will be described below.

Our work tries to cluster mobile users according to their mobile patterns. This is motivated by the inefficient computation to decide the profile replicas for each user. After clustering users into groups, profile replication can be conducted for each group. This will improve the execution efficiency as well as reducing the storage requirements. In this scenario, each member of the same group replicates her/his profile in the same databases. To perform clustering, we need to define the vector for each user and the similarity function. Call to mobility ratio (LCMR) at each zone is adopted as the basic element for constituting vectors. Specifically, each user is represented as a vector composed of a sequence of LCMRs, each of which is for the zone in a particular level in the hierarchy. The Minkowski distance (L_q), as defined below, has been adopted as the similarity function:

$$L_q = (|LCMR_{i1}\text{-}LCMR_{j1}|^q + |LCMR_{i2}\text{-}LCMR_{j2}|^q +\ldots+ |LCMR_{ik}\text{-}LCMR_{jk}|^q)^{1/q} \qquad (8)$$

Our approach allows clustering to be applied on some intermediate level of a hierarchy. It is observed that in some cases, clustering at higher level introduces more cohesive clustering, in addition to faster clustering due to fewer elements in each vector. For example, when $q=1$, it can be seen that the distance between user i and j measured on parent zone is always shorter because of the following inequation:

$$|(C_{i1}+ C_{i2})/M_i - (C_{j1}+C_{j2})/M_j| \leq |C_{i1}/M_i\text{-}C_{j1}/M_j| + |C_{i2}/M_i\text{-}C_{j2}/M_j| \qquad (9)$$

That is, user i and j have more similarities in mobile behaviors on parent zone ($LCA_{1,2}$). To constrain the number of groups, it may be more appropriate to perform clustering on some level other than the leaf level. We can then use the approach described in Section 3 on a per-group basis to determine the replication on the databases at and above the level in the hierarchy. However, since the calling frequencies (C_{ij}) at higher level are determined by the replication of its children zones, we have to first decide the replication of the databases below the level. We propose to adopt Phase-One algorithm in [7] for determining where to replicate for the nodes in the lower levels.

A database j should always replicate user i's profile if the following inequation is satisfied:

$$C_{ij}\, b_l > M_i\, b_u \qquad (10)$$

In other words, if $LCMR_{ij}$ (i.e., C_{ij}/M_i) $> b_l/b_u$, the decrease of lookup cost is more than the increase of update cost even if the parent of j also replicates user i's profile. In [7], R_{max} is defined to be b_l/b_u, and phase one of their algorithm picks up those databases with $LCMR$s greater than R_{max} in a bottom manner.

Our algorithm also proceeds in two phases. Let L_c be the level in the hierarchy where clustering is to be conducted. In the first phase, for each mobile user, a bottom up traversal in the hierarchy up to level L_c-1 is performed to determine the placement of the profile on a database only if its $LCMR > R_{max}$. Then we cluster the users into groups based on their $LCMR$s. After the first phase, let K'' be the maximum number of databases that store the profile replicas for each member in a group. In the second phase, we use the dynamic programming approach described in Section 3 to perform RA(r, N-K'') for each group, if $K'' < N$.

We are still left out with the problems of how to choose the level in the hierarchy for clustering and how clustering should be conducted. As described before, the clustering algorithms in the literature can be classified into two kinds: hierarchical clustering and partitioning. While hierarchical clustering tries to achieve the best clustering by continuously splitting the groups until the result is satisfactory, the partitioning approach aims to accomplish the best clustering for a given cardinality. A straightforward approach is to first use some hierarchical clustering approach on each level in the hierarchy in a bottom up fashion. If the number of groups obtained in a level is not small enough, the next higher level is tried. This procedure continues until the groups are cohesive and the number of groups is reasonably small. Once the level and the ideal number of groups are decided, partitioning is followed.

Up to now one may wonder the usefulness of incorporating clustering because clustering tends to take a long time (approximate time complexity is $O(n^3)$ for agglomerative-nesting algorithm, where n is the number of vectors [8]). We argue that the first phase of our approach can be conducted less often, while the second phase is performed more frequently as shown below. The rationale behind such an arrangement is that user's mobile behavior should be stable within a certain long period of time. Such a period determines the interval between the adjacent invocations of the first phase of our algorithm. The second phase of our algorithm, which can be conducted more often, is then used to fine-tune the replication assignment.

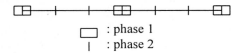

☐ : phase 1
| : phase 2

5. Conclusions

This paper investigates the location replication problem in a hierarchy of databases. With some simplification, we propose a dynamic programming approach for solving this problem. To further reduce the overhead of storage requirements and execution complexity, we incorporate clustering techniques which group mobile users with similar mobility behavior. Several issues are to be addressed in the future through careful performance evaluation. To name a few:

1. How does the dynamic programming approach perform under various parameter settings?
2. How does the level of clustering in the hierarchy impact the quality of replication assignment?
3. How often should clustering be performed in a dynamic environment?

References

[1] M. J. Berry, and G. Linoff, Data mining techniques: for marketing, sales, and customer support, John Wiley & Sons, 1997.
[2] H. Harjono, R. Jain, and S. Mohan, "Analysis and simulation of a cache-based auxiliary user location strategy for PCS," Proc. of Int. Conf. on Networks for Personal Communication, 1994.
[3] A. K. Jain, and R.C. Dubes, Algorithms for clustering data, Prentice-Hall, 1988.
[4] R. Jain, Y-B. Ling, C. Lo, and S. Mohan, "A caching strategy to reduce network impacts of PCS," IEEE Journal on Selected Areas in Communications, 12(8):1434-1444, Oct.1994.
[5] R. Jain, and Y-B. Ling, "A auxiliary user location strategy employing forwarding pointers to reduce network impacts of PCS," Wireless Network, 1:197-210, 1995.
[6] R. Jain, "Reducing traffic impacts of PCS using hierarchical user location database," Proc. of the IEEE int. conf. on Communcations, 1996.

[7] J. Jannink, D. Lam, N. Shivakumar, J. Widom, and D.C. Cox, "Efficient and flexible location management techniques for wireless communication systems," Wireless Networks, 3:361-374, 1997.

[8] L. Kaufman, and P. J. Rousseeuw, Finding groups in data: an introduction to cluster analysis, John Wiley & Sons, 1990.

[9] P. Krishna, N. H. Vaidya, and D. K. Pradhan, "Static and dynamic location management in mobile wireless networks," Journal of Computer Communication, 19(4), March 1996.

[10] S. Mohan, and R. Jain, "Two user location strategies for personal communication services," IEEE Personal Communications, 1(1): 42-50, 1994.

[11] R. T. Ng, and Jiawei Han, "Efficient and effective clustering methods for spatial data mining," Proc. of Int'l Conf. on VLDB, 1994

[12] E. Pitorua, and I. Fudos, "Tracking mobile users using hierarchical location databases. Technical Report DCS-97-10, Department of C.S., University of Ioannina, 1997.

[13] E. Pitoura, and G. Samaras, Data management for mobile computing, Kluwer academic publishers, 1998.

[14] G.D. Ramkumar, and A. Swami, "Clustering data without distance functions," IEEE Data Engineering Bulletin, 21(1):9-14, Mar. 1998.

[15] N. Shivakumar, and J. Widom, "User profile replication for faster location lookup in mobile environments," Proc. of Int. Conf. on Mobile Computing and Networking (Mobicom'95), 161-169, October 1995.

[16] J. Z. Wang, "A fully distributed location registration strategy for universal personal communication systems," IEEE Journal on Selected Areas in Communications, 11(6): 850-860, August 1993.

Distributed Control of Mobile ATM Networks Using CORBA

R. Radhakrishna Pillai, Maitreya Rangnath, Rahul Agrawal and Weiguo Wang
Kent Ridge Digital Labs
21 Heng Mui Keng Terrace
Singapore 119613
{pillai, maitreya, rahul, wwang}@krdl.org.sg

Abstract. This paper reports the design, implementation, and performance evaluation of a CORBA based distributed control architecture for mobile ATM networks. The distributed control architecture makes use of open signalling to manipulate the various network resources to realize network services such as call control, multicast, and mobility management. Open signalling provides the flexibility and ease in creating new network services as opposed to standard signalling approaches such as the ATM Forum signalling. The network control architecture interworks with the ATM Forum signalling. The performance of the prototype implementation is being evaluated to understand the effect of CORBA latencies on the signalling performance.

1   Introduction

Wired networks are evolving towards the use of Asynchronous Transfer Mode (ATM) as a transport mechanism because of its support for bandwidth-intensive applications, its ability to carry different media types, and its ability to guarantee Quality of Service (QoS). Wireless ATM (WATM) networks are expected to extend the capabilities of ATM transport to the wireless end user, in addition to providing mobility support [15]. WATM is gaining importance as a result of developments in sophisticated portable equipment with multimedia capabilities. The wide applicability of such equipment in diverse environments from classrooms and conventions, to industrial facilities and hospitals, has fueled the demand for a network infrastructure that supports mobile multimedia communications. WATM has two major components: the *Radio Access Layer* which deals with the wireless issues at the lower layers, concerning MAC and radio resource management; and the *mobile ATM protocol extensions* tackling issues pertaining to the higher layers such as location management and handover. This paper focuses on signalling and control in WATM to fulfil the latter requirements.

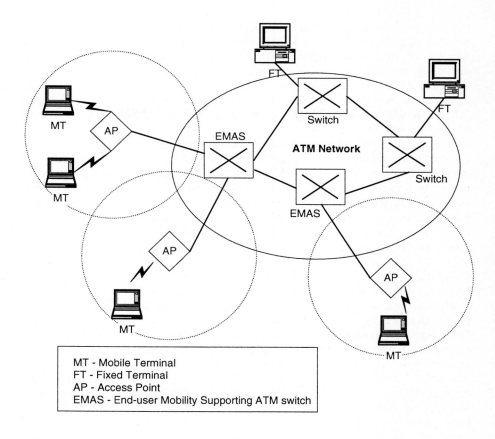

Fig. 1. A typical ATM network with wired and wireless hosts

A typical wireless ATM network scenario is shown in Figure 1. Communication can take place between mobile terminals (MT) and corresponding fixed terminals (FT). The backbone ATM network consists of several ATM switches. The ATM switch with mobility features will be called the End-user Mobility Supporting ATM Switch (EMAS). The Access Point (AP) serves as a multiplexer/demultiplexer for a number of mobile terminals sharing a port on the EMAS. The EMAS distinguishes different mobile terminals attached to the same AP using different virtual path identifier (VPI) values on its wired port. Each AP is comprised of a single port transceiver serving a group of portable mobile ATM terminals within its radio cell.

Signalling software is required in WATM for call setup and release, and to support handover and location management. Appropriate signalling is required to handle path extension, path re-routing, and QoS re-negotiation in the case of a handover. Specific signalling protocols and entities are also required to track and discover the location of mobile terminals. There are various options and approaches to signalling: one may use separate signalling protocol sets for the wired and wireless networks [13], or the same set of protocols [14]. Handover and location management may be realised by extending the UNI and NNI signalling protocols [1]. ATM switches can be controlled by open interfaces like the General Switch Management Protocol (GSMP) [10].

The basic problem with traditional network signalling is that protocols and algorithms are tightly coupled with the network architecture. *Open signalling*[1] (or *opensig*) however, does not prescribe to having standardized algorithms or protocols. Instead, it advocates the use of standard *interfaces* for resources such as switches, end-terminals and other network entities. By using these "open" interfaces, third party software developers can implement appropriate algorithms to access these network resources and to create new network services. In other words, open signalling conforms to the principle of separating interfaces from algorithms.

Using the opensig concepts, a distributed control architecture for WATM is proposed in this paper. The viability of this architecture is established by way of an implementation of a proof-of-concept prototype for our wireless ATM research project. Application of open signalling in WATM to deal with scalable flows using QoS controlled handoff has been reported in [22] Our approach differs from the previously explored architectures, because it explores the usability of different algorithms for end-to-end connection management between wired and wireless networks, point-to-multipoint and multipoint-to-multipoint connection setup between wired and wireless terminals, exploitation of multicast connection setup for handoff, and QoS re-negotiations for handoff. These aspects of signalling have not been explored in detail in the ATM Forum specifications and in the previous work on open signalling. Furthermore, our architecture has added provisions for supporting the ATM Forum UNI signalling, so that UNI-based mobile terminals can have access to the core open signalling network without modifications. This is achieved through the use of a signalling gateway that translates between open signalling and UNI signalling. Similar gateways could be employed for inter-working with PCS-based terminals. In this way, the architecture provides a platform for interworking between different signalling systems. A set of experiments is being carried out to understand the effect of CORBA latencies on the signalling performance. The preliminary results are reported in this paper.

---

[1] Open signalling is under standardization by the IEEE project 1520 on Programming Interfaces for Networks (http://www.ieee-pin.org)

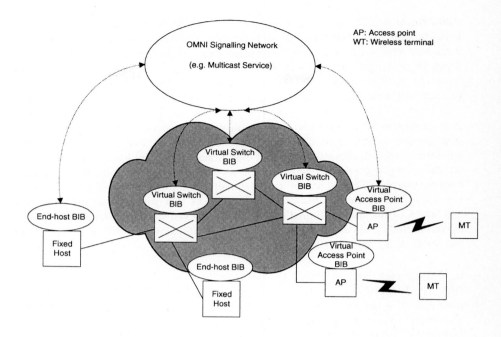

Fig. 2. Signalling in OMNI requires distributed interaction with BIBs

2 The Distributed Control Architecture

Initial efforts that went into the design of this binding architecture focused on modeling the network and multimedia computing resources only. The distributed control architecture builds on this previous endeavor in two ways. Firstly, resources are modelled in a more generic manner to incorporate characteristics of both the wired and wireless networks. Secondly, the architecture is extended to include basic network control services for multicast connection management and mobility management. As described later, these services provide a seamless and integrated signalling solution for wireless ATM. This software architecture has been termed

the *Open Multimedia Network Infrastructure* (OMNI) and follows a distributed object-oriented computing paradigm. In this paradigm, the network's resources and resources of end-terminals and devices, are modelled as a set of objects with well-known interfaces distributed across the broadband network. Based on the opensig programming model therefore, the *act* of multimedia network service creation requires the run-time distributed access and manipulation of these objects.

To further illustrate the concepts, Figure 2 shows the distributed nature of the OMNI software architecture. Consistent with the programming model, OMNI comprises a set of Binding Interface Base (BIB) objects populated across an ATM network, and a set of distributed algorithms that provide the service abstraction. As the figure shows, distributed algorithms provide a multicast service that allows the setup of multicast virtual connections for streaming user data between multiple hosts. In setting up these multicast virtual connections, resources are reserved through call invocations made to the BIB objects of each network entity involved.

It is important to note that with open signalling, object-to-object communication (via method call invocations) forms the entire basis of signalling activities in a network. This is a departure from the traditional telecommunications approach of standardizing specialized signalling protocols, with each protocol fulfilling a specific purpose. The tenet of open signalling is similar to object technology because it emphasizes on the design of interfaces that will abstract the behaviour and states of resources. "Signalling" is thus achieved by higher-level entities that make method call invocations to those interfaces, thereby controlling the behaviour and states of the resources.

In OMNI, each network entity has resources that are typically associated with a BIB. The BIB provides a software layer for accessing hardware features and logical resources of a network entity in a well-defined manner. Objects in the BIB have "common" interfaces that are defined by an implementation-independent Interface Definition Language (IDL). Having common interfaces provides a standard manner for entities implementing distributed algorithms to make call invocations to the BIB objects. In the OMNI software architecture, BIBs are also associated with wireless ATM resources. For example, the *Virtual Access Point BIB* contains interfaces that models the functionalities in the radio hardware and provides methods to control and manage radio resources and wireless link capacity.

In order to support multimedia network computing, *End-host BIBs* must also be associated with end-terminal devices and multimedia resources. Fixed hosts have BIB objects that allow device states to be accessed. These *virtual devices* model the functionalities of physical and logical devices in a host, such as network interface card, MPEG-1 video encoder and decoder, microphone and speaker devices. The BIBs have equivalent *VirtualCapacity* interfaces that abstract the CPU and media processing capacities of the end-hosts. The fact that Figure 2 does not indicate BIBs associated with mobile hosts is more a design rather than an implementation issue. These portable devices are often characterized by limited processing and power capabilities. Hence, it would be beneficial to situate the mobile host BIBs on the network as proxies that perform various functions on behalf of the mobile hosts. In general, such network proxies may relieve processing-limited mobile devices from executing complex functions, and help reduce the amount of communication and air-interface bandwidth required [4], [20]. The Binding Interface Bases, by themselves, are a passive representation of resource states. Network services, on the other hand, require the activity of resource reservations and distributed state manipulation [6]. A collection of basic control services is needed to provide the core functions for a distributed call control system. These services include resource management, group management, routing, and connection management. Together, they form the necessary distributed algorithms implemented as software agents that reside in a network domain. A network domain can be defined as a specific group of interconnected switches and hosts which the software agents have control over. The connection manager is responsible for setting up, modifying, and releasing a virtual connection with a specified Quality of Service between two hosts or network nodes. The route manager computes the optimal route between two hosts or network nodes.

Figure 3 depicts how the basic control services interact with BIBs distributed across the network domain to provide network services. [11] Provides a comprehensive description of the multicast connection service using the above mentioned agents. We focus on how the same solution can be used to support mobility-enhanced call control and management. The intention is to highlight the distributed control architecture from the standpoint of providing a seamless support for wireless ATM host access.

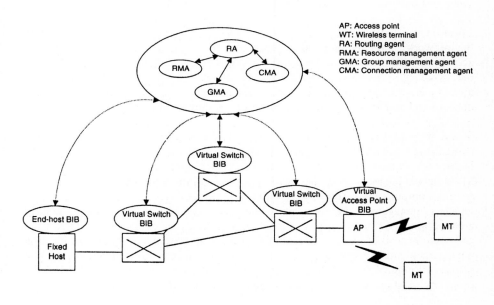

Fig.3. Interaction between basic control algorithms and BIBs

2.1 Handover

As a MT moves from one AP coverage area to another, the handover process maintains connectivity with the network by transferring the active, ongoing connections of the MT from one cell to the other. The handover process requires a signalling mechanism and a redeployment of network resources to reroute connections to the new AP. With our proposed distributed control architecture, handover is achieved by introducing a Handover Agent that resides on the AP or EMAS. The Handover Agent (HA) is responsible for coordinating the handover process between the wireless portion (MT-AP) and the wired network. By interfacing with the MECAM, the HA makes use of the connection management and route management services for re-routing VCs.

2.2 Location Management

The proposed distributed control architecture addresses location management in two areas: *location registration* and *call delivery*. The group management agent (GMA) maintains a database of multicast connection groups, and associations between MTs and their current physical locations. Apart from the responsibility of multicast group management, the GMA supports location queries and updates. Given a host name, the GMA must be able to resolve and return the current location of the host. In a mobile environment however, the association between host name and location is transient, and should therefore be treated separately [11]. The host-addressing scheme should not couple host identification with host location.

Location registration procedure is initiated when a MT reports its current location to the network, authentication takes place and the location databases are updated accordingly [2]. It occurs when the MT first powers-up and attaches to the AP, or in the event of a handover, when the MT attaches to the new AP. Upon MT attachment, the AP provides a temporary address to the MT for identification purpose and updates the location manager on the current MT location.

In the event of a call setup request to the MT, the mobility enhanced call manager (MECAM) is involved in the call delivery procedures to locate the MT. MECAM queries the location manager, which in turn examines the location database for the MT's current location. Once the location is obtained, the MECAM can proceed with routing computation, resource reservation and connection setup. The discussion on location management further shows the advantages of the distributed control architecture based on opensig. The location procedures are explicitly separated from call setup instead of an integral part of the call setup procedure. Should the location management strategy change, only the location manager is affected and not the rest of the call control entities. In general, this modular advantage is possible with the proper delineation of interfaces and responsibilities of software entities.

3 An Experimental Testbed

An experimental ATM testbed has been setup to examine the operability of the OMNI distributed software architecture, to validate the interworking between UNI-based end-terminals across the OMNI signalling network, and to conduct performance measurements and analysis of the call control system.

Each ATM switch has an associated switch controller PC. Virtual Switch BIB agents reside on the switch controller PCs, abstracting the behavior and states of the ATM switches and exposing them as interfaces to the distributed basic control services. The basic control services invoke the Virtual Switch BIB interfaces to perform connection setup and resource reservation. The advantage of having a separate switch controller PC and moving most of the signalling intelligence out of the switch, is to exploit the external processing capacity of the PC, particularly when connection volume increases or as signalling software becomes more advanced [16]. The OMNI basic control service agents such as CMA, RMA and MECAM are implemented as CORBA objects on one of the switch controllers or on a third party CORBA server. Although CORBA has been used in the implementation of OMNI, this should not preclude the use of other distributed computing platforms like DCOM and Java to implement the proposed architecture.

Performance measurements were obtained for a multicast connection setup and release at the CMA and MECAM. Hence, values obtained for the CMA are a subset of the values indicated for the MECAM. The CMA makes CORBA calls to the Virtual Switch BIB agents at the switch controllers to setup VCs. The mean connection setup time using the Virtual Switch BIB was 29.2 ms for Switch 1 (unicast connection) and 37.4 ms for Switch 2 (multicast connection with two leaves). This translates in to a call handling capacity of 0.12 million calls per hour (for calls with one unicast connection per call) and to 0.096 million calls per hour (for calls with one multicast connection with two leaves per call). However, the higher layer CORBA entities such as CMA, MECAM, RM etc. further increase the call setup/release delays as shown in Table 1.

Table 1. Average delays introduced by CORBA objects

Module	Average Delay (msec)
Mecam Call Setup	108.5738
Mecam Call Release	86.0492
CMA	93.0984
RMA	15.4918

These performance figures are slightly more compared to the corresponding figures for a call control using pure UNI/PNNI signalling. However, this approach for controlling the network using open signalling is more flexible compared to the UNI/PNNI based signalling. Certainly, performance improvements can be attained in a number of ways. One approach is to introduce concurrency into the CMA. Instead of performing the setup process sequentially on every switch on the path (as it is done now), a concurrent connection algorithm is used to setup VCs in the switches in [16,19]. Rather than make synchronous CORBA calls, a deferred synchronous model is used so that the CMA delegates the setup to each Virtual Switch BIB agents, and the agents make callbacks to the CMA when their task is finished. Another optimizing approach is to reduce the number of expensive CORBA calls made. For instance, when setting up a multicast channel in a switch, only a single CORBA call is required if the *SwitchFabric* BIB interface allows for multiple parameters to be specified in a single method call.

4 Conclusion

The design, implementation, and preliminary performance measurements of a CORBA based distributed control architecture for a WATM network is reported in this paper. The call control system with mobility features has been implemented and the viability and flexibility of the architecture has been demonstrated on this architecture using the open signalling concepts. A signalling gateway has been implemented and the interworking between the open signalling and the ATM Forum UNI signalling is demonstrated. In future, using appropriate signalling gateways, the proposed architecture could form a key component for interworking between different signalling systems such as PCS, ATM Forum UNI etc. In addition to realising the call control and mobility management in a flexible way using open signalling concepts, the project also aims at understanding the effect of CORBA latencies on the signalling performance. Though the preliminary performance figures are slightly more than the corresponding figures for call control using pure UNI/PNNI signalling, this approach for controlling the network using open signalling is more flexible compared to the UNI/PNNI based signalling.

Future work involves an in-depth performance measurement and analysis of the proposed architecture, the integration of the call control system with wireless hardware, and a study of the effect of wireless link characteristics on the signalling performance. Several important issues need to be further addressed - in particular, performance optimization and scalability of the software architecture and prototype implementation.

Acknowledgments

The authors acknowledge the contributions of the Wireless ATM Research Project team members Adrian Yau, Kenneth Soo, Li Hong Yi, Kok Seng, Bobby Jose, and He Sha.

References

1. Acharya, A., Bakre, A., Raychaudhuri, D.: Design and Prototyping of Location Management and Handoff Protocol for Wireless ATM Networks. Proceedings of ICUPC (1997) 213-217
2. Akyildiz, I. F., Ho, J.: On Location Management for Personal Communications Networks. IEEE Communications Magazine (Sept. 1996) 138-145
3. The ATM Forum: ATM User-Network Interface Specifications, Version 3.1. Prentice-Hall (1995)
4. La Porta, T.F., Sabnani, K., Gitlin, R.D.: Challenges for Nomadic Computing: Mobility Management and Wireless Communications. ACM Journal of Nomadic Computing, Vol. 1, No. 1 (1996)

5. Lazar, A.A., Lim, K.S., Marconcini, F.: Realizing a Foundation for Programmability of ATM Networks with the Binding Architecture. IEEE Journal on Selected Areas in Communications, Special Issue on Distributed Multimedia Systems, No. 7, (1996) 1214-1227
6. Lazar, A.A., Lim, K.S.: Programmability and Service Creation for Multimedia Networks. Proceedings of Fifth International Symposium on High Performance Distributed Computing, New York (1996)
7. Lazar, A.A., Bhonsle, S., Lim, K.S.: A Binding Architecture for Multimedia Networks. Journal of Parallel and Distributed Computing, Vol. 30, No. 2, (1995) 204-216
8. Lazar, A.A., Lim, K.S., Marconcini, F.: Binding Model: Motivation and Description. CTR Technical Report #411-95-17, Columbia University (1995)
9. Li, H.Y., Ngoh, L.H., Wang, W.G., Jose, B., Lee, K.S.: Supporting Soft Handover in Wireless ATM Networks Using Mobility Enhanced Multicast Service. Proceedings of First International Workshop on Wireless Mobile ATM Implementation, Hangzhou (1998)
10. Newman, P., et al.: Ipsilon's General Switch Management Protocol Specification ,Version 1.1. RFC 1987 (1996)
11. Ngoh, L.H., Li, H.Y., Wang, W.G.: An Integrated Multicast Connection Management Solution for Wired and Wireless ATM Networks. IEEE Communications Magazine (Nov 1997) 52-59
12. Pillai, R.R., Jose, B., Lee, K.S.: Interworking Between Different Access Signalling Systems Across an ATM Backbone Network. 4th Symposium on Interworking (1998)
13. Prathima Agrawal, Hyden, E.,. Krzyzanowski, P.,   Mishra, P., Srivastava, M.B., and Trotter, J.A.: SWAN: A Mobile Multimedia Wireless Network. IEEE Personal Communications (April 1996)
14. Rauhala, K. (Editor): ATM Forum BTD-WATM-01.07, Baseline Text for Wireless ATM Specifications (April 1998)
15. Raychaudhuri, D., Wilson, D.: ATM-based Transport Architecture for Multiservices Wireless Personal Communication Networks. IEEE Journal on Selected Areas in Communications, Vol. 12, No. 8 (1994) 1401-1413
16. Tam, M. T., Wang, W.G., Lazar, A.A.: A Comparative Study of Connection Setup on a Concurrent Connection Management Platform. Proceedings of IEEE Open Architecture and Network Programming (1998)
17. Tennenhouse, D. L. and Wetherall, D. J.: Towards an Active Network Architecture. ACM SIGCOMM Computer Communication Review, Vol. 26, No. 2, 5-18
18. Toh, C-K.: Wireless ATM and ad-hoc networks – Protocols and architectures. Kluwer Academic Publishers (1997)
19. Veeraraghavan, M., Kshirasagar, M. M., and Choudhary, G. L.: Concurrent ATM Connection Setup Reducing Need for VP Provisioning. Proceedings of IEEE Infocom (1996) 303-311
20. Ramjee, R. et al.: User Agent Migration Policies in Multimedia Wireless Networks. Proceedings of IEEE Infocom-98 (1998) 1147-1155
21. Acharya, A., Li, J., and Raychaudhury, D.: Primitives for Location Management and handoff in Mobile ATM Networks. The ATM Forum Contribution 96-1121 (1996)

22. Campbell, A.T., Liao, R. R.-F, and Shobatake, Y.: Delivering Scalable Flows Using QoS Controlled Handoff. The ATM Forum Contribution 97-0341 (1997)

New Thoughts on Effects of TCP Slow Start and FEC Coding in WATM Access Networks

Fraser Cameron[1], Moshe Zukerman[1], and Maxim Gitlits[1]

[1] The University of Melbourne, Department of Electrical and Electronic Engineering,
Parkville, Victoria, 3052, Australia
f.cameron@usa.net

Abstract. This paper takes a fresh look at coding parameters optimisation, TCP operation and adaptive modulation in the context of Wireless ATM (WATM) link dimensioning subject to meeting specified Quality of Service (QoS) requirements. The authors take into consideration a comprehensive set of teletraffic issues including: (1) effects of retransmissions of erroneous packets using Automatic Repeat Request (ARQ) protocols, (2) modulation efficiency (3) Forward Error Correction (FEC) redundancies, and (4) effect of traffic burstiness on loss and delay. Bit Error Rate (BER) parameters, obtained for a range of realistic situations by simulation, are optimized to obtain maximal efficiency over the dimensions of coding and modulation gain. In this paper the authors use the results to show that adaptive modulation, where modulation efficiency is dynamically optimized, provides better efficiency and/or QoS than the same system with FEC for both the ARQ and transparent cases. We present new thinking on perceived performance difficulties of TCP over wireless links.

1. Introduction

Personal and terminal mobility moving beyond 2000 requires ever better area coverage, improved signal quality and reliability as well as the ability to interface with wired Broadband Integrated Services Data Network (B-ISDN) multimedia networks supporting ATM. The advantages in transmitting fixed size information cells asynchronously across a network in accordance with the store and forward principle are that connection, bit rate, quality of service (QoS), and ubiquity of connection are allowed on demand. Since ATM provides inherent statistical multiplexing, network capacity is not wasted during low activity period, and a gain due to statistical multiplexing can be achieved [5]. This paper considers the operation of ATM over wireless links. The reader is further referred to [1] for further argument supporting the use of ATM in future networks.

Wired and wireless transmission differ in many respects. Perhaps the most important difference between wired and wireless (especially mobile) transmission is that the wireless case is very error prone. In the case of a transparent system (no retransmission), the two options to improve the Bit Error Rate (BER) and meet QoS requirements are to use Forward Error Correction (FEC) and/or to reduce the number of symbols in the transmitted constellation (decrease modulation gain). In non-transparent mode, an Automatic Repeat Request (ARQ) protocol is used to recover errors in addition to the above techniques.

Rectification of the high BER and the limited capacity of radio channels might suggest the inclusion of powerful error correction, equalisation, voice encoding and interleaving, however these impose their own complexity and delay limitations significantly affecting the performance of radio based ATM networks [10]. It is further clear that in wireless ATM networks, delay will be an important QoS requirement in addition to cell loss probability due to congestion. Delay will necessarily affect network dimensioning, traffic control mechanisms (such as Connection Admission Control (CAC) and congestion control) and add to an already complex set of QoS constraints.

This paper draws conclusions from implementation of the analysis developed in [4] and evaluates the benefit of an adaptive modulation scheme in WATM by simulating such a scheme using optimal dynamic modulation adjustment. The quanta of receiver constellation redundancy, and effect of FEC operation and overhead, is traded off against the resultant maximum channel capacity available for distribution between customers and the number of retransmissions by the higher layer protocols (link layer ARQ or end-to-end ARQ). We consider the effectiveness of each scheme in terms of efficiency (defined in Part 2) and draw conclusions about the effect of TCP action on the wireless access efficiency.

In determining optimal dimensioning and transmission parameters we must consider: (1) the connection traffic stream mean rate, and its level of burstiness; (2) the capacity of the overall link (the Modulation Gain); (3) the size of retransmitted block of data, ie. ARQ of a frame, packet or a single cell and hence the capacity allocated for retransmissions of erroneous blocks of data; (4) the capacity of the coding scheme; and (5) the capacity allocated for guaranteeing tolerable delay to avoid timeouts and congestion collapse.

The remainder of the paper is organised as follows: In Section 2 we describe the simulation process undertaken for evaluation; in Section 3 we describe the gains obtained through the use of adaptive modulation and assess the value of using both FEC and adaptive modulation. Finally we consider implications for the use of WATM over wireless channels, focussing on the perceived difficulty with TCP 'slow start'.

2. Simulating the Model

The basic idea of the analytical model is the separation between Queuing Based Efficiency (QBE) and Error Based Efficiency (EBE) [12]. To these concepts of efficiency we must add the concept of Modulation Efficiency (ME) which operates to indicate the proportion of the full rate capacity of the wireless channel that is currently available to data as a result of adaptive modulation.

	Throughput	Required Capacity
ARQ	Accepted error free raw data.	ARQ retransmission plus FEC and Modulation overheads.
Video	Accepted error free raw data.[1]	FEC and Modulation overheads.

Table 1. Our definitions for throughput and required capacity used for EBE calculation.

The QBE is defined as the ratio between the utilised capacity (including user data and overhead) required to provide an error bounded data rate, and the overall channel capacity, related to the additional capacity required to handle burstiness in the traffic. In this paper, for ARQ (data) systems, we approximate the utilisation of the single server model fed by the real trace to be 37.85%. For video use, stricter parameters were selected to achieve a utilisation of 27.5%.

The EBE is defined as the ratio between the mean raw data rate and the raw data rate plus all overheads associated with error corrections and retransmission of erroneous blocks of data, namely, FEC, and ARQ, multiplied by the normalised ME. We assume independence of QBE and EBE so that overall Efficiency, or simply, Efficiency, which is the ratio between the mean raw bit rate generated by the customer and the channel capacity, is calculated by multiplying the QBE by the EBE (which includes the ME). The remainder of this paper contains conclusions drawn from extensive simulation of differing EBE cases.

For transparent transmission (for example the case of real time services where there is no transmission of erroneous messages) optimisation is given by selecting the maximum ME to satisfy QoS for a given level of SNR. By contrast, for the case of services requiring retransmission of erroneous messages by the higher layer protocols (link layer ARQ or end-to-end ARQ), retransmissions need to be considered when deriving the optimal ME. Therefore additional capacity is required to allow for retransmissions of erroneous blocks of data (cells, packets or TCP windows) and there is a clear trade-off between the level of ME (channel capacity) and the expected number of retransmissions. Given a set modulation constellation, the required channel capacity for retransmissions is a also function of the size of the ARQ block size, FEC type and rate R chosen.

Simulations used in this paper were developed using the Matlab Communications Toolbox [8]. The wireless environment is a Varying Rayleigh Fading Channel (VRFC) in which the parameters were varied randomly with uniform distribution. The simulation uses Coherent Phase Shift Keying (MPSK) which was preferred since it is a simple, representative scheme, and the preferred modulation scheme for future WATM networks has not yet emerged. The analysis presented is, however, equally relevant for High Level Modulation including Enhanced Data rates for GSM Evolution (EDGE) [6] which uses Quaternary Offset QAM (Q-O-QAM). This approximation is justified since the analysis is independent of modulation scheme

---

[1] Normally video throughput will also include erroneous bits, but in this case we choose to exclude them to provide further insight into picture quality as a function of the SNR.

3. Impact of FEC and Adaptive Modulation on Utilisation

In this section we present numerical results displaying the strong connection between efficiency and Modulation Gain. We will demonstrate the imperative for the use of adaptive modulation in systems with highly variable noise levels such as WATM. Figure 1 shows results of BER as a function of Signal-to-Noise Ratio (SNR) for a variety of constellation sizes in our simple MPSK modulation scheme.

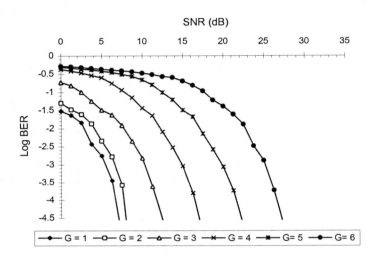

Fig. 1. BER for MPSK in VRFC with no coding simulated by MATLAB

Adaptive Modulation with no FEC Coding

Video data is an example case of a real time service where there is no retransmission of erroneous messages. In this case there is less wasteful retransmission, however, transmission at worse than set threshold BERs cannot be tolerated. Since large error rates can cause visible errors or even frame loss in video streams, threshold acceptable loss rates are set in real systems, usually with BER of $10^{-4} - 10^{-6}$. Figure 2 shows the link utilisation for such data not satisfying the QoS bound as zero to show clearly the 'acceptable' transmission. Using a threshold of 10^{-5} (a representative figure for medium compression transmission) we get utilisation characteristics for the video stream for dynamic G. The dynamic modulation gain is simply the maximum of any trace at any SNR meaning giving optimal efficiency over all values of SNR.

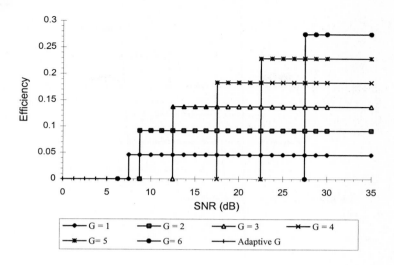

Fig. 2. Comparison of efficiency of Video transmission over VRFC amongst modulation gains for the transparent system as a function of SNR conforming to a QoS requirement of BER = 10^{-5}

When ARQ is taken into account we observe that the delay in transmission of a packet experiences a severe degradation at a threshold SNR level. This level varies with the number of symbols in the constellation. The threshold effect means that delay rapidly rises with decreasing SNR, for the fixed case, quickly becoming infinite as SNR reduces. This effect is reflected in the overall efficiency of each modulation constellation. For larger G there is a higher maximum efficiency but this is paid for via a higher SNR at which delay becomes infinite. Hence, as for the video case, the adaptive modulation scheme (which is simply the maximum at any SNR of any Modulation Gain in Figure 3) is preferable since it captures the efficiency gain of higher G and the SNR range of low G.

Increased blocksize implies an earlier onset of the rapid utilisation deterioration and increased delay. It is shown in the results of [4] that the gradient of efficiency degradation (that is the rapidity with which the utilisation decays with decrease in SNR) is an increasing function of blocksize. Since the mobile environment is characterised by sudden and extreme variations in noise, this reinforces the preferable nature of the smaller blocksize.

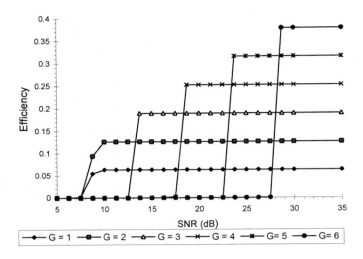

Fig. 3. Comparison amongst modulation gains for uncoded MPSK system with ARQ by constellation size of efficiency (EBE and QBE) for ARQ block size of 53000 bytes

FEC Optimisation

We now evaluate the use of FEC in our adaptive modulation system. FEC is used to improve Bit Error Rate (BER) and is of value in reducing ARQ retransmission for data services. FEC rates may be optimised using the methods set out in [7]. We conservatively assume independent (non-correlated) bit error in the system after modulation and simulate the MPSK system using a VRFC as before, now including a selection of code rates and types. FEC codes simulated included a simple convolutional code with constraint length L=3 as well as Reed Solomon (RS) RS(127,84), RS(127,64), and RS(127,42) codes. A soft decision Viterbi decoder was used for the convolutional code.

In [11] a model of the General Packet Radio Service (GPRS), currently undergoing standardization, was simulated. It was observed there that in this selective repeat ARQ GSM system [2], optimal performance was offered by the less powerful $R = \frac{3}{4}$ punctured convolutional code than other ($R = 4/5, 3/4, 1/2$ and $2/3$) codes with increased redundancy.

For the wireless case, the tradeoff between FEC redundancy and ARQ Selective Repeat retransmission gave an optimum FEC rate point at $R = \frac{3}{4}$. Our simulations consider a more comprehensive set of parameters and includes an important optimization across SNR. In Figure 4, we find a tendency for the less powerful FEC codes to give enhanced efficiency over most SNRs. In fact, in both the ARQ and transparent system, the only advantage in our simulated system was at extreme noise situations.

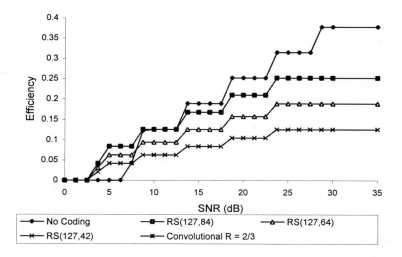

Fig. 4. Efficiency comparison amongst coding schemes for a MPSK system over a VRFC channel with ARQ for ARQ block size of 53000 bytes

The simulations assumed optimal dynamic modulation considered earlier and sought to quantify the efficiency gain to be made from the addition of FEC to the system. *The results show that a FEC with low R yet extreme gain is required to increase efficiency in such an adaptive scheme over the uncoded case* suggesting that simple FEC schemes of the type likely to be found in wireless terminals and handsets with constrained delay and complexity allowances may not be of benefit to an adaptive WATM system. However, we note in high loss situations, delay is minimized by the use of increasingly powerful FEC codes as noise worsens.

A comparison of FEC optimization against *G* leads us to discover that optimization over Modulation Gain in a system with adaptive modulation gives equal or better performance than optimization over FEC in a system with fixed modulation for all SNR values.

TCP Slow Start in WATM

The 'slow start' problem has been identified in the literature as one of the significant challenges of WATM [3]. Some authors have commented that a problem with ATM over wireless links is that the window protocol mechanisms built into TCP are designed to avoid network congestion and do not take account of characteristics of the wireless environment (which was not a consideration in the design of TCP). Hence cell loss on any link of the network – which TCP assumes is wired, having low BER – must be as the result of network congestion rather than an errored packet. In the situation of a cell loss in the network, the action of TCP is to reduce throughput in order to alleviate congestion including reducing window size – the 'slow start' phenomenon. The concern of commentators is that this mechanism, designed to alleviate congestion, would be of concern in the lossy wireless environment resulting in needlessly compromised utilisation by the incorrect assumption that the network was wired. An example is [3] where the concern is that 'slow start' may be wasteful in the case of Go Back N retransmission.

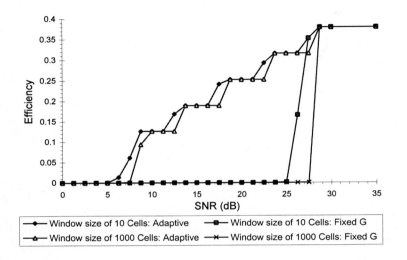

Fig. 5. Comparison of overall Transmission Efficiency (EBE and QBE) between adaptive and fixed modulation for uncoded MPSK system with ARQ TCP window size equal to 530 and 53000 bytes. There is an assumption of a 1/n salvage rate at the receiver for Go Back N and the packet size was 5 cells. The fixed case is $G = 6$

In the absence of a reliable AAL layer below TCP that performs end-to-end ARQ, our results suggest the contrary – for the fixed modulation case – reduction in window size is of benefit in increasing efficiency in the Go Back N case due the utilisation penalty for larger window sizes. If the window is reduced, Go Back N will require fewer packets to be retransmitted over the wireless link, reducing delay and increasing efficiency at the data link level. Since Go Back N requires end-to-end (not just wireless link) retransmission of all subsequent packets to the errored packet, and there is a sliding window, larger window size is similar to the retransmission of larger ARQ block sizes. So, for no retransmission, there can be no error in the window (equivalent to specification of blocksize = window) in our paper.

Figure 5 demonstrates the argument. In this case we analyse the Go Back N system with varying window size. As SNR decreases and error increases, the action of the protocol is to reduce TCP end-to-end window size, and thus throughput, due to the high proportion of overhead to data in smaller packets. Figure 5 shows the dramatic gain in lower SNRs for the fixed modulation case achieved as a result of reduction of window size from 53000 bytes (200 packets) to 530 bytes (2 packets). Although our simulation does not take TCP overhead into account in determining efficiency, it is clear that the utilisation curve for the fixed case with smaller window goes to zero at a lower SNR, showing that a reduction in window size gives an increased throughput in cases of high noise. Thus, although TCP reduces the window size assuming network congestion, it is also carrying out the correct action for wireless cell loss.

We note that our maximum window size is large one (packet size is 5 ATM cells). For a inter-continental link this is a realistic size window for bit rate of 20Mbs and for a inter-capital Australian link this is realistic for the somewhat higher data rate of 200Mbs.

For the case of adaptive modulation, the action of the transmitter is to move from one constellation to another when error becomes significant. In this case TCP decreases window size with associated utilisation benefits until the transmitter chooses a modulation constellation with greater redundancy, lower efficiency and lower packet error. The TCP window can then increase in response to the new conditions. Hence, TCP acts to 'cushion' the transfer between MEs. For the smaller window size, Figure 5 shows that the system is able to transmit using lesser modulation redundancy for the same SNR as the system with the larger window size. This gives significant efficiency and coverage gains.

Another option, considered in [9] suggests the implementation of an additional small block ARQ in a specific Wireless Data Link Control Layer (rather than end-to-end ARQ) to deliver a better quality channel over the wireless link to the higher layer protocols. This small block, low level ARQ has the effect of 'fooling' higher layers into believing that the physical layer is a higher quality than it is, thus avoiding inefficiencies in retransmission of larger blocks at higher levels. This approach indirectly encapsulates the efficiency benefit of smaller blocksize retransmission for WATM identified in this paper.

5. Conclusions

This paper considers the tradeoff of providing QoS for WATM at both the physical (modulation) and data link level (ARQ and FEC). It also considers the effect of the introduction of lower level ARQ (AAL). We show that the use of FEC with associated delay and complexity constraints can be avoided without violating the QoS bound. Our results show that that adaptive modulation offers significant efficiency and coverage gains over the fixed system when ARQ is considered and that in many instances an adaptive modulation system renders FEC redundant. We leave the implementation of the adaptive change of modulation parameters for another paper, however our findings suggest that preference should be given to systems that adaptively change their parameters according to the instantaneous level of interference and noise. We further observe that (1) the TCP assumption of a wired network, and the 'slow start' problem in particular, may not be a difficulty in wireless networks (2) that reduction in TCP window size has a beneficial effect in wireless transmission and (3) that even for certain realistic SNR conditions, the wastage due to errors can be very high because of retransmission.

6. References

[1] H ArmbrÜster, 'The Flexibility of ATM: Supporting Future Multimedia and Mobile Communications', (1995) *IEEE Personal Comm*, 76.

[2] G Brasche. 'Analysis of Multi-Slot MAC Protocols proposed for the GSM Phase 2+ General Packet Radio Service', (1997) *IEEE VTC* 1295.

[3] J Cain and D McGregor, 'A recommended error control architecture for ATM networks with wireless links', (1997) 15(1) *IEEE J Select Areas Comm* 16.

[4] F Cameron, M Zukerman and M Gitlits, 'Wireless Link Dimensioning and Transmission Parameters Optimisation', (1999) *Multiaccess, Mobility and Teletraffic*.

[5] L Cuthbert, L Sapanel, 'ATM-The Broadband Telecommunications Solution', (1993) 29 *IEEE Telecomm*.

[6] Ericsson, 'EDGE Feasibility Study Work Item 184; Improved Data Rates through Optimised Modulation', (1997) (Working Paper, SMG #22, Preliminary version 0.1).

[7] P Hiew, M Zukerman and M Gitlits, 'WATM Operation Based on Effect of FEC Code Rate and ARQ Retransmission' (1998) *IEEE VTC*.

[8] The Math Works Inc, *Communications Tool Box for use with MATLAB and SIMULINK* (1996).

[9] D Raychaudhuri *et al*, 'WATMnet: a prototype wireless ATM system for multimedia personal communication', (1997) 15(1) *IEEE J Select Areas Comm* 83.

[10] M Schwartz, 'Network Management and Control Issues in Multimedia Wireless Networks' (1995) *IEEE Personal Comm* 16.

[11] D Turina, 'Performance Evaluation of a Single-Slot Packet Data Channel in GSM', (1997) *IEEE VTC* 544.

[12] M. Zukerman, P Hiew and M Gitlits, "FEC code rate and bandwidth optimisation in WATM networks", in D. Everitt and M. Rumsewicz (eds.), Multiaccess, Mobility and Teletraffic: Advances in Wireless Networks, Kluwer, Boston, 1998.

[13] M Zukerman, P Hiew and M Gitlits, "Teletraffic Implications of a Generic ATM Wireless Access Protocol", *IEEE Globecom '97*.

A Centralised Cellular Database
to Support Network Management Process

Fabrizio Verroca[1], Carlo Eynard[1], Giorgio Ghinamo[1], Gabriele Gentile[1],

Riccardo Arizio[1], and Mauro D'Andria[2]

[1]CSELT – Via G. Reiss Romoli, 274 – 10148 Torino Italy
{fabrizio.verroca, carlo.eynard, giorgio.ghinamo, gabriele.gentile, riccardo.arizio}@cselt.it

[2] Telecom Italia Mobile – Via Nisio, 57 – Roma Italy
mdandria@tim.it

Abstract. A solution for cellular network data management is described which has been applied to the mobile network of Telecom Italia Mobile (TIM). The environment is particularly defying due to the characteristics of high development of the network and the very rapid growth still under way that requires a significant updating process.

1.   Introduction

This paper describes a cellular network database defined for the biggest European cellular operator Telecom Italia Mobile. The technical solution is based on a common data layer and data access services have been implemented using Oracle Stored Procedures, Packages, relational views, snapshots in order to meet Data Layer principles starting from the data level. The various systems interfacing the database and the main applications based on it are also briefly described, showing the benefits of chosen architectural and technical solutions. Such applications are automatic solutions for Network Creation, Service Assurance, Network Management and Work Force Management.

2.   Network Management Processes and network database

The network management processes are based on the knowledge of network configuration. These processes can be partitioned into two main groups:
- *Network Creation* that starts with planning; evolves with scheduling, designing and terminates with realisation;
- *Operation & Maintenance* of network elements (alarms management, work force and provisioning).

A rapid and easy access to network information can increase efficacy and efficiency of network processes. Technical information about network configuration is currently available from many different local data sources but there is the need of storing it in a logically centralised operational database: the *Network Database* is the unique reference for network inventory and catalogue.

The Network Database was designed following a Data Layer Architecture. Many different operational applications need to share data stored in the Network Database. The main goal was therefore to separate application logic and data access functionality providing a set of data access services. With this SW architecture it is possible to provide independence of information from logical data schema and from physical location of data. Transparent enforcing of business rules and integrity constraints, uniform and common interfaces between data and applications are also ensured.

With such management network architecture, loading and maintenance of data are the keys for TIM's tasks efficiency. Data in the Network Database must be aligned with local data in element manager systems. Specific audit procedures ensure the alignment so that the Network Database describes the actual network.

3   Network Database: main concepts

The Network Database is a relational database; the design has been developed with the Oracle Designer/2000, based on entity relationship modelling.

The Network Database was designed to support network management processes such as network creation, network management, operation & maintenance, service assurance.

The Network Database stores information about different network technologies such as TACS, GSM, DCS 1800, Intelligent Network and SDH Transport Network, providing a corporate and uniform perspective of network resources.

3.1 Main concepts

There are two main kinds of information in Network Database:

- The *Network Catalogue:* it provides a physical description of different types of network element and network infrastructure basic components that can be installed in the network. A description is given in terms of dimensions, functional and electric characteristics. The Network Catalogue also stores a set of configurations, describing the usual aggregations of basic components in more complex ones;
- The *Network Inventory:* it's the set of occurrences describing the actual physical resources (network elements, infrastructures) and logical resources (circuits, SDH path, routes) installed over the network. In the database, the physical resources are linked to the respective typological descriptions stored inside the catalogue.

3.1.1 Physical location and network topology

The Network Database stores information about network topology and physical location for each network element: a description of the network locations is provided in terms of addresses, geographical co-ordinates and other more detailed information about each site. For every network element the network connectivity is stored; for a selected BTS, the Network Database provides the controlling BSC and MSC.

From an organisational point of view, each network element is related to the corresponding managing territorial unit.

The distribution of network resources in the country is necessary for network planning. In the cellular planning process, the location of BTSs is a fundamental piece of information.

Moreover, an easy access to information about the addresses and geographical co-ordinates for each network element support the work force management and all tasks about operation and maintenance.

3.1.2 Network resources

The configuration of physical and logical resources is fundamental for all network design processes. Design processes can be divided in Switching network design, Cell planning, Transport network design.

Switching network
The switching network is composed of two different networks: signalling network and phone network. The topology of these two networks can be the same in some parts and different in some others. The design of these two networks has to integrate and optimise both of them.

Information about network configuration and traffic measures can support the designer to develop network plans. Traffic measurements and network configuration processing applications can propose an optimal network configuration under a profile of performances and management costs.

The Network Database supports an optimal design because it owns information about routing tables, routes between nodes and network consistence. Moreover, the Network Database stores information about the approved projects.

Cell planning
The process of access radio network design can be divided into the following tasks:
Electromagnetic coverage of land;
Dimensioning of radio channel;
Frequency planning
Connection with the switching network
Cell planning is a particularly critical process. The insertion of new BTS requires analyses on electromagnetic coverage, frequency planning, co-channel interference. The Network Database provides the necessary information to support the process and stores the results at the end of project.

Transport network

The transport network provides the transmission links between cellular network elements. The logical resources of transport network are path VC-12 (2 Mb/s) and they are supported by optical links STM (155 Mb/s). The <u>Network Database</u> describes the transport network configuration; this information can be used to design and optimize the transport network, conforming to technical and economical criteria.

3.1.3 Physical and logical topography of network elements

Each network element is partitioned in many single components, such as, for example, cards; a network element is furthermore linked to the network infrastructures located in a site. A description is provided for physical infrastructures like racks, shelves and slots where each single component is set up. From a logical point of view, the hardware and software components of the network elements are aggregated into functional blocks. The access to this kind of information may be useful for maintenance and for alarm resolution tasks because operator can localize the single element in terms of functional block, position in site and network element. Topography information is necessary to design new network element or extend it. With CAD application it is possible to process topography information, in terms of design.

3.1.4 Catalogue

The Network Catalogue provides a physical and functional descriptions of the network elements that are installable in the network.

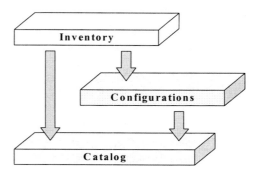

Fig. 1. Relationship between Inventory, Catalogue and Configuration

Each item in network inventory has a link with one or more items of the network catalogue, in particular with the typological descriptions.

The network configurations are the rules to aggregate single components or functional blocks or network elements. The physical configuration is done by aggregation of physical component typology; the functional configuration is done by aggregation of function components. Figure 1 shows the relationships between inventory, catalogue and configurations. Figure 1 shows that the catalogue is an independent element of Network Database, but the configuration set is based on the catalogue and the inventory is based on both configuration set and catalogue. Due to this data architecture, a data administrator is needed that has the authorisation to introduce new configurations or new topologies inside the catalogue. The user of the catalogue is generally a planner or designer as shown in figure 2.

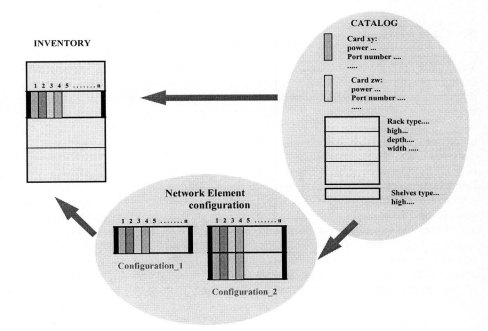

Fig. 2. How a designer can use catalogue.

4   Resource's state in Network Database

For every resource in the database, there is information about its state in the network. This information is associated with resource's life cycle. Life cycle starts with planning task and terminate with dismissing task. In this way in Network Database there are information about network evolution in smart and large term. The states that a resource can have are:

- PLANNED
- PROGRAMMED
- INSTALLED
- ACTIVATED
- DEACTIVATED
- DEINSTALLED

The information details about network resources (logical and physical) depend on the states in which they are. There are more information for resources in the *activated* state than resources in other states. For example a resource that has a *planned* state is described with less details than a resource in the *activated* state.

5 Case Method

The Network Database conceptual model has been designed with Oracle Designer/2000. This software is a CASE tool that allows to design data flow diagrams, process diagrams and *entity relationship model*. In addition it is possible to translate a conceptual scheme in a logical and physical scheme in a semiautomatic way. In our experience this has proven to be particularly useful since several companies have been involved in the Mobile Network Database Project in the different tasks and phases; the choice of a unique unambiguous repository that contain both conceptual and logical scheme has been a winning point.

End users must perceive the philosophy of the model and appropriate communication with them should be sought as a key to Database success. The entity relationship models have been used for many years to help top executives, directors, managers and others that already possess a deep understanding of their business. In this case we would give Network Database access and updating to all TIM operators of different experience and skills and it is essential to use unambiguous language, no abbreviations, and no jargon, to achieve this wide understanding. For example it is recommended that you don't even use the word entity with an end user.

6 Network Database software architecture

The Network Database has been designed following a **Data Layer Architecture**. Many different operational applications need to share data stored in the Network Database. The main goal is therefore to separate application logic and data access functionality. A set of data access services is provided in order to obtain independence from logical data schema, independence from physical location of data, transparent enforcing of business rules and integrity constraints, uniform and common interfaces between data and applications.

The Oracle 7.3 DBMS platform has been chosen as database server level. Data access services have been implemented using Oracle Stored Procedures and Packages, relational views and Oracle Snapshots in order to meet Data Layer principles starting from the data server level.

The client graphical user interface has been developed using Oracle Developer/2000. The PL/SQL code on client side directly invokes Data Layer access services in order to communicate with the database. Other external applications accessing to Network Database are interfaced in different ways depending on their technology and access requirements; in any case the interaction with the Network Database is finally performed using the data access services.

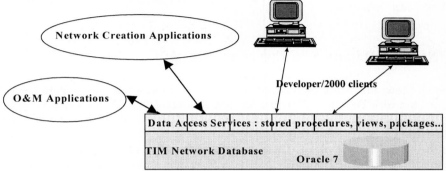

Fig. 3. TIM Network Data Layer

Once a uniform Data Layer is built, new applications can be developed using Data Access Services. An application under development shows in a Desktop GIS environment network elements, logical links and buildings geographically positioned in the landbase. A CAD environment supporting the Network Planning process is under development. The physical infrastructures like racks, shelves and slots where each single network element is set up will be graphically designed and positioned . A light version of this application, integrated with Desktop GIS environment, provide a browse functionality graphically showing racks, shelves and slots schematics.

All these systems are built on top of Network Data Layer using Data Access Services in order to communicate directly or indirectly (via interfaces) with Network Database. The Developer/2000 graphical user interface will be soon available on WEB using Oracle Network Computing Architecture (NCA) products like Oracle Web Developer/2000 Cartridge.

New services at a higher level can now be built on top of basic Data Access Services in order to provide access from other kinds of applications. Oracle 8 Enterprise Server and NCA-compliant products will be our reference software architecture main components.

The Network Database is a common repository of network data shared among different systems; therefore we would like it to become completely open. In the near future we expect to interface systems working around the Network Database that use CORBA/IIOP technology to communicate with other systems.

For this reason we would like to use Java to implement our data access services and CORBA to enable non-Oracle systems to communicate with Network Database using IIOP technology instead of SQL and SQL*Net. The idea is to use Java for new services and CORBA connectivity to communicate with new applications. We will not use Oracle 8 object types but we will continue to use relational data structure until object-oriented model will be fully supported. We are very interested in Java implementation of services that we today implement in PL/SQL.

Once the Network Inventory Database is available to users and systems, we could easily develop new systems able to provide data analysis functionality based on information stored in the Network Inventory Database and other data sources. A Data Mart having as a source Network Database and standard traffic measurements is at present under definition.

7 Network Database hardware architecture

Figure 4 shows the two-level architecture chosen as the hardware architecture for the Mobile Network Database. The first level is the server. In particular the Network Database is using server SUN Enterprise 4000 with 6 processors, 150 Gbyte mirrored and DBRM Oracle 7.

The second level is the client. There are two kinds of client; the first one is a light client with only Oracle Developer 2000 and it has only alphanumeric operations; the second one is a PC with Windows NT, Oracle Developer 2000 and with Microstation Bently (CAD) and Geographics (GIS).

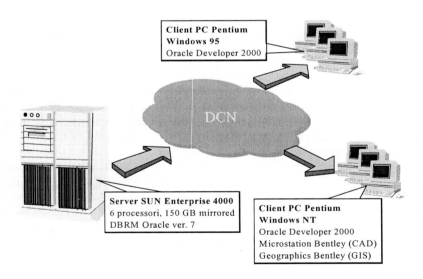

Fig. 4. Two levels architecture

Inside the Network Database there is a sites digital map; with CAD it is possible to position the network element on the map. In this way it is possible to obtain graphical details about size and room occupation of network elements. With GIS is possible to identify all the links between network elements and geographic positions of network elements.

Clients use the Data Communication Network (DCN) to communicate with the server, namely a WAN used by all management systems.

In the future Network Database hardware architecture shall evolve to a three-level architecture as shown in figure 5. In this case the first level is the server, but the second is a WEB server Unix/NT with Esri, Bentley and Oracle publishers. Three kinds of client are foreseen in the third level:

- client PC with Windows NT with Oracle Developer 2000, Microstation Bentley (CAD) and MapObjects/Arc view (GIS)
- client PC/Unix with Browser HTML
- client PC laptop with Browser HTML.

In this way it is possible use the Network Database from any PC with a Browser HTML.

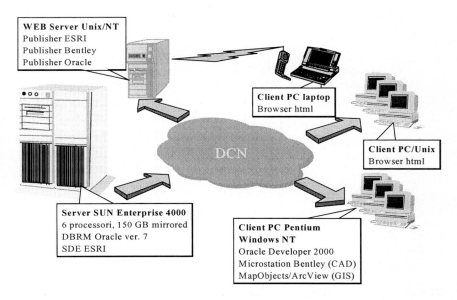

Fig. 5. Three levels architecture

This is very useful for employees working on the field with their PC laptop that can communicate retrieving and updating information from the Data Base, with a GSM terminal equipment connected to the laptop.

8   Network management architecture

In the figure 6, we describe the Network management Architecture, where the Network database is inserted. The Network Database has to compare his own information with the data of the Network Management Systems, using special SW routines, to update the stored data to the new real time configuration.

The Network Database reads the cell planning data and the switching Network information from the GSM Network Management System. The data about the logic and physical resources of the transport Network are available in the Transport Network Management System. Enhanced Management Systems store data about the single element topography, in terms of functional blocks and HW devices.

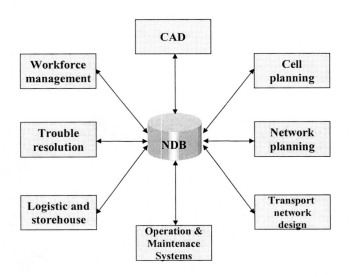

Fig. 6. Network management architecture

The Network design and planning tools can find the managed Network data in the Network Database.

At present, the following design tools are in use in TIM:

1. radio access Network: a tool is used for cell planning
2. BTS BSC MSC connection network: a tool find out the optimal locations of the nodes and dimensions of the links.
3. switching Network (inter MSC network): the interconnection links between MSC are dimensioned and optimised by a SW tool.
4. transport Network: a tool evaluates the configuration of the logical and physical resources.

When the management approves the proposed designs, the calculated data have to be stored in the Network Database.

The Network database is an information source for some other management tools supporting some particular operation and maintenance processes. These tools may support the sharing of scheduled work orders among the areas of the company and the different skilled workers. Some enhanced communication systems, as electronic mail and mobile equipment, may make easier the remote management of skilled workers distributed in the country.

Some examples of this kind of tools used in TIM are:

1. Trouble Ticketing Resolution
2. Work force management
3. Work order management
4. spare parts and warehouse management

A CAD is available to visualise data concerning the topography of the network premises and nodes.

In this way the maps concerning the localisation together with the logical and physical architecture of each network element are available.

Any changes on the logical and physical configuration of the nodes must be registered in the Network database, using the CAD interface, to store always the actual configuration of the network elements.

9   Interfaces between applications and Network Database

In order to define the SW interface between a general tool and the Network Database the following analyses have to be conducted:

1. defining the domain of the interesting data
2. defining the users requirements on the data
3. comparison of the different technology solutions solving that particular problem.

A careful analysis of the tool (or the system) deployment and their use in the company processes has to be conducted, in order to solve the first and the second items.

At first, the domain of the exchanged data is defined by the data models mapping of the two systems. In order to design a performing systems interface, the data requirements have to be defined. For every single information the following features have to be detailed:

1. CRUD (Create, Read, Update, Delete) rights on the single information
2. access frequency
3. updating time requirements.

With such analysis it is possible to define the set of technological solutions that could be used for interface implementation. Different solutions could be adopted depending on the data flow between Network Database and the system to interface (one-way, bi-directional interface), the communication needs (synchronous or asynchronous), the software implementation of systems, the amount of data involved and so on. As mentioned above, the Network Database is a common repository of network data shared among different systems; therefore its was designed to be completely open from the accessibility point of view .

In many cases, a Database-to-Database interface was built, using Data Access Services provided by the Data Layer (using stored procedures and views for direct access or Oracle snapshots for read-only replicas). Some legacy system has been interfaced via ASCII file but, in any case, the final interaction with Network Database is performed using Data Access Services.

10 Conclusions

The experience of specifying and making operative a network database for Telecom Italia Mobile highly developed network has shown the following evidences.

The presence of a centralised database containing complete and updated network configuration and making data available for several applications and environments represents fundamental step for the automation of the mobile operator processes and for the integration of tlc management systems.

A careful study must be performed in order to identify which contents and for which company entities are needed to be shared in the common database.

Particular attention should be paid to the definition of an appropriate Conceptual Scheme that is also flexible enough in order to allow future qualitative growth of database contents.

A key aspect is also the choice of an appropriate HW/SW architecture, particularly related to geographical reference aspects.

The technical knowledge of the system and its evolution, the study of network management processes, the definition of precise rules for consultation and especially for database updating are fundamental for a smooth adoption of the database itself and its development and improvement, continuing to represent also with time passing a key reference for the operating company.

References

1. M. Mouly, M.B. Pautet: The GSM System for Mobile Communications – International Standard Book 1992
2. Batini, Ceri, Navate: Conceptual Database Design – An Entity/Relationship Approach. The Benjiamin/Cummings Publishing Company, Inc. 1992
3. R. Barker: Oracle Case Method: Entity Relationship Modeling. Addison-Wesley Publishing Company 1990
4. Atzeni, Ceri, Paraboschi, Torlone: Basi di Dati: concetti, linguaggi e architetture. McGraw-Hill 1996

Security of Current Mobile IP Solutions

Stuart Jacobs

GTE Laboratories Inc.
40 Sylvan Road Waltham, MA 02454 USA
sjacobs@gte.com

Abstract. Due to the operation of IP's addressing and routing algorithms, mobile nodes (such as notebooks, portable workstations and palmtop computers) cannot currently participate, while roaming without being reconfigured, in tactical wired and wireless networks, strategic networks or the Internet. A node's IP address encodes the network access point to which the node is connected. This prevents IP packets from reaching the node if it moves to a new location and tries to connect to its home network from within a different network. Changing the IP address of a node when it moves is not possible while keeping existing transport level connections open. This change requires the termination of all current network activity and the user making a number of configuration changes followed by rebooting of the node.

There are a number of proposed solutions for supporting mobile nodes. Leading approaches are: Mobility Support in IPv4, Route Optimized Mobile IP for IPv4, and Mobility Support in IPv6 that are compatible with the TCP/IP protocol suite. This paper addresses the security needs for IP mobile hosts in the commercial world, the security capabilities and deficiencies of these solutions, and proposed solutions for identified security deficiencies.[1]

1 Introduction

The use of portable computing devices has mushroomed in the last few years. These devices range from 18-ounce personal digital assistants (PDAs) to workstation class notebook computers at under 7 pounds. With service providers deploying wireless communications systems in larger numbers, covering ever increasing areas, people are taking their computers on the road. At the same time organizations are making increased use of wireless LAN technologies to allow their employees to roam throughout a company facility and maintain connectivity with the corporate network infrastructure. Along with these network and computing changes, organizations are rapidly adopting the same networking model and protocol suite as used in the Internet, namely the Internet Protocol (IP) suite of protocols.

[1] Prepared through collaborative participation in the Advanced Telecommunications/Information Distribution Research Program Consortium sponsored by the US Army Research Laboratory under Cooperative Agreement DAAL01-96-2-002.

Unfortunately, the IP protocol suite has been designed with the assumption that computers (end nodes) rarely change their physical point of network attachment. Manual reconfiguration, until now, has been considered a sufficient approach for dealing with those cases when an end node moves from one physical point of network attachment to a different point. Manual reconfiguration is an error-prone procedure that the typical user does not have the skills or desire to carry out. After reconfiguration the node has a completely different network address (identity) from that previously used to reach the node.

There is considerable work being done to transparently support wired portable end nodes and wireless mobile end nodes on IP-based networks. The problem is that a node's IP address encodes the network access point to which the node is connected. This prevents IP packets from reaching the node if it moves to a new location and tries to connect to its home network from within a different network. Changing the IP address of a node when it moves is not possible while keeping existing transport level connections open. This change requires the termination of all current network activity and the user making a number of configuration changes.

The Internet Engineering Task Force (IETF) is the organization chartered with developing/refining the protocols for the Internet and performs this work primarily through the efforts of working groups. One such group is focusing on the issue of supporting mobile nodes within IP networks and has evolved a number of protocols which will support mobile nodes in IP (version 4 and version 6) based networks.

Unfortunately, as current work progresses on support for seamless mobile computing, today's networks are under attack. These attacks take many forms and are directed at different network functional layers. Wireless data links are vulnerable to eavesdropping, traffic analysis and denial-of-service attacks (jamming); wired data links are less vulnerable but not immune. IP network layer attacks take the form of denial-of-service (intentional misuse of the Address Resolution Protocol (ARP) and unsecured packet routing information modifications) and traffic analysis. Consequently, any approach supporting mobile nodes cannot afford to ignore security threats. This paper focuses on the security capabilities and deficiencies of the three IETF Mobile IP working group solutions.

2 General Mobility

IPv4 Mobile IP (MIPv4) [11] enables end systems and intermediate systems to move from one IP network to another. A Mobile Node (MN) is assigned a long-term IP address (home address) on a home network and is administered in the same way as a stationary node with a "permanent" IP address. When away from its home network, a "care-of address" (COA) is associated with the MN and reflects the MN's current point of network attachment.

MIPv4 uses protocol tunneling to hide an MN's home address from intervening routers between the MN's home network and its current location. The tunnel terminates at the MN's care-of address. At the care-of address, the original packet is removed from the tunnel and delivered to the MN. Figure 1 depicts the MIPv4 routing of packets. A Home Agent (HA) attracts and intercepts pack-

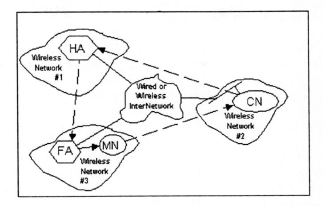

Fig. 1. *MIPv4 Packet Routing Path. All CN packets for MN must travel through HA at MN home network.*

ets that are destined to the home address of any of its registered MNs using proxy and gratuitous ARP mechanisms. An MN and a Foreign Agent (FA) exchange packets without relying on standard IP routing mechanisms; they simply bypass their normal IP routing mechanism when sending packets to each other by using their respective link-layer Media Access Control (MAC) addresses. MIPv4 basically operates as follows:

- FAs and HAs advertise their presence via Agent Advertisement messages on each IP network/subnet for which they provide mobility services.
- An MN receives Agent Advertisements and determines whether it is on its home network or a foreign network.
- When the MN detects that it is located on its home network, it operates without MIPv4 services. When returning to its home network, the MN deregisters with its HA, through exchange of Registration Request and Reply messages.
- When an MN detects that it has moved to a foreign network, it obtains a COA on the foreign network. The COA can either be determined from an FA's advertisements (an FA COA), or by some external assignment mechanism such as the Dynamic Host Configuration Protocol (DHCP) [6] (a co-located COA).
- The MN operating away from home registers its new COA with its HA through exchange of Registration Request and Reply messages between the MN and the HA.
- Packets sent to the MN's home address by a Correspondent Node (CN) are intercepted by the MN's HA, tunneled by the HA to the MN's COA, received at the tunnel endpoint, and finally delivered to the MN.

- In the reverse direction, packets sent by the MN are delivered to their destination using standard IP routing mechanisms, not necessarily passing through the HA.
- Should the MN move from one foreign network to another foreign network, any packets tunneled to the prior foreign network are lost.

IPv4 Route Optimized Mobile IP (ROMIPv4) [7] [9] extends the operation of the MIPv4 protocol allowing optimization of packet routing from a CN to an MN. The protocol extensions of ROMIPv4 provide a means for CNs to cache the binding (i.e., COA) of an MN and tunnel their own packets directly to the MNs COA, bypassing the MN's HA. These extensions also allow packets in transit, while an MN moves between networks, to be forwarded to the MN's new COA.

A CN optimizes its own communication with MNs by maintaining a "binding cache" containing the COAs of MNs. When sending an IP packet to an MN, if the CN has a binding cache entry for the MN, then it tunnels the packet to the cached COA using the encapsulation techniques described for HAs in MIPv4. Figure 2 shows the HA tunneling the initial CN packet to the FA followed by CN direct routing of follow-on packets to the MNs COA. In the absence of a cached

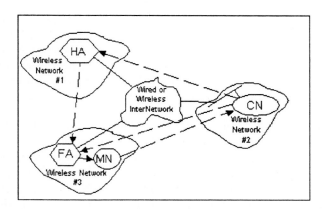

Fig. 2. *ROMIPv4 Packet Routing Path. Only first CN packet for MN must travel through HA, all following CN packets travel directly to MN current network.*

COA entry, packets destined for an MN are routed to the MN's home network in the same way as any other IP packet, and are then tunneled to the MN's current COA by the MN's HA. The original sender of the packet may be informed of the MN's current COA, giving the sender an opportunity to cache the COA. A node creates a binding cache entry for an MN only when it has received and authenticated the MN's mobility binding. Likewise, a node updates an existing binding cache entry for an MN only when it has received and authenticated the MN's new mobility binding (via a binding update).

ROMIPv4 provides for the MN's previous FA to be reliably notified of the MN's new mobility binding, allowing packets in transit to the MN's previous FA to be forwarded to its new COA. This notification also allows any packets tunneled to the MN's previous FA from CNs, with out-of-date cached COA entries for the MN, to be forwarded to its new COA.

During registration with a new FA, the MN and the FA establish a Security Association (SA). When the MN later registers with a new FA, the MN uses this SA as part of the notification to the previous FA that the MN has moved. The notification may include the MN's new COA, allowing the previous FA to create a binding cache entry for the MN. The FA will then forward any tunneled packets for the MN that arrive at this previous FA. ROMIPv4 identifies four methods that an MN can dynamically establish an SA with an FA when it registers with that FA:

1. The HA chooses a registration key, and returns a separate encrypted copy of the key to the FA and to the MN in its Registration Reply message.
2. The MN and the FA execute a Diffie-Hellman key exchange protocol [5] as part of the registration protocol.
3. The MN includes its public key in its Registration Request to the FA, the FA chooses the registration key and returns a copy of it encrypted with the MN's public key.
4. The FA includes an MD5 digest [12] of its public key in its Agent Advertisement messages. The MN includes a copy of this digest in its Registration Request, and the FA adds its full public key to the Registration Request when relaying it to the HA. The HA then chooses the new registration key and returns a separate encrypted copy of the key to the FA (using this public key) and to the MN (using its security association with the MN) in its Registration Reply message.

When an FA receives a packet tunneled to itself, it examines its visitor list for an entry for the destination MN. If a visitor list entry is found, the FA delivers the packet to the MN using MAC addressing mechanisms. The MN is the source of Binding Update messages sent to CNs that are communicating with the MN. Any CN that has no binding cache entry for an MN, will send normal, untunneled packets to the MN by the normal routing in the Internet using the MN's permanent address. When the HA receives a packet for a traveling MN, it tunnels the received packet to the destination MN based on its cached mobility binding. The MN may decide to send a Binding Update message to the originator of the packet so the originator will create a binding cache entry for that MN. Future packets sent by this node to the MN will be tunneled to the MN and not need the involvement of the HA.

When a node receives a Binding Update message, it verifies the authentication in the message, using the SA it shares with the MN. The authentication data is found in the Route Optimization Authentication extension. If the authentication succeeds, then the binding cache entry is updated for use in future transmissions of data to the MN.

IPv6 Mobile IP (MIPv6) [8] incorporates many of the features found in ROMIPv4. Some of the major functional differences between MIPv6 and ROMIPv4 are:

- MIPv6 uses IP version 6, as defined in [4], as its network protocol rather than IP version 4.
- A MN's HA and CNs learn and cache the MN's binding (i.e., COA) through use of a set of new IPv6 destination options defined for Mobile IPv6.
- MIPv6 complies with the Security Architecture defined in [1] and packets that include a Binding Update or Acknowledgment option must include an IPv6 Authentication header [2] in order to protect against forged Binding Updates and Binding Acknowledgments, thereby eliminating the need for a Mobile IP specific message authentication mechanism to establish an SA.
- A MN usually acquires its COA according to the methods of IPv6 Neighbor Discovery [10].
- The HA uses proxy Neighbor Discovery to intercept any IPv6 packets addressed to the MN's home address on the home subnet instead of using proxy ARP as in MIPv4 and ROMIPv4.
- The HA tunnels each intercepted packet to the MN's primary COA via encapsulating the packet using IPv6 encapsulation [3], addressed to the MN's primary COA.
- CNs use an IPv6 Routing header (instead of IPv6 encapsulation) to route packets to the traveling MN using the COA contained in their local Binding Cache or just received Binding Update.
- Every IPv6 MN is able to perform IPv6 decapsulation [3], whereas only MNs that used co-located COAs had to support this capability in ROMIPv4 and MIPv4.
- MIPv6 eliminates the use of Foreign Agents (FAs). If a packet arrives at the MN's previous default router (e.g., the MN moved after the packet was sent), the router will encapsulate and tunnel the packet to the MN's new COA using IPv6 encapsulation addressed to the MN's new primary COA.

Since foreign network routers should be sending periodic multicast Router Advertisement messages, the MN should have frequent opportunity to check if it is still able to reach its current default router, even in the absence of other packets to it from the router. On some network interfaces, the MN may also set its network interface into "promiscuous" receive mode, so that it is able to receive all packets on the link.

3   Mobility Requirements

As the use of mobile nodes becomes more common, a number of security-related requirements become vital:

Authentication and Integrity. The receiver of a message should be able to ascertain who the actual originator of the message is, thereby negating an intruder from masquerading as a legitimate source of the message in question.

The majority of networks mobile nodes visit, will be wireless nets which are subject to eavesdropping and unable to control actual attachment via physical controls.

When an MN receives an Agent Advertisement message, the MN needs to know it comes from a valid FA. Without authentication a hostile FA could easily masquerade as a legitimate FA and present a denial-of-service threat (as well as other privacy and integrity threats) by:

- issuing registration reply messages stating the MN registration request is denied,
- duplicating packets tunneled to the MN and possibly also packets sent by the MN, and
- forwarding MN registration requests to an address other than that of the MN's HA, or discarding MN registration requests, causing the MN to never receive a registration reply from its HA.

Any messages sent between MNs, HAs and FAs that affect how IP packets are routed MUST be received at the destination exactly as sent by the message source. Failure to validate the integrity of these types of messages allows a hostile node to modify these messages while in transit. Modification could easily result in an MN's attempt to register at a foreign network being denied or the registration occurring but packets destined for the MN being mis-routed/lost.

Authorization. When an MN wants to attach to a foreign network, the FA needs to know the authentic identity of the MN. The actual decision to allow the attachment is an authorization question which the FA cannot answer unless it knows, with some defined degree of assurance, that the MN is who it says it is. The organization which owns/operates a network should have the ability to decide who may attach to the network and what network resources may be used by the attaching node. Access control (authorization) at a foreign network being visited by an MN is critical within a mobile node context. Networks supporting visiting MNs need the ability to decide which MNs are allowed visiting rights. These networks also need a mechanism by which access control information may be defined, stored, validated and applied to requested MN visits. A commercial IP mobility protocol needs to address the mechanism(s) by which a network node obtains authorization information and guidelines to ensure interoperability between different implementations.

Nonrepudiation. The sender of a message should not be able to deny falsely that it originated a message at a later time. When an MN visits a foreign network the MN will consume network resources. From the perspective of the organization responsible for the visited network, a record of what resources are consumed by the visiting MN needs to be kept for performance management and accounting/billing purposes. The FA must have a way of identifying which MN consumed what resources such that the owner of the MN cannot deny the visit or resources consumed.

Key Management. The only method available to enforce authentication, integrity and nonrepudiation accurately is by using some form of cryptography; which requires the distribution/exchange of encryption key information amongst message senders and receivers. Strong authentication, integrity and nonrepudiation mechanisms are based primarily on the use of cryptographic algorithms. Modern algorithms base their security capabilities on the use of a key, or keys, which allows the algorithm(s) to be publicly available so long as the keying information is kept and distributed in a private manner.

One method for distributing the key information is to load it into each node manually. This is fine for a small number of nodes but runs into administrative problems. Page 29 of [13] highlights this problem by noting that if a separate key is used for each pair of nodes for authentication purposes, the total number of keys increases rapidly as the number of users increases. N users requires N(N-1)/2 keys. Individual key pairs amongst a 1000 nodes would require 499,500 keys, where each key must be kept and distributed in a secure manner. It quickly becomes apparent that a manual key distribution approach is not feasible for use in IP mobility except with a very small number of nodes. A truly viable solution for Mobile Nodes must scale well to large numbers of mobile nodes by providing a secure dynamic key distribution function.

4 Current Mobile IP Deficiencies

This section evaluates how the security capabilities and mechanisms of MIPv4, ROMIPv4 and MIPv6 map to the security criteria established in the preceeding section. The security issues and risks relative to authentication, authorization, nonrepudiation and key management follow.

Authentication: MIPv4 does not describe how manual establishment of SAs between MN, FA and HA is accomplished. The risk of a hostile FA masquerading as a legitimate FA and presenting a denial-of-service threat exists by using non-authenticated FA Advertisements and the optional nature of SAs between HA - FA and MN - FA. Both MIPv4 and ROMIPv4 rely on ARP, which does not provide any authentication so a wireless Home network is vulnerable to MN traffic stealing by having a hostile node on the wireless network. ROMIPv4 is an improvement over MIPv4 since SAs are required between MNs, CNs, FAs, and HAs but there are key distribution problems. The ROMIPv4 approach of allowing an HA to manage its SAs using a single "master" key by computing a node-specific key, MD5(node-address, master-key, node-address), can result in a Hostile node eavesdropping on communications between HAs, FAs, MNs and CAs for a period of time. An eavesdropping Hostile node can see many of the node addresses used, thereby gaining an advantage in deducing the master key value. MIPv6 requires SAs between MNs and Default Routers, as defined by IPsec Security Architecture [1], and use IPv6 Authentication header [2]. However, efficient key distribution/establishment between MNs and Default Routers is still an open issue.

Authorization: MIPv4, ROMIPv4 and MIPv6 are all silent regarding authorization, beyond including an FA registration denial code of "administratively prohibited", and thereby fail to address how an FA may ascertain the legitimacy of visiting MNs. All three leave authorization implementation to developers without providing guidelines

Nonrepudiation: MIPv4, ROMIPv4 and MIPv6 FA visitor list entries do not record the actual duration of the MN visit or the amount network resources consumed. The result is no mechanism for logging visiting MN resource consumption, and an owner/operator of the visited network is unable to track network resource utilization

Key Management: The MIPv4 default key management approach that all MNs, HAs and FAs are required to support is a manual distribution mechanism. MIPv4 requires a unique secret key as part of each existing SA between MNs and HAs (mandatory), MNs and FAs (optional), and FAs and HAs (optional). This approach would require three secret keys to exist for the mandatory and optional SAs covered by only one MN, HA and FA. If one considers, for example:

− five (5) wireless networks which support mobile nodes,
− each network containing a single combined FA-HA node and 20 MNs,
− 10 of the MNs in each network visits 3 of the other networks over a 4-hour period.

at the end of the 4-hour period 254 secret keys would be required, with each of these keys loaded prior to MNs going mobile. Those MNs not preloaded with keys would have to remain on their home networks. This is a very small scale scenario. When we look at proposed large commercial scenarios containing hundreds of HAs and FAs with 1,000s to 10,000s of MNs, the number of keys that are needed is far too huge to handle via a manual key distribution manner.

ROMIPv4 proposes four approaches for dynamically establishing authentication keys for Registration Request, Reply and Binding Update messages. Throughout the discussion of the four approaches, ROMIPv4 does not address key establishment with CNs beyond the requirement of a manually-established SA.

The HA as a Key Distribution Center (KDC): The approach of using the HA as a KDC, requires:

− the HA have a secret key based security association with the MN,
− the HA have a secret key based security association with the FA, and
− the HA to generate, encrypt and distribute Registration keys for use by the FA and MN.

This approach requires the use of three separate secret keys for one MN to register with one FA. When scaled to large networks we are facing the need for thousands of secret keys, two thirds of which are manually distributed and one third generated, encrypted and distributed dynamically as MNs register on foreign networks. An HA, supporting 100 MNs who roam to new foreign networks every 2 minutes, is faced with having to generate, encrypt and distribute as many as 3000 secret keys per hour (1200 milliseconds for each new key). These HA functions of generating, encrypting and distributing the MN-FA secret keys are in addition to all other HA activities. Can an HA perform these KDC functions on top of its responsibilities for handling traffic being tunneled to roaming MNs? Also this approach does not deal with the trust relationship that must exist between the MN and the FA for access control and non-repudiation. A trusted third party is necessary for the FA to trust the MN and the HA from an identity standpoint.

Diffie-Hellman Exchange between MN and FA: This approach allows MNs and FAs to establish registration keys by executing the Diffie-Hellman key exchange algorithm [5] as part of the MN's registration. Using the Diffie-Hellman algorithm allows the MN and its FA to establish a registration key without any pre-existing mobility security associations. One is still faced with the problem of manually distributing secret keys between MNs and HAs. Also this approach does not deal with the trust relationship that must exist between the MN and the FA for access control and non-repudiation. A trusted third party is necessary for the FA to trust the MN from an identity standpoint.

MN Public Key: With this approach the FA is charged with generating the new registration key and returning a copy of it encrypted with the MN's Public Key, received in a MN Public Key extension. However the FA has no way of verifying if the public key received from the MN is valid for that MN since there is no authentication associated with the Public Key sent by the MN. This approach also does not deal with the trust relationship between the MN and the FA for access control and non-repudiation. Again a trusted third party is necessary for the FA to trust the MN from an identity standpoint.

FA Public Key: The only real difference between this approach and that of using the HA as a KDC is that the HA uses an unauthenticated Public Key from the FA for encrypting the newly generated registration key being sent to the FA rather that an existing secret key security association between the HA and the FA. The inclusion of an MD5 digest of the FA's public key in a Registration Key Request Public Key Digest extension only establishes that the public key supplied by the FA in the FA Public Key extension is the same as received by the MN in an Agent Advertisement message.

MIPv6 Key Management: MIPv6 session key establishment between MNs and Default Routers currently requires a pre-established security relationship. A mechanism is necessary that avoids the need for a possibly time-consuming negotiation between these routers and MNs for the purpose of obtaining the session key, which under many circumstances would only be used once. MIPv6 currently is relying on the work of the IETF IP Security (IPSEC) Working Group to define this function. Currently IPsec work only addresses the dynamic establishment of session keys for secret key type cryptosystems.

5 Conclusions

MIPv4 and ROMIPv4 certainly provide support for mobile and portable end nodes in small IP-based networks in a relatively benign environment (especially given the lack of authentication of the ARP protocol). The network size directly impacts the effort to support a manual key distribution process in MIPv4. Therefore the use of MIPv4 should primarily be limited to use in intranets within a single organizational facility.

ROMIPv4 also provides support for mobile nodes in small IP based networks. Authentication has been improved in ROMIPv4 over that found in MIPv4. However, authorization is still not adequately addressed. The use of ARP by ROMIPv4 again limits ROMIPv4 use to a relatively benign environment, such as within a wired intranet. Key distribution has been improved over MIPv4 but still fails to provide a strong method of assuring trust between nodes. MIPv6 resolves some of the security issues found in MIPv4 and ROMIPv4 such as:

- Use of the IPv6 Neighbor Discovery mechanism (in conjunction with the IPv6 Authentication Header) instead of unauthenticated ARP and proxy ARP, and
- Mandatory authentication of all Binding Update and Binding Acknowledgment options.

The major problem with MIPv6 is that it requires the use of IPsec at the network layer. IPsec has primarily focused on secret key cryptosystems and symmetric key management and has yet to encompass public key technology for authentication and key/certificate management. A key component of IPsec is its use of multiple messages to negotiate an SA between two nodes. The network traffic resulting from the SA negotiation may be a small cost for secure associations that last from anywhere between minutes up to days. This approach results in a significant amount of network overhead to support an SA that may persist for less than 1500 milliseconds.

A number of approaches exist, [14], [15] and [16], for addressing the security problems in Mobile IP. The [14] approach introduces a Key Distribution Center mechanism but does not address the fundimental issue of trust relationships amongst the communicating parties. The IPsec approach presented in [15] uses public keys but adds additional overhead in using secret key session keys for IPsec ESP secured tunnels. The public key based authentication approach presented in [16] provides for trust relationships amongst the communicating parties without introducing the overhead that the [15] method includes. A similar approach to [16] could be used with MIPv6.

Use of public keys contained in Digital Certificates (DCs) issued by trusted third parties, Certificate Authorities (CAs), provides the key ingredient for establishing trust relationships between HAs, MNs and FAs. When an FA receives a message from an MN, the FA is able to validate the digital signature using the MN's public key. If the FA shares the same CA as the MN, the FA can easily authenticate the MN's DC by using the CA's public key already in the FA's possession. Should the FA and the MN not use the same CA, the FA can establish a trust hierarchy path between the FA's CA and the CA of the MN. The converse is true for MNs authenticating digital signatures from FAs and the same is true between HAs and FAs. The use of CAs allow Mobile IP aware systems to establish strong trust relationships to base authentication, access control and non-repudiation decisions on.

A number of issues still require further research. Which asymmetric public key algorithms are the most efficient for use in portable computing devices frequently powered by batteries? RSA [17] is one candidate, yet other public key algorithms exist and need to be studied. What are the necessary and appropriate fields in a Digital Certificate (DC) which is used to identify a machine? Are there mechanisms that can be used to protect the private key of a machine that does not require a human to enter a passphrase every time the private key needs to be decrypted? Should Certificate Revocation List (CRL) entries for DCs that apply to machines be stored in the same CRL as those CRL entries for DCs that apply to humans? How often should DCs be checked against CRLs? All of these issues have a direct impact on the performance of public key based authentication.

References

1. Atkinson, R., "Security Architecture for the Internet Protocol", RFC 1825, August 1995.
2. Atkinson, R., "IP Authentication Header", RFC 1826, August 1995.
3. Conta, A., Deering, S., "Generic packet tunneling in IPv6 specification", Internet Draft, draft-ietf-ipngwg-ipv6-tunnel-02.txt, June 1996. Work in progress.
4. Deering, S., Hinden, R., "Internet Protocol version 6 (IPv6) Specification", RFC 1883, December 1995.
5. W. Diffie, W., Hellman, M. E., "New directions in cryptography", IEEE Transactions on Information Theory, IT-22(6):644-654, November 1976.
6. Droms, R., "Dynamic Host Configuration Protocol", RFC 1541, October 1993.
7. Johnson, D., Perkins, C., "Route Optimization in Mobile IP", Internet Draft, draft-ietf-mobileip-optim-07.txt, November 1997. Work in progress.
8. Johnson, D., Perkins, C., "Mobility Support in IPv6", Internet Draft, draft-ietf-mobileip-ipv6-06.txt, August 1998. Work in progress.
9. Perkins, C., Johnson, D., "Registration Keys for Route Optimization", Internet Draft, draft-ietf-mobileip-regkey-00.txt, November 1997. Work in progress
10. Narten, T., Nordmark, E., Simpson, W.A., "Neighbor Discovery for IP version 6 (IPv6)", RFC 1970, August 1996.
11. Perkins, C., editor, "IP Mobility Support", RFC 2002, October 1996.
12. Rivest, R., "The MD5 Message-Digest Algorithm", RFC 1321, April 1992.
13. Schneier, B., "Applied Cryptography 2nd Edition", Chapter 22 pp. 513-514, John Wiley and Sons Inc., 1996.
14. Sanchez, L., Troxel, G., "Rapid Authentication for Mobile IP", Internet Draft, draft-ietf-mobileip-ra-00.txt, November 1997. Work in progress.
15. Zao, J., Condell, M., "Use of IPSec in Mobile IP", Internet Draft, draft-ietf-mobileip-ipsec-use-00.txt, November 1997. Work in progress.
16. Jacobs, S., "Mobile IP Public Key Based Authentication", Internet Draft, draft-jacobs-mobileip-pki-auth-00.txt, August 1998. Work in progress.
17. Rivest, R.L., Shamir, A., Adleman, L., "A method for obtaining digital signatures and public-key cryptosystems", Communications of the ACM, 21(2):120-126, February 1978.

The views and conclusions contained in this document are those of the author and should not be interpreted as representing the official policies, either expressed or implied, of the Army Research Laboratories or the U.S. Government.

An Active Database Framework for Adaptive Mobile Data Access *

Shiow-yang Wu and Chun-Shun Chang

Department of Computer Science and Information Engineering
National Dong Hwa University
Hualien, Taiwan, R.O.C.
showyang@csie.ndhu.edu.tw,
http://ravel.csie.ndhu.edu.tw/

Abstract. The ability to *adapt to changes* is among the most important issues in mobile information systems. We argue that active database system is the software architecture of choice as the foundation for adaptive mobile information services. We propose a modular framework and system architecture for building active mobile information systems by integrating off-the-shelf rule systems and database packages. For intelligent adaptation, a common *mobile event interface* is employed to detect the status changes. The rule system plays the role of a reactive component for making proper decisions in response to the changes. A general *database interface* ensures seamless integration of the rule system with any number of ODBC compliant database systems for flexible information access. We suggest implementation strategies and present performance results to demonstrate the feasibility of the proposed framework.

1 Introduction

In mobile computing environment, a mobile host is constantly subject to resource availability, changing mobile support stations and connection status, as well as terrain and weather. To cope with such a demanding environment, the ability to adapt to changes is among the most important system issues [5, 14]. Rudimentary mechanism for limited adaptation such as the power management facilities and "doze mode" operation on some portable devices are far from satisfactory. In many cases, optimal adaptation depends on both the resource and environment constraint, as well as the current status of operation. It may require instant and complex decision to be made on the fly.

As a motivating example, imagine the scenario in which a mobile user on a moving vehicle is approaching a mountain area where radio signal is expected to be weak or completely blocked. According to the current road and traffic condition and also from the speed and direction of the vehicle, no mobile support station will be available for the next half an hour before the vehicle passing

---

* This paper was partially supported by the National Science Council, Taiwan, R.O.C., under project NSC 86-2213-E-259-004.

through the mountain area, into the famous "semiconductor valley".[1] For assisting the user who must finish his/her work within half an hour for an important business meeting, the underlying information system has several choices. The easiest way is to take no specific action and run the risk of sudden disconnection, unfinished work, and a failed business trip. On the other hand, a highly adaptive system can sense the current situation, deduce key constraint mentioned above, and take the initiative in preparing for disconnected operation. Our goal is to apply intelligent techniques for adaptation in mobile information systems. In particular, we have identified the active database system concept as the building block for intelligent adaptation.

Active database systems have been shown to provide traditional databases with many desirable features [15]. For mobile information management, we found the active concept to be a power tool for intelligent adaptation. In particular, the event-driven interface is a natural candidate for sensing the resource availability as well as changes in the operating environment. The rule inference mechanism equips the system with sufficient arsenal to make intelligent decision and effective responses to any possible situation (such as intermittent disconnection). In this paper, we propose a modular framework for building adaptive mobile information systems based on the active database architecture.

Our framework is modular in the sense that a general software architecture is proposed to construct mobile information systems from existing enterprise databases using off-the-shelf rule systems and DBMS packages. Existing data can be used for active rule inference without any change to the DBMS. More specifically, we provide a *mobile event interface* as the active front-end. The detection and delivery of mobility, resource, and environment events enables an information system to be aware of current environment status and resource constraint. We construct a *database interface* on top of the widely accepted Open Database Connectivity (ODBC) standard [7] for seamless integration of rule languages with different database systems. This facilitates rule-based reasoning over any number of databases with ODBC driver support. A prototype implementation of our framework using CLIPS [2] and several PC database packages is reported in Section 6.

The rest of the paper is organized as follows. Section 2 enumerates research work on adaptation in mobile computing to position our work among others. Section 3 presents the proposed framework and the software architecture for its realization. Section 4 discusses the mobile event interface. Section 5 describes how we achieve easy access to multiple databases with the database interface. Section 6 provides our experience in prototype implementation and evaluation. Section 7 concludes the paper.

2 Related Work

Data management is emerging as one of the most promising area in mobile computing [1, 3, 9]. The need for adaptation is quickly identified as essential

---

[1] This is an imaginary scenario, therefore we avoid using any real place or name.

[5, 14]. Similar ideas have been discussed under terms like context-aware [12], application-aware [8, 11], and adaptive [4] information systems. However, related issues have rarely been addressed from a software engineering point of view. Among the few exceptions is the work done at CMU on both application-transparent and application-aware adaptation [10]. The advantage of application-transparent adaptation [6] is that no changes are needed to existing applications. However, such strategy is necessarily application-independent which cannot take advantages of any application-specific feature for optimal adaptation. On the other hand, the potential improvement offered by the application-aware adaptation may very well come with higher complexity and software development cost. Our main contribution is to provide a modular framework for an event-driven rule abstraction on top of existing information systems. With easy integration of off-the-shelf software packages without changes, and the rule system as a responsive component, we offer the benefits of both worlds.

3 System Architecture

Our design is driven by the following considerations. For dynamically responding to changes, a reactive component is mandatory. We extend the active database concept to satisfy this requirement. For resource and environment awareness, an *event subsystem* can be used to detect the changes and trigger the reactive component. The framework must allow easy access to databases of different types and vendors to cope with the heterogeneity of mobile computing. Finally, it is impractical to require transformation of existing data or modification to existing DBMS softwares. The framework should require minimal changes to existing systems. To summarize our design objectives:

1. A flexible event interface for responsive mobile computing.
2. A general mechanism to integrate event delivery with rule inference mechanism to enable the rule system as a reactive component.
3. Seamless integration of rule languages with database systems such that the inference power of the rule system can be used for intelligent adaptation.
4. Multiple and heterogeneous databases access by conforming to standards.
5. Reuse of off-the-shelf rule languages and database packages such that all current investment can be preserved and no data reformation is required.
6. The framework should be modular such that major components can be easily upgraded or even replaced to satisfy user demand.

We suggest an extended active database architecture consisting of four modular components for constructing client side mobile information systems:(1) a mobile event engine, (2) a rule system, (3) a database interface, and (4) a database system which is composed of a DBMS and a DB cache. Fig. 1 illustrates the components and their integration. Fig. 2 depicts the software architecture for the realization of our framework. The main idea is the shared event interface and database interface to allow easy integration of any rule system (such as CLIPS, OPS5, ...) with multiple database systems (such as Microsoft Access, DB Maker, ...). Details are discussed in the following sections.

338

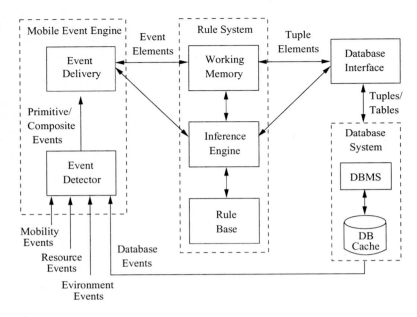

Fig. 1. A modular framework for building adaptive mobile information systems.

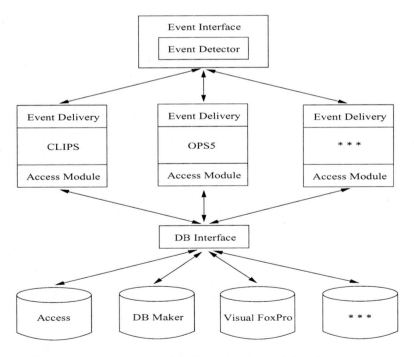

Fig. 2. Software architecture for building adaptive mobile information systems.

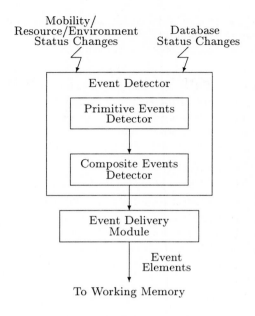

Fig. 3. The event interface.

4 Event Interface

The mobile event engine is the key component for resource and environment awareness. In additional to the traditional database and temporal events [15], we suggest the inclusion of mobility, resource, and environment events. Whenever a mobility variable (such as location, speed, etc.), the availability of a resource or the status of an environment variable has changed to a critical level, a corresponding event is triggered. These events are detected by the *event detector*. An event that is detected directly from a status change is called a *primitive event*. Primitive events can be combined to form *composite events*. When an event is detected, the *event delivery module* is responsible for transforming the event into an *event element* which is in exactly the same format as a *working memory element* of the rule system. In this way, the event engine can be easily integrated with the rule system without any change to the rule execution semantics or run-time system. The only modification to the rule system is a simple syntactic extension for users to specify the events of interest. Fig. 3 illustrates the structure of our event mechanism.

4.1 Mobile Event Specification

We classified the status changes in mobile hosts or the environment into three categories:

1. changes that are related or induced by the mobility of the mobile host;
2. changes in resource availability;
3. other status changes in the operating environment.

Events of the first two types usually occur with associated changes in certain measurable values such as the location change, low in battery power, and so on. The third type of event is for signaling other situations that may require immediate attention such as being in the process of hand-off. We use the names *mobility events*, *resource events*, and *environment events* for obvious reasons.

Mobility and resource events are specified in two forms:

> **On** $\langle Variable\_Name \rangle$ $\langle Op \rangle$ $\langle Value \rangle$
> **On** $\langle Variable\_Name \rangle$ **Level** $\langle Level \rangle$

The $\langle Variable\_Name \rangle$ can be the name of a mobility variable (such as **Location**, **Speed**, and **Direction**) or a resource variable (such as **Power**, **Memory**, and **Bandwidth**). The $\langle Level \rangle$ is currently defined to be either **High**, **Normal**, or **Low**.[2] The first form is for fine grain detection of the status change of the named variable while the second form is for testing the current availability level. For example, the resource event

> **On Bandwidth** < 10

will be triggered when the current bandwidth is lower than 10 Kb/sec. Similarly, the event

> **On Power Level** Low

will be triggered when the remaining battery power is lower than a predefined level.

Environment events are simply specified as:

> **On** $\langle Condition \rangle$

where $\langle Condition \rangle$ could potentially be any situation of interest but we limit it to include only **Hand-off** at present.

Mobility, resource and environment events are primitive events which can be further combined into composite events using arbitrary combination of the logical connectives **AND** and **OR**.[3] The occurrences of both primitive and composite events are detected by the event detector and delivered to the rule system by the event delivery module. It is important to note that, regardless of the rule system of choice, the event specification and detection module are shared among all rule languages as indicated in Fig. 2. In other words, all events are specified using the same set of syntax and detected with the same set of library modules. No porting or re-implementation is needed on any specific rule system. This is a good example of our modular design. The only thing that is rule-system dependent is the event delivery module, since events must be converted into a form understood by the inference engine of the corresponding rule system.

---

[2] It is certainly desirable to have user-defined levels, which are included in our plans for the immediate future.

[3] We excluded negation because activating a rule on the non-existence of an event is in general not in accordance with the semantics of active database rules.

4.2 Event Delivery

The separation of event detection and delivery is to:

1. support uniform event interface;
2. allow code sharing on common functionality;
3. enable easy integration of event mechanism with any rule system of choice.

Whenever an event is detected, it is presented in a standard format. The event delivery module of a particular rule system is to convert all detected events into event elements which are in the form of working memory elements of the corresponding rule system. In this way, the inference engine of the rule system can be used directly without modification to react to any event occurrence. Event elements are kept in working memory until either removed explicitly by an action of a rule or until the end of the current inference session. An inference session begins when the rule system is triggered by certain event occurrences and ends when no rule is executable. Note that a separate event delivery module must be developed for each rule system since different rule systems have different formats for working memory elements. Nevertheless, the structure and functionality of the module are the same across rule systems. It is therefore quite straightforward to port the event delivery module to suit a rule system of choice.

5 Database Interface

The database interface is responsible for integrating rule system with DBMS such that the tuples in the database can be used directly by the rule system for reasoning and the actions of a rule can perform arbitrary database operations. We also must have the system interact with multiple and heterogeneous databases without modification to existing databases and DBMS packages. Our approach is to separate the database interface into a rule-system dependent *access module* and a *common database interface module* built on top of the ODBC standard.[4] The access module provides a set of access functions as an extension of rule actions for database access. Tuples accessed from the databases are converted into *tuple elements* which are in the form of working memory elements of the rule system. Data generated within the rule system can also be saved into databases by the access functions. The access module is necessarily rule-system dependent because different systems have different language syntax and data formats. The common database interface module, on the other hand, is rule-system and DBMS independent. It is used to access one or more databases which may be built by DBMS packages from different vendors as long as the packages support ODBC. The structure and relationship between various components described above are depicted in Fig. 4.

---

[4] Any open database connectivity standard could be used in here. ODBC is chosen for accessing PC-based databases that are readily available on our machines.

Rule System

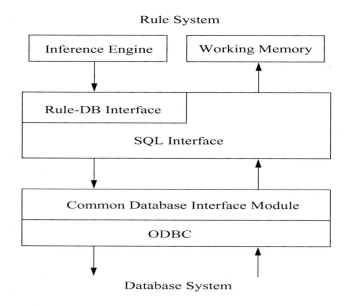

Fig. 4. The database interface.

5.1 Access Module

The design of the access module must satisfy two seemingly conflicting goals. It must be flexible and powerful enough to allow arbitrary database operations. At the same time, it must be simple and easy to use so that rule programmers with little knowledge about databases can still use it without any difficulty. Furthermore, it is desirable to have a common approach to database access to maintain a reasonable extent of uniformity across the access modules of different rule systems. We therefore provide two sets of functions for each access module:

1. *SQL interface*, for power users who want the full control and flexibility of database access; and
2. *Rule-DB interface*, for general rule programmers who may not know much about SQL.

The SQL interface provide a direct way of manipulating databases from rule actions using the SQL language. Each access function accepts a database name and an SQL statement. The programmer is free to use arbitrary SQL statements but is also responsible for their correctness.

The rule-DB interface consists of a **Load** and a **Save** function. The **Load** function accepts a database name and a table name. It reads the table from the designated database and inserts the tuples into working memory of the rule system. Tuples are inserted as elements of the working memory class with the same name as the table name. The **Save** function saves all elements of a working memory class into the table that bears the corresponding name.

Since access module is rule-system dependent, the syntax of both the SQL interface and rule-DB interface functions must be designed in the style of the corresponding rule system.

5.2 Common Database Interface Module

The access functions discussed above are necessarily rule-system dependent. Their functionality, however, are system independent. This is why a common database interface is possible and desirable. The interface can also be made independent of the underlying DBMS packages if a standard interface exists such that the actual database calls can be issued in a common format. We choose ODBC for such purpose. More specifically, we provide a shared library of functions that: (i) perform the necessary data conversion and aggregation; and (ii) issue ODBC calls to accomplish the desired functionality. In this way, we can access not only different databases with the same interface, but also multiple databases at the same time. The same interface can be used with any access module of the chosen rule system to communicate with any number of databases as illustrated in Fig. 2. No modification is required on either the existing databases or the underlying DBMS packages. This facilitates easy integration of existing data into the mobile information system as well as the objective of modular design.

6 Prototype Implementation

We have built a prototype system for evaluating the feasibility and potential of our framework. A Windows95 PC was chosen as the implementation platform since most of the existing portable computers are PC-based. Because of the space limit, we only discuss the database interface.

For the rule system, we chose wxCLIPS [13], a Windows version of the well-known CLIPS [2] expert system tool. For the database systems, any package with ODBC driver support would do. We selected Microsoft Access, Visual FoxPro, and DBMaker for their immediate availability on our machines.

The rule-DB interface is implemented by two functions: **LoadTable** and **SaveTemplate**, both in CLIPS syntax. The **LoadTable** is for loading database tuples into the rule system while **SaveTemplate** is for saving CLIPS data objects back to the database. The SQL interface is also implemented by two functions: **SQLtoFACT** and **SQLdo**. This is for power users who can use arbitrary SQL statements for better control over database operations.

The common database interface module is implemented by providing a layer of abstraction on top of ODBC. The layer is designed to hide the complexity of ODBC API so that the access functions could be implemented more easily.

For performance evaluation, we constructed a set of student databases using three different DBMS packages and wrote a rule program in CLIPS for computing GPA. Fig. 5 demonstrates the performance difference between using the CLIPS system alone and using the CLIPS integrated with a database (Visual

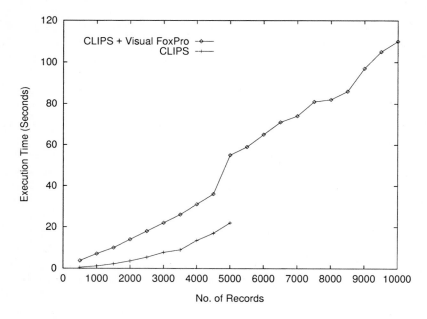

Fig. 5. Rule system (CLIPS) vs. database-enabled rule system (CLIPS + Visual Fox-Pro).

FoxPro). It is conceivable that without the additional overhead, the CLIPS system should be more efficient when the volume of data is small. However, the benefit of using database reveals itself when the data volume becomes larger. In particular, while the CLIPS system can only handle up to 5000 records before saturating the system resource, our implementation can handle a potentially unlimited number of records. We note that the processing time grows linearly with data size, which demonstrates the efficiency of our prototype implementation.

Fig. 6 compares the performance of the SQL interface and the rule-DB interface. The SQL interface is clearly more efficient. However, the rule-DB interface is much easier to use since it does not require prior knowledge about SQL.

Fig. 7 illustrates the performance of the database interface and also demonstrates the ability of our implementation to integrate the CLIPS system with different DBMS packages. All three packages exhibit linear growth of execution time with increasing data size, which indicates the limited overhead of our approach and the prototype implementation.

The performance results suggest that it is possible to achieve modularity and flexibility without loss of functionality and efficiency. We provide an easy integration mechanism to allow immediate extension of existing rule systems and database systems into adaptive mobile information systems. The integration can be achieved with low software development cost and good performance.

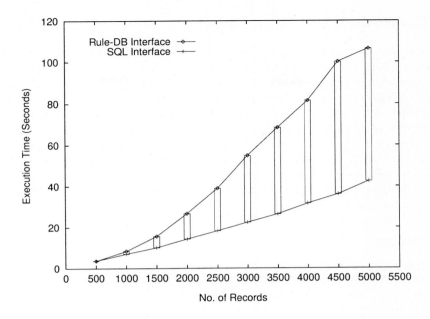

Fig. 6. SQL interface vs. rule-DB interface.

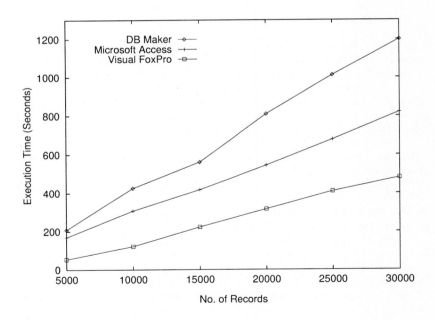

Fig. 7. Performance comparison of using different database packages.

7 Conclusions and Future Work

We proposed an active database framework for building adaptive mobile information systems. The key to intelligent adaptation is a mobile event interface and the integration of rule system with databases. Modularity is achieved through software architecture and techniques that can easily integrate off-the-shelf system components with existing data. A prototype implementation and evaluation results demonstrate the feasibility and potential of our approach.

This work is part of an ongoing project at National Dong Hwa University, Hualien, Taiwan, R.O.C. The goal is to develop necessary infrastructure, middleware, and software technologies for responsive mobile computing. We plan to apply the technologies on an experimental hospital information system and a campus information system.

References

[1] B. Bruegge and B. Bennington. Applications of mobile computing and communications. *IEEE Personal Communications*, 3(1), February 1996.

[2] Lyndon B. Johnson Space Center. CLIPS: A tool for building expert systems. (http:// www.jsc.nasa.gov/~clips/CLIPS.html).

[3] T. Imielinski and B. R. Badrinath. Wireless mobile computing: Challenges in data management. *Comm ACM*, 37(10):19–28, October 1994.

[4] T. Imielinski and S. Vishwanathan. Adaptive wireless information systems. Technical report, Department of Computer Science, Rutgers University, 1994.

[5] R. H. Katz. Adaptation and mobility in wireless information systems. *IEEE Personal Communications*, 1(1):6–17, 1994.

[6] J. J. Kistler and M. Satyanarayanan. Disconnected operation in the Coda file system. *ACM Transactions on Computer Systems*, 10(1):3–25, February 1992.

[7] C. Lambert. ODBC: Architecture, performance, and tuning. ODBC Product Group, Microsoft Corporation, 1995.

[8] Brian D. Noble, M. Satyanarayanan, Dushyanth Narayanan, James Eric Tilton, Jason Flinn, and Kevin R. Walker. Agile application-aware adaptation for mobility. In *16th ACM Symposium on Operating System Principles*, 1997.

[9] E. Pitoura and B. Bhargava. Building information systems for mobile environments. In *Third International Conference on Information and Knowledge Management*, pages 371–378, November 1994.

[10] M. Satyanarayanan. Mobile information access. *IEEE Personal Communications*, 3(1), February 1996.

[11] M. Satyanarayanan, B. Noble, P. Kumar, and M. Price. Application-aware adaptation for mobile computing. *Operating System Review*, 29, January 1995.

[12] B. Schilit, N. Adams, and R. Want. Context-aware mobile applications. In *IEEE Workshop on Mobile Computing Systems and Applications*, Santa Cruz, CA, U.S., December 1994.

[13] Julian Smart. wxCLIPS. (http:// web.ukonline.co.uk/julian.smart/wxclips/).

[14] T. Watson. Application design for wireless computing. In *IEEE Workshop on Mobile Computing Systems and Applications*, Santa Cruz, CA, U.S., December 1994.

[15] J. Widom and S. Ceri. *Active Database Systems: Triggers and Rules for Advanced Database Processing*. Morgan Kaufmann, San Francisco, California, 1996.

Design and Implementation of a Mobile Application Support System

Ching-Hong Leung, Kin-Man Cheung, Kin-Ho Yan, and Tin-Fook Ngai

Department of Computer Science
The Hong Kong University of Science & Technology
(hong@cs.ust.hk, csgerman@cs.ust.hk, ngai@cs.ust.hk)

Abstract. A high-performance mobile application support system is developed and set up at the Computer Science Department of HKUST. The system provides both transparent mobility support over cellular wireless computer networks and mobile application programming interface with which a mobile application can identify its current network location. The system incorporates a number of substantial enhancements beyond the mobile-IP protocol. A mobile host always monitors signal qualities from all reachable base stations and uses these information to decide when and to which base station it should hand off. This allows a mobile client application always maintaining the highest possible data transfer rate with servers on the wired network. Moreover, the system automatically caches data packets in nearby base stations in an attempt to avoid packet losses during hand-off and to reduce hand-off latency. Early experience showed that the system supports mobility very well and most often data caching in nearby base stations is not necessary.

1 Introduction

The objective of this work is to design and implement a mobile application support system over cellular wireless computer networks. The system consists of a network sub-layer which provides transparent permanent connections to mobile clients moving freely between the networks. A mobile application programming interface is also provided therefore a mobile client application can identify its current network location and invokes any location-dependent tasks.

A cellular wireless computer network covers multiple overlapping or disjoint spatial regions called cells. Each cell is covered by a wireless base station (access point) attached to the wired backbone of the computer network. A mobile host (MH) can connect to the network via wireless link to a base station in the same cell. When a mobile host moves from one cell into another cell, it needs to change its wireless link from one base station to another base station in order to maintain its network connection. This process is called handoff. During handoff, network routing information needs to be modified therefore network messages sent to the MH will be correctly directed to the new base station, then forwarded to the MH via the wireless link.

A number of network routing schemes [1, 2, 3, 4, 6, 7, 8] has been proposed to support transparent handoff.

Perkins et al [2] proposed the IETF Mobile-IP standard to address the mobile routing problem at the network layer. In the Mobile-IP scheme, each mobile host (MH) belongs to one home network and has its permanent home IP address. A station machine in the home network is designated as the home agent of the mobile host. When the mobile moves to other cells and is connected to a different network, a station machine in the attached network is designated as the foreign agent of the mobile host. When a host elsewhere wants to communicate with the mobile host, its home IP address is used and data packets are routed to its home network. At the home network, the home agent captures all data packets sent to the mobile host and redirect them to the current foreign agent of the mobile host using IP-in-IP encapsulation. When the foreign agent receives these redirected IP-in-IP packets, it will forward the original IP data packets to the mobile host via the associated wireless access point. Under this scheme, the home agent must keep track of the current foreign agent of the mobile host. During handoffs, control messages must be exchanged between the mobile host, its new foreign agent and home agent to update all necessary location and routing information.

In the Daedalus project at UC Berkeley, Balakrishnan et al [1] proposed a similar handoff scheme as the Mobile-IP. In addition to the redirection of data packets to the current foreign agent, the home agent multicasts the data packets to potential future foreign agents in the neighboring cells. The most recent data packets are cached in these potential foreign agents. When the mobile host later moves into one of those predicted neighboring cells, the corresponding foreign agent will send its cached data packets to the mobile host to make up any data packets lost during handoff.

In this work, we designed and implemented an enhanced handoff scheme for our mobile application support system. The scheme is similar to the Daedalus scheme in the sense that it also multicasts IP-in-IP data packets and caches the data packets in foreign agents of targeted neighboring cells. The major enhancement we have made is a practical decision maker that intelligently decides when to handoff, which foreign agents to cache data packets and which access points to connect to in an overlapping cell environment. The decision maker helps to maintain the best possible network connection (in terms of bandwidth) of a mobile host. We have set up a cellular wireless computer network and implement our mobile application support system within our department to evaluate the performance of the enhanced handoff scheme.

In this paper, we describe the design and implementation of our mobile application support system. Section 2 gives the details of the design of the application support system, especially of its handoff scheme. Section 3 describes our actual implementation. Section 4 reports our evaluation results and early experience with the system. Section 5 concludes this study.

2 Design of the Mobile Application Support System

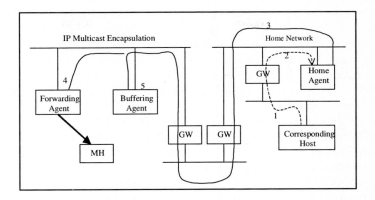

Fig. 1. Data packet routing to a mobile host.

Figure 1 shows how our mobile application support system routes a data packet from a correspondent host (CH) to the mobile host (MH).

1. Any CH sends out an IP packet to MH using the permanent home IP address of the MH.
2. The IP packet is routed to the home network where the home agent (HA) resides.
3. The HA traps the corresponding IP packet using Proxy ARP, then encapsulates the packet inside a multicast-IP header and multicasts the encapsulated packet using the multicast-IP address assigned to the MH.
4. Since the foreign agent (FA) to whose network the MH is currently attached has already joined the IP multicast group of the MH, it receives the encapsulated packets. The FA then strips the multicast-IP headers to retrieve the original IP packets and sends them to the MH through the access point in its network.
5. In some selected neighboring cells, the potential future foreign agents are designated as buffering agents (BAs) of the MH. These BAs have also joined the IP multicast group of the MH and receive copies of the encapsulated packets. Unlike the FA, after retrieving the original IP packets these BAs store the most recent IP packets inside their local buffers.

When the MH moves from one cell to another cell, the handoff operation is simple: The new FA is first asked to join the MH's IP multicast group and then the old FA is asked either to leave the group or to become a BA. If the new FA itself is already a BA before handoff, the handoff operation is even simpler because the new FA has already joined the multicast group.

The above routing scheme has two major advantages over the IETF Mobile-IP. First, the HA is no longer required to keep track of the current foreign agent of the MH. During handoff, an agent simply joins the MH's IP multicast group to become the MH's FA or BA and automatically receives all data packets sent to the MH. This considerably reduces the number of control messages being exchanged, thus the handoff latency. Second, the FA and BAs receive redundant copies of the encapsulated IP-in-IP packets via multicast. Such data redundancy helps to safeguard any potential loss of packets during handoff.

In our design, the mobile application support system should keep track of the current location of a MH and determines when and how a MH should handoff to a different access point. Each MH has a decision maker to perform these functions autonomously.

In order to help identifying the current location of a MH, every access point periodically broadcasts beacon messages which carry the access point's identity. By listening to the beacon messages, a MH not only can determine its current network location but also can determine which access points it can connect to and the qualities of the corresponding receiving signals.

By interpreting the presence and quality of the beacon signals, the decision maker determines the best access point that the MH should connect to and decide when a handoff should be initiated.

The decision maker uses the following three heuristic rules:

1. The absence of beacons within some fixed time interval implies that either the MH is no longer in the corresponding cell or the corresponding wireless link is too congested or noisy.
2. Stronger beacon signal strength implies that the MH is closer to the corresponding access point.
3. Decreasing beacon signal strength level over time implies that the MH is moving away from the corresponding access point. Similarly, increasing signal strength level implies that the MH is moving towards the corresponding access point.

When the MH consistently receives beacons from an access point with high and increasing signal strength level, the access point is a favorable candidate of connection. The decision maker chooses the agent associated with the most favorable access point as the MH's current foreign agent (FA). Agents associated with less favorable access points are chosen as the MH's buffer agents (BAs).

The decision maker continuously monitors the beacons and determines the best possible connection. Whenever the best connection identified is different from the current connection, the MH initiates the handoff procedure to establish the best connection.

For overlapping cells and relatively slow MH movements, the decision maker likely picks a current BA to be the new FA. In other words, a MH likely handoffs to one of its BAs. In this case, the new FA has the recent data packets already stored in its buffer during handoff. These buffered data packets will be sent to the MH immediately after the handoff to make up any lost packets during handoff.

It has been well studied that TCP/IP performance degrades significantly due to packet losses over wireless links.[4] Our mobile application supporting system is designed to avoid or reduce the number of packet losses during handoff. The TCP/IP performance can be improved in two ways:

1. The number of retransmissions during handoff is reduced.
2. The network connection would not experience long temporary disconnections due to handoffs. This prevents the TCP protocol from mistakenly interpret handoffs as network congestions and unnecessarily invoking its congestion control mechanism to slow down the network traffic.

3   Implementation

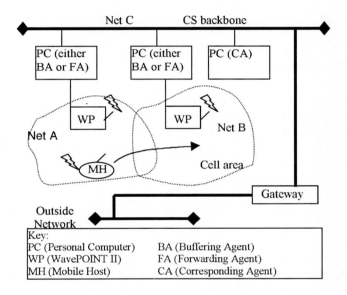

Fig. 2. Configuration of the mobile application support system.

Figure 2 shows the overall system architecture, both hardware and system, of our mobile application support system in the Computer Science Department at HKUST.

We have created three separate networks (indeed sub-networks) with different network IP addresses. Within each network, there is a Pentium II 233MHz PC which serves both as the router between the network and the common network backbone (the CS department's LAN) and as an MH agent in that network. Two Lucent's WAVEPOINT II wireless access points are attached to two of the three networks separately to create two overlapping wireless cells. (The third network without access point serves as the home network of the mobile hosts.) Mobile hosts are Pentium 150MHz laptop computers equipped with Lucent's WaveLAN PCMCIA wireless network cards. The WaveLAN wireless system uses Direct Sequence Spread Spectrum technology operating at the frequency of 2.4GHz with raw data bandwidth of 2Mbit/s [10]. In addition to ethernet supports, the WaveLAN network card allows a user to gather wireless signal quality measurements such as the wireless signal strength level, the silence level of the wireless medium and the signal quality of the last wireless packet received. All PCs and the mobile hosts run the Linux 2.0.33 operating system.

Our mobile application support system consists of three classes of system daemons: the MH daemons, the HA daemons and the FA/BA daemons running on the mobile hosts, home agents and forwarding/buffering agents respectively. Network routing and redirection is made in the network layer mostly under the control of these daemons. The Linux 2.0.33 kernel has also been enhanced to allow extraction of IP packets from encapsulated multicast IP packets.

3.1 MH Daemons

Every mobile host runs a MH daemon to choose the most appropriate FA and BA(s) for the MH and to decide when and which access point to handoff. The MH daemon regularly monitors the beacon signals and their signal qualities. For each access point whose beacon signals have been received, the MH daemon uses the following simple scoring algorithm to evaluate the appropriateness of an access point connection:

1. If no beacon is received from the same access point within the last period, its score is decremented.
2. If the received signal strength is above some predetermined threshold, its score is incremented. value.
3. If the signal strength from the same access point has been increased (decreased) in the last several periods, its score is incremented (decremented).

The score value of each access point connection is limited within a certain range. Once the score reaches its allowed maximum (minimum) value, it will no longer be incremented (decremented).

The MH daemon chooses the agent associated with the access point with the highest score to be the FA of the MH. In case of ties, the current FA is preferred. Next a current BA is preferred. If the chosen FA is different from the current FA, the MH daemon initiates handoff to the newly chosen access point by sending a request to the chosen FA.

Besides the selection of FA, the MH daemon chooses the agent(s) associated with the access point(s) with the second highest scores to be the BA(s) of the MH. In case of ties, the current FA or BA is preferred. If the chosen BA is not a current BA, the MH daemon sends a request to the agent to invite it to be the MH's BA.

3.2   HA Daemons

Every potential home agent runs a HA daemon. The HA daemon is responsible for processing registration requests from MHs and for redirecting data packet to the current FAs of its registered MHs.

When a MH first enters the mobile application support system, it must register with the agent associated with its home network. That agents becomes its HA. Upon receiving a registration request from a MH, the HA daemon records the MH's information and assign a multicast IP address to the MH.

The HA daemon uses the proxy ARP and tunneling network facilities to capture and redirect IP packets sent to its registered MHs. Whenever the network router makes an ARP request to obtain the hardware address of one of its registered MH, the HA replies with its own hardware address. Thus any IP packets sent to the permanent home address of the MH will then routed to the HA instead.

The HA daemon sets up tunnels [11] for its MHs. The tunnel interface provided by the kernel automatically encapsulates received IP packets with a new IP address header. The encapsulated packets are then resent and routed to its new destination. For each registered MH, the HA daemon establishes a tunnel to redirects its IP packets to its multicast IP address.

3.3   FA/BA Daemons

The FA/BA daemons act as the agents of a MH in networks other than its home network. When a MH handoffs to an agent, the MH daemon sends a handoff request to the FA/BA daemon of the agent. If accepted, the agent becomes the MH's FA. On the behalf of the MH, a FA daemon invites FA/BA daemons of selected agents to be the BA daemons of the MH. Once a FA/BA daemon becomes a FA or BA daemon of a MH, the daemon gets the MH's multicast IP address from its MH daemon and adds the agent to the multicast group.

When a FA or BA receives multicast IP-in-IP data packets from the HA of one of its associated MH, its network layer strips off the multicast IP header to retrieve the original IP data packets. For FA daemons, the data packets are then forwarded to the corresponding MHs; for BA daemons, the most recent data packets are stored in local buffers for the MHs. For better performance, all data packets are buffered and forwarded in the OS kernel. Separate threads are used to control data forwarding and buffering for each associated MH.

Data packet forwarding to the MH is automatically done by the kernel. The FA/BA daemon enables (disables) the data forwarding by adding (removing) the corresponding route in the agent's routing table.

Because the Linux 2.0.33 kernel cannot handle multicast IP-in-IP data packets, we modified the kernel to allow selectively recovery of IP packets from multicast IP-in-IP packets. A list of multicast IP addresses of all active MHs is maintained in the kernel. If the multicast IP address of an incoming IP packet matches one on the list, the kernel checks if the packet is an IP-in-IP packet. If so, the kernel retrieves the original IP packet and returns it to the lower network layer for routing.

4 Experiments and Evaluation

Experiments were conducted to evaluate the mobile application support system, especially the effectiveness of the handoff decision and the benefits of additional buffering of data packets in BAs.

Table 1. Signal strength levels at 2 test locations.

	Access Point A	Access Point B
Station A	26 ~ 28	15 ~ 17
Station B	6 ~ 9	23 ~ 25

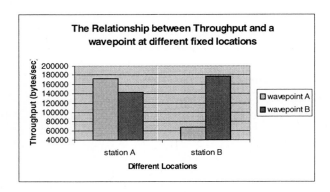

Fig. 3. Data throughputs at different locations.

Experiments were first performed to understand the relationship between wireless signal strength and data throughput. Two random locations at where the wireless signal strengths from the two wavepoints are significantly different were chosen. Table 1 shows the signal strengths measured at these two locations, Station A and Station B. The FTP program was used to transfer a large data file to the MH at one of these two locations via one of the wavepoints. The corresponding data throughputs were measured. Figure 3 shows the results. As expected, at both stations, the connection that has stronger signal strength gave higher data throughput. At Station A, if the MH is connected to Wavepoint A, the data throughput was 170KB/s, compared to 140KB/s if it is connected to Wavepoint B. At Station B, the difference is more significant. When the MH is connected to Wavepoint B, the data throughput was nearly 180KB/s, compared to only 65KB/s when connected to Wavepoint A. It should note that data throughput does not only depend on the signal strength of the corresponding

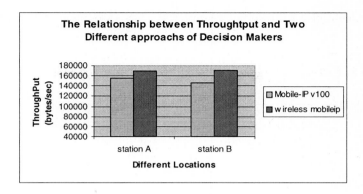

Fig. 4. Comparisons of two routing/handoff schemes.

connection, but is also affected by the presence of signals from other access point. The data throughput is not proportional to the signal strength level either.

Experiments were then performed to compare our handoff decision scheme with a Mobile-IP implementation, the Linux mobile IP v100 [5]. First the Linux mobile IP v100 was installed. The MH was moved to each of the above locations and the corresponding data throughput using FTP was measured. The experiment were repeated several times and at other locations. Then the entire experiment was repeated using our mobile application support system instead of running the Linux mobile IP v100. Figure 4 shows the results. Under our handoff decision scheme, the MH was able to consistently connect to the link with the strongest signal strength and delivered the best data throughput. The data throughputs at Station A and Station B were both 170KB/s which are closely to the best data throughputs achievable at these locations (170KB/s and 180KB/s respectively). In contrary, the data throughputs obtained using the Linux mobile IP v100 varied significantly depending on which access point the MH was connected during the moment of measurement. The average throughputs were low. The results show that our handoff decision scheme is effective and always maintains the best wireless connection.

The second set of experiments was conducted to evaluate the effectiveness of the additional data buffering in BAs.

The MH was placed at the location Station B and explicitly triggered to handoff from a weak signal connection (i.e. via access point A) to a strong signal connection (i.e. via access point B). Sequenced UDP data packets were continuously sent to a client on the MH over the network at the rate of one packet per every 20 ms. The client timestamped and recorded all UDP data packets received, including their sequence numbers. The FA/BA daemons were instrumented to send special system packets to the MH to mark the handoff period. Based on the client's record of UDP packet received, the total numbers of packets sent and the numbers of lost packets before handoff, during handoff and after handoff were counted respectively. The experiment was repeated 30 times.

Table 2. Packet loss probability before, during and after handoff at Station B

	average packet loss probability
Before handoff	0.017
During handoff	0.007
After handoff	0.006

Table 2 shows the average probabilities of packet losses before, during and after handoff respectively when the new FA did not buffer any data packets. From the table, one can observe that the packet loss probability dropped from 1.7% with the weak connection before handoff to 0.6% with the strong connection after handoff. The packet loss probability during handoff is lower than that before handoff but close to that after handoff. This shows that, even without additional buffering of packets in the new FA, there is no extra packet loss due to the handoff operation.

We can explain this almost lossless handoff by our system design. When a MH handoffs from one access point to another access point, it is in the overlapping region of the two cells. It is receiving packets from both access points. Because the new FA is already a designated BA before handoff, it has joined the multicast IP group of the MH. Our handoff procedure ensures that the new FA begins to forward data packets to MH before the old FA stops forwarding data packets. The chance of packet loss is very small.

We expected to see lower packet loss probability during handoff when duplicated packets were buffered at the new FA and resent to the MH. However, probably due to small sample in the experiments, no significant difference was observed when the new FA always buffered the most recent 2 packets.

5 Conclusions

We have implemented and set up a high-performance mobile application support system that provides both transparent mobility support over cellular wireless computer networks and mobile application programming interface (API) with which a mobile application can identify its current network location.

Compared to the IETF Mobile-IP standard, our system has incorporated a few major enhancements in its handoff and routing scheme. Each mobile host (MH) has assigned a permanent multicast IP address when it first registers with its home agent (HA). Subsequent communications between the home agent and its current foreign agent (FA) and buffering agents (BAs) use this multicast IP address. A new FA does not need to register with the HA. It only needs to join the multicast group. This simplifies the handoff procedure and reduces the handoff latency. Each MH runs a a MH daemon. Based on signal qualities monitored by the MH, the MH daemon intelligently chooses the best access point for connection, determines when to handoff and predicts which agents to be connected next. The MH daemon invites those potential new FA candidates to be buffering agents (BAs) of the MH. By joining the multicast IP group of the MH, the BAs receive data packets sent to the MH and always store the most recent data packets in their local buffers. When the MH later handoffs to a BA, the BA sends its buffered data packets to the MH to compensate any packet loss during the handoff.

Experiments were conducted to evaluate the mobile application support system. Our handoff scheme performs well and a MH is always able to connect to the best wireless link to provide the highest network throughput to its clients while moving between the wireless cells. While the prediction of potential FAs and the early multicast group membership of the BAs are found useful, early experience shows that buffering of recent data packets at the BAs is not effective in our system.

6   References

[1] H. Balakrishnan, R. H. Katz and S. Seshan, Handoffs in Cellular Wireless Networks: The Daedalus Implementation and Experience. Computer Science Division, UCB, U.S.A., Wireless Personal Communications 4: 141-162, 1997.

[2] C. E. Perkins and Sun Microsystems, Mobile IP, IEEE, 1997.

[3] A. V. Bakre and B. R. Badrinath, Implementation and Performance Evaluation of Indirect TCP, IEEE Transactions on Computer, vol. 46, No. 3, March 1997.

[4] H. Balakrishnan, R. H. Katz, S. Seshan and V. N. Padmanabhan, A Comparison of Mechanisms for Improving TCP Performance over Wireless Links, Computer Science Division, UCB, U.S.A., August 1996.

[5] A. Dixit and V. Gupta, Mobile-IP for Linux (ver. 1.00), Dept. of Computer Science, State University of New York, Binghamton. N.Y., May 23 1996.

[6] D. A. Maltz and D. B. Johnson, Protocols for Adaptive Wireless and Mobile Networking, Computer Science Department, Carnegie Mellon University, 5000 forbes Avenue, Pittsburgh, PA., Feb 1996.

[7] J. Stone, M. G. Baker, S. Cheshire and X. Zhao, Supporting Mobility in MosquitoNet, USENIX Technical Conference, San Diego, CA., January 1996.

[8] L. Tftode and R. Caceres, Improving the Performance of Reliable Transport Protocols in Mobile Computing Environments, IEEE Journal on selected areas in communications, vol. 13, No. 5, June 1995.

[9] D. Verworner, H. Bohme, M. Beck, M. Dziadzka, R Magnus and U. Kunitz, Linux Kernel Internals. Addison Wesley Longman, English, 1996.

[10] Wavelan documents, Lucent Technologies Corp. (http://www.wavelan.com)

[11] R. Woodburn and D. Mills, A Scheme for an Internet Encapsulation Protocol (RFC-1241) (ftp://ftp.ust.hk/pub/rfc/rfc1241.txt)

Proposition of an Identification Service on a Hybrid WLAN with Mobiles Stations

Christian SOUTOU, Thierry VAL, Fabrice PEYRARD, Jean-Jacques MERCIER

Université de Toulouse II,
IUT 'B', Groupe de recherche ICARE
1, Place Georges Brassens
31703 Blagnac
{soutou, val, peyrard, mercier}@iut-blagnac.fr

Abstract. This article describes the identification protocol on a hybrid Wireless Local Area Network (WLAN) with mobile and fixed stations. Our objective is to add decision elements to optimize the routing in such a system. Our protocol is based on the use of distributed reception tables in mobile stations. This protocol has been developed in Java.

1 Introduction

Day after day, the number of computers connected to a network is getting larger and larger. The current tendency to mobility is clearly identified with the portable phone success [7]. This infatuation is equally obvious in most computer equipments at LAN or WAN level. Mobile information systems require adequate protocols. In local networks, the mobility of computers entails the work out of architectures based on original topologies, the use of wireless medium (especially radio) and adequate protocol development. Databases (centralized or distributed) are well suited to offer services to lower-level protocols for wireless systems. The applications of these systems are various (notebooks, domotic, goods and person security systems, ...).

2 Network topology

The LAN topology we are developing is based on a two-level hybrid architecture (wire and wireless) [6]. Fixed stations (FS) consist of computer equipments which are connected to the LAN backbone and communicate only by wire link.

The computer equipments we call Radio Stations (RS) are either Mobile Stations (MS) which communicate only *via* radio, or Base Stations (BS), which are connected to the backbone LAN and which communicate via radio or wire links. The base stations make the link between the two kinds of medium. An example of possible topology of this hybrid-network architecture of a is illustrated in figure 1.

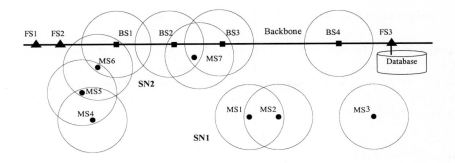

Fig. 1. Network topology

In order to allow communications between MS (Notebooks, Palmtops...), we have chosen a Spread Spectrum radio medium [1] with frequency hopping in the 2,4 GHz European band. This medium offers a baud rate up to 1 Mbps, in a 100-meter range. To obtain better baud rates between FS, larger ranges and to reduce costs, we also use an Ethernet wire backbone. This wire backbone permits the connection of fixed equipment (desktop computers, servers ...). The topology of such a network is dynamic. Indeed, according to the mobility and the position of MS, several kinds of communications are possible :

- pure wire communication via backbone LAN (between BS and FS, FS or BS between them);
- wireless communications (between BS and MS into range ; for example see figure 1 between BS1 and MS6, between MS into range, for example: between MS1 and MS2);
- hybrid communications in which some particular cases are studied, especially the relay (for example : MS4 can communicate with MS6 via MS5);
- several sub-networks can exist (for example : sub networks SN1 and SN2);
- a station can also exists by itself (for example MS3);
- several links can be concurrent to reach an equipment (for example : BS2 or BS3 to reach MS7).

In order to establish a communication without disconnection to MS, radio redundancy areas between BS cells are used in each necessary place. The range of radio transmitters is approximately 100 meters, but can hugely vary according to the obstacles to be crossed (wall, floor, ceiling, metallic cupboards...). To increase the range to several cells, we can offer a LLC 3 service [2] between two communicative entities, by a selective flooding technique and relay by wireless station (BS or MS) [5].

In order to respond to these specifications, our protocol includes a service of within-radio-range station identification.

3   Identification Protocol

Routing is well known in layer 3 of the OSI model, but for hybrid network, this architecture routing is outdated so it is interesting to propose additional concepts. Our protocol includes the identification of radio stations within range, so that resources are better exploited through location and allocation. As the wireless stations are aware of the stations within range, network flooding due to diffusion can be partly avoided.

3.1   Identification

So that radio station RS can permanently know their neighbors within range, each of them (MS or BS) emits an identification frame by radio diffusion (see Figure 2). This frame is received by every RS within range. This Identification message (ID) is emitted at regular time interval, but this interval can be different for each mobile station. This period is said to be selfadaptative and can vary according to the speed and the trajectory of mobile stations. The identification frame includes three fields :
- the address source. Each station is identified on the local system by a unique address;
- the frame type (here ID as IDentification);
- the period corresponds to the time interval between two ID frame emissions.

Our protocol allocates short identification periods to very mobile stations. On the other hand, long periods will be allocated to other mobile stations (less mobile than the previous ones). This principle allows the number of identification messages to be minimized.

@source station	Nature of Frame = ID	Period

Fig. 2. Identification frame structure

The principle of our identification protocol is quite similar to the beacons of the IP protocol [8] which fit to WAN. Nevertheless, periods of our ID messages is much lower than the mobile IP protocol due to the high baud rate offered by our radio interfaces (2,454 GHz-2,474 GHz). This is useful to provide a fine and fast localization in small cells. The BER of communications into our cells is better than the IP mobile one, particularly in domotic environments.

3.2   Reception tables

Each radio station includes a 3-field reception table (see Figure 3). Each row of this table concerns a station to reach.
- the first field contains the identifier of the station into range;
- the second field contains the station's last reception time;
- the third field contains the emission period of this station.

	1	2	3
	@station into range	last reception	period of the station into range
1			
2			
...			
j	SRj	Ti[2,j]	Ti[3,j]
...	...		

Fig. 3. Reception table of a radio station

3.3 Arrival of a mobile station

The arrival of a mobile station into a radio station reception coverage area entails :
- As soon as the ID message is emitted by the mobile station a new row is created in the wireless station table and in the other stations tables within range;
- As soon as the ID message is emitted by the wireless station, a new row is created in the table of the incoming mobile station and in the other wireless station tables.

The figure 4 describes an example of hybrid network which includes one base station SB1 and two mobile stations MS1 and MS2 at three moments t0, t1, t2 so that t1-t0=t2-t1 (these moments have been chosen to facilitate our running example).
- At t0 the MS1 station is out of the BS1 station reception area which already includes MS2.
- At t1, the MS1 station emits an ID message. We suppose that the emission periods are P for BS1, P1 for MS1 (P1=t1-t0), P2 for MS2 (P2=2P1). We have P < P1 < P2. At t0, the moment of the last ID message emitted by BS1 is t (t ≤t0).

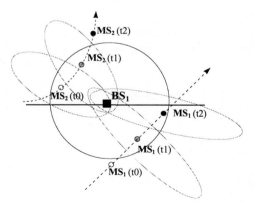

Fig. 4. Arrival of a mobile station

The arrival of the mobile station MS1 in the coverage area of a BS1 entails :
- As soon as the ID message from MS1 is emitted, a new row is created in the BS1 wireless station table and in the other station tables within range (here none);
- As soon as the ID message from the BS1 station is emitted, a new row is created in the table of the incoming mobile station (here the MS1 station table) and in the other wireless station tables within range (here the MS2 station table). The row includes the BS1 identifier, the reception time of the ID message and the period. In our example we have t+jP because we consider there will be j ID messages emitted by BS1 during P1 (P1>P).

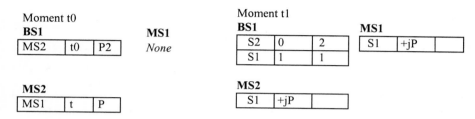

Fig. 5. Reception tables

3.4 Departure of a mobile station

The periodic emission of identification messages by radio stations entails the updating of second and third fields of the reception tables for each radio station receiving these messages. The departure of a mobile station from a reception area is detected by the radio station after examination of its reception table. If the identification message of the mobile station is not received by the radio station during the granted period (the MS one) then the communication between these two stations is lost and the row in the reception table of the wireless station is deleted. Row j (concerning a BSj mobile station) of the reception table T of a RSi radio station is deleted if : current time > T[1,j]+T[2,j]

Figure 6 illustrates the departure of the MS2 station from the cell of the BS1 station. The BS1 radio station emits j identification messages between [t0, t1], j other messages are emitted between [t1, t2]. Between moment t1 and t2, MS2 leaves the BS1's cell. Consequently, we can decompose the number j of identification messages emitted by BS1 between these two moments. We call j1 the number of identification messages until the departure of MS2 from the cell, and j2 the number of identification messages until t2, with j=j1+j2.

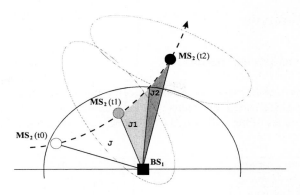

Fig. 6. Departure of a mobile station

In the time interval t2-t1, the reception table updating were :
- MS1 has emitted only one identification message received by BS1 at moment t2 (P1=t2-t1). So the second field of the row concerning MS1 in the reception table of BS1 is updated (see the asterisk in Figure 7);
- MS1 has received j identification messages emitted by BS1. The last updating of BS1 reception table is triggered by the identification message received (at moment t+2j because P < P1 and t1-t0=t2-t1 see the double asterisk in Figure 7);

The rows deleted in reception tables are (Fig. 7) :
- after t2 the condition current time > t0 +P2 is checked therefore the row concerning MS2 is deleted in the BS1 table.
- at time t2 the condition t2 > t1 + j1 * P + P is checked because t2 = t1 + (j1+j2)*P therefore the row concerning BS1 is deleted in the MS2 table.

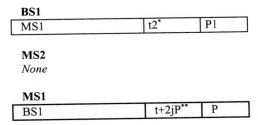

Fig. 7. Reception tables after moment t2

4. Prototype

4.1 Description of hardware

Our experimental model is composed of portable and fixed PC equipped with a radio interface (ISA card and antenna). The wire interface is a traditional Ethernet. The characteristics of the radio cards (ISA or PC-card) are summed up Figure 8.

Frequency bandes	2,452 GHz – 2,474 GHz
Radio techhnology	Spread Spectrum
Spread Spectrum method	Frequency Hopping
Emission power	100 mW
Range	200 m (free space)
Data rate	1,6 Mbits/s
Number of channels	15
Certifications	ETSI ETS 300.328 in USA, CE EMC-EEC in Europe

Fig. 8. Characteristics of radio cards

4.2 Choice of a communication protocol

Our network radio cards are delivered by the manufacturer with drivers for NetBEUI, IP and IPX protocols. In order to evaluate the behavior of this hardware, we developed a LLC protocol by using the low level primitives of these radio cards. The temporary unavailability of these primitives provided by the manufacturer, led us to choose the IP protocol to carry out our tests. The (UDP) datagram mode of IP was choosen because :

- it offers communications without connection (in our network, the path of frames can be variable according to the station mobility);
- it offers communications without acknowledgement (in our network, the protocol can manage acknowledgements from end to end).

For these reasons the UDP mode is very useful for communications between the mobiles.

4.3 Implantation of the protocol

The protocol was implemented in Java to allow the portability of the code between the various operating systems (Windows 95, Windows NT, Solaris). We have defined two Java classes related to this protocol. The " Frame " class (see Fig. 9) contains :the definition of the frame structure used; and the construction and extraction primitives of the frame fields; emission and reception primitives of a frame. The " Table " class (see Fig. 11) contains the definition of the reception table structure used; the management primitives of the tables (create, update, delete rows of reception tables).

```
public class Frame
{
        private                              Private variable
              String chframe = "", chn = "", cht = "";
              int tframe;
        public
              String src = "", des = "", type = "", period = 0;
              long n = 0;
              int t = 0, lframe;                    Public variables
              byte frame[];

        public Frame (int lg)
        {
              . . .
        }
        public void DoFrame ()
        {
              . . .
        }                                        Public methodes
        public void UndoFrame ()
        {
              . . .
        }
        public void SendFrame (DatagramPacket pk, DatagramSocket sc)
        {
              . . .
        }
        public DatagramPacket ReceiveFrame (DatagramSocket sc)
        {
              . . .
        }
}
```

Fig. 9. Frame class

An example of the use of frame emission using UDP sockets is described as follows.

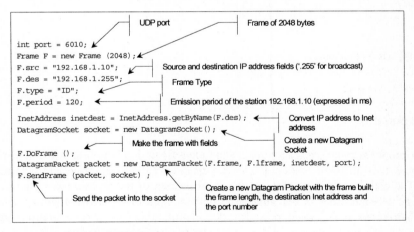

Fig. 10. Example of UDP frame emission

```
public class Table
{
        public Table ()                          Constructor
        {
            String srinrange = "" ;
            Int lastemission =0 ;
            Int srperiod = 0;
        }
        public void Arrival (String src, Int srperiod)
        {                                 Insert a row in the reception table with current time
            ...
        }
        public void Departure (String src)
        {                                 Delete a row in the reception table
            ...
        }
        public void Updating (String src, Int srperiod)
        {                                 Update a row in the reception table
            ...                           (current time and last period)
        }
}
```

Fig. 11. Table class

Figure 12 describes the line of the program code corresponding to the arrival of the mobile station (in our example 192.168.1.10). The method "ReceiveFrame" contains a call for the "Arrival" procedure. The method "ReceiveFrame" is executed for each station receiving a frame.The two methods "Departure" and "Updating" are called at each station level and are independent from frame reception.

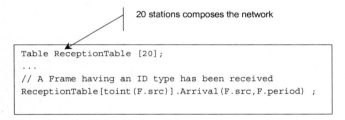

```
                                  20 stations composes the network

Table ReceptionTable [20];
...
// A Frame having an ID type has been received
ReceptionTable[toint(F.src)].Arrival(F.src,F.period) ;
```

Fig. 12. Using a reception table

5.   Conclusion

This paper proposes a service for mobile station identification in a hybrid WLAN. This network uses two different mediums : a wire medium called backbone and a radio medium. The cellular topology requires the identification of the mobile radio stations within range of each other in real time. The development of a particular protocol to manage distributed data tables provides the identification of mobile stations in reception cells. We have implemented our protocol of identification in Java.

On the basis of this work we will use identification tables to manage mobile station affectation to radio stations in order to have a better communication control. We are thinking of using affiliation tables distributed in radio stations (base stations or mobile stations). We plan to create a centralized or distributed database in fixed stations. This database will allow :

- to represent the global and dynamic topology of the network (position and number of stations,. evolution of the identification period, ...) ;
- to store an historic of particular events (communication loss, roundup of under-networks, breakdowns, ...) ;
- to manage identification problems according to the mobile and the cell in which it can be found at a given time (goods and person security applications)

At the same time, performance tests (by OPNET [3] simulation or on a real site [4]) will be undertaken on our experimental network to analyze the impact of the use of data contained in the database. Thereafter the database processes will be really implanted only in case of better performances (optimization of transit times, bandwidth, routing).

References

[1]   IEEE Standard Wireless LAN (P802.11-96/49A-49E), 1996.

[2]   VAL T., MISSON M., FREITAS A., " Using LLC type 1 and LLC type 3 services to communicate through a hybrid network with mobile devices ", Proceedings of the IEEE GLOBECOM'92, Orlando, Florida, Dec. 1992.

[3]   MIL 3, Inc., Opnet Modeler Version 3.5, vol. 1..12, Washington, Usa, 1997.

[4]   PEYRARD F., VAL T., MERCIER J.J., "A software platform of protocol specification, validation and simulation based on Estelle/Opnet co-operation", Proceedings of CFIP'97, Liège, Belgium, 1997.

[5]   PEYRARD F., VAL T., MERCIER J-J., " Simulation of ad-hoc WLAN with or without relay", accepted to IEEE ICUPC'98, Florence, Italy, 1998.

[6]   VAL T., MISSON M., " CASSIOPEE : a hybrid wireless LAN consisting of an infrared cellular network and a token backbone LAN ",Proceedings of the IEEE ICUPC'93, Ottawa, Canada, 1993.

[7]   KHAN F., ZEGHLACHE D., "Voice Clipping and Data Delay Analysis of Multiple Access for Wireless PCN", Proceedings of the IEEE GLOBECOM'96, London, England, 1996.

[8]   SENEVIRATNE A., "Convergence of Internet and Cellular Technologies : Threats and Challenges", Seminar LAAS laboratory, Toulouse, France, October 1998.

A Dynamic Navigation System Based on User's Geographical Situation

Toshihiko Hamano[1], Hiroki Takakura[2] and Yahiko Kambayashi[1]

[1] Department of Social Informatics, Kyoto University
[2] Department of Electrical Engineering, Kyoto University
Yoshida-Honmachi Sakyo Kyoto, 606-8501, Japan
{thamano, takakura, yahiko}@kuis.kyoto-u.ac.jp

Abstract. With remarkable advances of portable computers, users can move around various places with computers in order to achieve their objectives. This paper discusses a dynamic route navigation system which can cope with various kinds of users' situations, e.g., objectives, profiles, current locations, histories of activities and surrounding status of users. Based on these situations, the system continuously generates users' action plans in order to navigate to places where the users should visit. In order to obtain the situations effectively, a hierarchical wireless network model is proposed. By utilizing the mobile network, users can acquire information around them and interact with their surroundings. Functions of geographic database systems are employed to visualize the action plans effectively on the small sized display of portable computers. As an example of proposed system, this paper shows navigation system for shopping district where various kinds of shops and many people exist. How to cope with dynamic change of user's situations in shown for this particular example.

1 Introduction

With recent technological advances on computer systems, wireless networks and global positioning systems, many route navigation systems are developed. Car navigation systems and hand-held navigation systems are their typical examples. Conventional route navigation systems, however, lack ability to cope with dynamic change of users' situations. Therefore they cannot change navigation dynamically, and also cannot provide users optimal action plans and routes. Users are required to reenter their situations by hand when unexpected incidents occur. The navigation cannot be performed in realtime. This paper discusses a method to perform realtime route navigation for dynamic situation change. The system is named as NaviArea. In order to perform dynamic route navigation for situation change at every moment, it is required to continuously acquire users' situation, e.g., objectives, profiles, current positions and histories of user activity.

Existing route navigation systems[1, 2] use Global Positioning Systems (GPS) or infrared beacon systems in order to obtain users' locations. Although they can obtain users' current position, velocity and direction of movement, there is no ability to communicate each other and other information on users' situations is not obtained. In order to acquire information which a mobile computer does not have, the computer is usually connected to Internet (WWW[6]) by cellular phone. Internet has already become essential facility for computer society, so it is natural for mobile environment to utilize Internet. Considering speed of network, cost for communication and security issues, however, mobile users cannot use Internet for all possible purposes. Even if ultra-speed networks, e.g., giga bits backbones are utilized, the networks cannot have enough bandwidth to support all user's communications. Most part of the communications include user-specific information such as user's current position, payment for something. Such information should not be transfered on Internet in order to keep privacy.

This paper proposes a hierarchical wireless network model to acquire users' situations in realtime. By introducing the model to NaviArea, navigation service can be provided in the area covered by its networks. The area supported by NaviArea is referred as NaviArea Space. Users move around NaviArea Space, while they acquire various kinds of information and interact with their surroundings in order to achieve their objectives. Different from many existing systems, NaviArea is designed to avoid utilization of Internet whenever possible. Most of communications are performed among users and surrounding hosts in order to generate dynamic navigation. Short range networks are utilized for local communications and communications which should attend to securities. By receiving broadcasts of middle range networks in order to acquire local information to which depends the area users belong, increase of network traffic can be restrained. Only in the case that required information cannot be available, the system connects to Internet by cellular phone.

In NaviArea, there are many hosts which broadcast information and support peer-to-peer communication between a user and a host. Compared with ubiquitous computing[3, 4, 5] where many computers are distributed over many locations in the real world, our system distributes host computers within the range of wireless network and does not integrate all kinds of human activity information related to privacy. Each host supports users' activities in its covered area and provides information which relates to the area. If users want to access other kinds of information in NaviArea Space, they utilize global network, i.e., Internet. With growth of computing society, it is, however, considered that the difference between mobile computing and ubiquitous computing will vanish. By increasing the number of computers in the society and diversifying roles played by the computers, mobile computing and ubiquitous computing will be unified in the future.

After an action plan is determined, the result is represented as a map. Many route navigation systems widely utilize maps to explain routes effectively, since maps can be considered a good interface between users and systems. Because of the limited size of portable computers, understandable maps should be generated. Depend on the users' situation, scales of map, items which should be displayed and many other factors are changed. In order to generate arbitrary maps dynamically, our system employs the functions of geographic database systems[7, 8, 9, 10].

Rest of the paper is organized as follows. Section 2 discusses basic technologies utilized by NaviArea. Section 3 shows an example of NaviArea. In Section 4, outline of geographic database is explained. Functions of NaviArea are discussed in Section 5.

2 Basic Technologies of NaviArea

Users move around a certain limited area with some objectives. The users are equipped with portable computers in order to access to network services provided by NaviArea. In order to cope with the following problems discussed in the introduction, NaviArea utilizes three kinds of networks.

1) Speed of networks
   For some specific information, communication speed of global networks is not enough.
2) Interactivity through networks
   Interaction between users and systems require high-speed bilateral communication.
3) Privacy issues
   Data related to users' privacy cannot be broadcasted through global networks.

Network of NaviArea consists of the following hierarchy(Figure 1).

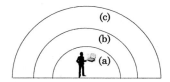

Fig. 1. Hierarchical Network Environment

(a) Short range network
    By this network, a user can acquire precise information on the status around him. This network is mainly utilized for peer-to-peer communication between two computers, e.g., a customer and a shop. Due to the peer-to-peer communication, this network is superior in security.
(b) Middle range network
    By broadcasting various kinds of information on the network, many users can receive them, e.g., advertisement of shops, traffic report, at the same time. Because this network cannot receive user's requirements, the user has to access to the short range network in order to get required information.
(c) Global range network (Internet)
    If a user cannot find out some necessary information, the user access to this network.

These three networks have different characteristics and can be accessed simultaneously.

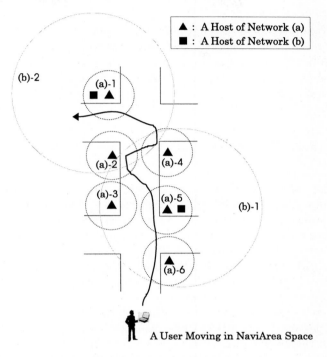

Fig. 2. A user moving in NaviArea Space

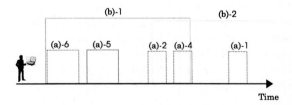

Fig. 3. Change of network to which a user belongs according to the user's movement

In short or middle range networks, there is only one host that provides location-specific information. In order to retrieve information to which current user's position does not relate, the user needs to access to the global network.

By assigning different bands of frequencies to these three networks, a user can simultaneously send and receive all information covered by the networks.

For each kind of networks, however, it is difficult to make strict distinction among cells. In order to avoid interference among cells, several frequencies are assigned to each network.

In case of short and middle range networks, a user needs not utilize telephone line. Therefore the user is charged when he access to the global range network.

As shown in Figure 2, a user moves around the area and repeats connection to and disconnection from networks. By referring various kinds of information, the user achieves his objectives.

3   Outline of NaviArea

As an example of our route navigation system, this paper supposes the case that many users move around area where various kinds of shops exist, e.g., shopping district. Usually users feel difficulty to find out a shop which sells their desired goods. If many shops offer the same goods, users may want to choose a shop based on a certain condition, e.g., the lowest price. If users do not have enough time to look for the goods, they want to know the nearest shop from their current position. In order to support such users' activities, this paper proposes a route navigation system which treats user's profile, geographic conditions, etc. Figure 4 shows the outline of NaviArea. A user carries with a portable computer, e.g., PDA, which manages user's profile and geographic databases. In the profile, objectives of user's activity such as goods to buy and things to look for are described. Time restriction and financial condition are also described in the profile. The portable computer keeps user's current position by using positioning systems, e.g, GPS. The computer stores user's activity, such as purchasing goods, into action history.

NaviArea utilizes hierarchical wireless network. Hosts are located in each shop. The middle range network provides various kinds of information. For example, shop A sells a commodity for 150 dollars. Store B opens from 10 a.m. to 5 p.m. Users usually acquire shops' information, such as commodities, stocks, prices and sales, from this middle range network. The short range network is used direct communication between a user and a shop, e.g., payment by electronic money. This network is superior to keep privacy due to the peer-to-peer communication. Since broadcast is performed on the middle range network, broadcast cannot contain realtime information. Users utilize the short range network in order to get fresh information of a shop. The global range network is utilized for acquiring information outside of NaviArea Space.

By utilizing all those information above, NaviArea generates optimal shopping plan and creates routing map on the portable computer. According to the action history and change of other information, shopping plan is dynamically changed.

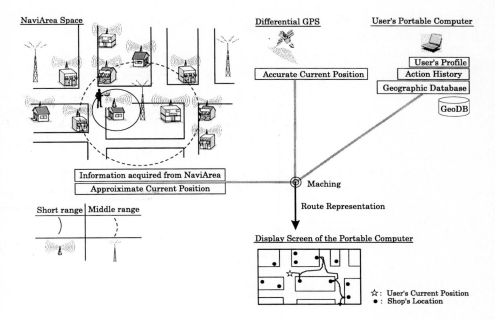

Fig. 4. The entire image of the system

4   Geographic Database

NaviArea utilizes maps dynamically generated by applying the theory of geographic database systems[7, 8, 9, 10]. Geographic data supported by NaviArea are previously stored in geographic database explained below.

4.1   Dynamic Map Synthesis

Although paper maps which are designed for a specific purpose can be considered to visualize required information effectively, many of them are designed for general purposes. They cannot have enough ability to be utilized by NaviArea.

On the contrary, computers can generate more suitable maps dynamically by combining information for more specific purposes. This is called dynamic map synthesis, which is one of the most important concepts on geographic databases. The dynamic map synthesis is executed in two steps. In the first step, a system submits queries to database. In the second step, a system calculates balances of answers from database and displays selected geographic objects on a map. After that users acquire visualized results as maps with keeping legibility.

In traditional geographic information systems, the systems conventionally have image pictures as map data. Maps are presented as superposition and joining of the images as shown in Figure 5. Because maps are prepared to support various kinds of utilization in advance, users may feel difficulty to find out geographic entities which they really need.

Geographic database systems, however, do not store maps but generate maps suitable for given possible queries instead.

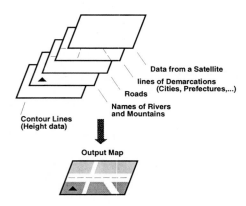

Fig. 5. Traditional geographic information systems

4.2 Geographic Database Systems

In geographic databases, each geographic entity such as roads, buildings, bridges, boundaries of cities and so on is stored as a geographic object. Each geographic object has geometric data such as points, lines and areas in form of an ordered set of coordination values. Maps are dynamically generated by combination of geographic objects in the following way. First, only required geographic objects are extracted from geographic database according to some conditions such as users' situation. Next, a form to present them on maps are determined. An overview of geographic database systems is shown in Figure 6. In this way, geographic database systems can generate maps which are understandable for users.

The features of geographic database systems are as follows.

- The representations of maps provided by the systems can be changed dynamically according to users' requirements: required objects can be displayed at the arbitrary scale and the arbitrary area in the required displaying form.
- By changing parameters of currently displayed maps, users can control displaying style of maps easily and freely.
- The geographic objects to be displayed as components of maps are dynamically changed according to users' requirements. Therefore the systems must adjust the amount of displayed objects considering with limitations of a display device.

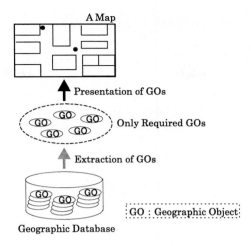

Fig. 6. An overview of geographic database systems

These features above are effective for portable computers which have displays of limited size. Compared with conventional geographic information systems, geographic database needs to store only primitive data in advance. Because the amount of data is small, this method is good for portable computers which storage capacity is small.

As discussed above, the geographic database can generate any scale of maps on which only required geographic objects are presented. NaviArea also takes this advantage of the geographic database. Combined the database with decision factors discussed in the next section, NaviArea dynamically generates optimal action plan in order to achieve users' objectives. The plan is visualized as maps in which route to places where users should visit.

More detailed discussion on geographic database systems are discussed in [7, 8, 9, 10].

5   Realtime Route Navigation

5.1   Decision Factors for Action Plan

As shown in Figure 7, first step to generate route navigation is collecting conditions for selecting a route. In this section, decision factors which affect to decide action plans are explained. By matching these decision factors with geographic information, the system generates optimal action plans for achieving user's objectives in realtime.

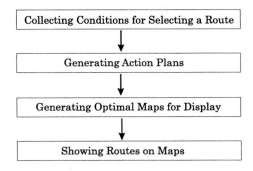

Fig. 7. Basic Flow for Route Navigation

[User's Profile]

User's profile describes user's personal information, user-dependent conditions as follows,

- Time restriction
- Financial restriction
- Objectives with targets
    - priority of targets
    - alternatives to targets
    - dependency among targets

According to user's activities, user's profile iwill be updated.
Table 1 shows one example of user's profile related to objectives.

Table 1. An example of user's profile

Objectives	Target	Priority	Alternatives	Dependency
shopping	VCR recorder	1	-	3
shopping	Watch	2	-	-
shopping	VCR tape	3	-	1
lunch	Italian	4	5	-
lunch	Fast Food	5	4	-

If a user purchases a certain commodity, the user's profile is changed. For example, if the user buys VCR recorder, his budget is decreased and priorities of targets are changed, i.e., a target (VCR recorder) is removed from the table and priority of VCR tape becomes 1st. According to the change of user's profile, action plan is dynamically changed.

[Information Acquired from Networks]

As discussed in Sections 2 and 3, from networks of NaviArea, a user acquires information which relates current position of the user. Short and middle range networks can send realtime information, e.g., shop A offers special sale from 3 p.m.

[Current Position of Users]

By identifying network to which a user belongs, approximate user's current position and direction of his movement can be acquired. In case that differential GPS is utilized, accurate information can be retrieved. These data are utilized to generate routing maps and to decide action plan.

[Histories of User's Activities]

User's activities such as visited shop, purchased goods are stored in history. This history is also utilized to decide action plan. For example, a store which has been visited is removed from the routing map.

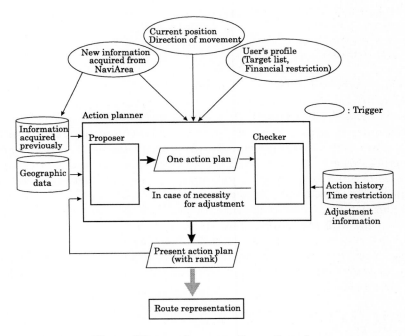

Fig. 8. Diagram for generating action plan

5.2 Generation of Action Plan

Utilizing decision factors, action plan is dynamically generated and updated. Figure 8 shows mechanism for generating action plans. When decision factors are changed, such as acquirement of new information from NaviArea, the change of user's current location or the modification of user's profiles, action planner receives the change as a trigger and generates new action plans. Output action plans are send to the route representation module and also are feedbacked as conditions for next plan generation.

It is possible that action planner generates several candidates for action plans. In this case, each plan is assigned rank and the highest plan is displayed on the portable computer.

5.3 Route Representation

Based on generated action plans, resulting routes are displayed on maps. The maps are generated and displayed dynamically by utilizing geographic database systems. Routes are represented in two kinds of forms as follows.

- Detailed route from user's current position to next place where the user should visit.
- Outline route which links all places based on current action plan.

6 Conclusion

This paper discussed a method that can generate realtime route navigation, NaviArea. By taking account of user's and his surrounding situation, the navigation is dynamically changed. Hierarchical wireless network model was proposed in order to acquire user's situation to support user's interaction with his surroundings and to keep privacy. NaviArea generates user's action plans by considering various conditions, e.g., user's current position, user's profile, user's action history and geographic information. In order to visualize generated action plans, NaviArea employs the concept of geographic database systems. The geographic database systems can generate any map appropriately and have flexibility to cope with the change of situation.

This paper assumed route navigation for shopping as an example of NaviArea. Because NaviArea will be practically utilized in combination with electronic money. In order to realize hierarchical wireless network, utilization of the following devices is planned.

- Short range network : wireless LAN or infrared LAN which consumes less electric power.
- Middle range network : wireless LAN which can cover wider area than above.
- Global range network : Point-to-Point Protocol utilizing portable communication equipment, e.g., cellular phone and personal handy-phone systems.

Currently, the utilization of these devices restricts the performance of NaviArea. It is, however, supposed that the devices can support much wider area and faster network speed in the near future, and that NaviArea can be effectively utilized in various applications.

Acknowledgment

This work is supported by the Grant-in-Aid for Scientific Research on Priority Areas (A), Advanced Database Systems for Integration of Media and User Environments, of the Ministry of Education, Science, Sports and Culture of Japan.

References

1. Sue Long, Dietmar Aust, Gregory D. Abowd and Kris Atkeson, "Cyberguide: Prototyping contextaware mobile applications", *Proceedings of ACM CHI'96 Project Note*, 1996.
2. Katashi Nagao, "Agent Augmented Reality: Integration of the Real World and Information Worlds via Software Agents", *Journal of Information Processing Society of Japan*, Vol.38, No.4, pp.257-266, 1997.
3. Mark Weiser, "Some computer Science issues in ubiquitous computing", *Communications of the ACM*, Vol.36, No.7, pp.86-96, 1993.
4. Roy Want, Andy Hopper, Veronica Falcao and Jonathan Gibbons, "The active badge location system", *ACM Transactions on information Systems*, Vol.10, No.1, pp.91-102, 1992.
5. Mik Lamming and Mike Flynn, "Forget-me-not: intimate computing in support of human memory", *In Proceeding of the FRIEND21 International Symposium on Next Generation Human Interface*, 1993.
6. R. Fielding, J. Gettys, J. Mogul, H. Frystyk, T. Berners-Lee, R Cailliau, J. Groff and B. Pollermann, "World-Wide Web: the information universe", *electronic networking: research, applications and policy 1 2*, pp.52-58, 1992.
7. M. Arikawa, H. Kawakita and Y. Kambayashi, "Dynamic Maps as Composite Views of Varied Geographic Database Servers", *Proc. of 1st Int'l Conf. on Applications of Databases (Witold Litwin, Tore Rische Eds.)*, Lecture Note in Computer Science 819, Springer-Verlag, pp.142-157, Jun. 1994.
8. M. Arikawa, H. Kawakita and Y. Kambayashi, "An Environment of Generating Interactive Maps with Compromises between User's Requirements and Limitations of Display Devices", *Journal of the Geographic Information Systems Association*, Vol.2, pp.21-32, Mar. 1994.
9. Takashi Kuroda, Hiroki Takakura, Masatoshi Arikawa and Yahiko Kambayashi, "Use of Object Co-Existence Relationships for Generation of Virtual Hypermedia Maps", *Proceedings of International Symposium on Digital Media Information Base*, Vol.2, pp.20-28, 1997.
10. Ken'ichi Horikawa, Masatoshi Arikawa, Hiroki Takakura and Yahiko Kambayashi, "Dynamic Map Synthesis Utilizing Extended Thesauruses and Reuse of Query Generation Process", *Proceeding of the 5th International Workshop on Advances in Geographic Information Systems (ACM-GIS'97)*, pp.9-14, 1997.

Summary of Panel Discussion: Future of Mobile Computing — Convergence of Research and Applications

Wang-Chien Lee

GTE Laboratories Incorporated, 40 Sylvan Road, Waltham, MA 02451, USA
wlee@gte.com

In the panel discussion session of International Workshop on Mobile Data Access, an enthusiastic audience was invited to join the panel of experts, Prof. Dik Lun Lee (Hong Kong University of Science and Technology, Hong Kong), Dr. Radhakrishna Pillai (Kent Ridge Digital Labs, Singapore), Dr. Hiroki Takakura (Kyoto University, Japan) and Mr. Stuart Jacobs (GTE Laboratories, USA) to explore several important issues relating to the data access aspect of mobile computing.

What are the existing and emerging applications?

The panel members believe that integrated voice and data communication for mobile users, mobile multimedia applications, high speed internet access, navigational and location dependent enquiry systems, navigation systems or guide systems for pedestrian, and systems and applications to support road warrior activities are important applications for mobile computing. Through discussions, systems embedded in automobiles are also identified as an important application for mobile computing.

What are the killer applications?

All existing network applications are moving to mobile applications. In addition, new applications that are specific to mobile environments like navigational applications will be deployed. All ubiquitous applications (i.e., applications that are able to access information at any time, in any form from anywhere) are going to be the killer applications. In addition, ubiquitous applications that can be used from simple, light-weight terminals will be more prominent among killer applications. Moreover, the web on the mobile network and seamless roaming are also identified as important killer applications.

What does the industry need from research?

Voice/handwriting recognition systems, adaptive user interface, and distributed system technologies need more research. Also, the industry needs Mobile IP that will scale to millions of mobile users, and robust mechanisms to protect the networks and assure consumers of authentication and privacy for their information. Moreover, there are several issues that need to be resolved in wireless networks: (1) the challenges in combining "mobility," "wireless" and "QoS guarantees," (2) mobility across heterogeneous wireless systems and the middleware needed to hide the differences among different underlying networks from the application, (3) mobile-aware applications and adaptation to different network conditions.

How do we map research onto the existing communication facility (e.g., Internet, GSM, wireless LAN, etc)?

When the heterogeneous nature of different networks is not considered, it is easy to map the research onto the existing communication facility. Very often, each one of these networks tries to solve the problems in mobile computing in a different way (e.g., internet access in GSM, multimedia over GSM, GPRS etc). The solution for one network may neither be applicable nor be efficient in another network. The panel members thought if we can make wireless networks and the Internet interoperable and protocols exist for negotiating the hardware constraints of the client, we can develop applications mostly independent of the underlying network.

What sorts of collaboration are needed?

Panel members thought that protocols and APIs should be standardized to make applications less dependent on the network. However, more collaborative effort is still required to develop both network infrastructure and applications. Industry should take the lead in providing the infrastructure. Research consortia need to be established with clearly defined goals.

What is the future?

The panel members believe that the future of mobile computing is toward a single transparent network with both wired and wireless segments where the mobile computing applications and networks will converge.

A Web Solution to Concurrency Awareness in Shared Data Spaces

Jens Thamm, Stephan Wilke, and Lutz Wegner

Universität Gh Kassel, FB Mathematik/Informatik, D-34109 Kassel, Germany
{injt, wilke, wegner}@db.informatik.uni-kassel.de

Abstract. Computer Supported Collaborative Work (CSCW) must present a shared workspace to co-operating users. This implies having a suitable engine at the client side which permits setting a focus on the shared data. Any concurrent activities of other users which happen to stretch into this viewport must also be made visible. Furthermore, the client must provide mechanisms for moving among the data (objects) and for making one's presence known. On the server side, a globally consistent state of the data must be maintained through an extended transaction concept. Here we present a description of a very compact, yet extensible solution to this task. It involves a standard Web browser with a small applet (less than 3 KB) as interface generator, and an object-relational database engine as server. The server uses a Tcl-based navigational language and drives the interfaces for the clients via stream socket connections.

1 Introduction

As we are moving towards a networked society, technologies for *Computer-Supported Cooperative Work* (CSCW) will be the greatest challenge for the information industry in the next decade. CSCW can be classified according to a time-space taxonomy [2, 3], as shown in Figure 1 below.

	place	
	same	different
time — same	learning theatre, control centre, ...	virtual meeting room, synchronous collaboration
time — different	computer lab, internet café, ...	anytime anyplace, asynchronous collaboration

Figure 1. CSCW modes

Here, we concentrate on support of synchronous collaboration, i.e. the same time/ different place mode which is generally considered the most promising, yet most difficult form of CSCW. It applies to many areas, like shared authoring, trading, scheduling, crisis management, and distance maintenance.

Synchronous CSCW, also called *synchronous groupware*, can again take on various forms. Baecker et al. [2] mention desktop conferencing systems for collaborative work across workstations, like e.g. in Xerox PARC's Colab project [13] or with shared screens, for which e.g. Rendezvous [11] is a toolkit. Other examples are electronic meeting and decision rooms, like e.g. GMD's DOLPHIN [9], or media spaces, like Ishii's TeamWorkStation [6].

Today's systems are usually a combination of these forms. All of them adhere to a relaxed WYSIWIS model (What You See is What I See) to establish a common ground for discourse. They differ in what can be shown, how communication between users occurs and how much each participant is aware of each others location, activities, focus of attention, etc.

Here we shall concentrate on describing our techniques of providing a database managed visualized shared object space. The approach makes use of the fact that many applications have users navigate within highly structured object spaces (documents, maps, floor plans, multimedia lectures, routing diagrams, scheduling tables). Views of this space (views in the database as well as in the interface sense) can be distributed synchronously, augmented by a suitable interaction paradigm. This paradigm, called *finger operations*, highlights objects of interest within the shared object space and permits manipulations of objects relative to these fingers which belong to participating (human) users or autonomous agents.

Locations of fingers, their movements, and changes inflicted on objects can be signaled by means of operation transmission to a central server which performs the transaction and broadcasts the visual operations needed for display update to all those collaborators who need to be aware of it.

This paper describes in detail the interplay between Web-based user interfaces and an object-relational server which supports concurrency awareness using the above mentioned finger paradigm. The solution draws heavily on Tcl-enabled browsers but other applet solutions, e.g. Java based, are equally feasible.

The remainder of this paper is organized as follows. We start with our definition of concurrency awareness and give an example in the next Section. Then we present the client-side solution in Section 3. This is continued for the server side in Section 4 which also gives a description of the navigational language and some code fragments. Section 5 reviews our solution and indicates where further research is needed. Users are also invited to connect to our server `http://www.db.informatik.uni-kassel.de/~escher/tcldb/escherClient.html` to get a feeling for the shared workspace even though some of the concurrency awareness features are not operational yet.

2 Structured Application Spaces and Concurrency Awareness

Collaboration scenarios which are mainly based on video conferencing and whiteboards, i.e. pure view sharing, have collaborators remain detached from the objects of discourse, their structure and fine-grain interrelation. As a supplement to these techniques, we suggest navigation amongst and manipulation of the objects which in most case will have a complex structures on their own. To remain independent of particular representations and to be applicable across a wide area of domains, we propose a general complex object data model as a suitable base for the collaboration network.

More precisely, the model is a graph where nodes represent objects and edges express whole-parts relations and links to shared subobjects. In many cases, collections of complex objects just form a tree. This is e.g. the case for the registration table (Figure 2 below), which permits students to register for courses of their choice.

In this example, the collection of complex objects forms a nested relational table

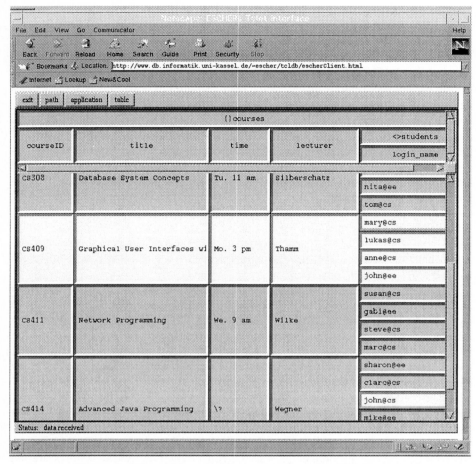

Figure 2. View of shared object space through a Web browser

which also has a very intuitive visualization.

Shaded (colored) areas within this visualization correspond to cursors which point to complex or atomic (elementary) objects. In case of this example, one cursor points to the course CS409, while another points to student John in CS 414.

Each cursor in the table has its counterpart in the schema above. In a collaborative environment, cursors reflect activities and bookmarks of other users, e.g. one person changing the lecturing time for a course, another person subscribing to a course. To avoid confusion with the more common use of the term cursor (screen cursor), we follow the practice of our database editor ESCHER [15, 17, 18, 19, 20] and call this pointer a *finger*[1].

By convention, each user may have several fingers placed over several tables, yet only one of them can be active at any time.

---

1. The terms cursor and pointer usually relate to widgets in windowing systems; in fact we will drag a mouse cursor to initiate movements of the finger.

Within a graph, a finger corresponds to a node in the graph. On the implementation level, a finger corresponds to the (invariant) address of the node, in OODB-speak to the object identifier (OID) of the object. In the strict hierarchical model, it can also be seen as the path from the root of the object tree to the sub-object to which a finger currently points. In Figure 3 we have depicted the path corresponding to the finger on the students list of course CS 409 with more solid lines for the nodes.

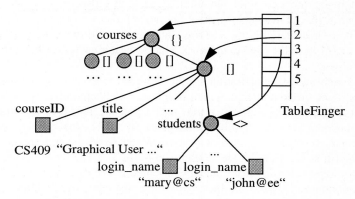

Figure 3. Object tree with stack for a table finger.

As we shall see in Section 4, going into a complex object, e.g. to the first registered student within a set of listed participants, corresponds to a push operation because it places the new address on the stack. Similarly, escaping from an atomic or complex object to the enclosing object is called a pop operation. Table 1 in Section 4 gives an overview of the more common finger operations.

The reason we advocate a strongly structured data space is that for visual browsing large distances can be traveled on the outer levels, yet at any time, details can be accessed by descending into lower nodes. Similarly, with zooming techniques a bird's view of the space is possible which blurs finer details like lower level entries or turns pictures into thumbnails.

Figure 2 shows slide bars at the side of the nested table. This implies that the object space is larger than what will fit onto a screen. This is a very common situation and has considerable performance consequences because large quantities of display data are transferred to the client and formed into a widget tree even though the viewport shows only a fraction thereof. Note also that placement of this viewport on the total data space is independent of where the user has placed a finger. It rather corresponds to a situation where someone has picked and reserved an item but is looking for another possibly better suited one.

Rodden [12] has investigated and extended this model of spatial awareness in more detail. His model includes people, information and other computer artifacts as objects, but does not consider nested objects. He lists the 16 possible modes of awareness including 6 overlaps based on the two subspaces of objects we mentioned above and for which he uses the terms *nimbus* and *focus* [12, p.88]

• The more an object is within your nimbus, the more aware it is of you.
• The more an object is within your focus, the more aware you are of it.

Technically speaking our finger technique then promotes sharing a nimbus. Equally important is sharing a focus (what we prefer to call a viewport because the term focus usually relates to that widget which receives the input), i.e. telling someone else to direct his view to the same things which are visible to oneself. The latter can be achieved through the former by first placing a finger into one's focus and then telling others to direct their focus to the newly installed nimbus.

Fortunately, the most common situation is that both subspaces coincide, i.e. a user has his window placed in such a way that his active finger — or a large part of what is visible of it — is centered in the window. Indeed, much of the display activity at the client side stems from the need to redraw a window as it must follow the movements of the active finger.

Finally, synchronous collaboration not only implies viewing data, but also manipulating them in an ordered fashion which is not very well supported by Web technologies. What is needed is an augmented transaction concept. This is in accordance with a long-standing demand which holds that the classical ACID-properties transactions are too limiting for complex applications, in particular in visual environments. In the words of Korth at the 1995 VLDB conference [7, p. 3]: „The recent evolution of the transaction model is a shift from machine-oriented concepts to human-oriented concepts." He continues [7, p.4]: „In this environment, the metric of TPS, transactions per second, is not the issue. Rather the quantity to be maximized is *human information transfers per second* (HITS)". In his views this might lead to an evolution of the ACID properties to something of the following:

- Atomic → structured, but flexible
- Consistent → mostly consistent, with exceptions clearly noted
- Isolated → cooperative, negotiated
- Durable → auditable trail of responsibility

In our opinion the main change is giving up isolation in favor of concurrency awareness. To achieve this awareness, ESCHER's finger paradigm appears as a good starting point.

In short, the extended transactional model also includes the usual reading and writing access modes with prevention of read/write and write/write conflicts. Access is provided when a finger can be placed onto the object. However, under certain circumstances it is feasible to read (look at) a larger object while at the same time subobjects are updated or deleted as long as the presence of the updater is known and made visible. Similarly, reading of uncommitted data is permissible as lang as the reader is made aware (and has acknowledged) that the contents of these fields may change. On the other hand, rollbacks in visual environments can be very distracting as state changes may occur which alter the display in an unpredictable way. Avoiding them all together, however, puts users at the mercy of others unless holding limits (3 minutes is a common time limit in airline reservation systems) are imposed and visualized. More details on the notion of negotiated transactions can be found in [18] but are omitted here.

3 Client-side Solution

Modern forms of CSCW activities will connect arbitrary users, agents and sites. Connections will be spontaneous and often short lived. Users and agents will migrate from site to site, e.g. for electronic shopping, negotiating with other users for sharing resources, chatting, etc. In these forms of interaction, it is very unlikely that users want to tie themselves to specific application software, order it, receive it over the net or on a CD, install it and run the application with large client-side application specific programs. This is even more true if the client is „thin", i.e. some form of network box.

Rather, users expect to join CSCW activities through their Web browsers. This does **not** imply that interaction is restricted to viewing pages which are either statically pre-generated or produced on-the-fly from a database at the server. Due to the enhancement of browsers, some of the activities can take place on the clients machine using what is commonly called an *applet*.

In essence, an applet is a script which is interpreted and executed by a virtual machine within the client's address space. Because they appear in the context of browsers and other interface related applications, they must have strong GUI generating features. Common scripting languages for this purpose are Java [1] and Tcl [5, 10] with their respective plug-ins for browsers like Netscape 4.0

Here, we demonstrate our solution based on Tcl/Tk, were applets are called Tclets[1], but other solutions based on commonly available plug-ins are equally possible. Regardless of the particular language, all solutions must be based on the concept of a safe interpreter or else the applet could run havoc and take over the client's machine. Rules for safe interpreters require e.g. that the applet may not

- access the file system (or only very restricted areas like /tmp),
- make use of libraries (`package require`)
- execute system commands via calls of exec
- grab and hold the focus
- connect via sockets to other servers except the one which shipped the original page.

As it turns out, these rules do not restrict our solution scheme but it should be stressed that, of course, no low-level database activities (e.g. client transaction logging) can happen on the client side. However, for our CSCW purposes this is not necessary and the solution we developed (see Figure 4 below) is surprisingly simple, although some of the details are tricky.

We start by providing a straight-forward HTML-page as an entry point for accessing the server which supports the desired CSCW activities. The page contains the usual greetings and a reference to the Tclets which for the example below reads like

```
<embed type="application/x-tcl"
 width=600 height=500
 src="escherClient">
```

This tells the browser, that a Tcl-script is to be loaded from the file `escherClient` on the Web-server's directory from which the Web-page came. It also provides an initial window size. Of course, provisions must be made for having the Tcl-plug-in (the Tcl execution engine) ready. If not, it can be downloaded from a Tcl server, such as `http://sunscript.sun.com/products/plugin.html`, in case the Web-browser sees a Tcl-reference for the first time.

This transfers a Tcl-file to the client. The file, less than 3 KB in total, performs essen-

---

1. pronounce „Ticklets".

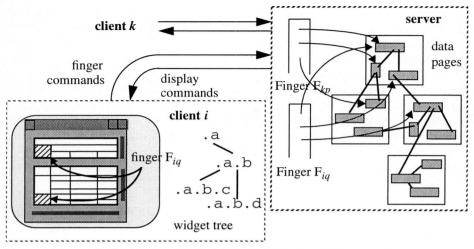

Figure 4. Distribution scheme and command passing

tially three tasks:
- it creates some elementary widgets (a few menus and a few buttons) for start-up selections
- it establishes a socket connection (by default: Internet domain stream sockets)
- it enters a "read command/eval command" loop.

With these three elements in place, the server can start to feed the client with application specific display code. In essence, these are plain Tcl/Tk commands for
- creating widgets (including label texts, border width, colors, fonts,...),
- defining their behavior (bindings),
- packing them, etc.

What is sent is exactly the same as a host would execute in generating a GUI interface on its own. Note that we are not sending the CSCW database data per se but rather display code with embedded data much in the same spirit as a PostScript printer receives printing code which ultimately displays the print image and thus the actual data.

Execution of this code creates a widget on the client machine with all the desirable features of a modern GUI: availability of all kinds of events, timed events for animation, multi-level bindings and tags for group behavior, entry widgets, scrolling, inclusion of pixel images, various geometry managers, etc.

User events are caught by the Tcl/Tk widget and the call-back routines tied to these widgets, say a label corresponding to an atomic field or a frame corresponding to a tuple or set of tuples, are invoked. The contents of these command scripts contain socket send commands which permit transmitting information about the event to the server. Note that the contents of these messages, augmented by actual parameters, have been determined by the server itself when it had sent the Tclet to the client.

In particular, the messages can contain data and commands in a language which the client does not understand or ask for privileges which the client cannot grant. The exact format is free and can be determined by the server. To avoid unnecessary parsing, it seems reasonable to use our existing database interface and implementation language, called TclDB [15], rather than defining a new interface protocol language. This language is an extension of Tcl geared towards navigational access to a nested object-relational database. A summary of this language is given below in Section 4.

As a different alternative one could consider sending the events to the server, i.e. mouse clicks with button id and coordinates. We investigated this alternative with the concept of a shadow display tree which would be a clone of the client side tree. However, this solution seemed overly complex because the interface events must eventually be translated into semantically meaningful actions within the object space, so it seems more natural to transmit these translation right away. Secondly, maintaining n display trees for n concurrent users requires quite large amounts of memory and absorbs a fair amount of computing power which would better be put into database operations. Thirdly, it is not trivial to maintain concurrent copies of widget trees for different types of base graphics systems.

4 Server-side Solution

The server consists of two fairly large units:
- a database engine
- a display and interaction server (mediator).

The database engine could be any object-relational DBMS. For the time being we use our own development, called ESCHER, which currently is a single-user database editor based on the nested relational data model [18]. Its lower three levels are Record Manager, Data Manager and Object Manager and are written in C. The first two handle typeless storage with a software based pointer swizzling concept. The third level knows DBMS types and provides a navigational interface to the data which operates with the fingers as described above and depicted in Figures 3 and 4.

In order to provide something like methods which can be attached to objects and attributes, we provided a wrapper around the Object Manager functions, written in an extension of Tcl, called TclDB. TclDB scripts can manage most of the ESCHER interaction, open tables and schemes, do the usual insert, delete, cut&paste and some limited forms of declarative queries using path expressions. With the full programming power of Tcl included, it is of course a full fledged programming language. Table 1 below gives a brief overview and should be self-explanatory.

In short, the server then has the following structure. It starts offering socket connections on a previously agreed port to any client willing to connect with it. In Tcl this is very easy:

```
socket -server server_accept $port_number
```

The command contains the name of the routine to call when the connection has been established, here `server_accept`. Its parameters are supplied automatically.

```
proc server_accept {cid addr port} {
    fileevent $cid readable "server_handle $cid"
    fconfigure $cid -buffering none
    ...
    client_start $cid
}
```

Table 1. Basic set of TclDB-commands

Command	Remark
escher	command having to do with the ESCHER database:
boot *path*	get database going, returns 0/1
shutdown	shut database down, returns 0/1
list applications	dbms is organized into applications, returns list of appl's
list schemes	~ list of schemes (table schemes) defined for an appl.
list tables	~ list of tables defined for an application
application	
select *name*	change to another application, returns application *name*
new *name*	creates a new application, returns *name* of new appl.
delete *name*	removes an application from database, returns *name*
table	command having to do with one or more tables:
open *name*	open a database table given by *name*, returns Tcl table
-id *tid*	id. *tid*, either system chosen or user defined with -id *tid*
list	return *name*1 *tid*1 *name*2 *tid*2 ...
-long	or same in longname version
close *tid*	close a table, returns *tid*
new *name scmname*	create new table with new *name* and existing *schema*
delete *name*	delete a table from an application, returns *name*
finger	command having to do with finger (cursor) generation
fork *fid*	create a new finger from existing finger *fid*, return either
-id *newfid*	system chosen *newfid* or user defined with option -id
free *fid*	release finger *fid*
list	list all existing fingers, returns *fid1 fid2* ...
-table *tid*	list fingers in a particular table *tid*, returns *fid1 fid2* ...
fid **push -first**	with an existing finger *fid* move on first (default)
-last	enclosed object, resp. move finger on last encl. object
-where *predicate*	move finger on object satisfying *predicate*, returns 0/1
path	move finger along path including attributes and indexes
fid **pop**	move finger *fid* to enclosing object
fid **go -first**	move finger from one object (tuple, attribute) to
-last	first (last) object within enclosing complex object
-back	to previous object (above, to left)
-next	to next object (below, to right)
-forcedup	to previous object (above) in an attribute regardless
-forceddown	of tuple boundaries, same to next object (below) in ...
-where *predicate*	first object which fulfills the *predicate*, returns 0/1
path	move finger along a *path* incl. attributes, indexes
fid **get** [*path*]	return value on which finger rests, optionally extended
	by path starting with finger position

Table 1. Basic set of TclDB-commands

Command	Remark
fid **type** [*path*] *fid* **attr** [*path*]	return type of object on which finger sits return attribute name of attribute on which finger sits

fid **set**
    value [*path*]
    -tonull [*path*]
    -toempty [*path*]
	
	set value for atomic object on which finger *fid* sits
	set complex object to database null
	turn a set-valued object into an empty set

fid **insert**
    -before [*path*]
    -after [*path*]
	inserts a null-object
	before finger *fid* and move *fid* onto element
	after finger *fid* and move *fid* onto element

fid **delete** [*path*]	delete object to which finger *fid* currently points and move *fid* to predecessor or to successor or, if neither exists, to enclosing object
fid **on -first** **-last**	return true iff finger *fid* on first element of collection return true iff finger *fid* on last element of collection
fid **isempty** [*path*] *fid* **isnull** [*path*] *fid* **isatomic** [*path*] *fid* **iscomplex** [*path*]	return true iff finger *fid* on an empty collection return true iff finger *fid* on a database null value return true iff finger *fid* on an atomic value return true iff finger *fid* is on a complex value

fid **istype -set** [*path*]
    -tuple [*path*]
    -list [*path*]
	return true iff finger *fid* on a set value
	... on a tuple value
	... on a list value

As can be seen, the server manages the reading end of the socket by file events calling a procedure `server_handle` which reads from the socket and interprets incoming requests. These requests contain some protocol specific commands for displaying tables and schemes and for other global tasks. The majority of the requests in the collaborative phase, however, will be TclDB commands supplemented with actual parameters as provided by the call-back routines attached to widgets and triggered by events relating to these widgets.

Next the server calls `client_start` and lets the user choose a specific collection of tables and schemes, which is called an **application** in ESCHER terms. Applications are stored as (meta-)tables within a special application, called **system**, much like a catalog in most DBMS. The procedure below shows nicely how TclDB opens these tables and their schemas and iterates over their contents turning the names into a list. Those commands shown in boldface are TclDB commands explained in Table 1 above.

Procedure `metaSelectFrame` (not shown here) turns the given list into a complete widget (a selection box) which is piped to the client who displays it with a generic routine `form_show` which is part of the initial Tclet.

```
proc client_selAppl {cid} {
  escher application select system
  set l {}
  set t [table open "APPLICATIONS.tbl"]
  set f [finger fork $t.root]
  iterate $f {lappend l [$f get]}
  table close $t
  set f [metaSelectFrame Application $l \
      "a list of tables to choose from" selappl]
  global out
  puts $cid "$out \n form_show $f"
}
```

Eventually the user has made her choice of table(s) and this choice is returned to the server via the server's reading end of the socket. It is parsed by `server_handle` and, based on the first argument, alternative `seltable` is chosen which starts display generation for the selected table.

```
proc server_handle {cid} {
  if {[gets $cid request] < 0} {
    close $cid
  } else {
    set args [lrange $request 1 end]
    switch [lindex $request 0] {
      start {
        set path [lindex $args 0]
        if [catch {escher boot $path} res] {
          client_error $cid „couldn't boot '$path'\n$res"
          return
        }
        client_selAppl $cid
      }
      ...
      seltable {
        set appl [lindex $args 1]
        client_showTable $cid [lindex $args 0] $appl
      }
    }
  }
}
```

This production of the table display is broken up into several routines. On the outermost level, `client_showTable` makes sure the application is set and calls `packTable` which in turn calls other procedures to generate frames and labels for sets (nested tables), tuples and atomic fields.

```
proc client_showTable {cid table appl}{
  escher application select $appl
```

```
set f [packTable $table]
global out
puts $cid $out \n form_show $f"
}
```

The actual building routine is complicated due to the variable size constraints for nested tables. It produces only one of several possible display styles. Below we show the part which produces an atomic field. Note that the display is generated by finger operations, thus [$f get] returns the value which the finger (variable) f points to at the moment.

```
if [$f isatomic] {
  puteval "label $id -text {[$f get]}\
    -width \$attWidth($path)\
    -anchor w\
    -font \$font(data) -bg \$bg\
    -bd 5 -padx 5 -pady 5"
  puteval "bindtags $id {$id Data Label . all}"
  return $id
}
if [$f istype -tuple] {
  puteval "frame $id -bd 0 -bg \$bg"
  ...
```

Finally, puteval is responsible for appending the produced commands to out which is either sent to a client and evaluated there or evaluated locally, e.g. for debugging purposes.

```
proc puteval {cmd} {
  global out
  append out „$cmd\n"
}
```

Other interesting points, in particular bindings enabling and disabling, are omitted here. As we progress in our implementation, readers will be able to inspect this code at the given URL.

5 Discussion

For CSCW activities over shared data spaces, three approaches seem feasible.
- a replicated, distributed database with added concurrency awareness
- a centralized database with display sharing
- a centralized database with operation passing

If the application is installed in the traditional way and if the client has proper file access, the first approach is a suitable solution. In particular, if data are fairly static and are pre-distributed, e.g. a shopping catalog or a multi-media lecture on a CD-ROM, bandwidth can be saved. For the sporadic collaboration over the Web which we envision, this is too static.

The second approach is like a X-Windows solution scaled up to work for the Web.

This also implies immediately its weakness: too high bandwidth and too much computing power requirements to work for more than a dozen displays.

The third approach describes what we have devised. Operation passing can again be subdivided into database operation passing versus display command passing. We advocate display command passing for the server-to-client communication, but database command passing based on our finger paradigm rather than pure event passing for the client-to-server direction. This solution requires a smaller client with less privileges which is better suited to a Web environment. To stress the point we like to emphasize that our solution doesn't need a special execution engine but runs nicely on the standard Tcl plug-in.

However, to run successfully, a number of technical problems must be solved. They concern

- smart display clipping to avoid transfers of large widget sets
- object identifier to widget identifier translations to bridge the name spaces
- multi-threaded management of multiple fingers to signal concurrency awareness
- safety aspects to avoid malignant command substitutions.

A more general issue is whether TclDB as a proprietary navigational interface to an object-relational DBMS editor is a good choice for client-server communication. Alternatives would be e.g. dialects of SQL or object-oriented query languages, in particular Java extensions like JDBC and SQLJ [8]. Also, if access and collaboration are based on Web browsers, it would be nice to include Web-based (unstructured) information sources. Both issues are of a fundamental nature and there is an on-going struggle for Web-DBMS connectivity standards [8] which we cannot settle here.

For the subdomain of Web-based CSCW, we still like to argue in favor of using Tcl. Firstly, Tcl's typeless nature, which only knows strings as data elements, is an ideal base for distributed applications where pointer values are meaningless. Secondly, Tcl's socket command is a marvel of simplicity as compared to the raw UNIX system programming interface. Thirdly, Tcl/Tk's asynchronous nature with file events governing the arrival of data blends much better into the communication concept as developments in C or C++.

Open research issues in our proposal are performance aspects, in particular during the initial widget tree building phase. Also, extending the transaction concept for CSCW activities not only gives up isolation in favor of concurrency awareness, as shown in this paper, but also involves even more subtle extensions, like negotiations [18], incomplete but not aborted operations, signalling of pending or hung actions, etc. For these CSCW modes, intuitive and appealing visualizations must be developed.

References

1. K. Arnold and J. Gosling. The Java Programming Language, Addison-Wesley, 1996
2. Ronald M. Baecker, Jonathan Grudin, William A.S. Buxton, and Saul Greenberg: Groupware and Computer-Supported Cooperative Work, Introduction to Chapter 11 of „Readings in Human-Computer Interaction: Toward the Year 2000", 2nd ed., Morgan Kaufmann, San Francisco, CA, pp. 741-753
3. C.A. Ellis, S.J. Gibbs, and G.L. Rein: Groupware - Some Issues and Experiences, CACM 34:1 (Jan. 1991) 38-58

4. Nita Goyal, Charles Hoch, Ravi Krishnamurthy, Brian Meckler, and Michael Stone. Is GUI Programming a Database Research Problem?, Proc. 1996 ACM Int. Conf. on Management of Data, Montreal, Canada, June 4-6, 1996, SIGMOD Record 25:2 (June 1996) 517-528

5. Mark Harrison and Michael McLennan: Effective Tcl/Tk Programming, Addison-Wesley, Reading, Mass., 1998

6. H. Ishii, M. Kobayashi, and K. Arita: Iterative Design of Seamless Collaboration Media: From TeamWorkStation to ClearBoard, Comm. ACM 37:8 (August 1994) 83-97

7. Henry F. Korth: The Double Life of the Transaction Abstraction: Fundamental Principle and Evolving System Concept, Proc. 21st VLDB, Zurich, Switzerland, Sept. 11-15, 1995 (U.Dayal, P. Gray, S. Nishio eds) 2-6

8. Susan Malaika: Resistance is Futile: The Web will assimilate your Database, IEEE Bull. of the TC on Data Engineering, Vol. 21, No. 2 (June 1998) 4-13

9. Gloria Mark, Jörg M. Haake, and Norbert A. Streitz: Hypermedia Structures and the Division of Labor in Meeting Room Collaboration, Proc. of the ACM 1996 Conference on CSCW, Boston, Mass. (November 1996) 170-179

10. John K. Ousterhout: Tcl and the Tk Toolkit, Addison-Wesley, Reading, Mass., 1994

11. J. F. Patterson, R. D. Hill, S.L. Rohall, and W.S. Meeks: Rendezvous: An architecture for synchronous multi-user applications. Proc. of the Third Conf. on CSCW (Los Angeles, CA. (October 1990) 317-328

12. Tom Rodden: Populating the Application: A Model of Awareness for Cooperative Applications, Proc. of the ACM 1996 Conf. on CSCW, Boston, Mass. (November 1996) pp. 87-96

13. Mark Stefik, Gregg Foster, Daniel G. Bobrow, Kenneth Kahn, Stan Lanning, and Lucy Suchman: Beyond the Chalkboard: Computer Support for Collaboration and Problem Solving in Meetings, CACM 30:1 (Jan. 1987) 32-47

14. J. Thamm, S. Thelemann, and L. Wegner: Visual Information Systems - A Database Perspective, Proc. DMS '96 Third Pacific Workshop on Distributed Multimedia Systems Hong Kong Univ. of Science and Technology, June 25 - 28, 1996 (David Du and Olivia R. Liu Sheng eds.) Knowledge Systems Institute, Skokie, IL (1996) 274-285

15. Jens Thamm and Lutz Wegner: What You See is What You Store: Database-Driven Interfaces, Proc. 4th IFIP 2.6 Working Conference on Visual Database Systems, L'Aquila, Italy, May 27-29, 1998, Yannis Ioannidis and Wolfgang Klas (eds.) 69-84

16. M. Venkatrao and M. Pizzo: SQL/CLI - A New Binding Style For SQL, SIGMOD Record 24:4 (Dec. 1995) 71-77

17. L. Wegner: ESCHER - Interactive, Visual Handling of Complex Objects in the Extended NF^2-Database Model, Proc. IFIP TC-2 Working Conf. on Visual Database Systems, Tokyo, Japan, April 1989, T.L.Kunii (Ed.), Elsevier North-Holland, Amsterdam (1989) 277-297

18. L. Wegner, M. Paul, J. Thamm, and S. Thelemann: A Visual Interface for Synchronous Collaboration and Negotiated Transactions, Proc. Advanced Visual Interfaces (AVI'96), Gubbio, Italy, May 27-29, 1996, T.Catarci, M.F.Costabile, S.Levialdi, G.Santucci (Eds), ACM Press (1996) 156-165

19. L. Wegner, S. Thelemann, S. Wilke, and R. Lievaart: QBE-like Queries and Multimedia Extensions in a Nested Relational DBMS, Proc. Int. Conf. on Visual Information Systems, Melbourne, Australia, 5-6 February 1996, C. Leung (Ed.) 437-446

20. D. Wilke, L. Wegner, and J. Thamm: Database-driven GUI Programming, Proc. Int. Conf. on Visual Information Systems (Visual'97), San Diego CA (Dec. 1997) 205-214

Structured Message Management for Group Interaction

Sozo Inoue and Mizuho Iwaihara

Department of Computer Science and Communication Engineering
Kyushu University
6–1 Kasuga-Koen, Kasuga-Shi, Fukuoka 816-8580, JAPAN
Email: {sozo, iwaihara}@c.csce.kyushu-u.ac.jp

Abstract

In a collaborative working environment, process automation is necessary in the sense that (a) to show a flow of work items to be done, which is particularly important for assisting complex human tasks, (b) to show current status of each task to other participants, such as announcing which task is completed or continuing. More advanced functionalities which current process automation systems lack are: (c) support for ad-hoc and/or unstructured tasks such as discussions, decision making, and (d) collaboration of different teams, in which participants may not share all the process information, especially when carrying out negotiations. These requirements are universal to any types of collaborative work environments.

In this paper, we propose a new model for management of process information through message communication, as a basis for solving the above requirements. In our model, messages, such as E-mails or primitive user actions, are basic elements of our model, and *message groups (m-groups)* are introduced to compose a hierarchical structure on messages. We show a method for process automation through m-group templates, and discuss adding transactional properties to m-groups.

1 Introduction

Through the rapid growth of global computer network, it is becoming important to support various kinds of collaborative work among people and computers. One of the important areas for collaborative work support is process automation. In the following, we show an example of process and message management.

A process is a set of activities, and every activity is recorded by a message, and messages are added to a message sequence. A *process class* is a set of processes of the same functionality, having a unique *process class name*. Process class names can be "Review Design," "Modify Design," "Test Unit," "Schedule And Assign Tasks." For software development and maintenance processes, there are several standardized definitions, such as ISO/IEC 12207 Software Life Cycle Processes[6] and ECMA TR/55[3], and we can import process class names from them.

A message is created by a member, having E-mail-like information such as body (text/voice/video), and date. Each message may have a collection of *handles*, which is a set of links to design/document documents (Figure 1).

Casual messages such as comments will be freely created and linked to other messages. However, formal messages such as design transfer forms, error reports, should be regulated and monitored by rules.

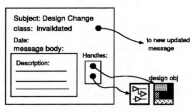

Fig. 1. Message format

Introducing *message classes* to represent the sender's intention of each message is useful. Message classes such as **support**, **objection**, **question** can be created, where each class name corresponds to intentions of messages, as in the graphical issue based information system (gIBIS)[4].

Figure 2 shows an example of process and message classes, where Modify_Design, Modify_Code, and Review_Design are process classes and items shown in the boxes are message classes. Process classes are taken from the benchmark software process example[9], which is used for software process description languages, and we added necessary message classes.

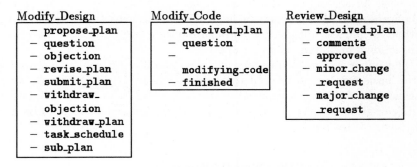

Fig. 2. An example of message classes

In a collaborative working environment like the above, process automation is necessary in the following aspects:

(a) to show the flow of work items to be done, which is particularly important for assisting complex human tasks,

(b) to show the current status of each task to other participants, such as announcing which task is completed or continuing,

(c) to provide support for ad-hoc and/or unstructured tasks such as discussions, decision making, and

(d) to enable collaboration of different teams, in which participants may not share all the process information, especially when carrying out negotiations.

These requirements are universal to any types of collaborative work environments. To deal with (a), workflow management systems (WfMSs) are effective. However, today's WfMSs do not deal with the above points (c) and (d) of structured message management. For example, the advanced workflow models of [5] and [11] assume strictly hierarchical (tree) task structures. However, in contrast to workflow tasks, message structures are often more complex, where directed acyclic graphs (DAGs) are appropriate. That is because a group of messages for resolving a problem should be shared by two different processes if the two processes require resolution of the problem.

As for (b), incorporating transactional semantics to process/message management is effective, to distinguish what is a successful finish (commit) from an unsuccessful finish (abort) of tasks or discussions. Current structured message management systems are devoid of such a transaction support.

In our previous approach[7], we have proposed a method for adding transactional dependencies to message links, in which each message has commit/abort states, so that various types of advanced transaction models[10] can be utilized in structured message management. However, in [7] we have not reached to the point of integrating the mechanism for composing message structures with the rules for adding transactional properties. In this paper, we propose a new model for management of process information through message communication, as a basis for solving the above requirements (a)–(d). M-groups are introduced to compose a DAG structure on messages, as an extension of [7]. We show a method for process automation through m-group templates, and discuss adding transactional properties to m-groups.

This paper is organized as follows: In Section 2, we introduce *m-group*, which is the basis for our structured message management. In Section 3, we define transactions of message communications, and introduce m-group templates which specify m-group structures. Section 4 is a conclusion and we summarize the contributions of this paper.

2 Message Groups (M-Groups)

In this section, we introduce *message groups (m-groups for short)* for supporting advanced message management.

2.1 M-Groups and m-group classes

In this section, we define m-groups and m-group classes. We use m-groups to model both process classes and message classes.

An *m-group class* of name C has its *class template $Temp(C)$*. We will define $Temp(C)$ in Section 2.2.

An *m-group instance* or simply *m-group* consists of its unique name S, message body *body(S)*, class name *Class(S)*, *child m-group set* (*child m-groups* for short) $CG(S) = \{S_0, S_1, \ldots, S_k\}$. *body$(S)$* represents a message object, such as text or video data, where a null value is allowed.

A child m-group set $CG(S) = \{S_0, S_1, \ldots, S_k\}$ is a possibly-empty set of m-group names. Each m-group S_i is called a *child* m-group of S. A *descendant* m-group is a child m-group or a child of a descendant m-group. We put a restriction such that an m-group cannot be a descendant m-group of itself. Let $\mathcal{MG}$ be the set of the whole m-groups. $\mathcal{MG}$ can be represented as a directed acyclic graph (DAG); namely one m-group can be shared by multiple parent m-groups. There will be the following advantages by allowing m-groups to form a DAG structure.

- Two different organizations, or two different teams within a large organization often collaborate and negotiate various agendas. In such cases, messages exchanged between those teams might be regarded differently in each team, and the classification and evaluation of each negotiation/discussion should be different according to teams. In such cases, each message should belong to different m-groups of those teams.
- There are situations such that one message has multiple meanings and it is more appropriate for the messages to belong to multiple groups. DAG structures can express such situations.

2.2   M-group class templates

We introduce *t-expressions* to represent nested structures of both m-group templates and m-group instances. Each term in a t-expression has a label n, called *t-name*. T-names are used as a tag to associate a template with its instance. A *terminal symbol* is either an m-group class name or instance name.

A t-expression on t-name n and terminal symbols $T_0, \ldots, T_k$ is defined as follows:

1. A term $n\!:\!T_i$ is a t-expression, where T_i is a terminal symbol.
2. A term $n\!:\!\langle e_1, e_2, \ldots, e_k \rangle$ is a t-expression called an *AND-group*, where each e_i is a t-expression.
3. A term $n\!:\![e_1, e_2, \ldots, e_k]^+$ is a t-expression called a *+-group*, where each e_i is a t-expression.
4. A term $n\!:\![e_1, e_2, \ldots, e_k]^*$ is a t-expression called a **-group*, where each e_i is a t-expression.

Now we define m-group templates. An *m-group template $\mathcal{T}(C)$* for an m-group class C is a tuple $[Child(C), Texp(C), Dep(C)]$, where $Child(C)$ is the *child m-group class set* of C, $Texp(C)$ is the *t-expression* of C, whose terminal symbols are in $Child(C)$, and $Dep(C)$ is the *dependency set* of C. We will define $Dep(C)$ in Section 3.2.

If $Child(C)$ is an empty set, then the class C is called a *simple* m-group class. We allow $Child(C)$ to contain class C itself, so that m-group instances can have an arbitrary depth of nesting. However, the depth of nesting must be finite.

The t-name of the outermost term of $Texp(C)$ is called the *root t-name* of $Texp(C)$. Each t-name can appear only once in template t-expression $Texp(C)$ for t-tames to be used as unique labels of terms in $Texp(C)$.

Example 1. Figure 3 shows two m-group templates for class **task** and class **question**. A single circle, such as **task_unit** and **question** represents an m-class, which also has its own template (template for **task_unit** is not shown). A box, such as **finished** and **transfered** represents a *simple* message class, which can have no child m-groups. The class name of each child m-group symbol is associated with its t-name, such as **q:question**.

Each template contains **root**, **abort**, **commit** m-classes depicted by double circles. In Section 3, we introduce transactional events on m-groups, and these child m-classes are intended to represent the root, commit and abort events of the root m-group. Simple m-groups do not have such child m-classes and they assumed to be committed right after they are created. The labeled edges represent transactional dependencies.

The template for **s:task** contains a +-group, which in turn contains **u:task_unit** and **q:question**. In the following, we associate +-groups the semantics such that an arbitrary positive number (≥ 1) of child m-groups of those classes in a +-group must be created. In this example, the +-group is intended to represent that several subtasks or questions must be initiated to carry out one task (we need at least one question or subtask before the root task terminates). One question may be raised to raise a question about the root task, and if the task turns out to be inappropriate to be done, then the task may be transfered without initiating a subtask, and an m-group of class **t:transfered** is created to indicate the conclusion.

*-groups are similar to +-groups, but *-groups are allowed to have no child m-groups. In Figure 3, an instance for **r:task_report** may be created, but it is optional. □

Now we define instances of m-group classes. An m-group *instance* S of an m-group class C is a tuple $[CG(S), Texp(S)]$ such that $CG(S) = \{S_0, S_1, \ldots, S_k\}$ is a set of child m-groups where $Class(S_i) \in Child(C)$, and $Texp(S)$ is a t-expression on terminal symbols $\{S_0, S_1, \ldots, S_k\}$ such that a t-name can appear multiple times in $Texp(S)$ but each m-group name S_i can appear only once.

A template t-expression $Texp(C)$ and its instance t-expression $Texp(S)$ must satisfy the following conditions 1–4:

1. If there is a term $n:S_i$ in $Texp(S)$ and $n:C_i$ in $Texp(C)$ having the same t-name n, then $Class(S_i) = C_i$.
2. If there is an AND-group term $n:\langle e_1, e_2, \ldots, e_k \rangle$ in $Texp(S)$, then there is an AND-group term of the same t-name $n:\langle e'_1, e'_2, \ldots, e'_k \rangle$ in $Texp(C)$ such

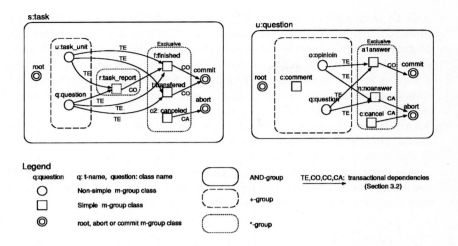

Fig. 3. M-group templates

that e_i and e'_i $(i = 1, \ldots, k)$ have the same t-name. **AND**-groups can be used to represent predefined flows, such as A must be followed by B.

3. If there is a +-group term $n : [e_1, e_2, \ldots, e_k]^+$ in $Texp(S)$, then $k \geq 1$ and there must be a +-group term of the same t-name $n : [e'_1, e'_2, \ldots, e'_m]^+$ in $Texp(C)$ such that for each $e_i(i = 1, \ldots, k)$ there is a t-expression $e'_j(1 \leq j \leq m)$ where e_i and e'_j have the same t-name.

4. If there is a *-group term $n : [e_1, e_2, \ldots, e_k]^*$ in $Texp(S)$, then either (a) the term has no e_i or (b) $k \geq 1$ and there is a *-group term of the same t-name $n : [e'_1, e'_2, \ldots, e'_m]$ in $Texp(C)$ such that for each $e_i(i = 1, \ldots, k)$ there is a t-expression $e'_j(1 \leq j \leq m)$ where e_i and e'_j have the same t-name.

Example 2. Figure 4 shows an example of instances of template **task**. Two m-groups of names S_1 and S_5 are instances of **task**, and S_2, S_3, S_4, S_6 and S_7 are child m-groups. Each bold line shows a root-child relationship. The m-group S_4 of class **question** is shared by two parents S_1 and S_5, and the instance is depicted as a DAG. This example can be interpreted as a question which is common to both tasks is raised, and an answer for the question is required to complete those tasks. $\square$

An informal description of how m-group instances are created and maintained is described as follows:

- First, an m-group S is created by a human participant, the system, or a software agent, with $body(S)$ containing a message and $Class(S)$ specifies S's class.

- New m-groups are added to $CG(S)$ as a child of S as the activities of S proceed. Classes of new child m-groups are regulated by the template $T(C)$.
- M-groups can be created before actual activities begin, to indicate participants what is the goal of the activities or how it should be done. Succeeding activities will fill the pre-created m-groups. For example, choosing a child of class **task_report** before proceeding a **task** m-group indicates that a report is expected at the end of the m-group.
- An arbitrary finite length of flows can be represented by using recursive templates, that is, a class definition for C which includes C itself as its child or descendant. An instance for C will be able to include a finite depth of a nested structure involving C. For instance, the template **question** of Figure 3 contains **question**, meaning that a discussion triggered by a question may contain another question in the course of the discussion.

3 Transactional Dependencies in M-Groups

3.1 Transactional events of m-groups

In this section, we discuss a scheme for giving transactional properties to m-groups, and show a method for assigning transactional dependencies to m-group instances using class templates.

We introduce transactional events on m-groups such that each m-group has four types of events root, active, commit and abort.

Our main motivation to introduce transactional events to m-groups is to clarify the effectiveness of each m-group. In the traditional sense of transactions, commit means a successful update of the database and abort means a failure and, an aborted transaction must have no influence on the database.

However, as for coordinating collaborative work, we often encounter the necessity of clarifying what is the goal of each activity and whether the goal is achieved or not. In that case, it is effective to introduce the notion of transactions to represent success/failure of each m-group.

We conceptually use the term *commit* of an m-group S, if S finished and produced desired results, and we use the term *abort*, if S finished but has not produced desired results. We assume that cancel, failure or any types of outcome of S which failed to deliver predefined results is considered as abort.

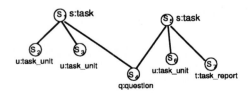

Fig. 4. M-group instance

We adopt the following guidelines for managing transactions of m-groups:

- M-group class templates should be designed to clarify what is the success/failure of an m-group. Child m-groups representing successful and failed results should be created within each template. Each successful (resp. failed) results should cause commit (resp. abort) of the root m-group.
- "Desired results" are represented by child m-groups which have transactional dependencies to the commit node of S's template.
- Although predefined templates are useful, those templates should be customized at runtime.

Now we define that each m-group S produces the following types of *transactional events*.

1. $r(S)$: (*root*) $r(S)$ occurs when m-group S is created.
2. $t(S)$: (*active*) $t(S)$ occurs when a child m-group S' of S has an event of type $r(S'), t(S'), c(S')$ or $a(S')$.
3. $a(S)$: (*abort*) $a(S)$ occurs when a child m-group of class **abort** is created as a child of S.
4. $c(S)$: (*commit*) $c(S)$ occurs when a child m-group of class **commit** is created as a child of S.

We assume that abort or commit of an m-group occurs when a simple child m-group of class **abort** or **commit** is created by a user or the system.

We call an m-group S is *terminated* if the last transactional event of S is either $a(S)$ or $c(S)$. Likewise, we call an m-group S is *not terminated* if the last transactional event of S is either $r(S)$ or $t(S)$.

3.2 Notations for transactional dependencies

We utilize two useful primitives $e_1 < e_2$ and $e_1 \rightarrow e_2$ to specify dependencies between transactional events, which are proposed by Klein[8], and also discussed in [1].

- $e_1 < e_2$: (precedence) If both event e_1 and event e_2 occur, then e_1 must precede e_2. There is no constraint on the possibility of occurrence of e_1 or e_2.
- $e_1 \rightarrow e_2$: (occurrence) If event e_1 occurs, then event e_2 must also occur. There is no constraint on the order of occurrences between e_1 and e_2. $\square$

We use conventional propositional logic symbols $\wedge$ (and), $\vee$ (or) , $\Rightarrow$ (implication) on transactional events of m-groups.

We define notations *Atomic, Exclusive, AA, CC, CO, AC, CA* and *TE* which are useful macros for declaring dependencies on both template and instance level dependencies. Here notations AA, CC, AC and CA are extended from [7] to deal with m-group structures.

Suppose that a t-expression $Texp(C)$ has t-names $n_1, \ldots, n_k$. The dependency set $Dep(C)$ for class C is a set of terms of the forms: $Atomic(n_i)$, $Exclusive(n_i)$, $AA(n_i, n_j), CC(n_i, n_j), CO(n_i, n_j), AC(n_i, n_j), CA(n_i, n_j)$ or $TE(n_i, n_j)$, where $1 \le i, j \le k$ and $i \ne j$. The semantics of these terms are defined in the following:

- $Atomic(n_i)$: Suppose that n_i is a t-name of an AND-, +- or *-group and $n'_1, \ldots, n'_m$ are the t-names which are elements of n_i. Then $Atomic(n_i)$ is a declaration of $a(n'_i) \rightarrow a(n'_j)$ and $c(n'_i) \rightarrow c(n'_j)$ for each pair n'_i and n'_j $(1 \le i, j \le m, i \ne j)$.
- $Exclusive(n_i)$: Suppose that n_i is a t-name of an AND-, +- or *-group and $n'_1, \ldots, n'_m$ are the t-names which are elements of n_i. Then $Exclusive(n_i)$ is a declaration of $c(n'_i) \rightarrow a(n'_j)$ for each pair n'_i and $n'_j (1 \le i, j \le m, i \ne j)$.

In the following definitions, suppose that n_i and n_j are t-names of terms $n_i : C_i$ and $n_j : C_j$ in $Texp(C)$.

- $AA(n_i, n_j)$: (abort dependency) Declaration of $a(n_i) \rightarrow a(n_j)$.
- $CC(n_i, n_j)$: (commit dependency) Declaration of $c(n_i) < c(n_j)$.
- $CO(n_i, n_j)$: (commit occurrence) Declaration of $c(n_i) \rightarrow c(n_j)$.
- $AC(n_i, n_j)$: Declaration of $(c(n_j) \rightarrow a(n_i)) \land (a(n_i) < c(n_j))$.
- $CA(n_i, n_j)$: Declaration of $c(n_i) \rightarrow a(n_j)$.
- $TE(n_i, n_j)$: (terminate) Declaration of $(c(n_i) < c(n_j)) \land (a(n_i) < c(n_i))$.

Note that n_i and n_j can be the root t-name of $Texp(C)$. If n_i is the root t-name, then events such as $a(n_i)$ and $c(n_i)$ are considered as abort and commit events of an instance of class C itself.

Declaration of $Atomic(n_i)$ gives n_i the constraint that all the child m-group instances of n_i must commit if a child m-group of S commits, and must abort if a child m-group of S aborts.

Declaration of $Exclusive(n_i)$ gives n_i the constraint that if a child m-group of n_i commits, then any other child m-group must abort.

Declaration of $AA(n_1, n_2)$ gives C the constraint that n_2 must abort if n_1 aborts. This is equivalent to the well-known abort dependency[1]. Declaration of $CC(n_1, n_2)$ gives C the constraint that n_1 and n_2 can commit together only if n_1 commits before n_2 commits. This corresponds to the commit dependency. Declaration of $AC(n_1, n_2)$ gives S the constraint that n_2 cannot commit before n_1 aborts. The declaration of $CA(n_1, n_2)$ gives S the constraint that n_2 must abort if n_1 commits. Declaration of $TE(n_1, n_2)$ gives S the constraint that n_1 must either commit or abort before n_2 commits. This can be used to represent that n_1's termination is required for n_2's commit.

We assume that C is imposed a constraint of the conjunction of all the dependencies in $Dep(C)$. Namely each dependency in $Dep(C)$ must be satisfied.

Example 3. Let us consider the templates in Figure 3. We depict pair-wise transactional dependencies using edges between two m-groups and assign group-wise dependencies *Exlucsive* and *Atomic* on AND-, +- and *- groups.

The TE dependencies coming into **finished** and **transfered** m-groups of **task** represents that each **task_unit** and **question** must either commit or abort before the m-group **finished** or **transfered** commits. If **finished** or **transfered** commits, then the **task** m-group must commit, due to the dependences of type CO which are coming into the commit node. An *Exclusive* dependency is set on ∗-group which contains **finished**, **transfered** and **canceled** m-groups. Hence only one of them can commit. □

Now we consider instance level dependencies. There are two ways to define transactional dependencies to m-group instances:

- **(template-defined dependencies)**: An m-group instance S of a certain class C is automatically assigned dependencies according to $Dep(C)$ of the template of C.
- **(user-defined dependencies)**: Users may put a certain dependency on an m-group instance S in an ad hoc manner.

To declare template-defined dependencies, we assume that dependencies are assigned to m-group instances of class C in the following way:

1. Suppose that $Dep(C)$ includes a dependency $Atomic(n_i)$ (resp. $Exclusive(n_i)$) where n_i is a t-name for an AND-, +- or ∗-group having elements $\{n'_1, \ldots, n'_k\}$. Also suppose that $S' = \{S'_1, \ldots, S'_m\}$ is the set of child m-groups of S such that the t-name of each S'_j is in $\{n'_1, \ldots, n'_k\}$. Then $Atomic(S')$ (resp. $Exclusive(S')$) should be imposed. Here, $Atomic(S')$ is interpreted as the t-names $\{n'_1, \ldots, n'_k\}$ in the original definition are replaced with instance names $\{S'_1, \ldots, S'_m\}$.
2. If $Dep(C)$ includes a dependency of type $AA(n_i, n_j)$ (likewise for CC, CO, AC, CA, or TE), a dependency $AA(S_i, S_j)$ should be imposed for each S_i and S_j such that S_i and S_j have the same t-names n_i and n_j, respectively. Here, $AA(S_i, S_j)$ is interpreted as the t-names n_i and n_j in the original definition are replaced by instance names S_i and S_j.

3.3 Rules for transactional dependency specifications

Now we discuss how a transactional dependency set $Dep(C)$ should be designed. We introduce the following rules in assigning transactional dependencies.

Rule1 Events $c(S)$ and $a(S)$ must be after the root event $r(S)$.

Rule2 Each child m-group S' must terminate before its parent S terminates. Namely, the following dependency shall be imposed between each m-group S and its child m-group S'.

$$(c(S') < c(S)) \wedge (c(S') < a(S)) \wedge (a(S') < c(S)) \wedge (a(S') < a(S))$$

Rule3 Each transactional dependency should be imposed within child m-groups of a certain m-group.

Rule4 If a child m-group S' is designated as a success (resp. failure) of the root S, then the dependency $c(S') \rightarrow c(S)$ (resp. $c(S') \rightarrow a(S)$) should be imposed. Namely, a commit of the child S' causes commit/abort of the root S.

Rule1 implies that an m-group can commit after every child m-group of the m-group has committed or aborted. That is, an m-group can have a result only after all the child m-groups are successfully or unsuccessfully terminated.

Rule2 imposes that a termination of an m-group S requires termination of all the children of S. In other words, if a root m-group is requested to abort, then all the child m-groups must terminate (commit or abort) before the root aborts. Participants in those child m-groups should be notified and requested to terminate those children.

Rule3 is introduced to assume that each dependency is included in an m-group. **Rule4** is introduced to clarify what is the success/failure of each m-group, by tying "success" ("failure") message classes to "commit" ("abort").

Arbitrary created transactional dependencies may become unsatisfiable. For this problem, we can use restrictions shown in [7] for keeping satisfiable dependencies.

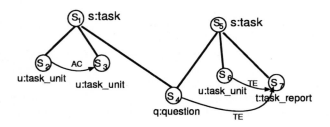

Fig. 5. Transactional dependencies on m-groups

Example 4. Figure 5 shows an instance of class **task** where template-defined dependencies are assigned. The TE dependencies between S_4, S_6 and S_7 are introduced by the template of **task**.

Let us suppose that the AC dependency from S_2 to S_3 was introduced by a user. This dependency puts the constraint that **task_unit** S_3 can commit only after S_2 aborts. Therefore it can be interpreted as **task_unit** S_3 is an alternative for S_2 and it can be employed only if S_2 failed. □

4 Conclusion

In this paper, we proposed a new model for structured message management, based on m-groups. The following is the advantages of our model:

- Since each m-group includes a message and the class of each m-group represents the functionality or purpose of the message, it is easy for members to understand the context of discussions/tasks. Created m-groups are useful for outsiders or newcomers who need to understand past records of communications.
- Software agents can also utilize informations from m-groups to understand the current status of user communications.
- By introducing transactions on m-groups, which m-groups are still active, have committed, or have aborted are clarified. Thus confusions among members caused by misunderstanding of termination of discussions/tasks can be avoided.
- M-groups can represent both freely produced, less constrained discussions and well order-constrained, hierarchically structured and prescribed tasks, by using transactional dependencies.

References

1. P. Attie, M. P. Singh, A. Sheth, and M. Rusinkiewicz, "Specifying and Enforcing Intertask Dependencies," *Proc. the 19th VLDB*, pp. 134–145, 1993.
2. Q. Chen and U. Dayal, "A Transactional Nested Process Management System," *Proc. Int. Conf. Data Engineering*, 1996.
3. ECMA and NIST, "Reference Model for Frameworks of Software Engineering Environments," Draft Edition 3 of Technical Report ECMA TR/55 and NIST Special Publication 500-201, 1993.
4. J. Conklin and M. L. Begeman, "gIBIS: A Hypertext Tool for Exploratory Policy Discussion," *ACM Trans. Office Information Systems*, Vol.6, No.4, pp.303-331, Oct 1988.
5. L. Liu and C. Pu, "Methodological Restructuring of Complex Workflow Activities, " *Proc. 14th Int. Conf. Data Engineering*, pp. 342–350, California, 1998.
6. ISO/IEC 12207, Information Technology – Software Life Cycle Processes, 1995.
7. M. Iwaihara, S. Inoue, and H. Matsuo, "On Unifying Message and Transaction Management for Collaborative Design Work," *Proc. Int. Symp. Digital Media Information Base (DMIB'97)*, Nara, pp. 300–304, Nov. 1997.
8. J. Klein, "Advanced Rule Driven Transaction Management," *Proc. COMPCON*, 1991.
9. M. I. Kellner, et al., "Software Process Modeling Example Problem," *Proc. 6th Int. Software Process Workshop*, pp.19–29, 1990.
10. K. Ramamritham and P. K. Chrysanthis, "*Advances in Concurrency Control and Transaction Processing*," IEEE Computer Society Executive Briefing, 1997.
11. M. Reichert and P. Dadam, "ADEPTflex –Supporting Dynamic Changes of Workflows Without Loosing Control," *Journal of Intelligent Information Systems, to appear.*

Group Activity Database
for Groupware Evolution

Hiroyuki Tarumi[1], Tetsuya Matsuyama[2], Yahiko Kambayashi[1] *

[1] Graduate School of Informatics, Kyoto University
[2] Department of Information Science, Kyoto University

Abstract. This paper proposes a new type of database for collaborative work. Known types of databases for collaborative work are databases of shared data and those of process data. A new type proposed in this paper is Group Activity Database (GADB). It contains history of group communication, which is used to analyze collaborative work. With a GADB, evaluation, user modeling, reengineering, simulation, and team awareness support will be helped. Evolution of groupware is supported by these activities. We adopt agent-based groupware architecture in order to realize open and distributed groupwork management. With this architecture, communication logs among agents or between agents and users are captured by a GADB for analysis.

1 Introduction

Research of *CSCW* (Computer Supported Cooperative Work) has been active for over ten years. So-called *groupware* products have been developed, e.g., enhanced e-mail systems, bulletin board systems, workflow or business process support systems, shared editors and hypermedia, collaborative writing systems, video conferencing systems, etc.

From the viewpoint of databases, two kinds of them have been important for CSCW. One is the type of databases that contain shared data on which the collaborative work is applied. This kind of database includes shared hypermedia systems[13, 20], repository database for software development (e.g., [14]), etc.

Databases of the other type contain *process data*. For example, a workflow management system may have a database that contains workflow process definitions and status of workflow cases.

In this paper, we propose a new category of databases for new age groupware: *Group Activity Database (GADB)*. It is purposed to support evolution and deployment of groupware systems.

2 Group Activity Database

An ideal GADB should be able to capture all histories of group activities. Histories include communication logs among groupwork participants, supporting

---
* {tarumi,matuyama,yahiko}@kuis.kyoto-u.ac.jp

software modules, and environments (outside of the working group and supporting system) as well as other system logs.

The purpose of GADB is mainly analyses of groupwork. Analyses benefit groupware designers and users in the following ways.

1. Evaluation:
   The data indicates how the groupware system is used, how people behave with the system, and how the work has changed in terms of efficiency. Designers and users can evaluate the groupware system based on these data.

2. User Modeling:
   Groupware design depends strongly on the user model, which abstracts user behaviors, e.g. when the user starts processing tasks, in what order, and when finishes them. The log data tell us other informal user behaviors like forwarding task requests to another person, etc. According to these data, the designer can improve the quality of user models in order to fit them to the reality.

3. Reengineering:
   Like user modeling, processes can also be remodeled based on the log data. For example, skipping or reversing the task processing order often occurs in reality. Professionals can sometimes find process bottlenecks from the log data. These findings can give a better process definition. This is so-called *business process reengineering (BPR)*.

4. Simulation:
   After reengineering design, the new business process should be validated prior to implementation. Simulation is one of the promising tools of validation. To enhance the reality of simulation, user models obtained from the log data would be useful.

5. Team Awareness:
   Team awareness[18] is a very important concept in cooperative work. It means enabling people to be aware of how and what other team members are doing. In order to support team awareness, visualizing the current status of other members and communications among them is important. The log data, especially very recent data, can be given to the visualizing process. It shows users what task each member is doing, how many backlogs each member has, etc.

A process database may also contain log data (e.g., EvE[5]). For example, workflow case status data are log data that indicate when and by whom these cases have been processed. In this sense, a workflow database can be regarded as a GADB. However, we insist that an exclusive database for the purpose of group activity record should be prepared. Reasons are as follows:

- A workflow database is dedicated to the workflow tasks managed by the system. Other informal communications are ignored.
- Basically, most of workflow databases cannot record histories that ignored the formal process definitions. For example, skipping or reversing the processing order may not be able to be recorded correctly.

- Sometimes a worker is concurrently doing jobs for multiple business processes. If workflow databases are used, the worker's activities are recorded separately on each database, so that user modeling would be difficult.

The next discussion is how to implement a GADB. The most difficult problem is capturing log data of all group activities that may be separately managed. We do not think that a GADB is applicable to all current groupware products. We assume agent-based groupware. It is not only to realize GADB, but because agent-based groupware has many promising features as the next generation groupware. The next section describes the agent-based groupware.

3 Agent-based Groupware

3.1 Features

In this paper we use the word "agent" in the following sense. An agent is a software module that is a surrogate for a user, or implements functions for an aspect of group activities (cost optimization, mediation of people, etc.). Agent can communicate with another agent by exchanging messages.

Agent-based Groupware is an architecture of groupware consisting of multiple agents. Multi-agent systems are very suitable to implement groupware due to the following features.

1. Openness:
   This basic feature means that it is widely applicable to large companies that have many divisions, joint ventures, loosely organized groups like those of alumnus/alumna or volunteers, and virtual enterprises. Concretely it means that the groupware satisfies the following conditions:
   - Each user can belong to multiple workgroups concurrently. To realize this, supporting functions are needed to enable users to concurrently take part in multiple business processes[8], and also personal tasks[9].
   - It positively utilize wide area networks like the Internet, intranets, and extranets.
   - Inter-organizational security issues are consciously maintained.
   - Distributed management is possible. It is important to allow each manager of divisions or sub-organizations to manage her or his group in her or his own way.
   - The system accepts the cultural differences among different sub-groups. For example, each sub-group has its own glossaries[18], constraints in schedule, job priorities, and management styles.
2. Scalability:
   It should be possible to append new elements to the system, or remove elements from it. It should also be possible for the system to run efficiently regardless of its size.
3. Evolution:
   It should be dynamically adaptable to exceptional events as well as to accept evolutionary process refinement or reengineering.

3.2 Existing Examples

The number of already existing agent-based groupware is not so many, but some of them are already in use.

Pan, et al. gave a very early example[17]. They give a framework of agent-based enterprise modeling. A enterprise is modeled with many discrete elements, each of which is an IA (Intelligent Agent) or a PA (Personal Assistant). The system was applied to a semiconductor fabrication process, in which case examples of IAs are machine control and monitoring processes. A PA can also be regarded as an agent that interfaces a user and IAs.

ADEPT project applied a multi-agent technology to the BT company's customer quote business processes[11, 12]. In its architecture, each division involved in the business process is represented as a group of agent (agency). They claim that agent architecture has the following benefits.

- Process management and resource management are conducted at the same time with one architecture.
- Exception handling is easy.
- It has robustness and scalability thanks to distributed architecture.

MACIV project in Portugal adopted a multi-agent technology for the resource management of civil construction companies[4]. Construction companies have many sites all over the countries. The project settled LAN at each site and regards a site as an agent.

INA/LI is designed with a multi-agent architecture supporting both group and personal work[9]. With this architecture, the WorkWeb system was proposed [22]. It realizes dynamic adaptation of workflow to exceptional and unpredicted situations, like sudden absence of a worker. The adaptation process is designed with negotiations among workflow management agents and human interface agents. This paper also proposes the concept of *Business Process Tactics* in contrast to business process reengineering. Business Process Tactics means dynamic, case-based change of a process, while reengineering changes the process definition.

3.3 Our Position

In this research, our assumption on the agent-based groupware is like those found in [17] and [9]. An interface agent for each user is mandatory because we should maintain user models. Communications between a user and its interface agent should be recorded as well as communications among agents.

Fig. 1 shows the concept of GADB, capturing all communication logs among agents and those between agents and users.

3.4 Data Capturing

It is rather easy to record communications among agents because of very formal protocol definitions. Captured data items are, generally, like Message ID, source

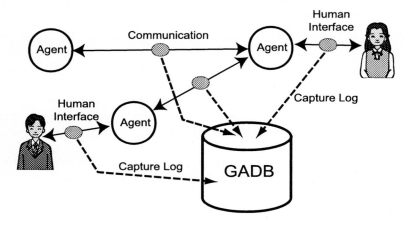

Fig. 1. Group Activity Database

and destination of messages, type of communication (task order, inquiry, cancellation, request for deadline extension, etc.), task name, time, priority value, deadline, etc. These data indicate history of processes.

Besides these data, there are more data items that depend on each application. At the time of agent design, a support system that can automatically define the database schema for application data should be given.

On the other hand, it is difficult to confirm correspondence of logged data of interaction between users and agents with group tasks, because interaction-level data are too fine-grained and including noisy information like meaningless mouse movement. The architecture of an user interface agent should be like Fig. 2.

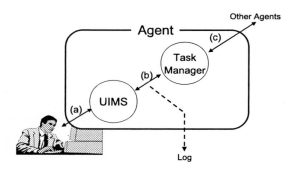

Fig. 2. Internal Agent Architecture to Take Interaction Logs

In this architecture, the concept of UIMS (User Interface Management Systems) is adopted. UIMS transforms device-level, machine-dependent UI operations into abstract level UI operations. It enables to get abstracted level interaction between user and the agent at (b).

Task Manager takes the role of user's surrogate. It may automatically answer requests from other agents. Hence communication logs between agents can be obtained at (c).

Logged data at (b) include:

1. Subset of logged data at (c).
2. User's manual input, like inputting a task description to his or her schedule management agent in case that the task is ordered off-line.
3. Information request from the user to the agent, and its answer.
4. Active message from the agent to the user, e.g. an urging message.

Note that logged data which appear at (c) but do not appear at (b) are those related to user requests resolved at the agent internally.

3.5   Requirements to GADB

A GADB is used both at the time of simulation and runtime operation. In both cases the same visualization feature can be utilized. However, at the time of simulation, it might be easier to acquire data because the simulation engine can simulate all agents and users on one machine.

GADB should be able to answer at least the following types of queries.

- For BPR and User Modeling
  - Give all log data related to a process.
  - Give all log data related to a worker, and sort them chronological order.
  - Give past tasks that could not keep deadlines.
  - Give a list of BPT activities that happened within a time period, or related to a given process.
  - Give all log data related to a given BPT activity.
  - Give all task requests that a given worker has at a given time.
- For Simulation
  - Give all task requests that a given worker has.
- For Visualization (at simulation and runtime)
  - Give all task requests that a group of workers have at the present time.
  - Give a list of workers involved with a given process.
  - The above queries with respect to a given past time.

4   Simulation

In this section, we will describe simulation functions in detail, which is one of the major applications of GADB.

4.1 Background

Business process simulation is an important key to solve problems in groupware design and deployment.

In the first author's experiences in developing and deploying office groupware systems based on asynchronous communication, like workflow systems and group calendar systems, he encountered difficulties as follows.

1. Difficulties in estimating its impact

   It is difficult for a groupware designer to make a quantitative estimation of the cost-effectiveness prior to the introduction of groupware to the business field. However, managers of groupware users require persuasive explanation of its impact before making up his or her mind to buy the groupware. Hence groupware designers are expected to explain the impact, although it is not easy. It is because the effect of (especially asynchronous type of) groupware is mainly in reducing communication loss or inefficiency, not in the main job (like document production) itself.

2. Difficulties in practical evaluation and test

   Another approach to solving the problem of giving a quantitative measurement of groupware impact is to test the groupware in the real business field. However, because groupware involves many people, it is also difficult to conduct the experimental use. Moreover, in case of large-scale open groupware, small experiments do not totally give the estimation of large-scale usage. In case of special groupware systems like those used in the situation of disaster, testing at the real field is intrinsically impossible.

3. Difficulties in predicting human behavior

   As Grudin pointed out[6], it is difficult for groupware designers to imagine how user behaviors change between before and after the groupware introduction. Hence they cannot design groupware with taking account of its usage and impact.

One of the most successful examples in solving these problems can be found in the development of POLITeam[19]. One of the goals of POLITeam is development of telecooperation systems that support the cooperation among the distributed governmental functions between Bonn and Berlin. In the development of POLITeam, an evolutionary development cycle was taken[25]. Thanks to this participatory development cycle including many interviews and workshops with users, users accepted the designed groupware very smoothly. However, this kind of development cycle is very difficult to take in usual cases. In case of POLITeam, there was a very strong background, the movement of capital city, which caused a feeling of crisis and focused all people's intention, so that it was possible to get all people's cooperation for interviews and workshops. POLITeam's case seems to be very exceptional.

Simulation gives another approach to overcoming difficulties in groupware development and deployment given above. Its most important advantage is that it does not need users' cooperation. By simulating new business processes, designers and users can evaluate the impact of the groupware introduction or changing business processes.

On the contrary, a problem of simulation is its reliability. As the third difficulty given above shows, human behaviors are very difficult to predict. Behaviors also vary person to person. For example, even in case of very simple workflow processing, it is very difficult to estimate when a particular person at a step of workflow finishes a task. This is because we cannot predict when the person really starts the task and how the person uses his or her time for the task (intensively or not). Personal behavior is a very important factor of business process simulation and they make simulation difficult and unreliable.

In spite of this problem, business process simulation has been one of the hottest topics in the research field of simulation systems. In the next subsection, business process simulation system models will be reviewed.

4.2 Business Process Simulation

The aim of business process simulation is to give data of newly introduced business processes in order to estimate the performance of new processes and to predict the behavior of the processes. Given data will help the *business process reengineering (BPR)* process.

The aims of BPR are, for example, to increase service level, to reduce total process cycle time, to increase throughput, to reduce waiting time, to reduce activity cost, or to reduce inventory cost. To achieve these goals, some techniques like combining duplicate activities, eliminating multiple reviews and approvals, processing in parallel, outsourcing inefficient activities, eliminating movement of work, etc. are applied. New business processes are validated by simulating random factors of the environment like customer arrivals[23].

A basic model of business process simulation consists of four elements[24]:

Entities Also called as flow objects, tokens, or transactions. These are the objects processed by resources. Customers, products, and documents are examples.

Resources These are objects that are used for adding value to Entities. Service representatives, automated process equipment, and transportation equipment are examples. They are allocated to activities.

Activities They are linked by connectors in order to represent the flow of entities through the simulation model.

Connectors They are used for linking processes and activities.

4.3 Our Approach

In our approach, simulation is performed on the agent-based groupware model. The general simulation model and categories can be interpreted on this model as follows.

- A *resource* is a pair of human and agent (user-interfacing agent, or personal assistant).

- *Connectors* are messages exchanged among agents.
- Because agent-based groupware is open, multiple processes should be simulated simultaneously. By simulation, interrelationship among processes should be able to be evaluated.

The objective of simulating agent-based groupware is to estimate the result of business process reengineering a priori. It is not different from the case of the general business process simulation. More detailed objectives are as follows.

- To estimate the impact of introducing agents. For example, to compare two cases: a case where resources are only human and a case where some or all resources are pairs of human and agents.
- To estimate the impact of changes of rules on some agents.
- To estimate the impact of process changes (e.g. activity order, resource assignment, etc.)
- To estimate the robustness of process against changes of randomly occurring events like interrupting jobs or absence of a person.
- To estimate the inter-dependency of two or more processes. For example, when the number of cases of a process increases, what effect will occur on other processes?

Introduction of rule-based agents and consideration of multiple processes make the simulation model more complex than usual business process simulation. Among them the most important factor is the behavior of resources (i.e. people) when multiple tasks are ordered from multiple processes. To model this factor, the order of beginning tasks and time distribution to tasks by a person. Below are some extreme models.

- Processing all tasks by first come first service basis.
- Processing tasks by the order of deadline.
- Distributing processing time evenly to all tasks.

Again, they are very extreme patterns and real people do not behave like these. By constructing user models with data from GADB, models of each person will be refined. Establishing user models is very important and inevitable task for the simulation.

The most important factor of simulation is to estimate when an activity will be finished. There are two approaches to the estimation.

- The finishing time is estimated relative to the deadline. For example, on the day of deadline, on the day before the deadline, on the next day of the deadline, etc.
- The finishing time is estimated as the time after some standard processing period from the beginning of the task.

The first approach is suitable to project-based[24] processes, like document writing and specification development. In this approach, dealing with multiple processes is not an important factor as long as the workload is not heavy. Required data only appear at the (c) part of Fig. 2. Important data items are type of communication, task or business process name, time, and deadline.

The second approach is suitable to production-based[24] processes like order fulfillment, claims processing, etc. Resources are supposed to be always fully assigned to tasks. At the time after a constant period from a task delivery, the task is supposed to be finished. In this approach, the order of beginning tasks is an important factor for simulation. User models described above are utilized. However, we should say these models are too simple to get reliable simulation results. We must acquire a lot of data before simulation. For example, a successful case of business process simulation took a long time and much cost to acquire reliable values for simulation[15].

5 Evolution

In this section we describe how groupware can evolve with simulation, tactics and reengineering techniques, utilizing group activity data. The order of evolutionary cycle steps is: (1) tactics, (2) reengineering, and then (3) simulation.

5.1 Business Process Tactics

As described earlier, Business Process Tactics (BPT) refers to activities that change process operation to dynamically adapt the process to exceptional cases. To show how BPT is possible is out of the focus of this paper. From the viewpoint of GADB, BPT is a very important source of data. BPT log will be used for later reengineering.

5.2 Business Process Reengineering

There are some research results in the BPR (Business Process Reengineering) field. Some of them are on the reengineering model[3, 1, 7], some applied knowledge technologies [10]. In ActionWorkflow[16] and Regatta[21], reengineering is represented as incremental re-definitions of a process definition. Borghoff discussed how two kinds of business processes can co-exist, those processes before and after the reengineering[2].

In our research approach, there are some approaches to BPR.

- From the log data of BPT, dynamic changes that often occur are found. These give hints for BPR.
- Visualized data in GADB show some hints for BPR. For example, bottlenecks of process flow.

5.3   Business Process Simulation

After reengineering design, simulation should be exercised. Simulation may have several stages.

1. **Initial simulation**: Total process is simulated with user model data that have been obtained from old processes. The new process should be validated with various settings of simulation parameters.
2. **Small introduction**: Before totally introducing the new process, it should be partially tested, if possible. This field test can involve small number of key persons and agents used at the previous simulation stage. At this stage, user models of key persons are verified. If their user models are different from those at the previous stage, the models are modified and the simulation should be retried.
3. **Beta testing**: If the small introduction stage was successful, the new process is totally introduced to the real field. New data with the new process are captured by a GADB. These new data should be compared to the data taken at the simulation stage. If user and process behaviors are much different from those supposed at the simulation stage, simulation should be retried with new data. According to the new simulation results, another reengineering will be sometimes necessary.

6   Conclusion

This paper proposes the concept of Group Activity Database (GADB), which is aimed at supporting groupware evolution, i.e. reengineering and simulation of business processes. It can also support team awareness functions if the data are visualized to group members.

We are now implementing the simulation engine and framework of GADB. Current design is based on usual RDB, but temporal database would also be suitable. Detailed specification of required queries and analyses and visualization of captured data are next important research issues.

Acknowledgement

Part of this work is supported by the Japanese Ministry of Science and Education, Grant-in-Aid for Scientific Research on Priority Areas (A), "Advanced Database Systems for Integration of Media and User Environments."

References

1. Bogia, D. P. and Kaplan, S. M.: Flexibility and Control for Dynamic Workflows in the wOrlds Environment. Proc. of Conf. on Organizational Computing Systems '95, ACM (1995) 148–159
2. Borghoff, U.M., Bottoni, P., Mussio, P., and Pareschi, R.: Reflective Agents for Adaptive Workflows. Proc. of the 2nd Int. Conf. and Exhibition on Practical Application of Intelligent Agents and Multi-Agents (PAAM'97), London, UK, (1997) 405–420
3. Ellis, C., Keddara, K., and Rozenberg, G. : Dynamic Change Within Workflow Systems. Proc. of Conf. on Organizational Computing Systems '95, ACM (1995) 10–21
4. Fonseca, J.M., de Oliveira, E., and Steiger-Garção, A.: MACIV, A DAI Based Resource Management System. Proc. of the 1st Int. Conf. and Exhibition on Practical Application of Intelligent Agents and Multi-Agents (PAAM'96), London, UK, (1996) 263–277
5. Geppert, A. and Tombros, D.: Logging and Post-Moretm Analysis of Workflow Executions based on Event Histories. Proc. of 3rd Int. Workshop on Rules in Database Systems (RIDS), Lecture Notes in Computer Science 1312, (1997) 67–82
6. Grudin, J.: Groupware and Social Dynamics: Eight Challenges for Developers. Comm. ACM 37(1) (1994) 92–105
7. Herrmann, T.: Workflow Management Systems: Ensuring Organizational Flexibility by Possibilities of Adaption and Negotiation. Proc. of Conf. Organizational Computing Systems '95, ACM (1995) 83–94
8. Holt, A.: Organized Activity and Its Support by Computer. Kluwer Academic (1997)
9. Ishiguro, Y, Tarumi, H., Asakura, T, Kusui, D, and Yoshifu, K : An Agent Architecture for Personal and Group Work Support. Proc. of Int. Conf. on Multi Agent Systems '96, (1996) 134–141
10. Jaeger, T. and Prakash, A.: Management and Utilization of Knowledge for the Automatic Improvement of Workflow Performance. Proc. of Conf. on Organizational Computing Systems '95, ACM (1995) 32–43
11. Jennings, N.R., et al.: Using Intelligent Agents to Manage Business Processes. Proc. of the 1st Int. Conf. and Exhibition on Practical Application of Intelligent Agents and Multi-Agents (PAAM'96) London, UK (1996) 345–360
12. Jennings, N.R., et al.: Agent-Based Process Management. Int. J. of Cooperative Information Systems 5(2-3) (1996) 105–130
13. Konomi, S., Yokota, Y., Sakata, K. and Kambayashi, Y.: Cooperative View Mechanisms in Distributed Multiuser Hypermedia Environments. Proc. of 2nd IFCIS Int. Conf. on Cooperative Information Systems (CoopIS'97) (1997) 15–24
14. Matsumoto, Y. and Ajisaka, T. : A Data Model in the Software Project Database KyotoDB. Advances in Software Science and Technology bf 2, Japan Society for Software Science and Technology (1990) 103–121
15. McGuire, F., Using Simulation to Reduce Length of Stay in Emergency Departments. Proc. of the 1994 Winter Simulation Conference (1994) 861–867
16. Medina-Mora, R., Winograd, T., et al.: The Action Workflow Approach to Workflow Management Technology. The Information Society 9 (1993) 391–404
17. Pan, J.Y.C. and Tenenbaum, J.M.: An Intelligent Agent Framework for Enterprise Integration. Trans. on Systems, Man, and Cybernetics 21(6) (1991) 1391–1408

18. Poltrock, S.E. and Engelbeck, G.: Requirements for a Virtual Collocation Environment. Proc. of ACM Int. Conf. on Supporting Group Work (Group'97) (1997) 61–70

19. Prinz, W. and Kolvenbach, S.: Support for Workflows in a Ministerial Environment. Proc. of Conf. on Computer Supported Cooperative Work (CSCW'96), ACM (1996) 199–208

20. Streitz, N.A., Geißer, J., Haake, J.M., and Hol, J.: DOLPHIN: Integrated Meeting Support across Local and Remote Desktop Environments and LiveBoards. Proc. of Conf. on Computer Supported Cooperative Work (CSCW'94), ACM (1994) 345–358

21. Swenson, K.D.: Visual Support for Reengineering Work Processes. Proc. of Conf. on Organizational Computing Systems, ACM (1993) 130–141

22. Tarumi, H., Kida, K., Ishiguro, Y., Yoshifu, K., and Asakura, T.: WorkWeb System — Multi-Workflow Management with a Multi-Agent System. Proc. of ACM Int. Conf. on Supporting Group Work (Group'97) (1997) 299-308

23. Tumay, K.: Business Process Simulation. Proc. of the 1995 Winter Simulation Conference (1995) 55–60

24. Tumay, K.: Business Process Simulation. Proc. of the 1996 Winter Simulation Conference (1996) 93–98

25. http://orgwis.gmd.de/projects/POLITeam/design/

Supporting Collaborative Work
by Process-Based Transaction Model

Tetsuya Furukawa[†], Haiyan Xu[‡], and Yihua Shi[††]

[†] Kyushu University, Japan
[‡] Fukuoka Institute of Technology, Japan
[††] Fukuoka Junior College of Technology, Japan

Abstract. Collaborative work presupposes information exchange among participants. In contrast, traditional transaction technologies allow concurrent users to operate on shared data, while providing them with the illusion of complete isolation from each other. To overcome this gap, this paper introduces a process-based transaction model, in which each subtransaction called a toolkit guarantees the consistency of transactions. Based on this transaction model, we discuss the correctness criterion of collaborative work formally and propose a concurrency control protocol and a recovery protocol to support collaborative work. The protocols permit users to exchange information with each other and to relieve the loss of result problem.

1 Introduction

Since sharing data is one of the most important characteristics of cooperative working environments, there has been growing interest in supporting collaborative work in advanced database applications like CAD/CAM and software engineering. To handle these applications, database researchers have concentrated mainly on developing advanced transaction models.

Traditionally, a transaction is the execution of database operations for which the database management system (DBMS) guarantees atomicity, consistency, isolation, and durability (*ACIDity*) properties [7, 10]. Application programs are responsible for the consistency of transactions. Both the consistency of schedules and the isolation property are ensured by concurrency control protocols based on serializability. Recovery protocols, on the other hand, take care of the atomicity and durability properties. However, the traditional transaction technology has the following problems in dealing with advanced database applications [5].

- Cooperation problem: In conventional DBMSs, serializability is the correctness criterion of concurrency control. In advanced database applications, transactions are long-lived. A long-lived transaction may access many data items in the course of its execution. The serializability of schedules severely restricts much cooperation by requiring the isolation of uncommitted transaction results. However, in cooperative working environments, there is a specific requirement to exchange the latest result among users during their activities. Blocking operations from reading the latest results over a significant period is a serious problem.

– Loss of result problem: A long-lived transaction is more easily interrupted by failures or deadlocks because of its long execution time. When a failure or deadlock occurs, a transaction has to be rolled back because of the atomicity property, undoing the effects of the transaction on the database. That is not acceptable for long-lived transactions because accumulated result will be lost if the transaction is aborted.

Using the semantics defined by each transaction, the notion of serializability can be weakened by extending the definition of equivalence between concurrent execution [1], or by describing the allowable interleaving among transactions [6, 8]. The nested transaction model provides a framework for decomposing a transaction hierarchically to decrease units of transactions which are required to be serializable or rolled back [11]. However, neither problem has been satisfactorily solved.

Adopting a process-centered approach, workflow management consisting of activities involving the coordinated execution of multiple performed by different processing entities, is emerging as a technique for modeling, executing, and monitoring such advanced applications [4]. Workflow management systems (WFMSs) use a process-centered (scheduler-based) approach, in which a task defines some work to be done. An abstract model of a task is a state automation whose behavior can be defined by providing its state transition diagram.

Although WFMSs are deployed to handle some real world applications, they still have several limitations [13, 15]. Some of these deficiencies are lack of a clear theoretical basis, undefined correctness criteria, limited support for concurrency control, and insufficient support for recovery. The transaction management approach, on the other hand, is based on a strong theoretical basis.

Our approach makes use of features of WFMSs to improve the modeling and execution support of transaction management. By associating states with data, in this paper, we introduce a process-based transaction model. Based on the transaction model, we propose a correctness criterion for collaborative work and show that the isolation property can be defined without depending on serializability. Based on the correctness criterion, a concurrency control protocol and a recovery protocol are proposed. The protocols allow users both to exchange their latest result as well as to relieve the loss of result problem.

The paper is organized as follows. Section 2 illustrates the method which makes subtransactions of process-based transactions responsible for consistency. Section 3 defines the correctness of schedules formally. In Section 4, a concurrency control protocol to ensure the correctness is proposed, permitting nonserializable execution. Section 5 introduces a recovery protocol which only aborts a part of a transaction when the transaction fails, and shows that the protocol makes the schedules cascading abort free.

2 Consistency of Databases

A fundamental problem with many transaction models is that they do not provide support for application-specified semantics, where transactions are modeled as a series of read and write operations on primitive data items in a database. The ultimate goal of concurrency control is to maintain the consistency of databases. In such models, a transaction is both the unit of consistency and the unit of work.

Application-specified semantics allows us to define the consistency of databases by associating states with data. The operations of a transaction can be divided to the sets of operations which maintain consistency of the database. If such sets of operations are the unit of consistency, serializability is no longer the correctness criterion of concurrency control. In this section, we introduce the toolkit providing the consistency.

Data in a database are *objects*. Each object o consists of two parts, the *entity part* $e_1(o), e_2(o), \cdots, e_m(o)$ and the *state part* $st_1(o), st_2(o), \cdots, st_m(o)$. The value of $e_i(o)$ is the ith aspect of o, such as a specification, a logic design, a netlist, or a result of simulation for circuit design. The value of $st_i(o)$ expresses the state of the corresponding entity $e_i(o)$ by the truth value, true when $e_i(o)$ is valid and false otherwise $(1 \leq i \leq m)$. Entities and states are atomic elements used to access databases, called data items.

Objects are classified according to their structure so that the objects in a class have the same types of entities. Relationships exist among objects: e.g., o_i is a component of o_j. Let $r(o_i, o_j)$ be a relationship between objects o_i and o_j named r. Thus, a database is expressed by a pair $\mathcal{DB}\langle O, R \rangle$ of a set of classified objects O and a set of relationships R.

For an object o, its entities are generated and updated step by step in order. For example, specifications of a circuit are given, a logic design is made from the specifications, and so on. Moreover, there may be conditions of objects to be generated or updated: an entity of an object cannot be valid if the corresponding entities of its component objects are not valid.

Definition 1. *The generation order* of an object represents the order of the entities of the object. Every entity has to be generated corresponding to its previous entity. *The precondition* of a state is a logic formula of states and relationships. Every state can be valid when its precondition is satisfied.

Although we assume that an entity has only one previous entity in a generation order, the results of this paper can be extended to the case where an entity can have multiple previous entities.

Example 1. Let $\mathcal{DB}_1\langle O_1, R_1 \rangle$ be such a database as $O_1 = \{o_1, o_2, o_3\}$ and $R_1 = \{comp(o_1, o_2), comp(o_1, o_3)\}$, where $comp(x, y)$ is the relationship that y is a component of x. Each object has four entities $e_1(o), e_2(o), e_3(o)$, and $e_4(o)$, which represent specification document, logic circuit data, netlist file, and simulation results, respectively. The entities have their states $st_1(o), st_2(o), st_3(o)$, and $st_4(o)$, which express o has completed these respective tasks.

The generation order of this example is illustrated in Figure 1. The precondition of $st_4(o_1)$ is $st_4(x) \wedge comp(o_1, x)$, while there is no precondition for the other states of o_1.

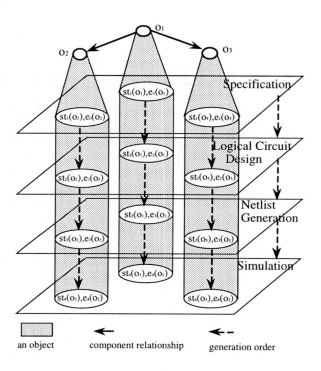

Fig. 1. Generation order

The consistency of a database requires that each state corresponds to the current value of its entity. For example, suppose logic circuit data $e_2(o_1)$ of Example 1 is changed because its simulation fails. Thus, $e_2(o_1)$ after the update is no longer the logic circuit data from which netlist file $e_3(o_1)$ was generated. If the value of $st_3(o_1)$ is still true, $\mathcal{DB}_1$ is not consistent.

By using states to express whether entities are valid, the consistency of a database can be defined formally.

Definition 2. A database is consistent if each state corresponds to the current value of its entity and the objects satisfy

- consistency in an object: if the state of an entity in an object is true, the state of the previous entity in the generation order is also true, and

– consistency among related objects: if the state of an entity in an object is true, the precondition of the state is satisfied.

An update of an entity must maintain the consistency of databases. We introduce below the toolkits to guarantee such consistency.

Definition 3. For an update of an entity $e_i(o)$ or a state $st_i(o)$, the toolkit of the update is organized by adding the following state operations.

– Update the state of $e_i(o)$: When $e_i(o)$ is updated, the old state of $e_i(o)$ has to be updated according to the current $e_i(o)$.
– Check the ability of state updates: The state $st_i(o)$ can be set to true when the preconditions of $st_i(o)$ are satisfied and the state of the previous entity in the generation order is also true.
– Propagate the update of the state: When the state $st_i(o)$ is set to false, the states of the subsequent entities in the generation order are set to false. Those states whose preconditions become not satisfied because of the updates are recursively set to false.

Example 2. For the database $\mathcal{DB}_1$, the toolkits include the following state operations to update the entities.

– $edit(x)$: edit the logic circuit $e_2(x)$ of object x
  precondition: *empty*
  state operations: set $st_2(x)$ according to $e_2(x)$ and set $st_3(x)$ and $st_4(x)$ false
– $netlist(x)$: generate the netlist file $e_3(x)$ of object x
  precondition: *empty*
  state operation: set $st_3(x)$ according to $e_3(x)$ and set $st_4(x)$ false
– $simulate(x)$: write the simulation result $e_4(x)$ of object x
  precondition: $st_4(y) \wedge comp(x, y)$
  state operations: set $st_4(x)$ according to $e_4(x)$, set $st_4(y)$ false for $comp(y, x)$
  if $st_4(x)$ is set to false, and recursively set $st_4(z)$ false for $comp(z, y)$

The state operations of $edit(x)$ and $netlist(x)$ maintain consistency in an object. The precondition of $simulate(x)$ assures that an object can be successfully simulated when all of its components have been so. The state operations of $simulate(x)$ set the states to false because the objects which have x as a component have not been simulated with the current x.

In order to discuss the concurrent execution of toolkits, each toolkit is presented as a sequence of read and write operations on data items in the rest of this paper. A toolkit of an entity reads the previous entity, the state of the entity, and the states appearing in the precondition; writes the entity and the state; and may write states of other entities.

Let $R(x)$ and $W(x)$ denote a read operation and a write operation on a data item x, respectively. Since a state has truth value, a write operation on a state x can be distinguished by its written value when the value to be written is known.

Let $W_T(x)$ and $W_F(x)$ be the write operations of true and false on a state x, respectively.

Example 3. The operations of the toolkits of $\mathcal{DB}_1$ are described as follows when the preconditions are satisfied.

- $edit(x)$:
  $R(st_1(x)), R(e_1(x)), R(e_2(x)), W(e_2(x)), W(st_2(x)), W_F(st_3(x)), W_F(st_4(x))$
- $netlist(x)$:
  $R(st_2(x)), R(e_2(x)), W(e_3(x)), W(st_3(x)), W_F(st_4(x))$
- $simulate(x)$:
  $R(st_3(x)), R(e_3(x)), \{R(st_4(y))$ for $comp(x,y)\}, W(e_4(x)), W(st_4(x))$,
  $\{$recursively $W_F(st_4(z))$ for $comp(z,x)$ if the value of $W(st_4(x))$ if false$\}$

Toolkits are write operations with some kind of triggers to maintain the database consistency. We conclude this section with the following theorem.

Theorem 4. *The execution of a toolkit maintains the consistency of the database.*

Proof. The state operations of a toolkit set the states of the objects so that the objects satisfy consistency both in an object and among related objects.

3 Process-based Transaction Model

In the conventional transaction model, a transaction is a sequence of read and write operations on data items. For advanced database applications, consistency of databases can be defined as discussed in Section 2, which allows us to introduce a process-based transaction model utilizing toolkits.

Definition 5. A toolkit transaction is that composed of operations of toolkits and read operations with a total or partial order.

For simplicity, we assume that a transaction has a total order, though the results of the paper can be easily extended to the case of partial orders.

The difference between the toolkit transaction model and the conventional transaction model is illustrated in Figure 2, where (a) is the conventional transaction model and (b) is the toolkit transaction model. The write operations of a conventional transaction are replaced with the corresponding toolkits in a toolkit transaction.

A concurrent execution of a set of transactions is called a schedule. When transactions are executed concurrently, the correct execution of the transactions is traditionally characterized by the following properties.

- *Atomicity:* All the operations of a transaction are executed, or none.
- *Consistency:* When a transaction is executed alone, the transaction takes the database from one consistent state to another (*consistency of transactions*); when a set of transactions is executed concurrently, the execution also maintains the consistency of the database (*consistency of schedules*).

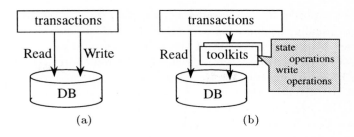

Fig. 2. Transaction model environment

- *Isolation:* Events within a transaction must be hidden from the other transactions running concurrently.
- *Durability:* The results of a committed transaction are made permanent in spite of failures.

In this section, we discuss the consistency and the isolation properties for toolkit transactions. The atomicity and the durability properties are related to the recovery problem as discussed in Section 5.

In the conventional transaction model, transactions are expected to satisfy the consistency of transactions. In other words, users have to organize a transaction so as to make the transaction consistent. If consistency of a database can be defined as shown in Section 2 and we adopt the toolkit transaction model, transactions are consistent without users' control.

Theorem 6. *A toolkit transaction is consistent.*

Proof. Suppose a transaction is executed alone in a consistent database. Theorem 4 shows that each toolkit of the transaction takes a consistent database to another consistent database. The toolkit transaction consequently results in a consistent database.

Let $T = \{T_1, T_2, \cdots, T_n\}$ be a set of toolkit transactions. *A schedule H over T* is the set of all operations of T_i, read operations of T_i and read and write operations of the toolkits of T_i, with total order $<_H$ such that $<_H$ preserves the total order of operations of T_i.

Two operations are said to conflict if they both operate on the same data item and at least one of them is a write operation. Thus, $R_i(x)$ conflicts with $W_j(x)$ while $W_i(x)$ conflicts with both $R_j(x)$ and $W_j(x)$. Two schedules H and H' over the same set of transactions are equivalent if they order conflicting operations in the same way.

If the transactions are consistent, a serial execution of the transactions maintains the database consistency, and each transaction retrieves data of a consistent database. If a schedule over a set of consistent transactions T is equivalent to a serial execution of T, the schedule is consistent. Such a schedule is called *serializable*. Usually the consistency of schedules and isolation of transactions are guaranteed by concurrency control protocols based on the serializability.

A process-based transaction model, i.e., the toolkit transaction model, assures a database of its consistency. If primitive level operations of toolkits are not executed concurrently, the database is always consistent because every toolkit takes the database from a consistent state to another consistent state. We call such schedule a toolkit level serial schedule. Toolkits can be executed concurrently if the consistency of the database is maintained.

Theorem 7. *For a set of toolkit transactions T, a schedule H over T is a consistent schedule if H is a toolkit level serializable schedule, i.e., H is equivalent to a toolkit level serial schedule.*

Proof. Suppose H is equivalent to a toolkit level serial schedule H'. Since H' is a serial execution of the toolkits, H' maintains the consistency of the database by Theorem 4. Thus, the equivalent schedule H is consistent.

Example 4. Figure 3 shows an example of a toolkit level serial schedule H_1 executed in database $\mathcal{DB}_1$ of Example 1 with the toolkits shown in Example 2, where t_i denotes the time of the execution. Since the primitive level operations of the toolkits are not executed concurrently, H_1 can be described with the toolkits as Figure 3 (a) while Figure 3 (b) shows the operations of H_1 in the primitive operation level.

Schedule H_1 of Example 4 is equivalent to neither serial executions $T_1 T_2$ nor $T_2 T_1$ due to $W_1(e_3(o_2)) <_{H_1} R_2(e_3(o_2))$ and $W_2(e_4(o_2)) <_{H_1} R_1(e_4(o_2))$. H_1 shows the difference between toolkit level serializable schedules and serializable schedules over transactions. In CAD/CAM applications, non-serializable executions such as H_1 are the essential cooperative works, where transactions refer to each other the latest intermediate results.

In order to solve this problem, we discuss the definition of the isolation property, which is guaranteed by serializability of transactions in conventional databases. In databases having consistency information, the isolation property of transactions is replaced with the following formal definition.

Definition 8. Let H be a schedule over a set of toolkit transactions T. H is equivalent to a schedule H' in which

- each transaction T in T is a *self-executed* if the entities accessed by T are not updated by other transactions in T until T is committed and if the states read or updated to true by T are not set to false until T is committed, and
- each transaction T in T is *retrieval consistent* if T retrieves data items of a consistent database.

The self-execution property separates entities from states. A transaction T_i is self-executed even if a false state read by T_i is updated to true by another

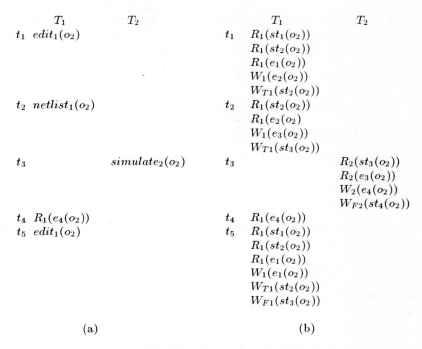

Fig. 3. Toolkit level serial schedule H_1

transaction T_j before T_i is committed. The work of a transaction is not disturbed by other transactions if the transaction is self-executed.

The isolation property of the conventional transaction model is performed by self-execution and retrieval consistency properties in the toolkit transaction model. Therefore, serializability is no longer the correctness criterion of schedules.

Definition 9. A schedule H over a set of transactions T is correct if

- each transaction of T is consistent,
- H is consistent,
- H is equivalent to a schedule H' where every transaction is self-executed, and
- every transaction in T is retrieval consistent.

Example 5. Schedule H_1 of the running example is a correct schedule because

- toolkit transaction T_1 and T_2 are consistent by Theorem 6,
- H_1 is consistent due to Theorem 7,
- T_1 and T_2 are self-executed by Definition 8, and

– both T_1 and T_2 are retrieval consistent since the databases retrieved by T_1 and T_2 are consistent by Theorem 7.

4 Reducing Lock Protocol

In this section, we propose a concurrency control protocol to ensure the correctness of schedules.

We use two kinds of locks, exclusive locks and shared locks on a data item x.

– When a shared lock is placed on x by a transaction, the other transactions can read x but cannot write x until x is unlocked.
– When an exclusive lock is placed on x by a transaction, the other transactions cannot read or write x until x is unlocked.

$Rl_i(x)$ and $Wl_i(x)$ denote a shared lock and an exclusive lock on x of transaction T_i, respectively. $Ru_i(x)$ and $Wu_i(x)$ denote the unlock operations by which T_i releases its shared lock and exclusive lock on x, respectively. We use $W_T l_i(x)$ as the lock operation for $W_{Ti}(x)$ and $W_F l_i(x)$ for $W_{Fi}(x)$.

Definition 10. The reducing lock protocol (RL protocol, for short) consists of the following rules.

1. A lock cannot be set on a data item x if x already has a conflicting lock.
2. A read operation $R(x)$ and a write operation $W(x)$ $(W_F(x), W_T(x))$ must be proceeded by the locking actions, a shared lock and an exclusive lock on x, respectively, i.e., $Rl(x) < R(x)$ and $Wl(x) < W(x)$ $(W_F l(x) < W_F(x),$ $W_T l(x) < W_T(x))$.
3. Exclusive locks $Wl(x)$, $W_T l(x)$, and $W_F l(x)$ are reduced into a shared lock $Rl(x)$ after the execution of the toolkit.
4. Every shared lock is released at the committed time of the transaction.

A schedule H over a set of transactions $\boldsymbol{T}$ is a reduced lock schedule (an RL schedule, for short) if locks and unlocks can be inserted to H so as to satisfy the reducing lock protocol.

Compared with the conventional strict 2PL protocol [3], RL protocol is less limited to lock data items as exclusive locks can be reduced to shared locks before unlock. For the recovery problem discussed in Section 5, we assume that shared locks are released at the committed time as for the strict 2PL protocol described in Rule 4. This assumption can be relieved for this discussion as the last lock action of a transaction must proceed the first release of shared lock of the transaction, like the ordinary 2PL protocol.

Example 6. Schedule H_1 is an RL schedule because locks and unlocks can be inserted according to RL protocol.

Some properties of schedule H can be got from the properties of the equivalent schedule of H. Toolkit level serial schedules are suitable to such equivalent schedules.

Lemma 11. *For an RL schedule H over a set of toolkit transactions T, there exists a toolkit level serial schedule equivalent to H.*

Proof. Let T' be the set of transactions consisting of one toolkit such that the toolkits appearing in T' also appear in T. An RL schedule H over T is a strict 2PL schedule over T' because it is the end of the toolkits that the exclusive locks are reduced to the corresponding shared locks. A strict 2PL schedule over T' is equivalent to a serial execution over T' [3], which can be regarded as a toolkit level serial schedule. Thus, for an RL schedule H over T, there exists a toolkit level serial schedule equivalent to H.

Using Lemma 11, we can prove that an RL schedule is both a consistent schedule and retrieval consistent, which leads us to the concluding theorem of this section.

Theorem 12. *An RL schedule H over a set of toolkit transactions T is correct.*

Proof. By Lemma 11, there is a toolkit level serial schedule H' equivalent to H. Since H' is consistent as shown in Theorem 7, equivalent schedule H is consistent. Every transaction of H' is self-executed because the exclusive locks still remain as the corresponding shared locks until the end of the transaction, which prevent the other transactions from writing the updated data items.

The shared locks also assure retrieval consistency of the transactions in H', because, at the beginning of a toolkit, the database is consistent as shown by Theorem 7, and the values of data items locked by the shared locks are unchanged. Thus, in the equivalent schedule H to H', every transaction is also retrieval consistent. Since a toolkit transaction is consistent as shown in Theorem 6, an RL schedule H over a set of toolkit transactions is a schedule over a set of consistent transactions. Hence schedule H is correct.

5   Recovery Protocol

When a transaction T is interrupted by a failure or falls into a deadlock, the partial effect of T on the database must be eliminated to guarantee the consistency of the database. In conventional databases, a transaction is consistent only if all of its operations are executed; that is, a transaction is a unit of consistency as well as a unit of work. When a failure or a deadlock occurs, the effects of uncommitted transactions have to be aborted since a transaction is the unit of atomicity.

Recovery protocol is used to ensure atomicity of transactions. In our toolkit transaction model, the consistency of transactions can be guaranteed by the toolkits. The effect of committing toolkits will not break the consistency of the transaction; i.e., the consistency of the schedule is maintained. This allows toolkits to be the unit of the atomicity.

Definition 13. The recovery protocol of a transaction for an RL schedule is the protocol that aborts the toolkit being executed.

As demonstrated in H_1, RL protocol permits users to retrieve the results of finished toolkits. In general, if a transaction T_i reads a data item which is written by an uncommitted transaction T_j, abortion of T_j leads to cascading abortion of T_i, even if T_i is committed. That is, it may make the loss of result problem badly and violate the durability property.

The recovery protocol for RL protocol, however, both assures the atomicity of toolkits and reduces the unit of the durability property from the transaction to the toolkit.

Theorem 14. *The results of a committed toolkit are made permanent in spite of failures by the recovery protocol for RL schedules.*

Proof. By Definition 10 of RL schedules, only the results of finished toolkits can be read by other transactions. The finished toolkits, however, are not required to be aborted by Definition 13 of recovery protocol for RL schedules. As a result, when the transactions are interrupted by a failure or fall into a deadlock, cascading aborts are avoided; thus, toolkits have the property of durability.

In conventional database management systems, avoidance of cascading aborts is obtained at the expense of reduced concurrency. Using this process-based transaction model, we solve the problems of both concurrency control and recovery efficiently.

6   Conclusions

In this paper, we have solved the problems of supporting collaborative work such as CAD/CAM databases in the following ways.

1. The method of composing process-based transactions, in which toolkits are responsible for consistency, was shown.
2. To ensure the correctness of collaborative work, a correctness criterion which makes use of the semantics of collaborative work was proposed.
3. To implement the correctness criterion, both a concurrency control protocol and a recovery protocol were introduced. The concurrency control protocol permits non-serializable cooperative executions in which transactions refer to each other the latest intermediate result. The recovery protocol relieves the loss of result problem.

Acknowledgment

This work is partly supported by the Grant-in-Aid for Scientific Research of the Ministry of Education, Science, Sports and Culture of Japan.

References

1. Agrawal, D., Abbadi, A. E., and Singh, A. K.: Consistency and Orderability: Semantics-Based Correctness Criteria for Databases, *ACM Trans. Database Syst.*, Vol. 18, No. 3, pp. 460–486 (1993).
2. Barghouti, N. S. and Kaiser, G. E.: Concurrency Control in Advanced Database Applications, *ACM Comput. Surv.*, Vol. 23, No. 3, pp. 269–317 (1991).
3. Bernstein, P. A., Hadzilacos, V., and Goodman, N.: *Concurrency Control and Recovery in Database Systems*, Addison-Wesley (1987).
4. Cichocki, A., Helal, A., Rusinkiewicz, M., and Woelk, D.: *Workflow and Process Automation: Concepts and Technology*, Kluwer (1998).
5. Elmagarmid, A. K. (ed.): *Database Transaction Models for Advanced Applications*, Morgan Kaufmann (1992).
6. Frrg, A. A. and Ozsu, M. T.: Using Semantic Knowledge of Transactions to Increase Concurrency, *ACM Trans. Database Syst.*, Vol. 14, No. 4, pp. 503–525 (1989).
7. Gray, J.: The Transaction Concept: Virtues and Limitations, *Proc. Int. Conf. on Very Large Data Bases*, pp. 144–154 (1981).
8. Garcia-Molina, H.: Using Semantic Knowledge for Transaction Processing in a Distributed Database, *ACM Trans. Database Syst.*, Vol. 8, No. 2, pp. 186–213 (1983).
9. Garcia-Molina, H. and Salem, K.: Sagas, *Proc. ACM SIGMOD Int. Conf. on Management of Data*, pp. 249–258 (1987).
10. Haerder, T., and Reuter, A.: Principles of Transaction-Oriented Database Recovery, *ACM Comput. Surv.*, Vol. 15 No. 4, pp. 287–317 (1983).
11. Nodine, M. H., Ramaswamy, S., and Zdonik, S. B.: A Cooperative Transaction Model for Design Databases, in [5], pp. 53–83 (1992).
12. Ramamritham, K. and Chrysanthis, P. K.: *Advances in Concurrency Control and Transaction Processing*, IEEE Computer Society Executive Briefing (1996).
13. Rusinkiewicz, M. and Sheth, A.: Specification and Execution of Transactional Workflows, in *Modern Database Systems* (Kim, W. (ed.)), Addison-Wesley (1994).
14. Weikum, G. and Schek, H.-J.: Concepts and Applications of Multilevel Transactions and Open Nested Transactions, in [5], pp. 516–553 (1992).
15. Worah, D., Sheth, A.: Transactions in Transactional Workflows, in *Advanced Transaction Models and Architectures* (Jajodia, S. and Kerschberg, L. (eds.)), Kluwer (1997).

A Cooperative Distributed Text Database Management Method Unifying Search and Compression Based on the Burrows-Wheeler Transformation

Kunihiko Sadakane   Hiroshi Imai

Department of Information Science, University of Tokyo
7-3-1 Hongo, Bunkyo-ku, Tokyo 113-0033, JAPAN
{sada,imai}@is.s.u-tokyo.ac.jp

Abstract. A new text database management method for distributed cooperative environments is proposed, which can collect texts in distributed sites through a network of narrow bandwidth and enables full-text search in a unified efficient manner. This method is based on the two new developments in full-text search data structures and data compression. Specifically, the Burrows-Wheeler transformation is used as a basis of constructing the suffix array (or, PAT array) for full-text search and of performing the block sorting compression scheme. A cooperative environment makes it possible to employ these new methods in a uniform fashion. This framework may be also used in future for the Web text collection/search problem. The paper first describes this method, and then provides preliminary computational results concerning I/O implementation of suffix arrays and performing the suffix sorting. These preliminary computational results indicate practicality of our method.

1 Introduction

We propose a text database management method for distributed cooperative environments. In a cooperative environment, each user works at his private space and his data are transferred to a common database shared by all users.

To search data from the common database, a search data structure is required. We treat text data such as source codes and documents. The suffix array (Manber and Myers [8]) or the PAT array (Gonnet, Baeza-Yates and Snider [6]) is a memory-efficient data structure for searching any substring of a text. The PAT array is used for text databases (Yoshikawa, Kato, Kinutani and Watanabe [11]) and we also use it for the common database. For full-text databases, the String B-tree (Ferragina and Grossi [5]) has good worst-case performance. However, its size is more than two times larger than the suffix array and therefore we use the suffix array.

To collect data of each user via narrow bandwidth networks, compression of data is necessary. Moreover, it is desirable that we could transfer a data structure for search at a low communication cost because a huge suffix array is constructed in the common database which is a very time-consuming task to overcome.

As a compression scheme, we propose using the Block sorting compression. The Block sorting is a general-purpose compression algorithm (Burrows and Wheeler [2]). It is suitable for text data and its compression ratio is better than the `gzip`. Though some compression algorithms achieve slightly better compression than the Block sorting, they require much CPU time and memory. Compression by the Block sorting takes more time than the `gzip`. However, decoding speed is fast enough for common use. Moreover, Sadakane [9] proposed a fast algorithm for the Block sorting compression.

In addition to good compression ratio and encoding/decoding speed of the Block sorting, we find its nice feature, which is the relation between encoding/decoding process and suffix array. In the encoder of the Block sorting, text symbols are permuted according to the suffix array. The permutation is called the Burrows-Wheeler transformation. In the decoder, the reverse transformation is computed and therefore the suffix array is also made. Using the interesting features of the Block sorting, we can newly unify search and compression in distributed environments. We transfer a text in compressed form and the common database server decodes it and gets the original text and its suffix array into memory and merges it into a large suffix array in disk (see Figure 1).

To realize our method, we have to overcome two difficulties. One is compression time for private data in local sites and the other is merging time in the common database server. Compression ratio of the Block sorting becomes better as the size of data grows. Each user should collect his data into one datum and compress it and send it to the server, that is a cooperative work. Because the size of data in the common database is huge, we have to incrementally update the database when new data arrives. The updating becomes an I/O algorithm using a disk. In this paper we show experimental results on suffix sorting on memory and we also propose a suffix array merging algorithm on disk. Our merging algorithm is faster than Gonnet et al. We find that our management method utilizing Sadakane's suffix sorting algorithm and a new merging algorithm proposed in this paper is practical for large text databases, for example Web search engines and genome databases, which are confirmed by experiments.

2 Text collecting method using the Burrows-Wheeler transformation

In this section we first explain the suffix array briefly and describe relationship between the Block sorting compression and the suffix array and modify the decoding algorithm. Next we propose a text collecting method unifying search and compression using the relationship. For a search data structure we use the suffix array and for a data compression scheme we use the Block sorting.

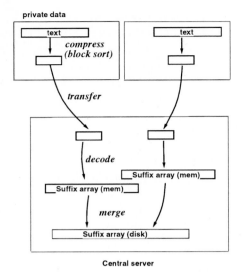

Fig. 1. Text collecting method

2.1 Suffix array

The suffix array is a memory-efficient data structure for searching any substring of a text. It is an array of indices. The indices represent suffixes of the text and they are sorted in lexicographic order of suffixes. A text T of length n is represented by $T[1..n]$ and its i-th suffix is $T_i = T[i..n]$. We assume that the text has a unique terminator \$, i.e. $T[n] = \$$. The suffix array of T is an array $I[1..n]$ and if $I[j] = i$ then the suffix T_i is lexicographically j-th suffix. Searching is done by a binary search on the array. Because each comparison in the binary search is string comparison, searching a string of length m takes $O(m \log_2 n)$ time. The suffix array requires only $5n$ bytes: n for T and $4n$ for I. Therefore it is suitable for large text databases.

2.2 The Block sorting and the suffix array

We use the Block sorting compression for transferring texts. The encoder of Block sorting consists of three processes: the Burrows-Wheeler transformation, move-to-front encoding and entropy coding. The Burrows-Wheeler transformation is the most time-consuming process and it is defined by lexicographical order of suffixes of a text. Therefore in the encoder the suffix array I of a text T is calculated. The transformation is a permutation of text symbols and its output $L[1..n]$ is defined as follows:

1. $i = 1$
2. $j = I[i] - 1$, if $j = 0$ then $j = n$

3. $L[i] = T[j]$, $i = i + 1$, if $i \leq n$ goto 2

Though the transformation takes much time, its reverse transformation from L to T is quickly computed in linear time by a radix-sort-like procedure [2].

1. $C[0..255] = 0$, for $i = 1$ to n $P[i] = C[L[i]] + +$
2. $sum = 0$
3. for $ch = 0$ to 255 $sum = sum + C[ch]$, $C[ch] = sum - C[ch]$
4. $i = pos$
5. for $j = n$ to 1
6. $\quad$ $I[i] = j + 1$, if $I[i] = n + 1$ then $I[i] = 1$
7. $\quad$ $T[j] = L[i]$, $i = P[i] + C[L[i]]$

In this code, *pos* is the index of terminator $. In the procedure, only step 9 is added to the original. The suffix array is implicitly made in the original procedure and therefore we simply output it to an array I. Therefore we can search any substring from a compressed text immediately the compressed text is decoded.

2.3 Collecting method

By using the Burrows-Wheeler transformation, we can unify search and compression of text databases in distributed cooperative environments. When a user sends data in his private database to other person, he compresses the data by the Block sorting and transfer it. Person who received the compressed data decodes it and simultaneously he gets the suffix array of the data and he can search any substring by using the suffix array. When a user sends data to the common database, the Block sorting compression is also used. The server of the common database decodes the compressed data into memory and merges it into a large suffix array in disk (see Figure 1). In the decoding step we can get the suffix array of the data and therefore it is not necessary to recompute the suffix array. A typical application of this method is a cooperative Web search server. HTML files in a Web server are collected by a search robot and they are compressed and transferred to the central server. By archiving and compressing the files communication cost is highly reduced. In the next section we describe suffix array merging algorithms.

3 Suffix array merging algorithm

In this section we describe two suffix array merging algorithms. One is Gonnet, Baeza-Yates and Snider [6] and the other is our straightforward merging algorithm. The algorithms merge a small suffix array of size m on memory into a large suffix array of size n on disk.

If we create a suffix array on disk from scratch, we can use an efficient algorithm of Crauser and Ferragina [4]. However, our method requires incremental creation of a suffix array, which is very suitable for the management of texts incrementally collected from cooperatively working sites. We define variables as follows: $T_M[1..m]$ is a text on memory, $I_M[1..m]$ is its suffix array, $T_D[1..n]$ is a text on a disk and $I_D[1..n]$ is its suffix array.

3.1 Gonnet, Baeza-Yates and Snider algorithm

First we describe the merge algorithm of Gonnet et al. The algorithm consists of two passes: counting and merging. A feature of the algorithm is sequential disk access.

Counting In the first pass, each suffix of T_D is read and its lexicographical order in I_M is calculated. We use an additional integer array $C[0..m]$. After the first pass, $C[j]$ represents the number of suffixes of T_D which are between $T_M[I_M[j-1]..m]$ and $T_M[I_M[j]..m]$ in lexicographic order.

1. $C[0..m] = 0$, $s = 1, e = r$ (r is a constant)
2. read $T_D[s..e]$ into memory
3. for each suffix of T_D in memory $T_D[i..e]$ ($s \le i < s + r/2$)
   (a) find j s.t. $T_M[I_M[j-1]..m] < T_D[i..e] < T_M[I_M[j]..m]$ by binary search
   (b) add 1 to $C[j]$
4. slide $T_D[s+r/2..e]$ to the first half of buffer, read $T_D[e+1..e+r/2]$ into the latter half of the buffer and goto step 3

Merging In the second pass, I_M is merged into I_D according to the array $C[0..m]$. The result is written to a new array $I'_D[1..n+m]$.

1. $i = 0, j = 0, k = 0$
2. $c = C[i]$
3. copy $I_D[j..j+c-1]$ to $I'_M[k..k+c-1]$ and let $k = k + c$
4. copy $I_M[i] + M$ to $I'_M[k]$ and let $k = k + 1$
5. $i = i + 1, j = j + c$, if $i \le n$ then goto step 2

The number of disk accesses of the algorithm is as follows. The number of read is n/B times for T_D and $4n/B$ times for I_D and the number of write is m/B times for T_D and $4(n+m)/B$ times for I'_D. Therefore the total is $(9n + 5m)/B$ times. Note that the size of character in a text is one byte, the size of elements of arrays is four bytes, B is disk page size and T_M is appended to the last of T_D.

To create a suffix array of a text of size n on disk, we have to divide the text into pieces of size m, sort them in memory and merge into disk. Therefore total number of disk accesses becomes

$$\frac{5m}{B} + \frac{9m + 5m}{B} + \frac{2 \cdot 9m + 5m}{B} + \cdots + \frac{(n-m) \cdot 9 + 5m}{B} = \frac{5n}{B} + \frac{9n(n-m)}{2Bm}$$

and time complexity becomes

$$O(m \log_2 m \cdot (m + \cdots + (n-m))) = O(n^2 \log_2 m).$$

This algorithm requires $9m + 4$ bytes memory (m bytes for T_M, $4m$ bytes for I_M and $4(m+1)$ bytes for C).

3.2 Our algorithm

Next we describe our straightforward merging algorithm. It is also a two-pass algorithm which consists of counting and merging. However, counting is performed by not traversing all suffixes of T_D but traversing those of T_M.

1. $i = 0, C[m] = n$
2. $s = I_M[i]$
3. find j s.t. $T_D[I_D[j-1]..n] < T_M[s..m] < T_D[I_D[j]..n]$ by binary search
4. $C[i] = j, i = i+1$, if $i \le m$ goto step 2
5. $C[i] = C[i] - C[i-1]$ $(i = n, \cdots, 1)$

The second pass is the same as Gonnet et al. However, by writing elements of a new array I'_D from right to left, we can overwrite I'_D to I_D and therefore temporary disk space is not required. Moreover, the array C is not necessary if the merging step is combined with the counting step. This algorithm requires only $5m$ bytes memory (m bytes for T_M and $4m$ bytes for I_M).

The number of disk accesses to create a suffix array of size n becomes as follows. One binary search requires $2 \log_2 n$ disk accesses and therefore merging a suffix array of size m into that of size n requires $2m \log_2 n$ disk accesses in the counting pass and $(8n + 5m)/B$ disk accesses in the merging pass. Therefore total number of disk accesses is

$$2m(\log_2 m + \log_2(2m) + \cdots + \log_2(n-m)) + \frac{5n}{B} + \frac{8n(n-m)}{2Bm} \le 2n \log_2 n + \frac{5n}{B} + \frac{8n^2}{2Bm}.$$

Time complexity is

$$O(m \log_2 n \cdot m \cdot \frac{n}{m} + (m + 2m + \cdots + (n-m))) = O(mn \log_2 n + \frac{n^2}{m}).$$

Roughly speaking, the time complexity is reduced by a factor of n/m, that causes practical speedup and it is confirmed by experiments. Though this algorithm performs binary searches and therefore random disk accesses occur, its time complexity is less than Gonnet et al. Furthermore, most of disk accesses by the binary searches are cached because we process suffixes of T_M in lexicographic order.

Theorem 1. *We assume that the size of disk cache is more than $2B(\lceil \log_2 n \rceil + 1)$ bytes and in each string comparison in binary searches the number of symbol comparison is less than B. When we merge a suffix array I_M of size m for a text T_M on memory into a suffix array I_D of size n for a text T_D on disk by our algorithm, the number of disk accesses is at most $4n/B$ for the suffix array I_D on disk and at most n for the text T_D on disk.*

Proof. First we show that all nodes in a binary search tree are read once from disk and therefore the number of disk accesses for T_D is at most n. We search all suffixes of T_M from the suffix array I_D in lexicographic order. Therefore traverse of nodes of the binary search tree is in-order. After a node u in the search tree is read, all nodes in two subtrees of the node are read. While the subtrees are traversed, the node u is in disk cache and after the traverses u is not accessed any longer.

Next we show that the number of disk accesses for I_D is at most $4n/B$. For any search path from the root to a leaf of the search tree internal nodes of the search tree are always in disk cache. Leaves of the search tree are read from left to right and adjacent leaves are consecutively accessed. Therefore total number of disk accesses is equal to the number of disk pages for I_D. Because integer is 32bit, the size of I_D is $4n$ bytes.

For example, if $n = 256M$, $m > 10M$ and $B = 8192$, $4n/B \ll n < m(\log_2 n + 1)$. Therefore the number of disk accesses is reduced by disk cache of size $2B(\lceil \log_2 n \rceil + 1)$ bytes.

4 Experimental results

We have experimented on making suffix arrays in memory and on disks. We use a Sun Ultra30 workstation (UltraSPARC-II 296MHz) with 1GB memory running Solaris 2.5.1 and Ultra60 (UltraSPARC-II 360MHz) with 2GB memory running Solaris 2.6. To perform binary searches on disk, we use the mmap(2) system call. The page size is 8192 bytes. Read size for a binary search is therefore $\log n \cdot 8192 \cdot 2 \le 512Kbytes$. In our merging algorithm suffixes of a text T_M in memory are processed in lexicographic order. Therefore in the next binary search almost the same elements of I_D are accessed and they are in disk cache. In the merging step, disk is sequentially accessed and therefore we do not use the mmap. Though we can execute our algorithm without any temporary disk, it is slow because of property of the mmap. Therefore we use temporary disk space in the merging step.

Texts used in our experiments are HTML files and Genome databases. The HTML files are collected to a search server and files are frequently updated. The Genome databases are also updated when new part of DNA sequences are analyzed. Both files are merged into a suffix array on disk. Because the files are very large, compression of the files is necessary to transfer.

4.1 Genome databases

Suffix sorting in memory First we have experimented on making suffix arrays in memory. If we have enough memory to store a suffix array of a text, we can use a fast string sorting algorithm (Bentley and Sedgewick [1]) and a fast suffix sorting algorithm (Sadakane [9]). The former requires $5m$ bytes memory and the latter requires $9m$ bytes memory to make a suffix array of size m. Bentley-Sedgewick algorithm can make larger suffix array than Sadakane's algorithm in limited memory. As for merging suffix arrays, algorithms of Gonnet et al. and ours require $9m$ bytes memory. If we sort suffixes and merge their suffix array into another suffix array on the same workstation, we need not consider memory requirements of both sorting algorithms. Moreover, Bentley-Sedgewick algorithm will become very slow if a text contains many repeated substrings. We use a measure of difficulty of sorting suffixes: average match length (AML). The AML of a text is defined as

$$\text{AML} = \frac{1}{n} \sum_{i=1}^{n} \text{lcp}(I[i-1], I[i])$$

where n is the length of the text, I is the suffix array and *lcp* is the length of the longest common prefix of two strings. The value varies among texts and if it becomes large, Bentley-Sedgewick algorithm becomes very slow. On the other hand, Sadakane's algorithm is not affected much by the AML.

Table 1 shows experimental results of suffix sorting time (*user* time) and AML of texts on the Ultra 30 workstation. The texts are taken from a genome database of human (`ddbjhum.seq`) [3]. The database is a text of about 400M bytes and it consists of sequences of ATCG and their explanations in English. We use its first 170M bytes and divide it into 17 files of size 10M bytes. They are numbered 0 to 16. In the table, AML represents the AML of a file, BS and Sadakane represent sorting time by Bentley-Sedgewick and Sadakane's algorithm respectively. Though Bentley-Sedgewick algorithm is slightly faster than Sadakane's algorithm when AML is small, it becomes very slow when AML is large. On the other hand, sorting time by Sadakane's algorithm is stable.

Table 1. sorting time and AML

file		sorting time (s)		file		sorting time (s)	
No.	AML	BS	Sadakane	No.	AML	BS	Sadakane
0	45.8	89.6	49.4	9	35.3	59.3	48.2
1	26.4	56.4	49.4	10	55.3	83.4	48.7
2	21.4	48.8	50.1	11	81.0	109.0	49.8
3	19.0	45.9	49.3	12	178.6	170.2	50.9
4	18.8	45.8	49.3	13	137.4	215.4	54.7
5	20.6	48.0	50.0	14	180.5	270.1	58.4
6	19.8	47.3	49.3	15	75.0	118.8	50.9
7	22.5	50.0	49.0	16	85.2	132.8	51.6
8	20.1	48.1	49.0				

Merging suffix arrays into disk Next we experimented on merging suffix arrays into disk on the Ultra60 workstation. Time is not *user* time but elapsed time measured by `rusage` command. First we merge the text database of human genome 10M bytes at a time.

Figure 2 shows merging time of BGS and our algorithm. Line graphs show totals of merging times of each merging step. A text is divided into pieces of size m and they are merged into the large suffix array on a disk one by one. The value of m is 10M, 20M, 40M, 80M and 160M bytes. In the figure, *BGS* shows total time of BGS and *Ours* shows total time of our algorithm. Total time of BGS is reduced as the m becomes large. The reason is as follows. The second pass is $O(n^2/m)$ time and it is inversely proportional to m. Though the first pass is $O(n^2 \log_2 m)$ time, in average case it depends on the number of symbol comparisons in string comparison functions. The number of symbol comparisons is proportional to the AML. We assume that two texts whose suffix arrays are merged have the same probability distributions of symbols. The first pass becomes $O((\text{AML}/m)n^2 \log_2 m)$ time and it is inversely proportional to m.

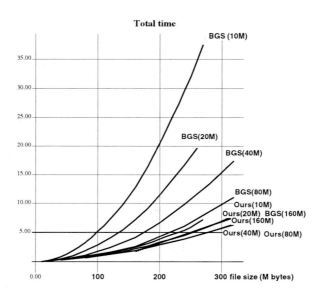

Fig. 2. Merging time

On the other hand, total time of our algorithm is not much affected. The first pass is $O(mn \log_2 n)$ time in the worst case and $O(\text{AML} \cdot n \log_2 n)$ time in the average. The latter does not depend on m.

The Ultra60 workstation has 2G byte memory. Our merging algorithms requires $5m$ byte memory and the rest of the memory is used for disk cache. Therefore many of accesses to the text T_D are cached. To examine effects of disk cache, we allocate a dummy space of size 1.5G on memory by using `mlock` function. Therefore we can use only 512M bytes. Table 2 shows merging time of our algorithm. The first row shows available memory and other rows show total time in seconds to make a suffix array of a text of size 240M. The value m, unit of merging, is 10M and 40M. Our algorithm becomes 2.98 times slower when

$m = 10M$ and 2.55 times slower then $m = 40M$ if available memory is 512M. In our algorithm the text T_D on disk is accessed randomly and therefore it becomes slower if available memory for disk cache is small. However, our algorithm is still faster than BGS.

Table 2. Available memory and merging time

main memory	ours(10M)	BGS(10M)	ours(40M)	BGS(40M)
2048M	5407.70	29678.6	3848.11	9870.68
512M	16119.7	46269.3	9816.64	21857.3

Our algorithm is fast when $m = 80M$ and it becomes slower when $m = 160M$. The reason is that suffix sorting in memory becomes slower as the m grows. We assume that sorting m suffixes takes $O(m \log m)$ time. A text of size n is divided into n/m pieces of size m and suffixes of each piece are sorted. Therefore sorting takes $O(n/m \cdot m \log m) = O(n \log m)$ time. Table 3 shows total sorting time for a text of size 320M. Sorting time of $m = 160M$ is about $\log_{10} 160 = 2.2$ times slower than that of $m = 10M$. However, if the text is compressed by the block sorting and we receive it by a compressed form, the sorting step is not necessary. In such case our algorithm becomes fast as m grows.

Table 3. Total sorting time

Unit of merge	10M	20M	40M	80M	160M
sorting time (s)	1444	1632	1814	2188	3123

4.2 HTML files

Table 4 shows sorting and merging time for HTML files on Ultra 30. We use HTML files which servers of University of Tokyo, Kyoto University, Osaka University and NTT (Nippon Telegraph and Telephone Corporation) have. The HTML files are collected by the *ODIN* [7]. Each column represents the size of compressed files, the size of original files, the size of files whose HTML tags are removed and their AML's, suffix sorting time by Bentley-Sedgewick algorithm and Sadakane's algorithm, sorting and merging time of BGS, and sorting and merging time of our algorithm. We first make a suffix array of files in University of Tokyo on disk and then merge that of files in Kyoto University, Osaka University and NTT. Note that the tar file for files of University of Tokyo are compressed from 111 M bytes to 22 M bytes by a Block sorting compressor bzip [10]. The columns of merge time show the time for making a suffix array of U. Tokyo and merging suffix arrays of other HTML files to disk. In the merge algorithms Sadakane's algorithm is used for sorting suffixes in memory. The table shows that AML of HTML files is very large and therefore sorting by the Bentley-Sedgewick algorithm becomes very slow. The table also shows that our merging algorithm is faster than the BGS algorithm.

Table 4. Sorting and merging time for HTML files

	U. Tokyo	Kyoto U.	Osaka U.	NTT
size of `.tar.gz`	28M	16M	10M	2.7M
size of `.tar`	111M	63M	41M	13M
size without tags	45M	26M	17M	3.4M
AML	779	481	441	123
sort time (BS) (s)	2016.9	729.1	439.5	28.2
sort time (Sadakane)	172.8	90.1	28.2	8.5
merge time (BGS)	302	874	888	724
merge time (ours)	337	503	222	128

5 Concluding remarks

We have proposed a text database management method for distributed cooperative environments. Our method can transfer full-text data in compressed form and the receiver can simultaneously obtain the original text and a search data structure called suffix array. The key idea of our method is using the Burrows-Wheeler transformation. The transformation is used in the Block sorting compression and it is defined by the suffix array of a text. We can obtain the original text and its suffix array from the compressed text.

Our method is applicable to large text databases such as Web search servers and Genome databases. In such cases databases are often updated. Therefore merging new data into a database is necessary. We also proposed a simple but efficient suffix array merging algorithm. The algorithm is faster than that of Gonnet, Baeza-Yates and Snider.

We experimented on suffix sorting and merging for HTML files and Genome databases. Both files have large AML's and therefore ordinary sorting algorithms take much time for sorting suffixes. We found that Sadakane's suffix sorting algorithm is effective in sorting such files. Concerning merging suffix arrays, our algorithm is faster than that of Gonnet, Baeza-Yates and Snider especially when merged texts are small and the difference becomes larger if we can use large disk cache. Therefore our merging algorithm is more applicable for frequent updating of large text databases.

Though our algorithm can merge suffix arrays, it cannot handle deletion of texts. As future works we develop a deletion algorithm for a suffix array and compare it with other data structure such as the String B-Tree.

Acknowledgment

We would like to thank Mr. Masanori Harada, who gave us HTML files of the ODIN and thank Dr. Akio Nishikawa, who helped us to obtain genome databases. The work of the second author was supported in part by the Graph-in-Aid for Scientific Research on Priority Areas (A), 'Advanced Database Systems for Integration of Media and User Environments' of the Ministry of Education, Science, Sports and Culture of Japan.

References

1. J. L. Bentley and R. Sedgewick. Fast algorithms for sorting and searching strings. In *Proceedings of the 8th Annual ACM-SIAM Symposium on Discrete Algorithms*, pages 360–369, 1997. http://www.cs.princeton.edu/~rs/strings/.
2. M. Burrows and D. J. Wheeler. A block-sorting lossless data compression algorithms. Technical Report 124, Digital SRC Research Report, 1994.
3. Center for Information Biology, National Institute of Genetics. DNA Data Bank of Japan. http://www.ddbj.nig.ac.jp/.
4. A. Crauser and P. Ferragina. External memory construction of full-text indexes. In *DIMACS Workshop on External Memory Algorithms and/or Visualization*, 1998. http://www.di.unipi.it/~ferragin/Latex/WSA.ps.gz.
5. P. Ferragina and R. Grossi. An external-memory indexing data structure and its applications. *Journal of the ACM*, 1998. (to appear).
6. G.H. Gonnet, R. Baeza-Yates, and T. Snider. New Indices for Text: PAT trees and PAT arrays. In W. Frakes and R. Baeza-Yates, editors, *Information Retrieval: Algorithms and Data Structures*, chapter 5, pages 66–82. Prentice-Hall, 1992.
7. M. Harada. ODIN. http://odin.ingrid.org/.
8. U. Manber and G. Myers. Suffix arrays: A new method for on-line string searches. *SIAM Journal on Computing*, 22(5):935–948, October 1993.
9. K. Sadakane. A Fast Algorithm for Making Suffix Arrays and for Burrows-Wheeler Transformation. In *Proceedings of Data Compression Conference (DCC'98)*, pages 129–138, 1998.
10. J. Seward. bzip, 1996. http://www.cs.man.ac.uk /arch/people/j-seward/bzip-0.21.tar.gz.
11. M. Yoshikawa, H. Kato, H. Kinutani, and M. Watanabe. The ParaDocs Document Database System and Visual User Interface for Information Retrieval. In *Advanced Database Systems for Integration of Media and User Environments '98*, pages 81–86. World Scientific Publishing, 1998.

Constructing Structured Document Views

Hiroyuki Kato, Masatoshi Yoshikawa

Graduate School of Information Science,
Nara Institute of Science and Technology,
8916-5 Takayama, Ikoma, Nara 630-0101, Japan

Abstract. We propose a database language to manipulate XML documents. The language is designed to meet the requirements for constructing XML document views with desired contents and logical structure. We also show an algorithm to derive DTDs for XML document view.

1 Introduction

Recently, DBMSs have been evolving by extending the types of values under their management. Structured documents are one of such important types. Managing structured documents in DBMSs yields benefits in that database functionality, such as concurrency control, access control and recovery, can be applied to document processing.

As with traditional databases, definition of structured documents as database views is required to keep logical data independence, We propose a database language to manipulate XML documents. One of the design goals of the database language is to meet the requirements for defining structured document views. We also give an algorithm to derive DTDs for views defined in the proposed language.

This paper is organized as follows. The remainder of this section gives, as preliminaries, an overview of XML and a database model we employ. Section 2 proposes our query language to manipulate XML documents in databases. Section 3 describes an algorithm to derive DTDs for views.

1.1 Preliminaries

The XML[4], developed under the auspices of the W3C, is a language to specify structured data including documents served, received and processed on the WWW. In XML world, tags called *elements* are embedded in document instances to specify logical structure of documents.

A DTD specifies order of occurrences of elements, so, in essence, it is a grammar for logical structure of a document. Elements are defined by *element declarations* in DTDs. An element declaration constrains the element's name and its *content model*. The content model are formed by a regular expression using child elements and some operators including sequence(" **,** "), repetition(" ***** ", " **+** ") and choice(" **|** ", " **?** "). Let r, r_1 and r_2 represent an element, and let ϵ represent nil value. Semantics of these operators are defined as follows:

```
<!ELEMENT article (title,author+,sec+)>
<!ELEMENT sec     (title,body)>
<!ELEMENT title   (#PCDATA)>
<!ELEMENT author  (#PCDATA)>
<!ELEMENT body    (#PCDATA)>
```

```
CREATE TABLE pubs(
  pub_date    DATE,
  1st_author  PERSON,
  paper       XML);
```

Fig. 1. A DTD of "paper" attribute.

Fig. 2. A database schema for publications.

- r_1, r_2 represents the sequence (concatenation) of r_1 and r_2.
- $r_1 \mid r_2$ represents the disjunction of r_1 and r_2.
- $r*$ represents the Kleene closure of r.
- $r+$ represents $r, r*$.
- $r?$ represents $r \mid \epsilon$.

We regard DTD as list of element declarations for simplicity. Figure 1 shows a DTD consisting of five element declarations in which **article**, **sec**, **title**, **author** and **body** elements are defined.

An element type has *element content* when elements of that type must contain only child elements (no character data), whereas an element type has *mixed content* when elements of that type may contain character data, optionally interspersed with child elements. In this paper, we will consider only element contents for simplicity.

The database assumed in this paper is possible to identify objects by OIDs, has IS_A hierarchy among types, and is a type extensible database which can be augmented by incrementally adding new abstract data types. The advantage of type extensible database are widely recognized[3]. In the following, we assume that the **XML** ADT is plugged in our database to manage XML documents. Because a DTD is a constraint for an XML document data, each database attribute associated with XML type has a DTD as its constraint. For example, the attribute "paper" in Figure 2 has the DTD in Figure 1.

2   A Database language to manipulate XML documents

In this section, we propose a query language, called **X-SQL**, over databases storing values of **XML** type. We adopt, from practical point of view, the syntax of SQL-92[1] which is an international standard. In type extensible object-relational database systems like PREDATOR[3], SQL can manipulate values of new domains by plugging-in corresponding ADTs to databases.

In XML, a DTD is a context-free grammar, and a document instance can be represented as a derivation tree of a context-free grammar[2]. Every non-terminal node of the tree is associated with logical structure of the document, and every leaf node of the tree is associated with contents of the document. Subsequently, we regard XML documents as ordered trees. For example, Figure 3 shows an ordered tree of an XML document which is conformable to the DTD in Figure 1.

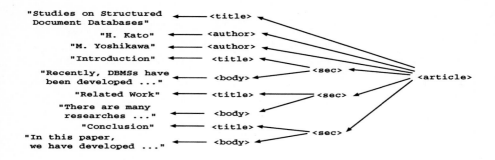

Fig. 3. An ordered tree representing an XML document.

We sometimes call the element corresponding to the root node in an ordered tree as *root element*, and elements corresponding to a node having leaf node as its child as *leaf element*.

In the rest of this section, we describe database language primitives to manipulate XML documents in extensional database (edb) and to define XML documents in intensional database (idb).

2.1 Manipulation of structured documents in edb

Manipulation of structured documents in edb consists of identifying subdocuments according to any logical structure and of specifying any relationships of logical structure. We introduce **ST^e-expression** as the former and two predicates, **include** and **precede over** as the latter.

Recall that we regard XML documents as ordered trees. Primitive relationships among nodes of trees are parent-child relationship and sibling relationship. Hence, primitives in manipulating logical structure of documents are *inclusion relation* as the parent-child relationship and *ordering relation* as the sibling relationship, between two logical structures. We define both ST^e-expression and the two predicates to have these functionality. By combining ST^e-expression and the two predicates, one can form expressions both of identifying subdocuments according to any logical structure and of specifying any relationships of logical structure.

We introduce ELEMENT type, defined as a subtype of the STRING type, to manage element names as its values. Each literal of values of the ELEMENT type is specified by an element name enclosed by '<' and '>'.

First, we define **ST^e-expressions** identifying subdocuments according to any logical structure.

Definition 1. Let A be a value or variable associated with **XML** type and let E be a value or variable associated with ELEMENT type. ST^e-expressions are formed as follows, recursively.

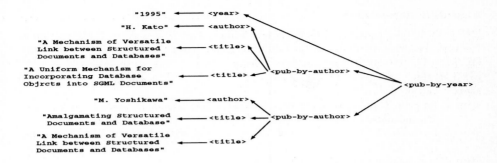

Fig. 4. An example of output documents by the sample query.

- A
- ST^e-expression$/E$
- ST^e-expression$//E$
- ST^e-expression$< E$
- ST^e-expression$<< E$

Note that, an ST^e-expression always begins with a value or a variable associated with **XML** type.

Definition 2. The semantics of ST^e-expressions are as follows. In this semantics, ST^e-expressions with E represent a ordered set with the occurrence order.

- A represents A itself.
- ST^e-expression$/E$ represents an ordered set of subtrees with element name E as their root, among child nodes of ST^e-expression.
- ST^e-expression$//E$ represents an ordered set of subtrees with element name E as their root, among descendant nodes of ST^e-expression.
- ST^e-expression$< E$ represents an ordered set of subtrees with element name E as their root, among left sibling nodes[1] of ST^e-expression.
- ST^e-expression$<< E$ represents an ordered set of subtrees with element name E as their root, among nodes preceding ST^e-expression.

Secondly, we introduce two predicates, named **include** and **precede over**, representing relationships of logical structure between given two (sub)documents. Let A_1, A_2 and A_3 be ST^e-expressions.

- A_1 **include** A_2 holds, if and only if A_1 can be modeled as subtrees with root nodes equivalent to parent nodes of A_2's trees.
- A_1 **precede** A_2 **over** A_3 holds, if and only if A_3 can be modeled as subtree containing sibling trees as A_1's being left sibling of A_2's.

---

[1] We assume our trees are with left-to-right ordering.

Algorithm deriveDTD

INPUT: InSQL as SQL representation of a query and $\mathcal{D}$ as a set of DTD associated with database attributes in the extensional database.

OUTPUT: deriveDTD (list of element declaration)

METHOD:

step 1 call procedure SQL2EDExpList(InSQL, nil).

step 2 for each E in D write deriveDTD with $E.l$ as a element name to declare and $E.r$ as content model of the element name.

step 3 for each of $\mathcal{D}$, element declarations related with deriveDTD add into deriveDTD.

step 4 remove duplication in deriveDTD.

step 5 concatenate content models of same element declarations with |, in deriveDTD

Fig. 5. Algorithm to derive DTD from queries.

2.2 Defining structured documents in idb

In this section, we describe how to define logical structure of XML documents in query results. In other words, we describe that, using subdocuments in edb as building blocks, how to define new logical structure of XML documents. For this purpose, we introduce constructors to define internal structure of XML documents as ST^i-expression. Because logical structure of XML documents are defined in DTDs, the constructors corresponds to those used in element declaration in DTDs. An element declaration consists of an element name and a content model of the element. Therefore, these constructors are broadly classified into two kinds. One includes functions and operators corresponding to operator used to form regular expressions in DTDs. Another includes a function to give a new element name to content model.

First, we introduce **ST_TEXT** type for explanatory convenience. The **ST_TEXT** type is a subtype of the **TEXT** and a supertype of the **XML** type. Values of the **ST_TEXT** type do not always have root elements, whereas values of the **XML** type always have root elements. Because of defining subtyping relationship based on domain-inclusion semantics, dom(XML) $\subseteq$ dom(ST_TEXT) holds[2]. Therefore, dom(ST_TEXT)−dom(XML) represents documents, each of which has no root element. Note that, adding root elements to values of the **ST_TEXT** type always results values of the **XML** type.

We distinguish **nil** from EMPTY. The **nil** represents a nil value, whereas the EMPTY represents a value of the ST_TEXT type. Because XML allows elements to have no contents, namely EMPTY, adding a root element to EMPTY yields a value of the **XML** type.

We now define ST^i-**expressions** to construct arbitrary logical structure using subdocuments stored in edb.

Definition 3. Let ST^e be a ST^e-expression and let E be a value or variable of the ELEMENT type, ST^i-expressions are formed as follows, recursively.

---

[2] For a given type t, dom(t) denotes the domain of t.

- ST^e
- ST^i-expression + ST^i-expression
- cat*(ST^i-expression)
- cat(ST^i-expression)
- ST^i-expression?
- ST^i-expression | ST^i-expression
- tagged(E, ST^i-expression)

We now describe three functions and three operators, associated with **ST_TEXT** type, as semantics of ST^i-expression, to construct internal structure of XML documents. These functions and operators correspond to operators used to form regular expressions which represent content model in DTD.

- For given two values of the **ST_TEXT** type, the operator "+" results a value of the **ST_TEXT** type which is the concatenation of the given values. This operator is associative and noncommutative. Because it is associative, we can view this operator as a polyadic operator and write, for example, $S_1 + \cdots + S_n$, where S_i is associated with the **ST_TEXT** type. The result of this operator is defined to be nil when operands include nil.
- For a given ordered set of values of the **ST_TEXT** type, aggregate functions, **cat*()** and **cat()**, result a value of **ST_TEXT** type.
  - **ST_TEXT cat*(set of ST_TEXT** $arg1$)
    results a value associated with the **ST_TEXT** type concatenating elements of input set in the same order as of the input. The result of this function is defined to be EMPTY when the input is nil.
  - **ST_TEXT cat(set of ST_TEXT** $arg1$)
    results same as **cat*()** except for the input as nil. The result of this function is defined to be nil when the input is nil.
- The unary operator "?" results the same value as its operand associated with the **ST_TEXT** type. The result of this operator is defined to be EMPTY when the operand is nil.
- The operator "|" results the same value, except nil value, as one of the its operands associated with the **ST_TEXT** type. If operands include plural values other than nil, this operator is undefined. Because it is associative, we can also view this operator as a polyadic operator.

Note that, results by applying these functions and operators not always have root elements, hence are associated with not the **XML** type but the **ST_TEXT** type. We now introduce the function, **tagged()**, which adds a root element to values of the **ST_TEXT** type, to be associated with the **XML** type.

- **XML tagged(ELEMENT** $arg1$, **ST_TEXT** $arg2$)
  add $arg1$ as root element to $arg2$ to be one value of the **XML** type. This function results nil when $arg2$ is nil.

```
SELECT tagged(<pub-by-year>, ye+cat*(p))
FROM
   ( SELECT tagged(<pub-by-author>, au+cat*(ti)) AS p, ye
     FROM    t, t.a/<author> AS au, t.a/<title> AS ti,
             t.a/<year> AS ye
     GROUP BY ye, au
     ORDER BY ti )
GROUP by ye
ORDER by ye, au
```

Fig. 6. Query example

```
<!ELEMENT pub-by-year  (year,pub-by-author*)>
<!ELEMENT pub-by-author (author,title*)>
<!ELEMENT year    (#PCDATA)>
<!ELEMENT title   (#PCDATA)>
<!ELEMENT author  (#PCDATA)>
```

Fig. 7. A derived DTD

3   Deriving DTD for structured document views

In many cases, DTDs for structured document views are not given a priori. Therefore, it is important to derive DTDs for views from view definition. DTDs for views are useful in many situations including optimization of queries on views.

Figure 5 shows an algorithm to derive DTDs from SQL queries defining views. For the purpose of our algorithm, forms of SQL queries could be limited to the following one without loss of generality:

```
SQL := SELECT S1 [AS A1], S2 [AS A2], ..., Sm [AS Am]
            FROM    F1, F2, ..., Fn
Fj   := SQL
```

As an example, assume XML documents like one in Figure 3 is stored in the attribute a of table t. Given such XML document, the query in Figure 6 outputs the XML documents in Figure 4. From the query in Figure 6, the algorithm **deriveDTD** derives the DTD in Figure 7.

References

1. C. J. Date and H. Darwen. *A Guide to The SQL Standard, 3rd ed.* Addison-Wesley, Reading, MA, 1993.
2. Gaston H. Gonnet and Frank Wm. Tompa. Mind your grammar: a new approach to modelling text. In *Proc. of the 13th International Conference on Very Large Data Bases (VLDB)*, pp. 339–346, September 1987.
3. Praveen Seshadri. Enhanced abstract data types in object-relational databases. *The International Journal on Very Large Data Bases*, Vol. 7, pp. 130–140, 1998.
4. World Wide Web Consortium. Extensible Markup Language (XML) 1.0. http://www.w3.org/TR/1998/REC-xml-19980210, February 1998. W3C Recommendation 10-February-1998.

procedure SQL2EDExpList(sql, D) result $EDExpList$
       D is a list of EDExp
       $EDExpList$ is a list of Element Declaration Expressions
       begin local variable
            E, E_1, E_2 are types of $EDExp$
            U is type of set of database attributes
       end local variable
  for each i from 1 to m
  $E \leftarrow$ ElementDeclareExp(S_i [AS A_i])   append E into D
  $U \leftarrow$ database attributes in $EDExp$
  for each a_i in U
   if a_i occur in the SELECT-clause of the FROM-clause F_j
   SQL2EDExpList(F_j)
   else
    for each E_1, E_2 in D
    if database attribute a_i occurring in $E_1.r$ also occur in $E_2.m$
    replace a_i in $E_1.r$ into $E_2.r$
    remove $E_2.r$ from D else
    replace a_i in $E_1.r$ into root element name in the DTD associated with a_i
  return D

procedure RegularExp(ST^{ei}-expression st) result regular expression of st
  if st is formed by cat(st') return RegularExp(st')+
   else if st is formed by cat*(st') return RegularExp(st')*
   else if st is formed by st'? return RegularExp(st')?
   else if st is formed by $st'_1+...+st'_l$ return RegularExp(st'_1),...,RegularExp(st'_l)
   else if st is formed by $st'_1|...|st'_l$ return RegularExp(st'_1)|...|RegularExp(st'_l)
   else if st is formed by tagged($element, st'$) return $elemet$
   else if st is formed by $st'/element$ return $element$
   else if st is formed by $st'//element$ return $elements$
   else if st is formed by $st' < element$ return $element$
   else if st is formed by $st' << element$ return $element$
   else return st

procedure ElementDeclareExp(S_i [AS A_i]) result $EDExp$
       S_i [AS A_i] is a select list item
         $EDExp$ consists of $EDExp.l$, $EDExp.m$ and $EDExp.r$
            $EDExp.l$ is element name to declare
            $EDExp.m$ is database attribute name
            $EDExp.r$ is regular expression
  if S_i is formed by tagged($element, s$)
  $EDExp.l \leftarrow element$
  if exists
  $EDExp.m \leftarrow A_i$
  $EDExp.r \leftarrow$ RegularExp(S_i)
  return $EDExp$

Fig. 8. Some procedures used in the algorithm **derivieDTD**

Temporal Objects for Spatio-Temporal Data Models and a Comparison of Their Representations*

Martin Erwig & Markus Schneider & Ralf Hartmut Güting
FernUniversität Hagen, Praktische Informatik IV
D-58084 Hagen, Germany
[erwig, markus.schneider, gueting]@fernuni-hagen.de

Abstract: We present a new approach to temporal data modeling based on the very general notion of *temporal object*. Moreover, we propose the database embedding of temporal objects by means of the *abstract data type* (*ADT*) approach. We consider the expressiveness of different temporal database embeddings, and we discuss the combination of temporal and spatial objects into *spatio-temporal objects* in (relational) databases. We explain various alternatives for spatio-temporal data models and databases and compare their expressiveness.

1   Introduction

In the past, in spite of many similarities, research in spatial and temporal data models and databases has largely developed independently.

Spatial database research [Gü94] has focused on modeling, querying, and integrating geometric and topological information in databases. For the modeling of spatial objects *spatial data types* (e.g. [SV89, SH91, GS95, Sc97]) have been identified as appropriate and efficient abstractions for modeling the geometric structure of spatial phenomena as well as their relationships, properties, and operations. We base our definition of spatial objects on the point set approach and on point set topology [Ga64]. A spatial object is assumed to be represented by a generally infinite point set with certain properties from which different structures like the boundary or the interior can be identified. There are mainly two reasons for this way of modeling: spatial objects modeled by the point set approach are efficiently implementable and can be easily embedded in a (relational) database. This leads us to the specific subclass of *linear spatial objects* where linearity is given through polygonal approximations. Moreover, the vast majority of optimization methods and indexing techniques builds upon such linear representations. Besides, this approach fits very nicely with our model of temporal objects.

Temporal database research [TCG+93] has concentrated on modeling, querying, and recording the temporal evolution of facts under different notions of time (valid time, transaction time) and thus on extending the knowledge stored in databases about the current and past states of the real world. Traditionally, temporal data has been modeled by tuple- or attribute-timestamped relations. This is a restricted view essentially preventing the treatment of *continuous* change of temporal data. In contrast, a more general

* This research was partially supported by the CHOROCHRONOS project, funded by the EU under the Training and Mobility of Researchers Programme, Contract No. ERB FMRX-CT96-0056.

view is offered by a (simplified) definition of a temporal object as a function mapping time to a certain codomain under some constraints, and this is the first contribution of our paper:

1. We present a very general model of *temporal objects* whose definition is based on the observation that anything that changes over time can be expressed as a function over time.

Currently, there are increasing integration efforts striving for a combination of space and time in "spatio-temporal data models and databases". We have already discussed evolving problems and have presented a first approach for a data model in [EGSV98]. A few other papers already exist that deal with the integrated modeling of space and time, for instance, [Wo94,YC93], but they do not address the embedding in databases.

This paper now views the topic from a rather fundamental perspective and additionally makes the following contribution:

2. We propose the database embedding of temporal objects in the spirit of the *abstract data type* approach applied to the integration of complex objects into databases [SRG83, St86].

In spatial database technology, for quite some time, spatial data types have been integrated as ADTs for attributes in relational schemas (e.g. [Gü88, SH91, Sc97]).[1] So far, temporal databases have been essentially based on atomic standard data types extended by an explicitly or implicitly given type for time. Tuples are associated with time stamps; each tuple describes the validity and the features of a fact or object. We show that temporal databases based on the ADT approach are more powerful than current ones and that a simple extension compensates this difference for a particular class of temporal objects.

3. We demonstrate the broad spectrum of integration options for temporal and spatial objects into *spatio-temporal objects* in (relational) databases and compare their expressiveness.

The variety of temporal and spatial data models offers many different possibilities for combining temporal and spatial objects into *spatio-temporal objects* in (relational) databases. We discuss this design space and explain different alternatives for spatio-temporal data models and databases. One of our main conclusions here is:

Spatio-temporal objects are special cases of temporal objects

We compare the expressiveness of the different temporal, spatial, and spatio-temporal data models. We focus on object representations and defer the treatment of operations and query languages to a subsequent paper. For spatio-temporal data models we establish a representation hierarchy. An interesting visualization of spatio-temporal objects for the linear case is a three-dimensional view in the form of *3D-polylines* for moving points and in the form of *polyhedra* for moving regions [EGSV98], respectively. We

---

1. It is widely known that spatial databases supporting the ADT approach can represent the same information as those decomposing spatial objects into a set of tuples in flat relations [BS77, Ro87].

show that, surprisingly, the polyhedra model is not comparable to any model of our hierarchy.

The rest of the paper is structured as follows: Sections 2 and 3 define a model for spatial and temporal objects and describe a representation for their use in databases. We also consider expressiveness of the different temporal modeling alternatives. Section 4 deals with the design space obtained when combining spatial and temporal objects. Various spatio-temporal data models are explained, and a number of relationships between the different models are shown. Section 5 concludes the paper.

2 Spatial Objects and Spatial Databases

2.1 Spatial Objects

Space is assumed to be composed of infinitely many points; it corresponds to the two-dimensional Euclidean space $\mathbb{R}^2$. Each spatial feature S is regarded as an arbitrary, possibly infinite, point set $S \subseteq \mathbb{R}^2$. We here take an ADT approach and use *spatial data types* for points and regions as appropriate abstractions of spatial phenomena. Elements of spatial data types are called *spatial objects*. The set of all spatial objects is denoted by SO = *Point* $\cup$ *Region* where *Point* and *Region* are the set of all point and region objects, respectively, and we also speak of the SO-model. Mathematical definitions of regions can be based on point set topology; to avoid application-specific anomalies we use regular closed sets and regularized set operations [Ti80, ES97]. For the implementation we need finite descriptions of point sets, and we employ *linear* approximations of spatial objects. The set of all *linear spatial objects* is denoted by $\overline{SO}$. Out of several implementation alternatives, our selection is to approximate regions by a type *Polygon* consisting of sets of polygons possibly with polygonal holes. The Points remain unchanged.

2.2 Representation of Spatial Objects in Databases

A *relation scheme R* is written as $R(A_1 : D_1, ..., A_n : D_n)$ where the A_i are the *attributes* of R. For a relation $r : R(A_1 : D_1, ..., A_n : D_n)$ holds: $r \subseteq D_1 \times D_2 \times ... \times D_n$. Tuples are described in the form $(A_1 = x, A_5 = b, ...)$; only the values of interest are shown.

Principally, there are two methods of integrating spatial objects into relational databases. The first method is to embed spatial objects directly as ADTs, i.e., a single attribute value contains a complete spatial object: $R(S : \alpha, ...)$ for $\alpha \in$ GEO = {*Point, Region, Polygon*}. This applies to the SO and $\overline{SO}$ model. The corresponding relational data models are called SO-REL and $\overline{SO}$-REL; they denote the set of relations with at least one attribute of a (linear) spatial data type. For simplicity we assume that each such relation has exactly one spatial attribute. The second method leads us to S-REL which denotes the set of relations modeling spatial features only with atomic standard attribute types. A polygon is represented as a set of tuples each storing the coordinates of two points representing a segment of the boundary representation of a polygon [BS77, Ro87].

A more detailed description of the SO/$\overline{SO}$-models and their representation in databases is given in the full paper [ESG97].

3 Temporal Objects and Temporal Databases

3.1 A Model of Temporal Objects

When defining a model for temporal objects one has to decide about a model of time. We choose – mainly for consistency with the spatial domains – time to be continuous, i.e., *time* = IR. Now anything that changes over time can be expressed as a function over time, i.e., the temporal version of objects of a type α is given by a function of type *time* $\rightarrow \alpha$, called a *temporal function*. The type of all (partial) temporal functions is simply:

$$\phi(\alpha) = time \rightarrow \alpha$$

We have to deal with representations that are computationally tractable. This means that for an arbitrary temporal function $f \in \phi(\alpha)$ we can determine the value of f at any time of its domain. Thus, we restrict $\phi(\alpha)$ to computable functions. It is also important to be able to compute values of the inverse function, i.e., ask for the times at which a temporal object took a specific value. Further restrictions result from the need to integrate temporal objects into the relational model and from compatibility with the chosen model for spatial objects. Thus, we restrict the domain of ϕ to finite sets of time points and intervals. For any type α that has a total order < (and equality =) we define the type of non-empty (open and closed) intervals over α as follows:

$$\iota(\alpha) = \cup \{\{[x, y],]x, y], [x, y[,]x, y[\} \mid x, y \in \alpha\} - \{\varnothing\} \text{ where}$$
$$[x, y] = \{a \in \alpha \mid x \leq a \leq y\},]x, y] = \{a \in \alpha \mid x < a \leq y\}, [x, y[= \{a \in \alpha \mid x \leq a < y\}, \text{etc.}$$

This way we can encode continuous parts of ϕ's domain by intervals, i.e., the domain of a temporal object is given by a finite set of pairwise disjoint intervals (any time point t can well be represented by a degenerated interval $[t, t] = \{t\}$.) We can now define the type constructor for *temporal objects* as:

$$\tau(\alpha) = \iota(time) \rightarrow \phi(\alpha) \qquad (= \iota(time) \rightarrow time \rightarrow \alpha)$$
$$\text{where } \forall \; \omega \in \tau(\alpha): \quad (1) \; \forall \, I, J \in dom(\omega) : I \cup J \notin \iota(time)$$
$$(2) \; \forall \, I \in dom(\omega) : dom(\omega(I)) = I$$

This means a temporal object ω is defined on a set of pairwise disjoint and non-adjacent intervals and associates with each interval of its domain a (partial) temporal function whose domain is just that interval. The set of all temporal objects is denoted by TO, and we also speak of the TO-model. There are at least two reasons for considering only *linear* temporal functions as a further restriction of temporal objects: (i) it is difficult to compute with general functions, and (ii) a linear temporal function has a straightforward representation, which is particularly important for the integration into relations: store the function values of the boundaries of intervals and use predefined interpretations for deriving function values for the interior of intervals.

In order to formalize the notion of linearity we consider argument types α that have a certain algebraic structure (we call these types *linear smooth*): there must be a non-trivial type $\Lambda(\alpha) \subseteq \alpha \rightarrow \alpha$ of functions on α for which two conditions hold: first, a scalar multiplication is defined, i.e., $\forall f \in \Lambda(\alpha), r \in$ IR: $r \cdot f : \alpha \rightarrow \alpha$ is a well-defined function (with $1 \cdot f = f$). Second, the function $\Delta : \alpha \times \alpha \rightarrow \Lambda(\alpha)$ yields for two values $x, y \in \alpha$ a function δ which captures the "difference" between x and y; in particular, $\delta(x) = y$ must hold. Then, by virtue of the scalar multiplication, values in the interior of an interval can be computed by δ. For instance, for $\alpha = \mathbb{R}$ the usual linear transition from x to y is captured by $\Delta(x, y) = \lambda x'.x' + (y\text{-}x)$ where scalar multiplication is defined as: $r\cdot(\lambda x'.x' + (y\text{-}x)) = \lambda x'.x' + r\cdot(y\text{-}x)$. The reason why Δ is defined to return a function and not simply a difference value is that the linear interpretation for $\alpha \in$ GEO is given by affine mappings (see Section 4), and for these the functional view is much easier to handle than the value approach.

Now the *linear temporal object* ($\overline{\text{TO}}$) model can be defined as a linear specialization of the TO-model (very much like $\overline{\text{SO}}$ is a specialization of SO). By $[t_1, t_2[$ we denote an arbitrary open, closed, or semi-open time interval, and we let $\|t\| = (t\text{-}t_1)/(t_2\text{-}t_1)$. We say that a temporal function f: *time* $\rightarrow \alpha$ is *k-piecewise linear* if:

$$\exists\, k \in \mathbb{IN}: dom(f) = \cup_{1 \le i \le k} I_i \text{ with } I_i = [t_1, t_2[\wedge \forall 1 \le i < j \le k: I_i \cap I_j = \varnothing$$
$$\wedge\, \forall\, I_i: |I_i| > 1 \wedge \forall\, t \in I_i: f(t) = (\|t\|\cdot\Delta(x, y))\,(x)$$
$$\text{where } x = \lim_{n \to \infty} f(t_1 + 1/n) \text{ and } y = \lim_{n \to \infty} f(t_2 - 1/n)$$

A k-piecewise linear function is always also $(k{+}1)$-piecewise linear. To get a canonical (and efficient) representation we look for minimal decompositions of intervals. Therefore, we say that f is *minimally decomposed* (or *maximally piecewise*, or just *k-piecewise*) if f is k-piecewise linear, but not $(k{-}1)$-piecewise linear. Then the *minimal decomposition* of f is defined as the partition $\pi(f) = \{(I_i, f|_{I_i}) \mid 1 \le i \le k\}$ where $f|_D = \{(x, f(x)) \mid x \in D\}$. Now the type of linear temporal objects is defined by the type constructor $\overline{\tau}$ as follows.

$$\overline{\tau}(\alpha) = \{\omega \in \tau(\alpha) \mid \text{(1) } \alpha \text{ is linear smooth}$$
$$\text{(2) } \forall\, I \in dom(\omega): |I| = 1 \vee \omega(I) \text{ is } k\text{-piecewise}\}$$

Note that we cannot simply restrict ω to be linear on each of its intervals, we rather have to refine this condition to finite partitions of each interval I because ω might have different linear behaviors on I. Therefore, we have used the notion of piecewise linearity. It is obvious that linear temporal objects are a strict subset of (general) temporal objects:

Lemma 3.1. $\overline{\text{TO}} \subset \text{TO}$.

3.2   Representation of Temporal Objects in Databases

The integration of temporal objects into relational databases can be done principally in two ways: temporal objects can be embedded directly as ADTs, i.e., a single attribute contains a complete temporal object: $R(O : \tau(\alpha), ...)$. This applies to the TO and $\overline{\text{TO}}$ models. The corresponding data models are called TO-REL and $\overline{\text{TO}}$-REL, and they denote the set of relations with at least one attribute being of a (linear) temporal object type. For simplicity we assume in the sequel that each such relation has exactly one temporal attribute.[2] In contrast, T-REL denotes relations with only atomic attribute types (including *time*). T-REL as defined below gives a unifying view on different traditional tuple-timestamped[3] models of temporal databases. Each temporal object is represented

---

2. The general case requires that the time domains of different temporal objects have to be "synchronized" by finding a common interval refinement when mapping to T-REL. This is not difficult, but makes the definitions longer.

by a set of tuples each storing a value of type α, a time stamp, and a flag B indicating the future value behavior: $R(A : \alpha, T : time, B : \{d, c, l\}, ...)$. B specifies the values in between two time stamps, i.e, given two tuples $(A = x, T = t_1, B = b, ...)$ and $(A = y, T = t_2, ...)$ of a relation $r \in$ T-REL where $\forall (T = t_3, ...) \in r: t_3 < t_1 \vee t_3 > t_2$, the value of A at any time $t_1 < t < t_2$, denoted by $A(t)$, is:

Interpretation	Definition	b	Name
completely undefined	$A^d(t) = \bot$	d	discrete
valid up to the next definition	$A^c(t) = x$	c	(stepwise) constant
changes continuously	$A^l(t) = (\|t\| \cdot \Delta(x, y))(x)$	l	linear

(In the informal model of [YC93] *spline interpolation* is suggested as another interpretation.) To be compatible with TO and $\overline{\text{TO}}$ we consider a further flag $C : \mathbb{B}$ for distinguishing closed and open intervals: $C = true \Leftrightarrow A$ is a valid value at T (otherwise, A is used only for deriving values in the interior of the preceeding and/or the following interval).

In order to compare T-REL with TO-REL and $\overline{\text{TO}}$-REL we define the temporal object represented by a relation from T-REL. Let $r = \{(A = a_1, T = t_1, B = b_1, C = c_1, ...),$ $..., (A = a_n, T = t_n, B = b_n, C = c_n, ...)\} : R(A : \alpha, T : time, B : \{d, c, l\}, C : \mathbb{B}, ...) \in$ T-REL be a (sub-) relation containing only tuples describing one temporal object (i.e., the projection to all attributes $\notin \{A, T, B, C\}$ yields a relation of a single tuple). First, we derive the set of temporal functions for the intervals represented in r:

$$\Phi(r) = \{\{(t, A^{b_i}(t)) \mid t_i < t < t_{i+1}\} \cup \{(t_j, a_j) \mid c_j = true, j \in \{i, i+1\}\} \mid 1 \le i < n\}$$

Next we have to map each interval to its corresponding temporal function. We get: $\{(dom(f), f) \mid f \in \Phi(r)\}$. Note that this is *not* yet the final temporal object, since there are, in general, more intervals in the T-REL representation than in the corresponding temporal object. Therefore, we have to normalize by merging temporal functions on adjacent intervals. This can be done by the function γ:

$$\gamma(\omega) = \begin{cases} \gamma(\{(I \cup J, f \cup g)\} \cup \omega') & \text{if } \exists \omega': \omega = \{(I, f), (J, g)\} \cup \omega' \text{ with } I \cup J \in \iota(time) \\ \omega & \text{otherwise} \end{cases}$$

Hence, the temporal object denoted by relation r is finally given by:

$$\sigma_T(r) = \gamma(\{(dom(f), f) \mid f \in \Phi(r)\})$$

For relations r that do not properly represent temporal objects $\sigma_T(r)$ is undefined, i.e., $\sigma_T(r) = \bot$.

Next we have to define the representation of a linear temporal object ω as a relation $r \in$ T-REL. Therefore, we first partition each interval of ω's domain into maximal subintervals so that the corresponding temporal function is linear on each of these subintervals. We obtain this through the minimal decomposition π. Note carefully, that we cannot represent "linear functions followed by a jump", but only jumps after stepwise

---

3. In contrast, attribute-timestamped models like that of [SS93] correspond more closely to the ADT view.

constant parts because we have spent for each interval only one attribute of type α. This means that we cannot represent a function that evolves linearly from x to y and continues with $z \neq y$. Thus, the representation function ρ described in the sequel is only partially defined.

Consider a k-piecewise temporal function f. Let $dom(f) = \cup_{1 \leq i \leq k} I_i$ with $I_i = [t_{i,1}, t_{i,2}]$, $x_i = \lim_{n \to \infty} f(t_{i,1}+1/n)$, and $y_i = \lim_{n \to \infty} f(t_{i,2}-1/n)$. If $x_i = y_i$, let $b_i = c$. Otherwise, if $y_i = x_{i+1}$, then $b_i = l$. Otherwise, $\rho''(f)$ (see below) is undefined. Then

$$\rho''(f) = \{(A=x_i, T=t_{i,1}, B=b_i, C=(t_{i,1} \in I_i)) \mid 1 \leq i \leq k\} \cup \{(A=y_k, T=t_{k,2}, B=d, C=(t_{k,2} \in I_k))\}$$

Now the relation representing any temporal function of a temporal object is given by:

$$\rho'(f) = \begin{cases} \{(A = f(t), T = t, B = d, C = true)\} & \text{if } dom(f) = \{t\} \\ \rho''(f) & \text{otherwise} \end{cases}$$

Finally, the relation representing a complete linear temporal object is:

$$\rho_T(\omega) = \cup_{(I,f) \in \omega} \rho'(f)$$

3.3 Expressiveness of Temporal Data Models

To compare the different models we use operations from the NF^2 relational model [SS86] to describe mapping bewteen them. Let $\nu[AS : A; f]$ be the *nest* operator that takes in addition to the set of attributes AS to be nested a function f that is applied to each resulting sub-relation r'. Then $f(r')$ is stored under the attribute A (instead of r'). Similarly, the *unnest* operator $\mu[A : AS; f](r)$ applies the function f to the value of attribute A of each of r's tuples and produces a relation of schema AS that is embedded into r.

Next we can compare the different temporal data models. First, we show that $\overline{TO}$-REL is more expressive than T-REL, but with two simple extensions T-REL becomes equivalent to $\overline{TO}$-REL. This means that the ADT approach is essentially equivalent to simple temporal relational models as far as linear temporal behavior is concerned. We also show that, in general however, TO-REL *is* more powerful than both $\overline{TO}$-REL and T-REL.

The difference between $\overline{TO}$-REL and T-REL lies essentially in the fact that one tuple in $\overline{TO}$-REL is represented by a set of tuples (= sub-relation) in T-REL. We can define two simple transformations to map between $\overline{TO}$-REL and T-REL. Any relation $r : R(A : \alpha, T : time, B : \{d,c,l\}, C : \mathbb{IB}, \ldots) \in$ T-REL can be transformed into an equivalent relation $s \in \overline{TO}$-REL simply by

$$s = \nu[\{A, T, B, C\} : O; \sigma_T](r)$$

Likewise, any relation $s \in \overline{TO}$-REL can be transformed into a T-REL relation r by:

$$r = \mu[O : \{A, T, B, C\}; \rho_T](s)$$

Let $\nu_T(\text{T-REL}) = \{\nu[\{A, T, B, C\} : O; \sigma_T](r) \mid r \in \text{T-REL}\} - \{\perp\}$, and let $\mu_T(\text{T-REL}) = \{\mu[O : \{A, T, B, C\}; \rho_T](r) \mid r \in \overline{TO}\text{-REL}\}$. Now we first have:

Theorem 3.1. $\nu_T(\text{T-REL}) \subset \overline{TO}\text{-REL}$.

Proof. Since σ_T is a total function, it is clear that each T-REL can be transformed into a corresponding $\overline{\text{TO}}$-REL. The fact that the inclusion is proper is grounded in the partiality of ρ_T: since each linear function followed by a jump cannot be represented by a T-REL, there are more $\overline{\text{TO}}$-RELs than T-RELs. □

There is an even more important difference between T-REL and $\overline{\text{TO}}$-REL that gets lost by lifting T-REL to the ADT-level of $\overline{\text{TO}}$-REL: non-temporal attributes in a $\overline{\text{TO}}$-REL exist independently from the domain of the temporal attribute. In contrast, an additional (implicit) rule would be needed to distinguish temporal attributes from non-temporal ones in T-REL. This reflects the fact that attribute-timestamped temporal models are, in general, more expressive than tuple-timestamped models.

If we extend T-REL by storing an additional α-attribute (and a second C-flag specifying the definedness at the end of intervals), we can actually represent all linear temporal objects in flat relations. Let us call such a model T^+-REL. (Of course, we have to redefine and extend the ρ_T and σ_T transformations, too.) Then:

Theorem 3.2. $\nu_T(T^+\text{-REL}) = \overline{\text{TO}}\text{-REL}$ and $\mu_T(\overline{\text{TO}}\text{-REL}) = T^+\text{-REL}$.

Still the ADT-approach is more general when we do not restrict ourselves to linear behaviors. As a direct corollary of Lemma 3.1 we obtain:

Theorem 3.3. $\overline{\text{TO}}\text{-REL} \subset \text{TO-REL}$.

4 Spatio-Temporal Data Types and Data Models

Now that we know how to model spatial and temporal objects and how to integrate them into databases we can consider their combination.

4.1 Landscape of Spatio-Temporal Data Models

A straightforward approach is indicated by the fact that τ is a type constructor: it is obvious to apply τ to types from GEO to immediately obtain *spatio-temporal objects* (STO). The types of this model comprise moving objects, i.e., MOV = $\{\tau(Point), \tau(Region), \tau(Polygon)\}$). Again we can restrict ourselves to linear objects, both for the temporal and the spatial component, and obtain the following models and types:

Model	linear component	Types
STO	—	$\tau(Point)$, $\tau(Region)$
$\overline{\text{S}}\text{TO}$	spatial	$\tau(Point)$, $\tau(Polygon)$
$\text{S}\overline{\text{T}}\text{O}$	temporal	$\overline{\tau}(Point)$, $\overline{\tau}(Region)$
$\overline{\text{S}}\overline{\text{T}}\text{O}$	spatial & temporal	$\overline{\tau}(Point)$, $\overline{\tau}(Polygon)$

Note that before we can apply $\overline{\tau}$ to either geometric type $\alpha \in$ GEO we have to ensure that these are all linear smooth. Therefore, we have to identify reasonable types $\Lambda(\alpha)$. The choice here is not unique, but for points arbitrary vector movements, and for regions and polygons *affine mappings* provide well-understood and general models of geometric transformations that are also amenable to scalar multiplication and to the difference operator Δ. Actually, scalar multiplication is already defined for both vectors and affine mappings. The Δ operation is defined for points as $\Delta(p, q) = \lambda p'.p'+(q-p)$ where "+" and "-" are usual vector addition and subtraction. Thus, Δ simply records the vector that translates p to q. The scalar multiplication is defined as $r \cdot (\lambda p'.p'+(q-p)) = \lambda p'.p'+r \cdot (q-p)$, and thus the intermediate positions of a point moving from p (directly) to q all lie on the straight line connecting p and q. For polygons (and regions) the difference is defined component-wise.[4] For two polygons we have: $\Delta(P, Q) = \lambda p.H \cdot p + v$ where the matrix

$$H = \begin{pmatrix} a & b \\ c & d \end{pmatrix} \text{ and the vector } v = \begin{pmatrix} v_x \\ v_y \end{pmatrix}$$

contain altogether six variables that are fully determined by three pairs of corresponding points from P and Q as follows. For each two corresponding points $p = (x, y)$ and $q = (x', y')$ we know:

$$x' = a \cdot x + b \cdot y + v_x \qquad \text{and} \qquad y' = c \cdot x + d \cdot y + v_y$$

For three different pairs of points we thus obtain six equations which are sufficient to compute the parameters a, b, c, d, v_x, and v_y. Scalar multiplication is defined as $r \cdot (\lambda p.H \cdot p + v) = \lambda p.(r \cdot H) \cdot p + r \cdot v$. Now we can also see why we do not take affine mappings for points, but just vector translation: since it is not possible to infer an affine transformation from just two points, it would be impossible to define Δ.

In the above table we have only listed ADTs. However, when we consider the integration into relations we can also as a further alternative distinguish the encoding of objects by a set of tuples. This applies to the spatial as well as to the temporal object part. We get the following eight modeling combinations where for each model we give its name and the attribute types[5] of spatio-temporal objects (see table below).

	TO		$\overline{\text{TO}}$		T (k snapshots)	
SO	$\tau(Region)$	STO	$\overline{\tau}(Region)$	$\overline{\text{STO}}$	$Region^{(k)}$	SOT
$\overline{\text{SO}}$	$\tau(Polygon)$	$\overline{\text{STO}}$	$\overline{\tau}(Polygon)$	$\overline{\overline{\text{STO}}}$	$Polygon^{(k)}$	$\overline{\text{SOT}}$
S (m segments)			$[\,\overline{\tau}(Line)^m\,]$	$\overline{\text{TOS}}$	$Line^{(k \cdot m)}$	ST

Apart from the already mentioned "full" ADT versions (i.e., spatial and temporal objects are both integrated as ADTs), the model SOT ($\overline{\text{SOT}}$) denotes a model where (linear) spatial objects are integrated into a tuple-timestamped temporal database: for each snapshot the currently valid version of the spatial object is stored. This is indicated by the exponent (k) expressing that there are k tuples representing all the k snapshots. Similarly, $\overline{\text{TOS}}$ denotes the model where spatial objects (i.e., polygons) are encoded by m tuples – for each segment one tuple –, and the temporal behavior is given by linear temporal objects. This means each evolving polygon is represented by m temporal objects storing the behavior of each segment. This seems to be a rather unrealistic model

---

4. We notice that the number of components cannot change for linear areas. So we cannot model the splitting or merging of regions.
5. We give only the type for areal objects; for points all entries in the first (second) column are $\tau(Point)$ ($\overline{\tau}(Point)$), and the third column always contains $Point^{(k)}$.

(mostly because temporal object models do not exist so far), however, SOT and $\overline{\text{S}}$OT are conceivable, since spatial object models do already exist. So these two models describe the option of simply combining existing database technology for spatial and temporal databases. We have omitted a possible model TOS of unconstrained temporal objects storing segment representations of polygons, since it seems to be rather difficult to "synchronize" arbitrary temporal line objects so that they always complement into a proper polygon. Finally, the most simple model that does not use ADTs at all is the ST model which represents a changing polygon by $k \cdot m$ tuples where m tuples representing one polygon snapshot get a common time stamp.

4.2   Expressiveness of Spatio-Temporal Models

All the different models presented above form a hierarchy which we will describe next. We obtain a representation hierarchy as shown on the right. An arrow from model A to model B means "A is less expressive than B", i.e., $A \subset B$. The edge labels serve as indices to the corresponding theorems. First, we combine and generalize results about spatial objects (see full paper) and of Theorem 3.1. Apart from aggregating spatial and temporal objects in an

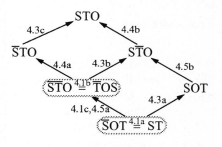

ST-REL separately (by means of v_S and v_T), we can also consider the quasi-simultaneous aggregation $v_{ST}(\text{ST-REL}) = v_T(v_S(\text{ST-REL}))$. μ_{T^+} is the extension of μ_T into a total function mapping to the extended representation ST^+-REL, and v_{T^+} is the corresponding extension of v_T. We also use $v_{ST^+}(\text{ST}^+\text{-REL}) = v_{T^+}(v_S(\text{ST}^+\text{-REL}))$. First, we can observe (see full paper):

Fact 4.1. $v_S(\text{S-REL}) = \overline{\text{S}}\text{O-REL}$ and $\mu_S(\overline{\text{S}}\text{O-REL}) = \text{S-REL}$.

Now we have:

Theorem 4.2.   (a) $v_S(\text{ST-REL}) = \overline{\text{S}}\text{OT-REL}$
(b) $v_{ST^+}(\mu_{T^+}(\overline{\text{T}}\text{OS-REL})) = \overline{\text{ST}}\text{O-REL}$
(c) $v_T(\text{ST-REL}) \subset \overline{\text{T}}\text{OS-REL}$
(d) $v_{ST}(\text{ST-REL}) \subset \overline{\text{ST}}\text{O-REL}$

Proof. Part (a) follows directly from fact 4.1. Part (b) deserves some explanations: First, we cannot simply apply v_S to $\overline{\text{T}}\text{OS-REL}$ because the spatial attributes are hidden in temporal objects, so we have to unpack them beforehand. However, we must be very careful here: since μ_T is not totally defined on $\overline{\text{T}}\text{OS-REL}$ (ST-REL is a true subset of $\overline{\text{T}}\text{OS-REL}$) we have to map to the extended representation ST^+-REL by means of the extended unnesting function μ_{T^+}. We then know: $\mu_{T^+}(\overline{\text{T}}\text{OS-REL}) = \text{ST}^+\text{-REL}$. Now we can aggregate the spatial objects and get (from part (a)): $v_S(\text{ST}^+\text{-REL}) = \overline{\text{S}}\text{OT}^+\text{-REL}$. Finally, we can aggregate the temporal objects and obtain (as a corollary of Theorem 3.2): $v_{T^+}(\overline{\text{S}}\text{OT}^+\text{-REL}) = \overline{\text{ST}}\text{O-REL}$. Part (c) follows directly from Theorem 3.1, and (d) follows from (b) and (c). □

We also have corresponding results for ST^+-REL:

Theorem 4.3. (a) $v_{T^+}(\text{ST}^+\text{-REL}) = \overline{\text{TOS}}\text{-REL}$
(b) $v_{ST^+}(\text{ST}^+\text{-REL}) = \overline{\text{STO}}\text{-REL}$

Theorems 4.2 and 4.3 express relationships of the flat relational model w.r.t. (linear) ADT models. Next we show relationships that result from the polygons being special cases of general regions.

Theorem 4.4. (a) $\overline{\text{SOT}}\text{-REL} \subset \text{SOT-REL}$
(b) $\overline{\text{STO}}\text{-REL} \subset \text{S}\overline{\text{T}}\text{O-REL}$
(c) $\overline{\text{STO}}\text{-REL} \subset \text{STO-REL}$

This theorem essentially follows from the fact that $\overline{\text{SO}} \subset \text{SO}$. Similarly, as a corollary of Lemma 3.1 we obtain the following result expressing that relations with linear temporal objects are less expressive than relations with general temporal objects:

Theorem 4.5. (a) $\text{S}\overline{\text{T}}\text{O-REL} \subset \overline{\text{STO}}\text{-REL}$
(b) $\text{S}\overline{\text{T}}\text{O-REL} \subset \text{STO-REL}$

And finally, as a corollary of Theorems 3.1 and 3.2, we obtain (note that part (a) is actually equivalent to Theorem 4.2 (c)):

Theorem 4.6. (a) $v_T(\overline{\text{SOT}}\text{-REL}) \subset \overline{\text{STO}}\text{-REL}$
(b) $v_T(\text{SOT-REL}) \subset \text{S}\overline{\text{T}}\text{O-REL}$
(c) $v_{T^+}(\overline{\text{SOT}}^+\text{-REL}) = \overline{\text{STO}}\text{-REL}$
(d) $v_{T^+}(\text{SOT}^+\text{-REL}) = \text{S}\overline{\text{T}}\text{O-REL}$

It is very instructive to imagine spatio-temporal objects as 3D-objects. Then the different models presented relate directly to different features and restrictions of 3D-objects. For instance, STO describes rather arbitrary volumes (or curves in the case of points), whereas $\overline{\text{STO}}$ is restricted to region objects with polygonal faces parallel to the x-y plane. $\text{S}\overline{\text{T}}\text{O}$ ($\overline{\text{S}\overline{\text{T}}\text{O}}$) restricts STO ($\overline{\text{STO}}$) further to straight translations and scalings plus rotations w.r.t. the t-axis (for points: translations only). Two severe restrictions of $\overline{\text{STO}}$ (that result from affine mappings) are: (i) the number of components cannot change, and (ii) the number of vertices of polygons cannot change. When considering linear representations (to facilitate efficient computations) and 3D-objects, we can also imagine moving regions being represented by *polyhedra*. It is then interesting to note that polyhedra are not comparable in expressiveness to $\overline{\text{STO}}$: polyhedra cannot represent rotations, but they can well model changes in the numbers of components and polygon vertices.

5 Conclusions

We have presented a new model for temporal objects and temporal databases that, in particular, offers quite different modeling options for spatio-temporal databases. The investigation of the relative expressiveness of the different models gives a clear picture of the relationships between these models. In particular, it can be seen that, compared with the traditional (flat) view of temporal databases, the ADT approach is more versatile and offers much more control over temporal behavior, even for linearly constrained objects. Future work should consider other specific spatio-temporal object models (such as polyhedra) in more detail.

References

[BS77]   R.R. Berman & M. Stonebraker. GEO-QUEL: A System for the Manipulation and Display of Geographic Data. *Computer Graphics*, vol. 11, pp. 186-191, 1977.

[EGSV98]   M. Erwig, R.H. Güting, M. Schneider & M. Vazirgiannis. Spatio-Temporal Data Types: An Approach to Modeling and Querying Moving Objects in Databases. *ACM Symp. on Geographic Information Systems*, 1998. To appear.

[ES97]   M. Erwig & M. Schneider. Vague Regions. *5th Int. Symp. on Advances in Spatial Databases*, LNCS 1262, pp. 298-320, 1997.

[ESG97]   M. Erwig, M. Schneider & R.H. Güting. Temporal Objects for Spatio-Temporal Data Models and a Comparison of Their Representations, Technical Report 225, 1997 (Revised Version 1998).

[Ga64]   S. Gaal. *Point Set Topology*. Academic Press, 1964.

[GS95]   R.H. Güting & M. Schneider. Realm-Based Spatial Data Types: The ROSE Algebra. *VLDB Journal*, vol. 4, pp. 100-143, 1995.

[Gü88]   R.H. Güting. Geo-Relational Algebra: A Model and Query Language for Geometric Database Systems. *Int. Conf. on Extending Database Technology*, pp. 506-527, 1988.

[Gü94]   R.H. Güting. An Introduction to Spatial Database Systems. *VLDB Journal*, vol. 3, pp. 357-399, 1994.

[Ro87]   J.W. van Roessel. Design of a Spatial Data Structure Using the Relational Normal Forms. *Int. Journal of Geographical Information Systems*, vol. 1, pp. 33-50, 1987.

[Sc97]   M. Schneider. *Spatial Data Types for Database Systems - Finite Resolution Geometry for Geographic Information Systems*. LNCS 1288, Springer-Verlag, 1997.

[SH91]   P. Svensson & Z. Huang. Geo-SAL: A Query Language for Spatial Data Analysis. *2nd Int. Symp. on Advances in Spatial Databases (SSD '91)*, pp. 119-140, 1991.

[SRG83]   M. Stonebraker, B. Rubenstein & A. Guttmann. Application of Abstract Data Types and Abstract Indices to CAD Data Bases. *ACM/IEEE Conf. on Engineering Design Applications*, pp. 107-113, 1983.

[SS86]   H.-J. Schek & M.H. Scholl. The Relational Model with Relation-Valued Attributes. *Information Systems*, vol. 11, pp. 137-147, 1986.

[SS93]   A. Segev & A. Shoshani: A Temporal Data Model Based on Time Sequences. Chapter 11 of [TCG+93], pp. 248-270, 1993.

[St86]   M. Stonebraker. Inclusion of New Types in Relational Data Base Systems. *2nd IEEE Int. Conf. on Data Engineering*, pp. 262-269, 1986.

[SV89]   M. Scholl & A. Voisard. Thematic Map Modeling. *1st Int. Symp. on the Design and Implementation of Large Spatial Databases*, pp. 167-190, 1989.

[TCG+93]   A.U. Tansel, J. Clifford, S. Gadia, S. Jajodia, A. Segev & R. Snodgrass. *Temporal Databases: Theory, Design, and Implementation*. Benjamin/Cummings Publishing Company, 1993.

[Ti80]   R.B. Tilove. Set Membership Classification: A Unified Approach to Geometric Intersection Problems. *IEEE Transactions on Computers*, vol. C-29, pp. 874-883, 1980.

[Wo94]   M.F. Worboys. A Unified Model for Spatial and Temporal Information. *The Computer Journal*, vol. 37, pp. 27-34, 1994.

[YC93]   T.S. Yeh & B. de Cambray. Time as a Geometric Dimension for Modeling the Evolution of Entities: A 3D Approach. *2nd Int. Conf. on Integrating GIS and Environmental Modeling*, 1993.

The Temporal Set-Theory, Tropology and Their Application in Spatiotemporal Modelling[*]

Agnar Renolen

Department of Surveying and Mapping
Norwegian University of Science and Technology (NTNU)
N-7034 Trondheim, Norway
e-mail: agnar@iko.unit.no

Abstract. In this paper we briefly introduce the basics of a proposed temporal set theory together with the associated tropology. In this theory, sets and attributes are expressed as functions over time, and we suggest how temporal attributes in general, and spatiotemporal attributes in particular, can be implemented based on this theory.

1 Introduction

The set-theory provide the most general and basic concepts of mathematics and applications of computer science. E.g. the most popular database model, the relational model is based on the set-theory. Undoubtedly, the neatness and the comprehensiveness of the set theory have been the key reason for the success of relational database management systems (RDMS) over the last two decades.

When the issue of temporal databases caught the interest of database researchers, it was natural to extend the relational model into a *temporal relational model*. However, we suggest that temporal databases should be based on a *temporal set-theory* rather than on existing snapshot database theory. In this paper, the most basic concepts of the temporal set-theory together with the associated *tropology* is proposed. The term tropology is introduced to denote the *study of changes* and stems from the Greek word *tropos* meaning to change or to turn. The ambition of this paper is not to present a complete theory, but to introduce a better framework that can be used to build better temporal and spatiotemporal data models.

The remainder of this paper is organized as follows: In the following section we define the time domain, and in Section 3 we introduce the temporal set theory. In Section 4 we develop a simple data model based on this theory, and finally we provide a discussion of implications and future research in the last section.

2 The Time Model

In this paper, we use the symbol $\mathbb{T}$ to denote the set of all times. We assume a continuous model of time that is isomorphic to the real numbers and the members of $\mathbb{T}$ are called *instants*.

---

[*] This work is sponsored by the Norwegian Research Council (NFR), project 31387

We also define a *metric* o n $\mathbb{T}$ which is a non-negative number $\delta(t_1, t_2)$ that computes the *duration* or *time difference* between any two instants t_1 and t_2:

$$\delta(t_1, t_2) = |t_2 - t_1|. \tag{1}$$

3 The Temporal Set Theory

3.1 Functions over Time

A function f over time is a function from the time domain $\mathbb{T}$ into some arbitrary codomain $\mathbf{A}$:

$$f : \mathbb{T} \to \mathbf{A}. \tag{2}$$

Functions of this type may in temporal databases be used to describe attributes of objects that is changing over time. Because we assert that such functions return a value even for times when the function is not defined, we introduce the symbol $\bot$ (null) which is used to indicate that an object did not exist at a some times. Thus, any domain $\mathbf{A}$ has a corresponding *temporal domain*

$$\mathbf{A}^T = \{f | f : \mathbb{T} \to (\mathbf{A} \cup \{\bot\})\} \tag{3}$$

which is the set of all functions with $\mathbb{T}$ as domain and $(\mathbf{A} \cup \{\bot\})$ as codomain.

To each function $f(t)$ we assign a *lifespan* $LS(f)$, which according to [3] [6] can be any subset of $\mathbb{T}$, representing the times at which the attribute is defined. Formally, we define the lifespan as a function from a temporal domain $\mathbf{A}^T$ into the power set $P(\mathbb{T})$,

$$LS : \mathbf{A}^T \to P(\mathbb{T}), \tag{4}$$

such that

$$LS(f) = \{t \in \mathbb{T} | f(t) \neq \bot\}. \tag{5}$$

In some cases, we restrict a lifespan to be a *connected* subset of $\mathbb{T}$, i.e. a *temporal interval*. A temporal interval can be identified by an ordered pair $\langle t_1, t_2 \rangle$ in $\mathbb{T} \times \mathbb{T}$, where $t_1 \leq t_2$. Since the distinction between lifespans and temporal intervals is important, we will define the set $2\mathbb{T}$ to be the set of all temporal intervals, and $P(\mathbb{T})$ to be the set of all lifespans. Thus $2\mathbb{T} \subseteq P(\mathbb{T})$. Note that we have given the symbol $2\mathbb{T}$ rather than $\mathbb{T}^2$ to avoid confusion with the bitemporal domain.

The *duration* of a lifespan, denoted $\|LS(f)\|$, is a non-negative number representing the amount of time during which the function existed. If the lifespan of a function contains only one instant, the duration is zero. The semantics of this is significant, since it allow us to represent instantaneous facts such as events (instantaneous changes) or snapshots (instantaneous states).

3.2 Temporal n-tuples and the Cartesian Product of Temporal Domains

Objects are described by a set of attributes. Since an object with n attributes comprises an n-tuple, temporal objects comprise of *temporal n-tuples*. Temporal objects also contain non-temporal attributes, but we treat these as constant-valued functions over time.

Let $\mathbf{A}_1, \ldots, \mathbf{A}_n$ be (non-temporal) sets, and let $\mathbf{B}$ be the Cartesian product

$$\mathbf{B} = \mathbf{A}_1 \times \cdots \times \mathbf{A}_n. \tag{6}$$

Then the Cartesian product of the corresponding temporal domains is the set of *temporal n-tuples* which are functions from $\mathbb{T}$ into the set $\mathbf{B} \cup \{\bot\}$. In other words,

$$(\mathbf{A}_1 \times \cdots \times \mathbf{A}_n)^T = \{f | f : \mathbb{T} \to (\mathbf{A}_1 \times \cdots \times \mathbf{A}_n \cup \{\bot\})\} \tag{7}$$

In the real world it may be the case that an attribute of an object, is not defined for the entire lifespan of that object. Moreover, attributes may also be maintained and updated for objects that does not logically exist. E.g. physicians may keep records of babies even before they are born.

However, for simplicity we will assert that no entry in a temporal n-tuple may exist unless the n-tuple itself exist. In other words, we introduce the following axiom:

$$LS(a_1) \cup \cdots \cup LS(a_n) \subseteq LS(\langle a_1, \ldots, a_n \rangle) \tag{8}$$

3.3 Temporal Sets

A set may contain a number of members. Over time, the set may receive new members while existing members may secede their membership. The members of a temporal set can be a non-temporal object, a function over time, or another set or temporal set. The same concept is described by [9] where a *valid time collection* provide the same functionality.

Formally, we also define a temporal set as a function over time: given any arbitrary domain $\mathbf{A}$ and the time domain $\mathbb{T}$, a temporal set τ can be described as a function from $\mathbb{T}$ into the power set $P(\mathbf{A})$

$$\tau : \mathbb{T} \to P(\mathbf{A}) \tag{9}$$

that for every time t in $\mathbb{T}$ returns a subset of $\mathbf{A}$ containing the elements that is a member of τ at that time. We use the notation

$$a \in \tau(t) \tag{10}$$

to indicate that the element a is a member of the temporal set τ at a time t. The *membership lifespan* of an element a with respect to a temporal set τ, denoted $LS(a \in \tau)$ is the set of times at which a is a member of τ. In other words,

$$LS(a \in \tau) = \{t \in \mathbb{T} | a \in \tau(t)\} \tag{11}$$

Following this definition, it is clear that the assertion

$$LS(a \in \tau) \subseteq LS(\tau) \tag{12}$$

must hold. Another assertion that may be introduced is that a set cannot contain dead members, in other words

$$LS(a \in \tau) \subseteq LS(a). \tag{13}$$

However, this axiom should only be optional, e.g. some members of, say, the GIS hall of fame, may no longer be alive.

It is now possible to define different types of Cartesian products and relations on temporal sets, in addition to traditional set operations such as union, intersection, difference, complement, cardinality functions, equality functions and so on. Also the extension into the bitemporal set-theory should be of interest to temporal database engineers. Due to space limitations, we cannot include these definitions here.

3.4 Updating a Temporal System and Tropology

So far, we have presented a machinery to represent a temporal system, but this system itself is static. Therefore, we need some kind of *evolution language* [7], to change and update this structure as time passes. According to [8], we introduce three types change operators. Let a and b be two elements with respect to some universe of discourse.

- The *constructor* of an element a is an unary or binary operation that creates a new element, and is denoted $\vdash$. An unary expression $\vdash a$ is read "the creation of a", while a binary expression $b \vdash a$ is read "b creates a", or "b spawns a".
- The *modifier* from one element a to an element b is a binary operator that establish a identity-preserving predecessor-successor relationship between two groups of elements, and is denoted $\mapsto$. The expression $a \mapsto b$ is read "a becomes b". In this case a and b must be two versions of the same object. Often, we want express causal relationships between objects or changes. E.g. that "an object a made b become c", can be expressed by the statement $a \vdash (b \mapsto c)$.
- The *destructor* of an element a is an unary or binary operator that destroys the element a, and is denoted $\dashv$. An unary expression $\dashv a$ is read "the destruction of a", while the binary expression $b \dashv a$ is read "b destroys a".

In general, we use similar expressions for sets that we presented above, i.e. to express the *assembly* or the *aggregation* of a collection of elements into a new set

$$(a_1, \cdots, a_n) \vdash \mathbf{A} = \{a_1, \ldots, a_n\}, \tag{14}$$

and the *dissolution* of an existing set (which does not mean the destruction of the members of the set),

$$\dashv \mathbf{A}. \tag{15}$$

We also de fine two membership operators for sets, these are *inclusion* which is denoted $\oplus$ and *secession* denoted $\ominus$. They are defined as follows:

$$\mathbf{A} \oplus a \equiv \mathbf{A} \mapsto (\mathbf{A} \cup \{a\}) \tag{16}$$

$$\mathbf{A} \ominus a \equiv \mathbf{A} \mapsto (\mathbf{A} \backslash \{a\}), \tag{17}$$

Related to these tropological operators and the lifespans of these, which are temporal intervals, a certain number of axioms should be defined. In order to express these, we use the relation *meets* between two temporal intervals [1]. If T_1 and T_2 are temporal intervals, then meets is defined by

$$T_1 \text{ meets } T_2 \equiv (T_1 \cap T_2 = \emptyset) \wedge (\neg \exists t \, (\sup T_1 < t < \inf T_2)). \tag{18}$$

As proposed in [2], the following two axioms must hold for the modifier:

$$LS(a) \text{ meets } LS(a \mapsto b) \tag{19}$$
$$LS(a \mapsto b) \text{ meets } LS(b) \tag{20}$$

For the creator, we have the two axioms

$$LS(\vdash a) \text{ meets } LS(a) \tag{21}$$
$$LS(b \vdash a) \quad \subseteq \quad LS(b) \tag{22}$$

while for the destructor, these two axioms must hold:

$$LS(\dashv a) \text{ meets } LS(a) \tag{23}$$
$$LS(b \dashv a) \quad \subseteq \quad LS(b) \tag{24}$$

4 A Temporal Data Model

4.1 Implementing Temporal Attributes

Different attributes of an object exhibit different types of behaviour. Given a function over time, we can identify at least three types of 'states' of that function. If f is a function over time, f is *dead* if $f(t) = \bot$, it is *static* if $\frac{d}{dt} f(t) = 0$ and it is *changing* otherwise. A function is *alive* if it is not dead (i.e. either changing or static).

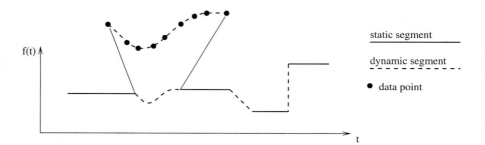

Fig. 1. Dynamic end static segments of a function.

Specifically, as illustrated in Figure 1, we may construct functions over time by using a series of alternating *static* and *dynamic segments* for the times where the function is alive. For times where the functions are in continuous change, the function may be implemented by a sequence of static segments with no duration called *data points* linked together with dynamic segments. This way, we can implement temporal attributes by a sequence alternating static and dynamic segments. Dynamic segments are also used to represent instantaneous changes. This way of implementing functions is slightly different from [4] who implement functions only using data points together with a flag that determines whether the point represent a gradual or instantaneous change since the previous data point.

Static segments are identified by an element of some domain $\mathbf{A}$ and a lifespan in $2\mathbb{T}$. Dynamic segments on the other hand are identified by two elements in $\mathbf{A}$, one for the initial state and one for the end state, together with two corresponding times in $\mathbb{T}$. Both dynamic and static segments may have a lifespan with zero duration.

4.2 Implementing Spatiotemporal Attributes

The concepts we have been describing above also applies to spatial entities. In this paper, we restrict ourselves to a two-dimensional Euclidean plane, $\mathbb{E}^2$. Thus, three types of *spatial atoms* my be defined:

- *point*—represents a 0-dimensional element. We define $\mathbb{S}_p = \mathbb{E}^2$ to be the set of all points.
- *curve*—represents a 1-dimensional element c which is a subset of $\mathbb{E}^2$ that is iso-morphic to the real numbers. We define $\mathbb{S}_c \subset P(\mathbb{E}^2)$ to be the set of all curves in $\mathbb{E}^2$.
- *region*—representing a 2-dimensional element r which is a subset of $\mathbb{E}^2$. We may identify two types of regions, simple regions which are connected subsets of $\mathbb{E}^2$, and complex regions which are not connected. We define $\mathbb{S}_r \subseteq P(\mathbb{E}^2)$ to be the set of all regions.

Then, the set of all spatial atoms $\mathbb{S}$ is defined as the superset

$$\mathbb{S} = \mathbb{S}_p \cup \mathbb{S}_c \cup \mathbb{S}_r, \tag{25}$$

and the corresponding set of *spatiotemporal atoms* becomes $\mathbb{S}^T$.

Worboys [10] defines a system of *ST-atoms* where each ST-atom is a right prism defined by the pair $\langle s, LS(s) \rangle$ where s is an element in $\mathbb{S}$, and $LS(s)$ is an element in $2\mathbb{T}$. Since these types of atoms cannot represent spatial objects that have a gradually changing extent, they correspond to the static segments of the spatiotemporal attributes. Thus we may call them *static ST-segments*. Then, we also need to define a set of dynamic segments of spatiotemporal attributes, called *dynamic ST-segments*. A dynamic ST-segment can be defined by two pairs $\langle s_1, t_1 \rangle$ and $\langle s_2, t_2 \rangle$ where s_1 and s_2 are elements of $\mathbb{S}$ and t_1 and t_2 are elements of $\mathbb{T}$ with $t_1 \leq t_2$. This gives us a system of six types of spatiotemporal segments as illustrated in Figure 2.

4.3 Explicit Tropology

In the spatial domain, interrelationships between static and dynamic segments can be more complex than the simple predecessor-successor relationships introduced above. E.g. a region may split into two or more smaller regions, or two or more regions may be joined to form a new bigger region. To accommodate this, we must allow the dynamic and static segments to have more than one predecessor and successor.

At least twelve different types of tropological relationships between simple objects can be identified (11 of them are described in [5]). These are as follows:

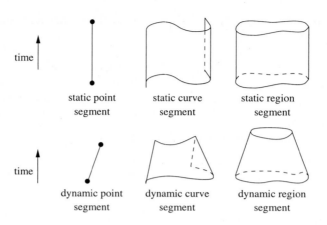

Fig. 2. Spatiotemporal segments

- *Create*: ⊢ *A*. An object is created.
- *Destruct*: ⊣ *A*. An object is destroyed.
- *Alterate*: $A \mapsto A'$. An object is modified.
- *Metamorphose*: $(\dashv A) \vdash B$. An object succeeds another object.
- *Divide*: $(\dashv A) \vdash (B, C)$. An object is divided into one or more pieces while the original object ceases to exist.
- *Merge*: $(\dashv (A, B)) \vdash C$. The opposite of merge. Two objects join to form a new object.
- *Deduct*: $(A \mapsto A') \vdash B$. An object is created from a part of another object.
- *Annex*: $(A \mapsto A') \dashv B$. The opposite of deduct, i.e. an object is included as a part of another object.
- *Spawn*: $A \vdash B$. Similar to deduct, but in contrast to deduct where the original object looses something that becomes a new object, the original object remains unchanged.
- *Swallow*: $A \dashv B$. Similar to annex and opposite to spawn. But in contrast to annex, the object that was swallowed does not become a part of the main objects which remains unchanged.
- *Reincarnate*: ⊢ *A*. This is simply another creation of an object, with the distinction that the object have existed before.
- *Compound*: $(A, (\dashv B), (C \mapsto C')) \vdash D$. An operation which is some sort of combination of split, deduct and spawn.

However, the reader may immediately recognize the possibility of more possible combinations, e.g. [5] also identifies a set of changes applying to sets (or composite objects).

5 Discussion

We have introduced the temporal set theory, and demonstrated its application in building temporal abstract data types. We have shown how to construct non-spatial attributes, spatial attributes and collections or sets as functions over time. We have also looked into the new research area that now seem to emerge from research in temporal GIS, which we have called *tropology*.

Our ultimate goal is to propose a model for an object-oriented temporal GIS, based on the object-oriented paradigm and the various aspects of evolution in an object-oriented database. The research presented in this paper, highly contributes to this goal.

We believe that, due to the wide range of applications of temporal GIS, we must strive for a common and comprehensive foundation and a general model for all these applications, whichever the temporal set-theory provides. Only this way, can we achieve many of the goals within GIS research today.

References

1. J. F. Allen. Maintaining knowledge about temporal intervals. *Communications of the ACM*, 26(11), November 1983.
2. J. F. Allen. Towards a general theory of action and time. *Artificial Inteligence*, 23(2), 1984.
3. J. Clifford and A. Croker. The historical relational data model (HRDM) and algebra based on lifespans. In *Proceedings, Third International Conference on Data Engineering*, 1987.
4. M. Erwig, R. H. Güting, M. Schneider, and M. Vazirgiannis. Spatio-temporal data types: An approach to modeling and querying moving objects in databases. Technical Report 224, FernUniversität Gesamthochschule in Hagen, 1997.
5. K. Hornsby and M. J. Egenhofer. Qualitative representation of change. *Lecture Notes in Computer Science*, 1329:15–33, 1997.
6. C. S. Jensen, J. Clifford, R. Elmasri, S. K. Gadia, P. Hayes, S. Jajodia, C. Dyreson, F. Grandi, W. Kafer, N. Kline, N. Lorentzos, Y. Mitsopoulos, A. Montanari, D. Nonen, E. Peressi, B. Pernici, J. F. Roddick, N. L. Sarda, M. R. Scalas, A. Segev, R. T. Snodgrass, M. D. Soo, A. Tansel, P. Tiberio, and G. Wiederhold. A consensus glossary of temporal database concepts. *SIGMOD Record (ACM Special Interest Group on Management of Data)*, 23(1):52–64, March 1994.
7. J.-B. Lagorce, A. Stockus, and E. Waller. Object-oriented database evolution. In F. N. Afrati and P. Kolaitis, editors, *Database Theory—ICDT'97, 6th International Conference*, volume 1186 of *Lecture Notes in Computer Science*, pages 379–393, Delphi, Greece, January 1997. Springer.
8. E. Rose and A. Segev. TOOSQL: A temporal object-oriented query language. *Lecture Notes in Computer Science*, 823:122–136, 1993.
9. A. Steiner and M. C. Norrie. A temporal extension to a generic object data model. Technical report, TimeCenter, May 1997. TR-15.
10. M. F. Worboys. A model for spatio-temporal information. In *5th International Symposium on Spatial Data Handling*, pages 602–611. IGU Commision on GIS, 1992.

TimeCube-Efficient Storage, Access and Analysis of Temporal (Historical) Data

Y. Ishii, T. Ishizaka, N. Mohan [†] **and J. Feng** [‡]

Beacon Information Technology, Inc., JAPAN
Ishii,Ishizaka,Mohan,Hyouketu@beacon-it.co.jp
Dalian University of Technology, China

Abstract. This paper introduces TimeCube-a technology product specifically designed for the analysis of master type data or dimensional data (such as customer information) which changes (in an aperiodic manner) over time. The application of time tested technology to original concepts from "unit of information and its three dimensionality", Y. Ishii , 1982.2 [1] and "Three Dimensional DBMS (3D-DBMS)", Y. Ishii, 1989.1.19 [2], has resulted in the development of TimeCube. TimeCube answers the increasing need in the IT marketplace for the efficient analysis of this distinct type of data. The focus is on analysis related to regenerating the data records at a previous instant of time, tracking the number and types of changes in the attributes for a record and examining the duration of particular states for the record. Beta testing is currently planned and/or already underway on various large customer sites in US, Japan and Australia for the future implementation of TimeCube.

1   Introduction

The efficient management of data is one of the most important challenges that organizations are facing today. In absence of the relevant knowledge, the foundations of many organizations are being weakened by their own information management systems that gather massive amount of data across various divisions and departments. Most conventional DBMS or Relational DBMS, which are the ones habitually used in information management systems, present SQL as a general query language for data retrieval and management. It has been observed that there is a special niche of application areas, such as "historical" personnel information in human resource applications, "historical" customer information in customer loyalty and retention applications, etc for which, in our opinion, SQL provides an insufficient level of support [3]. This is primarily with respect to ease of use and system performance. The records, which represent time-varying data, and can be referred to as time dimensional records must be efficiently stored and hence retrievable.

There are two ways of tackling these problems, one of which is to extend existing relational DBMS technology by implementing temporal query support. The other and more readily feasible option is to provide a specialized Database/Data

Warehouse server as a solid platform for doing information analysis in an integrated manner on historical dimensional data. In the same way as multidimensional database technology was a harbinger for problems in the areas of executive decision analysis/decision support, a few years ago, a new kind of system for analysis of this special type of data database is necessary for current customers. TimeCube has been developed as an all-inclusive database/date warehouse system for the automated collection, storage and querying of time-varying dimensional data [4].

2   Design objectives and assumptions

This section will list the design objectives of TimeCube, specifically features that should be included, and perhaps more importantly, those that will not be implemented (at the present stage). In order to provide for a coherent design for speedy implementation, the design objectives of TimeCube were considerably curtailed and certain overriding assumptions were also made. The following provides an incomplete list.

(1) Support for an abundance of temporal query functions

Many common temporal queries are either difficult to simulate in SQL, or require embedded SQL code within a procedural language. This is due to SQL's lack of support for the time dimension in its data model and query constructs. TimeCube should provide abundant temporal query functions to manage and query time-related data.

(2) Not a standard for all types of queries on all types of time-related data

The primary goal is a complete and elaborate product design that affords a speedy and practical implementation. There is no expectation on our part that the current design will be a standard for all time-related queries. However, the design will serve as a prototype for the future research and development of TimeCube.

(3) Simplicity and efficiency of temporal queries

Since TimeCube is designed specifically for the storage of historical data, the design must provide for the simple and efficient building of temporal queries.

(4) Support for only one time dimension, valid-time

Since TimeCube is designed for use with "master type data" or dimensional data and is based on the state model [5], it supports only one time dimension, valid-time. In contrast, TSQL endorses transaction-time and valid-time separately.

(5) Time-stamp to express the valid-time.

For the sake of simplicity, the time-stamp methodology is employed. For every change in the value of a History Enabled Field (HEF) of an object [6], a time-stamp or history record is automatically appended to TimeCube. TimeCube can then be conveniently used to query suchlike changes in historical data.

(6) Comprehensive support of time periods.

A period is an anchored duration of time, i.e., the portion of time delimited by two instants. Since instants and periods are dual, instants model state transitions, and periods model the time that a state is valid. There is a need to support queries on both these parameters. Refer to Section 4.1 for details.

(7) Support for multiple representations of time

SQL dictates a single representation for the time-stamp as year-month-day hour:minute:second. There is a need for different user-defined granularities, which TimeCube provides.

(8) Support for multiple languages

The use of TimeCube, internationally, necessitates multiple language and format support. With the help of user-defined formats, it is possible to easily support multiple languages and character sets.

(9) Support for temporal indeterminacy

Many applications require storing indeterminate information, or "don't know exactly when" type of information. Temporal indeterminacy correlates closely with time granularity. A time period with granularity of one day has an implicit temporal indeterminacy of 24 hours. TimeCube should provide support for temporal indeterminacy to permit fuzzy queries.

(10) Support for time zones

Since TimeCube will be used in international applications, there should be built in support for time zone function which can transform time zones accordingly.

(11) Support for Data Warehouse type functions

TimeCube should provide support for Data Warehouse functions, such as automated data collection and management to facilitate an online analytical processing environment.

(12) Support for temporal joins

TimeCube should provide support for temporal join to meet the requirement of complex applications. These refer to joins of tables with time constantly in consideration. Also, there should be support for joining TimeCube object files and other database tables etc..

(13) Support for set operations

TimeCube should support set operations, such as the product (object_and), sum (or), and difference (-) of sets of results obtained by querying.

(14) Support for multiple platforms

TimeCube is expected to be used in a variety of industries and application areas, hence there should be support for a multitude of platforms and environments.

3　TimeCube Data Model

Prior to delving into a detailed explanation of the TimeCube data model, it is appropriate to look back into an important but often overlooked facet, viz. the basic characteristics of the data stored within databases. It is necessary to carefully research the grain of the different types of data in order to ascertain the ideal tools for storing and managing it. All types of data can be broadly classified into three main categories: raw type data, aggregate type data, and master type

Name	Position	Department	Office	
T.,Yamada	Manager	Department1	Tokyo	
J.,Tanaka	Director	Department1	Osaka	
S.,Sato		Department1	Osaka	
H.,Kato		Department1	Osaka	
... ...				

(a)   Two-dimensional table without a time axis

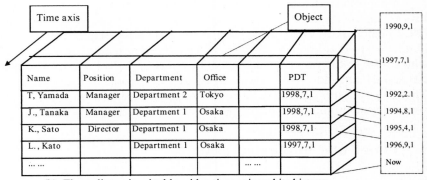

(b) Three-dimensional table with a time axis and its history
Figure 1 •Data model of TimeCube

(dimensional) data [7]. For the purposes of achieving OLAP, especially when data warehousing is being utilized, we recommend the usage of appropriate technology for these types of data [8]. With respect to master type (dimensional) data, one of the most important characteristics is Time. There are basically three accepted models of implementing time into data design, namely the snapshot model, event model and state model. With consideration to the need for ease of use and system performance, TimeCube is designed using the state model of time.

As shown in Figure 3, The data model or logical structure of the data to be managed in TimeCube is quite simple. Taking a personnel management master file as an example, first, we can imagine the file sans information about the time, such as the file on the first, July, 1997. The file can be easily represented as a two-dimensional table with the information fields on one dimension, and the records in the other like relational DBMS (See Figure 3(a)). Now, we can add the third axis, that of time to this two-dimensional table. The time axis automatically stores the information about the time period (Start-time, End-time) , in addition to the attribute values of all records in the file. When an attribute value of a field has been changed (such as an employee's promotion or office change) , a new record is appended to the file and the original record with the old information is added to a history of records. A collection of new and old records is referred to as a TimeCube object (See Figure 3(b)). A history record is only created for each TimeCube object when a change of an attribute or a field value occurs.

PD (A,U,D)	ID (After, Before)	PDT (YYYYMMDDHHMMSS)
A	After	YYYYMMDDHHMMSS
U	After	YYYYMMDDHHMMSS
D	Before	YYYYMMDDHHMMSS

Table 1 The map rule from PD and ID to Time-stamp

To implement the data model of TimeCube, each data record logically has a Processing Division (PD), Image Division (ID) and Processing Date and Time (PDT) before it is stored into a Data Warehouse. Processing Divisions include A (Add), U (Update) and D (Delete). Image Divisions consist of After and Before which refer to the time. A field called Time-stamp (PDT) is transformed from PD and ID and added to the data record after it is stored into a Data Warehouse. The map rule from PD and ID to Times-tamp is shown in Table 1. Which is very convenient and efficient to varied queries as described later.

4 TimeCube implementation

In this section, we will give a description of the actual implementation of the TimeCube design. We will provide details on the TimeCube system configuration, products that surround and are part of the TimeCube package that facilitate automated data detection, collection and management, and the platforms currently supported and those planned for in the future.

4.1 System components and configuration

As depicted in Figure 4.1, the major components of TimeCube are TCVista, TCAdmin, TCServer, Waha, Tracker and GATE/1, some system utilities and a variety of interfaces. We briefly describe below these components.

(1) TCVista

TCVista is the front-end query tool and interface for the actual users. It provides a convenient way to execute all the query functions that are supported by TimeCube. First, the initial login for connection to and disconnection from the server is achieved with TCVista. A host name, user name,and password are required for logging on to a TimeCube server. End-users can Edit/Delete a query condition by pointing and clicking the related items and selecting the required logical operands. Each query condition is associated with a view and can be saved to be for reuse at a later stage. A view can be specified as Private or Public. Only the user who originally created the query can use a Private view. On the other hand, various users on the network can share a Public view. An end-user can create or utilize a Private or Public view to perform the retrieval of data. The result can then be stored into a standard file format, which can be edited freely.

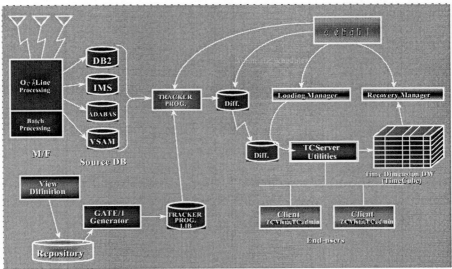

Figure 2□TimeCube™ System Configuration

(2) TCAdmin

TCAdmin is abridged from TimeCube Administrator. TCAdmin is used for managing and maintaining the system and user information, such as server system file information (TGCB), object file system information (TFCB), field definition information (TFDT), user, view and index information, etc. These attributes can be generated, updated or deleted using TCAdmin, which also master controls the log in to or log out a server, starting or stopping a server that provides services to the clients. TCAdmin is also used to backup or restore TimeCube as required.

(3) TCServer

TCServer is the actual server with the built in mechanism that provides all the services to the clients, such as query syntax check and interpretation/execution of the temporal queries posed. This is mainly a two-part main process, a query process and a data view process. The most important component is the scheduler for the various query and view process that constantly hit the server. A query or request is sent from a client via the RPC mechanism and TCServer is on standby to receive the request and respond to it using the necessary processes. If the request comes from a user, the main process for checking user's privileges, syntax and executing a query are initiated. Once completed, the result is returned to the client. If the request is from the DBA, the main process starts the view process for updating the view.

(4) Waha!

Waha! is abridged from Data WAre House Automation.This is a project running parallelly to the TimeCube project. It deals with the complex problem

of efficiently extracting data from the original databases and automating fully
the management and analysis of the data. Relevant components are employed
for TimeCube.

(5) Tracker and GATE/1

Tracker, as well as the other products related to GATE/1 [9], comprehensively address problems that are common in the data warehouse arena. A typical
scenario would be when large read-only databases are built, fed and administered to act as the foundation for a set of end-user tools that are specialized in
advanced query and data analysis functions.

(6) Utilities and interfaces

There are many utilities and interfaces built in or provided with TimeCube.
For example, TCApply, which is an efficient DB loader. It is used to insert
history data that is made available in Tracker acceptable format into a TimeCube
object file. TCUpd, is an object update tool, TCTrans is a tool to transform a
decompressed backup file into the Tracker format, which can be used to restore
a TimeCube, TCMaster is a project with which the records of a master file can
be add, update and delete. DBTrans-which can be used for code transformations
between different machines and code sets. Interfaces such as OLE2, API, ODBC,
Client etc. are also provided.

4.2 Management of Historical Data

Generally speaking, in traditional DBMS users store and manage historical data
using backups or snapshots taken at periodic intervals and/or by archiving all
the actual transactions in large files. This requires, in addition to a lot of disk or
tape space, a large amount of time to query and beneficially process. An efficient
and automated way of managing historical data is very important. The following
three methods are available to accumulate history data in TimeCube.

(1) Tracker

TimeCube files are addressing different goals: efficient support of complex
queries, simplification of the data model and history tracking. Such files must
be created by unloading data from the corporate databases, with a mapping
process that can sometimes be quite complicated (because of the different data
modeling strategies). In addition, maintaining the history of data requires a
method for tracking the changes that have occurred in the legacy data and
a method for propagating them to the target files. Allinformation about data
models, relationships among data, history, need to be maintained in a data
dictionary (the so called metadata). GATE/1 Tracker copes with precisely these
three problems, providing for automation of the mapping and unload process,
supplying tools for change capture and relying on metadata structures contained
in its repository. In combination with DBTrans and TCApply for efficient file
transfer and database loading, under a Data Warehouse type of architecture - a
TimeCube which stores and manages historical data from the same or different
machines is automatically created. The data processing and transformation can
be concisely represented as follows: [Source DB data] $\longrightarrow$ Tracker$\longrightarrow$ [Tracker

format data] $\longrightarrow$ DBTrans (optional) $\longrightarrow$ [target machine format data] $\longrightarrow$
TCApply $\longrightarrow$ [TimeCube object file]

(2) Log transformer

Log transformer is a tool that can convert original database log files into Tracker format data, based on the updated database information. Sometimes, such as when loading Windows NT's files from the Mainframe machine, DBTrans is needed to perform the code transformation between the different machines. The data processing and transformation can be concisely described as follows: [Source DB Log file] $\longrightarrow$ Log transformer $\longrightarrow$ [Tracker format data] $\longrightarrow$ DBTrans (optional) $\longrightarrow$ [target machine format data] $\longrightarrow$ TCApply $\longrightarrow$ [TimeCube object file]

(3) Csv2trackout

Csv2trackout is a program that can directly transfer CSV format files into TCApply input format files. For example, the contents of a CSV file in a spread-sheet form include PD, ID, PDT, primary key, and the values of fields. The data processing and transformation can be concisely represented as follows: [CSV format file] $\longrightarrow$ Csv2trackout $\longrightarrow$ [TCApply input form file] $\longrightarrow$ TCApply $\longrightarrow$ [TimeCube object file]

4.3   Platforms and current TimeCube implementation)

The current version (1.1) of TimeCube is specifically addressed to mimicking temporal databases, and the design objectives 1-11 have been implemented on the Windows NT (4.0) platform (Server functions) and Windows NT (4.0) or Windows 95 platforms (Client functions). The future versions 1.2 and 2.0 will realize the design objectives set out in 11-14 of Section 2. These are being designed and implemented concurrently and are expected to be released by the end of 1998. TimeCube is expected to provide support for time joins, set operations and Data Warehouse type functions. Also, multiple platforms, such as Windows NT, Windows 95 and UNIX (Solaris and/or HP), multiple language versions with English and Japanese are planned, and support for multiple interfaces including OLE2, API, ODBC, etc. will be also implemented.

5   Sample temporal queries

In this section we will briefly introduce some sample temporal queries that can be handled using TimeCube. As described above, TimeCube is provided with TCVista, a point and click query tool that a non-technical end-user can use it to build time-related queries without the requirement of learning programming skills. A more detailed explanation of the queries can be found in the related manual [6]. Let us take as an example, a personnel management system.Typical queries are illustrated as follows:

(1) Period specific query-It is limited to the period for which a particular condition remains true.

Ex: Who were the employees consecutively stationed at the Osaka office from 1996 to 1997?

Query syntax: Office = "Osaka" while ("19960101", "19971231")

(2) History query- It is based on the history value of a field .

Ex: Who are the employees that have been in the company for more than 25 years?

Query syntax: Age (Date of Joining) = 25 between (now)

(3) Length of period query-It is based on the length of the period during which a particular condition was/is satisfied.

Ex: Who are the employees that have a total experience of more than ten years of working abroad?

Query syntax: Total-time (Office ="Abroad") $\leq$ 10

(4) Event query-It is related to the changes of a field value based on the time when an event occurred .

Ex: Who are the employees promoted to Manager after 1990?

Query syntax: Change_time (Position = "Manager") $\leq$ 1990

(5) Combination query-It is the combination of above described queries and is connected using logicaloperands.

Ex: Who are the employees that have worked in Osaka and overseas?

Query syntax: Office = "Osaka" Object_and Office = "Abroad"

(6) Time granularity and fuzzy query-Many time granularity functions are provided in TimeCube. For example, Year, Month, Week, Date, Hour, Second, Millisecond, Microsecond etc. Also, user-defined (U1-U5) granularities can be used in query conditions. Furthermore, it is possible to place fuzzy conditions and perform fuzzy queries using TCVista.

In addition, TimeCube can also be used to read data when time or a period of time has been assigned and fetch information on the age, time or period when an event occurred/has been assigned.

6 Conclusions

TimeCube is a new type of Database/Data Warehouse System-a Time Dimensional Database/Data Warehouse which can collect and store time-varying data efficiently and automatically. In this paper, we have briefly introduced the design objectives and data model of TimeCube. We also give a detailed description of the implementation.of TimeCube, sample temporal queries and their applications. In comparison to relational DBMS, TimeCube addresses a specific niche application area. In order to service this area, all the tools and benefits such as a simple point and click query builder, TCVista, an automated system of accumulating and managing historical data, and above all ease of use and improved system performance are provided to the customers.

References

1. Ishii, Y., Software AG of Far East, Inc. "Unit of information and its three dimensionality" , 1982.2, IPSJ, Japan.

2. Ishii, Y., Software AG of Far East, Inc. "Three-Dimensional DBMS (3D-DBMS)" (original in Japanese),
3. Database Systems 69-8, 1989.1.19, Information Processing Society of Japan.
4. Snodgrass, R.T., The TSQL2 Temporal Query Language, Kluwer Academic publisher, Boston, 1995.
5. TimeCube Department, Beacon Information Technology, Inc., White Paper on TimeCube, Part I-Part II, 1997.
6. Ishizaka, T., "Time Related Data Warehouse System-Ti meCube" (original in Japanese), 1997.1, Beacon NEWS.
7. TimeCube Department, BIT, Inc., TimeCube Vista, TCadmin, and View control Ver.1.0, Manuals, 1997.
8. Ishii, Y., Beacon Information Technology, Inc. "Data Warehouse" (in Japanese), 1995, Japan Management Science Institute, Tokyo, Japan.
9. Selesta Ars S.p.a. -Rome, Gate/1-The Tracker Reference Manual version 1.0, 1997.

Proposal of Spatio-Temporal Indexing Methods for Moving Objects

Shogo Nishida, Hiroshi Nozawa and Naoki Saiwaki

Dept. of Systems and Human Science,Graduate School of Engineering Science,Osaka University,Toyonaka, Osaka 560-8531 JAPAN
nishida@sys.es.osaka-u.ac.jp

Abstract. This paper deals with spatio-temporal indexing methods for moving objects. Spatio-temporal indexing method gives a basis for data management structure for efficient search for large scale spatio-temporal data. In this paper, two types of indexing methods are proposed for managing spatio-temporal data for moving objects. Both methods are evaluated by computer simulation, and the merits and demerits of both methods are discussed.

1 Introduction

The management of spatio-temporal data is becoming increasingly important in many application fields such as Computer-Aided Design (CAD), Geographic Information Systems(GIS) and Virtual Reality(VR) systems. For spatial data management, much research has been done, and structures based on the space-partitioning have been proposed [1]. With these methods, spatial data are handled efficiently and spatial search, such as range search and nearest neighbors search, can be performed rapidly. However, these structures are designed only for managing spatial data with the temporal information. On the other hand, in temporal data structures [2, 3], only non spatial attribute-based temporal data are considered, and thus these structures do not provide efficient handling methods for spatio-temporal data. To manage spatio-temporal data efficiently, a new data structure is required.

Recently many studies have been conducted on spatio-temporal database [4, 5, 6, 7, 8, 9], and several types of data structures are proposed for managing fixed objects, which do not move in the space and change their states or repeat occurrence and extinction as the time goes on. [10, 11, 12] This type of data structure is expected to be useful for facilities management using three dimensional virtual space, because efficient data search is essential for realization of real-time response.

Here we extend the type of data and deal with a data structure for moving objects. We believe the importance of management of moving objects will be increased in near future. For example, emergency vehicles such as fire-suppression ones or mobile communication equipments may be picked as concrete examples of the moving objects. It is expected that efficient data structure for moving objects will be useful for management of emergency vehicles or mobile communication equipments.

In this paper, management of spatio-temporal data for fixed objects is surveyed first. Then, two types of indexing methods are proposed for managing spatio-temporal data for moving objects. Both methods are evaluated by computer simulation, and the merits and demerits of both methods are discussed.

2 Management of Spatio-Temporal Data for Fixed Objects

In this section, we consider four indexing methods for fixed objects to manage spatio-temporal data based on spatial partitioning [13, 14, 15]. The advantages and disadvantages of each method are discussed with respect to both the search efficiency and storage cost. The methods considered here are as follows:

2.1 MT structure

For each version, a distinct tree is constructed. Roots of the trees are managed by array or another tree. We call this the MT (Multi Tree) structure. (Fig.1(1)) The MT structure is suitable for a search for a single temporal version, because every temporal version of tree is stored separately. In many practical applications, the search for the current version is most often required. By using the MT, apparently, the search for the current temporal version is performed rapidly. However, when the access is not confined to the single temporal version, the searching time increases linearly by extending the time interval to be searched. From a viewpoint of storage space, the MT is extremely costly.

2.2 ST structure

Whole data is managed by a single tree. The tree is constructed based only on the location of data. Temporal information is treated as an attribute of each data. We call this the ST (Single Tree) structure. (Fig.1(2)) The ST is not suitable for a search for a single temporal version. In the ST structure, the temporal version information is not managed by the tree. Therefore, after the spatial search, temporal version information of each data should also be examined one by one. This implies the ST cannot perform a rapid spatial search for a single temporal version.

2.3 3DT structure

In general, N-dimensional spatial data with temporal information is considered as (N+1)-dimensional data. The partition of the data space is based on both

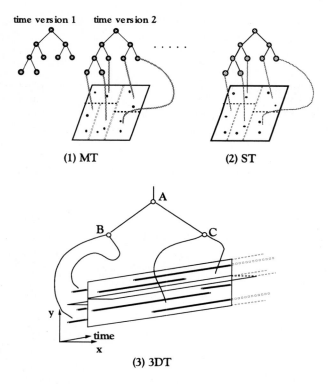

time version 1 time version 2

(1) MT **(2) ST**

(3) 3DT

Fig. 1. The MT, ST and 3DT structure.

the location and the temporal information of data. We call this the (N+1) Dimensional Tree (DT) structure. In the following sections, (N+1)-DT structure is treated as the 3DT for simplicity, by assuming two dimensional spatial data with temporal information. (Fig.1(3))

2.4 Adaptive Tree structure

Adaptive Tree structure (AT structure) is proposed to overcome the drawbacks of the ST, MT and 3DT structures. The ST tree is constructed based only on the spatial information of data, and temporal information is treated as an attribute of each data. Therefore, by using the ST, the search for narrow range of space is performed rapidly. However, search for broader range of space is not performed efficiently. On the other hand, the MT is constructed based only on the temporal information of data, and it has the same feature as the ST; that is, the performance becomes worse as the range of temporal search becomes broader. In general, tree structures have the property that the efficiency of search becomes worse as the area of searching becomes broader. The property cannot be avoided for tree structures.

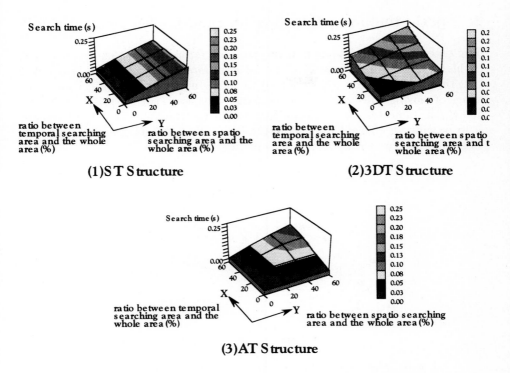

Fig. 2. Simulation results for range searching performance (CPU time).

Based on the above investigation, the AT structure is proposed [11, 12]. In this method, two data structures, that is, spatio data structure and temporal data structure is prepared in advance. Then, according to the demand of search, the method selects one of the data structures that is expected to search efficiently. In short, either spatio data structure or temporal data structure is selected adaptively depending on the demand of search.

Concretely, space partitioning for spatio data is done by using k-d tree [13]. On the other hand, temporal data are transformed into points in the occurrence / extinction plane, and these points are managed by tree structure.

Some of the simulation results are shown in Fig.2. The figure shows the performances of the spatio-temporal searching in the three dimensional plane, where X-axis and Y-axis indicate the ratio of temporal and spatio searching area toward whole area and Z-axis indicates CPU-time. It is confirmed that the performance of the AT structure is better than that of the ST and 3DT in the whole area from the figure.

3   Spatio-temporal Indexing Method for Moving Objects

Two types of spatio-temporal indexing methods for moving objects are proposed in this section. Here we ignore the volume of the moving objects and it is assumed that the moving objects are expressed by points approximately. Fig.3 shows an image of moving objects when the dimension of space is two. In this case, X-axis and Y-axis indicates the space and Z-axis indicates the time. The objective here is to provide an efficient data structure for moving objects as shown in Fig.3. The followings are the details of both methods.

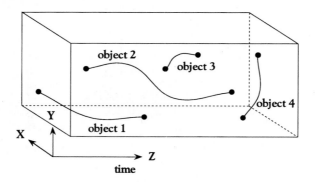

Fig. 3. Trajectories of moving objects in the spatio-temporal space.

3.1   Method 1

Method 1 is based on the AT structure mentioned in the previous section, and basically takes the same strategy as shown in Fig.4. Concretely, two data structures, that is, spatio data structure and temporal data structure are prepared in advance. Then, according to the demand of search, the method selects one of the data structures that is expected to search efficiently. In short, either spatio data structure or temporal data structure is selected adaptively depending on the demand of search.

3.1.1 Spatial Data Structure   Each object is moving in the spatio-temporal space, and trajectory of each object is projected on the spatial plane. For example, Fig.5 shows the projection of the trajectory of each object on the X-Y plane for the case of Fig.3. Here the MBR(Minimum Bounding Rectangle) for each trajectory is introduced as shown in the figure, and the centers of each rectangle is managed by tree structure. Space partitioning for spatial data is done by using k-d tree. Spatial data structure consists of two types of nodes, that is, internal nodes and leaves. An internal node has two children. The MBR value, which is expressed by the coordinates of two edges of MBR, is set to each

489

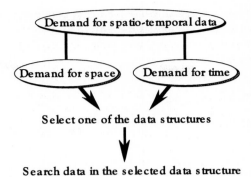

Fig. 4. Strategy of method 1.

internal node and leaf. Data are stored only in leaves. The maximum number of each leaf is called Capacity. Capacity is determined in advance before data structure is constructed. In the searching process, when arriving at an internal node, the pointer is determined by examining the MBR-value to decide whether to branch 'left' or 'right' child until arriving at a leaf. In this way, data are obtained from the tree structure.

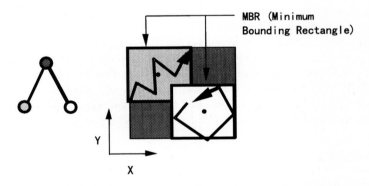

Fig. 5. Projection of the trajectory of each object on the X-Y plane.

3.1.2 Temporal Data Structure   Temporal data is usually treated as a segment in the time coordinate direction. For temporal data, significance exists in occurrence and extinction time. In the method, temporal data are transformed into points in the occurrence/extinction plane, and these points are managed by tree structures. In the occurrence/extinction plane, all points exist in the area below the line Y=X as shown in Fig. 6, since occurrence always exists before extinction. Partitioning of temporal data is done by using ternary trees recursively. (Fig. 6) Using some threshold value a, triangular data area is divided into three areas, that is, two triangular data areas and one square data area. Each triangular data area is divided into three areas recursively. Each square data area is managed by using k-d tree.

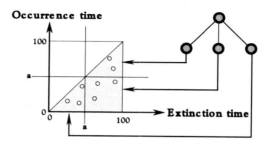

Fig. 6. Temporal data structure.

3.1.3 Selection Logic for Data Structure

In general, the search for narrow range of spatial data is performed rapidly by using the spatio data structure. In the same way, the search for narrow range of temporal data is performed rapidly by using the temporal data structure. Based on the above property, this logic adaptively selects either spatio data structure or temporal data depending on the demand of search. It is necessary for the logic to be simple enough since the total performance is directly affected by the selecting time, which is the time needed for selecting data structure.Here we adopt the logic to select the data structure whose ratio between search demand area and whole area is smaller as shown in Fig.7. This logic is simple, and it is correct when both temporal data and spatio data are uniformly distributed in the whole area.

3.2 Method 2

This method is considered to be a natural extension of 3DT structure mentioned in Section 2. The basic idea of the method is to manage the data as collection of piecewise linear lines in the spatio-temporal plane approximately and the center of each line is managed by k-d tree (Fig.8). Then the information of MBB (Minimum Bounding Block or , in other words, circumscribed cuboid) in the spatio-temporal plane is added to each leaf and node of the k-d tree as shown in Fig. 9. The concept of MBB is introduced in [4, 5], and the information is used to express the data area related to each leaf and node in our case. The concrete steps to construct the data structure and range search are as follows.

3.2.1 Construction of data structure

First, the trajectory of each object is expressed by piecewise linear lines. Then, the center of each line is

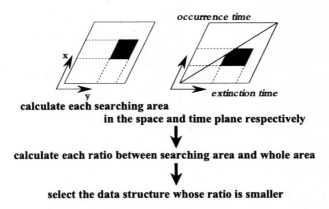

calculate each searching area
in the space and time plane respectively

↓

calculate each ratio between searching area and whole area

↓

select the data structure whose ratio is smaller

Fig. 7. Logic to select data structure.

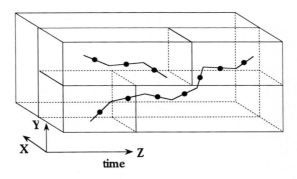

Fig. 8. Method 2.

calculated. Based on the center data of the piecewise lines, a k-d tree is created, where the capacity of each leaf is set to C. The MBB of each leaf of the k-d tree is calculated and the value is set to each leaf. In the same way, the MBB of each node of the k-d tree is calculated and the value is set to each node.

3.2.2 Range search for the data structure   The range to be searched is compared with the MBB of the node of the k-d tree. If the MBB of the node is included in the search range, then the search goes to the children of the node. If not, the search goes to another node. If the search comes to the leaf, the objects of the leaf are picked up.

4   Simulation Results

Computer simulations were carried out to evaluate the performance of the two methods mentioned in the previous section. Concretely the performance of Method 1 is compared with that of Method 2 by using Unix workstation. In the simulation

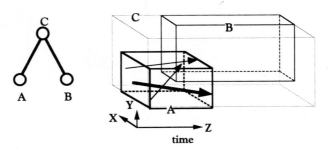

Fig. 9. MBB (Minimum Bounding Block) for each leaf and node.

cases, moving objects are expressed by the data of time-varying two-dimensional points $(X(t), Y(t))$ accompanied by occurrence and extinction. $X(t)$ and $Y(t)$ are expressed by

$$X(t + 1) = X(t) + k * Ux$$

$$Y(t + 1) = Y(t) + k * Uy$$

where Ux and Uy are randomly-generated values between -1.0 and 1.0 and k is a constant parameter . In the simulations, the total number of moving objects was 5000, and the leaf capacity C was 10 for both methods. Furthermore, the mean time between occurrence and extinction for the moving objects was 30% of the total simualtion time.

In the experiments, searching range was supposed to be cuboid in the spatio-temporal plane, whose values are varied from 1% to 20% of whole area. The performances of range searching for spatio-temporal data were tested 10 times, and the average value was used as the performance data. Fig.10 (a) and (b) show experimental results of range searching under the condition that ratio of spatial searching range is fixed to be 1% and 10% of the whole area, respectively. In the case of k=1, the performance of Method 1 is better than Method 2 for both experiments.In the case of k=10, however, the performance of Method 2 becomes better than Method 1. This results indicates that the performance of Method 1 is better than that of Method 2, when the movement of the objects in the space plane is relatively small. On the other hand, if the movement of the objects becomes large, then the performance of Method 1 becomes worse than Method 2. Fig.11(a) and (b) show experimental results for range searching under the condition that ratio of temporal searching range is fixed to be 1% and 10% of the whole area, respectively. For these cases, the same trand was observed as Fig.10(a) and (b).

Here it is supposed that k becomes zero. This is the special case for dealing with fixed objects, and in this case, Method 1 becomes AT structure and Method 2 becomes 3DT structure, respectively. As mentioned in Section 2, it has been already confirmed by computer simualtion that AT structure is better than 3DT structure for fixed objects. Therefore, it is very reasonable that Method 1 is better than Method 2 when k is small. On the other hand, the performance of spatial tree for Method 1 becomes worse as the value of k increases, because the information of the projection of the moving objects on the spatial plane has little meaning as the projection area increases. We think the experimental results are reasonable from these insights.

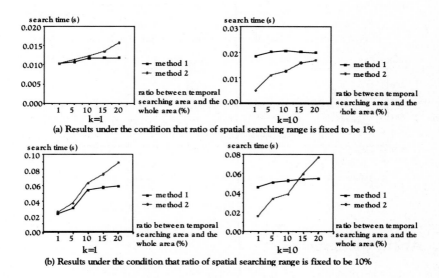

(a) Results under the condition that ratio of spatial searching range is fixed to be 1%

(b) Results under the condition that ratio of spatial searching range is fixed to be 10%

Fig. 10. Simulation Results for range search 1.

5 Conclusions

In this paper, two types of indexing methods are proposed for managing spatio-temporal data for moving objects. By computer simulations, the performance of both methods were evaluated quantitatively. Experimental results showed that the performance of Method 1 is better than that of Method 2, when the movement of the objects in the space plane is relatively small. On the other hand, if the movement of the objects becomes large, then the performance of Method 1 becomes worse than Method 2. It is also indicated that these results are reasonable by thinking of the physical meaning of both methods.

The important future works are to evaluate the performance of the proposed methods by using various data, to improve the methods to realize high performance, and also to extend the methods for handling spatio-temporal data in which both location and shape changes over time.

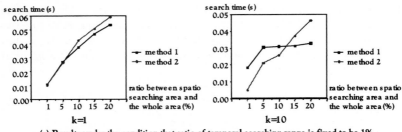

(a) Results under the condition that ratio of temporal searching range is fixed to be 1%

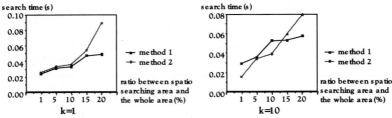

(b) Results under the condition that ratio of temporal searching range is fixed to be 10%

Fig. 11. Simulation Results for range search 2.

6   Acknowledgments

This work was partially supported by the Grant-in Aid for Scientific Research from the Japanese Ministry of Education, Science and Culture. (No.09230211)

References

1. H. Samet. *The Design and Analysis of Spatial Data Structures.* Addison-Wesley, 1989.
2. D.Lomet and B.Salzberg. Access Methods for Multi version Data. In *ACM SIG-MOD'89*, pages 315–324, 1989.
3. Wun R.Elmasri, G.T. J and Y-J. Kim. The Time Index: An Access Structure for Temporal Data. In *16th VLDB Conf.*, pages 1–12, 1990.
4. Y. Masunaga. An interval-Based Approach to a Spatial-Temporal Data Model for Virtual Collaborative Environments. In *CODAS*, pages 341–348, 1996.
5. Y. Masunaga. The Block-World Data Model for the Realization of Three Dimensional Virtual Work Space. In *DMIB'97*, pages 1–10, 1997.
6. S.Kuroki and A.Makinouchi. Design of the Spatio-Temporal Data Model Universe using Simprical Complexes. In *Report of SIG on Database Systems of the IPSJ, 96-DBS-109*, pages 221–226, 1996.
7. H.Arisawa T.Tomii and K.Salev. Design of Multimedia Database and a Query Language for Video Image Database. In *Int. Conf. on Multimedia and Computing and Systems*, pages 462–467, 1996.
8. Y.Kanamori S.Kawashima, M.Tabata and Y.Masunaga. Versioning Model of Image Objects for Easy Development of Image Database Applications. In *7th Int. Workshop on Database and Expert Systems Applications*, pages 194–200, 1996.

9. Y.Ishikawa and S.Uemura. SignatureCache: An Efficient Access Structure for Distributed Mediated Environments. In *Int. Symposium on Cooperative Database for Advanced Applications*, pages 384–387, 1996.

10. Y.Nakamura T.Teraoka, M.Maruyama and S.Nishida. The MP-tree: A Data Structure for Spatio -Temporal Data. In *the Fourteenth IEEE Phoenix Conference on Computers and Communications*, pages 326–333, 1995.

11. Naoki Saiwaki Atsuki Naka and Shogo Nishida. Spatio-Temporal Data Management for Highly Interactive Environment. In *6th IEEE International Workshop on Robot and Human Communication (ROMAN'97)*, pages 571–576, 1997.

12. Naoki Saiwaki Atsuki Naka and Shogo Nishida. An Adaptive Spatio-Temporal Data Management for Highly Interactive Environment. In *the DMIB'97*, pages 68–73, 1997.

13. J.L.Bentley. Multidimensional Binary Search Trees Used for Associative Searching. *Commun. ACM*, 18:509–517, 1975.

14. Y.Ohsawa and M.Sakauchi. The BD-tree – A new N dimensional Data Structure with Highly Efficient Dynamic Characteristics. In *IFIP Conf.*, page 539 544, 1983.

15. Y.Ohsawa Y.Nakamura, S.Abe and M.Sakauchi. A Balanced Hierarchical Data Structure for Multidimensional Data with Highly Efficient Dynamic Characteristics. *IEEE Trans. KDE*, 5:682,693, 1993.

Spatio-Temporal Data Management for Moving Objects Using the PMD-Tree

Yasuaki NAKAMURA, Hiroyuki DEKIHARA and Ryo FURUKAWA

Department of Computer Science Hiroshima City University
3-4-1, Ozuka-higashi, Asa-minami-ku,
Hiroshima, 731-3149, JAPAN
{nakamura, ryo-f}@cs.hiroshima-cu, deki@toc.cs.hiroshima-cu.ac.jp

Abstract. A spatio-temporal data structure, called the PMD-tree (Persistent Multi-Dimensional tree), has been proposed for managing the *live* intervals and locatoins of spatial objects. The PMD-tree provides efficient spatial and temporal searches not only for the current version of the data set but also the older versions of the data set. In the paper, novel concepts of time space bounding box (*TSBB*) and *motion list* are introduced to the PMD-tree to manage moving spatial objects efficiently. *TSBB* is an extended bounding box for a moving object that covers the trajectory of the object. As an object moves, a *TSBB* corresponding to the object is enlarged to enclose hte trajectory of the object. A *TSBB* is divided, when it becomes greater than a limit. A relation of an object and corresponding *TSBB*s are managed by a doubly connected linked list, called *motion list*. *TSBB*s are also managed by the PMD-tree. When a spatial and/or temporal query is given, *TSBB*s that intersect with the given spatio-temporal range are found by means of the PMD-tree. Then, tracing the *motion lists* of the *TSBB*s, the objects that satisfies the query can be found. Introduceing the concept of *TSBB* and *motion list* to the PMD-tree, moving objcets can be efficiently managed and be quickly found for spatio-temporal queries. By the series of simulation tests, the storage requirements and search performances are evaluated for several types of moving objects.

1 Introduction

The spatial data structures [1-12] have become very important in the fields of image processing, computer graphics, CAD, GIS (Geographic Information Systems), and so forth. Many spatial data structure [1-12] for multidimensional data have been proposed and some of them are applied to computer graphics, GIS, and facility management systems. In the data management by a spatial data structure, when data are deleted, the data are removed from the structure. Since the structure does not keep the older version data sets, it is impossible to access a past state of the data set.

Recently, several techniques [13-16] have been developed for managing not only the newest version of a data set but also the old versions of the data set. These structures provide accesses to the older version data sets. Resent researches [16,19] in the spatial data structure have developed spatio-temporal data structures that support spatial searches with time interval. We have also developed a spatio-temporal data structure called the PMD-tree [19]. The PMD-tree has properties that the sub-trees are always balanced and that the storage utilization rate is higher than 66.6%. Spatial queries such as the range search and nearest neighbor search with time interval can be performed efficiently and quickly by the spatio-temporal structures. However, these structures can manage only *static* objects that will not move. In other words, these spatio-temporal data structures manage *static* locations and *live* intervals of objects. They cannot manage the *dynamic* moving objects efficiently.

In the paper, we introduce novel concepts of time space bounding box (*TSBB*) and *motion list* to the PMD-tree to manage objects that may change their positions or shapes with time. A spatio-temporal proximity concept is introduced to search and manage moving or deforming objects. As the velocity of an object's motion is faster, the trajectory of the object's motion is split into more portions. Each portion is managed as a *TSBB* and the *TSBB*s are inserted into a PMD-tree as separate spatio-temporal data. The relations of these *TSBB*s and the object are managed by a doubly connected linked list, called the *motion list*. Spatio-temporal queries can be performed efficiently by the PMD-tree and *motion lists*.

In the following sections, representations of moving objects are given in 2. In sections 3 and 4, the PMD-tree and the management method of moving objects are described. The experimental results are shown in section 5.

2 Moving Objects

In the applications of geographic information systems (GIS), the background data such as roads, rivers, buildings and city boundaries do not change in a short time. However, in the systems such as monitoring and command systems for squad cars, ambulances, fire engines, or taxies, the locations of moving objects must be immediately managed and monitored to conduct the movements or to make motion plans. In managing the moving objects, the system must treat both types of data; *static* objects and *dynamic* moving objects. The velocity and direction of an object's motion are not always constant but they may change with time. Furthermore, deformation and rotation of objects are allowed. These make the position, direction, and shape of an object change with time.

(1) Motion of an object A location of an object is represented by $(X(t), Y(t), t)$ in two-dimensional case, where "t" is time, $(X(t), (Y(t))$ is a position of the object at "t". Usually, to record a motion, the locations of an object must be sampled. However, in the paper, we do not restrict an expression of the motion by the sampled locations but allow mathematical expressions representing a continuous motion. If an object prepares methods (in object-oriented sense) that determine the distance between the object and a point, and the intersection of the object and a rectangle, any expression of the

motion is allowed. If locations of an object are given at only sampled time, we assume the object moves a rectilinear motion with a constant velocity between consecutive sampled positions.

(2) Rotation of an object The direction of an object is also represented by $(\theta(t), t)$, where "t" is time, and $\theta(t)$ is a direction at "t". The direction can is represented mathematically or sampled values. However, the direction is not a primary search condition. We do not allow such queries without a spatial range that find objects whose directions are 45 degrees at time "T". Only proximity related query is accepted as primary search conditions.After finding objects by a spatial and temporal search using the PMD-tree, the direction of each object is checked.

(3) Deformation of an object The shape of an object is also defined by $(S(t), t)$, where "t" is time, and $S(t)$ is an expression of the object's shape at "t". We allow any form as an expression of $S(t)$, but the object must provide the functions that determine the distance between the object and a given point, and intersection of the object and a given rectangle at any time. If an object is rotating at a position, the centroid of the object may not move. In the case, the object is treated the same as a *static* object.

(4) Environments A huge number of spatial objects are managed by the systems. However, it is natural that most objects are assumed static and the number of moving objects is relatively small.

3   The Persistent MD-tree (PMD-tree) [19]

The PMD-tree (Persistent MD-tree)[19] is developed by making the MD-tree [12] persistent. Fig.1 shows a simple PMD-tree with two roots, R0 and R1, that consists of two versions of the MD-tree. In the section, structures and construction methods of the PMD-tree are described.

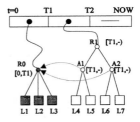

Fig.1 A example of PMD-tree

3.1   The MD and PMD trees

At first, a brief introduction of an MD-tree data structure is described. Fig.2 shows an example MD-tree. An MD-tree consists of two types of *nodes*; *leaf* and *internal node*.

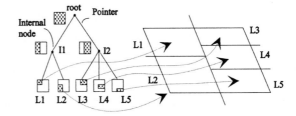

Fig.2 An MD-tree and correspondences of nodes and resions

An MD-tree consists of two types of *nodes*; *leaf* and *internal node*. Data objects are stored in only *leaves*. Each node corresponds to a (hyper-) rectangular region. The root corresponds to the entire data space. A child node corresponds to a sub-region of the parent region. If an object is inserted into a full *leaf* **L**, the corresponding region is split into two sub-regions such that at least half of objects in **L** are contained in each sub-region. Then a new *leaf* corresponding to one of the sub-regions is created, and objects in the sub-region are moved from **L** to the new *leaf*. In the MD-tree, since only the newest version remains, we cannot access any older version of the MD-tree.

On the other hand, as shown in Fig.1, a PMD-tree manages multiple roots of the MD-tree. A PMD-tree also consists of two types of node; *leaf* and *internal node*. An *internal node* and a ıleaf have two states: *live* and *dead*. A data object has also two states: *live* and *deleted* (or *dead*). A *live* interval is represented by time interval [T1, T2), where T1 indicates the time it was created, and T2 ($¿$ T1) indicates the time it was *deleted*. An interval [T1, -) means it is still ılive now. Each *node*, *leaf*, and object has a *live* interval (lifetime). Basically, when a datum is inserted into a full *leaf*, the *leaf* is split and new *leaves* are created to manage the datum in the *leaf* and new data. Then the *leaf* becomes a *dead leaf*. If an *internal node* is split or the region corresponding to an *internal node* is modified, the *node* becomes dead and a new *node* is created to manage the *live* children of the *dead node*.

Internal node and leaf An *internal node* **In** has the following fields;

$$NodeIn = \{Rect\_m, (Ts, Te), P\_array[4], L\_no, O\_no, O\_p, Rect\_c\},$$

where $Rect\_m$ is a rectangle which encloses all rectangles of the lower *nodes* of **In**, (Ts, Te) is the *live* time interval of **In**, $P\_array[4]$ is an array of child pointers, L_no is the number of *live* child *nodes*, O_no is the number of *dead* child *nodes*, O_p is a pointer to the old version node of **In**, and $Rect\_c$ is a circumscribed rectangle which encloses all the data in the sub-tree rooted with **In**. If Te of a node is '-', the node is *live* at present, and if Te has a value, the node is *dead*. In Fig.1, *dead nodes* and *leaves* are represented by gray circle and boxes.

A *leaf* **L** has the following fields;

$$LeafL = \{Rect\_m, D[C], E\_no, D\_no, Rect\_c\},$$

where $Rect\_m$ is a rectangle corresponding to *leaf* **L**, $D[C]$ is an array of pointers to the data, C is a capacity, E_no is the number of *live* data, D_no is the number of *deleted* data, and $Rect\_c$ is a circumscribed rectangle which encloses all the data in **L**.

3.2 Spatio Temporal Data Management by the PMD-tree

The data insertion using the PMD-tree is described in the section and an example is shown in Fig. 1. At first, a datum is inserted into an empty MD-tree. When

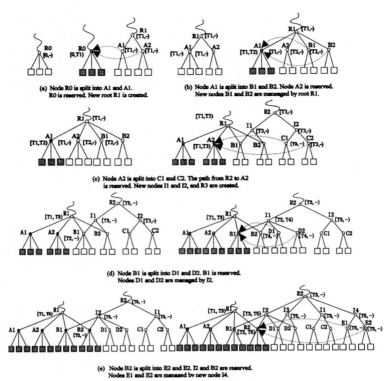

(a) Node R0 is split into A1 and A1. R0 is reserved. New root R1 is created.

(b) Node A1 is split into B1 and B2. Node A2 is reserved. New nodes B1 and B2 are managed by root R1.

(c) Node A2 is split into C1 and C2. The path from R2 to A2 is reserved. New nodes I1 and I2, and R3 are created.

(d) Node B1 is split into D1 and D2. B1 is reserved. Nodes D1 and D2 are managed by I2.

(e) Node B2 is split into E2 and E2. I2 and B2 are reserved. Nodes B1 and E2 are managed by new node I4.

Fig.3 A growing process of a PMD-tree

the first datum is inserted into an MD-tree at time 0, a new root **R0**[0,-) and a *leaf* bf L0[0,-) in the left part of Fig.1 are created. The datum is inserted into **L0**. Both **R0** and **L0** correspond to the entire data space. New data are also inserted into **L0** until the number of the data in **L0** is more than the capacity, C, of a leaf. If a datum is inserted into **L0** with C data, **L0** is split into two leaves, **L0**[0,-) and **L1**[0,-), by the leaf splitting algorithm [12] of the MD-tree. Then some of the data in **L0** and new datum are moved to **L1** such that both leaves have more than or equal to $C/2$ objects each. **L1** becomes a child of **R0**. If an object is inserted to a full leaf with one or two non-full siblings, the same adjustment technique [12] as the B-tree is applied to the MD-tree. Up to $3 \times C$ data are managed by the left MD-tree of Fig. 1.

In the PMD-tree, if the number of children of a node exceeds the capacity, the node becomes *dead* and two new nodes are created to manage the children of *dead* node .To make the MD-tree persistent, the node and leaf structures and the algorithms of the MD-tree are extended as follows in the PMD-tree.

(1) Although an *internal node* of an MD-tree can have at most three child *nodes*, an *internal node* of the PMD-tree can have at most four child *nodes* if at least one child is *dead*.

(2) If a *node* has three child *leaves*, when one of the child *leaves* of the *node* is split the *node* and three *leaves* become *dead*. Then four new *leaves* are created to store the data in three *leaves*.

(3) When the number of children of a *node* exceeds the capacity, the *node* becomes *dead*, then two new *nodes* are created to manage the *live* children of the *dead node*.

When $(3 \times C + 1)$-th datum is inserted into the left MD-tree in Fig.1, the *leaves* are split and four new *leaves* are created. Then the tree grows to the right one. Further growing processes are shown in Fig.3.

Data insertion and node splitting The following algorithm inserts a datum into a PMD-tree.

(1) By tracing from the root of the newest version tree to the lower nodes whose *Rect_m*'s include the centroid of a datum, find a leaf in which the datum will be inserted. If the leaf is not full, the datum is inserted.

(2) If the found leaf is full, the region of the leaf is split and new leaves are created by the MD-tree's algorithm [12]. The *live* data in the leaf are moved to the corresponding new leaves. When the parent, say **Ip**, of the leaf gets to have four leaves, **Ip** and old three child leaves become *dead*. Then two new nodes, which are new children of the parent of **Ip**, are created to manage two of four leaves each (see Fig.3(a-e)).

(3) If the number of the children of a node exceeds the capacity by the splitting, the node becomes *dead*, and new two nodes are created to manage the *live* children of the node (see Fig.3 (b), (c), and (e)).

(4) (3) is recursively applied to the parent of the new nodes. If the parent does not exist, a new root is created to manage the new *nodes*.

The formal procedures of the PMD-tree are described in [19].

4 Data Management of Moving Objects by The PMD-tree

4.1 Modeling of moving object

We assume an object has sufficient attributes that describe itself. In addition, each object has such methods (functions) that determine the distance from the object to a point, and the intersection of the object and a rectangle. The PMD-tree manages a time space bounding box (in short, *TSBB*) of an object. The spatial and/or temporal searches are carried out by the PMD-tree. Namely, at first, the proximity is examined based on the *TSBB* and a given point or rectangle, then the rigorous check between an object and the given point or rectangle is performed by using the method of the object.

Fig.4 shows an example moving object and *TSBB*s. The management mechanism of moving objects is shown in Fig.5. Object data are stored in ObjectDB, and the *TSBB* and centroid of an object are managed by separate structure called the *trace*. A *trace* includes *TSBB* that encloses the region an object occupies within a time interval and the trajectory of the centroid of the object. When an object is inserted in the system at time Ti, a *trace* with the bounding box and centroid of the object is created as shown in Fig.6.

The *trace* also contains a pointer to the corresponding object. The centroid is used to determine where, in the tree, a pointer to the *trace* is stored.

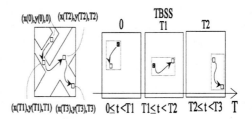

Fig.4 An MD-tree and correspondences of nodes and resions

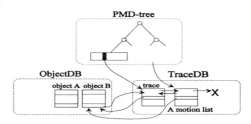

Fig.5 An MD-tree and correspondences of nodes and resions

The *trace* is inserted into a PMD-tree. The *TSBB* of the trace is used to determine the overlapping of a query range. As the object moves to a new position, the *TSBB* of the object is expanded such that it covers the region of the object within the interval, and the trajectory of the object's centroid is stored in the *trace*, as shown in Fig.6.

4.2 Motion list

As an object moves, the *TSBB* of a *trace* is enlarged. When the *TSBB* of a *trace* satisfies a condition at time Ti+1, the *trace*f becomes *dead* at Ti+1, then new *trace* is created to store the position and bounding box of the object at Ti+1. The old and new *traces* are connected by a doubly connected linked list. We call the list "*motion list*". *Motion lists* are managed by the separate structure called TraceDB. If an object does not move, no new *trace* is created. Several criteria for creating a new *trace* are tested in section 5.

The motion of an object is recorded as a time series of *traces*. In other words, the motion is split into sub-motions based on the criteria such as the length of a trajectory, or the longest side length of the *TSBB*. Fig.6 shows entries in a *trace* data structure and examples of *traces*. A trace may have a locus of the motion as a functional expression, curve, or series of sampled points.

4.3 Data management by the PMD-tree

A novel mechanism is introduced to the PMD-tree to manage moving spatial objects efficiently. Using Fig.6, the mechanism is described. When, at time Ti, a moving object, M, with the location $(X(Ti), Y(Ti))$ is inserted in the PMD-tree, a *trace* with *live* interval $[Ti, -)$ is created, where $[Ti, -)$ means the *trace* is created at Ti and still *live* at the present time. The position and *TSBB* of M, say $TSBB_M([Ti, Ti))$, are stored in the *trace*. Then, the *trace*, strictly *TSBB*, is managed by a PMD-tree. The motion of object M is tracked during interval $[Ti, Ti+1)$. Then the $TSBB_M$ of the *trace* is expanded as $TSBB_M([Ti, Ti+1))$ that covers the locus of M's motion. If $TSBB_M([Ti, Ti+1))$ satisfies a condition, the *trace* of M's motion is split at time $Ti+1$. The *trace* becomes *dead* at $Ti+1$. Then new *trace* with $TSBB_M([Ti+1,Ti+1))$ of M at $Ti+1$ is created and inserted into the PMD-tree. If $TSBB_{rmM}([Ti,Ti+1))$ does not satisfy the condition, the motion of M is still tracked until the $TSBB_{rmM}([Ti+1\ Ti+j))$, ($j \, ¿ \, 1$), satisfy the condition.

The condition of the trace splitting is based on the length of the locus, or the ratio of the *TSBB* and the region corresponding to a leaf. Since the *traces* of M's motion are managed as the *motion list* and each *trace* has a pointer to the corresponding object, the object can be obtained in a constant time from the *trace*.

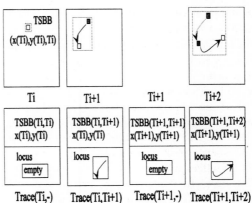

Fig.6 Object motion and traces

In the method, the faster an object moves, the more *traces* of the motion are created. If an object is frozen or just rotating at the same position, the *TSBB* does not grow and new trace is not created. The object is treated the same as a static object.

4.4 Spatial and temporal searches

In the method, the *traces* of a moving object are managed by the PMD-tree. When spatial temporal queries are given, objects are obtained by finding *traces* that intersect with a given spatio-temporal range. This intersection check can be performed as follows. At first, the PMD-tree finds *live* leaves whose regions intersect with the given spatial range and live interval intersect with the given period. The *traces* in the leaves may have intersections with the given range. Second, the *TSBB* of the *traces* are examined whether it intersects with the given time and space range. Third, the rigorous check of intersection is performed by the method each object has. In other words, each object must represent its behaviors completely by an equation, program, or sampled data. Furthermore, each object must provide such methods as deciding the proximity, intersection, inclusion and so forth.

Range search at time T: Find objects which intersect with a range R at time T.

1. Find a root of a PMD-tree whose *live* interval includes T.
2. (Perform a range search to find *traces* which intersect with R.)
    (a) Find *live* leaves at T whose circumscribed rectangles intersect with R.
    (b) Select *traces* in the leaves whose *live* intervals include T and *TSBB* intersects with R.
    (c) Apply rigorous check whether objects pointed by the selected *traces* intersect with R.
3. Return the pointers of objects

Range search with time interval: Find objects which intersect a range R during a given interval [T1, T2).

1. Find a root node of a PMD-tree whose *live* interval includes T2.
2. By tracing from the node to the *live* lower nodes at T2, find leaves whose *Rect_c*'s intersect with R.
3. For each leaf found, check whether its *live* interval intersects with [T1, T2).
4. If the leaf has non-empty intersection, then
    (a) select *traces* in the leaf whose *live* intervals intersect with [T1, T2).
    (b) S4.2: Apply rigorous check whether objects pointed by the selected *traces* intersect with R during [T1, T2).
    (c) S4.3 Collect objects whose *traces* intersect with R.
5. S5: For each old version nodes of the leaf, if the *live* intervals of the *nodes* intersect with [T1, T2), apply S2 to S4to the nodes, recursively.

5 Experimental Results

Using series of simulation tests, the storage requirements and search performances were evaluated for several types of moving objects. In the following, the PMD-tree based method (the proposed method) and the simplest method using the MD-tree are represented as PMD and MD, respectively. In MD method, all motions among the sampled positions are managed separately as vectors (directed lines) by using the single MD-tree, and time interval is treated as an attribute of a vector.

Table 1. Results of PMD-tree and MD-tree construction

(a) PMD-tree

No of initial data	No of Nodes	No of Leaves	No of total data	CPU time(sec)
5,000	2,045	3,416	18,541	0.47
10,000	3,364	6,071	35,928	0.95
50,000	15,884	27,986	179,982	6.58
100,000	32,202	56,455	334,615	15.88

(b) MD-tree

No of initial data	No of Nodes	No of Leaves	No of total data	CPU time(sec)
5,000	2,371	3,291	5,000	0.53
10,000	4,756	6,559	110,000	1.18
50,000	24,011	32,678	550,000	7.77
100,000	48,117	65,548	1,100,000	36.08

The statistics of the PMD-tree and MD-tree that manage moving objects are shown in Table 1. In the experiments, 10% of objects move with a rectilinear motion, and the positions are sampled 100 times. The speed of each object is given at random within the range (0, 1/2,500) per unit sampling time, where the side length of the entire square data space is equal to 1. The moving direction is also decided randomly. In PMD method, a *trace* is split when the locus length of an object's motion exceeds 1/2,000.

As shown in Table 1 (a), the total data (*traces*) is around 3.3 times as many as the initial data set. Table 1 (b), in the case of MD, shows the number of total data is equal to (11×initial data) (= (number of samples×0.1×initial data + initial data)). As the number of data (*traces*) in PMD is 1/3 less than that of MD method, the construction time is reduced to 88-44%. Usually, the storage requirement of the PMD-tree is almost 2.5 times as much as that of the MD-tree in data insertion cases [19], because any version of the MD-tree is preserved in the PMD-tree. However, in the experiments, since more *traces* are created in MD than in PMD, the total storage of PMD is approximately 15% less than that of MD.

Table 2. Search performances of the PMD-tree

(a) No of Visited Leaves

Search time	Search Area			
	1%	3%	5%	7%
0	8.5	24.7	48.7	79.0
20	10.9	26.1	47.1	74.4
40	10.7	25.4	45.7	70.5
60	10.3	24.3	44.2	69.3
80	10.0	23.8	43.9	66.8
100	9.4	21.3	38.9	61.0

(b) No of Visited Nodes

Search time	Search Area			
	1%	3%	5%	7%
0	23.3	38.3	57.4	80.2
20	22.1	35.7	52.3	73.1
40	22.1	35.6	53.9	72.6
60	22.6	36.2	52.4	73.5
80	22.3	35.7	53.4	72.7
100	21.1	32.8	48.6	67.6

Table 3. Search performances of the MD-tree

(a) No of Visited Leaves

Search time	Search Area			
	1%	3%	5%	7%
0	29.3	73.7	139.9	230.5
20	30.0	74.7	141.4	233.0
40	29.3	73.2	143.6	231.0
60	29.7	73.6	144.5	231.2
80	29.5	75.3	140.5	232.1
100	29.5	74.7	142.0	227.7

(b) No of Visited Nodes

Search time	Search Area			
	1%	3%	5%	7%
0	49.1	91.9	150.3	228.0
20	49.6	92.6	150.6	230.7
40	49.2	90.9	153.9	228.8
60	49.9	91.0	155.0	228.1
80	49.3	93.4	151.2	229.4
100	49.4	92.5	152.2	224.9

Tables 2 and 3 show the results of spatial searches at a past time. In the cases, the data set with 100,000 initial data is used. Since the spatial search performances in MD depend on the total number of data in the tree, the numbers of visited nodes are almost independent of the searched time and they are $O(\log(TN))$, where TN is the total number of data in the tree.

The total number of data is equal to 1,100,000 (= (11×initial data)). On the other hand, in PMD, the performances depend on the number of *live* data at a given time. The number of live data (*traces*) at a time is equal to 100,000 (= initial data) in PMD. Since MD has 11 times as much data as PMD, the numbers of visited nodes and leaves are 34 42% more than those of PMD. Namely, the search speed of PMD is 2 3 times faster than that of MD.

The same experiments of Table 1 are applied for the data sets with 1% of moving objects. As shown in Table 4, the total data in the PMD-tree is 60% of the MD-tree. The total amounts of storage are almost comparable in both cases.

Table 4. Results of PMD-tree and MD-tree construction

(a) PMD-tree

No of initial data	No of Nodes	No of Leaves	No of total data	CPU time(sec)
5,000	464	761	6,437	0.05
10,000	722	1,141	12,471	0.10
50,000	3,609	5,531	62,961	0.53
100,000	7,249	11,236	121,514	1.22

(b) MD-tree

No of initial data	No of Nodes	No of Leaves	No of total data	CPU time(sec)
5,000	440	602	10,000	0.05
10,000	870	1,198	20,000	0.10
50,000	4,322	5,979	100,0000	0.58
100,000	8,705	11,925	200,000	1.27

Tables 5 and 6 show the differences caused by the splitting rules of a *trace*. In the cases of Table 5, the rule that a trace is split if the longer side of the *TSBB* of a *trace* exceeds a given threshold is applied The threshold is equal to 1/2000. In Table 6, a *trace* is split if the *TSBB* of the *trace* becomes 1.2 times bigger than the are corresponding to the leaf in which the *trace* is included. In both cases, one percent of data is moving objects. The numbers of nodes, leaves, and total data (*traces*) in Table 6 are less than those in Table 5 in the cases the numbers of initial data are small. However, in Table 6, as the number of the initial data increases, the area of a *leaf* becomes small, then the number of *traces* increases faster. Consequently, the number of traces in the case of 100,000 initial data set of Table 6 is approximately 2 times as much as that of Table 5. Comparing Tables 4 (a) and 5, the case of Table 5 is slightly better. This is caused by the fact that all moving objects are moving with rectilinear motions. Further experiments should be done for more flexible motion than the rectilinear motion.

Table 5. Result of PMD-tree construction

No of initial data	No of Nodes	No of Leaves	No of total data	CPU time(sec)
5,000	417	684	6,237	0.05
10,000	710	1,134	12,208	0.08
50,000	3,574	5,441	61,850	0.53
100,000	7,053	10,848	119,083	1.25

Table 6. Result of PMD-tree construction

No of initial data	No of Nodes	No of Leaves	No of total data	CPU time(sec)
5,000	230	334	5,269	0.02
10,000	479	685	10,515	0.07
50,000	2,588	3,617	53,546	0.38
100,000	5,043	7,123	103,851	0.90

By the experiments, it is shown that the search performances of the proposed method are extremely higher than those of MD. Furthermore, these tests reveal that the proposed method can manage moving objects efficiently and the amount of storage increases at a small rate when the motion is slow. The time for updating the data structure for the data set of 100,000 with 10% moving objects is as fast as 158 msec. The spatial search with time interval can be performed in a few milliseconds if the time interval is short.

6 Conclusion

The PMD-tree has the novel properties that the tree corresponding to any time is always balanced, and that the storage utilization rate is higher than 66.6%. These properties guarantee the search performances are kept high and relatively independent of the total number and the distribution of data. By introducing the space time bounding box and the *motion list*, moving objects can be managed efficiently. The search performances are improved 3 times as much as those of a conventional method and the storage requirements are reduced to 1/11, in the best cases. Using the method, even if a moving object divides into several parts and they moves separately, we can manage the moving parts of the object by connecting the *traces* of the parts to the original. In the method, moreover, motions of an object are not restricted such as rectilinear motion with constant speed. We plan to apply the method to the monitoring and command systems for ambulances or squad cars.

References

1. Finkel, R, A., Bentley, J, L.: Quad Trees: A Data Structure for Retrieval on Composite Keys. Acta Informatica. 4. 1 (1974) 1-9
2. Bentley, J, L.: Multidimensional Binary Search Trees Used for Associative Searching. Commun. ACM. 18. 9 (1975) 509-517
3. Bentley, J, L., Friedman, J, H.: Data Structures for Range Searching Computing Surveys. 11. 4 (1979) 397-409
4. Robinson, J, T.: The K-D-B-tree: A Search Structure for Large Multidimensional Dynamic Indexes. Proc. ACM SIGMOD (1981) 10-18
5. Ohsawa, Y., Sakauchi, M.: The BD-tree -a New N-dimensional Data Structure with Highly Efficient Dynamic Characteristics. IFIP Conf. Paris (1983) 539-544
6. Nievergelt, J., Hinterberger, H., Sevcik, K, C.: The grid file: An adaptable symmetric, multikey file structure. ACM trans. on Database Systems. 9. 1 (1984) 38-71
7. Sellis, T., Roussopoulus, N., Faloutsos, C.: The R+-tree: A dynamic index for multidimensional objects. Proc. 13th Conf. on VLDB (1987)
8. Samet, H.: The Design and Analysis of Spatial Data Structure. Addison-Wesley (1989)
9. Gunther, O.: The design of the cell tree: an object-oriented index structure for geometric data bases. Proc. 5th Int. Conf. on Data Engineering (1989) 598-605
10. Lomet, D., Salzberg, B.: A robust multi-attribute search structure. Proc. 5th Conf. on Data Engineering (1989) 296-304
11. Bechmann, N., Kriegel, H, P., Schneider, R., Seeger, B.: The R*-tree: An efficient and robust access method for points and rectangles. 1990
12. Nakamura, Y., Abe, S., Ohsawa, Y., Sakauchi, M.: A Balanced Hierarchical Data Structure for Multidimensional Data with Efficient Dynamic Characteristics. IEEE trans. KDE. Vol.5. No.4 (1993) 682-694
13. Driscoll, J, R., Sarnak, N., Sleator, D, D., Tarjan, R, E.: Making Data Structure Persistent. J. Comp. & Syst. Sci. Vol. 38 (1989) 86-124
14. Sarnak, N., Tarjan, R, E.: Planar Point Location Using Persistent Search Tree. Commun. ACM. Vol. 29. No. 7 (1991) 669-679
15. Varman, P, J., Verma, R, M.: An Efficient Multiversion Access Structure. KDE. Vol. 9. No. 3 (1997) 391-409
16. Teraoka, T., Maruyama, M., Nakamura, Y., Nishida, S.: The MP-tree: An Efficient Data Structure for Spatio-Temporal Data. Proc. Int. Phoenix Conf. Computers and Communications (1995) 326-333
17. Comer, D.: The Ubiquitous B-tree. ACM Comp. Surveys. Vol. 11. No. 2 (1979) 121-137
18. Kamei, K., Nakamura, Y., Abe, S., Takeda, S., Tsukamoto, J., Kaga, T.: Highly Interactive Operator Workstation for Distribution Automation System Using Spatial Data Management. IEEE trans. Power Systems. Vol. 7. No. 1 (1992) 180-186
19. Dekihara, H., Nakamura, Y.: An Efficient Balanced Hierarchical Data Structure For Multiversion Accesses To Spatio-Temporal Data. Proc. EUSIPCO 98 (1998) 2205-2208

Implementing Sequoia 2000 Benchmark
on Shusse-Uo and Its Performance

Botao Wang, Hiroyuki Horinokuchi, Susumu Kuroki, Kunihiko Kaneko,
Akifumi Makinouchi

Department of Intelligent Systems
Graduate School of Information Science and Electrical Engineering
Kyushu University, Fukuoka, Japan 812-8581
{botaow, holyon, kuroki, kaneko, akifumi }@db.is.kyushu-u.ac.jp

Abstract. As an ODBMS, Shusse-Uo is built on Network Of Workstations (NOW). In Shusse-Uo, a storage manager based on distributed shared memory and a persistent programming language for object management are provided. In the paper, we introduce Shusse-Uo and discuss its features to deal with spatial data. Sequoia 2000 benchmark database is built on it. Performance tests of Shusse-Uo using Sequoia 2000 benchmark are performed. Some processing strategies are presented and the influences of clustering data on performance are analyzed, too. The results are compared with those of the related systems.

1   Introduction

The object-based approach appeared to offer substantial advantages over the traditional relational approach to build database systems. Object DataBase Management Systems (ODBMS) such as ObjectStore [1], O2 [1], and Versant [1] have gained a foothold in the commercial marketplace. Further, object-oriented model is combined with relational model. Such kind of systems is called ORDBMS [10]. Some systems have been implemented based on different approaches. They are Illustra ([2]), Paradise ([3][4][5]), and Monet ([6][7]). Some extensions are made according to applications and Sequoia 2000 benchmark [12] databases are built on them for performance tests.

In this paper, we will introduce the architecture of Shusse-Uo, an ODBMS, and discuss its features to deal with spatial data. Sequoia 2000 benchmark [12] is implemented by different approaches under the capabilities of Shusse-Uo. Some processing strategies for performance improvement are brought out. Some related systems are compared.

The remainder of this paper is organized as follows. Section 2 describes the architecture of Shusse-Uo. The spatial data management are presented in Section 3. Section 4 introduces spatial data processing strategies. The related work is introduced in Section 5. Performance test results using different approaches in Shusse-Uo are introduced and compared in Section 6. Finally Section 7 concludes the paper and describes the future works.

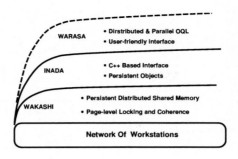

Fig. 1. Layers of Shusse-Uo (WARASA is currently under development)

2   Architecture of Shusse-Uo

As an ODBMS, Shusse-Uo is built using Distributed Shared Memory (DSM). Currently, it consists of two layers (See Fig. 1): **WAKASHI** [8] and **INADA/ODMG** ([9]). WAKASHI is a storage manager independent of data model. It has been tested by OO7 benchmark and competitive results were gotten [8]. INADA/ODMG is a database programming language for object data management.

2.1   WAKASHI

WAKASHI is a distributed object storage system. It runs on a distributed UNIX platform, which offers a loosely coupled computational environment. The main idea of WAKASHI is mapping: object persistence is provided by memory to disk mapping and global data sharing is supported by DSM mapping. In detail, disk mapping is realized by UNIX **mmap()** system call, the memory mapping and DSM mapping are realized in WAKASHI server by means of OS's paging mechanism. Fig. 2 shows the architecture of WAKASHI.

WAKASHI consists of 1) servers that run as a daemon process, and 2) a client library that is linked into user programs (client programs). The server performs data access control and transaction management. Page-level locking and cache coherence protocol are implemented. The client library provides communication interfaces between a client and the server on the client site. Both clients and servers are implemented as multi-threaded processes in order to exploit parallelism in a multi-processor environment. In WAKASHI, the basic storage unit is a heap. For each opened heap in a server, a corresponding thread is created. Each heap is a collection of pages. The data written in the heap has the same binary format as that written in memory.

Logically, the heap offers storage for objects without limitation on size and structure. In implementation, the maximum size is dependent on maximum file size of OS. In 32bit systems, the maximum heap size is 2GBs. However, in 64bit systems, the maximum size is 8192PBs. In 64bit system, it may be said that the

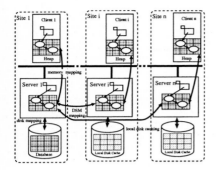

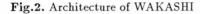

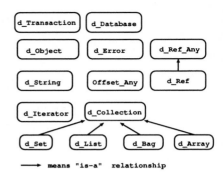

Fig.2. Architecture of WAKASHI

Fig.3. Utility classes of INADA/ODMG

mapping space is not practically limited. Since the emerging of 64bit computer such as DEC and SGI, the move to 64bit environment is inevitable. We have discussed extending database space in [11].

2.2 INADA/ODMG

INADA offers an application platform for building object databases with a database language for object management. The language provides the facilities to manage persistent objects with C++ based interface. An INADA program runs as a WAKASHI's client and it uses the client library provided by WAKASHI. INADA provides users with a library that allows the users to directly manipulate global persistent objects (i.e., persistent objects shared by different clients on different sites). In detail, it provides facilities to manipulate collections and to write distributed parallel programs [9]. ODMG93 C++ binding interface [13] is integrated into INADA and it is called INADA/ODMG. Fig. 3 shows the utility classes provided by INADA/ODMG library.

In INADA/ODMG, there are two types of heap: persistent heap and volatile heap. Both types of heap can be shared among distributed processes. Objects in a persistent heap exist all the time. Objects in a volatile heap just exist while the program that creates them is running.

For the space allocation of heap, the object with size bigger than the size of one page is stored in contiguous pages. When the sizes of objects are smaller than the size of one page, the objects belonging to the same size category are put into the same page if there are free spaces in this page. The size is categorized by the exponent of 2.

3 Dealing With Spatial Data

The Sequoia 2000 Project ([12]) explores the application of emerging database, network, storage, and visualization technologies to earth science problems, resulting in a "database-centric" metaphor for scientific computation. The Sequoia

2000 Storage Benchmark [12] uses real data sets and defines 11 queries. It is designed to represent the needs of engineering and scientific computing. The spatial data, like point and polygon, are defined and used.

3.1 Data Structure

Shusse-Uo is an ODBMS with the interface of ODMG/C++ binding [13]. It enables users to create arbitrarily complex objects like point and polygon. They are defined as classes in the database. The operators used to judge the spatial relationship of objects and the functions used to processing spatial data are defined as methods of classes. All the user-defined-classes in database are subclass of **d_Object** [13]. The query is compiled (currently hand-compiled) into INADA/ODMG C++ binding program and then compiled into binary running code.

3.2 Storage

In Shusse-Uo, the data are stored in heaps. The database space consists of all the heaps defined..The user can decide how many heaps should be created, and what kind of data is stored in which heap. A heap is considered as a clustering unit. In order to get better performance, this kind of physical database design has to be carefully done. The performance test results based on different clusterings are discussed in Section 6.

    d_Ref_Any [13] in INADA/ODMG is used to refer to objects in the database. Using **d_Ref_Any**, raster data can be stored in two heaps. It is shown in Fig. 4. One heap contains the attribute data such as width, length and so on. Another heap contains binary image data which are usually very large. The objects in the former heap are linked to the objects in the later heap. Another way to store raster image is to put these data into one heap. The former way (two heaps) is chosen here, because the pages storing attribute data are physically near. These data are saved in the tiles with same binary format as that in memory and are manipulated directly without format transformation.

3.3 Access Method

In order to efficiently access database, B+tree and R*tree are built up. The interface is template. B+tree is used to build index for traditional structured data. R*tree is designed to speed up the search for spatial objects based on their locations in a spatial space. We did some extensions on R*tree. The search results of R*tree can be grouped based on query semantic. Selectable filtering interface based on grouping is provided so that data refinement can become more faster. In Section 4.2, we will discuss this in detail.

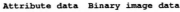

Attribute data Binary image data

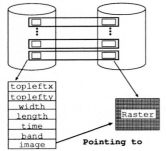

Fig.4. Storage structure of raster

Table 1. Results of different spaces

Unit: seconds

query 2	Cold	Warm	Hot
volatile heap	4.18	3.76	0.21
program memory	2.74	3.21	0.17
query 3	Cold	Warm	Hot
volatile heap	1.14	0.66	0.17
program memory	0.74	0.55	0.11

4 Processing Strategies

4.1 Dealing with Intermediate Results

When performing retrieval operations, some intermediate results should be stored. All the objects obtained as intermediate results are created and kept in the volatile heaps. The utilities provided by the system can be used by user here in the same way of the persistent heap. Because the heap is structured, extra data space and operations for object storage are necessary. At the same, since volatile heap is sharable too, the control for memory coherence is necessary.

But the intermediate results need not always to be sharable. For example, query 2 and query 3 clip the raster image first and then do other processing on the clipped data. The data size in the above queries is 2.08 MBs. With 4KBs page size, there are 520 pages. Because the clipped data at this step doesn't need to be sharable, management of storing such clipped data in heap with the control of memory coherence on it is overhead.

In order to decrease the above overhead, the intermediate results of raster are divided into two parts, the attributes data and raster data. The attributes data are created in a volatile heap, and the intermediate results of raster data are put into the program memory space directly. In this way, the INADA/ODMG utilities, such as **d_Bag** and **d_Iterator**, can still be used without extra programming and at the same time overhead can be decreased too.

Table 1 shows the performance comparison of query 2 and query 3 in different ways to put raster data.

4.2 Filtering Interface of R*tree

In Sequoia 2000 benchmark, query 6 finds all polygons that intersect a given rectangle and query 7 finds all polygons whose size is larger than a given size and within a given circle. Because operations in R*tree is based on Minimum Bounding Rectangle(MBR) of object, two steps are necessary for their evaluation: filtering and refinement. Filtering is processed in R*tree based on MBRs of

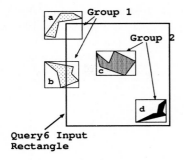

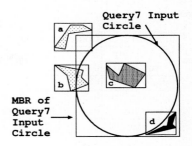

Fig.5. Grouping of R*tree of results(Query6)

Fig.6. Grouping of R*tree of results(Query7)

objects. The refinement gets the objects which meet the input condition based on the exact shape of objects. The time cost of refinement depends on the results of filtering.

Usually, filtering process using R*tree outputs the candidates of objects whose MBRs intersect a given rectangle. Fox example, as shown in Fig. 5, **a**, **b**, **c** and **d** are outputted because their MBRs intersect the input rectangle. However, objects **a** and **b** are classified differently from object **c** and **d**, because MBRs of **c** and **d** are inside the rectangle while the MBRs of **a** and **b** are not.

Observing this, we decided to change the filtering process of R*tree so that 2 groups of candidate objects are reorganized. One is **Group 1** whose MBRs intersect the edges of the rectangle, and another is **Group 2** whose MBRs are inside the rectangle. We can see that the **Group 2** objects are inside the rectangle and the refinement process is unnecessary. However, the **Group 1** objects need to be checked whether they really intersect the rectangle or not in the refinement process.

In query 6, only objects which intersect the rectangle are requested, so objects in **Group 1** need refinement. **Group 2** objects don't need refinement for the reason mentioned above.

But for query 7, all objects need refinement because the input for query 7 is circle. The MBR of the circle is used as input of R*tree. The objects inside the MBR are inside the rectangle but are not always inside the circle. For example, the object **d** in Fig. 6 is such a case. So grouping of the filtering process is meaningless.

Table 2 is the performance results based on different filtering strategy. We can find that it's better to choose two-group strategy in query 6 and choose one-group strategy in query 7. Table 3 shows the distribution of the objects inside and on the border of MBR for the query. By Table 3, we can find that the number of objects on the border is very small, so the I/O of reading polygon shape data for refinement can be saved greatly and query 6 greatly benefits from the grouping. There are overheads for searching R*tree in the way of grouping, because extra judging operations are needed while searching R*tree. It's CPU

Table 2. Results of Selectable Filtering Interface

Unit: seconds

query 6	Cold	Warm	Hot
One Group	3.82	2.62	0.26
Two Group	0.68	0.32	0.11
query 7	Cold	Warm	Hot
One Group	0.36	0.23	0.002
Two Group	0.54	0.26	0.003

Table 3. Distribution of the Objects Inside And on the Border of MBR

Unit: average number

query	inside	on border	total
query 6	440.0	0.0	440.0
query 7	53.5	0.2	53.7

overhead. That's the reason why results of two-group strategy of query 7 is worse. In summary, the rule for the query here to judge whether to use grouping method or not can be gotten as the following:

if the input of the query is the type of rectangle and is not the type of point, the two-group strategy should be used. Otherwise the one-group strategy should be used.

5   Related Work

The systems that were used for Sequoia 2000 storage benchmark can be classified into two categories. One is geographic information oriented systems, such as ARC-INFO, GRASS and IPW, which are introduced in [12]. Another one is the extension of the existing systems, Paradise [3][4][5] and Monet [6][7] are some examples. Because the formers are developed specially for processing geographic information and Shusse-Uo is an ODBMS for general database applications, following comparisons focus on the later two database systems on which sequoia 2000 database are built.

Paradise is an ORDBMS and it provides an extended-relational data model for the applications aiming at handling geographical applications . The built_in data types for spatial data management are provided. The spatial data types are associated with a set of spatial operators that can be accessed from an extended version of SQL. All the types are implemented based on Abstract Data Type (ADT).

Monet is a type- and algebra-extensible ORDBMS based on Binary Association Tables (BAT). It is table-oriented, too. For user-defined types, ADT facility is also provided. Its implementation strategy is "extensible-toolkit" approach. The support for new data types and accelerators is implemented through ADT interfaces.

Paradise uses extended built-in datatypes. Its capabilities of data processing is limited to its built_in datatypes. Monet has a good capability for extension of new datatypes and operations. To define the new operators, Monet system utility is used and the operators are added using dynamic linkage of C object-file or library.

Shusse-Uo is an ODMG [13]-based ODBMS, which is not limited to spatial applications. In our implementation of the benchmark, the database design is based on ODMG object database model and data structures. Users define their own objects as subclasses of **d_Collection** and **d_Object** and they allow flexible handling of complicated objects, such as spatial objects and spatial processing.

Paradise is based on the Client-Server model. In Monet, clients can either be normal applications doing function shipping or work with Monet systems in the way of peer-to-peer. In Monet server, **mmap()** is used same as in Shusse-Uo. There this function is used by the server to get data from disk, and **madivse()** is used to do buffer management. Shusse-Uo is based on the Peer-to-Peer model. Here besides getting data from disk by **mmap()**, data are mapped directly into database space and there are no data transfer between server and client and there are no overhead for copying data between buffers.

For very large data, Paradise chunks an array into subarrays and stores them in a file different from other data. The data compression is used for performance enhancement. Monet stores very large data in a file different from other data too. Decomposed storage model is used. Shusse-Uo can store very large data and normal size data together or in different files. No data compression is done in Shusse-Uo.

6 Results

All queries in the benchmark have been implemented in Shusse-Uo and our best results are compared with those of Monet which is supposed to show the best performance [7] compared with other systems [12]. The environment and results are listed in Table 6 and Table 4. Same as the other systems, the benchmark is performed by one user.

Note that the hardware environment of the both systems is very similar except that the clock time and the disk access performance of our system is a little slower. Though there are four CPUs in our system, because there is only one user here, only one thread is created on the client and there are no concurrent I/O requests, we can not benefit from the concurrency which can be expected by the multithread architecture mentioned earlier. As introduced in the paper [7], Monet is built based on multi-processors, and multithreads and shared-memory parallelism are used there.

The implementations based on different clustering approaches have been done and the result are listed in Table 4. Note that the operations of query 1 are creating and loading data and building index, although it is named "query 1". Since its results of all approaches are same, it is shown in Table 7.

For the definitions of cold, warm and hot, please refer to [7] and for the definitions of the queries, please refer to [12] for more details.

6.1 Different Clustering Approaches

Basically data clustering is used to improve locality of data. As introduced in Section 2.2, the objects with size smaller than the size of one page are put into same page according to their size categories. Because the size of data is variable, it's possible that the different type objects are put into the same page if there

Table 4. The Results of Different Clustering

Unit: seconds

	Clustering1			Clustering2			Clustering3			Clustering4		
	cold	warm	hot	cold	warm	hot	cold	warm	hot	cold	warm	hot
query2	2.92	4.04	0.17	2.74	3.75	0.17	2.74	3.21	0.17	2.74	3.21	0.17
query3	0.96	0.66	0.11	0.74	0.57	0.11	0.74	0.55	0.11	0.74	0.55	0.11
query4	0.24	0.16	0.08	0.22	0.15	0.08	0.21	0.14	0.08	0.21	0.14	0.08
query5	0.14	0.05	0.00	0.01	0.01	0.00	0.01	0.01	0.00	0.06	0.01	0.00
query6	2.49	0.96	0.11	0.94	0.46	0.11	0.68	0.32	0.11	1.67	0.37	0.11
query7	2.02	0.42	0.002	0.95	0.34	0.002	0.36	0.23	0.002	1.84	0.30	0.002
query8	2.65	1.98	0.09	1.20	0.54	0.09	0.88	0.36	0.09	1.86	0.43	0.11
query9	0.68		0.00	0.60		0.00	0.46		0.00	0.64		0.00
query10	4.7		0.38	4.60		0.39	2.7		0.37	3.76		0.38
query11	3.08	2.35	0.22	2.32	1.06	0.22	1.69	0.82	0.22	1.97	0.85	0.22

are stored in the same heap. The number of the heaps influences the locality of
data. Because **mmap()** is used in Shusse-Uo, main memory is used as cache.
The bigger the size of the total mapped data is, the more the memory is used.
This influences the performance of system, especially for large size of data.

In order to test the influences of different clustering strategies on performance, different clustering approaches have been tested. The results are listed
in Table 4. We tried four clustering plans:

- Clustering1: there are only one heap in database. All data are put into one
  heap.
- Clustering2: 4 heaps for each data type are defined. The data related to one
  data type are put together. For example, point data, point B+tree and point
  R*tree are put into one heap.
- Clustering3: 11 heaps are defined. In each heap, only the data in one specific
  type are stored. For example, point data, point B+tree and point R*tree are
  put into 3 different heaps. The locality is best.
- Clustering4: 9 heaps are defined. It is almost same as that of Clustering3,
  except that R*tree indexes (point, polygon, graph) are put into one heap.

6.2 Analysis of Results

According to the results listed in Table 4, some conclusions can be observed:

- The more the logical partition of data is, the higher the performance is.
  Within the capability of hardware, the more the number of heaps (logical
  partition of data) is, the higher the locality of data is. For example, in query
  6, polygon is used and its average size is 204Bs, and the size of R*tree is
  48Bs. The polygon with size smaller than 64Bs will be put into the same
  page as R*tree node if there are no clustering, like the case of Clustering2.

Table 5. Time cost of Query2

Unit: seconds

1st	2nd	3rd	4th	5th
2.73	2.57	2.53	3.12	3.99

Table 6. Environment of ShusseUo and Monet

Monet	Shusse-Uo
Sun Sparc 20	Sun Sparc 20
60Mhz	50Mhz
128MBs Memory	128MBs Memory
5 GBs	9 GBs
20MBs/s throughout	20MBs/s throughout
8.5 ms access time	Read:9.0ms,
	Write:10.5ms,

The average number of pagefault for query 6 is 89.6 in Clustering3 and 104.5 in Clustering2, where Clustering3 has a good locality than Clustering2.

The worst results were gotten in Clustering1 for its worst locality and mapping too much data unrelated to the query. On the other side, the best results were gotten in Clustering3 for its good locality and only mapping the data related to the query.

– The way of clustering data has a great influence on cold performance. The cold and warm results are different in different clustering approaches because the I/O is critical at these stages. The way of clustering has no influence on hot performance, because 'hot' is defined as memory operation. All the hot results are same in our different approaches.

The reason that warm result is worse than the cold result in query 2 is that page swapping occurred during the warm test. Because the values of input parameter of query 2 are changed randomly every time. The pages mapped into memory are always new and is kept in the memory by OS. The free and available memory space decreases fast. Here each piece of raster is stored as one 1600*2400 tile with pixel size 2Bs line by line with page size 4KBs. In this way, the memory used by query 2 each time is 16.64MBs for getting 26 200*200 clips data from 26 different rasters , and the total memory size is 128MBs. For query 2, usually from the 4th or 5th test, page swapping happened. The Table 5 is one procedure of query 2 testing, it records the time cost from 1st test to the 5th test.

6.3   Comparison with Monet

The environment and performance compared with Monet are listed in Table 6 and Table 7. In Monet, one piece of raster consists of mesh of titles. The tiles are adjusted to occupy one disk page, and from left to right, row by row[7]. The size difference between the data read in and the data actually used become very smaller, so the smaller memory is required. Though there are CPU overhead for format changing, swapping is avoided in query 2. In query 2, query 3 and query 4, intermediate results of raster is processed in memory not in volatile heap. In query 5, Quadtree is used in Monet and R*tree is used in Shusse-Uo. From query 6 to query 11 group filtering is selected according to the rule introduced in Section 4.2. The warm result can not be gotten in query 9 and

Table 7. The results of Monet and Shusse-Uo

Unit: seconds

query1	Monet			Shusse-Uo		
	raster: 590 point: 14.5 polygon: 107 graph:			raster: 1288 point: 278 polygon: 525 graph: 1121		
	cold	warm	hot	cold	warm	hot
query2	3.7	3.0	1.4	2.74	3.21	0.17
query3	0.87	0.75	0.30	0.74	0.55	0.11
query4	0.24	0.18	0.09	0.21	0.14	0.08
query5	0.09	0.08	0.00	0.01	0.01	0.00
query6	2.1	1.1	0.2	0.68	0.32	0.11
query7	0.51	0.39	0.01	0.36	0.23	0.002
query8	1.6	0.7	0.30	0.88	0.36	0.09
query9	1.4	0.2	0.00	0.46		0.00
query10	4.7		1.4	2.7		0.37
query11				1.69	0.82	0.22

query 10, because according to the definition of warm, the input parameter should be selected randomly. Using the islands data or not [12] influences greatly the measured time. The warm result of query 9 in Monet shows that the islands data was not be used. Query11 is implemented very easily using C++, so the query with recursive operation can be implemented easily in Shusse-Uo. Query11 is not tested in Monet. We summarize the attributes influencing performance of Monet and Shusse-Uo in the following:

- In Monet, Monet Interface Language (MIL) is provided for queries in a C-like syntax. The queries are translated into MIL programs which are interpreted. The interface of Shusse-Uo is ODMG/C++ binding, and the queries here are compiled into binary files directly.
- The **mmap()** is used by Monet server alone. The data is transfered between the server and clients. Shusse-Uo uses same address space between client and server, and so no data is transfered between them. The data is transfered only between servers. There is no format change, either.
- Monet provides buffer control using **madvise()** and the data is specially organized for optimal access inside the heap. For example, the Rtree got clustered spatially so that the adjacent rectangles are likely to be on the same memory page. In Shusse-Uo, the data with same size category are put into same page . Program memory for intermediate results and the selectable interfaces for R*tree are used here.

We think that the first two points are the reasons why our results are better than those of Monet. The last point is the different way to optimize DBMS.

7 Conclusion and Future Work

In this paper, we introduced Shusse-Uo, an ODBMS. We discussed the implementation of Sequoia 2000 benchmark with different approaches and compared the results with those of other systems. The strategies for dealing with intermediate results and filtering interface of R*tree are brought out for performance improvement and the influences of clustering data on performance are analyzed too. The experiment shows that Shusse-Uo can deal with multidimensional spatial data flexibly with good performance.

Experiments of parallel processing of Sequoia 2000 queries and multiuser sequoia 2000 benchmark are future work.

References

1. Alfons Kemper and Guido Moerkotte, " Object-Oriented Database Management", Prentice Hall Inc. 1994
2. Robin Bloor, Illustra and Informix-The Capabilities and its Integration with Informix DSA, Informix White Paper, March, 1996
3. Computer Sciences Department University of Wisconsin, Madison, Paradise Version 0.1 Reference Manual. 1994, January. http://ftp.cs.wisc.edu/paradise/papers
4. David J. DeWitt, et.al., "Client-Server Paradise",Proc. of VLDB 94
5. Jignesh Patel, JieBing Yu, et.al. , "Building a Scalable Geo-Spatial DBMS:Techn ology, Implementation, and Evaluation", Proc. of SIGMOD 97
6. Peter A. Boncz, Martin L.Kersten. "Monet: An Impressionist Sketch of an advanced Database System", Proc. of BIWIT 95
7. Perter A. Boncz, Wilko Quak, Martin L. Kersten, "Monet And Its Geographic Extensions", Proc. of EDBT 96
8. G.Yu, K.Kaneko, G.Bai, and A. Makinouchi, "Transaction Management for a Distributed Object Storage System WAKASHI-Design, Implementation and Performance", Proc. of ICDE 96, New Orleans, Louisiana, USA.
9. Kan Yamamoto, Multimedia Data Storage for the Object-Oriented Persistent Programming Language INADA, 1997, February. Master thesis, the Department of Intelligent Systems, Kyushu University, Japan
10. Krishna Kulkarni, Nelson Mattos, Anil K. Nori, Object-Relational Database Systems- Principles, Products, and Challenges, Tutorials-23rd Internatiolnal Conference On Very Large Data Bases, 1997
11. Botao Wang, Akifumi Makinouchi, Kunihiko Kaneko, Extending Database Space of Inada/ODMG for very Large Databases on 64 Bit Workstation, Proceedings of Eighth International Workshop on Database and Expert Systems Applications, September, 1997, France
12. Stonebreaker, M. et.al., "The SEQUOIA 2000 Benchmark", Proc. of 93 ACM SIGMOD Conference on Management of Data, 1993, Washington
13. R.G.G. Cattell, et.al., "The Object Database Standard:ODMG-93 Rel 1.2", Morgan Kaufmann Publishers, San Francisco, California Inc. 1996

A Spatiotemporal Query Processor Based on Simplicial Representation

Hiroyuki HORINOKUCHI[1], Botao WANG[1], Susumu KUROKI[1], and Akifumi MAKINOUCHI[1]

Department of Intelligent Systems
Graduate School of Information Science and Electrical Engineering
Kyushu University, Fukuoka, Japan 812-8581

Abstract. In spatial databases, efficient filtering of spatial objects using some index is a key issue to improve the retrieval performance. R*-tree is a well-known index which can manage points and rectangles. In R*-tree, objects are approximated by their MBRs and input region is also approximated by its MBR. And exact check is postponed to the refinement step. This paper propose a new approach to this filter. Input region as well as each of stored objects is managed by a R*-tree which allows more exact approximation of it and so enables more efficient filtering. This design is used in our spatiotemporal database system *Hawks* whose data model, called *Universe*, is based on the simplicial complex theory.

1 Introduction

There have been many researches on indexes for spatial databases. In GIS (Geographical Information System) area, for example, spatial indexes have been studied intensively and many indexes based on hash and tree have been proposed. For GIS applications, spatial queries such as point queries and range queries are processed. They are concerned with two dimensional spatial data, and these queries can be handled by tree indexes.

Databases for virtual reality and videos require more complex data management. The objects in the databases are not only static but also dynamic, i.e. they move. That is why spatiotemporal database systems and their indexes have become a recent research topic. A spatiotemporal database stores data having temporal attributes and spatial ones, as well. Such data is called spatiotemporal data. As the spatiotemporal data is more complex and its volume is more large, the importance of indexes increases.

For spatial databases, many kinds of indexes have been proposed. They can be divided into two groups in terms of data to be handled. One group includes K-D-B-tree [3] and SS-tree [2] which target points. The other includes R-tree [1] which can be used for both points and regions. In spatial databases, queries with regions as their condition are often required, so such a region based index is needed.

In spatiotemporal databases, the stored data as well as queries have spatiotemporal features. There are many types in such spatiotemporal queries and they have two constituents: *region* (including point and line) and *condition*. The region specifies the space which the specifying query is concerned with, and the condition describes the topological relationship between the given query region and objects in a database. For example, *a spatiotemporal point query* have 'a spatiotemporal point' as the region and 'intersection' as the condition. And this query retrieves all regions that intersect with the given point. Typical queries are listed as follows:

- Find those objects that intersect with a given region
- Find those objects that are contained in a given region
- Find those objects that contain a given region

Complex queries with complex condition can be made from these simple conditions and logical operators like *and*, *or*, and *not*. They are evaluated by calculating each constituent simple condition. This paper presents a new approach to evaluate such a simple spatiotemporal query using modified R*-tree.

The paper is organized as follows. In section 2, we discuss the issues in designing spatiotemporal index. And the spatiotemporal data representation model *Universe* [8, 9] is introduced. Then new design of spatiotemporal index is shown in section 3. This section presents how to implement the new index and how to use it to evaluate the spatiotemporal queries. Other related works are discussed in section 4. And finally section 5 concludes the paper with a future plan.

2 Spatiotemporal queries

In the spatiotemporal database system which is under development in our laboratory, named *Hawks*, a spatiotemporal data is represented using *Universe* data model which is based on a mathematical theory, simplicial complex. In this section, we introduce the Universe, the basic design of query processor, and the strategy how to use the spatiotemporal database index for efficient query evaluation.

2.1 Universe

In some spatiotemporal data models which have been proposed so far, the temporal dimension is less informative than the other spatial ones. For example, in Constructive Solid Geometry (*CSG*), moving objects in a three dimensional space are sampled periodically in time series. The resultant snapshots are linked each other and then stored in the database. These systems work using different spatial and temporal indexes. However, this approach may cause performance loss because of joining different treatments of spatial and temporal data.

Universe is a data representation model for spatiotemporal objects. Universe incorporates *simplicial complex* into the data model and is used to model shapes of objects in n-dimensional space where n is 2, 3, and 4. Tab. 1 shows n-dimensional simplex where n is 1 to 4. A simplicial complex is a set of those simplexes with some mathematical constraints. As a result, any dimension in the Universe has the first class citizenship.

Table 1. Dimensions and the corresponding simplexes

dimension	simplex
0	point
1	line segment
2	triangle
3	tetrahedra
4	4-simplex

2.2 Basic design of spatiotemporal query processor

The structure of our spatiotemporal index is similar to multi-dimensional R*-tree [6] except for the temporal axis. Any figure in a space with n axes forms a topological space where there is no difference between these axes. In other words, we do not distinct spatial and temporal axes.

Our basic design of spatial query processor is shown in Fig. 1 where a given query is processed in two steps: *filter* and *refinement*.

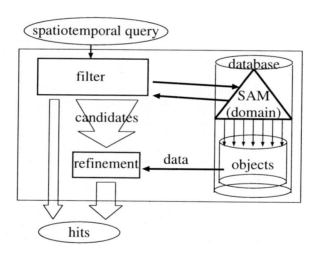

Fig. 1. Basic regional query processor

R*-tree and Minimum Bounding Rectangle To process spatiotemporal query efficiently, some additional structures for accessing data inside the spatiotemporal database and techniques for them are essential. Those structures are usually called Spatial Access Method (SAM) in spatial space. So we use *Spatiotemporal Access Method* as an extension of the SAM for spatiotemporal space and call it *SAM*, too. In our system, the multi-dimensional R*-tree is used for the SAM. R*-tree is one of the most efficient variants of R-tree.

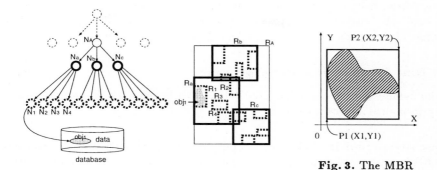

Fig. 2. An structure of R*-tree

Fig. 3. The MBR

Fig. 2 shows the logical figure of the R*-tree. The R*-tree is a kind of n-way-tree and its each node except the root has a number of child nodes within predefined range. A node has a region represented by *Minimum Bounding Rectangle (MBR)* and pointers referring to its child nodes. The MBR is the least rectilinear region that encloses a given area. An example of the MBR in two-dimensional world is shown in Fig. 3.

The region of a leaf node is a MBR of its corresponding object. And that of the non-leaf node is a MBR which encloses the union of its children's MBRs. Thus the region of the root node becomes a MBR of the domain where all objects exist. Since R*-tree makes use of MBR, it is independent from the exact shape representation of objects. In the query processing, MBRs of the R*-tree nodes and a MBR made from the given query region are compared, and only nodes whose MBR satisfies the given condition with the query region are searched for. When the traverse reaches to a leaf node, the object pointed to by the pointer becomes a candidate for the query.

Filter step: This step filters stored objects using the region and condition of a query and outputs a set of objects that may satisfy the given condition. These resultant candidates are piped to the successive step, the refinement. The MBR-based SAM serves as a filter which excludes all objects which do not fulfill the given condition and saves the cost of examining all the objects. This step usually outputs candidates as a set of OIDs, i.e. Object IDentifiers.

Refinement step: This step examines if each of the candidates given from the previous filter step satisfies the condition using the computational geometry. Although, this outputs the exact answer set, it costs because of the complexity of the calculations. This process involves not only CPU-time but also I/O to fetch objects from the disks. A well-known algorithm for this kind of geometric calculation is plane-sweep [10] which detects the intersection of two set of line segments with the order $O(n \log n)$ where n is the number of line segments. TR*-tree [13] is another approach to calculate intersection. TR*-tree has a R*-tree based structure which manages a set of trapezoids generated from objects. The complex calculation for intersection is decomposed into a number of simple traverse of the tree. Some comparisons show that TR*-tree algorithm outperforms the plane-sweep one.

2.3 Hint for efficient query processing

We did some experiments using SEQUOIA 2000 benchmark [5] and got a hint for performance improvement.

Query region and its MBR As stated in section 2.2, only MBRs of objects and MBR of query region are used in the filter step. Here we use *intersection* as the topological condition of query. Fig. 4 shows the typical intersections of MBRs in the two dimension which occurs in the filter. In this figure, five small rectangles *a* to *e* are MBRs of R*-tree leaf nodes.

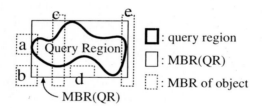

Fig. 4. query region, MBR(QR), and MBRs of objects in the R*-tree

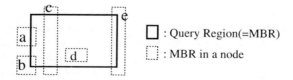

Fig. 5. query region and MBRs in the R*-tree

— When an arbitrary region like the area enclosed by the thick curve line is given to the query processor, the filter seeks for the objects which intersect MBR(QR), i.e. the MBR of the query region.

– When the processor given a window as in Fig.5, more techniques can be exploited. In this case, the object whose MBR has contained within the window entirely (like d) can escape from refinement.

On the contrary, when each dotted rectangle represents the MBR inside an intermediate node, all intersection tests executed at the descending nodes of d can be avoided.

Taking into consideration the above situations, we did some experiments in the SEQUOIA 2000 benchmark. One of its queries is a window query which is same as the latter situation. Tab. 2 shows the advantage of our intersection pattern selection in terms of query evaluation time for the cold, warm, and hot cases. The intersection test in the refinement step is done by comparing the faces of each candidate object to the query region. This selection mechanism can distinguish those objects which have no need to pass the refinement test.

Table 2. Distribute candidates into two sets. Time is in seconds

	cold	warm	hot
without selection	3.82	2.62	0.26
with selection	0.68	0.32	0.11

Rough approximation of the MBR The MBR of a query region is often much larger than the query region itself, because an object is not always axis-parallel rectilinear rectangle. When we compare MBR(QR) against a and d in the situation in Fig. 4, d seems to have more probability than a, because it is contained in the query region entirely. But this prediction is false. When the query region is not simple figure like window, removing such objects from the candidate set in the filter step is difficult while only one MBR is used to approximate the query region.

In the object approximation, using other figures such as convex hull, rotated MBR, minimum bounding n-corner, minimum bounding circle and so on have been proposed and compared in some experiments[11, 13]. Indeed, they can filter off some false hits, but its calculation costs considerably much larger compared to that of MBR.

Instead of using only one approximative figure to improve the filtering performance, we propose to organize a hierarchy of approximative region like R*-tree. The lower we descend in the tree, the more exact and more specific representations of object we can get.

3   Universe-based spatiotemporal query processor

Based on the previous observations, we designed a new query processing mechanism for the spatiotemporal database system Hawks. The basic two-step processor (refer Fig. 1) is also used for the new one. In the processor, filtering is performed with more accuracy by multi-level approximative structures of objects and query region.

3.1 Multi-level approximation of region

Each object in the domain space is also managed by a R*-tree. The lower we descend in the tree, the more accurate approximation we get. The idea of our filtering process is that we provide a tree structure with each of the objects in the space and only retrieve necessary parts of the object. And so that we may find if the object can fulfill given query's topological relationship or not.

As we use R*-tree to locate each object in the space, we use a R*-tree for each of object, too. Instead of the OID that resides in a leaf node of R*-tree for the domain, we store a pointer to the R*-tree that manages a corresponding object. As a result, the same number of SAMs as the stored objects are necessary. The basic structure is shown in Fig. 6. In the figure, the SAM(domain) shows the SAM of the object domain space and the SAM(obj) represents the SAM of object. Although the MBR of SAM(domain)'s leaf node and that of SAM(obj)'s root node are identical and one of them is not necessary, they are left untouched for the ease of explanation.

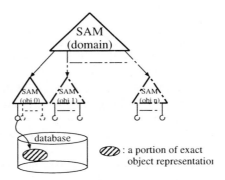

Fig. 6. New structure for domain and objects

3.2 Decomposition strategy

To construct a R*-tree for each objet, we decompose the object into a set of simplexes.

An example of decomposition for a 2-dimensional curving area is shown in Fig. 7 where the figure with thick outline is decomposed into 18 triangles sharing one edge each other. The triangles are managed by a R*-tree and are clustered as in Fig. 8 where 4 nodes *a*, *b*, *c*, and *d* have *five*, *three*, *five*, and *five* simplexes, respectively. This decomposition is a bit rough. The resolution of the decomposition depends on the target, and must have enough accuracy to prove its identity.

Fig. 7. Decomposition into simplexes

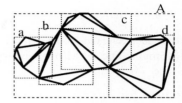

Fig. 8. Clustering a set of simplexes

The problem of this design is the storage cost for the simplexes of objects, if there are many. So it would be better to introduce some mechanism to reduce the size like a cell complex, i.e. a set of convex hull. How to decompose an object into simplexes is the key for the multi-level approximation, so we have to compare several decompositions as one of our future tasks.

3.3 Processing a spatiotemporal query

The strategy of traversing of the tree is quite identical to the previous filter-refinement scheme except that more complex comparison of SAM(object) and SAM(QR) is done in the filter step.

Filter The filter traverses not only the SAM(domain) but also the SAM(obj)s and SAM(QR). While descending the SAM(domain), there is no difference between previous two-step processor and this one. Its algorithm is shown in *FilterIS*. But when the traverse reaches to the root of some SAM(obj), we have to compare the SAM(obj) and SAM(QR). Although the traversing scheme for the SAM(domain) with many SAM(obj)s is same, the SAM(QR) is also traversed simultaneously. Its basic algorithm for the topological relationship *intersection* is described in *MoreFilterIS* shown below.

Using this multi-level approximation, the filter can pull only a portion of exact representation of object which may fulfill the given query topological relationship. This means that the processor can fetch only interesting part of exact object representation and reduce the complex calculation in the refinement.

This simple refinement algorithm finds one intersecting pair which will be piped to next step, refinement.

Refinement In this refinement, we examine the pairs of regions given from previous stage *filter* with complex mathematical based calculation. This step only tests the topological relationship based on simplex-simplex intersection, so it becomes much simpler than the plane-sweep algorithm when the dimension increased.

3.4 Query processing strategy

The tree is traversed in the depth-first way. Thus a LRU buffer for each of SAM(domain) and SAM(obj)s is necessary for caching tree nodes.

Basic idea for intersection test The main idea of this test is the comparison of the MBR(QR) and the MBR of each node in SAM(domain).

Procedure FilterIS collects all the objects whose MBR intersects MBR(QR).

```
FilterIS(O, Q)
  IF {O is an intermediate node,} THEN
    IF {O have intersection with Q,} THEN
      FOR {all of O's children,} DO
        FilterIS({child}, Q);
      END
    END
  ELSE
    IF {O has no need of refinement,} THEN
      {add the pointer to INSIDE};
    ELSE IF {O have to be refined,} THEN
      {add the pointer to BORDER};
    END
  END
```

In this procedure, O refers to a node of SAM(domain), Q refers to MBR(QR), and INSIDE and BORDER are list. The candidate nodes are inserted into two lists *INSIDE* and *BORDER*. *INSIDE* holds all OIDs of hits and *BORDER* has all OIDs that must have to be tested in the next *MoreFilterIS*.

```
MoreFilterIS(S, F)
  IF {S is intermediate node,} THEN
    IF {MBR(S) and MBR(F) have intersection,} THEN
      FOR {all of S's children,} DO
        MoreFilterIS(F, child);
      END
    END
  ELSE
    IF {F is intermediate node,} THEN
      MoreFilterIS(F, S);
    ELSE {do exact topological test against
```

```
      each simple figures of S and F,
      get each simplex from S and F, then
      return TRUE only when they have intersection.}
   END
END
```

In this procedure, S and F refer to SAM(obj) and SAM(QR), respectively. This algorithm traverses the trees in the depth-first way using the recursion. While descending one of the R*-trees, S and F are swapped one after the other so that both trees are descended simultaneously. This mechanism might have some work to refine. While descending the trees, the filter can limit the area to be searched and distinguish false hits without much computation cost.

Other types of query region Other types of query region are also processed in the very similar way.

- *Point* does not have the SAM(QR), and the only usable query condition is intersect. But when gathering all the objects which intersect a given point, tree traversing may reduce some intersection test between multi-dimensional objects and a point.
- *Window* does not need the SAM for the query region. However, the object decomposition improves the performance of query processing.
- *Outline of a region* also can be treated well without any difficulty in our index architecture.

4   Related works

Brinkhoff et al. proposed a design of spatial join processor [13] which influenced our design. Their processor is composed of three parts: *MBR-join* [12], *geometric filter*, and *exact geometry processor*. From the view point of architecture, the *MBR-join* and *geometric filter* correspond to our filter, and the *exact geometry processor* resembles to our refinement. The difference between theirs and ours is that we organize SAM(OBJ) and SAM(QR) not only to approximate their regions but also to manage their exact object representations.

For more efficient management of domain objects, each object is decomposed and clustered in our design. A similar technique is proposed in TR*-tree [13]. TR*-tree slices an object along a specified axis, and organizes those slivers into a R*-tree. The most different point between TR*-tree and our model is decomposition scheme. Main aim of our decomposition using simplex is to minimize the space of the regions in the intermediate nodes whose children do not cover. But it's difficult to achieve this target only by simply slicing objects.

In the 2-dimensional space, the triangulation scheme [7] proposed by Preparata et al. is very similar to our decomposition. But our decomposition is not applied only to objects in the domain but also to the query region. And we decompose the query region and the objects to get hierarchically clustered regions which are managed by R*-trees.

The z-order traversing [4] by Orenstein works in spatiotemporal space with a very simple manner. Divided Space is used like our MBR way, but it can not help geometry computations.

5 Conclusion

In this paper, we proposed a new spatiotemporal range query processor based on two step query processing with R*-tree. The test in SEQUOIA 2000 benchmark gave us important hint for the efficiency of query processing; Reducing the cost of refinement is the most important to the query processor.

The MBR can be used to get candidate objects easy and quickly with small storage. But using only single MBR for a query region and one for each object is too rough to get the qualified objects efficiently. We use the R*-tree to manage objects in domain space. In the similar way, we manage each object and query region using a R*-tree. A set of approximative regions represents more accurate figure of corresponding object than the MBR. Using those regions, the filter can reduce the candidates which can not fulfill given query condition at filter level. This leads to the considerably reduction of the I/O-cost in the refinement.

At last, the works to be done in near future are the design of the efficient decomposition scheme suitable for R*-tree and the investigation on more efficient algorithm of traversing trees of each object and query region.

Acknowledgment

We would like to thank the Workshop attendees of NewDB'98 in Singapore for their kind comments on this research. Their comments ware very useful to improve the quality of this paper. This research is supported in part by The Ministry of Education, Science, Sports and Culture, Japan under a Grant-in-Aid for Scientific Research on Priority Areas (Grant-No. 08244105)

References

1. A. Guttman. R-trees: a dynamic index structure for spatial searching. In *Proc. ACM SIGMOD Int. Conf. on Management of Data*, pages 47–57, 1984.
2. D. A. White and R. Jain. Similarity indexing with the SS-tree. In *Proceedings of the Twelfth International Conference on Data Engineering*, pages 516–523, 1996.
3. J. T. Robinson. The K-D-B-tree: A search structure for large multidimensional dynamic indexes. In *Proc. ACM SIGMOD Ann Arbor, USA*, pages 10–18, 1981.
4. Jack Orenstein. Spatial query processing in an object-oriented database system. In *Proceedings of the 1986 ACM SIGMOD*, pages 326–336, 1986.
5. Michael Stonebraker, Jim Frew, Kenn Gardels, and Jeff Meredith. The sequoia 2000 storage benchmark. In *Proceedings of the 1993 ACM SIGMOD*, pages 2–11, 1993.
6. N. Beckmann, H. Peter Kriegel, R. Schneider, and B. Seeger. The R*-tree: An efficient and robust access method for points and rectangles. In *Proceedings of the 1990 ACM SIGMOD*, pages 322–331, 1990.

7. Preparata F.P. and Shamos M.I., editors. *Computational Geometry.* Springer, 1985.
8. S. Kuroki and A. Makinouchi. Design of the spatio-temporal data model universe using simplicial complexes. *IPSJ SIG Notes(in Japanese)*, 109(37), 1996.
9. S. Kuroki, K. Ishizuka, and A. Makinouchi. Towards a spatio-temporal oql for the four dimensional spatial database system hawks. In *8th Int. Conf. and Workshop on Database and Expert Systems Applications*, page (to appear), 1995.
10. Shamos M. I. and Hoey D.J. Geometric intersection problems. *Proc. 17th Annual Conf. on Foundations of Computer Science*, pages 208–215, 1976.
11. T. Brinkhoff, H. P. Kriegel, and R. Schneider. Comparison of approximations of complex objects used for approximation-based query processing in spatial database systems. In *Ninth International Conference on DATA ENGINEERING*, pages 40–49, 1993.
12. Thomas Brinkhoff, Hans-Peter Kriegel, and Bernhard Seeger. Efficient processing of spatial joins using R-trees. In *Proceedings of the 1993 ACM SIGMOD*, pages 237–246, 1993.
13. Thomas Brinkhoff, Hans-Peter Kriegel, Ralf Schneider, and Bernhard Seeger. Multi-step processing of spatial joins. In *Proceedings of the 1994 ACM SIGMOD*, pages 197–208, 1994.

Implementing Class Library and Index for Managing Spatio-Temporal Data

Toshiyuki Amagasa   Masayoshi Aritsugi
Takayuki Tanaka   Yoshinari Kanamori

Department of Computer Science, Gunma University
1–5–1 Tenjin-cho, Kiryu 376–8515 Japan
{amagasa, aritsugi, tanaka, kanamori}@dbms.cs.gunma-u.ac.jp

Abstract. This paper describes a way of implementing a spatio-temporal conceptual data model which we have proposed as a class library on an object database system. The class library is composed of three classes: temporal, spatial, and spatio-temporal classes. As the temporal part of the class library, we exploit time-interval class that we have already developed for temporal data. In this paper, we first build a class for spatial concepts, and then integrate the class with the time-interval class. We also show some examples of spatio-temporal queries using the class library. Moreover, we investigate an indexing structure based on R*-tree for the class library so that any spatio-temporal query can be efficiently processed with it.

1   Introduction

Modeling image sequences and retrieving spatio-temporal objects from them by specifying their contents are important issues to today's database technology. It is necessary for many applications including medical image databases to handle image sequences. For this purpose, many researchers have studied on content description and retrieval of images [5, 7, 9, 11, 12, 14, 15, 16, 17].

In the retrieval of images containing objects, it is essential to model the objects appropriately. There are many researches employing minimum bounding rectangles (MBRs) to model objects in images. Let us consider, for example, CT images on cross section of liver on a patient (Fig. 1). In the figure, there are the liver, the main artery, and a cancer, and each of them is approximated with MBRs. In general, such images are recorded intermittently, and each image has time stamp at which it was recorded. We can employ MBRs and time stamps for specifying something like positions and sizes of objects and spatial relations between objects in querying on such image sequences.

We have proposed a spatio-temporal conceptual data model which enables us to model and query image sequences[5, 17]. In the model, we treat objects in images as MBRs. We also introduce MBCs (minimum bounding cuboids), which consist of MBRs with time intervals, in order to represent the valid time of objects. We can express an object's temporal change with a CMBC (composite minimum bounding cuboid) which is a sequence of MBCs. Main features of the

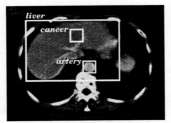

Fig. 1. An example of CT images

model are: (1) we can express spatio-temporal queries uniformly with intervals, (2) various kinds of spatial relations, such as topological, direction, and distance relations, are defined, and we can express queries using them, and (3) it does not depend on any specific application.

This paper describes a way of implementing the spatio-temporal conceptual data model as a class library on a commercial database system ObjectStore[13]. The class library is composed of three components: spatial classes (`Interval` and `MBR`), temporal classes (`TMInterval`, `CollectionTM`, and `CompositeTM`), and spatio-temporal classes (`MBC` and `CMBC`). We have already developed time-interval class library[2, 3], and in this work we employ it for temporal data. Hence, what we have to do is to implement spatial classes. Spatio-temporal classes can be constructed easily by combining spatial and temporal classes. For each class, we implemented all operations and relations as its methods.

Moreover, we investigate an indexing structure for the class library that enables us to process spatio-temporal queries efficiently. The index is based on the R*-tree[6]. One of the features of our index is that it stores not only spatio-temporal entities, such as MBCs, but also non-spatio-temporal values, such as areas of MBRs and durations in which MBCs were valid. In fact, these values are important and frequently used in some applications. For example, let us consider the above mentioned medical image databases. The area of a cancer and its changes with time are important for medical fields. If these values are not indexed, these values have to be computed from coordinates of MBCs when needed, which must cause large overhead.

The remainder of this paper is organized as follows. Section 2 overviews spatio-temporal conceptual data model. Section 3 describes class library based on the model. Section 4 introduces an indexing structure for the class library. Related work is compared with our work in Section 5, and Section 6 concludes this paper.

2   Modeling Spatio-Temporal Objects

In this section we describe briefly interval-based spatio-temporal representation of objects; a more detailed description including formal definitions of concepts can be found in [17].

We model an object appearing in an image with a minimum bounding rectangle (MBR). In the modeling, we assume that the status appearing in the image continues as it looks like by the time the next image is created. This assumption allows us to model an object with minimum bounding cuboids (MBCs) each of which consists of an MBR and the time interval.

Definition 1 *Let i_s and i_e be points on an axis of coordinates. Let us define an interval as a closed interval $i = (i_s, i_e)$.*

In this paper, the start and end points of a interval i are referred to as $i.sp = i_s$ and $i.ep = i_e$, respectively.

Definition 2 *Given object O, let $Ox = (Ox.sp, Ox.ep)$ and $Oy = (Oy.sp, Oy.ep)$ be its intervals, created by projecting it on x- and y-axes, respectively. The minimum bounding rectangle (MBR) of object O is defined as the domain (x,y) where*

$$Ox.sp \le x \le Ox.ep \land Oy.sp \le y \le Oy.ep \quad .$$

This is described as $(Ox, Oy; O)$ in this paper.

Definition 3 *Let the time interval in which $(Ox, Oy; O)$ is available be $Ot = (Ot.sp, Ot.ep)$. Let us define that the object's minimum bounding cuboid (MBC) is the domain (x, y, t) where*

$$Ox.sp \le x \le Ox.ep \land Oy.sp \le y \le Oy.ep \land Ot.sp \le t \le Ot.ep \quad .$$

This is described as $(Ox, Oy, Ot; O)$ in this paper.

One of the features of our conceptual model is that we not only express time intervals in which an object appears but time intervals in which the object does not. These time intervals are called *real-time intervals* and *null-time intervals*, respectively [2]. In the representation, an object in a null-time interval is modeled as a *null MBC* which consists of a *null MBR* with certain time interval. The null MBR and null MBC are described as $(\varepsilon, \varepsilon; O)$ and $(\varepsilon, \varepsilon, Ot; O)$, respectively.

To model dynamic changes of objects, including the objects' movement, expansion, contraction, appearance and disappearance, we introduce composite MBCs.

Definition 4 *Given an image sequence consisting of n images, each is numbered as i $(1 \le i \le n)$. Given object O, the MBC O_{mbc_i} of which is $(Ox_i, Oy_i, Ot_i; O)$. The object's composite MBC (CMBC) is defined as $\{O_{mbc_1}, O_{mbc_2}, \ldots, O_{mbc_n} \mid$*
$(\ldots((Ot_1 \text{ meets } Ot_2) \text{ meets } Ot_3) \ldots \text{ meets } Ot_n)\}$
where Ot_i meets Ot_{i+1} means $Ot_i.ep + 1 = Ot_{i+1}.sp$.

We use Allen's relations[1] between two intervals as a basis of all relations between intervals created by projecting objects on the x- or y-axis. We extended the relations so that we can express topological and direction relations and distances between objects appearing in an image[17].

There are eight kinds of topological relations between MBRs [12], namely, Disjoint, Meets, Insides, Contains, Overlaps, Equals, Covered_by, and Covers. Direction relations between objects, for example, above, left-below and so forth, are defined by combining two interval relations: one is along x-axis, and the other is along y-axis. One of the features of our model is that the direction relation between objects can be defined even in the case where the topological relation between the two objects is Contains[17]. We defined two types of distances between objects: distance between the centers of gravity and shortest distance between two objects[17].

3 Spatio-Temporal Class Library

3.1 Class Composition

In this section, we try to construct a class library for managing spatio-temporal objects. The library is based on the spatio-temporal conceptual data model. The model defines four concepts, namely, intervals, MBRs, MBCs, and CMBCs, and represents image sequences with these concepts. For the class library, we define four classes corresponding to the four concepts.

Our class library is composed of three components: spatial classes, temporal classes, and spatio-temporal classes. We employ the time-interval class library which we have implemented as the temporal classes[2, 3].

3.2 Class Definitions

Interval Class The Interval class has start and end points as its attributes. The definition of the Interval class is as follows:

```
class Interval {
private:
    int start;  // start point
    int end;    // end point
public:
    Interval(int s = 0, int e = 0);     // constructor
    ~Interval();          // destructor
    int startPoint();     // return the start point
    int endPoint();       // return the end point
    int duration();       // return the duration (|end - start + 1|)
    IntervalRelation* relation(Interval* u);
    PIntervalRelation* relationParam(Interval* u);
    Interval* intersection(Interval* u);
    Interval* cover(Interval* u);
};
```

The IntervalRelation and PIntervalRelation are classes which represent Allen's interval relations. In particular, the PIntervalRelation class represents extended relations which are introduced in our model, thereby we can represent the distance between two intervals as shown in [17].

MBR Class Since an MBR is composed of two intervals parallel to the x- and y-axes, the class MBR holds two Interval objects. In addition, we give an object identifier (OID) for the modeled object, of which type is integer, to this class.

```
class MBR {
protected:
    Interval* x;          // Int. on x-axis
    Interval* y;          // Int. on y-axis
    int id;               // the object id
public:
    MBR(Interval* ix, Interval* iy, int obj);
                          // constructor
    ~MBR();      // destructor
    Interval* x_interval();      // return the x
    Interval* y_interval();      // return the y
    int objectID();      // return the id
    int area();          // return the MBR's area
    Coordinates* gravity();      // return the center of gravity
    double distance(MBR *Q);
    double shortestDistance(MBR *Q);
    TopologicalRelation* topologicalRelation(MBR *Q);
    SpatialRelation* spatialRelation(MBR *Q);
    DirectionRelation* directionRelation(MBR *Q);
};
```

MBC class We can regard an MBC as an MBR from spatial viewpoint. On the other hand, we can regard an MBC as a time interval from temporal viewpoint. Thus, we let the MBC class inherit both the time-interval class (TMInterval) and the MBR class.

```
class MBC: public TMInterval, public MBR {
public:
    MBC(int s, int e, MBR* mbr);      // constructor
    MBC(TMInterval* ti, MBR* mbr);    // constructor
    ~MBC();      // destructor
};
```

CMBC class As described before, a CMBC is defined as a temporally ordered set of MBCs in which next neighbor MBCs are adjacent each other. Although we can define CMBC class which have a set of MBCs as its attribute, we employed the CompositeTM class[3] in order to achieve the restriction with ease.

```
class CMBC: public CompositeTM {
private:
    int id;      // the object id
    os_List<MBR*> mbrlist;      // list of references to MBR objects
public:
    CMBC();      // constructor
    CMBC(int obj, MBC* mbc);      // constructor
    ~CMBC();                       // destructor
    os_List<MBC*> mbcs();
    os_List<MBC*> real();
    os_List<MBC*> null();
    int objectID();      // return the id
    int cardinality();   // return the # of MBCs
    MBC select(int i);
    void append(MBC* mbc);
};
```

3.3   Query Examples

Here we use real image data. Figures 2 to 9 indicate CT images on cross section of liver of a patient. In Figures 2 to 3 we can see a cancer in the liver. The cancer moved to another place as shown in Figure 4, then it contracted with time, and finally it disappeared (Fig. 9) by radiotherapy.

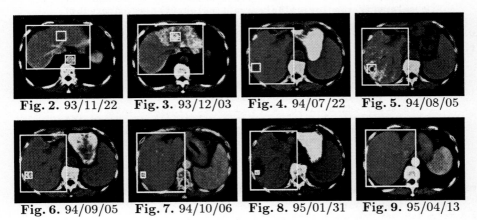

Fig. 2. 93/11/22   **Fig. 3.** 93/12/03   **Fig. 4.** 94/07/22   **Fig. 5.** 94/08/05

Fig. 6. 94/09/05   **Fig. 7.** 94/10/06   **Fig. 8.** 95/01/31   **Fig. 9.** 95/04/13

The liver and cancer are modeled with composite minimum bounding cuboids L_{cmbc} and C_{cmbc}, respectively. Note that each image is normalized as the patient's body size of 100×100 square.

$$
\begin{aligned}
L_{cmbc} = \{&((93/11/22, 94/07/21); ((11, 95), (8, 64); L)), \\
&((94/07/22, 94/08/04); ((4, 62), (11, 83); L)), \\
&((94/08/05, 94/09/04); ((6, 65), (12, 85); L)), \\
&((94/09/05, 94/10/05); ((4, 63), (12, 85); L)), \\
&((94/10/06, 95/01/30); ((3, 70), (9, 88); L)), \\
&((95/01/31, 95/04/12); ((6, 66), (10, 85); L)), \\
&((95/04/13, now); ((5, 71), (10, 82); L))\} \\
C_{cmbc} = \{&((93/11/22, 93/12/02); ((41, 64), (15, 29); C)), \\
&((93/12/03, 94/07/21); ((40, 64), (15, 30); C)), \\
&((94/07/22, 94/08/04); ((9, 22), (44, 68); C)), \\
&((94/08/05, 94/09/04); ((10, 23), (45, 70); C)), \\
&((94/09/05, 94/10/05); ((9, 20), (46, 69); C)), \\
&((94/10/06, 95/01/30); ((10, 20), (46, 69); C)), \\
&((95/01/31, 95/04/12); ((7, 14), (45, 67); C)), \\
&((95/04/13, now); ((\varepsilon, \varepsilon), (\varepsilon, \varepsilon); C))\}
\end{aligned}
$$

Some query examples using the class library are shown below. Each query is written in OQL[8]. We assume that the Cancer and Liver classes represent cancer and liver objects, respectively, and each of them is defined to be a subclass of the CMBC class in advance.

ex. 1 Find cancers occurred in the right part of the liver.

```
select c
from Cancer c, Liver l
```

```
where exists i in [1 ... c.cardinality()]:
    c.select(i).directionRelation(l.select(i)).x_relation() > 0 and
    (c.select(i).topologicalRelation(l.select(i)) == insides ||
    c.select(i).topologicalRelation(l.select(i)) == coveredby)
```

ex. 2 Find cancers that spread from the left part to the right part of the liver.

```
select c
from Cancer c, Liver l
where exists i in [1 ... c.cardinality()]:
    exists j in [1 ... c.cardinality()]:
    (c.select(i).directionRelation(l.select(i)).x_relation() > 0 and
    c.select(i).topologicalRelation(l.select(i)) == inside and
    c.select(j).directionRelation(l.select(j)).x_relation() < 0 and
    c.select(j).topologicalRelation(l.select(j)) == inside) and
    (c.select(i).relation(c.select(j)) == before or
    c.select(i).relation(c.select(j)) == meets)
```

ex. 3 Find the time at which the cancer on the liver disappeared.

```
select c1.mbcs().t
from (select c.mbcs() from Cancer c) c1, c2
where c1.x_interval() != 0 and c1.y_interval() != 0 and
    c2.x_interval() == 0 and c2.y_interval() == 0 and
    c1.relation(c2) == meets
```

As shown in these examples, we can express spatio-temporal queries with the class library using interval, spatial, topological and direction relations, and distance between objects. Note that we can express direction relations between objects even if they are overlapping each other in our model.

4 An Indexing Structure for the Class Library

4.1 Basic Index Structure

As shown so far, all spatio-temporal concepts are uniformly represented with intervals. This section introduces an indexing structure based on R*-tree[6] for handling interval data efficiently.

Vazirgiannis et al. proposed an R-tree based indexing structure for large multimedia data[18]. They experimented with the following schemes.

1. A simple spatial and temporal indexing scheme in which spatio-temporal objects can be handled with the two indexes:
   - a spatial (2D) index for spatial characteristics (id, x_1, x_2, y_1, and y_2 values), and
   - a temporal index for temporal characteristics (id, t_1, and t_2 values).
2. A unified indexing scheme consists of only one index: a spatial (3D) index for the complete spatio-temporal information.

Their results indicated that the latter is more efficient. Thus, we employ unified indexing scheme in this work. Let $O_{mbc} = (Ox, Oy, Ot; O)$ be a minimum bounding cuboid of object O. We determined the following four coordinates: x-axis ($Ox.sp$ and $Ox.ep$ values), y-axis ($Oy.sp$ and $Oy.ep$ values), t-axis ($Ot.stp$ and $Ot.etp$ values), and object id (O value).

4.2 Indexing Optional Values

In some applications, indexing some optional values in addition to the above mentioned values of coordinates can be useful. For example, areas of MBRs and durations of time intervals are important in medical image database applications. Let us consider a query "Find the time when the area of the cancer contracted to half compared with the area at 93/11/22." In processing such queries, areas of MBRs are necessary and they can be derived from spatial coordinates of MBRs. However, we cannot utilize the index for the processing. Instead, we must retrieve each cancer object and compute each cancer's area with the index. In this work, we intend to add two coordinates to our index: areas of MBRs and durations of time intervals.

We think that the index treating an object $O_{mbc} = (Ox, Oy, Ot; O)$ with the six coordinates, namely, x-axis $(Ox.sp, Ox.ep)$, y-axis $(Oy.sp, Oy.ep)$, t-axis $(Ot.stp, Ot.etp)$, object id (O), area axis $(Ox.dur \times Oy.dur)$, and duration axis $(Ot.dur)$. Consequently, the insertion procedure for the index needs some additional process that computes area and duration from the space and time coordinates. The search procedure becomes even more simple than the conventional one; when we query concerning optional values, it only searches the appropriate axes on the index.

Although indexing optional values improve performance of queries that use indexed values, this may affect performance of insertion. We confirm this with some results of experiments described in the following.

4.3 Performance Evaluation

We compared the performance of the index without optional values constructed on the four dimensions (4D) R*-tree with that of the index with optional values constructed on the six dimensions (6D) R*-tree (Figs. 10 and 11). We generated image sequences in the experiments where (1) there were n objects, (2) each object had 50 versions on average, and (3) intervals for the x-, y-, and t-axes of each version were uniformly distributed. We used a Sun Ultra 30 with UltraSPARC-II 296 MHz cpu and 128MB memory and ObjectStore 5.1.0 for the evaluation.

Figure 10 illustrates performance of insertion process. We varied the number of objects which appeared in each image. From the figure, we can see that the performance of the 6D R*-tree is worse than that of the 4D R*-tree. This is because the 6D R*-tree inserts objects with calculating area and duration.

Figure 11 shows performance of queries on duration. The 6D R*-tree performs better than the 4D R*-tree, because the 4D R*-tree has to examine each object and compute the duration on demand, while the 6D R*-tree does not need to do that but just processes range query on the duration axis.

5 Related Work

Vazirgiannis et al.[18] showed the unified scheme is more efficient than the scheme in which spatio-temporal objects can be managed with spatial index and temporal index separately.

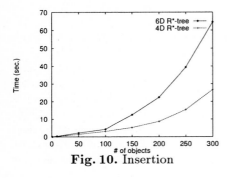

Fig. 10. Insertion

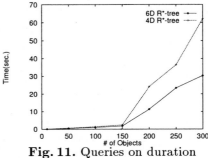

Fig. 11. Queries on duration

Horinokuchi et al. investigated an R*-tree based spatio-temporal indexing structure for the Universe data model[10]. They introduced a normalization process into R*-tree. The process improves efficiency of the index even if the axes of the index use some different kinds of units. The result is also useful for our index, because our index has event-axis whose unit has nothing to do with other axes, such as x- and y-axis.

Our index differs from theirs in one point, that is, we have introduced area- and duration-axes in addition to ordinary spatio-temporal axes. These values are often used in queries of some applications, and they can be processed with our index more efficient than others. In addition, we showed that introducing additional axes into R*-tree does not affect the performance on insertion seriously.

6 Conclusion

In this paper, we described a class library for modeling image sequences. The library is constructed on an object database system and is based on the spatio-temporal conceptual data model which we have proposed. We can describe and query contents of image sequences using the library. We employed CT images as an example of the actual application, and showed how we can model and query on image sequences. Furthermore, we proposed an indexing structure for the library. The index has additional axes expressing areas of objects (area axis) and durations of time intervals (duration axis) in addition to x-, y-, and t-axes. Therefore, we can process queries using such values efficiently. The effectiveness of the index was shown by some experiments.

Acknowledgements

We are grateful to Kimiko Sakurai for implementing our class library. We are also grateful to Prof. Tomio Inoue at the School of Medicine, Gunma University, for providing us CT images. This work was supported in part by the Ministry of Education, Science, Sports and Culture, Japan, under Grants-in-Aid for Scientific Research (Grant-No. 08244101 and 10680333), and in part by Nihon Sun Microsystems K.K.

References

1. J.F.Allen, "Maintaining Knowledge about Temporal Intervals," *Commun. ACM,* 26, pp.832–843, 1983.
2. T. Amagasa, M. Aritsugi, Y. Kanamori, and Y. Masunaga, "Interval-Based Modeling for Temporal Representation and Operations," *IEICE Trans. Info. & Syst.,* E81-D(1), pp.47–55, 1998.
3. T. Amagasa, M. Aritsugi, and Y. Kanamori, "Implementing Time-Interval Class for Managing Temporal Data," *Proc. Workshop on DEXA'98,* IEEE Computer Society, pp.843-849, Aug. 1998.
4. T. Amagasa, M. Aritsugi, and Y. Kanamori, "An Implementation of Interval Based Conceptual Model for Temporal Data," *IEICE Trans. Info. & Syst.* (to appear).
5. M. Aritsugi, T. Tagashira, T. Amagasa, and Y. Kanamori, "An Approach to Spatio-Temporal Queries – Interval-Based Contents Representation of Images – ," *Proc. DEXA'97,* LNCS 1308, pp.202–213, Sep. 1997.
6. N.Beckmann, H-P.Kriegel, R.Schneider and B.Seeger, "The R*-tree: An Efficient and Robust Access Method for Points and Rectangles," *Proc. ACM SIGMOD Conf.,* pp.322–331, 1990.
7. A.D.Bimbo, E.Vicario, and D.Zingoni, "Symbolic Description and Visual Querying of Image Sequences Using Spatio-Temporal Logic," *IEEE Trans. Knowledge and Data Engineering,* 7(4), pp.609–621, Aug. 1995.
8. R.G.G. Cattell and D.K. Barry, ed., "The Object Database Standard: ODMG 2.0," Morgan Kaufmann, San Francisco, California, 1997.
9. Y.F. Day, S. Dagtas, M. Iino, A. Khokhar, and A. Ghafoor, "Object-Oriented Conceptual Modeling of Video Data," *Proc. ICDE,* pp.401–408, 1995.
10. H. Horinokuchi, S. Kuroki, and A. Makinouchi, "Design and Implementation R*-tree for Spatiotemporal Index," Proc. IPSJ Symp. on Information Systems and Technologies for Network Society, pp.199–202, 1997.
11. Y. Masunaga, "The Block-World Data Model for a Collaborative Virtual Environment," *Proc. WWCA'98,* pp.309–324, Mar. 1998.
12. M. Nabil, J. Shephred and A.H.H. Ngu, "2D-Projection Interval Relationships: A Symbolic Representation of Spatial Relationships," *Proc. 4th Int. Symp. on Large Spatial Databases,* pp.292–309, Aug. 1995.
13. "ObjectStore C++ API Reference Release 5.0", *Object Design, Inc.,* Jul. 1997.
14. D. Papadias and T. Sellis, "Qualitative Representation of Spatial Knowledge in Two-Dimensional Space," *VLDB J.,* 4(3), pp.479–516, Oct. 1994.
15. D. Papadias, Y. Theodoridis, T. Sellis and M.J. Egenhofer, "Topological Relations in the World of Minimum Bounding Rectangles: A Study with R-trees," *Proc. SIGMOD Conf.,* pp.92–103, 1995.
16. J. Sharma and D.M. Flewelling, "Inferences from Combined Knowledge about Topology and Directions," *Proc. 4th Int. Symp. on Large Spatial Databases,* pp.279–291, Aug. 1995.
17. T. Tagashira, T. Amagasa, M. Aritsugi and Y. Kanamori, "Interval-Based Representation of Spatio-Temporal Concepts," *Proc. CAiSE'97,* LNCS 1250, pp.231–244, June 1997.
18. M. Vazirgiannis, Yannis Theodoridis, and Timos Sellis, "Spatio-temporal composition and indexing for large multimedia applications," *Multimedia Systems,* Vol.6, p.284–298, 1998.

A Spatiotemporal Data Management Method Using Inverse Differential Script

Yutaka Ohsawa and Kyungwol Kim

Saitama University, Japan

Abstract. According to popularization of the geographic information system (GIS), temporal data management has become very important. When GIS is used in daily work, the most frequently accessed data is the present data. Therefore, the access speed for the present data should not be lowered in spatiotemporal data management. Furthermore, the past data should also be able to be restored. This paper proposes a spatiotemporal data management method based on the geographic differential script file (GDSF) method. This method records changes in maps in the form of a graphical operation with a time print. When old data becomes necessary, the data is restored by applying the GDSF to the current map data. This paper describes a combination method of spatial data structure and the GDSF for expediting the excution of spatial retrieval.

1 Introduction

Geographic Information System (GIS) has been handling objects which distribute on two-dimensional planes or in three-dimensional space. Recently, however, the need has arisen to handle three or four-dimensional spatiotemporal data, which consists of conventional spatial axes and the time axis. For example, keeping construction history on a facility management system, the management of the history of building construction in a city, division and merge history of parcels in land register maps, and change of land use are examples of these needs.

Several methods are already proposed for spatiotemporal data management. One major methodology deals with spatiotemporal data as 4-dimensional data which consists of a 3-dimensional space and time axis[1][5]. This approach is suitable for the fields which need a continuous time axis, for example virtual reality. However, for facility management or land register use, changes occur occasionally, not continuously, in that case, continuous temporal management is not always necessary for GIS.

Teraoka, et.al [4] propose a method which records all history of growth of tree structure by data insertion and deletion. On this data structure, geographic data from any specified time can be retrieved in good time response. However, the data structure is somewhat bulky, because it contains not only the change but also stable data redundantly.

The data structure proposed in this paper intends to be used the second category temporal data, i.e. the data which has some duration of existence. The

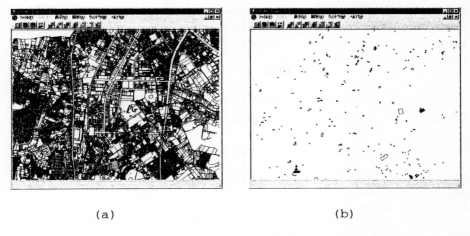

(a)   (b)

Fig. 1. Example of temporal data, (a) percels and houses in 1995, (b) difference between in 1995, and in 1996

data structure mainly manages the data corresponding to the present world, and it restores the past world by geometrical operation using differential script.

2 Spatiotemporal Map Management Using GDSF

Time based data is usually created by the following two methods; (1) During the operation of GIS in daily work, (2) by recreating a new map every specific period of time (for example, once a year).

With the spread of GIS use in daily work, temporal information created by the first method seems to have increased. By this method, the changes in the real world are reflected in GIS directly. The second method, however, is used mostly in tax administration in Japan (because, the tax is decided according to the state on January 1). Fig.1 shows an example how often changes occur in map data. This figure shows a rectangular area about 1.8 km in height, 2.4 km in width, about 3,200 parcels and 800 houses existing. Fig.1 (a) shows the state of the parcels and houses in 1995, and (b) shows the difference between 1995 and 1996.

In most cases, the present state is most important in GIS. The second most important is the difference between the present and near past states. Sometimes, a task to compare two specified times becomes necessary in statistical analysis, for example. That is to say, present data should be managed most effectively in time sequence data. Next, fast access to near past data should be considered, because near past data will be accessed more frequently than further past data.

The method proposed in this paper is based on the above analysis. The present data is managed on the center of the data structure, while past data is restored by applying a sequence of graphical operation commands to the present data. The command sequence describes the change from the present to past. Each command in the sequence has time print when the change (eg. house built, road constructed) had occurred.

3 Simple Temporal Information Management Using Geographic Differential Script File

3.1 Geographic Differential Script File

The GDSF, proposed by the authors in [2], is a file used in a method to manage and update map data in GIS. This method was designed to allow facilities to update geographic data that cannot be altered by users. The purpose of this method is to make map data available on CD-ROM, or in a network environment where ordinary users cannot alter the data on a server.

Imagine operations which revise an old map data set using a graphic editor (usually supplied as a function of GIS). The job is composed of a repetition of a series of actions: invoke a command (e.g. input an entity) by choosing from a menu, then input the coordinates of the vertices of the entity (e.g. polygon) by pressing a button on the pointing device. The GDSF is a set of graphic operation commands that corresponds to the series of the operations. In usual operation, the system actually alters the data set on the disc. In write prohibited circumstances, however, the users of the system cannot change the contents of the data set. In this case, the sequence of the change is written to a GDSF. To restore the modified data set, the system uses the original data and the GDSF. As the GDSF is composed by a series of edit commands, the modified data is restored by the system reading the graphic operation command one by one and applying it to the original data set.

As mentioned above, the GDSF records the invoked commands by the operator to the GIS. The commands are essentially insertion and deletion of the old data. The command, which the operator gives to the graphic editor, will hereafter be referred to as the graphic operation command.

Basic graphic operation command consists of the following;

1. add entity
2. delete entity
3. reshape entity
4. modify attribute (e.g. road name, building name)

Each graphic operation command composed by the following items;

(a) target layer
(b) kind of command (insert, delete, modify)
(c) shape and position
(d) time print (when the event occured, when the data was added to the database)

Map data is composed of several layers of data overlapping each other. The target layer shows which layer among them is being considered. The kind of command shows one of graphic operation command listed above.

The shape and position shows those of the entity to be added or to be deleted. The format of this information depends on individual entity. For example, if the entity is a point, only x and y coordinates are necessary to show them, and if the entity is a polyline (like a road), the shape and position are given by vertex number (N) and a vertex coordinate sequence (x1,y1,x2,y2,.....xN,yN).

In actual GIS, several kinds of time print are necessary. One is the time when the entity adds to the database, one is the time the entity appears in the real world, and another one is the time a building is registered to the city office. Then, temporal GIS must be able to handle multi time base. The proposed method manages temporal data by command sequence, so multi time data can easily be handled by this method by having several command sequences.

3.2 Restoring Old Dated Data by GDSF

Very simple time base management can be realized by strictly adhering to this method. That is, having a time print attached to each GDSF command, the map data of a specified point of time can be restored by applying the GDSF commands even though time prints are older than the specified date. However, by this simple method, the processing time of restoration is in proportion to the length of the command sequence in GDSF. In these cases, recovering the present state becomes a most time consuming task. This fact contradicts the objective of recovering the present state in the most efficiently manner. Fig.2 (a) shows the method.

Another method to manage temporal information by GDSF is to make a set of inverse commands of the GDSF and to apply it to the present data. The arrangement of the commands is also inverted from new to old order according to the time print. The base data of this method is the newest (present) data, and the specified time data is created by the inverse commands of the GDSF. This method always keeps the present state, so that no restoring process is necessary for the present state. Though restoration of the old state needs time in proportion to the length of the history, this is an acceptable characteristic. Fig.2 (b) shows the method. Then, the authors adopt the second method to manage the temporal data.

To make the method very simple, it is summarized as follows: a simple method is to make a GDSF file as a collection of graphic commands describing the difference from the present data is created, then apply the command until the specified time to be restored. This command sequence can be realized by a bi-directional list. When recording the differences occurring in daily work, add the command on the top of the list. Conversely, this can be done to apply the GDSF from the top of the list until the specified time to restore an old state. Simple stack can not adopt this process, because after restoring the old time data, the command sequence needs to be applied again (in this case, apply the inverse command) to the restored old data to obtain the present data, as shown in

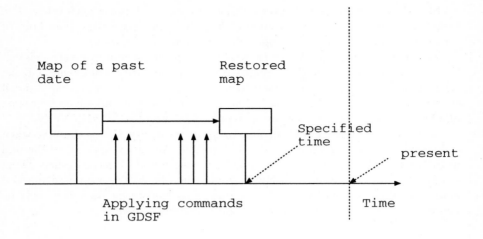

Map of a past date

Restored map

Specified time

present

Applying commands in GDSF

Time

(a) Restoring by simple GDSF

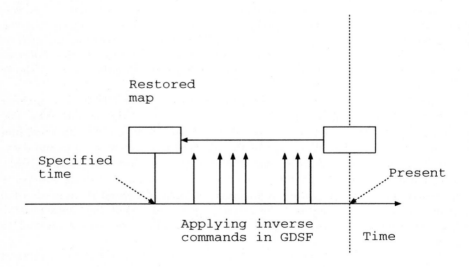

Restored map

Specified time

Present

Applying inverse commands in GDSF

Time

(b) Restoration from present data by inverse command

Fig. 2. Methods of restoring a map of a specified time

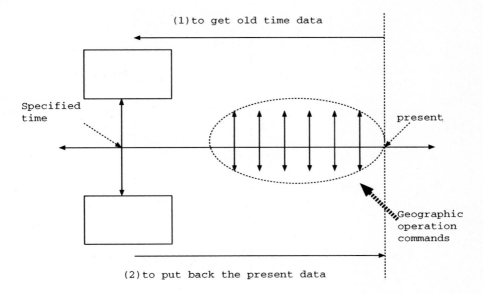

Fig. 3. Defect of simple method using GDSF

Fig.zu:fig3. The biggest defect of this simple method is very time consuming in two stages of restoration (one for getting old data, the other one for restoring to the original state). The feature "cherishing the present data" causes this.

Furthermore this simple method does not have contrivances to improve time efficiency in spatial retrieval. Usually, GIS handles big amount of data. Then, the GDSF can become too large to cover a whole area with a single bi-directional list. To improve time efficiency, some spatial indexes are necessary for GDSF list.

4   Spatiotemporal Data Structure Using GBD Tree

4.1   Basic GBD Tree

For the efficient handling of geographic data, spatial data structure is necessary. R- tree[6], R*-tree[7], and GBD-tree[2] are examples of this purpose. Several spatial data structures are based on hierarchical space division to reduce the amount of data which is concerned for spatial retrieval.

The GDSF structure mentioned above does not consider the efficiency in spatial retrieval. The GDSF should also have spatial structure for efficient retrieval. Though, any spatial structure can be adopted for this purpose, we chose to implement GBD-tree.

GBD-tree is a balanced multi-way tree structure similar to R-tree. However, its manner of region division differs from that of R-tree and its successor (e.g.

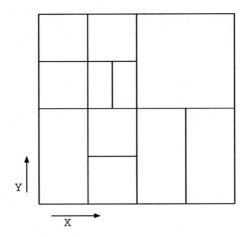

Fig. 4. Example of Regions Gotton by Successive Division

R*-tree). GBD-tree manages entities by two additional items of information: minimum bounding rectangle(MBR) and the center point of the MBR. The MBR is used for spatial retrieval, and the center point is used to determine in which cluster (or bucket) the entity belongs.

When a leaf node overflows by adding entities to the tree, the entities contained in the node are divided into two new leaf nodes according to the center point of the MBR of each entity. Each leaf node corresponds to a region on the map plane. And the shape of the region is always a square or a rectangle of which the length of the short edge is half of the long edge. In other words, the region is a rectangle made by successive division by x(horizontal) and y(vertical) axes alternatively. Samples of the divided regions are shown in Fig.4.

Each node in GBD-tree has an MBR, the number of child nodes, the pointers of the child nodes, and the information to express the position and the size of the divided region. In GDB tree, the position and the size of the divided region is restricted as the one which is explained above. The number of children is restricted by a given number K, like in R-tree.

When the number of entities in a leaf node exceeds K, the region of the leaf node is divided into two sub-regions under the condition that both sub-regions contain at least $K/3$ entities. Accompanying this, the entities in the leaf node are divided into two sub-regions, depending on the center point of the entity. Two new leaf nodes are created by this division.

The two leaf nodes are inserted into the parent node. When the parent node causes overflow, it is divided into two nodes again. The effect propagates towards the root node, like other known hierarchical dynamic data structures, e.g. B-tree and R- tree.

When spatial retrieval is made on the GBD-tree, the MBR is checked to

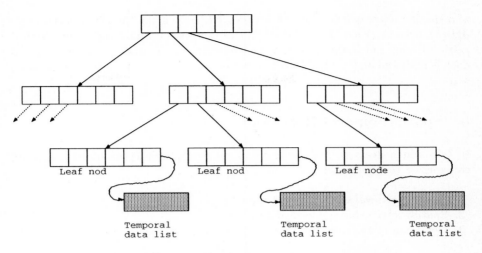

Fig. 5. Structure of GBD tree with temporal data

decide whether further dissension of the sub-tree is necessary or not. Only when the MBR of the node and the specified search area are overlapping is the sub-tree investigated.

4.2 Expansion of GBD Tree for Temporal Data Management

Using the same method as that of spatial data and temporal data (more precisely each GDSF command), the position of the leaf node where the data is stored can also be determined according to the center position of the MBR, then the data is stored in the determined leaf node. Each leaf node has a pointer to the priority queue for storing the temporal data. Temporal data is stored in the leaf node of the GBD-tree. The characteristic of GBD-tree of which mechanisms using to register data and to retrieve data are different is very important when to insert temporal data. The leaf node in which the temporal data is to be inserted is determined depending on the center position of the data. On the other hand, the node is not determined uniquely on R-tree and its successors because the data are divided by the shape of the MBR at the time that the division is invoked.

The priority of the queue is ordered by the time print from new to old. Fig.5 shows the concept of the structure. To distinguish the MBR of temporal data from that of present data (which is described in Sect.4.1), the MBR of the present data is denoted as MBRp, and the MBR of the temporal data is denoted as MBRt.

Retrieval from the queue is also required in order to restore the old timed data, In order to avoid omission of temporal data during spatial retrieval, each node of the GBD tree has the MBR of temporal data. When restoring the map of a specific date, spatial retrieval is executed, referencing the MBR of temporal data attached to each node. If the MBR of temporal data overlaps the specified retrieval area and if the node is a leaf node, then the queue storing temporal data is reviewed and applied to the command that is controlling the current data set.

5 Spatiotemporal Retrievals

In GIS which deals with discrete temporal events, the types of retrievals are categorized to the following:

1. Spatial retrieval of the present data
2. Spatial retrieval of a specified time data
3. Detection of the difference between two specified times.

The first type of retrieval is not temporal retrieval. Conventional GISes usually execute this type retrieval. The proposed data structure can execute the retrieval by simply not using the extension for temporal data, as described in [3]. There is no retrieval time loss by the extension. In the following two subsections, the other two types of retrievals are described.

5.1 Special Retrieval of Specified Time Data

The most typical spatial retrieval is range retrieval. Other spatial retrieval (for example, to find nearest neighbor) can also be executed by a combination of range retrieval. The following describes how to do range retrieval on the proposed data structure.

First, retrieval of the present data is done by the usual method of searching the GBD tree. Specifically, the overlap between the specified retrieval area and the MBRp on each node is inspected. If these two are overlapping, descend the tree and repeat the same check for all the child nodes. If the node is a leaf node, select the entities actually included in the specified range and add the entities to the result set. In this searching process, there is no overhead time caused by adding temporal information to the tree structure.

When a particular time (old date) is specified outside of the retrieval range, the priority queues attached to the leaf nodes are inspected. Range retrieval of a specified time is executed by the following steps, let the specified time be T and the specified range be R.

(1) empty the result set S.
(2) check whether MBRp or MBRt overlaps with R
(3) if they are overlapping and the node is not a leaf node, descend the tree and repeat the check for all child nodes.
(4) if they are overlapping and the node is a leaf node, copy the data in the leaf node to a working space W.

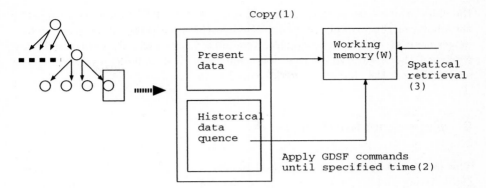

Copy(1)

Fig. 6. Steps of Spatiotemporal Retrieval

(5) apply the GDSF commands attached to the node whose time print is not older than T. This operation is executed on the data in the working space W. Add the result of W to S.

Fig.6 summarizes the steps of temporal retrieval. Every leaf node consists of two parts, the present data and the historical data queue. After having reached a leaf node, the present data part is copied to a working space W. Then the GDSF commands are applied until specified time. The contents in W are modified to the states of the specified time. Finally, spatial retrieval is performed on W.

The most important points of the method are in step (5). The first point is that the range retrieval with specified time is executed on a working space W, and there are no effects on the spatial data stored in the GBD tree. The second is that the influence of the operations by the GDSF commands is restricted within each leaf node. For example, a command to insert an entity has no effect on the other leaf nodes. When there is an insertion command on a priority queue of a leaf node, execution of this command has no effect on the results of the operation on the other nodes. In addition, if there is a deletion command on a priority queue of a leaf node, the object must exist on the same leaf node, because the GBD tree distributes entities to individual leaf nodes according to the center points. Also, deletion commands have no effect on other leaf nodes.

5.2 Detection of the Difference Between Two Specified Times

The comparison of two specified points in time is a frequently requested operation in spatiotemporal GIS. The proposed data structure can execute this type of operation easily.

Let two specified points in time be t1 and t2 ($t1 < t2$: t1 is older than t2). This type of retrieval, the step (1) in Fig.6 is not necessary, because the state of the present has no effect on the result. Fist, skip the historical data queue until the time print is newer than t2. Then, execute the GDSF commands stored in the queue in the working memory W while the time print of the command is newer than t1. When the steps have completed, the entities existing in W are a part of the result. To do this operation over the leaf nodes overlapping the specified area, the change can be detected in the area.

6 Experimental Results

The method described above is implemented on a SUN workstation by using C++. Using real data for experiment is very difficult, because map data contains private information, no city governments do not give permission to use their data. For that reason, the authors used an ordinal digital map published by Japan Map Center. To make temporal data, short line segments with time print were generated by a pseudo-random sequence.

The digital map data was inserted into the data structure as the present data. On the other hand, the short line segments with time prints were inserted as temporal data, therefore they were stored in the queues of the leaf nodes.

The digital map data contained about 12,000 entities (including points and polylines) , the number of generated short line segments was 6,000. Range searches using over specified date were executed using the digital map data.

Table 1. Retrieval Time of Range

normalized time	area size 0.002	area size 0.005	area size 0.01	area size 0.02
0.1	2.4	6.0	8.1	16.6
0.5	3.0	7.3	9.3	19.2
1.0	3.7	9.0	10.8	22.4

Table 1 shows the result. Each row shows the size of range in which area size is normalized by the area size of the map. Each column shows the specified date which is normalized by the time period between the present data and the oldest date.

The range retrieval of the present data is not affected by existence of temporal data. The range search using a specified time increases the retrieval time linearly to how many geographic operations are necessary to restore the data of the time. This is unavoidable under the method using the strategy which restores the old dated data by geographic operation commands.

7 Conclusion

This paper describes a new spatiotemporal data management method using differential script. The presented method requests no extra time consumption for spatial retrieval on the present data. To restore the old data, the method requires extra retrieval time depending on the length of history. These results meet the characteristics which were intended before designing the data structure.

Implementation of this data structure on actual GIS and theoretical analysis are future projects.

Acknowledgments

This study was supported in part by the Japanese Ministry of Education, Science, Sports and Culture, Grant-in- Aid for Scientific Research on Priority Areas "Advanced Database Systems for Integration of Media and User Environments", and Creative Basic Reserch #09NP1401: "Research on Multimedia Mediation Mechanism for Realization of Human-oriented Information Environments".

References

1. Donna Peuquet, Liujin Qian, "An Integrated Database Design for Temporal GIS", Proceedings of the Seventh International Symposium on Spatial data Handling, pp.21–31, Taylor & Francis, 1996
2. Yutaka Ohsawa, Kim Kyongwoel, "An Individual Management Method on a Distributed Geographic Information System", Proc. of '98 International Workshop on Advanced Image Technology, pp.105–110, 1998
3. Yutaka Ohsawa, Masao Sakauchi, "A New Type Data Structure with Homogeneous Nodes Suitable for a Very Large Spatial Database", Proc. of 6th International Conference on Data Engineering, pp.296–303, 1990
4. T. Teraoka, M.Murayama, Y.Nakamura, S.Nishida, "The Multidimensional Persistent Tree: A Spatio-temoral Data Management Structure Suitable for Spatial Search", Trans. IEICE, Vol.J78-D-II, No.9, pp.1346–1355, 1995
5. S.Kuroki, A.Makinouchi, "Representation of Spatial, Temporal, and Spatio- Temporal Data in the Topological Space Data Model Universe", IPSJ Tech. Report, 98-DBS-116(1), pp.133–140, 1998
6. A.Guttman, "R-trees: A Dynamic Index Structure for Spatial Searching", Proc. ACM SIGMOD Int. Conf. On Management of Data, pp.47–57, 1984
7. N.Beckmann, H.P.Kriegel, R.Schneider, B.Seeger, "The R*-tree: An Efficent and Robust Access Method for Points and Rectangles", Proc. of the 1990 SIGMOD, pp.322–331, 1990

Extracting Event Semantics from Video Data Based on Real World Database

Kiril Salev, Takashi Tomii, and Hiroshi Arisawa

Division of Electrical and Computer Engineering, Faculty of Engineering,
Yokohama National University, Japan
e-mail: {kitcho,tommy,arisawa}@arislab.dnj.ynu.ac.jp

Abstract. Video is considered the most effective medium for capturing events. There are two major approaches of representing video contents: the structured modeling approach and stratification. They require video to be divided into simple semantic units on top of which some structures are built to express high-level video semantics. Text is used to describe the necessary semantic units. A major problem of such an approach is that the descriptions tend to be incomplete and subjective. In addition, segmenting video sequences and describing their semantic contents is a tedious task.

In the present paper we define some low-level semantic primitives that can be detected automatically and are "semantics-free" from the viewpoint of event semantics. Further, we offer a methodology for describing event semantics and deriving it from the low-level primitives. We describe a prototype system based on the methodology and offer schema for its implementation based on the Real World Database. Our approach reduces the problem of video segmenting to simply performing a database query.

1 Introduction

Recent advancements in computer technology have made it possible complex multimedia data like computer graphics, images, video, etc. to be easily handled. As an important consequence therefrom, multimedia databases have developed significantly and many applications have become commercially available.

Practical value of multimedia databases is determined by the options they offer for representing, storing, and retrieving various kinds of media objects such as still images, voice, full-motion video, etc. Recently, there has been intensive research on image and video retrieval. Most of the efforts have been concentrated on so-called "content-based" retrieval, which aims at identifying objects or extracting content descriptions through various computer vision and image processing techniques on image features such as color, texture, shape, etc. Although there are widely accepted models for representing most of those features, it is also obvious that in case of a video movie, for example, some higher-level features cannot be extracted that way. For instance, even if we can recognize all objects involved in a video scene, we still cannot say what *is happening* in that scene. Still there is a need to provide database users with capabilities for effective handling and querying of such high level semantic features, that is, to represent the semantics of *events*.

Regarding events in the real world, video is considered the most effective medium for capturing them. At present, there are two major approaches of representing video contents: the structured modeling approach [16, 17] and stratification [4]. In the structured modeling approach, the video is divided into shots, representing the set of primitive concepts. On the other hand, in the stratification approach the video sequence is divided into a set of overlapping strata, each stratum representing only a single event, which can be easily described. In both cases text is used to describe manually the necessary semantic units and their contextual information. However, a major problem of such an approach is that the descriptions tend to be incomplete and subjective. In addition, the process of segmenting video sequences into shots/strata and describing their semantic contents is an arduous and tedious task. Automated tools are essential to help users in extracting primitive semantic units from the raw video material.

In the present paper we define some low-level semantic primitives that can be detected automatically and are "semantics-free" from the viewpoint of event semantics. Further, we offer a methodology for describing event semantics and deriving it from the low-level primitives. Our approach is based on the concept of Real World Database (RWDB) [3, 9]. It provides a total environment for capturing, modeling, and storing physical or logical objects from the real world. Captured data of any type is stored into a multimedia database in a uniform way. All data is stored as it is observed, enabling the creation and realistic representation of a virtual world using given media.

Existing automated systems [13, 15, 17] treat mainly the process of segmenting video sequences into shots, on the basis of cinematic editing rules, and do not deal with event semantics.

The paper is organized as follows. The next section is an introduction into the concept of RWDB. In section 3 we define the event semantic primitives and discuss semantic representation of events. Then, in section 4 design of a prototype system is addressed. Section 5 describes the database implementation of the prototype, and the last section concludes the paper.

2   Real World Database

The objective of RWDB is to provide total environment for capturing, modeling, and storing physical or logical objects from the real world. Everything in the real world could be modeled through it and any type of data could be accumulated. To achieve this goal, RWDB should include at least the four components listed below [3, 9]. The conceptual architecture of RWDB is shown in Figure 1.

2.1   Real World Capturer (RWC)

RWC captures the external shape of objects in the real world. Depending on the capturing devices, various types of spatial information can be obtained. For

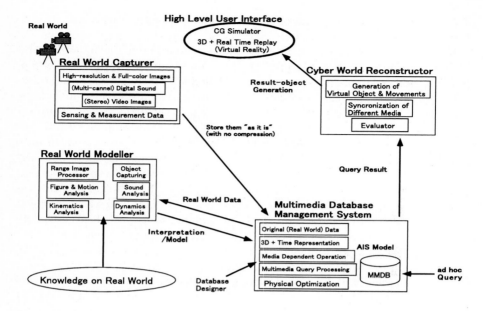

Fig. 1. Conceptual architecture of RWDB

example, by using a pair of video cameras we can get simultaneously frame sequences for the left-eye and right-eye views. Recent technology enables us to get a full-color, high quality digital image with no data compression (i.e. lossless.) However, it is very difficult to extract the complete surface model or motions (kinematics) model of an object from a frame sequence. On the other hand, there are several commercially available motion capturing systems but those can trace only a small number of marked points and considerable part of the original information (e.g. surface and texture) is lost. Finally, another type of input device is a 3D scanner by which we can get a complete surface (polygon) model of static objects. The practical solution is to get the above kinds of information and combine them into one model at the database level.

2.2 Real World Modeler

RWM is a set of tools, which analyze captured data and generate new information. For example, a tool called "outline chaser" catches the outline of an object in a certain video frame, and then traces it in the preceding and successive frames. Another tool called "point tracer" detects stereo pairs and calculates the range values for (specified) points in a pair of (left and right) frame images and makes a rough sketch of the 3D objects in the real world. Several algorithms for range image generation in the image processing area are discussed and evaluated in [1]. All results of the analysis are stored into the database preserving the correspondences to the original images.

2.3 Multimedia Database (MMDB)

MMDB is a database that treats a variety of data types like full texts, graphic drawings, bitmap images, and image sequences. The features of such data are quite different from the conventional DBMS's ones, because some of them are continuous and might very often occupy much more space than traditional data types. As to the data model, in order to integrate all types of data, it is essential to introduce simple primitives for describing real world entities and the associations between them. Moreover, for handling multimedia data the query language should involve a number of media-dependent operations for retrieving and displaying. For better intuitive understanding, the result of a query in RWDB creates a new "cyberspace". Relevant model for describing 2D or 3D data and multimedia query language MMQL for flexible retrieval was presented in [2].

2.4 Cyber World Reconstructor (CWR)

As discussed above, the result of an inquiry consists of various types of data such as frame sequences and 3D graphics data. In order to visualize the query result, RWDB should provide a "player" (viewer) of the result world. CWR is, in this sense, an integrated system of 3D computer graphics and 3D video presentation. Since modeling methods of objects in the fields of 3D graphics and VR systems are quite different from the database approach, new and unconventional solutions are necessary.

3 Semantic representation of events

Based on the RWDB concept, our goal is to offer a mechanism for semantic extraction of events from the raw video data. Particular considerations and examples, when necessary, will refer to manufacturing processes. In Section 4 we will discuss the reasons for such a choice but in general, the same methodology can be applied without significant changes to almost any other area.

When considering events, different levels of abstraction are applied depending on the user's objectives. For instance, in a car plant we can view as an event simply the screwing of a screw or the making of a whole car. In many cases such separation is strictly regulated. For example in the field of industrial engineering the same production process is considered at four different levels — production line, processes, elementary operations, and elementary movements, and there are strict hierarchical relations between them. An example is given in Figure 2.

Existing approaches [4, 12, 17] for representing video contents and expressing event semantics focus on handling such kind of relatively high-level information, assuming the existence of some primitive building blocks. However, there is a gap between the level of those primitive blocks and the features that can be detected automatically in the video data. To solve that problem, the necessary semantic units are described manually. That is quite a laborious task (as it has to be performed for each new video instance) and leads very often to incomplete and subjective descriptions.

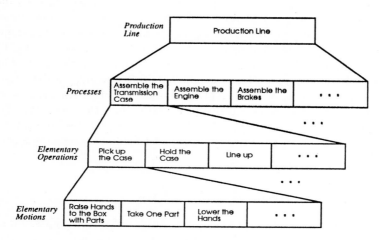

Fig. 2. Levels of a production process

Considering the example in Figure 2, it should be possible to extract elementary motions from a video of the production process by using our method. Recognizing events in a manufacturing process (and in the real world in general) and understanding the way things happen is of great importance. Most research efforts so far have been dedicated to the problems of shape and size capturing, and various approaches, matching algorithms, etc., have been developed. Compared to that, event detection and event modeling still remain underdeveloped. In some works computing trajectory of objects and modeling movements of objects are researched [7, 11] but event semantics is either not addressed or has to be expressed by the user when formulating queries.

The approach we offer here allows event semantics to be derived from automatically detectable video features and the process is as simple as performing a database query. In the following subsections we define primitives that are free of event semantics. Then, we describe how the transition is performed from those primitives to different kind of constructs, charged with event semantics.

3.1   Atomic units

Here we define the basic elements in our model. We introduce atomic units as simple primitives, which at the same time contain enough information for deriving the higher-level semantics.

Definition: We call an atomic unit (or AU) the tuple (T, P, O, S, R), where T is a time instant, P is a point in 3D space, O is a 3D object located in point P at the time instant T, S is a subject in relation R with the object O.

Atomic Unit 1	
T	3624
P	(+3.045, -0.071, +1.903)
S	'worker's hand in a white glove'
O	'screwdriver No. 8'
R	'touches'

Fig. 3. Example of atomic unit

R is a relation that can be observed and detected in a given point of time, independently from the preceding and succeeding time instances. Also, R is independent from the viewpoint in the 3D space. Examples of such relations are "touches", "is inside", "is close to", etc. Figure 3 shows an example of an AU instance.

Following from the definition, AUs don't have temporal duration. The reason for choosing such representation is that we assume all media to be in digital format, therefore (in case of time-dependent media) we have some sampling rate with clearly defined time instants and they determine the highest resolution at which media can be observed. In addition, the existing methods for automatic detection of video features are mainly frame-based. Since evolving in time is an essential characteristic of events, AUs cannot express it and can be regarded as semantics-free in the context of event semantics.

In some cases, some of the components of an AU instance may be omitted. For instance, if we want to specify just the existence of a subject at a given point of time and at a given location, then no values need to be specified for the object and relation components.

We can have several AUs at a given point of time. For instance, they may represent different objects, subjects, and/or relations. The problem of AU detection will be discussed in more detail in Section 4.

3.2   Model events

The basic idea of introducing model events is to form a part of the database that contains knowledge about the typical features of events and to use it for extracting event instances from the raw video data on the basis of the detected AUs.

A model event is defined as a directed graph $G_{ME} = \{N, TOR, TDR, SDR\}$, where

$$N = \{N_i\}, N_i \in \{S_i \times O_i \times R_i\};$$

$$TOR \subseteq \{Ni \times Nj\};$$

$$TDR \subseteq \{Ni \times Nj\};$$

$$SDR \subseteq \{Ni \times Nj\}.$$

N represents a set of nodes. Each node consists of a subject S_i, object O_i, and relation R_i between them. The meaning they represent is similar to the AUs, but in case of model event nodes, subject and object are generalized and refer to a class of subjects/objects in the AU's meaning. For instance, while in case of a model event node an example of subject value can be 'wrench,' in the AU it would be 'wrench No. 8.'

TOR is a set of one-way edges, representing temporal relations between nodes. The tuple $< N_i, N_j >$, representing the edge from N_i to N_j means that N_i is before N_j in time. If both $< N_i, N_j >$ and $< N_j, N_i >$ are presented, that means N_i and N_j are simultaneous. Since nodes, like AUs, are instantaneous, all possible temporal relations between them are 'before,' 'after,' and 'simultaneous.' In Section 4 another, more practical way of expressing the simultaneousness of AUs will be discussed.

TDR is a set of two-way edges representing temporal distance between nodes. In many cases it is not enough to define only the order of AUs, since the time between their occurrence is important, too. Temporal distance relations are labeled with minimum and maximum time limit values expressing these requirements. TOR and TDR are semantically independent — it is possible, for instance, to have some temporal distance requirement without relation to the order in which AUs are happening.

SDR is another set of two-way edges, representing spatial distance between nodes. As our considerations are about 3D space, spatial relations strongly depend on the viewpoint. In order to simplify our model, we consider a spatial relation only the 3D distance between nodes, because it is independent from the viewer's position. Two-way edges are labeled with the minimum and maximum distance required between the nodes.

An example of model event is shown in Figure 4. It represents the event "screwing of a screw", which consists of taking a screw from the box with screws, fixing the screw in some position, and then applying the screwdriver in the same position. Here we assume that if the worker's hand is inside the box of screws,

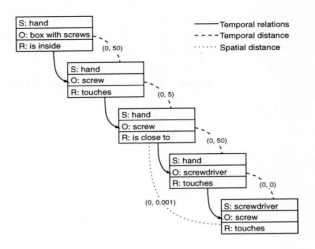

Fig. 4. Example of model event

then a screw is taken. Also, the requirement for a very small temporal distance between the second and the third node (see Figure 4) represents approximately the moment when the screw is released. Then its position should be the same where the screwdriver is applied, and that is the meaning of the spatial requirement between the third and the fifth node.

3.3 Correspondence between atomic units and model events

We introduce here event instances in order to represent the correspondence between AUs and model events.

An event instance represents the occurrence of an event in the real world and its semantics is expressed by some model event. The event instance can be visualized by playing the respective part of the video data or by some other tools included in the CWR part of RWDB.

Each event instance is determined by a set of AUs in the following way. Each model event node corresponds to exactly one AU from the set that matches the node components and satisfies all spatio-temporal relations included in the model event graph. Matching between AU and model event node holds if and only if: (i) the AU's subject/object values are elements of the class, represented by the respective subject/object values of the node; (ii) both the AU and model event node have the same value of their relation component. Spatio-temporal relations can be verified easily by using the values of time and place components of AUs.

Event instances develop in time and occupy some time interval that includes all AUs involved, i.e. the temporal closure of all time instants. There may be various algorithms for calculating it, depending on the specifics of the application field, but the topic is beyond the scope of this paper.

Therefore, the problem of extracting event semantic units from the raw video material is reduced to retrieving event instances from the multimedia database. The appropriate database schema and query execution is discussed in Section 5.

4   Design of a prototype system

In our current prototype of RWDB, the tools capable of detecting AUs are part of the RWM. One such tool, called 3D Chaser, was presented in [14]. It extracts the spatial coordinates of an object from a pair of stereo video frames, and traces that object in the preceding and succeeding frames. Then, by comparing the spatial locations of some specially selected objects, it can detect simple relations between them like "touch", "hold", etc. In such a way, the 3D Chaser generates series of AUs and stores them in the MMDB component of RWDB.

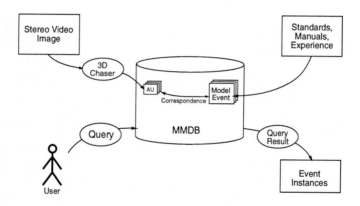

Fig. 5. Schema of the prototype system

On the other hand, model event definition has its theoretical foundations in the research presented in [8, 10]. It shows that object/event recognition can be done regardless of the existence of object representations by observing only some characteristic points of the object. In practice, events in each application area are happening according to some plan or scenario. A typical example is the field of production engineering, where all works and operations are strictly regulated by various standards and detailed directions. But similar examples can be found even in the everyday life — it is enough to mention the various instruction manuals, recipe books, or just some person's knowledge. All these can be used as a good and natural basis for defining model events. Figure 5 shows the general idea of the prototype.

One further step is to consider for each event not the whole sequence of AUs, but only some chosen characteristic points. The definition of model events allows events to be described precisely and in great detail. But from a practical viewpoint, that is not very convenient. Some simplification of the model event description is desirable. One way to achieve it is to adopt a more "optimistic" approach to the problem. That means to suppose some cause-and-effect relations exist at the low levels of consideration, and to skip that part of the description, supposing it always happens and there is no need to check it when looking for certain event in the database. In other words, we can skip the "effect" part of the description. For example, we can assume that if a plant worker takes the screwdriver, inevitably he/she is going to perform a screwing operation with it. Thus, the description of that operation in the model event can be reduced to the two simple events of taking the screwdriver and putting it back. In fact, such an approach is used in the example in Figure 5.

We call such characteristic points *event triggers*. Exploring particular methods for choosing event triggers is beyond the scope of the present paper, but noticeable improvements can be achieved even using only intuition and experience.

Another practical point is to use the temporal distance relation for expressing simultaneous model event nodes (instead of two temporal relation edges as defined in Section 3.2.) That would allow a more realistic definition of the relation "simultaneous", because in practice it may vary depending of the application area, user's objectives, etc.

Our considerations so far were based on a single-media video sequences. But the same approach can be used for AUs from various different media, provided that relevant automatic detection tools are developed. That would simplify the model event definitions and make them more reliable.

5 Database implementation

Here we will discuss in brief the data model and its application in organizing multimedia data, and in particular — model event and AU data. We use the AIS data diagram, which is not only powerful and intuitive, but also offers considerable advantages in representing information structures in multimedia applications. The basic ideas of AIS (Abstract Information Structure) were presented in [1, 2]. The AIS diagram, an extension of Chen's E-R diagram [5], is a notation of information structures of the real world. The design primitives of AIS diagram are entities and associations (Figure 6). AIS databases are built by these simple primitives and, in this sense, have a "flat" structure.

564

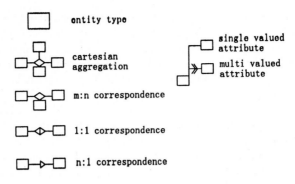

Fig. 6. AIS primitives

All these entities are grouped into entity types similar to the E-R model. The AIS diagram describes all entity types, relationship entity types, and component entity types graphically. We denote entity types, like in E-R diagrams, by rectangles, and associations between types — by lines. Relationship types are denoted by rhombuses or triangles, depending on the mapping cardinality between the entities.

Figure 7 shows the database schema of a database that provides the necessary environment for the work of the prototype discussed in section 4. It is depicted by using the AIS diagram.

There are two main entities in the diagram — *ModelEvent* and *AtomicUnit*. The structure of the model-event part includes the multi-valued attribute *ModelEventNode*, representing model event nodes, and *MESubject*, *MEObject*, and *MERelation* entities, representing the components of a model event node. *StartNode* and *DestNode* define the edges of the graph. The three types of edges are represented by the *TRelation*, *TDistance*, and *SDistance* entities. The last two have as attributes the minimal and maximal values of the distance. In addition, *ModelEvent* has as an attribute textual description of the event it represents.

On the other hand, *AtomicUnit* has a simpler structure. It represents the structure we discussed in section 3 (see Figure 3).

Finally, correspondence between model events and AUs is implemented by the entities *ClassObj*, *ComponentObj*, and *Relation*. The values of subject and object components in model events are of the same type. Separation to "subject" and "object" is imposed by semantic considerations. Depending on the context, the same thing (*ClassObj* entity value) may take the role of either subject or object. The same is valid for the AU components — in that case they are *ComopnentObj* values.

Event instances are generated by performing queries to the database. They are written by using the query language MMQL. It is of a functional type and

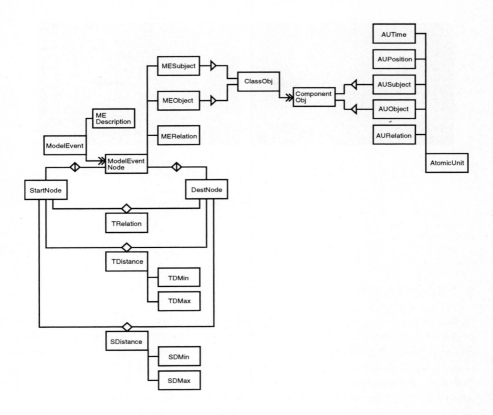

Fig. 7. Database schema, using the AIS diagram

is capable of following the links in the database schema in either direction. That allows arbitrary complex objects to be derived from the "flat" database. AIS diagram, together with the MMQL allows powerful and flexible data retrieval. Also, the language is suitable for parallel retrieval and computations, which is a major benefit if taking into account the huge size and complexity of multimedia data. The query result is in the form of structured data, called OE (Object Expression). Then it is visualized by the CWR. One example is shown in Figure 8. The left image and right image in the figure are parts of a stereo movie generated by the Video Image Player component of the CWR. Circles are added to the original movie for emphasizing worker's hands. More details about MMQL can be found in [2].

Left Image   Right Image

Fig. 8. Visualization of the query result

6 Conclusion

In this paper we have offered a new method for automatic detection of semantic primitives in video data, based on the RWDB concept. The proposed conceptual modeling approach allows event semantics to be derived from low level primitives, which can be detected automatically and do not involve event semantics. A design of a prototype system has been described and a database schema was offered for implementing the prototype. By using it, the semantic primitive definition becomes as simple as performing a query to the database. Further research should be focused on development and refinement of event detection techniques by taking into account other media types. Also, relevant database techniques should be developed on top of the event instances for expressing and handling higher-level event semantics.

Acknowledgements: A part of this research was supported by Scientific Research on Priority Areas: Research and Development of Advanced Database Systems for Integration of Media and User Environments.

References

1. Arisawa, H., Tomii, T., Yui, H., Ishikawa, H.: Data Model and Architecture of Multimedia Database for Engineering Applications. IEICE Trans. Inf. & Syst., Vol. E78-D No. 11 (1995.11) 1362–1368
2. Arisawa, H., Tomii, T., Salev, K.: Design of Multimedia Database and a Query Language for Video Image Data. Proceedings of the IEEE International Conference on Multimedia Computing and Systems in Hiroshima, Japan (1996.6) 462–467
3. Arisawa, H.: Considerations on Real World Data Modeling. IEICE Technical Report Vol. 96, No. 54, DE96-4 (1996) 19–24 (in Japanese)

4. Auguierre-Smith, T. G., Pincever, N. C.: Parsing Movies in Context. Proceedings of USENIX (1991) 157–168

5. Chen, P. P.: The Entity-Relationship Model Toward a Unified View of Data. ACM Trans. on Database Systems Vol. 1, No. 1 (1976) 1–49

6. Chua, T. S., Ruan, L. Q.: A Video Retrieval and Sequencing System. ACM Transactions on Information Systems Vol. 13, No. 4 (1995.10) 373–407

7. Dimitrova, N., Golshani, F.: Motion Recovery for Video Content Classification. ACM Transactions on Information Systems Vol. 13, No. 4 (1995.10) 408–439

8. Goddard, N.: The Perception of Articulated Motion: Recognizing Moving Light Displays. Ph.D. Thesis, Univ. of Rochester, Rochester, N.Y. (1992)

9. Imai, S., Salev, K., Tomii, T., Arisawa, H.: Modeling of Working Processes and Working Simulation Based on Info-Ergonomics and Real World Database Concept. Proceedings of the 1998 Japan-USA Symposium on Flexible Automation (1998.7) 147–156

10. Johansson, G.: Spatio-Temporal Differentiation and Integration in Visual Motion Perception. Psychol. Res. Vol. 38, No. 4 (1976) 379–393

11. Li, J. Z., Özsu, M. T., Szafron, D.: Modeling of Moving Objects in a Video Database. Proceedings of the IEEE International Conference on Multimedia Computing and Systems in Ottawa, Canada (1997.6) 336–343

12. Little, T. D. C., Ghafoor, A.: Interval-Based Conceptual Models For Time-Dependent Multimedia Data. IEEE Trans. on Knowledge and Data Engineering Vol. 5, No. 4 (1993) 551–563

13. Nagasaka, A., Tanaka, Y.: Automatic Video Indexing and Full-Video Search for Object Appearances. Visual Database Systems Vol.2, Elsevier Science Publishers, B. V., Amsterdam (1992)

14. Okui, H., Okamoto, Y., Imai, S., Tomii, T., Arisawa, H.: Motion Analysis for Designing Factory Work Database Based on Video Data. IPSJ SIG Notes Vol.98, No.58, 98-DBS-116(2) (1998.7) 241–248 (in Japanese)

15. Ruan, L. G., Smoliar, S. W., Kankanhalli, A.: An Analysis of Low-Resolution Segmentation Techniques for Animate Video. Proceedings of the 2nd International Conference on Automation, Robotics and Computer Vision, Singapore, CV-16.3 (1992.9) 1–5

16. Rubin, B., Davenport, G.: Structured Content Modeling for Cinematic Information. SIGCHI Bull. 21, 2 (1989) 78–79

17. Tonomura, Y.: Video Handling Based on Structured Information for Hypermedia Systems. Proceedings of the International Conference on Multimedia Information Systems, Singapore (1991) 333–344

18. Vazirgiannis, M., Boll, S.: Events in Interactive Multimedia Applications: Modeling and Implementation Design. Proceedings of the IEEE International Conference on Multimedia Computing and Systems in Ottawa, Canada (1997.6) 244–251

Structured Modeling for Video Databases[1]

Eunsook Ryu[*], Yonghun Kim[*], Mi-Young Lee[†], Kyuchul Lee[*]

[*] Dept. of Computer Engineering, Chungnam National University,
Taejon, KOREA, 305-764
{esryu, yhkim, kclee}@comeng.chungnam.ac.kr
[†] Dept. of Data Engineering, Computer & Software Technology Laboratory,
Electronics and Telecommunications Research Institute, Taejon, KOREA, 305-350
mylee@dbserver.etri.re.kr

Abstract. Video information is an important component of multimedia systems such as Digital Library, World-Wide Web (WWW), and Video-On-Demand (VOD) service system. However, since it is difficult to store and retrieve video data like traditional text data, new data models suitable for video information are required. Video information has hierarchical document structure inherently, so it is named "structured video document" in this paper. This paper proposes a data model, a query language, and indexing scheme for structured video documents in order to store, retrieve, and share video documents efficiently in collaborative work environment. In representing structured video documents, the object-oriented data modeling technique is used since the hierarchical structure information can be modeled as complex objects. We also define object types for the structure information. Our query language supports not only content-based retrieval but also structure-based retrieval, which means the queries based on the structure of video documents. In order to perform structure queries efficiently, as well as to reduce the storage overhead of indices, an optimized inverted index structure is proposed.

1   Introduction

Recently, the problem of how to store and retrieve multimedia information is becoming increasingly important with the advent of new applications such as Digital Library, World-Wide Web (WWW), and Video-On-Demand (VOD) service system. Especially, video is an important component of multimedia computing and communication environments, with applications as varied as broadcasting, education, and publishing. However, since it is difficult to store and retrieve video data like traditional text data, new data models suitable for video information are required. An early proposal was to divide a video document into segments, that is, contiguous frames. Recent approaches [2,3,5,7,8,9] have focused on the data model based on captions or annotations associated with logical video segments, and a corresponding query language and indexing video documents.

---

[1] This research was supported by ETRI (contract No. 98154) as a part of "Development of DBMS for Internet Multimedia Document" project.

However, most previous research doesn't support the rich data model for structured video data as well as an expressive query language and an efficient indexing scheme. For example, the query for searching a sports program, including the same scene with a specific scene of the news program on TV, can not be retrieved by only using physical indexing method. In this case, first of all, there should be hierarchical composition of video expressions with high-level semantic description such as program or scene. The semantic description of each program or scene can be obtained from the captions or annotations of video data. Then, the keyword list extracted from the semantic description should be provided for content-based video indexing in order to retrieve a query efficiently.

Therefore, new data model, query language, and indexing scheme based on DBMS are required to store video data, and to retrieve and share video documents efficiently. The following factors should be considered in the modeling of video data.

- Video data should be able to store and retrieve a specific scene instead of the whole content of video data. Therefore, it is desirable that video data be classified into semantic units such as program, scene and shot, arranged according to some logical structure.
- Query language, supporting not only content-based retrieval (the queries based on the captions or annotations of video data), but also structure-based retrieval (the queries based on the logical structure of video documents) should be provided.
- Indexing structure for video documents should be supported to perform content and structure queries efficiently, as well as to reduce the storage overhead of indices
- A meaningful scene often can be included in other video documents. Several users often can collaborate in the creation, update, insert, etc. of video documents, and access different fragments of a whole video document concurrently. Therefore, it is necessary to avoid data duplication and to share the same data content in collaborative work environment.

Video information has hierarchical document structure inherently, so it is named "structured video document" in this paper. This paper proposes a data modeling, query language, and indexing scheme for structured video documents. In representing structured video document, the object-oriented data modeling technique is used since the structure information has hierarchical characteristics. Our query language supports not only content-based retrieval, (the queries based on the captions or annotations of video data), but also structure-based retrieval, (the queries based on the logical structure of video documents). In order to perform structure queries efficiently, as well as to reduce the storage overhead of indices, the index structure proposed by Lee [4] is used. Therefore, we provide an optimized inverted index structure. This paper is organized as follows. In Section 2, object-oriented modeling of structured video document is described. The query language and query examples are presented in Section 3, and the indexing scheme for efficient accessing of structured video documents is described in Section 4. Finally, Section 5 presents the conclusions and comments about future work.

2 Object-Oriented Modeling of Structured Video Document

In this section, we describe the logical structure of video documents and define composite objects for the structure information. We also explain about the efficient retrieval scheme of hierarchical structure and sharing video data proposed in this paper.

2.1 Logical Structure of Video Documents

Video documents have a hierarchical logical structure like text documents. Fig. 1 represents composite objects for the logical structure of the video documents. We assume that the domain of video documents is for TV broadcasting. Video documents are composed of different semantic units such as program, scene and shot arranged according to some logical structure in our domain. In Fig. 1, a video document consists of several *programs* such as two advertisements, sports, and news. A *program* is composed of one or more *scenes*. For example, each news item such as sports, weather, and economy in news program can be regarded as *scene*, and several kinds of commercials in an advertisement program can become *scene*. One or more related *shots* are combined in a *scene*. For example, the cloud map of a weather forecast scene in a news program can be *shot*. *Scene* can be reorganized by collecting *shots* of interest. A *shot* may belong to several *scenes*, and a *scene* may belong to one or more *programs* repeatedly. For example, in Fig. 1, the two *B_scene*s of *Advertisement_program1* and *Advertisement_program2* represent the same commercial, and the *Shot15* of the *Sports_scene* in the news program refers to the *Shot15* of the sports program. A *shot* consists of one or more *frames* recorded contiguously. *Frame* represents the physical unit, and *shot, scene*, and *program* represent the logical unit of video documents in our domain. There is a *part-of* relationship between a child node and a parent node. In each composite object, the video document itself is the root of the hierarchy, and only the leaf nodes contain the contents of video data.

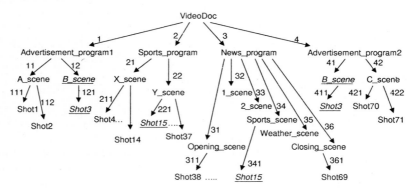

Fig. 1. Logical structure of video document

In this paper, we assume that the semantic description of each *program, scene*, and *shot* can be obtained from the captions or annotations of video data, and the keyword lists extracted from the semantic description are provided for content-based video indexing. Each object of hierarchical logical structure in Fig. 1 is defined as follows.

Definition 2.1: video document object, $V = (vid, Pt_i, C_i)$ where,
- *vid* is an object identifier of video document object.
- Pt_i represents a set of *program* objects P, $(Pt_i \in P)$, where t_i $(1 \leq i \leq n)$ means the sequence of object.
- C_i $(1 \leq i \leq n)$ represents the properties for video document objects.

Definition 2.2: program object, $P = (pid, St_i, C_i)$ where,
- *pid* is an object identifier of program object.
- St_i represents a set of *scene* objects S, $(St_i \in S)$, where t_i $(1 \leq i \leq n)$ means the sequence of object.
- C_i $(1 \leq i \leq n)$ represents the properties for program objects.

Definition 2.3: scene object, $S = (sid, Tt_i, C_i)$ where,
- *sid* is an object identifier of scene object.
- Tt_i represents a set of *shot* objects T, $(Tt_i \in T)$, where t_i $(1 \leq i \leq n)$ means the sequence of object.
- C_i $(1 \leq i \leq n)$ represents the properties for scene objects.

Definition 2.4: shot object, $T = (tid, F[i, j], C_i)$ where,
- *tid* is an object identifier of shot object.
- $F[i, j]$ represents frame sequence of video data, where $[i, j]$ $(1 \leq i, j \leq n)$ means the start position and length of frame sequence.
- C_i $(1 \leq i \leq n)$ represents the properties for shot objects.

2.2 Class Definition for Structured Video Document

Object-oriented DBMS technology can be used to define composite objects for the logical structure of video documents described in Section 2.1. In this section, the class hierarchy for structured video document is designed based on the object-oriented data model.

Fig. 2 illustrates the class hierarchy designed for a structured video document. The root class of video document structure is the class *VideoDocStructure*, which has two subclasses *VideoDoc* and *Fragment*. The class *VideoDoc* can have a subclass according to the kinds of video documents such as Drama, Concert and Cartoon. The properties defined in the class *VideoDoc* are inherited by its subclass. Every object of logical structure is defined as a class such as *Program, Scene* and *Shot*. The class *Program, Scene* and *Shot* are defined as the subclasses of the class *VideoStructure*.

On the other hand, the class *Program* is defined as the domain of the attribute *programs* defined in the class *VideoDoc*, and the classes *Scene* and *Shot* are defined as the domain of the attribute *scenes* and *shots*. The superclass of various kinds of multimedia data types such as text, graphic, image, audio, and video is *Media*. The class *VideoFragment*, defined as the domain of the attribute *frames*, has two superclasses *Fragment* and *Video*. The classes *VideoDocStructure, VideoStructure*,

Fragment, and *Media* are defined as abstract classes, which only define characteristics inherited by their subclass.

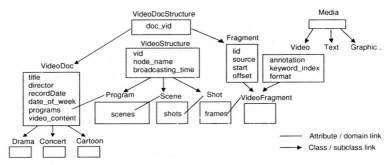

Fig. 2. The class hierarchy for structured video documents

The following class definitions are specified in compliance with the SQL3. In the definition of the class *VideoDocStructure*, the attribute *doc_vid* is declared for identifying a unique document. The methods *ancestor* and *children* defined in the class *VideoDocStructure* will be described in Section 2.3. In the definition of the class *VideoDoc*, the attribute *title*, *director*, and *recordDate* is a descriptive attribute, while the attribute *programs* represents the logical structure object, and has a *LIST* of *Program* as its domain. The attribute *video_content* has an object identifier of the video object containing the entire video content of a document. The method *GetVideoDoc* is also defined in the class *VideoDoc* in order to obtain the entire video document content at once. The attribute *scenes,* defined in the class *Program,* has *LIST* of *Scene* as its domain.

```
CREATE OBJECT TYPE VideoDocStructure
      (PROTECTED        doc_vid              String
       FUNCTION         ancestor (e1 String, e2 String) RETURNS String
       FUNCTION         children (e1 String, e2 String) RETURNS LIST (String));
CREATE OBJECT TYPE VideoDoc UNDER VideoDocStructure
      ( title           Text,
        director        Text,
        recordDate      Date,
        programs        LIST(Program),
        Video_content   Video
        FUNCTION        GetVideoDoc ( v1 Video ) RETURNS Video);
CREATE OBJECT TYPE Program UNDER VideoStructure
      ( scenes          LIST(Scene) );
```

The class *Media* is defined as follows. In the class *Media, start* and *end* are attributes for specifying start time and end time of each media data, and used to represent the temporal relationship. The attribute *position* is used for spatial presentation. The actual data of each media type is stored in the attribute *content* as a Blob(Binary large object) in our framework. To represent the temporal relationship between two media objects, the temporal relationship methods such as *equal, before, meets, during, overlaps, starts, finishes,* which simplify Allen's [1] 13 temporal relations, can be defined in the class *Media*.

```
CREATE OBJECT TYPE Media
    ( PUBLIC          start      Time,
                      end        Time,
      PRIVATE         content    Blob,
                      position   Point
      FUNCTION        meets(m1 Media, m2 Media) RETURNS BOOLEAN ... );
```

The following is the class *Video* defined in this paper.

```
CREATE OBJECT TYPE Video UNDER Media
    ( PRIVATE         keyword_index InvertedIndex,
                      annotation    Text,
                      format        String
      FUNCTION        contains(v1 Video, search_expr
                      Varchar(max_pattern_length) ) RETURNS BOOLEAN
      FUNCTION        overlay( v1 Video, v2 Video )   RETURNS Video
      FUNCTION        filter( v1 Video, a Attri )     RETURNS Video
      FUNCTION        frameSize( v1 Video, i Integer ) RETURNS Video
      FUNCTION        extract(v1 Video, a Attri)      RETURNS Video
      FUNCTION        equal( v1 Video, v2 Video )     RETURNS BOOLEAN
      FUNCTION        fadeIn( v1 Video )              RETURNS Video
      FUNCTION        fadeOut( v1 Video )             RETURNS Video
      FUNCTION        replicate( v1 Video )           RETURNS Video
      FUNCTION        playDuration( v1 Video, t Time ) RETURNS Video
      FUNCTION        forward( v1 Video, o Offset )   RETURNS Video
      FUNCTION        rewind( v1 Video, o Offset )    RETURNS Video );
```

As shown above, the attribute *annotation* is the description data for content-based retrieval. The attribute *format* represents video data format. The method *contains* searches whether the value of the attribute *annotation* contains given keywords. Other methods are media-specific methods. For example, the method *playDuration* is used for playing a video during a given time, and the method *equal* is used for testing whether two video objects are equal. Media-specific methods can be added to the class definition later.

2.3 Efficient Retrieval of Hierarchical Structure

In order to support the efficient retrieval of the structure object, we have to maintain the hierarchical information about the composite object of logical structure. In this paper, we provide two operations: *ancestor* and *children*. These operations are used for accessing ancestor and descendant objects fast without disk access. The number associated with each node in Fig. 1 is the node identifier (*NID*). We use the *NID* for the retrieval of the structure object. A *NID* of a node in a composite hierarchy is generated by concatenation of the children identifiers in the path from the root to the node. For example, the *NID* of the node, which is the first shot of the first scene of the second program in the logical structure in Fig. 1, is '211'. The definitions of *ancestor*, and *children* operation are as follows:

Definition 2.5: ancestor (node, k) = shift_right(NID(node), k) where,
– *node* : a node in a composite hierarchy of video document
– *k* : the level
– *shift_right* : shifting the *NID* of a child node *k* digits right

Definition 2.6: children (node, k) = shift_left(NID(node), k) where,
– *shift_left* : shifting the *NID* of a parent node *k* digits left

For example, the ancestor node at the 2-level backward for the node *Sports_program.X_scene.Shot4* in Fig. 1 can be obtained by shifting the '211' 2 digits right.

> ancestor(Sports_program.X_scene.Shot4, 2)
> = shift_right(NID(Sports_program.X_scene.Shot4), 2)
> = shift_right('211', 2) = 2 (Sports_program)

The children node at the 1-level forward for the node *Advertisement_program2.C_scene* in Fig. 1 can be obtained by shifting the '42' 1 digits left. The results are the *NID* of '42x' form.

2.4 Sharing Video Data

The actual video data should be contained in each leaf object, such as the shot in composite objects of Fig. 1. However, it may cause two problems. First, video data is duplicated if we store the actual data in every leaf node of the logical structure. For example, the leaf node *Sports_program.Y_scene.Shot15* in Fig. 1 has the same data with the leaf node *News_program.Sports_scene.Shot15*. It is necessary to avoid data duplication and to share the same data content. Secondly, retrieving the whole content of a document can degrade the performance seriously since we have to access every leaf object.

Therefore, in order to solve the problems, each leaf object should not contain actual data in our framework. Instead, the actual video data is stored as a Blob, and each leaf object contains the pointer to the original source data (i.e. Blob data) and the *start* position within the source data and the *offset* in bytes. This type of object is modeled as the class *Fragment*, which is a subclass of the class *VideoDocStructure* in Fig. 2. We provide the class *VideoFragment*, which is common subclass of the classes *Video* and *Fragment*. The attribute *doc_vid* in the class *VideoFragment* is inherited from *VideoDocStructure*. For example, the video document 'TV_video_doc' consists of several video fragment objects like Fig. 3 in our storage structure. We can find that two objects are the same objects, though they have the different *lid* in Fig. 3.

By treating video data in this manner, we can share video data on logical structure and enhance the performance in retrieving the whole content of video document. As a matter of fact, video data is stored in a compressed format. For that reason, the method *GetFrame*, which is capable of fetching any frame without regard for its data format, is also defined in the class *Fragment*.

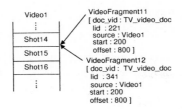

Fig. 3. Sharing of video data

3   The Query Language

This paper provides the following three types of queries that should be supported for structured video document.

– Attribute-based queries : queries based on attributes such as *title, recordDate*.
– Content-based queries : queries based on the captions or annotations of video data.
– Structure-based queries : queries based on the logical structure of video documents

We can also make more powerful mixed queries of the above three types. The syntax of the query language is specified in compliance with the SQL3 standard. The following shows a typical example query based on attributes. The query is "Select record date of a VideoDoc whose doc_vid is 'TV_video_doc'.".

> SELECT   *v..recordDate*
> FROM   *VideoDoc v*
> WHERE   *v..doc_vid = 'TV_video_doc'*

The following example shows a typical content-based query, "Select all scenes of a news program whose scenes contain 'weather' and 'rain'.". The condition *contains* searches the scenes containing both words.

> SELECT   *p..scenes*
> FROM   *VideoDoc v, v..programs p*
> WHERE   *p..node_name = 'News_program' AND*
>   *contains(p..scenes, 'weather' AND 'rain')*

The query expressions are extended to support efficient description of the logical structure of video documents in this paper. The extended query expressions are *component* and *list* expression proposed in [6]. The *component* expression allows navigation to ancestor and descendant nodes of a node through the logical structure of a video document. The syntax of *component* expression is *component(parameter)*, where *parameter* specifies the number of levels to navigate forwards or backwards, or a specific node. The *parameter*s are defined as follows:

– \$ (^) : leaf (root) node(s)
– * (/) : 0 or more levels forward (backward)
– + (-) : 1 or more levels forward (backward)
– > (<) : following(preceding) sibling nodes of a node
– <> : all sibling nodes of a node

- i (-i) : i levels forward (backward)
- i~j (-i ~ -j) : i~j levels forward (backward)

The *component* expression is implemented by using *ancestor* and *children* operations described in Section 2.3. It is defined as the method of the class *Fragment* of Fig. 2 and inherited by its subclasses. The following shows some examples of the *component* expression for the logical structure in Fig. 1.

- Advertisement_program2..component($) = {Shot3, Shot70, Shot71}
- X_scene..component(*) = {X_scene, Shot4, … Shot14}
- Weather_scene..component(-) = {News_program}
- Advertisement_program1..component(2) = {Shot1, Shot2, Shot3}

The *list* expression is designed to locate a specific portion of a list of nodes. Either L[i] or L[i:j] is a list expression, where L is a node name or *component* expression, and *i* and *j* are integers or character '$'. L[i] returns the *i*-th node, or the last node in the case of '$', from the list L. L[i:j] extracts the sublist of L starting at position *i* and ending at position *j*. Examples of the list expression are given below.

- News_program[2]..scene[$] : the last scene of the second news program
- Shot[1:3] : the first, the second, and the third shot
- News_program..component(1)[3] : the third scene at 1 level forward

Using our extended expressions, users can access each node of the logical structure. For example, the query, "Select the third item of the news program broadcasted at seven o'clock on Sunday evening", is expressed as follows.

> SELECT   *p..scenes[3]*
> FROM   *VideoDoc v, v..programs p*
> WHERE   *p..node_name = 'News_program' AND v..date_of_week = 'Sun' AND*
>   *p..broadcasing_time = '19:00:00'*

The query, "Select the following program of the sports program", can be posed as follows.

> SELECT   *p..component(>)[1]*
> FROM   *VideoDoc v, v..programs p*
> WHERE   *p..node_name = 'Sports_program'*

Using the extended query language proposed in this paper, we can make queries based on not only the document content or structure but also the combination of both document content and structure. The example query, "Select the sports program that includes the same scene with the news program's scene whose annotation contains 'basketball'.", is expressed as follows.

> SELECT   *q*
> FROM   *VideoDoc v, v..programs p q, p..scenes r*
> WHERE   *p..node_name = 'News_program' AND*
>   *q..node_name = 'Sports_program' AND*
>   *FOR SOME r..component($) AS x (contains(x, 'basketball')) AND*
>   *x..component(-) IN q..scenes..component(<>)*

By using temporal relationship methods defined in the class *Media*, we can also make the queries based on the temporal relationships between present objects. The following example shows a typical temporal relation query, "Select the program presented just before news program".

SELECT   q

FROM   *VideoDoc v, v..programs p q*

WHERE   *p..node_name = 'News_program' AND meets(q, p)*

The condition *meets(q, p)* in the above query is satisfied when there is a meets relationship between *q* and *p* objects. In other words, *q* is presented just before *p* without any gap.

4   Indexing Scheme for Structured Video Documents

In this section, we describe the indexing scheme which supports not only processing structure queries efficiently, but also the process of considerably reducing the storage overhead of indices [4]. A majority of information retrieval systems for efficient access of full-text data use the inverted index. In order to support direct node access for performing structure queries efficiently, it is also required to include all the index terms of nodes in the inverted index. The index terms are extracted from the annotations for video documents. In the hierarchical logical structure, leaf nodes are associated with data while internal nodes represent only structure relationships between document components. However, even though the internal nodes have no associated document data, the data at the subtrees must be considered as their data. That is, internal nodes must include all index terms of leaf nodes. In this case, the child nodes of a node can have some index terms in common like Fig. 4. The inverted list for any node in Fig. 4 are as follows:

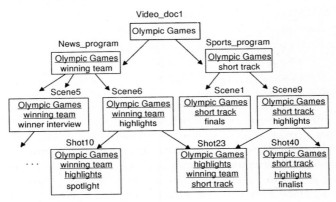

Fig. 4. Logical structure of video document with index term

- inverted_list(Olympic Games) = {Video_doc1, News_program, Sports_program, Scene5, Scene6, Scene1, Scene9, Shot10, Shot23, Shot40 }
- inverted_list(winning team) = { News_program, Scene5, Scene6, Shot10, Shot23 }
- inverted_list(short track) = { Sports_program, Scene1, Scene9, Shot23, Shot40 }
  inverted_list(highlights) = { Scene6, Scene9, Shot10, Shot23, Shot40 }

In Fig. 4, the common terms that are underlined become the index terms of the parent node. In other words, the common index terms of child nodes are promoted their parent nodes. For example, the *Scene5* and *Scene6* in Fig. 4 have the index term 'winning team' in common. This index term is promoted its parent node *News_program*. However, even though the common index term 'winning team' of the *Shot10* and *Shot23* is promoted *Scene6*, the term should not be eliminated in the *Shot23* because the *Shot40* does not have 'winning team' in common index term. In order to reduce the storage overhead of indices, we use optimized inverted index structure. That is, by eliminating common index terms from child nodes, only the parent node is possessed of the common index terms of child nodes. Then, the child nodes can avoid duplication of index terms. Fig. 5 shows index terms without duplication. The inverted list for Fig. 5 is as follows.

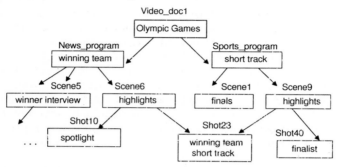

Fig. 5. Index terms without duplication

- inverted_list(Olympic Games) = {Video_doc1 }
- inverted_list(winning team) = { News_program, Shot23 }
- inverted_list(short track) = { Sports_program, Shot23 }
- inverted_list(winner interview) = { Scene5 }
- inverted_list(highlights) = { Scene6, Scene9 }
  inverted_list(finalist) = { Shot40 }

In this inverted index scheme, the index size decreases if the rate of promoted index terms from child nodes to parent nodes increases. The storage requirements are also minimized and the performance of accessing a node is enhanced. In this scheme, the index of a node is '*index[node]* $\cup$ *index[ancestors]* $\cup$ *index[children]*'.

The following shows the definitions of the class for index structure. The class *InvertedIndex* has two attributes: *term,* and *postings* which has *SET* of *Posting* as its domain. The class *Posting* is composed of the identifier of video document (*doc_vid*) and the identifier of a node (*vid*)

CREATE OBJECT TYPE InvertedIndex		*CREATE OBJECT TYPE Posting*	
(term	*String,*	*(doc_vid*	*String,*
postings	*SET(Posting));*	*vid*	*String);*

5   Conclusions

Video information is an important component of multimedia systems such as Digital Library, World-Wide Web (WWW), and Video-On-Demand (VOD) service system. Therefore, data model, query language, and indexing scheme based on DBMS are required to store video data, and to retrieve and share video documents efficiently in collaborative work environment.

This paper proposes object-oriented data model, extended query language, and indexing scheme for structured video document. We provide the logical structure of video documents and define composite objects for the structure information. We also explain about the efficient retrieval scheme of hierarchical structure, and the sharing of video data. Our query language supports not only content-based retrieval, but also structure-based retrieval, which means the queries based on the logical structure of video documents. In order to perform structure queries efficiently, we use indexing scheme that supports optimized inverted index structure. By using this indexing scheme, we can reduce the storage overhead of indices considerably.

More research remains to be done in this paper. The prompt and efficient presentation or browsing of video documents is required because of the temporal and spatial characteristic of video data. More expressive query operation, for example, such as *hyperlink network*, should be supported. Besides multimedia documents combined with multimedia data including text, audio, graphics, and images as well as video should be modeled.

References

1. Allen, J. F.: Maintaining Knowledge about Temporal Intervals. Comm. Of the ACM, Vol. 26, No. 11 (1983) 823-843
2. Hjelsvold, R., Midtstraum, R.: Modelling and Querying Video Data. Proc. of the 20th VLDB Conference (1994) 686-694
3. Jiang, H., Montesi, D., Elmagarmid, A. K.: VideoText Database Systems. Int. Conference on Multimedia Computing and Systems (1997) 344-351
4. Lee, K., Lee, Y. K., Berra, P. B.: Management of Multi-structured Hypermedia Documents: A Data Model, Query Language, and Indexing Scheme. Multimedia Tools and Applications (1997) 199-223
5. Oomoto, E., Tanaka, K.: OVID: Design and Implementation of a Video-Object Database System. IEEE Transactions on Knoweldge and Data Engineering, Vol. 5, No. 4 (1993) 629-643
6. Ryu, E., Lee, K.: A Multimedia Query Language for Handling Multi-Structure Information. Proc. of the Fifth Int. Conference on Database Systems for Advanced Applications (1997) 333-342
7. Smith, T. G. A., Davenport, G.: The Stratification System: A Design Environment for Random Access Video. In Workshop on Networking and Operating System Support for Digital Audio and Video (1992) 250-261
8. Weiss, R., Duda, A.: Composition and Search with a Video Algebra. IEEE MultiMedia, Vol. 2, No. 1, (1995) 12-25
9. Zhang, H., et al.: Automatic parsing and indexing of news video. IEEE Multimedia Systems, Springer-Verlag (1995) 256-266

Applying Unsupervised Fuzzy C-Prototypes Clustering in Motion-Based Segmentation

Supot Nitsuwat and Jesse S. Jin

School of Computer Science and Engineering
The University of New South Wales
Sydney 2052, AUSTRALIA
E-mail:{supotn,jesse}@cse.unsw.edu.au

Abstract. Recent technology in digital video processing has moved to "content-based" storage and retrieval. There is a strong demand to segment multiple moving objects in a video sequence so that a higher level task can be performed on the individual object. In segmentation, robust clustering is a necessary step which plays an important role in identifying regions. In this paper, we present a scheme for extracting moving objects. First, the dense optical flow fields are calculated to extract motion vectors. Surface fitting is performed over the parametric motion model. Then, an unsupervised robust fuzzy C-Prototypes clustering technique is applied to motion-based segmentation in the parameter space. Finally, the individual moving object and background can be represented in layers. Experimental results showing the significance of the proposed method are provided.

1   Introduction

Multimedia systems currently play an important role in our everyday life, ranging from home entertainment to finance and education. Of the many components of a multimedia system, the video clip is a dominant part. However, video data are voluminous, therefore the necessity for an effective and efficient visual data management system is required. Video processing, e.g., video indexing, is a promising technique of this storage and retrieval system that will replace the classical management systems (DBMSs) [Ahanger et al. 1996]. Video processing can be classified into two main groups, camera operation-based and content-based techniques. In the first category, the sequences of video first have to be segmented based on all image transitions (abrupt transitions or camera break, e.g., pan,zoom and gradual transitions, e.g., fade-in, fade-out, dissolve, wipe). The basic idea of this technique is to describe video units using a representative key frame [Smoliar et al. 1996]. This representation format relieves the user from the need to watch the entire video during browsing. However, in many video programs, there are plenty of shots. This means that the number of the representative key frames can be enormous. In addition, a key frame often fails to represent the dynamic and time varying content. These drawbacks have made researchers turn to new more effective techniques.

In the second group, researchers pay attention to identifying and representing video content via object features, e.g., colour, texture, shape, volume, motion, and edge features [Flickner et al. 1995]. The basic idea of this system is that if we can distinguish individual objects in the whole video sequences, and can track and identify them based on the information about each object, we would be able to capture the changes in content throughout the sequences [Ferman et al. 1997]. Among these object features, motion content has been used as a key index in video retrieval systems. Motion content is an important promising key for such a task. This requires a segmentation of moving objects. Because of involving moving objects, motion information is the most important cue for this task. By definition, motion-based segmentation is a process to be used for labelling pixels which associated with different moving objects based on motion information. Depending on the algorithms to be used, the segmentation can be performed separately or simultaneously with optical flow estimation. In this paper, parametric motion-based segmentation using optical flow vectors will be addressed.

Segmentation of the optical flow field has been studied by many researchers [Ayer et al. 1995,Chang et al. 1997, Hotter et al. 1996, Murray et al. 1987, Odobez et al. 1995, Sawhney et al. 1995,1996, Wang et al. 1994, Weiss 1996]. Amongst various techniques, segmentation by fitting the optical flow vectors into a 2-D motion model is the most attractive method. The main idea of this approach is to describe the motion of each object by a low dimensional parametric model, e.g., affine motion model. After calculating optical flow vectors, parameter estimation is performed in relation to this model. Several parameter estimation techniques, namely, the method of moments, the least-square method, the maximum-likelihood method, and the maximum a posteriori method have been used. For instance, in the affine clustering approach proposed by Wang et al. [1994], the optical flow field of each pixel was first estimated by using multi-scale coarse-to-fine algorithm based on a gradient approach. Then the affine parameters within each non-overlapped subregion were calculated by using the linear least square technique. The parameter fields which cover the same object were merged by using the k-means clustering technique. Finally, the regions were reassigned by using hypothesis testing. The process continued until a few number of points were reassigned. Instead of using fixed size block, Choi et al [1996] proposed the combination the optical flow field with the result of change detection in the preliminary segmentation step. A multi-stage segmentation method with a hierarchical motion model were presented, in which a uniform subregions were fit into a simple motion model and uniform regions were fit into a complex model. In [Cheong et al. 1996], zero-crossings of a wavelet transform were used in intraframe segmentation and probabilistic clustering in a mixture model for identifying moving object was proposed. Motion segmentation was obtained by the least square approximation of affine motion parameters using Gauss-Newton iterative optimization.

All of these researches involve three main components, namely,

– calculating the optical flow vectors;

- estimating motion parameters by regression and specifying the spatial support using clustering;
- representing moving objects by layers.

Among above-mentioned researches, Wang's algorithm has been frequently cited. However, this algorithm has its own drawback. In parameter estimation, it suffers from the sensitivity of the clustering procedure to the noise in the parameter space [Altunbasak et al. 1998, Ayer et al. 1995]. Even though the "merge and classify" technique has been used instead of using the adaptive *k*-means clustering [Borshukov 1997], the problem of the automatic extraction of an unknown number of clusters still be the main task that should be studied intensively. Therefore, the main propose of this paper is to present the robust clustering framework for motion-based segmentation that can be used to overcome these problems.

After calculating optical flow vectors from a pair of images, our approach estimates the motion parameters of the affine model by fitting this model to the optical flow field of each non-overlapped block using the linear least square technique. We then perform clustering over the parameter space, the most challenging step. We propose an unsupervised robust fuzzy c-prototype clustering method. It combines fuzzy clustering with robust statistical estimators proposed by Frigui and Krishnapuram [1996] for their intensity-based segmentation. In our work, we use optical flow vectors. The clustering regions that are corresponding to moving objects have been merged and the numbers of cluster have been extracted simultaneously. Finally, the moving objects are represented in layers.

This paper is organized as follows. Section 2 presents the procedures for calculating the motion parameters from the 2-D dense optical flow field. The unsupervised robust fuzzy C-Prototypes algorithm is presented in Section 3. The experimental results of applying the above technique on motion-based segmentation of synthetic and real images are presented in Section 4. Finally, Section 5 contains concluding remarks.

2 Motion Model Parameters Estimation from the 2-D Dense Optical Flow Field

Among many motion-based segmentation methods, segmentation by surface fitting of a 2-D motion model to the optical flow vectors is the most attractive one. After calculating optical flow vectors from a pair of images, the motion parameters were then estimated. In Wang and Adelson method [1994], the six-parameter affine motion model have been defined:

$$V_x = \theta_{(x,1)} + \theta_{(x,2)}x + \theta_{(x,3)}y \tag{1}$$

$$V_y = \theta_{(y,1)} + \theta_{(y,2)}x + \theta_{(y,3)}y \tag{2}$$

where

$$\theta_x = \{\theta_{(x,1)}, \theta_{(x,2)}, \theta_{(x,3)}\} \tag{3}$$

$$\theta_y = \{\theta_{(y,1)}, \theta_{(y,2)}, \theta_{(y,3)}\} \tag{4}$$

are the parameters of the affine motion model, which can be estimated over each non-overlapped rectangular region by the least means square regression. In these models, (V_x, V_y) denotes the x- and y- components of optical flow vector at the coordinate (x,y) of each patch. Different patches that belong to the same moving object are likely to have the same motion parameters. Therefore, the next step is to merge these patches into the same group by clustering technique. We propose an improved unsupervised robust fuzzy c-prototype clustering technique for this process.

3   An Unsupervised Robust Fuzzy C-prototypes Algorithm

The Unsupervised Robust Fuzzy C-prototypes Algorithm (URCP) proposed by Frigui and Krishnapuram [1996] integrates the advantages of fuzzy clustering and robust statistical estimators. The main reasons of why the combination is necessary can be described in the following. Firstly, by definition, the unsupervised clustering technique is a process that learns how to classify feature vectors directly from the current data. In motion-based segmentation, there are not many examples for training the clustering algorithm. Furthermore, the fuzzy clustering algorithm also overcomes the serious disadvantage of constrained memberships that performed deficiently when the feature vectors are contaminated by noise. Secondly, for robust characteristic of clustering algorithm, the performance of an algorithm should not be affected significantly by small deviations. It also should have a reasonable accuracy for the estimated model [Dave et al. 1997]. Therefore, the combination of these two disciplines presents a promising algorithm for clustering.

There are three major steps in the URCP algorithm, which will be described in the following sections. More details in each step can be seen in [Frigui and Krishnapuram 1996].

3.1   The Preliminary Clustering of the Feature Space

The robust C-Prototype (RCP) algorithm, as a generalization of the M-estimator [Frigui and Krishnapuram 1996], plays a major rule in the preliminary clustering of the feature space. This algorithm minimises the objective function,

$$\mathbf{J}_R(\mathbf{B}, \mathbf{U}, \mathbf{X}) = \sum_{i=1}^{G} \sum_{j=1}^{N} (u_{ij})^m \rho_i(d_{ij}^2), \tag{5}$$

subject to $u_{ij} \in [0,1]$, and $\sum_{i=1}^{G} u_{ij} = 1 \ \forall j$.

Here $\mathbf{X} = \{\mathbf{x}_j | j = 1, ..., N\}$ denotes a set of N feature vectors. In this case, they are estimated values of optical flow vectors $((\bar{V}_x, \bar{V}_y))$ that estimated by substituting motion model parameters into equations (1) and (2). G denotes the number of clusters. Constant $m \in [1, \infty)$ is a fuzzifier. Element d_{ij}^2 is the distance from feature vector $\mathbf{x}_j$ to the centroid of cluster β_i. $\mathbf{B} = (\beta_1, ..., \beta_C)$ is a C-tuple of cluster centroids. $\mathbf{U} = [u_{ij}]$ is the constrained fuzzy C-partition, where u_{ij} denotes the degree of membership of feature vector $\mathbf{x}_j$ in β_i. Finally, $\rho_i(.)$ denotes the lost function that can be used to introduce another robust weight function w_{ij}.

In this step, an initial number of clusters is assigned to G. This number should be larger than the expected maximum number of clusters in the feature space. The initial centroids of clusters are also assigned to $\mathbf{B}$. When iteration converges, i.e., the centroids of clusters are stable, the preliminary partitions of the feature space are generated and can be used in the next step.

3.2 The Unconstrained Robust C-Prototypes

Before merging similar clusters into the same group, the unconstrained RCP should be performed. In this stage, a feature vector can be shared by more than one group by relaxing the probabilistic constrain in equation (5). An entire dense region which has been split into several adjacent clusters after performing the RCP in the first step may be covered by these clusters simultaneously. This means that all clusters can be adjusted their shape freely.

3.3 A Cluster Merging Algorithm under a Robust Cluster Similarity

From the second step, one dense region may be covered by several clusters. Our next task is to select the "best" cluster for each region by merging the feature vectors from several clusters that cover the same region into the representative cluster. In [Frigui and Krishnapuram 1996], a robust cluster similarity has been used as a reliable measure of compatibility for this merging. The similarity measure between clusters i and j can be defined as

$$\mathbf{S}_{ij} = 1 - \frac{\sum_{x_k \in G_{ij}} | \mathbf{u}_{ik} - \mathbf{u}_{jk} |}{| \mathbf{G}_i | + | \mathbf{G}_j |}. \tag{6}$$

where $\mathbf{G}_i$ and $\mathbf{G}_j$ denote the set of all good feature vectors belonging to ith and jth cluster, respectively, $\mathbf{G}_{ij}$ denotes the set of all good feature vectors belonging to either cluster i or j, and $| \mathbf{G}_i |$ and $| \mathbf{G}_j |$ denote the robust cardinality of clusters i and j.

While performing this URCP algorithm iteratively, the optimum number of clusters are automatically adjusted. Finally, after no merging takes place the optimum number of clusters and members of each cluster are extracted.

4 Experimental Results

We have tested the URCP algorithm on both synthetic optical flow vectors and optical flow vectors that were generated from real image sequences. Because of the limitation of space we presented here only one result from each sequence.

4.1 Synthetic Optical Flow Vectors

In a synthetic optical flow field (Fig.1), vectors can be divided into four regions. Each region corresponds to a moving object. Firstly, we divide this vector field into non-overlapped 4x4 rectangular blocks. The motion model parameters are calculated by fitting each block to affine motion model (1) and (2). We then calculate the estimated values $(\bar{V}_x, \bar{V}_y)$ of each block from these parameters. These estimated values have been used as feature vectors in the next step, URCP clustering. Due to less noise, we can observe from feature space plotting (Fig.2) that the feature vectors of each group are clearly separated. We begin clustering the feature vectors by assigning ten feature vectors that settled in each group to the initial cluster centroids. Fig.3 shows the result after performing the preliminary clustering of the feature space. Fig.4 shows the result after performing the unconstrained RCP algorithm. Fig.5 shows final clusters after performing 15 iterations of the URCP algorithm. Finally, after mapping the clustered feature vectors back to the spatial space of the original image, Fig.6 shows each region that corresponds to a particular moving object.

 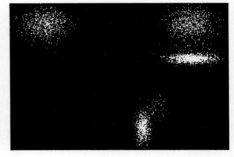

Fig. 1. The synthetic optical flow vectors   **Fig. 2.** The feature space of the estimated optical flow vectors

4.2 Optical Flow Vectors from Image sequences

The URCP clustering algorithm has also been applied to cluster the optical flow vectors generated from the popular real image sequence "flower garden". In the first step, we calculate the optical flow vectors using the Lucas and Kanade algorithm [1981]. This algorithm produced a 2-D dense optical flow field, Fig.(7).

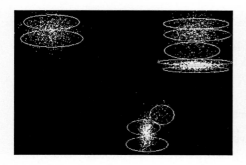

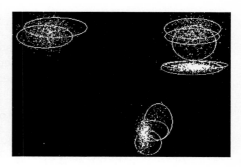

Fig. 3. Result of the RCP algorithm on feature vectors of synthetic optical flow vectors.

Fig. 4. Result of the unconstrained RCP algorithm on feature vectors of synthetic optical flow vectors.

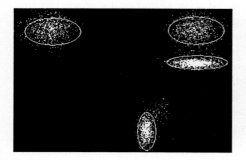

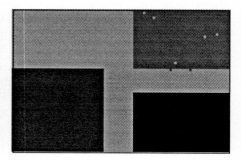

Fig. 5. Result after 15 iterations of the URCP algorithm on feature vectors of synthetic optical flow vectors.

Fig. 6. The segmented image of synthetic optical flow vectors

After dividing these vectors field into non-overlapped blocks, the motion model parameters are calculated. The estimated values $(\bar{V}_x, \bar{V}_y)$ of each block are used as feature vectors in the URCP clustering step. After merging, regions are extracted and represented in layers, as shown in Fig.11. Different regions represent different moving objects, except the dark region which represents the static object (the sky). The quality of regions depends strictly on the quality of optical flow vectors.

5 Conclusion

Motion-based segmentation plays an important role in dynamic scene analysis. In order to effectively and efficiently segment images with multiple moving objects, an unsupervised robust clustering technique is required. The technique should not only cluster the feature field into clusters but also extract the optimum number of clusters corresponding to the moving objects. In this paper, the unsupervised robust fuzzy C-Prototypes clustering technique has been applied to perform the parametric motion-based segmentation in the parameters space. The algorithm contains three steps, namely, the preliminary clustering of the feature space, the unconstrained robust C-Prototypes, and cluster merging algorithm under a robust cluster similarity. We have tested the technique on both synthetic data and real image sequence. The results show that the quality of the segmented image depends strictly on the quality of optical flow vectors. The post-processing of optical flow calculation is required. In this algorithm, we actually treated the motion model parameters as fixed parameters. Further research would focus on dynamic clustering technique, e.g., EM algorithm, which treats these parameters in the same way but is more robust and consumes less time than this algorithm.

Fig. 7. Optical flow vectors of the first two frames of the flower garden sequence

References

Altunbasak,Y. and Eren,P.E. and Tekalp,A.M.(1998). Region-based parametric motion segmentation using color information. *Graphical Models and Images Processing*, 60 (1), January, (1998), 13–23.

Ahanger, G. and Little, T. D. C.(1996). A Survey of Technologies for Parsing and Indexing Digital Video. *Visual Communication and Image Representation*, 7 (1), March, (1996), 28–43.

Ayer,S. and Sawhney,H.S.(1995). Layered representation of motion video using robust maximum-likelihood estimation of mixture model and MDL encoding. *Proceeding of the IEEE intl. conf. on computer vision and pattern recognition*,IEEE press, June, (1995).

Borshukov,G.D. and Bozdagi,G. and Altunbasak,Y. and Tekalp,A.M.(1997). Motion segmentation by multi-stage affine classification. *IEEE trans. on images processing*, 6 (9), September, (1997).

Chang,M.M. and Tekalp,A.M. and Sezan,M.I.(1997). Simultaneous motion estimation and segmentation. *IEEE transactions on Image Processing*, 6 (9), September ,1997.

Cheong,C.K. and Aizawa,K. and Saito,T. and Kaueko,M.K. and Harashima,H.(1996). Structure motion segmentation for compact image sequence representation. *Proceedings of the SPIE:Visual communications and image processing'96*, 2727, SPIE press, March, (1996), 1152–1163.

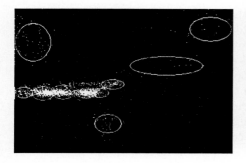

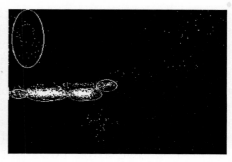

Fig. 8. Result of the RCP algorithmfrom on feature vectors of "flower garden" sequence.

Fig. 9. Result of the unconstrained RCP algorithm on feature vectors of "flower garden" sequence.

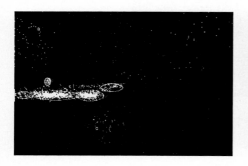

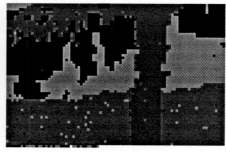

Fig. 10. Result after 20 iterations of the URCP algorithm on feature vectors of "flower garden" sequence.

Fig. 11. The segmented image of "flower garden" sequence

Choi,J.G. and Kim,S.D.(1996). Multi-stage segmentation of optical flow field. *Signal processing*, 54, (1996), 109–118.

Dave,R.N. and Krishnapuram,R.(1997). Robust clustering methods: A unified view. *IEEE Trans. on Fuzzy Systems*, 5 (2), May, (1997), 270–293.

Ferman, A. M. and Gunsel, B. and Tekalp, A. M.(1997). Object-based Indexing of MPEG-4 Compressed Video. *Visual Communications and Image Proceeding'97*, San Jose, California, (1997), 282–287.

Flickner, M. and Sawhney, H. and Niblack, Ashley, J. and Huang, Q. and Dom, B. and Gorkani, M. and Hafner, J. and Lee, D. and Petkovic, D. and Steele, D. and Yanker, P.(1995). Query by image and video content: The QBIC System. *IEEE Computer*, September, (1995), 23–31.

Frigui,H. and Krishnapuram,R.(1996). A robust algorithm for automatic extraction of an unknown number of clusters from noisy data. *Pattern Recognition Letters*, 17, (1996), 1223–1232.

Hotter,M. and Mester,R. and Muller,F.(1996). Detection and description of moving objects by stochastic modelling and analysis of complex scenes. *Signal processing:Image communication*, 8 (1996), 281–293.

Lucas,B.D. and Kanade,T.(1981). A iterative image-registration technique with an application to stereo vision. *DARPA Proceedings of Image Understanding Workshop*, 1981, 121–130.

Murray,D.W. and Buxton,B.F.(1987). Scene segmentation from visual motion using global optimization. *IEEE transactions on pattern analysis and machine intelligence*, PAMI-9 (2), March, (1987) 220–228.

Odobez,J.M. and Bouthemy,P.(1995). Direct model-based image motion segmentation for dynamic scene analysis. *Proceedings Second Asian Conf. on Computer Vision: ACCV'95*, (1995).

Sawhney,S. and H.Ayer,S. and Gorkani,M.(1995). Model-based 2D and 3D dominant motion estimation for mosaicing and video representation. *Proceeding of the IEEE intl. conf. on computer vision and pattern recognition*,SPIE press, June, (1995).

Sawhney,H.S. and Ayer,S.(1996). Compact representations of video through dominant and multiple motion estimation. *IEEE trans on pattern analysis and machine intelligence*, 18 (8), August, (1996), 814–830.

Smoliar, S. W. and Zhang, H. J.(1996). Video Indexing and Retrieval. In :*Multimedia Systems and Techniques,* edited by Borko Furht, Kluwer Academic Publishers, (1996), 495–516.

Wang,J.Y.A. and Adelson,E.H.(1994). Spatio-temporal segmentation of video data. *Proceedings of the SPIE: Image and Video Processing II*, 2182, February, (1994), 120–131.

Weiss,Y.(1996). Interpreting images by propagating Bayesian beliefs. *Technical paper of Media Perceptual Computing Lab., MIT*, (1996).

Author Index

Springer
and the
environment

At Springer we firmly believe that an
international science publisher has a
special obligation to the environment,
and our corporate policies consistently
reflect this conviction.
We also expect our business partners –
paper mills, printers, packaging
manufacturers, etc. – to commit
themselves to using materials and
production processes that do not harm
the environment. The paper in this
book is made from low- or no-chlorine
pulp and is acid free, in conformance
with international standards for paper
permanency.